THE COMPLETE WORKS OF THE *PEARL* POET

THE
COMPLETE WORKS
OF THE

Pearl

POET

Translated with an Introduction by
CASEY FINCH

Facing-page Middle English Texts Edited by

MALCOLM ANDREW AND RONALD WALDRON
CLIFFORD PETERSON

UNIVERSITY OF CALIFORNIA PRESS
BERKELEY   LOS ANGELES   OXFORD

University of California Press
Berkeley and Los Angeles, California

University of California Press, Ltd.
Oxford, England

Library of Congress Cataloging-in-Publication Data

The Complete works of the Pearl poet / translated with an introduction
  by Casey Finch ; facing-page Middle English texts edited by Malcolm Andrew,
  Ronald Waldron, and Clifford Peterson.
     p. cm.
    Includes bibliographical references.
    Contents: Pearl—Cleanness—Patience—Sir Gawain and the
Green Knight—Saint Erkenwald.
    ISBN 0-520-06874-2 (alk. paper).—ISBN 0-520-07871-3 (pbk. :
alk. paper)
    1. English poetry—Middle English, 1100–1500—Modernized versions.
    2. Gawain (Legendary character)—Romances. 3. Arthurian romances.
  I. Finch, Casey. II. Andrew, Malcolm. III. Waldron, Ronald.
  IV. Peterson, Clifford, 1942–   .
  PR1972.G35A345 1993
  829'.108—dc20

                                      92-6803
                                         CIP

Printed in the United States of America

9 8 7 6 5 4 3 2

The Middle English texts of *Pearl, Cleanness, Patience,* and *Sir Gawain and the Green Knight*, as well as the Glossary to these four poems, are reproduced from *The Poems of the Pearl Manuscript: Pearl, Cleanness, Patience, Sir Gawain and the Green Knight*, revised edition, edited by Malcolm Andrew and Ronald Waldron (Exeter: University of Exeter, 1987), and are used by permission of Malcolm Andrew and Ronald Waldron. The Middle English text of *Saint Erkenwald* is reprinted from *Saint Erkenwald*, edited by Clifford Peterson (Philadelphia: University of Pennsylvania Press, 1977), and is used by permission of Clifford Peterson.

Contents

Acknowledgments

This translated edition of the complete works of the *Pearl* poet gathers between two covers much of Malcolm Andrew and Ronald Waldron's edition of the four poems of the *Pearl* manuscript (along with many of their notes and their Glossary), and much of Clifford Peterson's edition of *Saint Erkenwald* (with a number of his notes). By no means does it replace these invaluable editions; and readers will have to consult Andrew and Waldron and Peterson for their illuminating introductions, emendations, bibliographies, textual notes, and other useful apparatuses. Above all, then, my thanks go to Malcolm Andrew, Ronald Waldron, and Clifford Peterson, each of them responsible in his way for producing the very finest editions of these poems available. If they had not allowed me to borrow so liberally from their work, this project would not have been possible.

I thank Marie Borroff, to whose magnificent translations of *Pearl* and *Sir Gawain and the Green Knight* I humbly and enviously refer the reader. For what she has taught me, the intellectual generosity she has displayed, and the insightful comments she has provided on my *Gawain* translation, I am most grateful. I thank Peter Bowen, the better half of innumerable conversations concerning the *Pearl* poet in general and this project in particular, whose astute understanding of *Sir Gawain* and *Saint Erkenwald* enhanced and deepened my own. I value his harsh advice as much as his tender friendship. My gratitude is due Robert Brentano (one of those rare teachers who positively transform students' lives), whose erudition, intellectual style, and encouragement were genuinely inspirational to me when I started out as a medievalist. For the improvement her intelligence and good sense brought to the book, I'm honored to acknowledge Margaret Denny. I send clusters of flowers, my deepest respect, and scores of thank-you notes to my brother, Mark

Finch—a superlative writer of fiction and a superior textual editor—whose hard work, keen eye, and intelligence brought remarkable improvement to this work when it was most desperately needed. I thank John Gesang of *Hawai'i Review* for his enthusiasm, sharp poetic sense, and very concrete help in promoting the project. My deep appreciation is due Sean Killean, an extraordinary poet, who read the *Gawain* translation with great sensibility and a steadily focused eye. My warm thanks go to Pamela Nicely, who read the translation of *Pearl* with acuity and intelligence and whose *every* suggestion was incorporated. I thank Paul Parish, my friend and finest teacher, who made significant improvements on my translation of the impossible *Pearl*; I am indebted to him both emotionally and intellectually. I want to express my weak-kneed gratitude to James Schamus for the support and the smart advice he has invariably given, in this and other projects. When I asked for his help, he was, as always, both responsive and enlightening. Thanks go to Peter Dale Scott, whose enthusiasms were as sincere as his criticisms were sharp. For his kind advice and warm telephone manner, I thank A. C. Spearing, one of the finest *Pearl* poet scholars. And finally, I would like to register my appreciation for the helpful advice of Melissa Spielman, whose reading of the *Pearl* translation was both scrupulous and canny.

Translator's Note

The most conscientious translation is self-negating. It seeks to become transparent, to introduce the audience to the original text, and then, like a matchmaker, to step quietly aside. It is also deeply paradoxical. It tells lies in order to tell the truth; it transforms and alters so that its original text—that infinitely delicate and mutable thing—may be carried across from one cultural space to another, from one time to another, more or less intact. Forever and acutely aware of its inevitable failure, of the way it sullies the delicate gift it was meant to deliver undamaged, translation is always ready to proclaim as examples of faithfulness its own techniques of infidelity. What is more, translation is uncomfortable about its status as criticism; but criticism it invariably is. It has interpreted the text with the most violent form of intervention, mediating absolutely between the original and the reader.

What is offered here is by no means a literal translation of these poems. (Literal prose translations are available and serve their purpose as extended glosses to the originals.) I have tried, instead, to convey a sense of the original *poetry*, that elusive blend of sound and sense that creates the complicated experience of art. These translations are intended to stand on their own as poems in Modern English, as alliterative and sometimes rhyming poetry. To this end, I have taken untold numbers of liberties with the texts. When I felt the sacrifice necessary (and all too often this meant that I had run up against my own limitations), I strayed from the syntax, the line order, the verb tense, the exact imagery of the original. Sometimes when the text's meaning was open-ended, I imposed interpretations by fiat, blurred a distinction, fudged a metaphor. Often enough, I would discover myself compelled to ignore a caesura, the precise name of a flower or an herb, an isolated apostrophe, or even what seemed the very unit of the sentence in the poet's text in order to render the translation poetically consistent and effective. At other times, I allowed myself enjambments that did not occur in the original, half-rhymes, or even identical rhymes where the original rhymes were pure. Indeed, the list of things lost from the original in this translation fairly staggers me. And I should add what will be obvious to readers who are familiar with the originals: I allowed myself the license to stray farther from the literal text of *Pearl*—of a form almost unmatched in English literature for its difficulty—than from the texts of the other poems.

I am deeply pleased, therefore, that this edition features, alongside these translations, texts of the original poems edited by three of the leading scholars of the *Pearl* poet. Peterson's edition of *Saint Erkenwald* and Andrew and Waldron's edition of *The Poems of the Pearl Manuscript* represent the very best editions available today (the best, indeed, that scholarship so far has generated). The presence of these editions of the original poems gives me encouragement that the reader will never be led astray by any liberties I might have taken in the translation. Instead, he or she will always have literally at hand the finest editions of the originals. And if the reader decides (as I would strongly encourage him or her to do) primarily to study the original text, then I hope the translation will prove useful whenever difficulties are encountered.

Something must be said of the metrical decisions I have made in this translation. While I have maintained the rhyme schemes and the alliteration of the originals throughout, there is a fundamental difference between the meter I have adopted for these translations and that of the original poems. *Sir Gawain and the Green Knight, Patience, Cleanness,* and *Saint Erkenwald* are characterized by the alliterative long line, divided by a caesura, composed of roughly four accented syllables—the first three of which alliterate—typically interspersed with from seven to nine unaccented syllables. (The line as a whole thus usually contains eleven to thirteen syllables.) *Pearl*, on the other hand, employs a shorter alliterative line, which is also divided by a caesura and made up of four accented syllables. But in *Pearl*, the accented syllables alliterate more loosely, and the line as a whole is interspersed usually with only four to six unaccented syllables. (*Pearl*'s line thus generally contains eight to twelve syllables.) Both the long-line and short-line forms, then, can be called different kinds of accented tetrameters, in which a wide variation is allowed in the number of unaccented syllables that fall between the stresses. Indeed, such metrical variation is responsible for much of the rhythmic modulation and beauty of the originals; and, understandably, many past translators of these poems have retained this aspect.

I am convinced, however, that these poems were intended to be performed before a live audience in one form or another, to be enacted in court as entertainments (certainly read aloud and perhaps even accompanied by music). And in their public and theatrical delivery— in whatever form—they would have gained an insistent rhythmic regularity that the text as it stands on the page does not convey. To my ear, at least, modern translations that use accented verse—that allow themselves, in other words, the wide variations in the number of unaccented syllables that occur in the original—while technically faithful, nonetheless lose the underlying rhythmic regularity that the original was meant to display.

I have decided, therefore, to adopt a fairly regular anapestic tetrameter for *Sir Gawain and the Green Knight, Patience, Cleanness,* and *Saint Erkenwald.* There are dangers with this meter, not least of which is the fact that it can tend to trivialize, to sound like children's narrative poetry or light verse. Still, I thought this meter, given the right modulation, could be resurrected for "high" poetry and, moreover, put to a distinct advantage. I hoped that anapestic tetrameter, deployed properly, would lend these translations a stately, "medieval" quality. I hoped, for instance, that the rigidity and "learnedness" of the form would in *Sir Gawain and the Green Knight* confer the same courtly dignity and sensitivity to decorum with which the poem's protagonist is so movingly concerned. And I hoped the meter, in turn, would recreate at the rhythmic level the sense of strict and unvarying religious piety that *Patience, Cleanness,* and *Saint Erkenwald* posit as ideals. At the same time, it seemed to me, the self-consciousness and artificiality of anapestic tetrameter would convey the sophisticated tone, running throughout *Gawain, Patience,* and *Cleanness,* of light, urbane burlesque. There are two ways, however, in which I sought to mitigate the anapestic meter. First, I continually varied the basic form with a number of devices: placing the alliteration on an unaccented syllable, interspersing trochees and iambs, creating feminine lines, and so forth. Second, in *Sir Gawain* I rendered the bob as an iamb, and the wheel as iambic trimeter. Thus every stanza of the Arthurian romance closes by breaking from the anapestic form, allowing the ear a little rest, as it were.

As for *Pearl,* I have rendered the shorter alliterative line of the original into iambic tetrameter, a verse form with a more venerable history in English.

Introduction

THE *PEARL* POET

Pearl, Cleanness, Patience, and *Sir Gawain and the Green Knight*—these titles, it must be borne in mind, are merely editorial—are to be found on folios 43–130 of a unique late fourteenth-century vellum manuscript, 118 mm wide and roughly 167 mm high, known as MS Cotton Nero A.x, Art. 3, now held in the British Library. Interspersed among these folios are various illustrations—thoughtlessly labeled crude by most critics—of scenes in the poems. *Saint Erkenwald* can be found in folios 72v–75v of another manuscript (really two separate manuscripts bound as one), known as British Library Ms. Harley 2250, and inscribed in the late fifteenth century. Harley 2250 also includes part of the *Stanzaic Life of Christ, De Sancto Martino*, the *Speculum Christiani, Themata Dominicalia, De Sancto Iohannes Baptisa, Saynt Elene*, other assorted lines in Latin and English, short prose and verse pieces, sermons, and narratives.

Little is known of the so-called *Pearl* poet or *Gawain* poet. Through the years, scholars have labored diligently to fix him or her by name or circumstance. Yet the list of candidates remains a long one.

Sir Israel Gollancz (1907), one of the great early editors of the *Pearl* poet, vigorously defended the received idea that the author was the "philosophical" Ralph Strode, the logician and tutor at Oxford in the 1360s whom Chaucer mentions in *Troylus and Criseyde*, despite the fact that Carleton F. Brown (1904b) had recently presented a number of objections to the theory. Several years later, a considerable scholarly debate developed over the proposal that the poet was "Huchown of the Awle Ryale" (see MacCracken). And after Henry L. Savage suggested a clerk in the house of Enguerrand de Coucy, Earl of Bedford, in 1926, in 1928 Oscar Cargill and Margaret Schlauch, arguing persuasively that

1

the poet had to be a clerk in the house of John Hastings, Earl of Pembroke, nominated both John Prat, a minstrel, and John Donne, a valet of the king's kitchen. In the 1930s, as if the waters were not muddied enough, C. O. Chapman (1932) marshaled convincing evidence that the author was John of Erghome; while Oakden (1930–35), in a study of the geography of *Sir Gawain and the Green Knight*, placed the poet in the house of John of Gaunt (257–61).

Finally, in 1956, Ormerod Greenwood advanced the name of Hugh Mascy (1–12), and variations on the name have since attained a certain currency. William Vantuono (1987) and Erik Kooper have proposed one John de Mascy (or Massey). Other critics put forward John de Massey, rector of Stockport in Cheshire, whom Hoccleve mentions in the early fifteenth century, and whom Clifford Peterson identifies with John Massey of Cotton in Cheshire (1974, and 1977, 15–23). Although this name in one form or another has become widely accepted, it should be stressed that it is still highly conjectural. Sadly, our poet remains anonymous.

Nor can we say conclusively that the same individual is responsible for all five poems. The idea of common authorship, more or less originated by Carl Horstmann in his 1881 *Altenglische Legenden* (265–75), has been disputed by scholars ever since. Carleton F. Brown, for one, scrutinizing the theology of *Pearl*, persuasively questioned the notion (1904b); and his study strengthened the earlier argument of J. T. T. Brown, based on metrical analysis, against a single author. In their 1925 edition of *Sir Gawain and the Green Knight*, J. R. R. Tolkien and E. V. Gordon argued that one person had written the four poems of the Cotton Nero manuscript (A.x)—*Pearl, Cleanness, Patience,* and *Sir Gawain and the Green Knight*—but considered it "very dubious" that the same poet was responsible for *Saint Erkenwald* (xviii). To this day, though their ranks are thinning, a significant number of critics—Ruth Morse (45–48), John W. Clark (1941, 1949), and Larry Benson among them— have continued to oppose the theory of common authorship. Nevertheless, it is now the prevailing opinion that all five poems were written by the same person. In his 1926 edition of *Saint Erkenwald*, Savage neatly and convincingly summarized the evidence gathered by previous scholars on similarities in vocabulary, alliteration, phraseology, passages, and style that seem to bind the five poems intimately (liv–lxv). Today, to the growing list of critics who agree in attributing the five poems to a single author may be added the name of Marie Borroff, a preeminent scholar and superior translator of *Pearl* and *Sir Gawain*. What is more, as we accrue knowledge of the Northwest Midlands dialect—probably from Cheshire and/or Lancashire—in which the five poems were written, the evidence continues to mount. The jury, however, is still out; we can no more absolutely attest to a common authorship for these five poems than we can name their author.

We are left, then, with a sketchy, more or less anonymous figure—an official of a provincial estate perhaps, a university-trained clerk, or a private chaplain—who seems to be responsible for five extraordinary moments in the supposed alliterative revival.

Nor do our uncertainties end there. For like the name of their author, the dates of these compositions remain a matter of guesswork. Still, chronological limits of some kind can be tentatively set. For instance, *Patience* seems to precede—because it apparently provides fodder for—at least a part of the 1377 B-text of Langland's great alliterative poem, *Piers Plowman*. *Pearl* seems to follow Boccaccio's 1360 *Olympia*, which may be its source or, at any rate, part of its background. *Cleanness* probably follows the 1356 French version of Mandeville's *Travels*. As for *Sir Gawain and the Green Knight*, scholars have placed its composition sometime after the foundation of the Order of the Garter in the 1340s (see Moorman 1977, 13–16, and Jackson, who assigns the year 1362). *Saint Erkenwald* was given the approximate date of 1386, first by Friedrich Knigge in 1885, then by Gollancz in 1922 (reprint edition, 1932). Both critics assumed the poem was an occasional composition accompanying the elevation by Robert Braybrooke, Bishop of London, into "first-class feasts of the days of the Conversion and Commemoration of St. Paul, and of the Deposition (April 30) and Translation (November 14) of St. Erkenwald" (Peterson 1977, 11). It must be noted, however, that the scrupulous Peterson, for one, has convincingly proposed a later date for the saint's legend (1977, 11–15). At any rate, exact chronological limits for the poems—much less a precise chronological sequence—continue to elude us.

SHARED CHARACTERISTICS OF THE POEMS

In the end, what can be said definitively of the *Pearl* poet paints a blurred and rather spectral portrait; in fact, our sense of the biographical person behind the works is limited to what little information the poems offer internally. But in the face of such obscurity, perhaps we should take to heart the resigned, good-humored advice of Sir Gawain himself before setting off on his grim journey to the Green Knight's Chapel:

"Why pule, complain, or pout?"
Said Gawain, showing zest,
"What destiny deals out
A man must put to test."

(562–65)

With the same simultaneously wistful and determined spirit, then, with a resolve to make do with what we have at hand, let us see what we can reconstruct of the poet from the poetry itself. We can begin by cataloging the significant characteristics of the *Pearl* poet.

There is—importantly for the theorists of common authorship—a characteristic use of periphrases for God within these five poems; indeed, the *Pearl* poet seems to make a habit of referring to God periphrastically rather than directly. Everywhere in the oeuvre, the presiding deity is referred to and invoked not simply as *God* or *Lord*, but rather by the rhetorically elaborate, circumlocutionary, and attributive trope known as *periphrasis*. In *Cleanness*, for example, God is called "He Who wrought all" (5), or "He Who put in people the power to see" (583). In *Pearl* we hear of the "world's Wielder" (736). *Sir Gawain*, for its part, figures for its divine overseer "He Who above / Rules the world" (2056–57). In *Saint Erkenwald*, the deity is called succinctly the "Maker of men" (283). And in *Patience*, God is "He Who made ears" (123), the "Wielder of wisdom" (129), and, in Jonah's elaborate description:

"the One Who the world once made,
He Who set all the stars in the sky, and the winds,
And made every man, all that moves, with a word!"

(206–8)

Such periphrases have a dual effect. On the one hand, they tend to highlight the sublime nature of God, to underscore His mysteriousness, and to locate Him emphatically *above* his creation. But on the other, they serve to personify the Creator, to bring Him down to earth, where He is articulated as a kind of builder or craftsman, indeed, a master poet. God is simultaneously ineffably divine and insistently human. And this, too, emerges as an identifiable characteristic of the *Pearl* poet.

Almost everywhere in the poems there is a fascination with food in general and with the formalities of banqueting in particular. In *Sir*

Gawain, the action begins at the Round Table in Camelot with a New Year's feast that is matched in its splendor only by the later extended feasting in Bertilak's castle. Significantly, in *Patience* the penance enforced by the King of Nineveh is dietary; he orders

> "That all bodies that bide in this borough with life—
> All the animals, adults, and all that are young,
> Every prince, every priest, every prelate as well—
> Shall fast as is fit for their false, evil deeds.
> Take each babe from the breast, though he bawls out and cries.
> Take each beast from the broom sage; he'll bite on no grass,
> Nor will pass to a pasture with plants there. And from
> Water holes keep the horse, and from hay keep the ox.
> We shall howl in the height of our hunger at once;
> Thus by Him will be heard every howl of pain!"
>
> *(387–96)*

Cleanness provides an extended disquisition on hospitality and banqueting. The parable of the wedding feast is twice, though very differently, recounted (33–47, 51–176); the hospitality of Abraham to God and of Lot to the angels is manifested in the haste and deference with which each welcomes them and arranges a meal; and there may be no moment in any of the poems as elaborate as the description of Belshazzar's feast. But perhaps the most vivid and moving image of banqueting comes at the close of *Saint Erkenwald*. There, as the judge's soul finally ascends from hell—where it had lingered " 'in a dark, chilly death . . . ever hungry for heaven's great feast' " (306–7)—and enters heaven, the corpse describes the scene:

> "At that supper my soul is seated right now!
> With the words and the water that wash away sin
> You have lit up a lamp in the lightless abyss!
> In a second my spirit was stricken with joy,
> And went forth to the feast where the faithful are served!
> By a guard she was greeted and guided along
> To a stall set aside, where she'll stay evermore!"
>
> *(332–38)*

For the *Pearl* poet, this banquet in heaven is no mere metaphor; it is a very real feast at which substantial souls enjoy palpable food.

The *Pearl* poet, too, shows a preference for the Old over the New Testament. To be sure, there is much here of the New Testament; the poet is, after all, a profoundly Christian writer. In *Pearl*, for example, the Maiden's retelling of Christ's parable of the vineyard constitutes a turning point in the debate; and the poem ultimately moves past debate altogether and into the pure and searing (re)vision of the apocalypse from Revelation. In *Cleanness*, as well, there are crucial moments drawn from Matthew and Luke. And Christ's sermon on the Beatitudes in Matthew forms an introductory and significant part of *Patience*. What is more, the Jewish and Christian texts are theologically ranged in a hierarchy in which the Old prefigures, and is fulfilled and perfected in, the New; and this schema tends implicitly to privilege the New Testament everywhere in the poems. Nevertheless, there is no doubt that the *Pearl* poet was more immediately and naturally attracted to the rousing stories and lurid details of the Old Testament, whose more starkly and prominently narrative fabric seems better suited to his sensibility than the parabolic style of the late antique Christian writers. Even in *Pearl*, a poem which is emphatically concerned with the mystery of Christ and which literally rehearses New Testament prophecy, almost every point in the central debate between the Dreamer and the Maiden pivots on material from the Old Testament: Isaiah, Psalms, and so forth. *Patience*, in turn, comprises what amounts to an imaginative translation of the Book of Jonah. And the homily *Cleanness* weaves together as negative exempla several Old Testament stories: the Fall and the Flood, God's visit to Abraham and Sarah, the destruction of the cities, Nebuchadnezzar's seizure of the holy vessels and conversion to God, and Belshazzar's feast.

Another striking characteristic of the *Pearl* poet is his sense—unmatched by his contemporaries—of the visual medium, his propensity for what today is called the cinematic, or special, effect. The power of the fourteenth-century lyricists surely lies in the intense emotional registers they were able to create; the intensity of Langland doubtless comes from his astonishing ability to mobilize afresh outmoded allegorical structures; and Chaucer's longevity is, above all, a function of his ability to appropriate literary conventions ironically and to populate them with new and surprising and indelible characters. But there is nothing, I think, in English literature quite like the *Pearl* poet's sense of the potentially miraculous nature of the *visual*. There is no blood quite so red as the blood that drops from Gawain's neck onto the white expanse of snow at the Green Chapel in *Sir Gawain and the Green Knight*.

There are few images at once so sharp and so disorientingly strange as the first vision of the Pearl Maiden on the opposite riverbank in *Pearl*. Indeed, everywhere in the *Pearl* poet we are confronted with arresting, almost overwhelming, visual effects. Consider the eerie, floating hand of God as it scratches the mysterious letters on the wall at Belshazzar's feast in *Cleanness*; the bright, flowing wound of Christ that is the source of the river in *Pearl*'s New Jerusalem; the talking head of the Green Knight at Arthur's court in *Sir Gawain*; or the detailed and vividly imagined belly of the whale in *Patience*. Perhaps the most striking special effect of all is the fast-motion decomposition—not unlike that of monsters and aliens in today's movies—of the judge's corpse in *Saint Erkenwald*:

> Of his visage all vestiges vanished at once.
> His body turned black as the blistering dirt,
> Just as dry as the dust when it's driven in swirls.
> For as soon as his soul had settled in peace,
> Then the corpse that had clothed her decayed, and was gone.
>
> *(342–46)*

This image of sudden, dusty dematerialization recalls the equally vivid image in *Cleanness* of the destruction of the cities as the snapping of an old and dried binding of a book:

> The cliffs and the crags were cloven apart,
> Like a book that is broken, whose binding explodes.
> When the black smoke of brimstone had bled everywhere,
> Those four cities had sunk; yes, they'd slipped into hell!
>
> *(965–68)*

Like the Old Testament cities of *Cleanness*, the corpse in *Saint Erkenwald* is at one moment fleshly and throbbing with life. At the next, it is crackled and dry, disintegrating instantly into dust.

There is also in the *Pearl* poet a concern—almost an obsession—with enclosed spaces and with miraculous resurrections from such enclosures. Noah's ark and Lot's tightly locked home, precariously protected from the angry crowd in *Cleanness*; the splendid and miraculously preserved coffin of the judge in *Saint Erkenwald*; the curtained bed in which Gawain sleeps late in Bertilak's castle in *Sir Gawain and the Green Knight*;

the earthly enclosure in *Pearl* in which the Maiden lies buried and "wrapped in rot" (22)—these kinds of enclosures, whether gravelike or protective, secure or precarious, form a recurring motif in the five poems. In *Patience*, the whale's belly in which Jonah is immured is perhaps the most elaborately and concretely realized of these gravelike enclosures. And whereas Jonah must grope his way *blindly* through the terrible, nauseating belly, the poet and the reader can see and sense with an awful clarity the nature of the enclosure in all of its visceral and symbolic detail. For like all such spaces in the oeuvre, this topos is a kind of trap, a proving ground planned by God, the locus of a moral test, and a holding tank for a prisoner slated for miraculous release and exultation.

What is more, the fanciful yet anatomically vivid description of the whale's belly exemplifies another characteristic of the *Pearl* poet: a passion for technical detail evident everywhere in the poems. For the *Pearl* poet, despite his avowed transcendentalism, despite his fascination with the beyond, is above all fundamentally *of* this world. His allegiance to the here and now animates every line. He is entranced by the colorful variety of the things of the earth, deeply concerned with the natural world (the changing seasons and the minutiae of the countryside, gardens thick with grass and herbs, the sunlit farmlands at harvest, the snowy forests of Wales, the raging depths of the sea) and with the artificial (the details of hunting, painting, sailing, cooking, armor, falconry, and military strategy, architecture, clothing, harvestry, jewelry, horsemanship, music, tapestry making, bookbinding, stained glass). Consider the description of Gawain donning his armor as he prepares to embark on his journey from Camelot:

He duly was dressed in a doublet from Tharsia.
A cape was clasped closely about him;
It was lined with a white and wonderful fur.
Two shoes made of steel were set on his feet.
On his legs servants lapped and tied lovely, bright greaves.
Polished knee-pieces, both perfectly made,
Were girded to the gear and with gold knots secured.
Cuisses, cunningly clasped, were placed
With new thongs on his thighs, which were thick and strong.
All was covered keenly with a coat of bright mail,
Which was wrapped around the rich cloth that he wore.
Then came braces, well burnished, on both of his arms,
And glorious, glistening gloves on his hands.

(571–83)

This marks a moment when all of the poem's narrative, theological, and symbolic machinery is temporarily suspended, left in abeyance, while the description lovingly and obsessively indulges in the immediate detail. It is helpful to recall here Auerbach's famous description of the excursus upon the origin of Odysseus's scar in the nineteenth book of the *Odyssey*. For what Auerbach articulates as the Homeric style—in which all phenomena are represented "in a fully externalized form, visible and palpable in all their parts, and completely fixed in their spatial relations" (6)—is also evident in the *Pearl* poet's magnificent description. The pleasure here clearly involves the sensual experience of the military accoutrements: the Tharsian doublet; the fur-lined cape; the glistening steel shoes, knee-pieces, and greaves; the formidable braces, the cuisses, the gloves. The sparkling, almost photographic, visual intensity with which the armor is described has the effect of putting aside for the moment all other considerations. We are faced with an absolute allegiance to the concrete, the same representational style that Auerbach finds in Homer: one in which details are determinedly placed in the foreground and "brought to light in perfect fullness [so] that a continuous rhythmic procession passes by, and never is there a form left fragmentary or half-illuminated, never a lacuna, never a gap, never a glimpse of unplumbed depths" (6–7).

There is yet another characteristic element common to all five poems. Frequently in the *Pearl* poet's work we encounter an urbane, slightly wry, slightly bitter, appreciation for the potential comedy of hardship, a sensibility that will make the best of a bad situation, even flirt with it, if a pleasure, however limited, can thus be had. Consider, for instance, this moment at the beginning of *Patience*:

> Since I'm personally placed by Dame Poverty's side,
> I must ply to Dame Patience, and play with them both. . . .
> For to love those two ladies and lavish them praise
> Is far better than blaming them both, which brings grief.
> If my destiny deems them, disdain is for naught.
>
> *(35–36, 47–49)*

The playfulness with which poverty is thus allegorized as a young lady with whom one might dally suggests a mind that is at once devoutly obedient to the unchallengeable will of God and yet resourceful, pragmatic, even ironic. For instance, although the lines at the poem's end warning the reader not to rail madly against the lot God has assigned him are otherwise typically didactic, their tone is far from simply edifying:

> Therefore, fight not so fiercely, sir! Follow your path,
> And be proven patient in pain and in joy!
> Because he who in haste very heatedly tears
> At his shirt must in sorrow just sew it again.
>
> *(524–27)*

To be sure, this passage shows an unswerving and deeply felt resignation to the inscrutable will of God; it is heartfelt, urgent, and pious. The words enjoin us to succumb in advance to what cannot be warded off. But they imply at the same time a sophisticated and realistic attitude that is neither entirely uncynical nor absolutely solemn. The concretization—in which the shredding and resewing of a single shirt embodies in miniature a complex spiritual and emotional response to suffering— is comic, even cartoonish; there is something genuinely funny about the poet's dramatization of impatience. And meanwhile, the lesson is folksy and wise: instead of compounding your hardship, you would serve yourself best by grinning and bearing it, by keeping your shirt on when the cold weather sets in. Calm down, take stock of things, above all, be practical; histrionics only make things worse.

One final characteristic shared by these five poems must be mentioned. Among the great Christian writers in the English language, the *Pearl* poet is most like Milton in consciously drawing upon earlier forms for his materials: hagiography, homily, dream vision, and Arthurian romance. Like Milton, too, he transforms and, at the same time, preserves the traditions he inherits. Even as it leaves its genre intact, *Saint Erkenwald* turns hagiography to purposes that are specifically and recognizably those of the *Pearl* poet. As insistently as they adhere to the conventional homiletic form, *Patience* and *Cleanness* modulate and personalize it by interjecting delightfully comic and quotidian touches. *Sir Gawain and the Green Knight*, for its part, burlesques even as it upholds the traditional codes of Arthurian literature that constitute its background. And there is nothing quite like the skillful amalgamation in *Pearl* of the modified Anglo-Saxon alliterative line and the newer, more cosmopolitan French technique of rhyming. *Pearl*, indeed, is the most palpable and unusual demonstration of the poet's habit of simultaneously sustaining and transforming the forms he receives. For within it, the allegorical form of the dream vision, even as it remains fundamentally unaltered, becomes at once theological debate, personal elegy, and *consolatio*.

We recognize this dynamic, for instance, in the lines toward the beginning of *Sir Gawain* in which the narrator is presented as a transmitter of popular tales:

Listen, then, to this lay if a little it please;
As they told it in town I'll retell it right now
    To you.
Most masterfully made,
This tale so tried and true,
With letters well inlaid,
Was recited hitherto.

(30–36)

On the one hand, the poem is an ongoing product of oral transmission: it will be told aloud to us as it was heard by the teller "in town." On the other hand, though, the poet reminds us that this particular episode in the stories of the knight has already been committed to a written literary tradition: it has already been "masterfully made" in "letters." The *Pearl* poet's rendering of *Sir Gawain and the Green Knight* is thus at the same time both oral and written, and it is acutely concerned with the differences and similarities between the two kinds of transmission. What is more, we confront here a characteristic literary self-consciousness; for the poet continually recognizes the nature, and belatedness, of his poetic function.

Indeed, it can be argued more generally that *Pearl, Cleanness, Patience, Sir Gawain and the Green Knight*, and *Saint Erkenwald* are, in fact, among the earliest instances of artistic self-reflexivity in English literature. For the *Pearl* poet's works are, above all, aware of themselves as revisions of earlier works, modifications, recontextualizations of preexisting literary orders. Though their "originals" may be timeworn, their treatments and contexts are wholly and almost anxiously new. How does the *Pearl* poet at once continue and cannily mitigate the traditions he inherited? In what way does he transform the materials handed down to him in order to inaugurate a wholly new form of art?

INCARNATIONAL ART

The best way to answer such questions, I think, is to recognize the significant part played in the oeuvre by parataxis. Auerbach's analysis of the narrative technique of the *Chanson de Roland* and the *Chanson d'Alexis* is quite pertinent here. For Auerbach, parataxis involves a "juxtapositive, and pro- and retrogressive method in which causal, modal, and even temporal relations are obscured. . . . Time and again there is a new start; every resumption is complete in itself and independent; the next is simply juxtaposed to it, and the relation between the two is often left hanging" (105). In *Patience*, for instance, each picture of Jonah—sleeping in the ship's hull, praying in the belly of the whale, preaching to the Ninevites—is framed and spotlighted like a painting in a gallery. Each episode is set apart, sharply delineated from those that surround it, in order to infuse it with the force of the emblematic; each image is highlighted to enhance its symbolic quality; each event operates as a separate, plastic instance of the kinds of spiritual abstractions—Impatience, Folly, Repentance—which the story mobilizes and articulates. Far from trying to smooth the edges of the story he has inherited from the Vulgate, the poet in *Patience* in fact sharpens them, rendering the narrative units even more abrupt.

The *récits* themselves are often painstakingly suited to this effect. The poet intrudes upon the narratives with a seemingly endless series of interruptions. The *Pearl* poet seldom hesitates to suspend the story's forward progress in order to linger on elaborate descriptions (of feasts, knightly armor, ships), to generate apostrophes ("O Lord, cold were his comfort and cares" [*Patience* 264]), to underscore ironies ("Thus the man, who in health / Fled from God, now in grief prays that God will approach!" [*Patience* 295–96]), to advise the audience ("But be careful your clothes are as clean as can be / And fair for the feast, lest you find yourself harmed" [*Cleanness* 165–66]), to declare oaths and make exclamations, to mention his source.

The effect of these episodic and interruptive devices is to achieve a halting, juxtapositive quality, to enact a paratactic mode that isolates units of meaning and makes them emblematic, ultimately constructing a story, conceived as, in Auerbach's words, "a string of autonomous, loosely interrelated events, a series of mutually quite independent scenes . . . each of which contains an expressive gesture. . . . The course of events is thus resolved into a series of pictures; it is, as it were, parceled out" (114–15). Perhaps the most powerful such moment in the oeuvre is that in *Patience* when Jonah, discovering himself in the belly of the whale, first prays and then sleeps. The episode is, in this respect, worth citing at length, worth pausing over and exploring:

> First he glides near the gills through the glistening slime;
> Then he goes down the gullet, whose girth he thinks vast,
> Always head over heel, always hurtling about,
> Till he breaches the belly, as big as a hall.
> To glean where he's gone, Jonah gropes in the dark.
> So he stood in the stomach, which stank like hell. . . .
> So in grief Jonah gave in. To God he cried:
> "O Prince of Your prophet, have pity on me!
> Though I'm foolish, fickle, and false in my heart,
> Yet to me, Lord, be merciful; mitigate wrath!
> Though I'm pitiful, puling, of prophets the worst,
> You are God, and all goodness and grace are Your own!
> On Your man have mercy, though mired in sin;
> Prove You're Lord through the length of the land and the sea!"
> Jonah crawled to a corner and crouched there, so that
> No defilement or filth could fasten on him.
> He stayed there, safe, although steeped in the dark;
> As he'd slept in the ship, Jonah slept in that whale.
> In the beast's giant belly he bides. Of the Lord
> And His deeds Jonah dreams for three days and nights,
> Of His mercy and might.
>
> *(269–74, 281–95)*

Each moment here, each word, is evenly weighted. The pacing of events is slow and deliberate; like actions in a ponderous religious ritual, every gesture is completed and put aside before the next is begun. In this way the scene as a whole is broken into sharply delineated parts. The trip down the gullet, the groping in the dark, the prayer, the three-days' sleep—each element is separated abruptly from the rest, ranged in an unmodulated rhythmic progression, and placed at the very center of a stage whose periphery is invisible. And just as parataxis here functions to isolate this moment from its narrative surroundings, the utter darkness itself serves to emphasize the extent to which each microevent is absolutely distinct from the others.

And it is precisely by being rendered discrete and cut off from its environment that every element here is infused with an extraordinary solemnity and uniqueness. Each gesture seems to hover in a profound and impenetrable void, with no simultaneity, no overlapping of detail and event. When we learn, for instance, that "Jonah had to have heard, as they hurried along, / The waves beating on the back of the boisterous, mad whale" (301–2), the detail comes as something of a shock. Swept up by the force parataxis exhibits to isolate and cut off events from one another, we had never imagined that such a scene would be noisy. And though noise there certainly is, the clamor is eerily inaudible, lost in the silence that seems to surround each word, each gesture, of Jonah's prayer. The paratactic modality that gives the story as a whole a picaresque quality has the force, in the scene at hand, of "string[ing] pictures together like beads" (115), as Auerbach puts it.

Moreover, the entire mise-en-scène of the poem, and what elements occupy it, are suggested in only the most rudimentary of narrative strokes. Of course, we are told, as if incidentally, of the ship, the sea, the ocean floor, the shore, the city of Nineveh, the woodbine. But on the stage before us these are mere props, isolated concretions that function not as synecdoches for the surrounding environment but as the totality of its accoutrements. Boat, belly, shore, city, vine—there is literally nothing else here. Each gesture of the poem, accordingly, is like that of professional wrestling in Roland Barthes's description: "What is thus displayed for the public is the great spectacle of Suffering, Defeat, and Justice. Wrestling presents man's suffering with all the amplification of tragic masks. The wrestler who suffers in a hold which is reputedly cruel (an arm-lock, a twisted leg) offers an excessive portrayal of Suffering; like a primitive Pietà, he exhibits for all to see his face, exaggeratedly contorted in an intolerable affliction" (1972, 19). And like professional wrestling, *Patience* as a whole and much of the entire oeuvre "is a sum of spectacles" which "offers excessive gestures, exploited to the limit of their meaning" (1972, 16).

For Auerbach, parataxis gives representational privilege to isolated gestures and events in vertical relation to their larger spiritual significations over "the horizontal, historical connections between events" (115) in relation to one another. The interconnectedness of things, their metonymy, is elided; parataxis is concerned not with the network of relations that binds events on earth one to another but with the isolation of events, with the proximity they enjoy to the realm of the transcendental, their nearness to the sky. In their paratactic modality, according to Auerbach, gestures, prayers, utterances, strokes of recognition, crises, desires, epiphanies, moments of clarity, "no longer have any reality, they have only signification" (115). But in the *Pearl* poet, parataxis functions not only to separate reality and signification but, paradoxically, to join them as well. The force of the story of Jonah lies precisely in its bringing together the concrete and the abstract, linking, for instance, the local fact of Jonah's impatience and the soteriological problem of Impatience in general. In the paratactic mode used by the *Pearl* poet, the utmost tension between the spiritual and the worldly, between heaven and earth ensues. Auerbach's analysis to the contrary, with parataxis in general, and with the *Pearl* poet in particular, reality and signification, event and meaning, seem to *coincide absolutely*. Jonah fully embodies, even as he "allegorically" represents, the problem of impatience.

On the one hand, then, there is never an instant in the poems when event and meaning function independently of each other; the tiny reality of the Dreamer's loss in *Pearl*, for instance, and the vast reality of Loss in general cannot ultimately be separated. For in that dream vision, the narrator's terrible situation embodies a condition that is poignantly universal. On the other hand, the stark separations of reality and signification, of earth and heaven, are everywhere marked and insistent; for what constitutes the dramatic force and emblematic potential of, for example, Gawain's test is precisely its uniqueness, its profound isolation from the possibilities of connectedness. Nor for that matter is Jonah's three-day "burial"—in its immediate manifestation at least—ontologically like Christ's. For while Christ's burial is superhuman and universalizing, Jonah's remains utterly individual. What is emphasized again and again is that which distinguishes the human and the divine, the individual and the universal.

How can we account for these paradoxes in the *Pearl* poet? I think Barthes's distinction between "classical" and "modern"—or what I will call "horizontal" and "vertical"—language will be helpful here, even if it will be necessary to discover the ways in which it is finally dismantled by the poems themselves. For Barthes, classical, horizontal language is above all relational: "In it, no word has a destiny by itself, it is hardly the sign of a thing, but rather the means of conveying a connection. Far from plunging into an inner reality consubstantial to its outer configuration, it extends, as soon as it is uttered, towards other words, so as to form a superficial chain of intentions" (1967, 44). Classical, horizontal language, then, is fundamentally earthbound and diacritical. Each moment in it, so far from being internally generated, from blazing forth in a sublime and isolated genesis, is ranged along a conventional plane that connects it with every other moment in a causal or metonymic relation. Each word, each unit of meaning, belongs properly to its environment; and accordingly, the totality of meaning is conceived holistically. Horizontal language, then, is above all a social thing, a rhetoric. Products of custom and usage, its elements are characterized by a kind of good-neighborliness, by the easy proximity and interrelatedness they enjoy with one another. Filled with civic purpose, ranged along a horizontality, it "is always reducible to a persuasive continuum, it postulates the possibility of dialogue, it establishes a universe in which men are not alone, where words never have the terrible weight of things, where speech is always a meeting with the others" (1967, 49). Horizontal poetry, accordingly—and here one thinks of the epics of antiquity—is acutely and concretely attuned to its situation, to its political context; it is functional, concerned primarily with the interconnectedness of things, with the contiguity of events on earth.

In modern, or vertical, language, by contrast, "what is attempted is to eliminate the intention to establish relationships and to produce instead an explosion of words" (1967, 46). What is intended is a series of abrupt and violent eruptions of pure utterance, moments that declare aloud their separation from one another, their sublime uniqueness, their proximity not to one another but to the sky. In vertical language,

> the Word shines forth above a line of relationships emptied of their content. . . . Connections are not properly speaking abolished, they are merely reserved areas, a parody of themselves, and this void is necessary for the density of the Word to rise out of a magic vacuum, like a sound and a sign devoid of background. . . . Fixed connections being abolished, the Word is left only with a vertical project, it is like a monolith, or a pillar which plunges into the totality of meanings. . . . The interrupted flow of the new poetic language initiates a discontinuous Nature, which is only piecemeal. At the very moment when the withdrawal of functions obscures the relations existing in the world, the object in discourse assumes an exalted place.
>
> *(1967, 46–50)*

The word in vertical language shines forth in a burning, unique brilliance. It leaps upward from a horizontality that would bind it to its civic and rhetorical duties, from the sheer interconnectedness of things, in order to assume an epiphanic quality. The vertical is, above all, romantic; for in it, "the bursting forth of the poetic word . . . institutes an absolute object; Nature becomes a succession of verticalities, of objects, suddenly standing erect, and filled with all their possibilities" (1967, 50). Its moments are fundamentally unrelated, adorned only "with the violence of their irruption" (1967, 50). And vertical poetry, accordingly, is full of a terrible sublimity; "it relates man not to other men, but to the most inhuman images in Nature: heaven, hell, holiness, childhood, madness, pure matter, etc." (1967, 50).

For Barthes, horizontal and vertical language tend to be mutually exclusive; by virtue of their implicit natures, each cuts off the possibility of the other. And Barthes's vertical language, in particular, refuses proximity to the horizontal because it refuses connectedness altogether. But in the *Pearl* poet, these seemingly antithetical modalities exist side by side. The characterization of the Pearl Maiden is perhaps the best example in the poems of the coexistence of both discursive modes.

For on the one hand, she seems to operate as a pure sign, removed from horizontal connections; she is vertical, epiphanic, and absolutely without plasticity. Many critics, characterizing her as a purely wooden type, an allegorical figure, are convinced that she exists primarily as an emblem; and they are, I think, responding appropriately to the symbolic transparency she surely displays. Certain aspects of her depiction indeed function as "empty" signs: the Pearl Maiden's face, gesture, speech seem often to "no longer have any reality, they have only signification" (Auerbach, 115). But on the other hand, she is undeniably a product of horizontal language. More than an "empty" allegorical symbol, she is also strikingly concrete—located and realized. She is instantly recognizable to the Dreamer, and her body itself is given an earthly particularity by being placed in a specific "garden" (9, *erbere*). For all her potential for sublime meaning, the Pearl Maiden remains distinctly individual.

Allegorical significance and individualized character, grandiose meaning and local event, vertical and horizontal language, in a word, heaven and earth: in the *Pearl* poet these are at once joined and strangely broken off from one another. A disturbing and paradoxical relation is established between the spiritual and the worldly, between what we can call, adopting I. A. Richards's terminology, vehicle and tenor. We have thrust upon us a pulsating sense of what simultaneously separates and joins the visible and the invisible orders.

The *Pearl* poet seems concerned primarily with demonstrating the profound contiguity between the divine and the human. Theodore Bogdanos's point is quite pertinent here: "Immaterial meaning is made to depend on the material qualities of the symbolic image and even to behave like them. . . . This complementarity is significant: From a theological standpoint, it is at the center of Christian mystery" (9). A deep Western tradition forms the background of this notion. During the medieval period it was especially reinforced, for example, by Paul's insistence in Romans (1:20) that the invisible order is known through the mediation of the visible, by the richly physical representations of the divine in Christian iconography and hagiography, and, especially, by the modality of accommodation—the use of graphic, earthbound stories to convey spiritual meanings—that structures the parables of Christ. Hugh of Saint Victor, for instance, elevates all five senses as "indispensable instruments of spiritual truth through their perception of the world's beauty"; Aquinas reaffirms "the value of sensible creation as a symbolic vehicle to knowing God"; and Augustine, "despite his Platonic leanings, sees the physical world sanctified and redeemed in God's act of the creation" (Bogdanos 7, 8, 7). However profoundly distinct the higher and lower realms remain, however passionate the medieval insistence on the disparity that separates the Creator and the fallen world, there is nevertheless an overarching sense of a shared ontological status that binds the entire universe. It is precisely this tradition that shapes the radical proximity of spiritual and human orders, of vertical and horizontal discourses, in the *Pearl* poet.

When we experience, for instance, that isolated, glowing image of the Pearl Maiden in the New Jerusalem, we are confronted with the mysteriously dual nature of the sign as it was conceived in the medieval period. Augustine, tapping into a vast tradition, distinguished two opposing functions of signs in *On Christian Doctrine*:

> Signs are either literal or figurative. They are called literal when they are used to designate those things on account of which they were instituted: thus we say *bos* [ox] when we mean an animal of a herd. . . . Figurative signs occur when that thing which we designate by a literal sign is used to signify something else; thus we say "ox" and by that syllable understand the animal which is ordinarily designated by that word, but again by that animal we understand an evangelist, as is signified in the Scripture, according to the interpretation of the Apostle, when it says, "Thou shalt not muzzle the ox that treadeth out the corn."
>
> (*2.10.15*)

It will be noted here that in its figurative usage a sign will nevertheless retain its primary literal meaning, for the figurative depends on the literal for its very existence. The Old Testament stories, though containing a number of figurative meanings, are, for medieval exegetes, first of all historical accounts of the tribe of Israel; without this grounding, "higher" meanings would be quite impossible. Aesthetically and theologically, as Bogdanos has it, the interplay "between divine tenor and human vehicle conveys a sense of divine mystery more convincing than any conceptual formulation" (3–4).

Moreover, the tense, interlocking relation of literal and figurative signs is analogous to the entire structure of salvation. For just as the figurative depends on the literal, just as the immaterial can be conveyed only through the material, so, as Augustine writes, "the Word of God was made flesh, by assuming that flesh in which itself also might be manifested to men's senses" (15.11.20). The act of incarnation fuses the divine and the human into an absolute contiguity. Similarly, the didactic purpose of the *Pearl* poet depends on the way in which literal and figurative poles of language are collapsed in his poetics. In the poems as well as in the created universe, according to Bogdanos, "two opposing natures are brought together in a dynamic relationship" (9). Barthes's supposedly opposed horizontal and vertical poles of discourse are brought furiously together. The *Pearl* poet's art is thus above all "incarnational art," its structure analogous to God's divine artifice. As Bogdanos and Schotter have argued, his work is finally a soteriological exercise.

But at the same time—and here, I believe, we reach the heart of the matter—the fundamental theological separation of the earthly and the divine, of horizontal and vertical language, is paradoxically underscored in this process. It is worth recalling, and accepting unquestioningly, the Pearl Maiden's words of Mary:

> "O courteous queen!" that fair one cried,
> And kneeled down with covered face.
> "O matchless mother, fairest maid,
> Whose great and lofty gift is grace! . . .
> For piety the pure are paid.
> But no usurpers see this place!
> The empress pure of paradise
> Rules hell and heaven flawlessly,
> And earth, yet does no man disgrace;
> For she is queen of courtesy."
>
> *(433–36, 439–44)*

This moment bears every mark of Barthes's vertical language; it separates itself from a horizontality that would bind it to earth; the Maiden's words move upward, isolated and epiphanic; and in her speech as a whole "the Word shines forth," adorned only "with the violence of [its] irruption" (1967, 46, 50). Moreover, the high place held in heaven by the Maiden functions finally to render Mary's position all the more awesome and unearthly. Even as we experience the earthly and the divine as echoes of one another, paired and therefore intimately related, we are made acutely aware of the vast difference that separates them. The Maiden and Mary, in a sense, form mirror images of one another; and, as in a mirror, the original and the reflection are at once alike and reversed.

In the *Pearl* poet we are faced, in fact, with the paradox and mystery of the incarnation at the very center of Christianity. Bogdanos's argument is particularly helpful here. Reminding us of Pseudo-Dionysius's notion that the symbol "reveals truth while veiling it," Bogdanos states:

> In bringing together such vastly different natures, the incarnational symbol holds the maximum metaphoric tension, because it is more than metaphor. It insists on a sacramental identity between its terms, which all levels of human perception contradict. Because the tenor is unknown and fundamentally inexpressible, the vehicle tends to engulf it with its own reality and define it totally in its own terms. Yet the human mind resists this engulfment, escaping at the same time into new vehicles and new analogical relationships between distant realities.
>
> *(11–12)*

The vehicle (the Pearl Maiden, say, as individual girl) functions by referring to a half-absent, half-present tenor (in this case, the redeemed soul); the tenor in turn functions by residing within and, at the same time, escaping the vehicle. This movement transforms the normal relation of vehicle and tenor, of Barthes's horizontal and vertical language, into an endless circle on which horizontal and vertical modalities are continually doubling back on one another, alike and yet different. The material and the immaterial are sumultaneously bifurcated and collapsed.

The aesthetic and theologic are played out in the oscillations of the earthly and the divine: the meaning of one is ultimately located, finds both its displacement and its image, in the other. The Christian in search of salvation finds himself continually shuttling back and forth across the meanings of the poems as they simultaneously separate and join heaven and earth, vertical and horizontal language, tenor and vehicle. What he learns is that the physical is both separate from and a part of the metaphysical. For if, as Bogdanos states, incarnational art "insists on the reality of the physical as a means of representing the spiritual, and if the spiritual is to be understood in terms of the physical, then the very qualities and distinguishing characteristics of the physical shape the spiritual meaning in our minds and they become part of it" (10). The master trope of the *Pearl* poet, then, is a form of synecdoche; from the widest perspective, all things in history and on earth are seen ultimately to form a part of the whole, not only of God's creation and plan but of God himself. It is the poet's purpose to embody this mystery in an aesthetic that is also, in its way, an analogous part of the created and redeemed universe.

We can move, then, if only a step or two, beyond Auerbach's great division of Western representation into two vast traditions for which the works of Homer and the Old Testament writers comprise the inaugural paradigms. For Auerbach:

> The two styles, in their opposition, represent basic types: on the one hand fully externalized description, uniform illumination, uninterrupted connection, free expression, all events in the foreground, displaying unmistakable meanings, few elements of historical development and of psychological perspective; on the other, certain parts brought into high relief, others left obscure, abruptness, suggestive influence of the unexpressed, "background" quality, multiplicity of meanings and the need for interpretation. . . .
>
> *(23)*

One recognizes here an earlier version of Barthes's division of language into horizontal and vertical modalities; clearly, the duality remains to our day a powerful way of articulating a very real distinction in modes of Western representation. But with the *Pearl* poet in mind, we can suggest that there is yet a third order of representation. For here we confront these two modes, the vertical and the horizontal, ranged in a relation to one another that is at once fused and polarized. Heaven and earth are pressed into a contiguity, even as they remain starkly separated. And naturally enough, the great paradigm for the intense and paradoxical relation that issues forth as incarnational art is to be found neither in Homer nor in the Old Testament but in the numinous parables of Christ.

SAINT ERKENWALD

Saint Erkenwald combines the theme, very common in hagiography, of the incorrupt body and the legend, beginning in the eighth century, of Pope Gregory the Great's successful prayers for the soul of the entombed Roman emperor Trajan (Hulbert 1918–19; Peterson 1977, 38–45). Trajan became "a type of the righteous heathen, the just man whose eternal soul was nonetheless condemned because of his lack of knowledge of the grace of God," and his tale appears in the *Divine Comedy*, in both the B- and the C-text of *Piers Plowman*, and in Jacopo della Lana's commentary on Dante, *Comedia di Dante degli Allagherii* (Peterson 1977, 39). For Peterson, "the bringing together of the incorrupt body theme and the Trajan-Gregory legend, and the naturalization of the resulting whole into England and its association with St. Erkenwald seem to be the work of this poet. What inspired the fusion of themes, if anything other than the poet's imagination, it is not possible to say" (1977, 42).

The poem might be characterized as a drama at the apex of which heaven and earth, the universal and the local, are brought momentarily, complexly, and miraculously together. The story narrates a particular moment in the life of a particular saint that, at the same time, encapsulates and registers the scope of salvation, the most grandiose and sweeping gesture within the Christian schema. The miracle by which the judge's soul is freed from his body and transported to the heavenly feast operates at once as a specified and microscopically located moment in the history of London and as an echo of the vast gesture of Christ's sacrifice on earth. For if in the incarnation, the divine is brought down to earth for the purpose of redemption, in *Saint Erkenwald* what is at once a reversal and a reiteration of this process occurs: the earthly, the utterly fallen, is raised, redeemed, and brought into contact— indeed, communion—with the divine. And if in *Saint Erkenwald* a particular act of salvation is miraculously manifested, this event at the same time reminds us of the larger incarnation of Christ, which opens up the possibility of universal salvation. The tension *and* the harmony thus created between individual event and universal significance, between micro- and macro-narrative, could hardly be greater. God more or less improvised the redemption of man—who was not necessarily programmed to fall (see *Cleanness* 237–40)—as a modified version of His original, overarching scheme of things; similarly, this individual redemption of the just judge exemplifies the ability of the overarching scheme of things to be modified, softened, reversed even, in the name of mercy.

And in the poem it is Saint Erkenwald's tears that embody most fully the coincidence of the particular and the universal, the individual soul's salvation and the general possibility of human salvation as a whole. The saint's tears are simultaneously the outpourings of human emotion and the waters of baptism, the expression of individual grief and the divine agency of salvation.

> First Saint Erkenwald's eyes at the edges grew wet;
> He was speechless, sighing and sobbing aloud,
> As he paused at that place till composure returned.
> Toward the body he bowed, then, and bathed it in tears,
> As he let out: "O Lord, sustain life in this man!
> For this corpse I would quickly acquire Your pure,
> Holy water, with which I would wet him, and say:
> 'You are born again, baptized, and brought to new life
> By the Trinity's truth; although truant, you're cleansed!'
> Though he dropped into death, I'd have done thus Your will!"
>
> *(311–20)*

Saint Erkenwald's words here are plaintive, the mood of his statement optative; for after all, the saint is issuing a prayer rather than a formal baptism. If he had holy water (which he doesn't), then he'd baptize the judge (which he can't). The moment is pathetic in the best sense of the word, and as such, it encapsulates the judge's situation as a whole; though he had lived a just and worthy life, the possibility of salvation was, and seems to remain, starkly unavailable to him.

But a miracle intervenes:

> All the while he'd wept, as he worded his prayer,
> And his tears to the tomb had been tumbling in streams.
> When one fell on its face, the corpse faintly sighed, . . .
> "Good bishop, you've blessed me and brought me from gloom,
> Have saved thus my soul from suffering death!
> Through the water you wept and the words that you used,
> You have bathed me in baptism, brought me new life."
>
> *(321–23, 327–30)*

At issue here is the distinction (which is ultimately transcended) between prayer and baptism; Erkenwald's tearfully stated desire for holy water miraculously transforms into holy water the very tears that the desire occasioned in the first place. Emotional expression becomes a sort of ritual performance; prayer becomes baptism. The theology here is at once intensely legalistic (for the ritual trappings must be in place to make the baptism valid) *and* malleable (for those trappings can be improvised for the occasion). The poem's crucial miracle is neither the preservation nor the animation of the corpse, as critics have sometimes suggested; rather, it is the movement by which Saint Erkenwald's individual prayer and tears become the universally applicable "words and . . . water that wash away sin" (333).

And while the poem thus orchestrates a kind of harmony between human emotion and divine plan, it also orchestrates a relation between the pagan past and the Christian "present." The story, after all, narrates a moment in the history of London during which Erkenwald, overseeing the renovation of Saint Paul's, continues the work of his predecessor, Augustine, in converting pagan England to Christianity. Erkenwald's renovation of the church and salvation of the judge's soul thus echo and literalize Augustine's conversion of pagan England to Christianity, renewing the past by reconstituting it as Christian, much as the New Testament seeks to reconstitute and thus to renew the Old. But as the pagan past is thus transformed and Christianized, at the same time the Christian present is informed by the values supposedly operative in the pagan past. Interestingly, in *Saint Erkenwald*, those values embody what would become the Renaissance humanism that elevated disinterestedness and reason over divine intervention as instruments of justice. Yet, in the poem, the pagan and "humanistic" justice that the judge meted out needs to be recognized and rewarded by a miraculous intervention. As with Saint Paul's Cathedral, the pagan past is reclaimed and renovated in the name of Christianity even as it confers its values upon the Christian scheme.

A Christian sense of history is thus evoked in which the past is radically modified even as it is honored and preserved. What is more, as in the opening lines of *Sir Gawain and the Green Knight*, in *Saint Erkenwald* we are given a sense of London in particular—first named "New Troy" (25)—and England in general as an extension and transformation of pagan origins. What is at work, then, is a very early manifestation of the kind of developing nationalism that would not find full expression until, for instance, Shakespeare's *Henry V*. But if this protonationalism looks forward to the fully fledged expressions in the Renaissance of an English sense of national identity, at the same time it is based on a conservative impulse—everywhere evident in the *Pearl* poet—that seeks to recapture the cultural spirit (and the very alliterative verse) that flourished before the Norman Invasion of 1066.

Pagan justice and Christian mercy, the past and the present: in *Saint Erkenwald* these are ranged together by a process that might well be called *translation*, the transformation and renewal of one language, one order of things, by another. For in *Saint Erkenwald* in particular and in the *Pearl* poet as a whole, translation—a kind of renovation—is an overriding concern. And in the story of the bishop of London, this renovation is expressed primarily as a process of naming and renaming. New Troy becomes London; in "Christ's mighty name" (16) old temples are rechristened as churches; Peter, James, and Margaret replace Apollo, Jupiter, and Juno as the names revered—in each case, naming or renaming is at work. So if *Saint Erkenwald*'s most overt sacramental gesture is baptism, the poem is also deeply concerned not only with the process of christening (and rechristening) that conventionally attends baptism but also with the more general problem of translation as a form of renewal. As in Belshazzar's feast in *Cleanness*, the central narrative problem seems at first to be literal translation; a miraculously preserved corpse is discovered buried under a dead language, in a coffin whose lid has

> a border embellished with bright, golden words,
> Which were runelike, unreadable, rare, and obscure.
> What they meant—although masterfully made and intact—
> No one knew; they could never pronounce them aloud.
> At length many learned men looked on those words,
> But they failed to find out what those figures meant.
>
> *(51–56)*

But once Erkenwald has made his interventions, the central issue turns out not to be literal translation—which, in fact, is quietly forgotten— but instead, the spiritual translation brought about by baptizing the judge's soul. It is worth remembering here that although the poet has inherited the legend of Trajan from a fairly popular literary tradition, including the *Divine Comedy*—a poem that insistently names names—in *Saint Erkenwald* the judge is left anonymous, as though as unnameable as the untranslatable words on his tomb. If the Londoners were deeply worried about the corpse's identity, the poem, like the saint, ultimately renders such concerns insignificant. The judge's name matters little; his soul is what counts. The story thus replaces the hunger for translation with the process of transcendence. But in the *Pearl* poet in general, as we shall see, the two operations can never be finally separated.

PATIENCE

Patience—perhaps the earliest of the five poems—recasts into homiletic form the Old Testament story of Jonah, framing the tale of the reluctant prophet's mission to the capital of the Assyrian empire as a negative exemplum of the virtue of patience. As the homily unfolds, the Christian reader (or hearer) gradually gains an appreciation of the complexities and contours of this elusive virtue or, rather, *poynt* ("tenet") (1). A subtle amalgam of pious subordination to the will of God and lighthearted, urbane, and playful resignation to daily life's necessities, the virtue of patience is articulated in the homily as a *poynt* one attains, like Jonah, only begrudgingly. In this way, the achievement of virtue is represented as an interior psychologic drama, a dialogue or battle which the Christian must wage and win within himself or herself in order to be prepared for redemption. A supreme tension is enacted within the soul between the search for and the achievement of salvation. And this dramatic tension within the soul is echoed in what I have called the dimension of reflexivity the poet creates between his role as speaker and his story. In *Patience*, in fact, reflexivity becomes the implicit dilemma of the poem's production. For the "translator" of the story and the story itself share essential attributes. A glance at the poem's relation to its primary source will serve as an illustration.

From the characteristically laconic Vulgate translation of the Jonah story, we learn only that the prophet, after receiving God's injunction to bear His message to the Ninevites, flees instead to Tarshish: "Et surrexit Jonas, ut fugeret in Tharsis a facie Domini" (Jonah 1:3) or, as I would translate the Latin translation: "And Jonah got up in order to take flight to Tharsis [and to flee] from the face of God." In the *Pearl* poet's "translation" of the Vulgate, by contrast, we are given a monologue that reveals in elaborate detail the immediate and ongoing condition of Jonah's mind:

"If I bow to His bidding and bring them His words,
And those townspeople take me, my troubles would start!
He Himself just now said they are sinful, each one;
If I tender such tidings, they'll take me at once,
Put me in prison, place me in stocks,
Confine me in fetters, and fling out my eyes!
Here's a marvelous message to meet them all with!
These are fine words to fling amongst foes in that town!"

(75–82)

Here, as on other occasions, the *Pearl* poet expands upon his source, articulating his character's psychological motivations where the original is silent. The poet simultaneously achieves several purposes by elucidating the reasons for Jonah's flight: anagogically, the relation of Jonah and Christ is underscored; dramatically, we enjoy a richer, more generously sketched, and certainly more bathetic character than the Vulgate offers; didactically, the irony is emphasized that Jonah exposes himself to greater perils in his attempt to flee lesser; and so on.

But above all, what the *Pearl* poet has supplied is a dimension of reflexivity absent from, or at any rate submerged in, the original; for at the levels of both style and narration, the poet develops as his central problem the issue of transmitting the word of God. This is quite overtly his artistic task as well as his art's expressed theme; the poem, above all, bears a message about Jonah's reluctant bearing of messages, forming an embellished translation of a story which is itself implicitly concerned with the problem of translation. *Translation*—etymologically, a "bearing across" of a message—constitutes the theme that affiliates Jonah and the narrator of *Patience*. Just as both bear sacred messages to their audiences, so each is in the literal sense a kind of translator.

Everywhere in *Patience*, in fact, we are confronted with the issue of bearing or translating the word of God; and this issue is always fraught with a special sense of urgency, even where it is overtly comical. This urgency is, above all, a function of the subtle parallels the speaker develops between the material of the story and its transmission. Again and again, the narrator's situation is implicitly compared with Jonah's:

For playmates Dame Patience and Poverty are.
I must suffer their sting, since I'm stuck with the two! . . .
For what good is it, grudging and grieving? What use?

If my lord, as he likes, on a lark sends me off,
Sends me riding or running to Rome on a chore,
What would grumbling get me but grief for my pains?
He would surely insist, though I squabbled and writhed;
And I'd suffer for sure, when I should have complied
Without fighting so fiercely the fate of my lot.

                    (45–46, 50–56)

The tone here of irony and light comicality is at once reinforced and undercut by the comparison the homilist draws between himself and the Old Testament prophet. The poem enacts, even as it narrates, the renewal of prophecy; it is thus an instance of what Perry Meisel calls "reflexive realism, the secret of virtually all strong artistic discourse," in which "narration and story coincide precisely but metaphorically, analogously rather than literally—a perfect equation of *récit* and *histoire* even as they are different. Reflexive realism narrates itself by narrating something else like it. . . . In reflexive realism, rhetorical and representational planes, *récit* and *histoire*, are doubles rather than twins" (46). We will discover this technique, transformed and deepened, in the metaphorical dimensions of *Cleanness* and *Pearl*.

CLEANNESS

For what has been considered its "disunity"—and too often without a full appreciation of the problems such a term involves—the critical literature surrounding the poems under discussion has almost unanimously judged *Cleanness* the weakest of the five. Charles Moorman's introduction to his edition of the four Cotton Nero poems serves both as summary and synecdoche of the reception the homily has experienced for years. For Moorman, as for most of its readers, *Cleanness* "seems at times diffuse, even long-winded. The poet here has almost too much material to handle, and the kind of amplification which was rigorously controlled in *Patience* occasionally seems digressive in [*Cleanness*]" (1977, 28). To be at once diffuse, long-winded, and digressive is, above all, to fail to have a center, a single, unifying intention. Scholars have thought that in *Cleanness* the sheer exuberance of homiletic performance somehow overwhelms the very reason for the homily: to warn, to exemplify, and ultimately to exhort.

Recently, however, critics have modified this view, looking behind what Andrew and Waldron call the "apparent farfetchedness" of

Cleanness's materials to discover the "unity-in-diversity" of the poem's design (21). It has come to be understood, for instance, that through subtle thematic modulations among the negative exempla the poet reiterates and, at the same time, deepens and transforms his centralizing definition of cleanness. An appreciation has developed for the function of the linking sections. The description, for example, of the purity of Christ's birth, which leads to the information that Christ broke bread with a supernatural neatness, far from being an extraneous and eccentric detail, serves a unifying function within the poem as a whole. It recalls the descriptions of the fall of Lucifer and of Adam where we learned that God's wrath is mitigated by a profound and eventually overwhelming mercy; it makes a distinction between human and supernatural cleanness in which each informs the other; and finally, more particularly, it links the stories of Abraham and Lot with those of Nebuchadnezzar and Belshazzar by reiterating and reshaping the poem's concern with politeness, table manners, hospitality, and the proper handling of vessels, holy or otherwise.

Another target of criticism in *Cleanness* has been its theology and, specifically, its representation of God. Assuming everywhere in the *Pearl* poet's work a sharp delineation between heaven and earth, between the spiritual and the carnal, that the poems themselves explicitly oppose, critics have pointed to certain infelicities in *Cleanness*'s God. Even A. C. Spearing—a critic insightful enough to note the poet's habit of synthesizing, rather than discriminating, moral and physical meanings—reflects this view when he judges God's exchange with the incredulous Sarah as it is transformed by the *Pearl* poet to be unsuccessful, or at least counterproductive, to the poem's larger meaning. Whereas God in the Vulgate responds to Sarah's denial with an august and majestic terseness—"Non est, inquit, ita: sed risisti" (Genesis 18.15)—*Cleanness*'s God is more colloquial, in Spearing's words, "familiar, intimate, and almost domestic" (1970, 60):

"Now forget it!" said God. "You've gone far enough!
For you laughed very low; but we'll leave it at that."

(669–70)

Spearing condemns this moment as inappropriate; for him, the poet's brilliant sense of the quotidian and his keen ear for the idiomatic—usually right and poetically vibrant—have here undermined his larger poetic purpose: "I think one might reasonably have doubts about the wisdom of his treatment of this particular moment, because the gain in realism surely involves a loss in suggestiveness—suggestiveness about what cannot be fully stated, the nature of the divine as it impinges on the human. In the speech just quoted, it seems to me that God has become man all too completely for the purposes of this particular story" (1970, 60). To his portrayal of God, as to the obstinate speech he gives Lot's wife, the poet has added an artistic touch "too delightfully comic for the mysterious import of the situation" (1970, 61).

Critics, then, often assume a fundamental incompatibility between the divine and the human in the *Pearl* poet and, accordingly, become ill at ease when they discover in *Cleanness* a God capable of boisterous, almost malicious rage, of poignant regret, or of colloquial, even quaint, expressions and attitudes. But since we encounter explicitly and consistently anthropomorphic constructions of divine reality throughout the poem, perhaps we would do well to accept such representations as a fundamental part of the poet's purpose. We would thus avoid accusing him of aesthetic infelicity and assume instead that if God in *Cleanness* is capable of quotidian gestures, that characterization is not a flaw in the poem but an inextricable part of its theological design. Far from agreeing that the poet portrays a God who "has become man all too completely for the purposes of this particular story," we should consider the possibility that the purpose of this particular story necessitates just such a conflation of the divine and human.

But in doing so we immediately confront a difficulty. For at the same time—and here we approach the very center of the poem—the impulse of so many critics to find a persistent irreconcilability between divine and human planes cannot be denied. The parable of the wedding feast that leads up to the first major exemplum is a case in point. There the host rages over the ill-clad guest:

> "Take him!" he cried,
> "Bailiff, now bind at his back both his hands,
> Fix fast on his feet fetters of iron,
> Stick him in stocks, and stow him away
> In my deepest of dungeons where dwells biting grief,
> Where weeping and woe, endless wailing and pain
> Live together—until he is taught how to dress!"
>
> *(154–60)*

Here is a frightening, physically vivid scene. The prisoner, helplessly bound and fettered, is displayed at first in the open, public, and brilliantly lit space of shame, only to be thrust into the dark, private cell reverberating with the sounds of his own gnashing agony. Indeed, the punishment meted out is so vividly realized, the judgment so grim and final, and the description of the tortures so lovingly specific in its details that the allegorical exegesis (itself unusual for the *Pearl* poet) of clothes as works seems unsatisfyingly remote and artificial:

> Of what kind are these clothes you must clothe yourself in
> To appear before that Prince in the proper attire?
> In a word: what you wear are the works you've performed;
> They're the love and the labors that lie in your heart.
>
> *(169–72)*

To be sure, this gloss provides an effect soothing in retrospect by restoring, albeit partially, our sense of the propriety of the cosmic system of rewards and punishments. It comes, nevertheless, far too late to restructure our response to the sufferings of the guest "clothed in the coarsest of rags" (135). Indeed, here as elsewhere in the poem, the vehicle threatens to overwhelm the tenor entirely. The "Creator of all" (212), we think, can have nothing in common with this fiercely unpredictable "rich man" (51)!

But we are wrong. And our response, I would argue, is completely in keeping with the poet's didactic purpose. In order to "look on our Lord" (28), we must dress ourselves in the cleanest of spiritual clothes; but to do so, we must first earn an understanding of the mysterious and profound relation of earthly and heavenly things, of the material and the immaterial. First, that is, we must literally dress appropriately; for, as Elizabeth Keiser argues, there is a "close connection between ideals of social decorum and the service of God, in both His heavenly and His earthly households" (64). And, as the poet insists again and again, God *is indeed* a kind of "rich man" (51) who "held a marriage feast meet for his male heir to have" (52).

PEARL

An appreciation of this dynamic provides an insight into the enigmatic dream vision, *Pearl*. It helps, as well, to understand the trouble with

either side of the great debate that has surrounded this poem since
Morris's edition of 1864: whether the poem is fundamentally elegiac
or allegorical. Recent critics have come to understand the coexistence
of these dimensions, along with several others, within the poem. For in
the image of the pearl, we confront a supreme mixture of physical and
spiritual meaning, of physical *as* spiritual meaning; and it is consequently
detrimental to our sense of the poem's richness to discount either the
elegiac or the allegorical dimension. The image marks perhaps the
finest example of the poet's incarnational art. As in *Cleanness*, the
overriding poetic in *Pearl* involves a eucharistic troping in which the
spiritual and the earthly are joined by being displaced onto each other.

Spearing's point is quite true: "the pearl symbol is not static but
dynamic: it develops in meaning as the poem extends itself in time,
and this development in meaning is coordinated with the developing
human drama of the relationship between the Dreamer and the Maiden"
(1966, 101). What begins in the poem's first line as a purely worldly
pearl becomes by its last the soul itself, and our growing comprehension
of the poem's mysteries through the course of reading is in this sense
perfectly analogous to the Dreamer's. But although our understanding
of the spiritual realm develops along with the Dreamer's, the transcen-
dental referent remains forever just beyond reach. Does the pearl finally
typify the soul? God? Newborn innocence? Significantly, the question
is left very much open. Simultaneously knowing and unknowable, the
pearl directs the Dreamer both to a full apprehension of his loss and
to a sense of the incompleteness of his apprehension. She is at once the
lost object of his desire and the powerful signifier of that desire,
representing both the possibility and, for fallen man, the impossibility
of transcending loss. Even as the spiritual and the worldly coincide in
the pearl symbol, they remain starkly separated.

And this is the case with the poem in general. The heavenly order
in *Pearl* is undoubtedly structured like the worldly; in fact, it resembles
a late medieval political state. Like a divinely sanctioned nation arranged
under its sovereign, heaven is cooperative, hierarchically ordered, and
theoretically unchanging. Each part within it has its fixed role, like the
limbs of a body. To the Dreamer's suggestion that the Maiden has
usurped her superiors by acceding as queen of heaven, she responds
with skillful, if conventional, rhetoric:

> "Should likened limbs each other dread?
> Should foot fight foot, or arm fight chest?

Is by your hand your head depressed
When wearing wondrous jewelry?"

(463–66)

The historically ubiquitous metaphor of the body politic—behind which
lies the notion of the universe as a series of successively larger bodies
or microcosms—has here the effect of gathering the vastness of heaven
into the confines of a single physical body, of incarnating and thereby
focusing the entire metaphysical order. All of heaven is rhetorically
transported to earth; indeed, it seems to walk about, embodied, wearing
jewelry or trinkets. Heaven, in fact, is a kind of Christian noble.

The metaphysical realm in *Pearl* is thus perceived and depicted as
an amplified chivalric order. The souls of the saved are depicted as
kings and queens. They live, as the Dreamer predicted, in a kind of
castle, timeless and monumental beyond measure, to be sure, but
nevertheless unmistakably late fourteenth century in its architectural
outlines. Mary, we are told, is the queen of courtesy. And here and
there in the poem, the emotionally fraught, conventional language of
courtly love surfaces. The Dreamer, for instance, in the depth of his
grief, pines as a young man would for a lost loved one:

A lovelorn, longing look I bear
For that precious pearl without a spot.

(11–12)

Or again, when Christ woos and marries the Maiden, He does so in the
words of a lover in medieval romance:

" 'Come hither, love, whom I will wed.
You're pure and precious certainly.' "

(763–64)

Of course, the purport of these words is fundamentally spiritual, and
their effect edifying for Dreamer and audience alike. They enact—and
beautifully so—the highest moment of Christian reality, the redemption
of the individual soul. Nevertheless, the dimension within them of
sexual affection and passion cannot fail to move and, perhaps, seduce
us; in *Pearl*, indeed, the union of the soul with Christ in its heavenly

salvation is just a little bit sexy. At any rate, it occurs within the codes of a medieval chivalric order. The spiritual and earthly orders are linked in a mysterious and intimate proximity.

Yet the very language in the poem that functions to underscore this proximity of the physical and the metaphysical indicates the unbridgeable difference between the two realms. The problem of the pearl's place in heaven, the focus of so much of the dialogue between the Maiden and the Dreamer, is a case in point. When he learns that the pearl has been married to Christ and crowned as the queen in bliss, the Dreamer protests:

> "Can this be true?
> Please ease your anger if I err.
> Are you the bride of heaven blue
> Whom people praise without a peer?
> From Mary, we believe, grace grew
> When, but a virgin flower, she bore
> Our Lord. Who wears her crown? In lieu
> Of what? A trait more fine and fair?"
>
> *(421–28)*

When the Dreamer later reiterates his complaint that by becoming queen of heaven the Maiden has received there " 'too dear a due [*date*]' " (492), she responds by punning on his word, at once deepening and transforming its meaning: "Unduly [literally, "without date or limit"] God grants dear largess" (493). The problem here involves the paradoxical idea of a hierarchy of equality in heaven, and the point is that heavenly hierarchy is profoundly different from its earthly counterparts in that it functions without the subordination that characterizes earthly power structures:

> "This court within our Lord's great land
> Accords with His arrangings.
> For all the souls that herein stand
> Are of their realm great queens or kings.
> No one would want another's land;
> We're pleased by neighbors' high holdings
> And would their crown and court expand,
> If we could ever cause such things.
> But she from whom Christ's good grace springs

Reigns over all in royalty.
No envy, though, by this she brings;
For she is queen of courtesy."

                    (445–56)

The soul in heaven thus participates in what Georges Bataille oxymo-
ronically calls a *unique relation*, a notion that the Dreamer finds almost
untenably paradoxical. Each soul is simultaneously king or queen—at
once supreme and unique—*and* part of the populace, that is, ranged
in a relational system. For on the one hand, as we know from the
Maiden's experience, the intimate and individual relation of the soul
to Christ in heaven is a kind of monogamous marital fusion of the soul
with God. But on the other hand, this relation is the same for each one
among the 144,000 souls in the New Jerusalem. Meanwhile, Mary reigns
over *all*, somehow displacing no one; her royalty shines above the others
even as the others are, for their part, no less royal. Heaven is thus a
kind of glorious polygamy; and the soul is simultaneously the center of
the heavenly system and just another cog within it, a queen and at the
same time a member of a harem.

Critics impatient with what they perceive as the Dreamer's stubborn-
ness or stupidity fail to see him as a figure of universal fallen conscious-
ness for which heavenly reality is ineluctably, if not unacceptably,
paradoxical. What is more, they fail to discover themselves in the
character of the Dreamer. But everywhere in *Pearl* an insistent paral-
lelism is established between the Dreamer as he confronts the vision,
and the audience as it confronts the poem. Like the Dreamer who
complains,

"Your story seems unreasonable!
God's righteousness rules all mankind
Or Holy Writ is a foolish fable!"

                    (590–92)

we have questioned the poem's orthodoxy—itself a problematic no-
tion—bringing to bear Scripture and tradition to refute the Maiden's
story. Like the Dreamer who wishes to wade across the river, we long
to penetrate the inner sphere of the poem, its final and finalizing
meaning from which we feel forever excluded. And like the Dreamer,
we have come slowly and imperfectly to an understanding of the dual

nature of the pearl itself; for it is at once a little girl (and the poem a kind of elegy) and an allegorical embodiment (what Bogdanos calls an image of the ineffable).

And it is our sense of this paradox, perhaps, that links us most intimately with the figure of the Dreamer. What the Dreamer finally learns or, rather, accepts is the impossible lesson of the heavenly simultaneity of identity and difference. The entire machinery of the poem responds to the question:

> "O pearl," I asked, "prepared in white,
> Are you my pearl for whom I've pined
> And hung my head each hopeless night
> When gall and grief my heart confined?"

> *(241–44)*

The answer is yes and no. For this is at once the same little girl restored and something utterly transformed, something "healed within this heavenly house" (271) and changed into a pearl of price.

The duality of the pearl, moreover, is never simply transcended. Indeed, dramatically, if not symbolically, the poem as a whole narrates rather the *failure* of transcendence. After all, in the end, the Dreamer is abruptly returned as it were to earth (or to consciousness?), reconciled to his loss but bereft nevertheless. And interestingly for a visionary poem, visionary immediacy is never really achieved. For though the Dreamer, granted a vision, has "passed over" into the realm of the otherworldly, there he nevertheless discovers himself starkly divided from the Pearl Maiden by the river whose source, curiously, turns out to be Christ's wound. It is as though Christ's blood—the very material and medium of man's redemption and therefore the vehicle for his reunion with God—also operates to enforce the separation. And when, at the poem's end, the Dreamer is granted the vision of the New Jerusalem, it turns out that the vision is, like the rest of the *Pearl* poet's works, deeply mediated by a prior text. For, as the Dreamer is at pains to point out, he sees not the New Jerusalem per se but instead *what John saw* when *he* saw the New Jerusalem: in a word, not a vision but a vision of a vision.

And it is this vision that registers the act of looking and, by extension, knowing, as a central problem in the poem. The Dreamer's gaze (like ours when we read the visionary poem) partakes of a moment when the veil of fallen consciousness has been temporarily lifted; yet at the same time it reinforces a sense of fallenness and mediation as humanity's essential condition by the Dreamer's unbridgeable distance from the city. His gaze conflates a fallen, imperfect perception of things together with a burning perceptual clarity. And however moving the visionary experience of *Pearl* might be, it is perhaps the fact that the vision nevertheless remains somehow incomplete—and abruptly cut short—that operates as the most compelling, because poignant, aspect of the poem.

SIR GAWAIN AND THE GREEN KNIGHT

Testimony to the poet's ability to master the most disparate forms, *Sir Gawain and the Green Knight* is justly esteemed as one of the finest Arthurian romances written in English. The fabric of the poem is a skilled and delicate interweaving of three traditional narrative elements: the beheading game, the exchange of winnings, and the temptation. In each Gawain is tested; and the reader, along with Gawain, is again and again lulled into complacency by the well-defined divisions that seem to separate the three story elements, only to discover the surprising way in which they impinge upon one another. The temptation scenes, for instance, appear to test only Gawain's chastity; but as the story unfolds, we come to understand the integral part they play in the beheading game with which the poem begins and ends. As Marie Borroff points out:

> The most dangerous temptation is that which presents itself unexpectedly, as a side issue, while we are busy resisting another. Gawain accepts the belt because he recognizes in it a marvelously appropriate device for evading imminent danger, "a jewel for his jeopardy." At the same time, his act may well seem a way of granting the importunate lady a final favor while evading her amorous invitation. Its full meaning as a cowardly, and hence covetous, grasping at life is revealed to him only later, and with stunning force.
>
> *(1967, ix)*

In fact, the entire story turns out to be framed by a still-larger story: Morgan le Fay's traditional enmity for the court of Arthur. Once again, what we thought the central issue, the very ground of the narrative, is displaced by a different conflict.

Like *Pearl*, *Sir Gawain* exhibits a number of structurally intricate patterns. It begins and ends, for example, with references to the sack of Troy and with the New Year season. Indeed, as Moorman points out, the three introductory elements—"the reference to the fall of Troy, the account of the founding of Britain by the Trojan Brutus, and the setting of the scene in Arthur's court"—are "almost verbally repeated in reverse order to round out and conclude the poem" (1977, 39). A number of motifs and touches are, in fact, carefully doubled in the course of the poem: Gawain's donning of his armor at Arthur's court and at Bertilak's castle, in both cases lovingly described; Gawain's leave-taking at Camelot and at Bertilak's castle; the Green Knight's spectacular departure from the hall and Gawain's, both attended by sparks; the two confession scenes; and so forth. It has often been noted, moreover, that the three hunting scenes embody in miniature the patterns at work in the poem as a whole. They are wrapped, as it were, around the three temptation scenes. We begin and end with the glorious violence of the chase in the natural world; and interposed among the grand descriptions of the hunt of the deer, the boar, and the fox are the comic, uncannily analogous, and almost claustrophobic bedroom scenes.

This structural balancing is, of course, in keeping with the theme of the balance and alternation of "bane and cheer" (19) which the poem's first "wheel" announces and which flows as an undercurrent through the entire romance. In the poem, the world is envisioned as a place given to vast oscillations:

> If this story ends sadly, though, suffer no shock;
> For with many drinks men are made merry and light,
> Although charging time changes, unchecked, all it touches;
> And the last things are less like the first than we wish.
>
> (496–99)

Indeed, this principle of unexpectedness and oscillation functions almost as a cosmic law, and it incorporates both the world of human rituals—"After Christmastime comes on the coldest of Lents" (502)—and the world of nature:

> But the season of summer comes suddenly on,
> When Zephyrus strokes every seedling and herb.

Fully pleased is the plant that can play in such wind;
After dawn, when the dew finally drops from his leaves,
He bathes in the beams of the bright summer sun.
But Harvest comes hurriedly, hastening him on,
Reminding him to ripen before arrival of winter.
With his droughts he drives the dust from the ground;
He fans that dust free from the face of the earth.
The wild, rising wind starts wrestling the sun.
The leaves from the linden alight on the earth.
The grass that was green turns to gray in the field;
All ripens and rots that had risen that spring.

(516–28)

The description is worth quoting at length not only for its intrinsic beauty but also for its function as a correlative of Gawain's psychological state. The internal and the external echo each other; and both are equally subject to the changing, cyclical nature of things.

It is within this continually changing order that Gawain is called upon to demonstrate—or fail to demonstrate, as the case may be—the virtue of loyalty, a kind of stability amid the vicissitudes of the evidently unstable cosmos. John Gardner has argued that the dramatic tension in *Gawain*—similar to that in the *Pearl*—is the conflict between human selfishness and the ideal of selfless courtesy; and here, as in the *Pearl*, the conflict is rooted in mutability, the condition of human existence within nature. The poet sets up the conflict at once, focusing in the opening lines (as he will do in the closing lines) on what Gardner calls the vanity of mortal kingdoms (70).

And this conflict, to be sure, lies at the center of the romance. But it would be slightly more accurate, I think, to say that the poem concerns the embodiment in the real political world of ideal codes of behavior, the transposition or translation into the world of heavenly virtues—an admittedly problematic, if not impossible, enterprise. For *Sir Gawain and the Green Knight* concerns, above all, the relation of a very real and individual knight to the chivalric and Christian ideals symbolized, for instance, in the pentangle depicted on Gawain's shield. Much criticism has pondered the precise nature of the five virtues—*fraunchyse, felaȝschyp, clannes, cortaysye,* and *pité* (652–54 of the original)—for which the pentangle stands; and the poem itself is often read, as Gardner's introduction demonstrates, as a drama in which the character of Gawain is tested and judged according to the degree to which he falls short of these ideals. And again, this is certainly the source of much of the local conflict and characterology of the poem.

But all along, what is thrown into question is the extent to which the virtues of the heavenly order can be reconciled with the worldly. We are deeply interested, of course, in the fate of the individual hero; at the same time, however, a number of poetic devices—a grandiose narrative technique, the use of traditionally symbolic situations (quests, temptations), and elements of the supernatural—alert us to the play of wider issues.

Primarily, I would argue, the poem narrates the testing of the chivalric system of behavior in order to articulate that behavior as an ideal *negotiation* between heavenly virtue and political reality. Reflexively, this negotiation is itself embodied in the poem through a series of worldly negotiations in which Gawain becomes engaged: with the Green Knight in the beheading game, with Bertilak in the exchange of winnings, and with the lady in the temptation scenes. In each, Gawain enters into—or tries to refuse—contracts, promises, quasi-feudal arrangements; and the drama of the poem, as well as its more symbolic dimensions, lies precisely in the nature of the problems attending these contracts, interestingly called *games*. The story of *Sir Gawain and the Green Knight* is, in fact, a triad of overlapping stories, each of which concerns the machinery of contract. It is their overlap that creates the tension, for Gawain enters into contracts which, by the nature of their terms, cannot all be completely honored. His individual "bad faith" is surely an issue worthy of the vast amount of discussion it has received in the critical literature, and as readers we must never push it from the center of the poem, where it belongs.

At the same time, however, *Sir Gawain* is concerned with the possibility of a specific system of relations among people—that is to say, with the very notion of the chivalric order—that echoes the fundamental relation of the individual soul with God. To honor a promise in the political arena is analogous to upholding a heavenly virtue on earth; and in the poem, when Gawain breaks his contract with Bertilak, it becomes impossible to distinguish the spiritual from the worldly dimension of his fault. Reminding us that "the moral term *Schuld* [guilt] has its origin in the very material term *Schulden* [to be indebted]" (194), Nietzsche underscores the problem of spiritual and worldly contracts: "To breed an animal with the right to make promises—is not this the paradoxical problem nature has set itself with regard to man?" (189). It is within the phenomenon of contracts that the heavenly and the worldly orders are conflated in the poem. And this problem is perhaps most evidently revealed in the puzzling final confession of Gawain at the Green Chapel.

Throughout the entire scene there is operating a fine mixture of the
language of business (and games) and the language of spiritual confession.
The Green Knight clearly behaves as a kind of businessman. When
Gawain threatens to answer with violence any further blows, the Green
Knight responds:

"Be less bellicose, bold man, nobody has erred;
No one here has behaved in a hostile, bad way.
What our covenant called for I've carried out here.
You've been paid what I promised; that's perfectly fair.
I release you at last from all lingering debts."

(2338–42)

At the same time, the Green Knight functions as a priest, and Gawain
as a confessing sinner; indeed, as J. A. Burrow points out, the scene
"follows closely the actual order of the confessional" (127). Gawain
restores the belt, and confesses:

"I succumbed here to cowardice, cared for my life,
And, becoming most covetous, keenly fell short
Of the loyalty, largess, belonging to knights.
Now I'm faulty and false, afraid for my life."

(2379–82)

This speech ends, as Burrow says, "with a general confession of full
guilt, a request for penance to be imposed, and a promise of future
amendment" (129–30):

"Profound's my perfidy.
But if I ever could
Regain your grace, I'd be
Most grateful, ever good."

(2385–88)

The Green Knight, for his part, assumes the role of confessor:

"Any harm I have had is hereby amended;
As you've fully confessed, you are fully absolved.

All your penance you paid at the point of my blade;
You're as free of your faults as you'd find yourself if
Since your birth you had been unbendingly pure."

(2390–94)

This moment recalls the "real" confession at Bertilak's castle in which Gawain

confessed his sins and was shriven at once.
For his major and minor sins, mercy he asked.
When he prayed of the priest to be piously cleansed,
He absolved Gawain certainly; safely he'd face,
Though it dawned the next day, dreaded doomsday itself.

(1880–84)

What has happened, I think, is a fusion of the heavenly and earthly realms into one, a complete conflation of the two orders. The poem finally depicts chivalry as what Andrew and Waldron call a "blend of manners, social obligation, and high religious ideals" (40). Where *Pearl* had evoked a sense of the simultaneous proximity and remoteness of the heavenly and worldly realms, *Sir Gawain* is concerned with establishing a middle ground, with imagining through the model of a chivalric order a political arena in which heavenly ideals are registered and confirmed on earth. This naturally involves a compromise of sorts; the two realms remain fundamentally incompatible. The heart of the drama derives precisely from this incompatibility; *Sir Gawain and the Green Knight* is the story, among other things, of the fault of a single knight, not an account of an idealized triumph. Nevertheless, embodied in the enigmatic confession scene at the Green Chapel is the poet's projection of a chivalric order that enacts on earth as nearly as possible the abstractions and perfect arrangements of heaven.

Pearl

The facing-page text is reproduced from *The Poems of the Pearl Manuscript: Pearl, Cleanness, Patience, Sir Gawain and the Green Knight*, ed. Malcolm Andrew and Ronald Waldron (rev. ed. University of Exeter, 1987).

I

Perle plesaunte, to prynces payė
To clanly clos in goldė so clere:
Oute of oryent, I hardyly saye,
Ne prouėd I neuer her precios pere.
So roundė, so rekėn in vche araye,   5
So smal, so smoþe her sydez were;
Queresoeuer I jugged gemmez gayė
I sette hyr sengeley in synglure.
Allas! I leste hyr in on erbere;
Þur3 gresse to groundė hit fro me yot.   10
I dewyne, fordolked of luf-daungere
Of þat pryuy perle withouten spot.

Syþen in þat spote hit fro me sprange,
Ofte haf I wayted, wyschande þat wele
Þat wont watz whyle deuoyde my wrange   15
And heuen my happe and al my hele—
Þat dotz bot þrych my hert þrange,
My breste in bale bot bolne and bele.
3et þo3t me neuer so swete a sange
As stylle stoundė let to me stele.   20
Forsoþe þer fleten to me fele.
To þenke hir color so clad in clot!
O moul, þou marrez a myry juele,
My priuy perle withouten spotte.

Þat spot of spysez mot nedez sprede,   25
Þer such rychez to rot is runne,
Blomez blayke and blwe and rede
Þer schyne ful schyr agayn þe sunne.
Flor and fryte may not be fede
Þer hit doun drof in moldez dunne,   30
For vch gresse mot grow of graynez dede;
No whete were ellez to wonez wonne.
Of goud vche goude is ay bygonne:
So semly a sedė mo3t fayly not,
Þat spryngande spycez vp ne sponne   35
Of þat precios perle wythouten spotte.

To þat spot þat I in speche expoun
I entred in þat erber grene,
In Auguste in a hy3 seysoun,
Quen corne is coruen wyth crokez kene.   40
On huyle þer perle hit trendeled doun
Schadowed þis wortez ful schyre and schene:

I

Pearl, O pleasure for a prince,
Enclosed in gold, so clean and clear,
I own that all the orient's
Fine pearls, though pure, provide no peer
So round, so rich, so wrapped in glints   5
Of light, so small, so smooth and dear.
In gems that I have judged, no hints
Are seen of her superior.
In a garden green with grass, my cheer
Was lost! It lunged to land. O lot!   10
A lovelorn, longing look I bear
For that precious pearl without a spot.

In the spot where she once sprang from me,   *Adam's loins?*
I've pined and prayed to glean that pure
And welcome one that wondrously
Brought happiness and health. But care,   15
All raging, racked me wretchedly;
And burning bitterness I bore.
Yet somehow there was sung to me
A sweeter song than chorister   20
Could ever chant; there came such cheer
In dreams of her, though wrapped in rot!
O earth, you rob a rich and rare
And precious pearl without a spot!

That spot with spices sweet was spread;   25
For riches there to rot were run.
But blooms of yellow, blue, and red
Still shimmered in the shining sun!   *humanized gem*
For flower or fruit will not fall dead
If grown against that pearl's grain.   30
From dying husks new husks are spread;
No wheat would else reach winnow-bin.
From good is every good begun.
So strong a single seed could not
But fructify; so flowers sprung   35
From precious pearl without a spot.

In that same spot where I had stayed
I gained a garden, gleaming bright,
When August wheat is harvested,
With sickles scythed, and stacked up tight.   40
Among the shrubs where she had sped—
Some stood in shade and some in light—

Gilofre, gyngure, and gromylyoun,
And pyonys powdered ay bytwene.
ȝif hit watz semly on to sene,   45
A fayrre flayr ȝet fro hit flot,
Þer wonys þat worþyly, I wot and wene,
My precious perle wythouten spot.

Bifore þat spot my honde I spennd
For care ful colde þat to me caȝt;   50
A deuely dele in my hert denned,
Þaȝ resoun sette myseluen saȝt.
I playned my perle þat þer watz penned,
Wyth fyrce skyllez þat faste faȝt.
Þaȝ kynde of Kryst me comfort kenned,   55
My wreched wylle in wo ay wraȝte.
I felle vpon þat floury flaȝt,
Suche odour to my hernez schot;
I slode vpon a slepyng-slaȝte
On þat precios perle withouten spot.   60

II

Fro spot my spyryt þer sprang in space;
My body on balke þer bod. In sweuen
My goste is gon in Godez grace,
In auenture þer meruaylez meuen.
I ne wyste in þis worlde quere þat hit wace,   65
Bot I knew me keste þer klyfez cleuen.
Towarde a foreste I bere þe face,
Where rych rokkez wer to dyscreuen.
Þe lyȝt of hem myȝt no mon leuen,
Þe glemande glory þat of hem glent,   70
For wern neuer webbez þat wyȝez weuen
Of half so dere adubbemente.

Dubbed wern alle þo downez sydez
With crystal klyffez so cler of kynde.
Holtewodez bryȝt aboute hem bydez   75
Of bollez as blwe as ble of Ynde;
As bornyst syluer þe lef on slydez,
Þat þike con trylle on vch a tynde;
Quen glem of glodez agaynz hem glydez,
Wyth schymeryng schene ful schrylle þay schynde.   80
Þe grauayl þat on grounde con grynde
Wern precious perlez of oryente;
Þe sunne bemez bot blo and blynde
In respecte of þat adubbement.

Gillyflower, ginger, and gromwell bred,
And peonies pleased with pure delight.
So sweet it was, all shining bright,   45
So fresh the fragrance of that plot,
I'm certain that it was the site
Of precious pearl without a spot.

Before that spot I hung my head;
My care had cut me to the core.   50
From wounds of woe within I bled.
Though reason bid me rage no more,
I suffered still; my sadness spread.
I knew of neither wisdom nor
The consolation Christ had bred.   55
My saddened soul still showed its sore;
I fell upon that grassy floor
Asleep, my ravaged senses shot,
And dreamed a swooning dream before
My precious pearl without a spot.   60

II

My soul soared from that spot to the sky,
While on the land my limbs lay still,
And with God's mercy hovered high.
Afaint, I floated from a hill,
Wandering I knew not where or why.   65
Sharp cliffs of stone stood tall and still
Above the trees I turned to spy.
Rich rocks were ranged along that hill.
Those stunning, stately stones would fill
A lea with light most ambient!   70
No man-made finery or frill
Was woven with such wonderment!

Each wide and wondrous way I traced,
Each cliff with clear and crystal side.
Below each, far-flung forests faced   75
The bowers about with boles blue-dyed.
The leaves, like lovely silver laced
With light, on limbs lay low and wide;
When rays of sun along them raced,
They shot out light from side to side.   80
The place, too, precious pearls supplied,
And gems and jewels of orient;
The sun itself is dim beside
The flame of that fair wonderment.

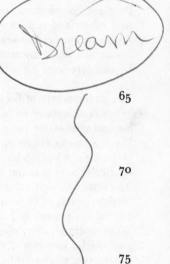

The adubbemente of þo downez dere   85
Garten my goste al greffe forȝete.
So frech flauorez of frytez were,
As fode hit con me fayre refete.
Fowlez þer flowen in fryth in fere,
Of flaumbande hwez, boþe smale and grete; 90
Bot sytole-stryng and gyternere
Her reken myrþe moȝt not retrete,
For quen þose bryddez her wyngez bete,
Þay songen wyth a swete asent.
So gracios gle couþe no mon gete   95
As here and se her adubbement.

So al watz dubbet on dere asyse
Þat fryth þer Fortwne forth me ferez
Þe derþe þerof for to deuyse
Nis no wyȝ worþé þat tonge berez.   100
I welke ay forth in wely wyse,
No bonk so byg þat did me derez.
Þe fyrre in þe fryth, þe feier con ryse
Þe playn, þe plonttez, þe spyse, þe perez;
And rawez and randez and rych reuerez, 105
As fyldor fyn her bonkes brent.
I wan to a water by schore þat scherez;
Lorde, dere watz hit adubbement!

The dubbemente of þo derworth depe
Wern bonkez bene of beryl bryȝt.   110
Swangeande swete þe water con swepe,
Wyth a rownande rourde raykande aryȝt;
In þe founce þer stoden stonez stepe,
As glente þurȝ glas þat glowed and glyȝt—
As stremande sternez, quen stroþe-men slepe, 115
Staren in welkyn in wynter nyȝt;
For vche a pobbel in pole þer pyȝt
Watz emerad, saffer, oþer gemme gente,
Þat alle þe loȝe lemed of lyȝt,
So dere watz hit adubbement.   120

III

The dubbement dere of doun and dalez,
Of wod and water and wlonk playnez,
Bylde in me blys, abated my balez,
Fordidden my stresse, dystryed my paynez.
Doun after a strem þat dryȝly halez   125
I bowed in blys, bredful my braynez;

In awe within those wondrous heights,   85
My soul from suffering found cure,
And from the fragrances of fruits
That filled the air found new ardor.
Between each branch flew birds with mates,
Both big and small, and bright and fair.   90
No zither strings with sharps and flats
Could capture such a canto's cheer;
For when they waved their wings their clear,
Unsullied song to the sky was sent!
No man might sweeter music hear   95
Than the warbling of that wonderment.

Through wondrous woods of wide array
Then forth by Fortune I was led.
No paint or pen could well portray
The beauty of that blessed abode.   100
I ventured forth, afresh and gay.
Neither rock nor rill lay in the road
I walked. Dear was each display
Of fruit tree, spice, and flowerbed.
Through leas and lanes, like golden thread,   105
A rippling river ran, resplendent.
I wandered to that winding bed
Of water. Lord, what wonderment!

Above that wondrous waterway
Rose banks of beryl, bold and bright.   110
The river ran without delay,
Singing softly and sailing straight
Along its lap where in array
Stones gleamed and glowed like glints of light
Through glass, like shining stars that sway   115
Above each sleeping head at night.
The stones along that shining site—
Soft emeralds, sapphires brilliant—
Lit that lea with lovely light.
Oh, welcome was that wonderment!   120

III

That wonderment, both far and wide,
Was decked with splendid den and dale;
I set my sorrows all aside
And soothed my grinding grief and gall.
I reached a radiant riverside,
My mind with welcome thoughts awhirl.   125

Þe fyrre I folȝed þose floty valez,
Þe more strenghþe of joye myn herte straynez.
As Fortune fares þeras ho fraynez,
Wheþer solace ho sende oþer ellez sore,   130
Þe wyȝ to wham his wylle ho waynez
Hyttez to haue ay more and more.

More of wele watz in þat wyse
Þen I cowþe telle þaȝ I tom hade,
For vrþely herte myȝt not suffyse   135
To þe tenþe dole of þo gladnez glade.
Forþy I þoȝt þat paradyse
Watz þer ouer gayn þo bonkez brade;
I hoped þe water were a deuyse
Bytwene myrþez by' merez made;   140
Byȝonde þe broke, by slente oþer slade,
I hoped þat mote merked wore.
Bot þe water watz depe, I dorst not wade,
And euer me longed ay more and more.

More and more, and ȝet wel mare,   145
Me lyste to se þe broke byȝonde,
For if hit watz fayr þer I con fare,
Wel loueloker watz þe fyrre londe.
Abowte me con I stote and stare;
To fynde a forþe faste con I fonde,   150
Bot woþez mo iwysse þer ware,
Þe fyrre I stalked by þe stronde;
And euer me þoȝt I schulde not wonde
For wo þer welez so wynne wore.
Þenne nwe note me com on honde   155
Þat meued my mynde ay more and more.

More meruayle con my dom adaunt.
I seȝ byȝonde þat myry mere
A crystal clyffe ful relusaunt:
Mony ryal ray con fro hit rere.   160
At þe fote þerof þer sete a faunt,
A mayden of menske, ful debonere;
Blysnande whyt watz hyr bleaunt;
I knew hyr wel, I hade sen hyr ere.
As glysnande golde þat man con schere,   165
So schon þat schene anvnder schore.
On lenghe I loked to hyr þere;
Þe lenger, I knew hyr more and more.

At each unsullied sight I sighed
With awe, my heart assuaged. For all
Whom Fortune's fickle fancies call—
Whether solace sent or sorrow sore, 130
Whether granted greatest bliss or gall—
Receive their measure more and more.

More mirth was mixed amidst that scene
Than I could properly portray.
Nor could an earthly heart sustain 135
A fraction of that fiery joy.
It seemed that paradise, unseen,
Was just beyond the waterway
That formed a barrier between
Myself and deep delight that lay 140
Within that city's walls. A way
Across that river, rich and rare,
I sought, though unsuccessfully,
While longing moved me more and more.

More and more and ever more 145
I pined and longed to penetrate
That fine and fresh abode. For fair
As was my side, far fairer yet
Did seem that sweet, opposing shore.
I searched to find a ford to let 150
Me cross. But the more I searched the more
Great dangers daunted me. Despite
My yearning for that place, sheer fright
Had hold of me; I hung before
That shimmering and sacred sight. 155
New matter moved me more and more.

More marvelous than man could tell
Rose ridges from that riverside;
Above that beauteous brook and dell
Climbed a crystal cliff with light supplied. 160
And seated below that citadel
Was a child, a maid of noble blood.
She wore all white. And very well
I recognized this marvelous maid!
Like glints of gold in wood inlaid, 165
So shone that fair one on the shore.
I doted on her face, delayed,
And the more I knew her, more and more.

[handwritten margin notes:] — human nature to see paradise 1st pt etc. — will & desire for more — don't appreciate what have — his daughter — compares daughter to naturals — wearing crown, pale ivory

The more I frayste hyr fayre face,
Her fygure fyn quen I had fonte,
Suche gladande glory con to me glace
As lyttel byfore þerto watz wonte.
To calle hyr lyste con me enchace,
Bot baysment gef myn hert a brunt.
I seȝ hyr in so strange a place—
Such a burre myȝt make myn herte blunt.
Þenne verez ho vp her fayre frount,
Hyr vysayge whyt as playn yuore:
Þat stonge myn hert ful stray astount,
And euer þe lenger, þe more and more.

IV

More þen me lyste my drede aros:
I stod ful stylle and dorste not calle;
Wyth yȝen open and mouth ful clos
I stod as hende as hawk in halle.
I hoped þat gostly watz þat porpose;
I dred onende quat schulde byfalle,
Lest ho me eschaped þat I þer chos,
Er I at steuen hir moȝt stalle.
Þat gracios gay withouten galle,
So smoþe, so smal, so seme slyȝt,
Rysez vp in hir araye ryalle,
A precios pyece in perlez pyȝt.

Perlez pyȝte of ryal prys
Þere moȝt mon by grace haf sene,
Quen þat frech as flor-de-lys
Doun þe bonke con boȝe bydene.
Al blysnande whyt watz hir beau biys,
Vpon at sydez, and bounden bene
Wyth þe myryeste margarys, at my deuyse,
Þat euer I seȝ ȝet with myn yȝen;
Wyth lappez large, I wot and I wene,
Dubbed with double perle and dyȝte;
Her cortel of self sute schene,
With precios perlez al vmbepyȝte.

A pyȝt coroune ȝet wer þat gyrle
Of marjorys and non oþer ston,
Hiȝe pynakled of cler quyt perle,
Wyth flurted flowrez perfet vpon.
To hed hade ho non oþer werle;
Her lere-leke al hyr vmbegon;

170
175
180
185
190
195
200
205
210

The more I mused on that maid's face,
And looked on her most lovingly,
The more I gained a special grace   170
I'd never known before. And I
Desired dearly some discourse
With her, but wonder took away
My speech, so stunning was that place,   175
So sharp the shock she did convey.
She started, then, to stare at me,
Her face, as ivory, pale and pure.
My heart was jarred with jolts of joy.
That marvel moved me more and more!   180

IV

More weight of woe I underwent;
I stood there still and dared not call.
With eyes alert and lips silent,
I hung as hushed as hawk in hall,
And felt that presence provident.   185
Transfixed, I feared what might befall
Lest I should lose my wonderment
Before I'd found a way to stall
This maid both mild and mystical.
I was with want and woe ensnared   190
When silently she rose, a small
And precious prize with pearls prepared!

There pearls prepared in pure array
Might mortal glean with God's good grace;
For, fresh as fleurs-de-lis in May,   195
She reached that running river's course.
All white she was: a white bouquet
With dearest dress, dainty amice,
And darling pearls. A dear display
Of mounted margeries, ablaze   200
With light, long sleeves, and lovely dress,
She shined like sunlight unimpaired.
Oh, lovely was that little lass,
A precious prize with pearls prepared!

She wore a crown, prepared with pearl   205
Of striking hue: no other stone
But pearly pinnacles awhirl
And flowers finely set. There shone
No ornament beside that furl
Of white, so wondrous and alone!   210

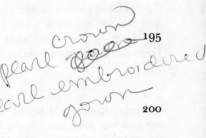

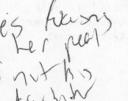

Her semblaunt sade for doc oþer erle,
Her ble more blaȝt þen whallez bon.
As schorne golde schyr her fax þenne schon,
On schylderez þat leghe vnlapped lyȝte.
Her depe colour ȝet wonted non   215
Of precios perle in porfyl pyȝte.

Pyȝt watz poyned and vche a hemme—
At honde, at sydez, at ouerture—
Wyth whyte perle and non oþer gemme,
And bornyste quyte watz hyr uesture.   220
Bot a wonder perle withouten wemme
Inmyddez hyr breste watz sette so sure;
A mannez dom moȝt dryȝly demme
Er mynde moȝt malte in hit mesure.
I hope no tong moȝt endure   225
No sauerly saghe say of þat syȝt,
So watz hit clene and cler and pure,
Þat precios perle þer hit watz pyȝt.

Pyȝt in perle, þat precios pyse
On wyþer half water com doun þe schore.   230
No gladder gome heþen into Grece
Þen I quen ho on brymme wore;
Ho watz me nerre þen aunte or nece:
My joy forþy watz much þe more.
Ho profered me speche, þat special spyce,   235
Enclynande lowe in wommon lore,
Caȝte of her coroun of grete tresore
And haylsed me wyth a lote lyȝte.
Wel watz me þat euer I watz bore
To sware þat swete in perlez pyȝte!   240

V

'O perle,' quoþ I, 'in perlez pyȝt,
Art þou my perle þat I haf playned,
Regretted by myn one on nyȝte?
Much longeyng haf I for þe layned,
Syþen into gresse þou me aglyȝte.   245
Pensyf, payred, I am forpayned,
And þou in a lyf of lykyng lyȝte,
In paradys erde, of stryf vnstrayned.
What Wyrde hatz hyder my juel vayned,
And don me in þys del and gret daunger?   250
Fro we in twynne wern towen and twayned,
I haf ben a joylez juelere.'

She stood as solemn as an earl.
Her skin was white as whalebone,
Her beauteous hair was loosely blown
About her shoulders, gold, unsheared.
Her skin gave off a shining tone: 215
A precious pearl with pearls prepared!

Prepared with pearl, pure filigree
At waist, wrist, and throat she wore.
No other shining stone had she.
But whiter still was what she bore   220
Upon her breast: a beauteously
Polished pearl! It was so pure
A man might meet eternity
Before he found its like. I'm sure
No man could by himself secure   225
The words to fit that finely flared
And precious piece; it glowed so pure,
A gem with precious pearls prepared!

Prepared with pearls of precious price,
She slowly neared that shining shore.   230
The happiest heart from here to Greece
Was mine; she'd reached that river rare!
Nearer to me than aunt or niece,
She made my mirth so much the more.
To me she turned her tiny face,   235
And deigned to bow, so dear, demure;
Then from her head that crown so pure
She doffed; and she to me declared
Great words of welcome. All my cheer
Was answering that pearl prepared.   240

V

"O pearl," I asked, "prepared in white,
Are you my pearl for whom I've pined
And hung my head each hopeless night
When gall and grief my heart confined?
Since losing you a lasting blight   245
Of care has come—it cuts, unkind!—
While you have lived a life most light
In paradise, left pain behind.
What fate has strangely here consigned
My pearl and punished me?" I swore,   250
"Since forced from you by fate unkind,
I've been, indeed, a joyless jeweler."

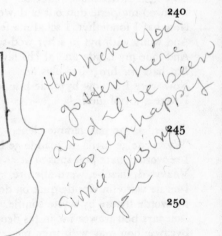

That juel þenne in gemmez gente
Vered vp her vyse with yȝen graye,
Set on hyr coroun of perle orient,   255
And soberly after þenne con ho say:
'Sir, ȝe haf your tale mysetente,
To say your perle is al awaye,
Þat is in cofer so comly clente
As in þis gardyn gracios gaye,   260
Hereinne to lenge for euer and play,
Þer mys nee mornyng com neuer nere.
Her were a forser for þe, in faye,
If þou were a gentyl jueler.

'Bot, jueler gente, if þou schal lose   265
Þy joy for a gemme þat þe watz lef,
Me þynk þe put in a mad porpose,
And busyez þe aboute a raysoun bref;
For þat þou lestez watz bot a rose
Þat flowred and fayled as kynde hyt gef;   270
Now þurȝ kynde of þe kyste þat hyt con close
To a perle of prys hit is put in pref.
And þou hatz called þy Wyrde a þef,
Þat oȝt of noȝt hatz mad þe cler;
Þou blamez þe bote of þy meschef;   275
Þou art no kynde jueler.'

A juel to me þen watz þys geste,
And julez wern hyr gentyl sawez.
'Iwyse,' quoþ I, 'my blysfol beste,
My grete dystresse þou al todrawez.   280
To be excused I make requeste.
I trawed my perle don out of dawez;
Now haf I fonde hyt, I schal ma feste,
And wony with hyt in schyr wod-schawez,
And loue my Lorde and al His lawez   285
Þat hatz me broȝt þys blys ner.
Now were I at yow byȝonde þise wawez,
I were a joyfol jueler.'

'Jueler,' sayde þat gemme clene,
'Wy borde ȝe men? So madde ȝe be!   290
Þre wordez hatz þou spoken at ene:
Vnavysed, forsoþe, wern alle þre.
Þou ne woste in worlde quat on dotz mene;
Þy worde byfore þy wytte con fle.
Þou says þou trawez me in þis dene   295
Bycawse þou may with yȝen me se;

That jewel then, with gems supplied,
Raised up her eyes, aglow and gray,
Replaced her regal crown, inlaid, 255
And solemnly began to say:
"O sir, you're certainly misled
To say your gem has gone away,
That basks in such a beauteous bed
As is this garden. Gracious, gay, 260
Forever here she'll frolic, play,
And laugh; no loss will threaten her.
All wealth, you'd see, would not outweigh
This joy, were you a gentle jeweler!

"But gentle jeweler, since you lose 265
Your joy because you lose a gem,
Your heart is much amiss. You amuse
Your mind with momentary whim.
For what you lost was but a rose
That flowered and finally failed in time. 270
But healed within this heavenly house,
And blessed, your beauteous pearl's become.
Though fate, you feel, has felled your gem,
It was from naught renewed. Its cure
You call a curse! Confused you seem 275
To be, but not a gentle jeweler."

A jewel she was, my gentle guest,
A jewel fine each gentle word.
"O richest one," said I, "to rest
You've laid the misery that marred 280
My peace. Your pardon I request;
I thought my pearl killed, not cured.
But now, by her pure presence blessed,
I'll stay with my sweet joy, assured
Of God's great laws, and praise the word 285
Of Him Who brought my bliss so near!
I'll wade this water, undeterred,
And be, indeed, a joyful jeweler."

"O jeweler," said that gem so clean,
"You jest! Or is this lunacy? 290
Three things you've said to me, I glean.
All three are false, pure foolery.
You speak not knowing what you mean;
Your words are thoughtless! Witlessly
You guess I'm in this garden green— 295
How little mortal eyes can see!—

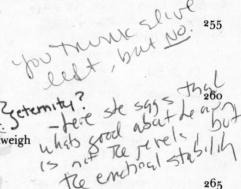

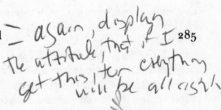

Anoþer, þou says in þys countré
Þyself schal won with me ryȝt here;
Þe þrydde, to passe þys water fre:
Þat may no joyfol jueler.   300

VI

'I halde þat jueler lyttel to prayse
Þat leuez wel þat he sez wyth yȝe,
And much to blame and vncortoyse
Þat leuez oure Lorde wolde make a lyȝe,
Þat lelly hyȝte your lyf to rayse,   305
Þaȝ Fortune dyd your flesch to dyȝe.
Ȝe setten Hys wordez ful westernays
Þat leuez noþynk bot ȝe hit syȝe;
And þat is a poynt o sorquydryȝe,
Þat vche god mon may euel byseme,   310
To leue no tale be true to tryȝe
Bot þat hys one skyl may dem.

'Deme now þyself if þou con dayly
As man to God wordez schulde heue.
Þou saytz þou schal won in þis bayly;   315
Me þynk þe burde fyrst aske leue—
And ȝet of graunt þou myȝtez fayle.
Þou wylnez ouer þys water to weue;
Er moste þou ceuer to oþer counsayl.
Þy corse in clot mot calder keue,   320
For hit watz forgarte at paradys greue;
Oure ȝorefader hit con misseȝeme.
Þurȝ drwry deth boz vch man dreue,
Er ouer þys dam hym Dryȝtyn deme.'

'Demez þou me,' quoþ I, 'my swete,   325
To dol agayn? Þenne I dowyne.
Now haf I fonte þat I forlete,
Schal I efte forgo hit er euer I fyne?
Why schal I hit boþe mysse and mete?
My precios perle dotz me gret pyne.   330
What seruez tresor bot garez men grete,
When he hit schal efte with tenez tyne?
Now rech I neuer for to declyne,
Ne how fer of folde þat man me fleme.
When I am partlez of perle myne,   335
Bot durande doel what may men deme?'

'Thow demez noȝt bot doel-dystresse,'
Þenne sayde þat wyȝt; 'why dotz þou so?

And claim that in this lovely lea
You'll linger long. You last aver
You'll wade this water easily.
You can't at all, my joyless jeweler!   300

VI

"That jeweler's not worth word of praise
Who trusts his mere and mortal eye.
He's destitute and disobeys
Who claims our living Lord could lie,
Our God Who's sworn your soul to raise   305
When Fortune deems your flesh should die!
Who warps His word our Lord dismays.
He tricks himself who trusts his eye
And thus betrays his pride. To try
To test each truth by proof, begrudge   *Have to have faith*   310
What mortal mind can't verify,
Is sin, O sir, which God will judge.

"Judge for yourself if you've transgressed
Your Lord by braying blasphemy. *→ saying impious things about the Lord*
You rant you'll reach this peaceful nest;   315
First ask for hospitality
And grace, for great is your request.
You wish to wade this stream. But be
Aware: to forge this way you first   *→ Adam & Eve*
Must sink beneath clay's canopy;   320
For even in the ecstasy   *have to be dead*
Of paradise did man misjudge.
So death must every mortal see
Before he sees the Lord, our Judge."

"If you so judge my sins," said I,   325
"My sorrow is the more severe;
Just when I gain what grievously   *beginning to realize that pearl will not bring him joy*
I'd missed, delight will disappear.
I lose what I had won. Oh, why
Does cherished pearl bring no cheer?   330
What good is wealth that makes men cry
When with it men must part for drear
And dreadful days? From here
To death, the world's wastes I'll trudge
Without my pearl, precious, pure.   335
Let mortal men my misery judge."

"You merely judge your deep distress
And nothing else," she said. "But why?

For dyne of doel of lurez lesse
Ofte mony mon forgos þe mo.   340
Þe oȝte better þyseluen blesse,
And loue ay God, in wele and wo,
For anger gaynez þe not a cresse.
Who nedez schal þole, be not so þro;
For þoȝ þou daunce as any do,   345
Braundysch and bray þy braþez breme,
When þou no fyrre may, to ne fro,
Þou moste abyde þat He schal deme.

'Deme Dryȝtyn, euer Hym adyte;
Of þe way a fote ne wyl He wryþe.   350
Þy mendez mountez not a myte,
Þaȝ þou for sorȝe be neuer blyþe.
Stynt of þy strot and fyne to flyte,
And sech Hys blyþe ful swefte and swyþe;
Þy prayer may Hys pyté byte,   355
Þat mercy schal hyr craftez kyþe.
Hys comforte may þy langour lyþe,
And þy lurez of lyȝtly fleme;
For, marre oþer madde, morne and myþe,
Al lys in Hym to dyȝt and deme.'   360

VII

Thenne demed I to þat damyselle:
'Ne worþe no wrathþe vnto my Lorde,
If rapely I raue, spornande in spelle:
My herte watz al with mysse remorde,
As wallande water gotz out of welle.   365
I do me ay in Hys myserecorde.
Rebuke me neuer with wordez felle,
Þaȝ I forloyne, my dere endorde,
Bot kyþez me kyndely your coumforde,
Pytosly þenkande vpon þysse: 370
Of care and me ȝe made acorde,
Þat er watz grounde of alle my blysse.

'My blysse, my bale, ȝe han ben boþe,
Bot much þe bygger ȝet watz my mon;
Fro þou watz wroken fro vch a woþe,   375
I wyste neuer quere my perle watz gon.
Now I hit se, now leþez my loþe.
And quen we departed we wern at on;
God forbede we be now wroþe;
We meten so selden by stok oþer ston.   380

Men often moan to lose the less
And lose what matters more thereby.
Much better, you should learn to bless
Your God, not grind your teeth and cry;
Wild anger wins not a watercress.
God will with suffering supply
Whomever He will. Although you cry   345
Like a doe deranged, refuse to budge,
And scratch and shout, you'll soon comply
To our Lord's will, our Life and Judge.

"Judge your God, His good indict!
His wondrous way He'll never lose.   350
Your view amounts not to a mite.
Though you should never wean from woes,
Still cease your loud complaints and spite,
And seek God's goodly grace. Expose
Yourself through precious prayer. Excite   355
Great mercy's might which overthrows
All sin and blessings free bestows.
For what of grace would God begrudge?
To men His mercy overflows.
All lies in Him, Your Lord and Judge!"   360

VII

That gem I answered as I judged:
"I'd neither God were wroth with me
Nor that in reckless rant I raged.
My heaving heart in agony,
As water from a well, deluged.   365
I recommend to God's mercy
My soul: Forgive my sacrilege
Of mourning most indulgently.
O show me your sweet sanctity.
With mercy, maid, remember this: 370
You racked my soul relentlessly,
On whom was based my only bliss.

"My bliss and bane have you been both.
But more a bane to me you've been.
For on each road and rutted path
I've never gained my pearl again.   375
To see it now my soul, in truth,
Feels one with her as we were when
Together! God, don't give us strife!
We meet so seldom by a stone   380

Þaʒ cortaysly ʒe carp con,
I am bot mol and manerez mysse;
Bot Crystes mersy and Mary and Jon,
Þise arn þe grounde of alle my blysse.

'In blysse I se þe blyþely blent,   385
And I a man al mornyf mate.
ʒe take þeron ful lyttel tente,
Þaʒ I hente ofte harmez hate.
Bot now I am here in your presente,
I wolde bysech, wythouten debate,   390
ʒe wolde me say in sobre asente
What lyf ʒe lede erly and late,
For I am ful fayn þat your astate
Is worþen to worschyp and wele, iwysse;
Of alle my joy þe hyʒe gate,   395
Hit is in grounde of alle my blysse.'

'Now blysse, burne, mot þe bytyde,'
Þen sayde þat lufsoum of lyth and lere,
'And welcum here to walk and byde,
For now þy speche is to me dere.   400
Maysterful mod and hyʒe pryde,
I hete þe, arn heterly hated here.
My Lorde ne louez not for to chyde,
For meke arn alle þat wonez Hym nere;
And when in Hys place þou schal apere,   405
Be dep deuote in hol mekenesse.
My Lorde þe Lamb louez ay such chere,
Þat is þe grounde of alle my blysse.

'A blysful lyf þou says I lede;
Þou woldez knaw þerof þe stage.   410
Þow wost wel when þy perle con schede
I watz ful ʒong and tender of age;
Bot my Lorde þe Lombe þurʒ Hys godhede,
He toke myself to Hys maryage,
Corounde me quene in blysse to brede   415
In lenghe of dayez þat euer schal wage;
And sesed in alle Hys herytage
Hys lef is. I am holy Hysse.
Hys prese, Hys prys, and Hys parage
Is rote and grounde of alle my blysse.'   420

VIII

'Blysful,' quoþ I, 'may þys be trwe?—
Dysplesez not if I speke errour—

Or well. Your words are weighed, high-flown,
While mine are motes and much amiss.
O mercy, Christ, Mary, John,
You are the base of all my bliss!

[handwritten: 3 theme of language]

"In blissfulness you bask and dwell,   385
But mourning's my unmerry mate.
My sorrow is insufferable;
This you've not cared to contemplate.
But since I'm in this stately dell,
I ask, would you, without debate,   390
To me your life here truly tell?
How is my lady, early, late?
It eases me that your estate
Is filled with such fine fruitfulness.
Serenity does satiate   395
This bower on which I base my bliss!"

"Now bliss be both your friend and guide,"
Responded she, both soft and clear.
"I welcome you to walk and bide
With me. Your worthy words are dear.   400
But bear in mind that boasting, pride,
And haughtiness are hated here.
My gracious Lord is loathe to chide.

[handwritten: traits of romance heroes]

To God just gentle ones come near;
When in His presence you appear,   405
Show only simple humbleness.
To Him is such demeanor dear,
Who is the base of all my bliss.

"A blissful life you say I've led;
You'd like to hear it; I'll oblige.   410
Now know that when your pearl fled,
I was too young, of tender age.
The Lord, our Lamb, through His Godhead,
Took me in merciful marriage
And crowned me queen. In bliss we wed.   415
For all eternity's endless age
I hold my Lord's high heritage;
Forever I am wholly His.
His love, esteem, and lineage
Are root and base of all my bliss."   420

VIII

"O bliss!" I cried, "Can this be true?
Please ease your anger if I err.

Art þou þe quene of heuenez blwe,
Þat al þys worlde schal do honour?
We leuen on Marye þat grace of grewe,
Þat ber a barne of vyrgyn flour.
Þe croune fro hyr quo moȝt remwe
Bot ho hir passed in sum fauour?
Now, for synglerty o hyr dousour,
We calle hyr Fenyx of Arraby,
Þat fereles fleȝe of hyr Fasor—
Lyk to þe quen of cortaysye.'   430

'Cortayse quen,' þenne sayde þat gaye,
Knelande to grounde, folde vp hyr face,
'Makelez moder and myryest may,   435
Blessed bygynner of vch a grace!'
Þenne ros ho vp and con restay,
And speke me towarde in þat space:
'Sir, fele here porchasez and fongez pray,
Bot supplantorez none withinne þys place;   440
Þat emperise al heuenz hatz—
And vrþe and helle—in her bayly;
Of erytage ȝet non wyl ho chace,
For ho is quen of cortaysye.

'The court of þe kyndom of God alyue   445
Hatz a property in hytself beyng:
Alle þat may þerinne aryue
Of alle þe reme is quen oþer kyng,
And neuer oþer ȝet schal depryue,
Bot vchon fayn of oþerez hafyng,   450
And wolde her corounez wern worþe þo fyue,
If possyble were her mendyng.
Bot my lady of quom Jesu con spryng,
Ho haldez þe empyre ouer vus ful hyȝe,
And þat dysplesez non of oure gyng,   455
For ho is quene of cortaysye.

'Of courtaysye, as saytz Saynt Poule,
Al arn we membrez of Jesu Kryst:
As heued and arme and legg and naule
Temen to hys body ful trwe and tryste,   460
Ryȝt so is vch a Krysten sawle
A longande lym to þe Mayster of myste.
Þenne loke: what hate oþer any gawle
Is tached oþer tyȝed þy lymmez bytwyste?
Þy heued hatz nauþer greme ne gryste   465
On arme oþer fynger þaȝ þou ber byȝe.

425

Are you the bride of heaven blue
Whom people praise without a peer?
From Mary, we believe, grace grew   425
When, but a virgin flower, she bore
Our Lord. Who wears her crown? In lieu
Of what? A trait more fine and fair?
And yet that royal queen's so rare,
In faith, the Phoenix of Araby   430
She's called, who flew from her Creator,
For she's the queen of courtesy."

"O courteous queen!" that fair one cried,
And kneeled down with covered face.
"O matchless mother, fairest maid,   435
Whose great and lofty gift is grace!"
She prayed and, lifting high her head,
Deliberately did me address:
"For piety the pure are paid.
But no usurpers see this place!   440
The empress pure of paradise
Rules hell and heaven flawlessly,
And earth, yet does no man disgrace;
For she is queen of courtesy.

"This court within our Lord's great land   445
Accords with His arrangings.
For all the souls that herein stand
Are of their realm great queens or kings.
No one would want another's land;
We're pleased by neighbors' high holdings,   450
And would their crown and court expand,
If we could ever cause such things.
But she from whom Christ's good grace springs
Reigns over all in royalty.
No envy, though, by this she brings;   455
For she is queen of courtesy.'

"Through courtesy, as Saint Paul said,
We crowd united under Christ,
As arm and leg and lifted head
Are bound together; this is best.   460
So every Christian soul to God
Is like a limb by Him possessed.
Should likened limbs each other dread?
Should foot fight foot, or arm fight chest?
Is by your hand your head depressed   465
When wearing wondrous jewelry?

So fare we alle wyth luf and lyste
To kyng and quene by cortaysye.'

'Cortaysé,' quoþ I, 'I leue,
And charyté grete, be yow among;
Bot my speche þat yow ne greue,   470
. . . .
Þyself in heuen ouer hyȝ þou heue,
To make þe quen þat watz so ȝonge.
What more honour moȝte he acheue   475
Þat hade endured in worlde stronge,
And lyued in penaunce hys lyuez longe
With bodyly bale hym blysse to byye?
What more worschyp moȝt he fonge
Þen corounde be kyng by cortaysé?   480

IX

'That Cortayse is to fre of dede,
Ȝyf hyt be soth þat þou conez saye.
Þou lyfed not two ȝer in oure þede;
Þou cowþez neuer God nauþer plese ne pray,
Ne neuer nawþer Pater ne Crede—   485
And quen mad on þe fyrst day!
I may not traw, so God me spede,
Þat God wolde wryþe so wrange away.
Of countes, damysel, par ma fay,
Wer fayr in heuen to halde asstate,   490
Oþer ellez a lady of lasse aray;
Bot a quene!—hit is to dere a date.'

'Þer is no date of Hys godnesse,'
Þen sayde to me þat worþy wyȝte,
'For al is trawþe þat He con dresse,   495
And He may do noþynk bot ryȝt.
As Mathew melez in your messe
In sothfol gospel of God almyȝt:
In sample He can ful grayþely gesse
And lyknez hit to heuen lyȝte.   500
"My regne," He saytz, "is lyk on hyȝt
To a lorde þat hade a uyne, I wate.
Of tyme of ȝere þe terme watz tyȝt,
To labor vyne watz dere þe date.

'"Þat date of ȝere wel knawe þys hyne.   505
Þe lorde ful erly vp he ros
To hyre werkmen to hys vyne,

Such are we bound, whom God has blessed,
As kings and queens in courtesy."

"Kind courtesy, it's my belief,"
I said, "you show and live among.   470
God grant ~~my speech~~ brings you no grief

.   .   .   .   .   .

But heaven seems to form a fief
Of which you're queen, though very young.
But higher is he whose heart's belief   475
Was steadfast, strong, whose flesh was stung
By penitential trials, whose tongue
Has told no lies! His soul, truly,
Would in this bower best belong,
Here crowned a king of courtesy!   480

IX

"Too freely comes that courtesy
Of which you speak, if truth you say.
Not two years old, on bended knee
You neither learned to praise nor pray
The Pater or the Creed's decree,   485
Yet queen were deigned within a day!
I can't accept this thoughtlessly!
If God had deigned you duchess, say,
Or countess, kind, then, is His way.
Or if God's grace had rendered you
Among the best, I would not bray.   490
But *queen*? That's far too dear a due!"

"Unduly God grants dear largess,"
That mild maid did me indict.
"No rift disrupts God's righteousness;
He renders only what is right,   495
As Matthew does in the Mass express.
In God's good gospel he did right
When parable did he profess:
'My realm is like a vintner's, great   500
With grapes that must be gained, despite
Their quality or health or hue.
One harvests at the season's height,
When vineyards are both dear and due.

" 'Dear workmen duly drew about   505
A great landlord,' the gospel goes,
'Who hired helping hands, worked out

And fyndez þer summe to hys porpos.
Into acorde þay con declyne
For a pené on a day, and forth þay gotz,   510
Wryþen and worchen and don gret pyne,
Keruen and caggen and man hit clos.
Aboute vnder þe lorde to marked totz,
And ydel men stande he fyndez þerate.
'Why stande ȝe ydel?,' he sayde to þos;   515
'Ne knawe ȝe of þis day no date?'

' " 'Er date of daye hider arn we wonne:'
So watz al samen her answar soȝt.
'We haf standen her syn ros þe sunne,
And no mon byddez vus do ryȝt noȝt.'   520
'Gos into my vyne, dotz þat ȝe conne:'
So sayde þe lorde, and made hit toȝt;
'What resonabele hyre be naȝt be runne
I yow pay in dede and þoȝte.'
Þay wente into þe vyne and wroȝte,   525
And al day þe lorde þus ȝede his gate,
And nw men to hys vyne he broȝte
Welneȝ wyl day watz passed date.

' "At þe date of day of euensonge,
On oure byfore þe sonne go doun,
He seȝ þer ydel men ful stronge   530
And sade to hem with sobre soun:
'Wy stonde ȝe ydel þise dayez longe?'
Þay sayden her hyre watz nawhere boun.
'Gotz to my vyne, ȝemen ȝonge,
And wyrkez and dotz þat at ȝe moun.'   535
Sone þe worlde bycom wel broun;
Þe sunne watz doun, and hit wex late.
To take her hyre he mad sumoun;
Þe day watz al apassed date.   540

X

' "The date of þe daye þe lorde con knaw,
Called to þe reue: 'Lede, pay þe meyny;
Gyf hem þe hyre þat I hem owe,
And fyrre, þat non me may reprené,
Set hem alle vpon a rawe   545
And gyf vchon inlyche a peny.
Bygyn at þe laste þat standez lowe,
Tyl to þe fyrste þat þou atteny.'
And þenne þe fyrst bygonne to pleny

Their wages. Pennies he proposed
Per day to persons, pious, stout.
They all agreed and all arose
To toil at their task throughout
His realm. They pruned his vineyard's rows.
He went to town, where idlers chose
To tarry late: a tardy crew.
"Why stand you still?" he said to those,   515
"You've doubtless heard of my dear due!"

" ' "For our dear due we'd here begun,"
They answered then that worthy lord,
"Awaiting work ere break of sun.
But no one has our work implored."   520
"Then work my vineyards, everyone!"
He called. They came to his accord:
"For all the work by dusk you've done,
I'll pay each man his right reward."
So over vines each person pored,   525
While he continued to accrue
More men to harvest his fine hoard
Till dusk was dearly overdue.

" 'When dearly due was evensong,
An hour ere the sun went down,   530
He met more men amidst a throng
And asked, "Why idle here, why frown?
You're stout who stand about, and strong."
"There was no work," they whined, "in town."
"Then gather my grapes, you yeomen young;   535
And do this deed till dusk comes down."
And soon the sun was overthrown.
Assembling all his sundry crew,
That patron paid each man his own
Fair wage that was so dearly due.   540

X

" 'Their dearly due did he bestow.
He roused his reeve: "This company
Has earned what honestly I owe.
And so that none reproaches me,
Align them all along a row;   545
A penny give each man as fee.
Start with the last to come; bestow
Exactly what all did agree."
Then those who'd done more drudgery

And sayden þat þay hade trauayled sore: 550
'Þese bot on oure hem con streny;
Vus þynk vus oȝe to take more.

'"'More haf we serued, vus þynk so,
Þat suffred han þe dayez hete,
Þenn þyse þat wroȝt not hourez two,   555
And þou dotz hem vus to counterfete.'
Þenne sayde þe lorde to on of þo:
'Frende, no waning I wyl þe ȝete;
Take þat is þyn owne, and go.
And I hyred þe for a peny agrete,   560
Quy bygynnez þou now to þrete?
Watz not a pené þy couenaunt þore?
Fyrre þen couenaunde is noȝt to plete;
Wy schalte þou þenne ask more?

'"'More, weþer louyly is me my gyfte—   565
To do wyth myn quatso me lykez?
Oþer ellez þyn yȝe to lyþer is lyfte
For I am goude and non byswykez?'
Þus schal I," quoþ Kryste, "hit skyfte:
Þe laste schal be þe fyrst þat strykez,   570
And þe fyrst þe laste, be he neuer so swyft,
For mony ben called, þaȝ fewe be mykez."
Þus pore men her part ay pykez,
Þaȝ þay com late and lyttel wore,
And þaȝ her sweng wyth lyttel atslykez,   575
Þe merci of God is much þe more.

'More haf I of joye and blysse hereinne,
Of ladyschyp gret and lyuez blom,
Þen alle þe wyȝez in þe worlde myȝt wynne
By þe way of ryȝt to aske dome.   580
Wheþer welnygh now I con bygynne—
In euentyde into þe vyne I come—
Fyrst of my hyre my Lorde con mynne:
I watz payed anon of al and sum.
Ȝet oþer þer werne þat toke more tom,   585
Þat swange and swat for long ȝore,
Þat ȝet of hyre noþynk þay nom,
Paraunter noȝt schal to-ȝere more.'

Then more I meled and sayde apert:
'Me þynk þy tale vnresounable;   590
Goddez ryȝt is redy and euermore rert,
Oþer holy wryt is bot a fable.

Spoke out, "We sweated in our chore;   550
All day we drudged on bended knee.
We think that thus we've earned the more.

" ' "We've labored more than these men here,
And sweated in the sun all day.
Yet men who've worked an hour mere   555
Are paid the same as us. Why, pray?"
Then said that lord to laborer:
"I don't condone your great dismay.
These goods now gather. Go in cheer.
A penny paid, you said, per day   560
Was fair. Why whimper now? Why bray?
That was the wage to which you swore;
Agreements men must not betray
With men! Why ask you now for more?

" ' "Moreover, isn't it my right   565
To put my pennies where I please?
On sinfulness you've set your sight.
No fellow I unfairly fleece."
And so,' Christ said, 'shall I requite:
Those last shall be the first to rise;   570
The first shall last receive their right.
I call a crowd, but patronize
A few!' His mercy multiplies
For those arriving late and poor.   *Forgiving*
For souls the more amiss there lies   575
God's mercy, which is much the more.

"More merry mirth have I here won,
More bounteous bliss has come to me
Than in the world would anyone
Receive by labor rightfully.   580
Although the day was nearly done
Before I worked the vine, yet He
Rewarded me at once. Thus none
Was paid before the Lord paid me.
Though others worked more worthily,   585
And chopped and sweated in their chore,
Yet none received his fief and fee
Nor might for many years or more."

Then more did I speak out my mind.
"Your story seems unreasonable!   *questioning again*   590
God's righteousness rules all mankind
Or Holy Writ is a foolish fable!

In sauter is sayd a verce ouerte
Þat spekez a poynt determynable:
"Þou quytez vchon as hys desserte,
Þou hyȝe Kyng ay pertermynable."
Now he þat stod þe long day stable,
And þou to payment com hym byfore,
Þenne þe lasse in werke to take more able,
And euer þe lenger þe lasse þe more.'   595

                                                        600

XI

'Of more and lasse in Godez ryche,'
Þat gentyl sayde, 'lys no joparde,
For þer is vch mon payed inlyche,
Wheþer lyttel oþer much be hys rewarde.
For þe gentyl Cheuentayn is no chyche,   605
Queþersoeuer He dele—nesch oþer harde:
He lauez Hys gyftez as water of dyche,
Oþer gotez of golf þat neuer charde.
Hys fraunchyse is large: þat euer dard
To Hym þat matz in synne rescoghe—   610
No blysse betz fro hem reparde,
For þe grace of God is gret inoghe.

'Bot now þou motez, me for to mate,
Þat I my peny haf wrang tan here;
Þou sayz þat I þat com to late   615
Am not worþy so gret fere.
Where wystez þou euer any bourne abate
Euer so holy in hys prayere
Þat he ne forfeted by sumkyn gate
Þe mede sumtyme of heuenez clere?   620
And ay þe ofter þe alder þay were,
Þay laften ryȝt and wroȝten woghe.
Mercy and grace moste hem þen stere,
For þe grace of God is gret innoȝe.

'Bot innoghe of grace hatz innocent: 625
As sone as þay arn borne, by lyne
In þe water of babtem þay dyssente.
Þen arne þay boroȝt into þe vyne.
Anon þe day with derk endente
Þe niyȝt of deth dotz to enclyne.   630
Þat wroȝt neuer wrang er þenne þay wente
Þe gentyle Lorde þenne payez Hys hyne.
Þay dyden Hys heste; þay wern þereine;
Why schulde He not her labour alow?

In Psalms you shall the saying find,
Indeed quite indisputable,
'By You are *earned* rewards assigned,   595
O cherished King unchangeable!'
If one worked more in toil and trouble
Yet you're rewarded first, then for
Less work more wealth is payable.
So more is less and less is more!"   600

XI

"But *more* and *less* within this site
Are one," replied that righteous maid.
"Though differently does He requite,
Here equally each one is paid.
What He allots, though harsh or light,   605
Here equally each gift is weighed.
As water from a wondrous height
Flows freely in a fine cascade,
So freely at our feet is laid
Each gift; who loved the Lord in life   610
With precious prizes thus is paid,
For God's good grace is great enough.

"Enough, I pray, poor sir! You prate
I've hardly earned my penny here.
You claim I came to work too late,   615
Have not deserved this heaven dear.
What man was ever born so great,
So pious and so pure in prayer,
That never did he demonstrate
His gross unworthiness to near   620
God's realm? The more men age the more
They do what's wrong and right rebuff.
God's grace alone will guide them here;
For *that* His grace is great enough.

"But graced enough are innocent   625
And newborn babes in God's design.
By being baptized they are sent
To that true Landlord's trellised vine.
When quickly day, with darkness blent,
Is made by death's dark night supine,   630
Then those who kept quite innocent
Are given pay by God divine.
They kept His law and dear design;
Why wouldn't He their work approve,

Ȝys, and pay hym at þe fyrst fyne?   635
For þe grace of God is gret innoghe.

'Inoȝe is knawen þat mankyn grete
Fyrste watz wroȝt to blysse parfyt.
Oure forme fader hit con forfete
Þurȝ an apple þat he vpon con byte;   640
Al wer we dampned for þat mete
To dyȝe in doel out of delyt
And syþen wende to helle hete,
Þerinne to won withoute respyt.
Bot þeron com a bote astyt;   645
Ryche blod ran on rode so roghe,
And wynne water; þen, at þat plyt,
Þe grace of God wex gret innoghe.

'Innoghe þer wax out of þat welle,
Blod and water of brode wounde.   650
Þe blod vus boȝt fro bale of helle,
And delyuered vus of þe deth secounde;
Þe water is baptem, þe soþe to telle,
Þat folȝed þe glayue so grymly grounde,
Þat waschez away þe gyltez felle   655
Þat Adam wyth inne deth vus drounde.
Now is þer noȝt in þe worlde rounde
Bytwene vus and blysse bot þat He withdroȝ,
And þat is restored in sely stounde;
And þe grace of God is gret innogh.   660

XII

'Grace innogh þe mon may haue
Þat synnez þenne new, ȝif hym repente,
Bot with sorȝ and syt he mot hit craue,
And byde þe payne þerto is bent.
Bot Resoun, of ryȝt þat con not raue,   665
Sauez euermore þe innossent;
Hit is a dom þat neuer God gaue
Þat euer þe gyltlez schulde be schente.
Þe gyltyf may contryssyoun hente
And be þurȝ mercy to grace þryȝt;   670
Bot he to gyle þat neuer glente
As inoscente is saf and ryȝte.

'Ryȝt þus I knaw wel in þis cas
Two men to saue is God—by skylle:
Þe ryȝtwys man schal se Hys face,   675

Indeed, and all their dues consign? 635
For that, God's grace is great enough.

"Enough it's known that humankind
Was wrought to live in rich delight.
But our first father that gift resigned;
With apple red he ruined that right. 640
By that disgrace we all are damned
To die a joyless death in blight,
And be by heat of hell confined,
To rot there robbed of all respite.
But remedy arrived, so bright! 645
Rich blood ran down that rood so rough
And water pure. As proved that sight,
The grace of God is great enough!

"Enough flowed forth from that great well!
Both blood and water from that wound 650
Saved howling souls from heinous hell,
And dreary second death deponed.
Baptismal waters, truth to tell,
Flowed freely from that fierce-cut wound
And washed away that guilt so well 655
In which Adam's full fold was drowned.
Since then our sin has been dethroned;
All are blessed by God's great love
Since that bright hour of bliss. Profound
Is God's good grace and great enough! 660

XII

"Good grace enough might those men have
Who, sorrowed by their sins, repent,
Who suffer grief, and cry and crave
In pain, all patient, penitent.
But reason's strength will surely save 665
Those ones whose souls are innocent.
The grim decree God never gave
That good should suffer punishment.
The guilty by contrition bent
Can gain His grace and great delight. 670
But he who held all innocent,
His innocence is safe by right.

"That reason's right! Regard the case
When God saved two good souls by skill.
The penitent shall see His face 675

say it was Adam who braved it
not Eve

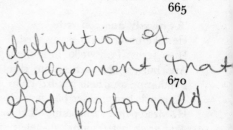

definition of judgement that God performed.

Þe harmlez haþel schal com Hym tylle.
Þe sauter hyt satz þus in a pace:
"Lorde, quo schal klymbe Þy hyȝ hylle,
Oþer rest withinne Þy holy place?"
Hymself to onsware he is not dylle: 680
"Hondelyngez harme þat dyt not ille,
Þat is of hert boþe clene and lyȝt,
Þer schal hys step stable stylle":
Þe innocent is ay saf by ryȝt.

'The ryȝtwys man also, sertayn,   685
Aproche he schal þat proper pyle--
Þat takez not her lyf in vayne
Ne glauerez her nieȝbor wyth no gyle--
Of þys ryȝtwys sayz Salamon playn,
Hym Koyntyse oure con aquyle;   690
By wayez ful streȝt He con hym strayn,
And scheued hym þe rengne of God awhyle,
As quo says, "Lo, ȝon louely yle:
Þou may hit wynne if þou be wyȝte."
Bot hardyly, withoute peryle,   695
Þe innocent is ay saue by ryȝte.

'Anende ryȝtwys men ȝet saytz a gome,
Dauid, in sauter, if euer ȝe seȝ hit:
"Lorde, Þy seruaunt draȝ neuer to dome,
For non lyuyande to Þe is justyfyet."   700
Forþy to corte quen þou schal com
Þer alle oure causez schal be cryed,
Alegge þe ryȝt, þou may be innome,
By þys ilke spech I haue asspyed.
Bot He on rode þat blody dyed,   705
Delfully þurȝ hondez þryȝt,
Gyue þe to passe, when þou arte tryed,
By innocens and not by ryȝte.

'Ryȝtwysly quo con rede,
He loke on bok and be awayed   710
How Jesus Hym welke in areþede,
And burnez her barnez vnto Hym brayde.
For happe and hele þat fro Hym ȝede
To touch her chylder þay fayr Hym prayed.
His dessypelez with blame "Let be!" hym bede   715
And wyth her resounez ful fele restayed.
Jesus þenne hem swetely sayde:
"Do way, let chylder vnto Me tyȝt;
To suche is heuenryche arayed":
Þe innocent is ay saf by ryȝt.   720

And grace on innocents shall fall.
As David in the Psalter says:
'Who'll climb, O Lord, Your lofty hill
Or walk within Your holy place?'
At once he answered thus that call: 680
'Whose hands did neither harm nor ill,
Whose breast was ever pure and bright;
His steps will stay steadfast and still.'
For innocents are safe by right.

"But righteous souls as well will gain   685
That castle's wondrous walls if, while
They lived, they lived not all in vain
Nor gave their neighbors grief or guile.
One penitent did wisdom gain;
So Solomon did in script reveal: 690
When Wisdom to God's wide domain
Guided that good and guileless soul,
He might have said, 'This merry knoll
You'll have if heartily you fight.'
The penitent must see great peril;   695
But innocents are saved by right.

"Of righteous men did David speak
In the Psalms, if yet you've gleaned that guide:
'Do not to court Your servants take;
They'll prove not pure or justified.'   700
When to that court you wander, weak,
Where all your treacheries are tried,
And you your righteousness invoke,
This passage proves you'll be denied.
But He that high on the rood's wood died,   705
Whose body bled both day and night,
Will only judge you justified
By innocence and not by right.

"Who righteously reads Scripture's word
Will glean in it good guidance, aid,   710
And read how Christ with good folk fared;
They brought their babies at their side
To seek what solace from Him soared.
Though for His precious touch they prayed,
Christ's disciples access barred.   715
'Stay back from Jesus Christ!' they bade.
'Let them approach,' the Lord then said.
'To children will I dole delight.
For so is heaven high arrayed.'
The innocent are safe by right.   720

XIII

'Ryȝt con calle to Hym Hys mylde,
And sayde Hys ryche no wyȝ myȝt wynne
Bot he com þyder ryȝt as a chylde,
Oþer ellez neuermore com þerinne.
Harmlez, trwe, and vndefylde,   725
Withouten mote oþer mascle of sulpande synne:
Quen such þer cnoken on þe bylde,
Tyt schal hem men þe ȝate vnpynne.
Þer is þe blys þat con not blynne
Þat þe jueler soȝte þurȝ perré pres,   730
And solde alle hys goud, boþe wolen and lynne,
To bye hym a perle watz mascellez.

'This makellez perle þat boȝt is dere,
Þe joueler gef fore alle hys god,
Is lyke þe reme of heuenesse clere—   735
So sayde þe Fader of folde and flode—
For hit is wemlez, clene, and clere,
And endelez rounde, and blyþe of mode,
And commune to alle þat ryȝtwys were.
Lo, euen inmyddez my breste hit stode: 740
My Lorde þe Lombe, þat schede Hys blode,
He pyȝt hit þere in token of pes.
I rede þe forsake þe worlde wode
And porchace þy perle maskelles.'

'O maskelez perle in perlez pure,   745
Þat berez,' quoþ I, 'þe perle of prys,
Quo formed þe þy fayre fygure?
Þat wroȝt þy wede he watz ful wys;
Þy beauté com neuer of nature—
Pymalyon paynted neuer þy vys,   750
Ne Arystotel nawþer by hys lettrure
Of carped þe kynde þese propertéz;
Þy colour passez þe flour-de-lys,
Þyn angel-hauyng so clene cortez.
Breue me, bryȝt, quat kyn offys   755
Berez þe perle so maskellez?'

'My makelez Lambe þat al may bete,'
Quoþ scho, 'my dere Destyné,
Me ches to Hys make, alþaȝ vnmete
Sumtyme semed þat assemblé.   760
When I wente fro yor worlde wete
He calde me to Hys bonerté:
"Cum hyder to Me, My lemman swete,

XIII

"Right then Christ called his servants mild
And told them all no one would win
His cherished kingdom but as a child:
For that alone allows you in.
Those harmless, dear, and undefiled,   725
Those spotless and without all sin,
Will reach this castle unreviled;
Without delay they're welcomed in
To all the love that lies herein.
This gem the jeweler to secure,   730
Sold all his store, both wool and linen,
To buy this pearl, precious, pure.

"This precious pearl, pure and dear,
That jeweler gave his goods to gain;
Like heaven high, it's bright and clear,   735
The world's Wielder did maintain.
For it is good and gives off cheer;
Its roundness cannot ever wane.
The righteous own it, and sincere;
And long upon my breast it's lain.   740
My Lord the Lamb, Who once was slain,
Has placed it here to reassure
My peace. Forsake this world insane,
And buy that pearl, precious, pure."

"O precious pearl," said I, "so pure,   745
You bear on breast a pearl of price!
Who formed your gown and fair figure?
For surely he was shrewd and wise.
Your beauty's never known in nature;
Pygmalion never painted your face;   750
Nor did Aristotle your
Angelic virtues ever trace.
Your skin's like fleurs-de-lis; and grace
Abounds in your demeanor dear!
O say, I plead, what pious place   755
Do you hold here, my pearl pure?"

"Our Lamb so pure," that pearl said,
"Endeared me to His destiny
As wife, although unwarranted
Such wonder once appeared to be.   760
For when I from the world fled
He granted me the greatest glee:
'Come hither, love, whom I will wed.

For mote ne spot is non in þe."
He gef me myȝt and als bewté;   765
In Hys blod He wesch my wede on dese,
And coronde clene in vergynté,
And pyȝt me in perlez maskellez.'

'Why, maskellez bryd þat bryȝt con flambe,
Þat reiatéz hatz so ryche and ryf,   770
Quat kyn þyng may be þat Lambe
Þat þe wolde wedde vnto Hys vyf?
Ouer alle oþer so hyȝ þou clambe
To lede with Hym so ladyly lyf.
So mony a comly onvunder cambe   775
For Kryst han lyued in much stryf,
And þou con alle þo dere outdryf,
And fro þat maryag al oþer depres,
Al only þyself so stout and styf,
A makelez may and maskellez.'   780

XIV

'Maskelles,' quoþ þat myry quene,
'Vnblemyst I am, wythouten blot,
And þat may I with mensk menteene,
Bot "makelez quene" þenne sade I not.
Þe Lambes vyuez in blysse we bene,   785
A hondred and forty þowsande flot,
As in þe Apocalyppez hit is sene:
Sant John hem syȝ al in a knot.
On þe hyl of Syon, þat semly clot,
Þe apostel hem segh in gostly drem,   790
Arayed to þe weddyng in þat hyl-coppe,
Þe nwe cyté o Jerusalem.

'Of Jerusalem I in speche spelle.
If þou wyl knaw what kyn He be—
My Lombe, my Lorde, my dere Juelle,   795
My Joy, my Blys, my Lemman fre—
Þe profete Ysaye of Hym con melle
Pitously of Hys debonerté:
"Þat gloryous Gyltlez þat mon con quelle
Withouten any sake of felonye,   800
As a schep to þe slaȝt þer lad watz He,
And, as lombe þat clypper in hande nem,
So closed He Hys mouth fro vch query,
Quen Juez Hym jugged in Jerusalem."

You're pure and precious certainly.'
Beauty, bliss, He vouchsafed me,   765
And with His blood washed what I wore.
He crowned me queen in virginity
And robed me in these pearls pure."

"O purest pearl, as bright as flame,
In royalties so rich and rife,   770
What kind is He, that lofty Lamb
Who took you for His trusted wife?
Higher than others did you here climb
To lead with Him this gracious life,
Though many a dear and worthy dame   775
For Christ has lived in lasting strife.
But all those souls you've soared above;
Their dear delight you must defer
When all alone you are His wife.
A peerless pearl, so precious, pure."   780

XIV

"I'm purest pearl," averred that queen,
"Unblemished and without a blot;
And that I may with grace maintain.
But *peerless?* No, I said that not!
We're all dear brides in the Lamb's demesne,   785
All hundred forty thousand that
In the Apocalypse are seen.
Saint John saw all that sinless lot:
In vision strange on Sion's height,
Apostle John saw all and some   790
Of those virgins their nuptial night
In joyous New Jerusalem.

"Jerusalem's true tale I tell,
Conveying just what kind is He:
My Jewel, Lamb, and Lord as well,   795
My blessing, bliss, and ecstasy.
Isaiah does of great God tell,
His cleanness and His clemency,
How He was killed upon a hill
When falsely charged with felony.   800
And though He lived quite guiltlessly,
As sheep in shearers' hands succumb
He kept His peace when heinously
Jews judged Him in Jerusalem.

'In Jerusalem watz my Lemman slayn   805
And rent on rode with boyez bolde,
Al oure balez to bere ful bayn
He toke on Hymself oure carez colde;
With boffetez watz Hys face flayn
Þat watz so fayr on to byholde.   810
For synne He set Hymself in vayn,
Þat neuer hade non Hymself to wolde;
For vus He lette Hym flyȝe and folde,
And brede vpon a bostwys bem;
As meke as lomp þat no playnt tolde   815
For vus He swalt in Jerusalem.

'In Jerusalem, Jordan, and Galalye,
Þeras baptysed þe goude Saynt Jon,
His wordez acorded to Ysaye.
When Jesus con to hym warde gon,   820
He sayde of Hym þys professye:
"Lo, Godez Lombe as trwe as ston,
Þat dotz away þe synnez dryȝe
Þat alle þys worlde hatz wroȝt vpon.
Hymself ne wroȝt neuer ȝet non,   825
Wheþer on Hymself He con al clem.
Hys generacyoun quo recen con,
Þat dyȝed for vus in Jerusalem?"

'In Jerusalem þus my Lemman swete
Twyez for lombe watz taken þare,   830
By trw recorde of ayþer prophete,
For mode so meke and al Hys fare.
Þe þryde tyme is þerto ful mete,
In Apokalypez wryten ful ȝare:
Inmydez þe trone, þere sayntez sete,   835
Þe apostel John Hym saȝ as bare,
Lesande þe boke with leuez sware
Þere seuen syngnettez wern sette in seme.
And at þat syȝt vche douth con dare,
In helle, in erþe, and Jerusalem.   840

XV

'Thys Jerusalem Lombe hade neuer pechche
Of oþer huee bot quyt jolyf
Þat mot ne masklle moȝt on streche,
For wolle quyte so ronk and ryf.
Forþy vche saule þat hade neuer teche   845
Is to þat Lombe a worthyly wyf.

"In drear Jerusalem He died   805
Between two thieves—men bad and bold—
For crimes we cast was crucified.
Thus Adam's felony He felled.
To Him were wicked whips applied
And to His holy face! Behold,   810
For sins we sowed our Maker died!
In righteousness He reconciled
Our fault. And for our failing fold
He waned on cross all wearisome;
Just as a lamb was our Lord felled   815
In joyless, sad Jerusalem.

"Jerusalem, Jordan, Galilee—
John baptized souls within each zone.
Isaiah's words with John's agree;
For, judging Jesus, John made known   820
By privilege of a prophecy:
'Behold God's Lamb, steadfast as stone,
Who from foul sin will mankind free,
Though sin is thickly overgrown.'
Our sinfulness was not His own;   825
Yet for those sins did He succumb.
His origin is never known
Who died in drear Jerusalem!

"Jerusalem saw my Love submit.
Isaiah's words and John's compare: 830
'The Lord is like a lamb.' They fit:
'Our Lord,' both add, 'is fine and fair.'
A third time, too, does Holy Writ
The same sagacious point declare.
John saw Him once. The saints did sit   835
Around Him, ranged upon a chair.
Christ opened up the book that bore
The seven seals. All were struck dumb
At such a sight. On earth was fear,
In hell, and high Jerusalem.   840

XV

"Jerusalem's lovely Lamb was white;
To stain Him nothing could contrive.
On that soft fleece no spot could sit;
With richest wool it was full rife.
Just so each unstained soul is fit   845
To be that Lamb's worthy wife.

And þaȝ vch day a store He feche,
Among vus commez nouþer strot ne stryf,
Bot vchon enlé we wolde were fyf—
Þe mo þe myryer, so God me blesse!
In compayny gret our luf con þryf,   850
In honour more and neuer þe lesse.

'Lasse of blysse may non vus bryng
Þat beren þys perle vpon oure bereste,
For þay of mote couþe neuer mynge   855
Of spotlez perlez þat beren þe creste.
Alþaȝ oure corses in clottez clynge,
And ȝe remen for rauþe wythouten reste,
We þurȝoutly hauen cnawyng;
Of on dethe ful oure hope is drest.   860
Þe Lombe vus gladez, oure care is kest;
He myrþez vus alle at vch a mes.
Vchonez blysse is breme and beste,
And neuer onez honour ȝet neuer þe les.

'Lest les þou leue my talle farande,   865
In Appocalyppece is wryten in wro:
"I seghe," says John, "þe Loumbe Hym stande
On þe mount of Syon ful þryuen and þro,
And wyth Hym maydennez an hundreþe þowsande,
And fowre and forty þowsande mo.   870
On alle her forhedez wryten I fande
Þe Lombez nome, Hys Faderez also.
A hue fro heuen I herde þoo,
Lyk flodez fele laden runnen on resse;
And as þunder þrowez in torrez blo—   875
Þat lote, I leue, watz neuer þe les.

'"Nauþeles, þaȝ hit schowted scharpe,
And ledden loude alþaȝ hit were,
A note ful nwe I herde hem warpe,
To lysten þat watz ful lufly dere.   880
As harporez harpen in her harpe,
Þat nwe songe þay songen ful cler,
In sounande notez a gentyl carpe;
Ful fayre þe modez þay fonge in fere.
Ryȝt byfore Godez chayere   885
And þe fowre bestez þat Hym obes
And þe aldermen so sadde of chere,
Her songe þay songen, neuer þe les.

Each day new crowds does He admit;
For favors, though, we never strive.
Each one He brings we would were five.
The more the merrier in bliss!   850
In endless throngs our love will thrive;
Our love grows more and never less.

"Our love's no less when others bring
Their bliss to us. On every breast
A pearl is strung; no strife can spring   855
Among the souls who share that crest.
Though on our corpses dirt clods cling
And mortals mourn our death, distressed,
One death to us did knowledge bring
And all our raging wrongs redressed.   860
So by that Lamb were we all blessed.
He brings us mirth with every Mass.
Each one is with kind bliss caressed,
Yet others' honors are never less.

"The less to think the tale a lie,   865
Take Revelation's words: 'Along
With the Lamb, I saw on Sion high
A hundred thousand virgins throng
And four and forty thousand nigh!
I saw that on each forehead shone   870
The Lamb's and Father's names. The sky
Then issued forth a fearful song:
A sound like rivers, raging, strong,
Or hurly-burly from abyss
That lashed out loud and lasted long;   875
O Lord that sound was never less!

" 'Never less, it sounded sharp;
But although loud and long that roar,
Those virgins' voices did it usurp.
They sang a note, both strong and dear.   880
As heavenly as humming harp
Was the song they sang, assured and clear.
Never did it wane or warp;
They chanted long that canto's cheer.
Before God's throne, to which were near   885
The beasts that bowed in lowliness,
Before the elders, all austere,
They sang that song and never less.

'"Nowþelese non watz neuer so quoynt,
For alle þe craftez þat euer þay knewe,   890
Þat of þat songe myȝt synge a poynt,
Bot þat meyny þe Lombe þat swe;
For þay arn boȝt, fro þe vrþe aloynte,
As newe fryt to God ful due,
And to þe gentyl Lombe hit arn anjoynt,   895
As lyk to Hymself of lote and hwe;
For neuer lesyng ne tale vntrwe
Ne towched her tonge for no dysstresse.
Þat moteles meyny may neuer remwe
Fro þat maskelez mayster, neuer þe les."'   900

'Neuer þe les let be my þonc,'
Quoþ I, 'my perle þaȝ I appose;
I schulde not tempte þy wyt so wlonc,
To Krystez chambre þat art ichose.
I am bot mokke and mul among,   905
And þou so ryche a reken rose,
And bydez here by þys blysful bonc
Þer lyuez lyste may neuer lose.
Now, hynde, þat sympelnesse conez enclose,
I wolde þe aske a þynge expresse,   910
And þaȝ I be bustwys as a bose,
Let my bone vayl neuerþelese.

XVI

'Neuerþelese, cler, I yow bycalle,
If ȝe con se hyt be to done;
As þou art gloryous withouten galle,   915
Withnay þou neuer my ruful bone.
Haf ȝe no wonez in castel-walle,
Ne maner þer ȝe may mete and won?
Þou tellez me of Jerusalem þe ryche ryalle,
Þer Dauid dere watz dyȝt on trone,   920
Bot by þyse holtez hit con not hone,
Bot in Judée hit is, þat noble note.
As ȝe ar maskelez vnder mone,
Your wonez schulde be wythouten mote.

'Þys motelez meyny þou conez of mele,   925
Of þousandez þryȝt so gret a route;
A gret ceté, for ȝe arn fele,
Yow byhod haue, withouten doute.
So cumly a pakke of joly juele
Wer euel don schulde lyȝ þeroute,   930

" 'No less they were! No mortal throat,
For all the skills the singer knew,
Could sing that sonorous song's first note,   890
Unless he joined that joyous crew.
From earthly sin they stand remote;
As fine first fruits to God they're due.
And with the Lamb they're one, devout,   895
Most like the Lord in looks and hue,
And never tell a tale untrue.
Among them there is no distress,
No single soul who would ensue
To leave the Lord. They're never less.' "   900

"Nevertheless, then let me thank
My pearl," said I, "although I pose
More questions now to you whose link   *not trusting*
With Christ is intimate. He chose
Your hand! In sinfulness I'm sunk,
But you're a fine and fresh new rose   *his daughter → rose (995)*
Abiding by this blissful bank.
Your love and life you'll never lose.
But now I beg you to excuse
Impertinence. This plea address: 910
Although I'm wretched, rife with woes,
I beg your knowledge nevertheless.

XVI

"Lady, nevertheless I call
Upon your help, should you condone.
You're great and glorious, all in all.   915
To me now make your knowledge known.
Have you no well-wrought castle wall?
Don't you demesne and manor own?
Jerusalem has towers tall: *still looking*
There David ruled on regal throne.   *for material*
But that's not near this wooded zone;   *greatness*   920
Judea boasts that bounteous plot.
Unmatched are you beneath the moon;
Your house should be without a spot.

"Those spotless souls of which you tell,   925
A throng of thousands you're throughout;
Your city must be sizable
And wide! It wouldn't be allowed
That strong and sparkling citadel
These wondrous virgins were without.   930

And by þyse bonkez þer I con gele
I se no bygyng nawhere aboute.
I trowe alone ȝe lenge and loute
To loke on þe glory of þys gracious gote.
If þou hatz oþer bygyngez stoute,   935
Now tech me to þat myry mote.'

'That mote þou menez in Judy londe,'
Þat specyal spyce þen to me spakk,
'Þat is þe cyté þat þe Lombe con fonde
To soffer inne sor for manez sake,   940
Þe olde Jerusalem to vnderstonde,
For þere þe olde gulte watz don to slake.
Bot þe nwe, þat lyȝt of Godez sonde,
Þe apostel in Apocalyppce in theme con take.
Þe Lompe þer withouten spottez blake   945
Hatz feryed þyder Hys fayre flote;
And as Hys flok is withouten flake,
So is Hys mote withouten moote.

'Of motez two to carpe clene,
And Jerusalem hyȝt boþe nawþeles—   950
Þat nys to yow no more to mene
Bot "ceté of God" oþer "syȝt of pes"—
In þat on oure pes watz mad at ene;
With payne to suffer þe Lombe hit chese;
In þat oþer is noȝt bot pes to glene   955
Þat ay schal laste withouten reles.
Þat is þe borȝ þat we to pres
Fro þat oure flesch be layd to rote,
Þer glory and blysse schal euer encres
To þe meyny þat is withouten mote.'   960

'Motelez may so meke and mylde,'
Þen sayde I to þat lufly flor,
'Bryng me to þat bygly bylde
And let me se þy blysful bor.'
Þat schene sayde: 'Þat God wyl schylde;   965
Þou may not enter withinne Hys tor;
Bot of þe Lombe I haue þe aquylde
For a syȝt þerof þurȝ gret fauor.
Vtwyth to se þat clene cloystor
Þou may, bot inwyth not a fote;   970
To strech in þe strete þou hatz no vygour,
Bot þou wer clene, withouten mote.

But by this bank that I now stroll
I see no city here about. *Can't see heaven*
You've reached this dell, I have no doubt,
From far away to find this plot.
If you've a castle, keen and stout, 935
Please show me now that special spot." *Proof?*

"That spot's within Judea's zone
Of which you speak," she said to me.
"Our Lord the Lamb did there atone
With death our dire villainy. 940
As '*Old* Jerusalem' it's known;
From sin the Son there set us free.
The *New* Jerusalem was shown
To John within an ecstasy.
That lofty Lamb with all His glee 945
Has led us to that lovely lot.
And as we show no treachery,
That city is without a spot.

"There are two separate spots, you glean,
Both called 'Jerusalem,' which might
Become confused; that name can mean
'City of God' or 'Peace's Sight.' *literal →* *anagogical* 950
In one the lofty Lamb did clean
Through death our deep and dire blight.
The other stands by men unseen; 955
There peace ensues without respite.
Thereto our fleeting souls take flight
When death has come and corpses rot.
There lasting love and pure delight
Come to that throng without a spot." 960

"My spotless maiden, mild and bright, *I won't to go to Heaven.*
Let's find that precious place, I plea;
O guide me to its glorious height,"
I said then to that fleur-de-lis.
"Such access God does not think right, 965
And won't allow," she said to me.
"The Lamb, although, with fleece so white,
Did in His graciousness agree *got a sneak preview*
To let you stand apart and see *as it is*
From far away that city's plot; 970
But in that city's streets can be
The clean alone, without a spot.

XVII

'If I þis mote þe schal vnhyde,
Bow vp towarde þys bornez heued,
And I anendez þe on þis syde   975
Schal sve, tyl þou to a hil be veued.'
Þen wolde I no lenger byde,
Bot lurked by launcez so lufly leued,
Tyl on a hyl þat I asspyed
And blusched on þe burghe, as I forth dreued,   980
Byȝonde þe brok, fro me warde keued,
Þat schyrrer þen sunne with schaftez schon.
In þe Apokalypce is þe fasoun preued,
As deuysez hit þe apostel John.

As John þe apostel hit syȝ with syȝt,   985
I syȝe þat cyty of gret renoun,
Jerusalem so nwe and ryally dyȝt,
As hit watz lyȝt fro þe heuen adoun.
Þe borȝ watz al of brende golde bryȝt,
As glemande glas burnist broun,   990
With gentyl gemmez anvnder pyȝt,
With bantelez twelue on basyng boun,
Þe foundementez twelue of riche tenoun;
Vch tabelment watz a serlypez ston,
As derely deuysez þis ilk toun   995
In Apocalyppez þe apostel John.

As John þise stonez in writ con nemme,
I knew þe name after his tale.
Jasper hyȝt þe fyrst gemme
Þat I on þe fyrst basse con wale—   1000
He glente grene in þe lowest hemme.
Saffer helde þe secounde stale;
Þe calsydoyne þenne withouten wemme
In þe þryd table con purly pale;
Þe emerade þe furþe so grene of scale;   1005
Þe sardonyse þe fyfþe ston;
Þe sexte þe rybé. He con hit wale
In þe Apocalyppce, þe apostel John.

Ȝet joyned John þe crysolyt,
Þe seuenþe gemme in fundament;   1010
Þe aȝtþe þe beryl cler and quyt;
Þe topasye twynne-hew þe nente endent;
Þe crysopase þe tenþe is tyȝt;
Þe jacynght þe enleuenþe gent;
Þe twelfþe, þe tryeste in vch a plyt,   1015

XVII

"To see that spotless city, stride
Along this river's running bed.
I'll lead you there along this side   975
Till to a lofty hill you're led."
No longer would I wait or bide;
I slipped along light leaves outspread
Till that great citadel I spied.
I saw—as, moving forth, I sped   980
Along the stream, near a high hill's head—
A city bright as the sun thereon,
As I'd in Revelation read,
Described by the Apostle John.

Just as John had seen that site,   985
I saw that scene, that famous zone:
Jerusalem as from a height
Descended down to me alone.
Of burnished gold it was, as bright
As glints of gleaming glass, and prone   990
To radiate rich rays of light.
Twelve great tiers along it shone,
All twelve as steps arranged. Each stone
Was differently composed thereon,
As was announced in that well-known   995
Apocalypse of Apostle John.

As John has called those gems by name,
I recognized each rock I eyed.
Green jasper was the gem that came
Along the lowest level, wide   1000
And fine and flickering its flame.
The next was sapphire that I spied.
Chalcedony, of great acclaim,
Adorned the third with pomp and pride.
Of emerald was the fourth step's side.   1005
The fifth sardonyx had thereon.
The sixth was ruby, as descried
Apocalypse of Apostle John.

John said that shining chrysolite
The seventh step adorned. He found   1010
The eighth was beryl, blue and bright.
The ninth with topaz did abound.
The tenth was chrysoprase, so right.
The next with jacinth gems was crowned.
The twelfth, which doles such dear delight,   1015

Þe amatyst purpre with ynde blente.
Þe wal abof þe bantels bent
O jasporye, as glas þat glysnande schon.
I knew hit by his deuysement
In þe Apocalyppez, þe apostel John.   1020

As John deuysed ȝet saȝ I þare:
Þise twelue degrés wern brode and stayre;
Þe cyté stod abof ful sware,
As longe as brode as hyȝe ful fayre.
Þe stretez of golde as glasse al bare,   1025
Þe wal of jasper þat glent as glayre.
Þe wonez withinne enurned ware
Wyth alle kynnez perré þat moȝt repayre.
Þenne helde vch sware of þis manayre
Twelue forlonge space, er euer hit fon,   1030
Of heȝt, of brede, of lenþe to cayre,
For meten hit syȝ þe apostel John.

XVIII

As John hym wrytez ȝet more I syȝe:
Vch pane of þat place had þre ȝatez,
So twelue in poursent I con asspye,   1035
Þe portalez pyked of rych platez,
And vch ȝate of a margyrye,
A parfyt perle þat neuer fatez.
Vchon in scrypture a name con plye
Of Israel barnez, folewande her datez,   1040
Þat is to say, as her byrþ-whatez;
Þe aldest ay fyrst þeron watz done.
Such lyȝt þer lemed in alle þe stratez
Hem nedde nawþer sunne ne mone.

Of sunne ne mone had þay no nede;   1045
Þe Self God watz her lombe-lyȝt,
Þe Lombe her lantyrne, withouten drede;
Þurȝ Hym blysned þe borȝ al bryȝt.
Þurȝ woȝe and won my lokyng ȝede;
For sotyle cler noȝt lette no syȝt.   1050
Þe hyȝe trone þer moȝt ȝe hede
With alle þe apparaylmente vmbepyȝte,
As John þe appostel in termez tyȝte.
Þe hyȝe Godez Self hit set vpone.
A reuer of þe trone þer ran outryȝte   1055
Watz bryȝter þen boþe þe sunne and mone.

Was amethyst with blue inwound.
The wall above those walks ran round
With jasper gems that clung thereon.
I'd read of all in the renowned
Apocalypse of Apostle John.   1020

What John had watched I witnessed there!
Those twelve long steps rose steep and sheer.
That city soared, a solid square!
In length and height did it adhere
To its full breadth. Its streets were fair   1025
And gold! Its walls were jasper, clear
As egg-glaze, white; while everywhere
Did prized and precious gems appear.
That cherished site gave off such cheer!
Twelve furlongs' length it ran upon;   1030
Twelve furlongs' depth, both far and near.
So measured all Apostle John.

XVIII

What John had seen I there did see.
That city's sides each had three gates;
Thus twelve there were. Wrought wondrously   1035
Upon those doors were precious plates;
Each had a mounted margery,
And each a name that consecrates
Israel's twelve sons handily.
In turn each gate communicates,   1040
According to their births' true dates,
The oldest to the last. A boon
Of light that city radiates;
It needed neither sun nor moon.

There the sun and moon supplied   1045
No glow, for God alone was light,
The Lamb their lantern glorified;
That city shone and glimmered bright.
Through tall, transparent walls I spied
Great houses with unhindered sight.   1050
A wondrous throne, well edified,
Stood there, steadfast in its might.
Just as John did truly write,
High God Himself adorned that throne.
A river ran from Him, so bright   1055
It outshone both the sun and moon!

Sunne ne mone schon neuer so swete
As þat foysoun flode out of þat flet;
Swyþe hit swange þurȝ vch a strete
Withouten fylþe oþer galle oþer glet.   1060
Kyrk þerinne watz non ȝete,
Chapel ne temple þat euer watz set;
Þe Almyȝty watz her mynster mete,
Þe Lombe þe sakerfyse þer to refet.
Þe ȝatez stoken watz neuer ȝet,   1065
Bot euermore vpen at vche a lone;
Þer entrez non to take reset
Þat berez any spot anvnder mone.

The mone may þerof acroche no myȝte;
To spotty ho is, of body to grym,   1070
And also þer ne is neuer nyȝt.
What schulde þe mone þer compas clym
And to euen wyth þat worþly lyȝt
Þat schynez vpon þe brokez brym?
Þe planetez arn in to pouer a plyȝt,   1075
And þe self sunne ful fer to dym.
Aboute þat water arn tres ful schym,
Þat twelue frytez of lyf con bere ful sone;
Twelue syþez on ȝer þay beren ful frym,
And renowlez nwe in vche a mone.   1080

Anvnder mone so gret merwayle
No fleschly hert ne myȝt endeure
As quen I blusched vpon þat baly,
So ferly þerof watz þe fasure.
I stod as stylle as dased quayle   1085
For ferly of þat frech fygure,
Þat felde I nawþer reste ne trauayle,
So watz I rauyste wyth glymme pure.
For I dar say with conciens sure,
Hade bodyly burne abiden þat bone,   1090
Þaȝ alle clerkez hym hade in cure,
His lyf wer loste anvnder mone.

XIX

Ryȝt as þe maynful mone con rys
Er þenne þe day-glem dryue al doun,
So sodanly on a wonder wyse   1095
I watz war of a prosessyoun.
Þis noble cité of ryche enpresse
Watz sodanly ful, withouten sommoun,

The sun and moon shine not so sweet
As that rich river ran and flowed.
It swiftly swept through every street,
So free from filth was every road.   1060
No temple stood in that retreat,
No church or chapel ever showed;
In the Almighty do they meet,
Their Lamb, their Sacrifice Who strode
On earth and second life bestowed.   1065
All doors are open night and noon.
No one reaches that rich abode
Who sports a spot beneath the moon.

The moon has in that land no might;
She cannot with such brightness vie.   1070
And since there's never known dark night
Why should she sail through the sky?
If set beside the shining light
That glistens there, both low and high,
The sun and planets, although bright,   1075
Would dim and darken to the eye.
Twelve trees are growing tall nearby
That stream, with fruits of life bestrewn.
Twelve times a year they fructify,
So much renewed as is the moon.   1080

So much beneath the moon no frail
And mortal heart could well endure!
I saw that city, grand in scale;
So fine and fierce was its allure,
I stood as still as startled quail.   1085
I neither knew discomfiture
Nor suffered from the least travail.
With radiance was I ravished, pure!
So I dare say, with conscience sure,
Had mortal body borne that boon   1090
The greatest clerks could find no cure
For that mere man beneath the moon.

XIX

Just as the mighty moon will rise
Before the shining sun is down,
So then, before my blissful eyes,   1095
There formed a crowd. Within that town
Those precious virgins, each a prize,
Together went. With great renown

Of such vergynez in þe same gyse
Þat watz my blysful anvnder croun.   1100
And coronde wern alle of þe same fasoun,
Depaynt in perlez and wedez qwyte;
In vchonez breste watz bounden boun
Þe blysful perle with gret delyt.

With gret delyt þay glod in fere   1105
On golden gatez þat glent as glasse;
Hundreth þowsandez I wot þer were,
And alle in sute her liuréz wasse.
Tor to knaw þe gladdest chere.
Þe Lombe byfore con proudly passe   1110
Wyth hornez seuen of red golde cler;
As praysed perlez His wedez wasse.
Towarde þe throne þay trone a tras.
Þaȝ þay wern fele, no pres in plyt,
Bot mylde as maydenez seme at mas,   1115
So droȝ þay forth with gret delyt.

Delyt þat Hys come encroched
To much hit were of for to melle.
Þise aldermen, quen He aprochad,
Grouelyng to His fete þay felle.   1120
Legyounes of aungelez togeder uoched
Þer kesten ensens of swete smelle;
Þen glory and gle watz nwe abroched;
Al songe to loue þat gay Juelle.
Þe steuen moȝt stryke þurȝ þe vrþe to helle   1125
Þat þe vertues of heuen of joye endyte.
To loue þe Lombe His meyny inmelle
Iwysse I laȝt a gret delyt.

Delit þe Lombe for to deuise
With much meruayle in mynde went.   1130
Best watz He, blyþest, and moste to pryse,
Þat euer I herde of speche spent;
So worþly whyt wern wedez Hys,
His lokez symple, Hymself so gent.
Bot a wounde ful wyde and weete con wyse   1135
Anende Hys hert, þurȝ hyde torente.
Of His quyte syde His blod outsprent.
Alas, þoȝt I, who did þat spyt?
Ani breste for bale aȝt haf forbrent
Er he þerto hade had delyt.   1140

Each virgin gathered in the guise
That my pure pearl wore: with crown   1100
Just as my gentle gem's, and gown
Of precious pearls, all pure and bright.
And on each shimmering breast there shone
A precious pearl of pure delight.

With great delight they gathered near   1105
Those glasslike gates that glowed, inlaid:
A hundred thousand throng, all dear,
All dressed in pearls, a fine parade.
It's hard to say who had most cheer.
Then came the lofty Lamb, displayed   1110
In precious pearls, each pure and clear,
And seven golden horns. Arrayed,
Those virgins formed an accolade
Before His throne. They showed no spite;
But meek and mild as a maid   1115
At Mass they went with great delight.

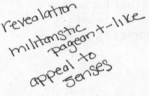
revelation militaristic pageant-like appeal to senses

His coming brought delight, too dear
For merely a mortal man to tell.
For when that lofty Lamb drew near
The elders at His feet all fell.   1120
Fine angels came, each casting clear
And strong incense of sweetest smell.
Anew that company did cheer
That Jewel; their song did grow and swell.
That sound could sink through earth to hell,   1125
That the virtues hailed from heaven's height.
I loved that lofty Lamb as well
As all the rest, with dear delight.

Shared delight

Delightful, dear enough to daze,
Was that wise Lamb. In wonderment   1130
I held Him worthier of praise
Than all on whom much speech is spent.
All white He was, so wise His ways,
So mighty and magnificent.
A wound, still wet, was there, ablaze.   1135
Below His heart His skin was rent;
And from the wound bright blood was sent.
"Great God," I thought, "Who's done this spite?
A breast should be with sorrow bent
Before it finds in this delight."   1140

The Lamb turning pt

who did this?

The Lombe delyt non lyste to wene;
Þaȝ He were hurt and wounde hade,
In His sembelaunt watz neuer sene,
So wern His glentez gloryous glade.
I loked among His meyny schene   1145
How þay wyth lyf wern laste and lade;
Þen saȝ I þer my lyttel quene
Þat I wende had standen by me in sclade.
Lorde, much of mirþe watz þat ho made
Among her ferez þat watz so quyt!   1150
Þat syȝt me gart to þenk to wade
For luf-longyng in gret delyt.

XX

Delyt me drof in yȝe and ere,
My manez mynde to maddyng malte;
Quen I seȝ my frely, I wolde be þere,   1155
Byȝonde þe water þaȝ ho were walte.
I þoȝt þat noþyng myȝt me dere
To fech me bur and take me halte,
And to start in þe strem schulde non me stere,
To swymme þe remnaunt, þaȝ I þer swalte.   1160
Bot of þat munt I watz bitalt;
When I schulde start in þe strem astraye,
Out of þat caste I watz bycalt:
Hit watz not at my Pryncez paye.

Hit payed Hym not þat I so flonc   1165
Ouer meruelous merez, so mad arayd.
Of raas þaȝ I were rasch and ronk,
Ȝet rapely þerinne I watz restayed,
For ryȝt as I sparred vnto þe bonc,
Þat brathþe out of my drem me brayde.   1170
Þen wakned I in þat erber wlonk;
My hede vpon þat hylle watz layde
Þeras my perle to grounde strayd.
I raxled, and fel in gret affray,
And, sykyng, to myself I sayd: 1175
'Now al be to þat Pryncez paye.'

Me payed ful ille to be outfleme
So sodenly of þat fayre regioun,
Fro alle þo syȝtez so quyke and queme.
A longeyng heuy me strok in swonc,   1180
And rewfully þenne I con to reme:
'O perle,' quoþ I, 'of rych renoun,

That Lamb's delight might no man glean;
Though wounded there, His face betrayed
No suffering. No sign was seen
Of lingering pain; His look conveyed
Sheer joy. I saw that crowd; serene   1145
It looked, with lasting life repaid.
And soon I saw my sweetest queen;
I'd thought she'd stood by me, not strayed.
Much mirth was mine to see my maid
Among that crowd. She was so white   1150
And wonderful, I longed to wade
That river rare with rich delight.

No longer mourning loss

XX

Delight then dazed my ear and eye;
I stood there, stupid, stultified.
The more I saw that maid nearby   1155
The more I pined to reach her side;
And thinking nothing would deny
My way, I swelled with silly pride,
And vainly, madly, vowed to try
To swim that stream although I died   1160
Before I crossed that river wide!
Before I reached such ecstasies,
A beckoning told me to bide:
My plan did not my true Prince please. — *God wouldn't want him to*

Displeased that I should have the gall   1165
To cross that stream, my steps He stayed.
Although I heeded not that call,
My walk was wondrously delayed;
For when I reached that river all
My dream did flit away and fade!   1170
I woke just where I first did fall
Asleep; on that same spot I laid
Where first my precious pearl had strayed.
My mind was marred with agonies,
But sighing to myself I prayed: 1175
"Let be whatever that Prince please!"

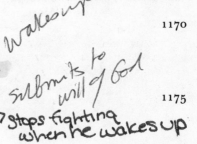

Wakes up
submits to will of God
stops fighting when he wakes up

Deeply displeased was I to be
Exiled from that realm so bright,
So rich and rife in royalty.
Swooning with gall and grief, in plight,   1180
I piteously began to plea:
"O pearl—precious, prized, and right—

So watz hit me dere þat þou con deme
In þys veray avysyoun!
If hit be ueray and soth sermoun   1185
Þat þou so strykez in garlande gay,
So wel is me in þys doel-doungoun
Þat þou art to þat Prynsez paye.'

To þat Pryncez paye hade I ay bente,
And ȝerned no more þen watz me geuen,   1190
And halden me þer in trwe entent,
As þe perle me prayed þat watz so þryuen,
As helde, drawen to Goddez present,
To mo of His mysterys I hade ben dryuen.
Bot ay wolde man of happe more hente   1195
Þen moȝte by ryȝt vpon hem clyuen;
Þerfore my joye watz sone toriuen,
And I kaste of kythez þat lastez aye.
Lorde, mad hit arn þat agayn Þe stryuen,
Oþer proferen Þe oȝt agayn Þy paye.   1200

To pay þe Prince oþer sete saȝte
Hit is ful eþe to þe god Krystyin;
For I haf founden Hym, boþe day and naȝte,
A God, a Lorde, a frende ful fyin.
Ouer þis hyul þis lote I laȝte,   1205
For pyty of my perle enclyin,
And syþen to God I hit bytaȝte,
In Krystez dere blessyng and myn,
Þat in þe forme of bred and wyn
Þe preste vus schewez vch a daye.   1210
He gef vus to be His homly hyne
Ande precious perlez vnto His pay.
                        Amen.   Amen.

How dear is what you've done for me
In showing me this shining sight;
For if you've really gained delight   1185
And wear that garland, it would ease
My days within this dungeon's blight
To know that you the pure Prince please!"

Had I to please that Prince been bent,
Not craved more than was granted me,   1190
But stood there, still, obedient
To my pure pearl's true decree,
I might have been to great God sent
And shown there still more mystery.
But mortals, madly, are intent   1195
On making more than rightfully
Is theirs. Gone was my greatest glee.
I stood, exiled from ecstasies.
O Lord, he's lost who foolishly
Turns not to You Whom he should please!   1200

To please that Prince, to be contrite,
Can all good Christians still incline.
For He is near, both noon and night,
Our God, our Lord, and Friend. For mine
Was a fair fortune when on height   1205
For my pure pearl I swooned, supine.
Since then I've stayed both true and right.
So with Christ's blessings, free and fine,
Which in the form of Bread and Wine
Many a mortal daily sees,   1210
Oh, may we serve Him well and shine
As precious pearls our Lord to please.
                    Amen   Amen

Cleanness

The facing-page text is reproduced from *The Poems of the Pearl Manuscript: Pearl, Cleanness, Patience, Sir Gawain and the Green Knight,* ed. Malcolm Andrew and Ronald Waldron (rev. ed. University of Exeter, 1987).

Clannesse whoso kyndly cowþe comende,
And rekken vp alle þe resounz þat ho by riȝt askez,
Fayre formez myȝt he fynde in forþering his speche,
And in þe contraré kark and combraunce huge.
For wonder wroth is þe Wyȝ þat wroȝt alle þinges   5
Wyth þe freke þat in fylþe folȝes Hym after—
As renkez of relygioun þat reden and syngen,
And aprochen to Hys presens, and prestez arn called;
Thay teen vnto His temmple and temen to Hymseluen,
Reken with reuerence þay rychen His auter,   10
Þay hondel þer His aune body and vsen hit boþe.
If þay in clannes be clos þay cleche gret mede;
Bot if þay conterfete crafte and cortaysye wont,
As be honest vtwyth and inwith alle fylþez,
Þen ar þay synful hemself, and sulpen altogeder   15
Boþe God and His gere, and Hym to greme cachen.
He is so clene in His courte, þe Kyng þat al weldez,
And honeste in His housholde, and hagherlych serued
With angelez enourled in alle þat is clene,
Boþe withinne and withouten in wedez ful bryȝt;   20
Nif He nere scoymus and skyg, and non scaþe louied,
Hit were a meruayl to much, hit moȝt not falle.
Kryst kydde hit Hymself in a carp onez,
Þeras He heuened aȝt happez and hyȝt hem her medez.
Me mynez on one amonge oþer, as Maþew recordez,   25
Þat þus of clannesse vnclosez a ful cler speche:
'Þe haþel clene of his hert hapenez ful fayre,
For he schal loke on oure Lorde with a leue chere';
As so saytz, to þat syȝt seche schal he neuer
Þat any vnclannesse hatz on, auwhere abowte;   30
For He þat flemus vch fylþe fer fro His hert
May not byde þat burre þat hit His body neȝe.
Forþy hyȝ not to heuen in haterez totorne,
Ne in þe harlatez hod, and handez vnwaschen.
For what vrþly haþel þat hyȝ honour haldez   35
Wolde lyke if a ladde com lyþerly attyred,
When he were sette solempnely in a sete ryche,
Abof dukez on dece, with dayntys serued?
Þen þe harlot with haste helded to þe table,
With rent cokrez at þe kne and his clutte traschez,   40
And his tabarde totorne, and his totez oute,
Oþer ani on of alle þyse, he schulde be halden vtter,
With mony blame ful bygge, a boffet peraunter,
Hurled to þe halle dore and harde þeroute schowued,
And be forboden þat borȝe to bowe þider neuer,   45
On payne of enprysonment and puttyng in stokkez;
And þus schal he be schent for his schrowde feble,

Cleanness: who would clearly acclaim her with praise
And rehearse all the reverence she rightly demands
Will soon find fitting phrases and forms for the task.
But to praise the impure would be painful and hard.
He Who wrought all is righteously wrathful, incensed,   5
If a votary's vile and has villainous ways.
For consider God's servants who sing and who read,
Who approach His presence as priests of the church,
And who take to His temple, entrusting their lives.
If they piously preach; if, approaching His altar,   10
They bring forth His beauteous body with awe;
If they're pure; then they're plenteously paid by the Lord.
If their faith, though, is false, if they fail to be true,
If, appearing pious, they're poisoned within,
Then they're sinful themselves, and they surely defile   15
Both our God and God's vessels and goad Him to wrath.
For so clean in His court is the King of all things,
And so fair to His folk, that He's faithfully served
By the angels who, inside and outside all pure,
Are bedecked with brilliance in bright, glowing robes.   20
If the Lord were not loathe to see lying and wrong,
That would be a great wonder! It wouldn't occur!
Jesus Christ made this clear in His discourses once
When He blessed with bliss the Beatitudes eight.
I've in mind one among those whom Matthew records;   25
In a discourse on cleanness he clearly insists:
"They are blissful and blessed whose breasts are pure;
They will look on our Lord and be light in their hearts!"
Matthew says that such sight won't be seen by the bad,
Or by any who anywhere on them have filth.   30
He Who's flung every filth very far from His heart
Cannot bear that a blemished body be near!
So don't hasten to heaven in hideous clothes,
Nor the robes of a rogue, nor with rough, filthy hands;
For how would a holder of high place react   35
If a rogue who was wretched and rough came right up,
While he solemnly sat on a splendid throne
Above dukes on a dais, all daintily served,
If that rogue in a rush came right up to the bench,
Dressed in wretched old rags and in ripped, filthy hose,   40
With his tunic torn and his toes sticking out?
He'd be ousted for any or all of these things!
With rebukes he'd be blasted and banished at once;
He'd be hurled to the hallway, heaved from the court,
Forbidden to bide there or bother that lord,   45
Or be placed in a prison, and put into stocks.
Thus disgrace he would get for his garments' bad state,

Þaȝ neuer in talle ne in tuch he trespas more.
And if vnwelcum he were to a wordlych prynce,
Ȝet hym is þe hyȝe Kyng harder in heuen;   50
As Maþew melez in his masse of þat man ryche,
Þat made þe mukel mangerye to marie his here dere,
And sende his sonde þen to say þat þay samne schulde,
And in comly quoyntis to com to his feste:
'For my boles and my borez arn bayted and slayne,   55
And my fedde foulez fatted with sclaȝt,
My polyle þat is penne-fed and partrykez boþe,
Wyth scheldez of wylde swyn, swanez and cronez,
Al is roþeled and rosted ryȝt to þe sete;
Comez cof to my corte, er hit colde worþe.'   60
When þay knewen his cal þat þider com schulde,
Alle excused hem by þe skyly he scape by moȝt.
On hade boȝt hym a borȝ, he sayde, by hys trawþe:
'Now turne I þeder als tyd þe toun to byholde.'
Anoþer nayed also and nurned þis cawse: 65
'I haf ȝerned and ȝat ȝokkez of oxen,
And for my hyȝez hem boȝt; to bowe haf I mester,
To see hem pulle in þe plow aproche me byhouez.'
'And I haf wedded a wyf,' so wer hym þe þryd;
'Excuse me at þe court, I may not com þere.'   70
Þus þay droȝ hem adreȝ with daunger vchone,
Þat non passed to þe place þaȝ he prayed were.
Thenne þe ludych lorde lyked ful ille,
And hade dedayn of þat dede; ful dryȝly he carpez.
He saytz: 'Now for her owne sorȝe þay forsaken habbez;   75
More to wyte is her wrange þen any wylle gentyl.
Þenne gotz forth, my gomez, to þe grete streetez,
And forsettez on vche a syde þe ceté aboute;
Þe wayferande frekez, on fote and on hors,
Boþe burnez and burdez, þe better and þe wers,   80
Laþez hem alle luflyly to lenge at my fest,
And bryngez hem blyþly to borȝe as barounez þay were,
So þat my palays plat ful be pyȝt al aboute;
Þise oþer wrechez iwysse worþy noȝt wern.'
Þen þay cayred and com þat þe cost waked,   85
Broȝten bachlerez hem wyth þat þay by bonkez metten,
Swyerez þat swyftly swyed on blonkez,
And also fele vpon fote, of fre and of bonde.
When þay com to þe courte keppte wern þay fayre,
Styȝtled with þe stewarde, stad in þe halle,   90
Ful manerly with marchal mad for to sitte,
As he watz dere of degré dressed his seete.
Þenne seggez to þe souerayn sayden þerafter:
'Lo! lorde, with your leue, at your lege heste

Though he didn't do damage in deed or in word.
If he were so unwelcome to that worldly prince,
God in heaven on high would be harsher by far! 50
Bear in mind the rich man who, from Matthew we know,
Held a marriage feast meet for his male heir to have.
He sent forth a summons: "Assemble them all!
They shall dine at my dais, well dressed for the feast.
My bulls, my boars, and my birds are made fat; 55
They'll be succulent, certainly, slaughtered and cooked.
My poultry and partridges, pen-fed and fat,
Cranes most sweet, dainty swans, and succulent quail
Are prepared to perfection; they'll please every guest.
Therefore come to my court; quickly come while it's hot!" 60
When they heard they'd been hailed to the house of that lord,
They came up with excuses, declining the feast.
One, pleading he'd purchased some property, said:
"I must see my estate, and settle affairs."
Another said, "No," and announced this excuse: 65
"I have yearned for yoked oxen and yesterday bought
For my servants the same, and must sojourn home now;
As they ply to the plow I am pledged to take charge."
"On my word, I've just wedded a wife," said the third.
"So excuse me at court; I can't come right now." 70
Without manners those men to the messengers spoke,
Each refusing to fare to the feast at the hall.
Angered and grieved upon getting the news,
The lord spoke of the slight he'd received with great wrath:
"They'll be sorry they slighted me, sad they refused; 75
This is wickedness worse than the wicked Gentiles'.
Therefore move out, my men, to the main thoroughfares,
To the city's four sides, and surround the whole place.
Hail there whomever you happen to meet,
All and one: men and women, the wealthy and poor. 80
Ask each one if he's willing to wend his way here.
And as barons then bring them all back to my house
Till my fine hall is filled for the feast I will give.
Those asked first, I have found, were unfit to be guests."
His retainers toured the entire countryside, 85
And beckoned all bachelors back to the court.
Hastening on horse came a host of young squires.
And finally on foot came both freemen and serfs.
When they fared to that feast they were feted with pomp,
Were received by the steward and seated at once 90
By the marshal. Each man, in a mannerly way,
Was arranged by his rank (as is right and fit)
In his seat. Then the servants said to their lord:
"We have gone out as ordered and gathered these men;

And at þi banne we haf broȝt, as þou beden habbez,   95
Mony renischche renkez, and ȝet is roum more.'
Sayde þe lorde to þo ledez, 'Laytez ȝet ferre,
Ferkez out in þe felde, and fechez mo gestez;
Waytez gorstez and greuez, if ani gomez lyggez;
Whatkyn folk so þer fare, fechez hem hider;   100
Be þay fers, be þay feble, forlotez none,
Be þay hol, be þay halt, be þay onyȝed,
And þaȝ þay ben boþe blynde and balterande cruppelez,
Þat my hous may holly by halkez by fylled.
For, certez, þyse ilk renkez þat me renayed habbe,   105
And denounced me noȝt now at þis tyme,
Schul neuer sitte in my sale my soper to fele,
Ne suppe on sope of my seve, þaȝ þay swelt schulde.'
Thenne þe sergauntez, at þat sawe, swengen þeroute,
And diden þe dede þat watz demed, as he deuised hade,   110
And with peple of alle plytez þe palays þay fyllen;
Hit weren not alle on wyuez sunez, wonen with on fader.
Wheþer þay wern worþy oþer wers, wel wern þay stowed,
Ay þe best byfore and bryȝtest atyred,
Þe derrest at þe hyȝe dese, þat dubbed wer fayrest,   115
And syþen on lenþe bilooghe ledez inogh.
And ay as segges serly semed by her wedez,
So with marschal at her mete mensked þay were.
Clene men in compaynye forknowen wern lyte,
And ȝet þe symplest in þat sale watz serued to þe fulle,   120
Boþe with menske and with mete and mynstrasy noble,
And alle þe laykez þat a lorde aȝt in londe schewe.
And þay bigonne to be glad þat god drink haden,
And vch mon with his mach made hym at ese.
Now inmyddez þe mete þe mayster hym biþoȝt   125
Þat he wolde se þe semblé þat samned was þere,
And rehayte rekenly þe riche and þe poueren,
And cherisch hem alle with his cher, and chaufen her joye.
Þen he bowez fro his bour into þe brode halle
And to þe best on þe bench, and bede hym be myry,   130
Solased hem with semblaunt and syled fyrre,
Tron fro table to table and talkede ay myrþe.
Bot as he ferked ouer þe flor, he fande with his yȝe—
Hit watz not for a halyday honestly arayed—
A þral þryȝt in þe þrong vnþryuandely cloþed,   135
Ne no festiual frok, bot fyled with werkkez;
Þe gome watz vngarnyst with god men to dele.
And gremed þerwith þe grete lorde, and greue hym he þoȝt.
'Say me, frende,' quoþ þe freke with a felle chere,
'Hov wan þou into þis won in wedez so fowle?   140
Þe abyt þat þou hatz vpon, no halyday hit menskez:

As you bid we have brought here before you today   95
From the streets all these strangers; yet still there is room."
Said that man to his men, "Well, then, march out again
Wide and far in the fields to fetch me more guests;
To the gorse heaths and groves go and gather more folk;
Go and welcome all walks of life, welcome them all;   100
Whether feeble or fierce, they will find open arms.
Be they wan, one-eyed wastrels or wondrously fit,
Be they halting or hale, healthy or sick—
I would crowd my court with their company now!
All those ones, though, who wouldn't my welcome accept,   105
Who denounced me ignobly, will never again
Find themselves being served any supper of mine,
Nor sipping my soup, though they suffer their deaths!"
At that speech the sergeants to serve him went out,
And dutifully did as he ordered them all: 110
Filled his palace with plenty of people. All sorts
(Although some didn't spring from a sanctioned, true bond!),
Whether worthy or worthless, were well treated there.
Most prominently placed were those people best dressed;
They were seated, as suited their stations, on the dais,   115
While the lower guests lined the length of the board.
Thus each guest, as his garment was gorgeous or poor,
Either rich or rough, by that ranking was placed.
They provided the purest a plenteous meal;
All the same, though, the simplest were served just as much.   120
All made merry with minstrelsy, meat, and good cheer;
By that lord they were lavished with lovely amusements.
All began to be glad—there was good food and drink—
And each guest soon grew gay with the guest at his side.
In the midst of the meal, the master decided   125
That he'd see the assembly he served at his feast
To enhearten, make happy the high and the low,
Be attentive to all, and to teach them good cheer.
So he went on his way to the wide hall below.
There he bid the best at the benches be gay.   130
After talking to those, he continued along
From table to table; he talked to each guest.
But he gleaned soon a guest there whose garments were all
Most unsuited for such an occasion as this,
In that company clothed in the coarsest of rags   135
(From the field they were fouled, neither festive nor pure),
A bold fellow unfit to be found with good men.
At that guest the host grew very angry and said
With ferocity, "Friend, now be frank! By what ruse
Did you get by the guardpost in garments so rude,   140
So unfit for a festival, foul and torn?

Þou, burne, for no brydale art busked in wedez.
How watz þou hardy þis hous for þyn vnhap to neȝe
In on so ratted a robe and rent at þe sydez?
Þow art a gome vngoderly in þat goun febele;   145
Þou praysed me and my place ful pouer and ful gnede,
Þat watz so prest to aproche my presens hereinne.
Hopez þou I be a harlot þi erigaut to prayse?'
Þat oþer burne watz abayst of his broþe wordez,
And hurkelez doun with his hede, þe vrþe he biholdez;   150
He watz so scoumfit of his scylle, lest he skaþe hent,
Þat he ne wyst on worde what he warp schulde.
Þen þe lorde wonder loude laled and cryed,
And talkez to his tormenttourez: 'Takez hym,' he biddez,
'Byndez byhynde, at his bak, boþe two his handez,   155
And felle fetterez to his fete festenez bylyue;
Stik hym stifly in stokez, and stekez hym þerafter
Depe in my doungoun þer doel euer dwellez,
Greuing and gretyng and gryspyng harde
Of teþe tenfully togeder, to teche hym be quoynt.'   160
Thus comparisunez Kryst þe kyndom of heuen
To þis frelych feste þat fele arn to called;
For alle arn laþed luflyly, þe luþer and þe better,
Þat euer wern fulȝed in font, þat fest to haue.
Bot war þe wel, if þou wylt, þy wedez ben clene   165
And honest for þe halyday, lest þou harme lache,
For aproch þou to þat Prynce of parage noble,
He hates helle no more þen hem þat ar sowlé.
Wich arn þenne þy wedez þou wrappez þe inne,
Þat schal schewe hem so schene schrowde of þe best?   170
Hit arn þy werkez, wyterly, þat þou wroȝt hauez,
And lyued with þe lykyng þat lyȝe in þyn hert;
Þat þo be frely and fresch fonde in þy lyue,
And fetyse of a fayr forme to fote and to honde,
And syþen alle þyn oþer lymez lapped ful clene;   175
Þenne may þou se þy Sauior and His sete ryche.
For feler fautez may a freke forfete his blysse,
Þat he þe Souerayn ne se, þen for slauþe one;
As for bobaunce and bost and bolnande priyde
Þroly into þe deuelez þrote man þryngez bylyue.   180
For couetyse and colwarde and croked dedez,
For monsworne and mensclaȝt and to much drynk,
For þefte and for þrepyng, vnþonk may mon haue;
For roborrye and riboudrye and resounez vntrwe,
And dysheriete and depryue dowrie of wydoez,   185
For marryng of maryagez and mayntnaunce of schrewez,
For traysoun and trichcherye and tyrauntyré boþe,
And for fals famacions and fayned lawez;

Sir, you show no respect! I assure you, my friend,
To your woe you arrived at this wedding feast here
In these rags which are ripped up and rent at the sides!
You are saucy and insolent, sneaking in here.   145
My title you treated with true disregard
When my place you approached disrespectfully, man!
Do you pray that I'll prattle, praising such clothes?"
By such fury that fellow was frightened at once;
He heavily hung down his head to the ground,   150
So afraid evil fate would befall him anon
That he quivered wordlessly, waited in awe.
The lord spoke out loudly by lifting his voice.
This he told to his torturers: "Take him!" he cried,
"Bailiff, now bind at his back both his hands,   155
Fix fast on his feet fetters of iron,
Stick him in stocks, and stow him away
In my deepest of dungeons where dwells biting grief,
Where weeping and woe, endless wailing and pain
Live together—until he is taught how to dress!"   160
Jesus Christ thus compares heaven's kingdom on high
To a marriage feast; many are summoned to come.
Indeed, all are invited, both evil and good,
To that feast if at font they have first been baptized.
But be careful your clothes are as clean as can be,   165
And fair for the feast, lest you find yourself harmed
When approaching that Prince Who has parentage high:
As He hates hell itself, our Lord hates the unclean.
Of what kind are these clothes you must clothe yourself in
To appear before that Prince in the proper attire?   170
In a word: what you wear are the works you've performed;
They're the love and the labors that lie in your heart.
If they're found to be fair, to be fine and well meant,
Well fitting in form for your foot and your hand,
If the bulk of your body is beauteously clothed,   175
Then you'll see our Savior Who sits on His throne.
But the errors are ample which exclude us from bliss,
From the sight of our Savior: sloth is one;
And for pompousness, pride, and puffed-up self-love
Any sinner is thrust down the throat of the fiend.   180
For bold cunning, deeds crooked, and covetousness,
For dark perjury, drunkenness, death-dealing acts,
And for stealing and squabbling your soul may be lost,
For robbery, ribaldry, and rank, hurtful lies,
For depriving of dowry, disinheriting widows,   185
For marring good marriages, meeting with thieves,
For treachery, tyranny, treason as well,
For false defamation and fraudulent laws—

Man may mysse þe myrþe þat much is to prayse
For such vnþewez as þise, and þole much payne,   190
And in þe Creatores cort com neuermore,
Ne neuer see Hym with syȝt for such sour tournez.
Bot I haue herkned and herde of mony hyȝe clerkez,
And als in resounez of ryȝt red hit myseluen,
Þat þat ilk proper Prynce þat paradys weldez   195
Is displesed at vch a poynt þat plyes to scaþe;
Bot neuer ȝet in no boke breued I herde
Þat euer He wrek so wyþerly on werk þat He made,
Ne venged for no vilté of vice ne synne,
Ne so hastyfly watz hot for hatel of His wylle,   200
Ne neuer so sodenly soȝt vnsoundely to weng,
As for fylþe of þe flesch þat foles han vsed;
For, as I fynde, þer He forȝet alle His fre þewez,
And wex wod to þe wrache for wrath at His hert.
For þe fyrste felonye þe falce fende wroȝt   205
Whyl he watz hyȝe in þe heuen houen vpon lofte,
Of alle þyse aþel aungelez attled þe fayrest:
And he vnkyndely, as a karle, kydde a reward.
He seȝ noȝt bot hymself how semly he were,
Bot his Souerayn he forsoke and sade þyse wordez: 210
'I schal telde vp my trone in þe tramountayne,
And by lyke to þat Lorde þat þe lyft made.'
With þis worde þat he warp, þe wrake on hym lyȝt:
Dryȝtyn with His dere dom hym drof to þe abyme,
In þe mesure of His mode, His metz neuer þe lasse.   215
Bot þer He tynt þe type dool of His tour ryche:
Þaȝ þe feloun were so fers for his fayre wedez
And his glorious glem þat glent so bryȝt,
As sone as Dryȝtynez dome drof to hymseluen,
Þikke þowsandez þro þrwen þeroute,   220
Fellen fro þe fyrmament fendez ful blake,
Sweued at þe fyrst swap as þe snaw þikke,
Hurled into helle-hole as þe hyue swarmez.
Fylter fenden folk forty dayez lencþe,
Er þat styngande storme stynt ne myȝt;   225
Bot as smylt mele vnder smal siue smokez forþikke,
So fro heuen to helle þat hatel schor laste,
On vche syde of þe worlde aywhere ilyche.
Ȝis, hit watz a brem brest and a byge wrache,
And ȝet wrathed not þe Wyȝ; ne þe wrech saȝtled,   230
Ne neuer wolde, for wylfulnes, his worþy God knawe,
Ne pray Hym for no pité, so proud watz his wylle.
Forþy þaȝ þe rape were rank, þe rawþe watz lyttel;
Þaȝ he be kest into kare, he kepes no better.
Bot þat oþer wrake þat wex, on wyȝez hit lyȝt   235

Any person's deprived of that praiseworthy bliss,
And his soul will suffer for such vices as these, 190
Never come to the court of the Creator at all,
Nor at last be allowed there to look on our God.
But I've hearkened and heard from the highest of clerks
And have read much of righteousness, rich and pure:
It's reported the Prince of high paradise is 195
Fully angered with all that is evil and wrong.
But in truth not one text ever told me that God
Ever punished a part of His precious works,
Nor avenged any vices, vileness, or sin,
Nor was half so hastily heated with wrath, 200
Nor so suddenly set upon seeking revenge
As He punished impurity, practiced by fools.
Faced with grime, He forgets His forgiving, light ways
And rises in rancor to revenge Himself then.
His wrath first was thus fired: the fiend proved to be 205
(Although high up in heaven and held in esteem,
Of all other angels ordained the most fair)
Ungrateful for gifts he'd been given by God;
He beheld his own beauty, was blinded to others'.
And, forsaking his Sovereign, spat forth these words: 210
"Past the peaks, near the polestar, I'll place my high throne,
And become like the King, the Creator of all!"
At these rank words God raged in His wrath upon him;
To the deep he was driven by dreadful decree.
And though moderate, merciful, measured in wrath, 215
The Lord that day lost of His legions a tenth.
Though the fiend was fond of his fine, lovely clothes—
Which glowed with a gleaming, glorious light—
At the moment our Maker was moved to rage,
He threw down a thousandfold throng, all turned black. 220
All those fiends from the firmament fell through the air,
In a sweeping wind swirled like snow in a gust,
And were hurled down to hell like a hive aswarm.
Thus the fiendish folk huddled for forty long days,
Till the tempest had taken its terrible course. 225
As when strained meal smokes from a sieve, even so
Down to hell from high heaven that heinous cloud dropped;
All over the earth that mist evenly hovered.
It indeed was a drastic, a dire revenge!
Yet the act was not angry, nor the archfiend ashamed; 230
For the devil disdained to be done in by God,
Or to pray for His pity—so proud he remained!
Though the punishment pained him, his repentance was small;
He abided in badness, though banished to hell.
Or consider the sentence next suffered by men 235

Þur3 þe faut of a freke þat fayled in trawþe,
Adam inobedyent, ordaynt to blysse.
Þer pryuély in paradys his place watz devised,
To lyue þer in lykyng þe lenþe of a terme,
And þenne enherite þat home þat aungelez forgart;   240
Bot þur3 þe eggyng of Eue he ete of an apple
Þat enpoysened alle peplez þat parted fro hem boþe,
For a defence þat watz dy3t of Dry3tyn Seluen,
And a payne þeron put and pertly halden.
Þe defence watz þe fryt þat þe freke towched,   245
And þe dom is þe deþe þat drepez vus alle;
Al in mesure and meþe watz mad þe vengiaunce,
And efte amended with a mayden þat make had neuer.
Bot in þe þryd watz forþrast al þat þryue schuld:
Þer watz malys mercyles and mawgré much scheued,   250
Þat watz for fylþe vpon folde þat þe folk vsed,
Þat þen wonyed in þe worlde withouten any maysterz.
Hit wern þe fayrest of forme and of face als,
Þe most and þe myriest þat maked wern euer,
Þe styfest, þe stalworþest þat stod euer on fete,   255
And lengest lyf in hem lent of ledez alle oþer.
For hit was þe forme foster þat þe folde bred,
Þe aþel aunceterez sunez þat Adam watz called,
To wham God hade geuen alle þaſ gayn were,
Alle þe blysse boute blame þat bodi my3t haue;   260
And þose lykkest to þe lede, þat lyued next after;
Forþy so semly to see syþen wern none.
Þer watz no law to hem layd bot loke to kynde,
And kepe to hit, and alle hit cors clanly fulfylle.
And þenne founden þay fylþe in fleschlych dedez,   265
And controeued agayn kynde contraré werkez,
And vsed hem vnþryftyly vchon on oþer,
And als with oþer, wylsfully, upon a wrange wyse:
So ferly fowled her flesch þat þe fende loked
How þe de3ter of þe douþe wern derelych fayre,   270
And fallen in fela3schyp with hem on folken wyse,
And engendered on hem jeauntez with her japez ille.
Þose wern men meþelez and ma3ty on vrþe,
Þat for her lodlych laykez alosed þay were;
He watz famed for fre þat fe3t loued best,   275
And ay þe bigest in bale þe best watz halden.
And þenne euelez on erþe ernestly grewen
And multyplyed monyfolde inmongez mankynde,
For þat þe ma3ty on molde so marre þise oþer
Þat þe Wy3e þat al wro3t ful wroþly bygynnez.   280
When He knew vche contré coruppte in hitseluen,
And vch freke forloyned fro þe ry3t wayez,

Through the fault of our forefather. Failing in truth,
Adam drastically disobeyed. Dealing him joy,
God had planned for his place within paradise; man
Was to dwell in delight for a destined time there,
Then inherit the home that the high angels lost.   240
Through the urging of Eve, though, an apple he ate.
Violating a law that the Lord had declared
With a penalty placed on it, openly stated.
Both are parents of people thus poisoned and fallen,
For that fruit was forbidden that they foolishly touched.   245
Their doom is the death destined for all.
Yet God's mood was both measured and moderate then,
For a matchless maiden amended that doom!
But all things that were thriving, the third time God raged,
Were destroyed in a show of unmeasured revenge.   250
For the folk had grown filthy, unfit and impure,
Made their way in the world without any lords.
Both in form and in face far the fairest of all,
Far the best, the most blissful, most blessed with life,
The most stalwart and sturdy that stood on two feet,   255
And the longest of life that have lived here below:
These folk were the first to move forth on the earth,
Of their ancestor, Adam, the offspring most fair.
To him God had once given the greatest of things:
All the bliss without blame that a body could have.   260
The offspring of Adam were equally blessed
(Since that first age no finer, no fairer have lived).
Not one law was laid down by the Lord in those days
But to keep to the course nature calls for in all.
They defiled their flesh, though, with filthy deeds,   265
And practiced impious, repugnant, bold acts.
With their vile perversions they voided their seed,
And, both loathsome and lecherous, lusted for others
With such foulness the fierce fallen angels themselves
Came in droves to debauch the daughters of men   270
And, lustful and loathsome, to lay with them there.
They begat with their gruesome acts giants on them.
Those men were the mightiest men on the earth.
They were feared for their fierceness and famous for strength;
Yes, the meanest among them gained marvelous fame;   275
The most harmful was hailed as the highest of all.
Thus evil erupted all over the earth.
And among many men those ways multiplied fast,
Till that race had corrupted the rest of mankind.
The Right One, Who wrought all, was enraged at the sight.   280
When He saw that sinning had swarmed through the land,
That each soul had strayed from the straight, narrow path,

Felle temptande tene towched His hert.
As wyȝe wo hym withinne, werp to Hymseluen:
'Me forþynkez ful much þat euer I mon made,   285
Bot I schal delyuer and do away þat doten on þis molde,
And fleme out of þe folde al þat flesch werez,
Fro þe burne to þe best, fro bryddez to fyschez;
Al schal doun and be ded and dryuen out of erþe
Þat euer I sette saule inne; and sore hit Me rwez   290
Þat euer I made hem Myself; bot if I may herafter,
I schal wayte to be war her wrenchez to kepe.'
Þenne in worlde watz a wyȝe wonyande on lyue,
Ful redy and ful ryȝtwys, and rewled hym fayre,
In þe drede of Dryȝtyn his dayez he vsez,   295
And ay glydande wyth his God, his grace watz þe more.
Hym watz þe nome Noe, as is innoghe knawen.
He had þre þryuen sunez, and þay þre wyuez:
Sem soþly þat on, þat oþer hyȝt Cam,
And þe jolef Japheth watz gendered þe þryd.   300
Now God in nwy to Noe con speke
Wylde wrakful wordez, in His wylle greued:
'Þe ende of alle kynez flesch þat on vrþe meuez
Is fallen forþwyth My face, and forþer hit I þenk.
With her vnworþelych werk Me wlatez withinne;   305
Þe gore þerof Me hatz greued and þe glette nwyed.
I schal strenkle My distresse, and strye al togeder,
Boþe ledez and londe and alle þat lyf habbez.
Bot make to þe a mancioun, and þat is My wylle,
A cofer closed of tres, clanlych planed.   310
Wyrk wonez þerinne for wylde and for tame,
And þenne cleme hit with clay comly withinne,
And alle þe endentur dryuen daube withouten.
And þus of lenþe and of large þat lome þou make:
Þre hundred of cupydez þou holde to þe lenþe,   315
Of fyfty fayre ouerþwert forme þe brede;
And loke euen þat þyn ark haue of heȝþe þretté,
And a wyndow wyd vponande wroȝt vpon lofte,
In þe compas of a cubit kyndely sware;
A wel dutande dor, don on þe syde;   320
Haf hallez þerinne and halkez ful mony,
Boþe boskenz and bourez and wel bounden penez.
For I schal waken vp a water to wasch alle þe worlde,
And quelle alle þat is quik with quauende flodez,
Alle þat glydez and gotz and gost of lyf habbez;   325
I schal wast with My wrath þat wons vpon vrþe.
Bot My forwarde with þe I festen on þis wyse,
For þou in reysoun hatz rengned and ryȝtwys ben euer:
Þou schal enter þis ark with þyn aþel barnez

He grew angered and grieved at the grim spectacle
And said to Himself, as a stricken man would:
"That I formed man at first I fiercely regret. 285
Therefore death, therefore doom, to the doers of sin!
I will lay waste the lands! All that lives on the earth,
All the bountiful beasts, all the birds and the fish,
Every soul I supplied, every spark of life:
All shall die certain death and be driven from earth! 290
I am grieved that I gave them life's goodness and shall
Ever warily watch their wicked, foul deeds!"
But one loyal man lived in those lust-ridden times.
He was proper and pious and pure in his heart,
And lived out his life in the love of our God. 295
By going with God his grace was increased;
His name was Noah, known everywhere.
He had three sons, all thriving, three daughters-in-law.
The first son he named Shem; the second was Ham;
And Japheth the joyful was the name of the third. 300
Now our God in His anger and grief came to Noah;
Speaking wild, bitter words, our Lord warned that good man:
"Now the end of the flesh on the earth is at hand;
Yes, the last of all life I'll allow, indeed cause.
I am wrathful at wrongs that are rampant on earth, 305
For foulness and filth have fired My wrath.
I'll assuage with destruction My sharp, stinging rage;
All the provinces, people, will perish at once.
Therefore build now a boxlike boat, a strong ark
Made of trees that you truly plane. Tighten the planks. 310
Provide it with plenty of pens for the beasts,
And caulk it with clay till secure, watertight.
Daub on the deck and deep sides all the joints.
The dimensions you'll make it shall measure this way:
You shall cut fifty cubits across for its breadth. 315
Three hundred you'll hew for its hull-length, I say.
Make it high—it shall have for its height fifty cubits.
On its hull I would have you hew out with care
A window, quite wide, a square cubit in size.
In its hull, too, you'll hew out a hole for a door; 320
Inside it stables and stalls you shall build,
Long passages, and pens. Make plenteous gates.
For I'll waken the waters and wash clean the earth
And lash out all life with a long-lasting flood:
All the creatures that crawl or cut through the air, 325
All that breathe in life's breath I will break in My wrath!
But this promise, this pledge, I provide for you now:
Since with reason you've reigned and been righteous and good,
You shall enter the ark with all of your sons,

And þy wedded wyf; with þe þou take   330
Þe makez of þy myry sunez; þis meyny of aȝte
I schal saue of monnez saulez, and swelt þose oþer.
Of vche best þat berez lyf busk þe a cupple,
Of vche clene comly kynde enclose seuen makez,
Of vche horwed in ark halde bot a payre,   335
For to saue Me þe sede of alle ser kyndez.
And ay þou meng with þe malez þe mete ho-bestez,
Vche payre by payre to plese ayþer oþer;
With alle þe fode þat may be founde frette þy cofer,
For sustnaunce to yowself and also þose oþer.'   340
Ful grayþely gotz þis god man and dos Godez hestes,
In dryȝ dred and daunger þat durst do non oþer.
Wen hit watz fettled and forged and to þe fulle grayþed,
Þenn con Dryȝttyn hym dele dryȝly þyse wordez.
'Now Noe,' quoþ oure Lorde, 'art þou al redy?   345
Hatz þou closed þy kyst with clay alle aboute?'
'Ȝe, Lorde, with Þy leue,' sayde þe lede þenne,
'Al is wroȝt at Þi worde, as Þou me wyt lantez.'
'Enter in, þenn,' quoþ He, 'and haf þi wyf with þe,
Þy þre sunez, withouten þrep, and her þre wyuez;   350
Bestez, as I bedene haue, bosk þerinne als,
And when ȝe arn staued, styfly stekez yow þerinne.
Fro seuen dayez ben seyed I sende out bylyue
Such a rowtande ryge þat rayne schal swyþe
Þat schal wasch alle þe worlde of werkez of fylþe;   355
Schal no flesch vpon folde by fonden onlyue,
Outtaken yow aȝt in þis ark staued
And sed þat I wyl saue of þyse ser bestez.'
Now Noe neuer styntez—þat niyȝt he bygynnez—
Er al wer stawed and stoken as þe steuen wolde.   360
Thenne sone com þe seuenþe day, when samned wern alle,
And alle woned in þe whichche, þe wylde and þe tame.
Þen bolned þe abyme, and bonkez con ryse,
Waltes out vch walle-heued in ful wode stremez;
Watz no brymme þat abod vnbrosten bylyue;   365
Þe mukel lauande loghe to þe lyfte rered.
Mony clustered clowde clef alle in clowtez;
Torent vch a rayn-ryfte and rusched to þe vrþe,
Fon neuer in forty dayez. And þen þe flod ryses,
Ouerwaltez vche a wod and þe wyde feldez.   370
For when þe water of þe welkyn with þe worlde mette,
Alle þat deth moȝt dryȝe drowned þerinne.
Þer watz moon for to make when meschef was cnowen,
Þat noȝt dowed bot þe deth in þe depe stremez;
Water wylger ay wax, wonez þat stryede,   375
Hurled into vch hous, hent þat þer dowelled.

And your wife as well and the wives of your sons—   330
In the boat you'll have built you shall bring them. For eight
Of men's souls I will save thus, not sparing the rest.
Of each beast that has breath you shall bring forth a pair.
Of each clean kind you'll enclose seven pairs.
Prepare of the impure one pair of each kind.   335
I'll preserve thus the seed of each species on earth.
Each male with its mate shall be mutually paired;
Thus pair by pair each will please its own mate.
With what food you can find you shall furnish the ark
To sustain both yourself and your sojourners, too."   340
So that good man goes out, just as God has ordained,
All in dread of danger; he dares not refuse.
When the boat has been built, all obediently done,
God descends and He solemnly says to the man:
"Have you answered My orders now, Noah, each one?   345
Have you caulked and secured with clay the boat?"
"By Your leave," says that loyal man, "Lord, yes I have.
The task given me, God, as You gave me the wisdom,
I have answered." "Then enter the ark with your wife,"
God says. "Take your sons and your daughters-in-law.   350
All the animals also—they'll enter the boat.
Seal yourselves soundly inside that ark;
For seven days hence I will send to the earth
A rushing, harsh rain and a raging, cold storm.
It will wash from the world the works of black filth.   355
No flesh will be found on the face of the earth.
But you eight will escape in the ark you have built;
With the seed of all species: I'll save that as well."
From that time Noah continues his work
Until all are, as ordered, accordingly stowed.   360
Very soon came day seven; the ship was filled
With the animals, every kind earth could supply.
The abyss was then broken. The banks began flooding;
Every spring poured forth strong, endless streams' overflow.
No bank went unbroken; each burst, giving way.   365
The sea started swelling, ascending on high.
Clouds were tossed up and torn into tatters and shards.
The rain began rushing through rifts in those clouds;
It fell forty days till the flood finally stopped,
Overwhelming each wood and each wide, open field.   370
When the waters washed over the world below,
Every mortal thing met with the meanest of deaths.
There was piteous pleading when the plight was made known
That a death in the deeps was the doom all would have.
That flood overflowed; it forever increased   375
As it washed away walls, seizing women and men.

Fyrst feng to þe flyȝt alle þat fle myȝt;
Vuche burde with her barne þe byggyng þay leuez
And bowed to þe hyȝ bonk þer brentest hit wern,
And heterly to þe hyȝe hyllez þay haled on faste.   380
Bot al watz nedlez her note, for neuer cowþe stynt
Þe roȝe raynande ryg, þe raykande wawez,
Er vch boþom watz brurdful to þe bonkez eggez,
And vche a dale so depe þat demmed at þe brynkez.
Þe moste mountaynez on mor þenne watz no more dryȝe,   385
And þeron flokked þe folke, for ferde of þe wrake.
Syþen þe wylde of þe wode on þe water flette;
Summe swymmed þeron þat saue hemself trawed,
Summe styȝe to a stud and stared to þe heuen,
Rwly wyth a loud rurd rored for drede.   390
Harez, herttez also, to þe hyȝe runnen;
Bukkez, bausenez, and bulez to þe bonkkez hyȝed;
And alle cryed for care to þe Kyng of heuen,
Recouerer of þe Creator þay cryed vchone,
Þat amounted þe mase His mercy watz passed,   395
And alle His pyté departed fro peple þat He hated.
Bi þat þe flod to her fete floȝed and waxed,
Þen vche a segge seȝ wel þat synk hym byhoued.
Frendez fellen in fere and faþmed togeder,
To dryȝ her delful destyné and dyȝen alle samen;   400
Luf lokez to luf and his leue takez,
For to ende alle at onez and for euer twynne.
By forty dayez wern faren, on folde no flesch styryed
Þat þe flod nade al freten with feȝtande waȝez;
For hit clam vche a clyffe, cubites fyftene   405
Ouer þe hyȝest hylle þat hurkled on erþe.
Þenne mourkne in þe mudde most ful nede
Alle þat spyrakle inspranc—no sprawlyng awayled—
Saue þe haþel vnder hach and his here straunge,
Noe þat ofte neuened þe name of oure Lorde,   410
Hym aȝtsum in þat ark, as aþel God lyked,
Þer alle ledez in lome lenged druye.
Þe arc houen watz on hyȝe with hurlande gotez,
Kest to kythez vncouþe þe clowdez ful nere.
Hit waltered on þe wylde flod, went as hit lyste,   415
Drof vpon þe depe dam, in daunger hit semed,
Withouten mast, oþer myke, oþer myry bawelyne,
Kable, oþer capstan to clyppe to her ankrez,
Hurrok, oþer hande-helme hasped on roþer,
Oþer any sweande sayl to seche after hauen,   420
Bot flote forthe with þe flyt of þe felle wyndez.
Whederwarde so þe water wafte, hit rebounde;
Ofte hit roled on rounde and rered on ende;

Many fled from the flood, tried to find a safe place.
Many women ran wildly with wailing, young babes.
All left the flat lowlands to look for high ground,
Where they ran in a rush while the raging rain fell.   380
All for naught! For the noisy storm, inevitably,
Went on raging and roaring. Rain rose up until
It had filled the fields and flooded each nook;
Each dale lay deep in the deadly, cold rain.
Though the highest of heights was heavy with rain,   385
Still the folk there flocked in their fear and their dread.
Afloat on that furious flood were wild beasts;
Some hoped they were heading for high ground, not death.
Some from high places howled to heaven in fear.
Others woefully wailed and whimpered and cried.   390
To those high places hares and swift harts clambered fast;
With the bucks and the bulls and the badgers they ran.
In their care they cried out to the King of the sky;
In their plight they piteously pleaded for aid.
But confusion increased; the Creator's mercy   395
With His pity had passed for the people He loathed.
When the flood to his feet had finally swelled,
Each sinner was certain he'd suffer his death.
In that flood every friend joined a friend to embrace,
To endure there his doom and to die arm in arm.   400
Lovers took leave of their loves; they must part.
All had ended forever; they would ever be sundered.
Thus no flesh, when the forty days finally had passed,
Was left stirring; that strong flood had struck down all life.
Over cliffs it had climbed fifteen cubits at least;   405
Than the highest of hills it rose higher by much.
In the mud all that moved was to mold transformed.
All sank and succumbed, for no struggling availed.
But the fortunate family, afloat in the ship
Of Noah—who knew well the name of our Lord—   410
Yes, all eight in the ark, even as the Lord wished,
Were kept safe from the storm that surrounded them all,
Though their boat ever bounced about on the waves.
Near the clouds it was cast, over countries it sailed,
As it went on its way over water for days.   415
Over deeps it was driven, in danger it seemed,
Without mizzen or mast, without means of bowline,
Without capstan or cable to clasp to an anchor,
Without hurrock or hand-helm hasped to a rudder,
Without swelling, wide sails for searching out ports.   420
In the winds as they warred the ark wandered along,
Went wherever the water would waft it about.
It would roll around and would rear on its end.

Nyf oure Lorde hade ben her lodezmon hem had lumpen harde.
Of þe lenþe of Noe lyf to lay a lel date,   425
Þe sex hundreth of his age and none odde ʒerez,
Of secounde monyth þe seuentenþe day ryʒtez,
Towalten alle þyse welle-hedez and þe water flowed;
And þryez fyfty þe flod of folwande dayez;
Vche hille watz þer hidde with yþez ful graye.   430
Al watz wasted þat wonyed þe worlde withinne,
Þat euer flote, oþer flwe, oþer on fote ʒede,
That roʒly watz þe remnaunt þat þe rac dryuez
Þat alle gendrez so joyst wern joyned wythinne.
Bot quen þe Lorde of þe lyfte lyked Hymseluen   435
For to mynne on His mon His meth þat abydez,
Þen He wakened a wynde on watterez to blowe;
Þenne lasned þe llak þat large watz are.
Þen He stac vp þe stangez, stoped þe wellez,
Bed blynne of þe rayn: hit batede as fast;   440
Þenne lasned þe loʒ lowkande togeder.
After harde dayez wern out an hundreth and fyfté,
As þat lyftande lome luged aboute,
Where þe wynde and þe weder warpen hit wolde,
Hit saʒtled on a softe day, synkande to grounde;   445
On a rasse of a rok hit rest at þe laste,
On þe mounte of Ararach of Armene hilles,
Þat oþerwayez on Ebrv hit hat þe Thanes.
Bot þaʒ þe kyste in þe cragez were closed to byde,
ʒet fyned not þe flod ne fel to þe boþemez,   450
Bot þe hyʒest of þe eggez vnhuled wern a lyttel,
Þat þe burne bynne borde byhelde þe bare erþe.
Þenne wafte he vpon his wyndowe, and wysed þeroute
A message fro þat meyny hem moldez to seche:
Þat watz þe rauen so ronk, þat rebel watz euer;   455
He watz colored as þe cole, corbyal vntrwe.
And he fongez to þe flyʒt and fannez on þe wyndez,
Halez hyʒe vpon hyʒt to herken typyngez.
He croukez for comfort when carayne he fyndez
Kast vp on a clyffe þer costese lay drye;   460
He hade þe smelle of þe smach and smoltes þeder sone,
Fallez on þe foule flesch and fyllez his wombe,
And sone ʒederly forʒete ʒisterday steuen,
How þe cheuetayn hym charged þat þe chyst ʒemed.
Þe rauen raykez hym forth, þat reches ful lyttel   465
How alle fodez þer fare, ellez he fynde mete;
Bot þe burne bynne borde þat bod to hys come
Banned hym ful bytterly with bestes alle samen.
He sechez anoþer sondezmon, and settez on þe douue,
Bryngez þat bryʒt vpon borde, blessed, and sayde: 470

If not guided by God, they'd have gone to their deaths!
Noah's life was quite long. To relate truth, he had,   425
Ever since the ascent of his six-hundredth year,
In the second month seen fully seventeen days
When the floods began falling and flowing from high.
For thrice fifty days following, the flood covered the earth;
Every hill remained hidden by high, raging waves.   430
All that floated or flew or on foot roamed the earth
Was destroyed by the storm as it swirled about;
What remained was the mighty ark, moved on the waves;
Each species was stowed away safely within.
When our Sovereign decided to stop the great flood,   435
To remember His mercy, be moderate with Noah,
He awakened a wind; and the waters withdrew.
All the lakes' water levels were lowered at once.
He stopped up the springs and He sealed every well.
At His word all the waters were walled up and ceased;   440
The oceans, once single, were sundered apart.
All this happened the hundred-and-fiftieth day
That the boat had been blown about by the storm,
Where the water and wind chose to wash it about.
It alighted one lovely day, lodged in the ground;   445
On a rising, vast rock the boat rested at last,
On Mount Ararat's height—in Armenian hills—
Which in Hebrew is hailed as the high, mighty Thanes.
Though the craft was thus caught in the crags hard and fast,
The vast lakes were not lowered, nor lessened the flood.   450
Just the highest of hills had their heads above waves;
On board they beheld the bare earth all around.
Noah pondered and peered through his porthole at once.
He sent forth a sentry to search for dry land:
The dark raven, rank and rebellious in heart.   455
He was colored like coal, coarse and untrue.
He flies on his flight. As he floats on the winds,
That bird swoops high, soars up to scan all the lands,
And cackles and croaks: there's carrion near!
It is cast on a cliff and it catches his eye.   460
When he smells its scent, he descends there at once
Till he falls on the foul flesh, filling himself.
In his greed he forgets what the good man has said,
What the captain commanding the craft has enjoined.
Just as long as he locates food, little he cares   465
How his fellows are faring. He flies off alone.
Back on board the beasts were embittered; and Noah
In his rage at the raven ranted and cursed.
For a traveler truer he takes up the dove.
As he brings out that bird, Noah blesses her well: 470

'Wende, worþelych wyȝt, vus wonez to seche;
Dryf ouer þis dymme water; if þou druye fyndez
Bryng bodworde to bot blysse to vus alle.
Þaȝ þat fowle be false, fre be þou euer.'
Ho wyrled out on þe weder on wyngez ful scharpe,   475
Dreȝly alle alonge day þat dorst neuer lyȝt;
And when ho fyndez no folde her fote on to pyche,
Ho vmbekestez þe coste and þe kyst sechez.
Ho hittez on þe euentyde and on þe ark sittez;
Noe nymmes hir anon and naytly hir stauez.   480
Noe on anoþer day nymmez efte þe dowue,
And byddez hir bowe ouer þe borne efte bonkez to seche;
And ho skyrmez vnder skwe and skowtez aboute,
Tyl hit watz nyȝe at þe naȝt, and Noe þen sechez.
On ark on an euentyde houez þe dowue;   485
On stamyn ho stod and stylle hym abydez.
What! ho broȝt in hir beke a bronch of olyue,
Gracyously vmbegrouen al with grene leuez;
Þat watz þe syngne of sauyté þat sende hem oure Lorde,
And þe saȝtlyng of Hymself with þo sely bestez.   490
Þen watz þer joy in þat gyn where jumpred er dryȝed,
And much comfort in þat cofer þat watz clay-daubed.
Myryly on a fayr morn, monyth þe fyrst,
Þat fallez formast in þe ȝer, and þe fyrst day,
Ledez loȝen in þat lome and loked þeroute,   495
How þat watterez wern woned and þe worlde dryed.
Vchon loued oure Lorde, bot lenged ay stylle
Tyl þay had typyng fro þe Tolke þat tyned hem þerinne.
Þen Godez glam to hem glod þat gladed hem alle,
Bede hem drawe to þe dor: delyuer hem He wolde.   500
Þen went þay to þe wykket, hit walt vpon sone;
Boþe þe burne and his barnez bowed þeroute,
Her wyuez walkez hem wyth and þe wylde after,
Þroly þrublande in þronge, þrowen ful þykke.
Bot Noe of vche honest kynde nem out an odde,   505
And heuened vp an auter and halȝed hit fayre,
And sette a sakerfyse þeron of vch a ser kynde
Þat watz comly and clene: God kepez non oþer.
When bremly brened þose bestez, and þe breþe rysed,
Þe sauour of his sacrafyse soȝt to Hym euen   510
Þat al spedez and spyllez; He spekes with þat ilke
In comly comfort ful clos and cortays wordez:
'Now, Noe, no more nel I neuer wary
Alle þe mukel mayny on molde for no mannez synnez,
For I se wel þat hit is sothe þat alle seggez wyttez   515
To vnþryfte arn alle þrawen with þoȝt of her herttez,
And ay hatz ben, and wyl be ȝet; fro her barnage

"Now fly forth, worthy fowl, and find us a home.
Over level seas look; if you locate dry land,
Return here to tell us your tidings of joy.
Though that fowl was false, you'll be faithful and good."
So she whirled over water on wings that were swift,　　　475
Never dared to come down; but all day she flew on.
When she saw no dry site that would serve as a home,
The dove circled and searched for the ship, which she found
After dark. She flew down to its deck, where she perched.
Noah tenderly took her to lodge for the night.　　　480
Some time later he took her and told her to fly,
To search the vast sea for a site of dry ground.
So she soared through the sky while scouting for land
Until night, when to Noah she nimbly returned.
Then one evening arrived; she alighted from high　　　485
And patiently perched on the prow of the ark.
In her beak she had brought a branch of olive—
On it green leaves were growing, so graceful and fine—
Of salvation a sign that was sent by our Lord,
A pact of the peace He now pledged with the beasts!　　　490
There was bliss in that boat where there'd been only fear;
In that craft, caulked with clay, they were comforted well!
On the first of the first month that falls in the year,
On a fine morning—fresh and fair—all the men
Gaily laughed aloud and, while looking, could see　　　495
That the waters had waned and the world had dried.
Each person piously praised the Lord,
But they kept to the craft till He called them forth.
They were gladdened to get, then, from God a command
To alight on the land. He'd delivered thèm all!　　　500
The door smoothly and swiftly they swung open wide.
That family fared slowly forth on the ground;
With their wives the men walked. Now the wild beasts came;
In the thickest of throngs they went thrusting their way.
Of each kind that was clean Noah kept back one beast.　　　505
He rightly and righteously raised up an altar,
Where he solemnly sacrificed such as were clean
Of creation's creatures; God craves nothing else.
When those beasts were burning and blazing, when smoke
Brought the scent of the sacrifice soaring to Him　　　510
Who can send to destruction or save all of life,
The Lord called out to comfort; He courteously
Addressed Noah: "Now know that I'll never again
Curse the earth and those on it for any man's sins.
For I see that men's senses are set upon evil,　　　515
Are to thriftless things thrown by the thoughts in their hearts.
So they've been, so they'll be. From his birth, it is clear,

Al is þe mynde of þe man to malyce enclyned.
Forþy schal I neuer schende so schortly at ones
As dysstrye al for manez dedez, dayez of þis erþe.   520
Bot waxez now and wendez forth and worþez to monye,
Multyplyez on þis molde, and menske yow bytyde.
Sesounez schal yow neuer sese of sede ne of heruest,
Ne hete, ne no harde forst, vmbre ne droȝþe,
Ne þe swetnesse of somer, ne þe sadde wynter,   525
Ne þe nyȝt, ne þe day, ne þe newe ȝerez,
Bot euer renne restlez: rengnez ȝe þerinne.'
Þerwyth He blessez vch a best, and bytaȝt hem þis erþe.
Þen watz a skylly skyualde, quen scaped alle þe wylde,
Vche fowle to þe flyȝt þat fyþerez myȝt serue,   530
Vche fysch to þe flod þat fynne couþe nayte,
Vche beste to þe bent þat bytes on erbez;
Wylde wormez to her won wryþez in þe erþe,
Þe fox and þe folmarde to þe fryth wyndez,
Herttes to hyȝe heþe, harez to gorstez,   535
And lyounez and lebardez to þe lake-ryftes;
Hernez and hauekez to þe hyȝe rochez,
Þe hole-foted fowle to þe flod hyȝez,
And vche best at a brayde þer hym best lykez;
Þe fowre frekez of þe folde fongez þe empyre.   540
Lo! suche a wrakful wo for wlatsum dedez
Parformed þe hyȝe Fader on folke þat He made;
Þat He chysly hade cherisched He chastysed ful hardee,
In devoydynge þe vylanye þat venkquyst His þewez.
Forþy war þe now, wyȝe þat worschyp desyres   545
In His comlych courte þat Kyng is of blysse,
In þe fylþe of þe flesch þat þou be founden neuer,
Tyl any water in þe worlde to wasche þe fayly.
For is no segge vnder sunne so seme of his craftez,
If he be sulped in synne, þat syttez vnclene;   550
On spec of a spote may spede to mysse
Of þe syȝte of þe Souerayn þat syttez so hyȝe;
For þat schewe me schale in þo schyre howsez,
As þe beryl bornyst byhouez be clene,
Þat is sounde on vche a syde and no sem habes—   555
Withouten maskle oþer mote, as margerye-perle.
Syþen þe Souerayn in sete so sore forþoȝt
Þat euer He man vpon molde merked to lyuy,
For he in fylþe watz fallen, felly He uenged,
Quen fourferde alle þe flesch þat He formed hade.   560
Hym rwed þat He hem vprerde and raȝt hem lyflode;
And efte þat He hem vndyd, hard hit Hym þoȝt.
For quen þe swemande sorȝe soȝt to His hert,
He knyt a couenaunde cortaysly with monkynde þere,

To gross malice the mind of each man is inclined.
Not again will My grief and My anger cause Me
To annihilate all till the end of time.   520
Now go forth, be fruitful, and fill with your kind
All the earth; and great honor you'll earn in this way.
In succession the seasons won't cease. All will come:
Both the hail and the heat, both the hotness and shade,
Both the sweetness of summer and the sharp, winter wind,   525
Both the night and the noon. With each new year shall come
A great cycle unceasing. Of such are you king!"
Our Lord blessed every beast as He bade it go forth.
As bidden, each beast went abroad on the earth:
Every fowl with feathers flew through the sky;   530
To the flood the fin-waving fishes returned;
To the grasses, growing and green, went the beasts.
And the reptiles, writhing, wriggled away.
To the field and furrow went foxes and polecats.
To the heaths went the harts, and hares went to leas.   535
To lairs ran the lions and leopards at once.
To the highest of heights flew the hawks and eagles.
To the water went all of the web-footed birds.
Thus each species sped for the spot that was fit.
All the earth was thus owned by the four men alive.   540
Oh how awesome the anger, how endless the rage,
That the Father on folk that He fashioned ordained!
Whom He cherished He chastised as churls. He destroyed
All the villains who vilely violated His laws.
So beware! If to worship that One you desire,   545
And to come to the court of the King of bliss,
Don't be found in the filth of the flesh, which cannot
By the world's vast waters be washed or erased.
For men are so mean that, no matter how high,
If they're stained with their sins these will show to their grief;   550
If they're sporting a speck or a spot they will lose
Any sight of the Sovereign Who sits upon high.
Those who come to the court of that King must be pure,
Must be polished perfectly, pure as a beryl
That is sound on all sides, without seams anywhere,   555
Without blemish or blot as the beauteous pearl.
When the Sovereign Who sits on high sorely repented
That He'd ever created on earth humankind—
Which had fallen to filth—He fiercely avenged.
When finally all flesh that He'd formed was destroyed,   560
He was grieved that He'd given the gift of their lives.
When the storm finally ceased, though, it seemed to Him harsh;
Sorry He'd struck out so savagely then,
He a covenant courteously cast with mankind,

In þe mesure of His mode and meþe of His wylle,   565
Þat He schulde neuer for no syt smyte al at onez,
As to quelle alle quykez for qued þat myȝt falle,
Whyl of þe lenþe of þe londe lastez þe terme.
Þat ilke skyl for no scaþe ascaped Hym neuer.
Wheder wonderly He wrak on wykked men after,   570
Ful felly for þat ilk faute forferde a kyth ryche,
In þe anger of His ire, þat arȝed mony;
And al watz for þis ilk euel, þat vnhappen glette,
Þe venym and þe vylanye and þe vycios fylþe
Þat bysulpez mannez saule in vnsounde hert,   575
Þat he his Saueour ne see with syȝt of his yȝen.
Alle illez He hates as helle þat stynkkez;
Bot non nuyez Hym on naȝt ne neuer vpon dayez
As harlottrye vnhonest, heþyng of seluen:
Þat schamez for no schrewedschyp, schent mot he worþe.   580
Bot sauyour, mon, in þyself, þaȝ þou a sotte lyuie,
Þaȝ þou bere þyself babel, byþenk þe sumtyme
Wheþer He þat stykked vche a stare in vche steppe yȝe—
Ȝif Hymself be bore blynde hit is a brod wonder;
And He þat fetly in face fettled alle eres,   585
If He hatz losed þe lysten hit lyftez meruayle:
Trave þou neuer þat tale—vntrwe þou hit fyndez.
Þer is no dede so derne þat dittez His yȝen;
Þer is no wyȝe in his werk so war ne so stylle
Þat hit ne þrawez to Hym þro er he hit þoȝt haue.   590
For He is þe gropande God, þe grounde of alle dedez,
Rypande of vche a ring þe reynyez and hert.
And þere He fyndez al fayre a freke wythinne,
With hert honest and hol, þat haþel He honourez,
Sendez hym a sad syȝt: to se His auen face,   595
And harde honysez þise oþer, and of His erde flemez.
Bot of þe dome of þe douþe for dedez of schame—
He is so skoymos of þat skaþe, He scarrez bylyue;
He may not dryȝe to draw allyt, bot drepez in hast:
And þat watz schewed schortly by a schaþe onez.   600
Olde Abraham in erde onez he syttez
Euen byfore his hous-dore, vnder an oke grene;
Bryȝt blykked þe bem of þe brode heuen;
In þe hyȝe hete þerof Abraham bidez:
He watz schunt to þe schadow vnder schyre leuez.   605
Þenne watz he war on þe waye of wlonk Wyȝez þrynne;
If Þay wer farande and fre and fayre to beholde
Hit is eþe to leue by þe last ende.
For þe lede þat þer laye þe leuez anvnder,
When he hade of Hem syȝt he hyȝez bylyue,   610
And as to God þe goodmon gos Hem agaynez

For His mood became measured; He'd mellowed His wrath.   565
He would wipe out the world all at once nevermore,
Nor destroy, for the sin in men's souls, all life,
For as long as all lands were to last by decree.
God never forgot the agreement He made,
Though He's certainly slain many sinners since then.   570
Thus the world was wiped out for wicked men's deeds.
Many folk by God's fury were frightened that time,
All because of that cursed, unclean, wicked sin
Which is venomous, vicious, and vile withal,
And sullies the soul with its sickening thoughts.   575
Those who sin thus won't see our Savior at last.
As He hates stinking hell, our Lord hates vile sins.
But at night or at noon there is nothing He hates
More than lechery, lustful and loathsome and gross!
Of such deeds evildoers shall die without hope.   580
So remember this, man, though you're mean and impure,
Though you babble and bear yourself badly in life:
He Who put in people the power to see
Was not born Himself blind. That would be a strange thing!
It could hardly occur that His hearing should fail   585
Who has fittingly fixed on each face the two ears!
Do not trust any tale without truth that you hear.
There's no secret so small He can't see it with ease.
No one is so wary, so wily in sin,
But he's found out before he has fashioned such thoughts.   590
He's the great, searching God; He's the ground of all deeds;
And He sees into secrets, the seat of desire.
When He finds in a fellow fairness within,
And a heart that is holy, He blesses that man
And sends him a vision; he sees our Lord's face!   595
The impure and impious He punishes, though;
And in dooming—for deeds that are dark—sinful men,
He's repulsed by their practices, put off so much
He can't bear to hold back. No, He bursts forth to kill!
This same ire was evidenced amply one time.   600
On the earth in the olden time Abraham once
In the shade of a soaring oak sat near his door.
There were beating down burningly beams of the sun.
By that oak, in that awful heat, Abraham stayed,
For he sought there the shade of the shining, green leaves.   605
Then he noticed three noblemen, nearing his house.
Just how fine and fair were those foreigners there
Will be obvious after the end of the tale.
For when Abraham under the oak sees them come,
And beholds them, he hastens and hurries right up.   610
As to God he goes up and greets them with cheer.

And haylsed Hem in onhede, and sayde: 'Hende Lorde,
Ȝif euer Þy mon vpon molde merit disserued,
Lenge a lyttel with Þy lede, I loȝly biseche;
Passe neuer fro Þi pouere, ȝif I hit pray durst,   615
Er Þou haf biden with Þi burne and vnder boȝe restted,
And I schal wynne Yow wyȝt of water a lyttel,
And fast aboute schal I fare Your fette wer waschene.
Resttez here on þis rote and I schal rachche after
And brynge a morsel of bred to baume Your hertte.'   620
'Fare forthe,' quoþ þe Frekez, 'and fech as þou seggez;
By bole of þis brode tre We byde þe here.'
Þenne orppedly into his hous he hyȝed to Saré,
Comaunded hir to be cof and quyk at þis onez:
'Þre mettez of mele menge and ma kakez;   625
Vnder askez ful hote happe hem byliue;
Quyl I fete sumquat fat, þou þe fyr bete,
Prestly at þis ilke poynte sum polment to make.'
He cached to his covhous and a calf bryngez,
Þat watz tender and not toȝe, bed tyrue of þe hyde,   630
And sayde to his seruaunt þat he hit seþe faste;
And he deruely at his dome dyȝt hit bylyue.
Þe burne to be bare-heued buskez hym þenne,
Clechez to a clene cloþe and kestez on þe grene,
Þrwe þryftyly þeron þo þre þerue kakez,   635
And bryngez butter wythal and by þe bred settez;
Mete messez of mylke he merkkez bytwene,
Syþen potage and polment in plater honest.
As sewer in a god assyse he serued Hem fayre,
Wyth sadde semblaunt and swete of such as he hade;   640
And God as a glad gest mad god chere
Þat watz fayn of his frende, and his fest praysed.
Abraham, al hodlez, with armez vp-folden,
Mynystred mete byfore þo Men þat myȝtes al weldez.
Þenne Þay sayden as Þay sete samen alle þrynne,   645
When þe mete watz remued and Þay of mensk speken,
'I schal efte hereaway, Abram,' Þay sayden,
'Ȝet er þy lyuez lyȝt leþe vpon erþe,
And þenne schal Saré consayue and a sun bere,
Þat schal be Abrahamez ayre and after hym wynne   650
With wele and wyth worschyp þe worþely peple
Þat schal halde in heritage þat I haf men ȝarked.'
Þenne þe burde byhynde þe dor for busmar laȝed;
And sayde sothly to hirself Saré þe madde:
'May þou traw for tykle þat þou teme moȝtez,   655
And I so hyȝe out of age, and also my lorde?'
For soþely, as says þe wryt, he wern of sadde elde,
Boþe þe wyȝe and his wyf, such werk watz hem fayled

And as one he welcomes them well: "Noble lord,
If your sovereignty's servant deserves such honor,
By your leave, a little here linger, I pray.
With your say, I'd beseech you to sit here until   615
You have stayed with your servant in shade, gotten rest.
I will furnish you fast. Fine water now
I will find and bring forth; your feet I will wash.
Therefore wait by this wondrous oak while I go;
I will bring you a bit of bread for your strength."   620
"Now go forth," they said. "Fetch those fares you suggest.
Meanwhile we'll wait by this wide trunk of oak."
To his house he hurried. He hastened to Sarah
And commanded she move at that moment in haste:
"From three measures of meal make me good cakes.   625
Under hot ashes heave them. Be hasty, be quick!
But first fan hot the fire. Some food I will kill.
We'll make stew in a snap, in a second or two!"
So he carried a calf to his cow shed where he
Had it slaughtered and skinned by his servant at once.   630
It was tender, not tough; in no time it was boiled.
Thus he got for his good guests together a meal.
With good manners he makes himself bareheaded then,
And lays on the lawn a lovely, clean cloth,
Where politely he leaves them unleavened, hot cakes.   635
For their bread he brings them some butter in haste
And pours them appropriate portions of milk.
He serves them the stew and some soup in good bowls.
A steward's respect that man showed to his guests;
With a manner both mild and meek he behaved.   640
God, as his guest, was gladdened at heart.
He was pleased, and praised in His pleasure His friend.
Therefore, hovering, hoodless, that host oversaw
The meal for those men who are matchless in strength.
They said as they sat in the shade, three in one—   645
When the meal was removed—in a mannerly way:
"Dearest Abraham, afterwards I will return,
Well before your life's flame has flickered its last.
Then shall Sarah conceive you a son, newly born;
He'll be Abraham's heir, and he'll afterwards have   650
Noble offspring. All will be honored at last
With the heritage high that I've held out to men."
Sarah, hanging back, hiding behind the door, laughed,
And softly said to herself in her mirth:
"Do you madly imagine we'll make us an heir,   655
Although I am so old, as is also my lord?"
Indeed, Scripture says so: both were certainly old,
And they'd long ago left off such leisurely play.

Fro mony a brod day byfore; ho barayn ay bydene,
Þat selue Saré, withouten sede into þat same tyme.   660
Þenne sayde oure Syre þer He sete: 'Se! so Saré laȝes,
Not trawande þe tale þat I þe to schewed.
Hopez ho oȝt may be harde My hondez to work?
And ȝet I avow verayly þe avaunt þat I made;
I schal ȝeply aȝayn and ȝelde þat I hyȝt,   665
And sothely sende to Saré a soun and an hayre.'
Þenne swenged forth Saré and swer by hir trawþe
Þat for lot þat Þay laused ho laȝed neuer.
'Now innoghe: hit is not so,' þenne nurned þe Dryȝtyn,
'For þou laȝed aloȝ, bot let we hit one.'   670
With þat Þay ros vp radly, as Þay rayke schulde,
And setten toward Sodamas Her syȝt alle at onez;
For þat cité þerbysyde watz sette in a vale,
No mylez fro Mambre mo þen tweyne,
Whereso wonyed þis ilke wyȝ, þat wendez with oure Lorde   675
For to tent Hym with tale and teche Hym þe gate.
Þen glydez forth God; þe godmon Hym folȝez;
Abraham heldez Hem wyth, Hem to conueye
Towarde þe cety of Sodamas þat synned had þenne
In þe faute of þis fylþe. Þe Fader hem þretes,   680
And sayde þus to þe segg þat sued Hym after:
'How myȝt I hyde Myn hert fro Habraham þe trwe,
Þat I ne dyscouered to his corse My counsayl so dere,
Syþen he is chosen to be chef chyldryn fader,
Þat so folk schal falle fro to flete alle þe worlde,   685
And vche blod in þat burne blessed schal worþe?
Me bos telle to þat tolk þe tene of My wylle,
And alle Myn atlyng to Abraham vnhaspe bilyue.
The grete soun of Sodamas synkkez in Myn erez,
And þe gult of Gomorre garez Me to wrath.   690
I schal lyȝt into þat led and loke Myseluen
If þay haf don as þe dyne dryuez on lofte.
Þay han lerned a lyst þat lykez me ille,
Þat þay han founden in her flesch of fautez þe werst:
Vch male matz his mach a man as hymseluen,   695
And fylter folyly in fere on femmalez wyse.
I compast hem a kynde crafte and kende hit hem derne,
And amed hit in Myn ordenaunce oddely dere,
And dyȝt drwry þerinne, doole alþer-swettest,
And þe play of paramorez I portrayed Myseluen,   700
And made þerto a maner myriest of oþer:
When two true togeder had tyȝed hemseluen,
Bytwene a male and his make such merþe schulde come,
Welnyȝe pure paradys moȝt preue no better;
Ellez þay moȝt honestly ayþer oþer welde,   705

They had been truly barren for years up till then,
For Sarah was seedless for some time before.   660
Our Sire as He sat there said, "Look, Sarah laughs,
Not accepting the story I said would come true.
Does she hold that My hands would find hard any task?
Still that promise I pledge to uphold. I'll return
Very soon to this site, and see that all's done.   665
I will send then to Sarah a son and an heir."
Suddenly Sarah came, swearing that she
Had not laughed, even once, at what had been said.
"Now forget it!" said God. "You've gone far enough!
For you laughed very low; but we'll leave it at that."   670
They rose up and readied themselves to depart;
Toward Sodom they set their sight at once.
For that city stood near; it was set in a vale
Not two miles from Mambre where Abraham dwelled.
That man went on the way, for his words could explain   675
Where that city was set as he showed the way there.
God that way goes, with that good man behind,
For he comes to escort them courteously.
Near the sin-ridden city of Sodom, the Father
Begins throwing them threats for unthinkable sins.   680
To the one who was with Him He waxed in His rage:
"Can I hide My heart from so humble a man,
From his person keep pent up the plan I have formed?
He's the chief of the children I've chosen as Mine;
From him people shall populate plenteously.   685
Since this chief's many children are chosen as blessed,
It behooves him to hear of the heights of My wrath.
I will tell My intent to this trusty man now.
A great sound comes from Sodom; it sinks in My ears.
And Gomorrah's meanness moves Me to wrath.   690
I am nearing there now and will know for Myself
If they're really as wretched as rumors suggest.
There's a lust they have learned that I like not at all;
In their flesh they have found this gross fault, far the worst.
Every male's vile mate is a man like himself;   695
And, with one like a woman, two wickedly join.
I in private provided a practice for them;
What I sanctioned was sweet, and it sought nature's way.
It was good," said God, "because guided by love.
Two paramours' play I portrayed then Myself.   700
I made thus a manner, a means to make love,
In which two, when together, would take such delight—
And I mean here a man with his mate, his true wife—
That in paradise pleasure would prove hardly more,
All as long as their loving's unlewd. I ordained   705

At a stylle stollen steuen, vnstered wyth sy3t,
Luf-lowe hem bytwene lasched so hote
Þat alle þe meschefez on mold mo3t hit not sleke.
Now haf þay skyfted My skyl and scorned natwre,
And henttez hem in heþyng an vsage vnclene.   710
Hem to smyte for þat smod smartly I þenk,
Þat wy3ez schal be by hem war, worlde withouten ende.'
Þenne ar3ed Abraham and alle his mod chaunged,
For hope of þe harde hate þat hy3t hatz oure Lorde.
Al sykande he sayde: 'Sir, with Yor leue,   715
Schal synful and saklez suffer al on payne?
Weþer euer hit lyke my Lorde to lyfte such domez
Þat þe wykked and þe worþy schal on wrake suffer,
And weye vpon þe worre half þat wrathed Þe neuer?
Þat watz neuer Þy won þat wro3tez vus alle.   720
Now fyfty fyn frendez wer founde in 3onde toune,
In þe cety of Sodamas and also Gomorre,
Þat neuer lakked Þy laue, bot loued ay trauþe,
And re3tful wern and resounable and redy Þe to serue,
Schal þay falle in þe faute þat oþer frekez wro3t,   725
And joyne to her juggement, her juise to haue?
Þat nas neuer Þyn note, vnneuened hit worþe,
Þat art so gaynly a God and of goste mylde.'
'Nay, for fyfty,' quoþ þe Fader, 'and þy fayre speche,
And þay be founden in þat folk of her fylþe clene,   730
I schal forgyue alle þe gylt þur3 My grace one,
And let hem smolt al unsmyten smoþely at onez.'
'Aa! blessed be Þow,' quoþ þe burne, 'so boner and þewed,
And al haldez in Þy honde, þe heuen and þe erþe;
Bot, for I towched haf þis talke, tatz to non ille   735
3if I mele a lyttel more þat mul am and askez.
What if fyue faylen of fyfty þe noumbre,
And þe remnaunt be reken, how restes Þy wylle?'
'And fyue wont of fyfty,' quoþ God, 'I schal for3ete alle
And wythhalde My honde for hortyng on lede.'   740
'And quat if faurty be fre and fauty þyse oþer:
Schalt Þow schortly al schende and schape non oþer?'
'Nay, þa3 faurty forfete, 3et fryst I a whyle,
And voyde away My vengaunce, þa3 Me vyl þynk.'
Þen Abraham obeched Hym and lo3ly Him þonkkez: 745
'Now sayned be Þou, Sauiour, so symple in Þy wrath!
I am bot erþe ful euel and vsle so blake,
For to mele wyth such a Mayster as my3tez hatz alle.
Bot I haue bygonnen wyth my God, and He hit gayn þynkez;
3if I forloyne as a fol Þy fraunchyse may serue.   750
What if þretty þryuande be þrad in 3on tounez,
What schal I leue of my Lorde—if He hem leþe wolde?'

That they do such in secret and silently, too;
Then the flame of love's fire could be fanned up so high
That all evils on earth could not end such delight.
But they've altered My orders, ignored what is right.
They couple uncleanly and cling to gross acts. 710
For their sins I am set to smite them at once.
Thus for ever and ever is everyone warned."
Abraham was awestruck and altered by grief
At this promise of punishment, painful and dire.
He said, as he sighed aloud, "Sir, by Your leave, 715
Shall the sinful and sinless both suffer as one?
Would my Lord ever like it if laws should decree
That the wicked and worthy as one shall be paid?
Would You weigh with the worst those ones whom You love?
Could the Maker of man ever mete out such deeds? 720
If You found there just fifty true friends in that town,
On the sidewalks of Sodom, the sites of Gomorrah,
Never lacking Your laws, always loving Your word,
Who in reason were righteous and ready to serve,
Would You end them for the errors that others had done? 725
Shall they share in the suffering sinners have earned?
Such was never Your notion! No, never will You
Be ungracious or grim as our God, or unfair!"
"If I find there that fifty," the Father said,
"Who are free from that filth, I'll refrain, as you ask; 730
Through My grace, I'll forgive them their guilt one and all.
I will let them off lightly and leave them in peace."
"Now God, You are gracious and good," said the man.
"All is held in Your hand, both high heaven and earth.
Therefore don't be displeased if I dare to ask more, 735
If for instance I ask, though I'm ashes and dust:
What if five of that fifty proved false? Would You then—
If the rest were righteous—be wrathful or mild?"
"If just five of that fifty proved false, I'd back down;
I'd withhold My hand from hurting one man." 740
"What if forty were faultless, though filthy the rest?
Would You still destroy them and strike out their lives?"
"I'd defer—if just forty were faultless—my wrath,
Though unpleased, I would put aside punishment then."
He bowed humbly, and heartily thanked the Lord: 745
"Blessed Savior, You easily slough off Your wrath!
I'm but earth, full of evil, but ashes all black,
And unsuited to speak with a Sovereign so high.
I've begun, though, with God, Who's not angered as yet;
If I foolishly falter, forgive me, O Lord. 750
Must I think, if a throng of just thirty were there
Without sin, that You'd slay them for sins of the rest?"

Þenne þe godlych God gef hym onsware:
'Ʒet for þretty in þrong I schal My þro steke,
And spare spakly of spyt in space of My þewez,   755
And My rankor refrayne four þy reken wordez.'
'What for twenty,' quoþ þe tolke, 'vntwynez Þou hem þenne?'
'Nay, ʒif þou ʒernez hit ʒet, ʒark I hem grace;
If þat twenty be trwe, I tene hem no more,
Bot relece alle þat regioun of her ronk werkkez.'   760
'Now, aþel Lorde,' quoþ Abraham, 'onez a speche,
And I schal schape no more þo schalkkez to helpe.
If ten trysty in toune be tan in Þi werkkez,
Wylt Þou mese Þy mode and menddyng abyde?'
'I graunt,' quoþ þe grete God, 'Graunt mercy,' þat oþer;   765
And þenne arest þe renk and raʒt no fyrre.
And Godde glydez His gate by þose grene wayez,
And he conueyen Hym con with cast of his yʒe;
And als he loked along þereas oure Lorde passed,
Ʒet he cryed Hym after with careful steuen: 770
'Meke Mayster, on Þy mon to mynne if Þe lyked,
Loth lengez in ʒon leede þat is my lef broþer;
He syttez þer in Sodomis, Þy seruaunt so pouere,
Among þo mansed men þat han Þe much greued.
Ʒif Þou tynez þat toun, tempre Þyn yre,   775
As Þy mersy may malte, Þy meke to spare.'
Þen he wendez his way, wepande for care,
Towarde þe mere of Mambre, mornande for sorewe;
And þere in longyng al nyʒt he lengez in wones,
Whyl þe Souerayn to Sodamas sende to spye.   780
His sonde into Sodamas watz sende in þat tyme,
In þat ilk euentyde, by auṅgels tweyne,
Meuand mekely togeder as myry men ʒonge,
As Loot in a loge dor lened hym alone,
In a porche of þat place pyʒt to þe ʒates,   785
Þat watz ryal and ryche so watz þe renkes seluen.
As he stared into þe strete þer stout men played,
He syʒe þer swey in asent swete men tweyne;
Bolde burnez wer þay boþe with berdles chynnez,
Ryol rollande fax to raw sylk lyke,   790
Of ble as þe brere-flour whereso þe bare scheweed.
Ful clene watz þe countenaunce of her cler yʒen;
Wlonk whit watz her wede and wel hit hem semed.
Of alle feturez ful fyn and fautlez boþe;
Watz non aucly in ouþer, for aungels hit wern,   795
And þat þe ʒep vnderʒede þat in þe ʒate syttez;
He ros vp ful radly and ran hem to mete,
And loʒe he loutez hem to, Loth, to þe grounde,
And syþen soberly: 'Syrez, I yow byseche

God in His graciousness gave this reply:
"If that throng were just thirty, they'd thrive one and all.
They'd be spared, for My spite would then slacken at once,   755
All My rancor and wrath put to rest by your words."
"Were there twenty in town, would they too have to die?"
"I would grant grace to all, if it gladdens your heart.
If that twenty were true I'd take pity on all;
From my rage I'd release all the region at once."   760
Then Abraham answered, "Lord, only one speech;
Then I'll plead that You pity those people no more.
If there're ten within town who are trustworthy, pure,
Will You mellow Your mood, and their mending allow?"
"That I'll grant you," said God. "You are gracious!" said he.   765
Abraham afterwards asked Him no more;
Our God he let go on the paths by Himself.
But he watched as God walked on His way to the town.
As he looked where the Lord was fast leaving him there,
With a care-ridden cry he called to Him thus: 770
"By Your leave, gentle Lord, my kin Lot lives in town;
If You'd condescend kindly, consider Your man.
For in Sodom Lot stays. A poor servant of Yours,
Among those men whom You're mad at he lives.
When You strike down that city, assuage Your wrath.   775
That meek man in Your mercy and mildness spare!"
As he walks on his way, he is weeping in grief;
Back to Mambre he makes his way, moaning aloud.
He lay all night long, sadly lingered at home,
While the Sovereign to Sodom sent spies on their way.   780
Thus His signal to Sodom was sent at that time.
For two angels that evening arrived in the town.
The two humbly there hastened as handsome young men;
Lot, by a lodge door, was lingering then.
On a seat by the city gates sat that good man.   785
He was royal and rich, like that region itself.
As Lot stared at the street, at the sinners at play,
He beheld both those handsome men, hastening forth.
They were beardless youths, beautiful both to behold.
They had long hair, like lovely, luxurious silk,   790
And their skin, where it showed, was as soft as a rose.
Their eyes shimmered and shined with a soft, lovely light.
What they wore was white; they were wondrously fair.
They were faultless in feature, as fine as could be.
After all they were angels, in every way fair!   795
When he saw those two sojourners stepping right up,
Lot rose very rapidly, running their way.
To greet them with grace to the ground he bowed,
And said very solemnly, "Sirs, I implore:

Þat ȝe wolde lyȝt at my loge and lenge þerinne.   800
Comez to your knaues kote, I craue at þis onez;
I schal fette yow a fatte your fette for to wasche;
I norne yow bot for on nyȝt neȝe me to lenge,
And in þe myry mornyng ȝe may your waye take.'
And þay nay þat þay nolde neȝ no howsez,   805
Bot stylly þer in þe strete as þay stadde wern
Þay wolde lenge þe long naȝt and logge þeroute:
Hit watz hous innoȝe to hem þe heuen vpon lofte.
Loth laþed so longe wyth luflych wordez
Þat þay hym graunted to go and gruȝt no lenger.   810
Þe bolde to his byggyng bryngez hem bylyue,
Þat watz ryally arayed, for he watz ryche euer.
Þe wyȝez wern welcom as þe wyf couþe;
His two dere doȝterez deuoutly hem haylsed,
Þat wer maydenez ful meke, maryed not ȝet,   815
And þay wer semly and swete, and swyþe wel arayed.
Loth þenne ful lyȝtly lokez hym aboute,
And his men amonestes mete for to dyȝt:
'Bot þenkkez on hit be þrefte what þynk so ȝe make,
For wyth no sour ne no salt seruez hym neuer.'   820
Bot ȝet I wene þat þe wyf hit wroth to dyspyt,
And sayde softely to hirself: 'Þis vnsaueré hyne
Louez no salt in her sauce; ȝet hit no skyl were
Þat oþer burne be boute, þaȝ boþe be nyse.'
Þenne ho sauerez with salt her seuez vchone,   825
Agayne þe bone of þe burne þat hit forboden hade,
And als ho scelt hem in scorne þat wel her skyl knewen.
Why watz ho, wrech, so wod? Ho wrathed oure Lorde.
Þenne seten þay at þe soper, wern serued bylyue,
Þe gestes gay and ful glad, of glam debonere,   830
Welawynnely wlonk, tyl þay waschen hade,
Þe trestes tylt to þe woȝe and þe table boþe.
Fro þe seggez haden souped and seten bot a whyle,
Er euer þay bosked to bedde, þe borȝ watz al vp,
Alle þat weppen myȝt welde, þe wakker and þe stronger,   835
To vmbelyȝe Lothez hous þe ledez to take.
In grete flokkez of folk þay fallen to his ȝatez;
As a scowte-wach scarred so þe asscry rysed;
With kene clobbez of þat clos þay clatrez on þe wowez,
And wyth a schrylle scharp schout þay schewe þyse wordez: 840
'If þou louyez þy lyf, Loth, in þyse wones,
Ȝete vus out þose ȝong men þat ȝore-whyle here entred,
Þat we may lere hym of lof, as oure lyst biddez,
As is þe asyse of Sodomas to seggez þat passen.'
Whatt! þay sputen and speken of so spitous fylþe,   845
What! þay ȝeȝed and ȝolped of ȝestande sorȝe,

At my house as your host I would have you remain.   800
As your servant I'd serve you. Please stay at my house,
And with water I'll wash your weary feet there.
In my cottage I'll cater you; come for the night!
In the morning tomorrow you'll move off, refreshed."
But they turned down his true invitation; they wished   805
Just to stay where they stood in the street until dark,
Where they'd linger, lodging alone, out of doors.
For the heaven on high was the house that they craved.
Lot persisted and pleaded so pleasantly though,
That they gave in, agreed that they'd go, as he asked.   810
Noble Lot to his lodgings led them at once.
(They were royally arrayed, for his riches were great.)
Lot's wife, in her way, gave them welcome at first,
And his daughters, both dear, deftly welcomed the guests.
They were meek, pretty maidens, not married as yet.   815
They were certainly seemly, sweet, and well dressed.
Lot quickly looked through his lodgings and called
To his men there to make a meal for the guests.
Then said Lot, "Mind you, leave unleavened the food;
Do not serve them with salt, or bread leavened at all."   820
I believe, though, that Lot's wife still leavened their bread;
She was spiteful and spoke to herself in low tones:
"So these fellows are fussy and fine in their tastes!
Should all sup without salt in their sauce just for them?"
So she served up well salted the sauce to those guests,   825
This despite the clear speech Lot had spoken to her.
And she scornfully spoke to them, showing her ire.
Why such mad, wretched manners? She maddened the Lord.
As they sat and were served up their supper that day,
Those two guests were gay; they were gladdened at heart.   830
Till they washed they both waxed with a wonderful cheer.
The table and trestles were tilted away.
They had sat after supper the shortest of times,
When the city was stirred up and swarming nearby.
Those who weapons could wield, both the weak and the strong,   835
On all sides then assailed them to seize the two men.
All the folk in a flock began forcing the gate;
Like the sound of a sentinel, shouting broke out.
With their clubs those men crazily cudgeled the walls,
And shrilly and sharply they shouted these words: 840
"Hear us, Lot, if you love your own life! Hear us well!
Those same two, whom you've taken in, turn over now!
They will learn of our love-ways; our lust is inflamed!
That's the custom we keep with those coming to Sodom."
What! They spewed out and spoke of such sickening filth!   845
What! They shouted such scandalous, sin-ridden words

Þat ȝet þe wynd and þe weder and þe worlde stynkes
Of þe brych þat vpbraydez þose broþelych wordez.
Þe godman glyfte with þat glam and gloped for noyse;
So scharpe schame to hym schot, he schrank at þe hert.   850
For he knew þe costoum þat kyþed þose wrechez,
He doted neuer for no doel so depe in his mynde.
'Allas!' sayd hym þenne Loth, and lyȝtly he rysez,
And bowez forth fro þe bench into þe brode ȝates.
What! he wonded no woþe of wekked knauez,   855
Þat he ne passed þe port þe peril to abide.
He went forthe at þe wyket and waft hit hym after,
Þat a clyket hit cleȝt clos hym byhynde.
Þenne he meled to þo men mesurable wordez,
For harlotez with his hendelayk he hoped to chast: 860
'Oo, my frendez so fre, your fare is to strange;
Dotz away your derf dyn and derez neuer my gestes.
Avoy! hit is your vylaynye, ȝe vylen yourseluen;
And ȝe are jolyf gentylmen, your japez ar ille.
Bot I schal kenne yow by kynde a crafte þat is better: 865
I haf a tresor in my telde of tow my fayre deȝter,
Þat ar maydenez vnmard for alle men ȝette;
In Sodamas, þaȝ I hit say, non semloker burdes;
Hit arn ronk, hit arn rype, and redy to manne;
To samen wyth þo semly þe solace is better.   870
I schal biteche yow þo two þat tayt arn and quoynt,
And laykez wyth hem as yow lyst, and letez my gestes one.'
Þenne þe rebaudez so ronk rerd such a noyse
Þat aȝly hurled in his erez her harlotez speche:
'Wost þou not wel þat þou wonez here a wyȝe strange,   875
An outcomlyng, a carle? We kylle of þyn heued!
Who joyned þe be jostyse oure japez to blame,
Þat com a boy to þis borȝ, þaȝ þou be burne ryche?'
Þus þay þrobled and þrong and þrwe vmbe his erez,
And distresed hym wonder strayt with strenkþe in þe prece,   880
Bot þat þe ȝonge men, so ȝepe, ȝornen þeroute,
Wapped vpon þe wyket and wonnen hem tylle,
And by þe hondez hym hent and horyed hym withinne,
And steken þe ȝates ston-harde wyth stalworth barrez.
Þay blwe a boffet inblande þat banned peple,   885
Þat þay blustered, as blynde as Bayard watz euer;
Þay lest of Lotez logging any lysoun to fynde,
Bot nyteled þer alle þe nyȝt for noȝt at þe last.
Þenne vch tolke tyȝt hem, þat hade of tayt fayled,
And vchon roþeled to þe rest þat he reche moȝt;   890
Bot þay wern wakned al wrank þat þer in won lenged,
Of on þe vglokest vnhap euer on erd suffred.
Ruddon of þe day-rawe ros vpon vȝten,

That the wind and the world and the weather themselves
Still stink from the sin that they spoke of that day!
At that shouting Lot shudders; he shivers with fear.
He is shot through with shame; and he shrinks in his heart,   850
Well aware of the ways of those wicked, vile men.
Never before has he felt a misfortune like this.
"Alas," says Lot, as he quickly gets up.
He goes to his gates where are gathered those men.
What! He walks up, not worrying what they will do;   855
He goes straight through the gate to those grumbling, vile men,
Walking forth to confront that fiendish, mad crowd.
And the latch as he left was relocked at his back.
To those men he spoke measured and mild, thoughtful words
(Thus he sought to dissuade them from such evil ways):   860
"You are acting too oddly, my old, noble friends!
Now abandon such braying; don't bother my guests.
Now for shame! With such sins you'd be shaming yourselves.
Though you're justly called gentlemen, jokes such as these
Are shameless. I'll show you more natural ways.   865
I have two daughters, treasures in truth, in my house.
Both are maidens, unmarried to men to this day.
If I say so, in Sodom they're surely the best.
They have reached now their ripeness; they're ready for men.
To be with such beckoning beauties would please.   870
I'll give you those graceful, young girls. They'll be yours!
With them make any mirth; but don't menace my guests."
Those vile, dark villains then vaunted aloud;
Back to Lot they threw loudly their lewd, sinful words:
"Aren't you fully informed you're a foreigner here?   875
You're a churl! If we chose we would chop off your head!
Who enjoined you as justice to judge our deeds?
You as commoner came here, though carrying wealth."
Thus they threw words, threatened, and thronged at his door.
That crowd began crushing him, crying in rage.   880
Through the gate ran those guests, and they grabbed Lot.
But those young men emerged and managed to seize
Their host; to his house they hauled him at once.
They firmly fastened with fetters the gates,
And cursed that crowd with a crashing, loud din,   885
So that blindly as Bayard it blundered around.
By the lodging of Lot those men longed to make sport,
But all night they got nothing: no, none of their wants.
So they crawled and crept away, crying and grim;
Since they relished some rest, those men roamed from that place.   890
Those who stayed in that city were shocked soon enough
By the saddest destruction that struck on the earth.
When the red, dawning rays of light rose in the sky,

When merk of þe mydnyʒt moʒt no more last.
Ful erly þose aungelez þis haþel þay ruþen,   895
And glopnedly on Godez halue gart hym vpryse;
Fast þe freke ferkez vp ful ferd at his hert;
Þay comaunded hym cof to cach þat he hade,
'Wyth þy wyf and þy wyʒez and þy wlonc deʒtters,
For we laþe þe, sir Loth, þat þou þy lyf haue.   900
Cayre tid of þis kythe er combred þou worþe,
With alle þi here vpon haste, tyl þou a hil fynde;
Foundez faste on your fete; bifore your face lokes,
Bot bes neuer so bolde to blusch yow bihynde,
And loke ʒe stemme no stepe, bot strechez on faste;   905
Til ʒe reche to a reset, rest ʒe neuer.
For we schal tyne þis toun and trayþely disstrye,
Wyth alle þise wyʒez so wykke wyʒtly devoyde,
And alle þe londe with þise ledez we losen at onez;
Sodomas schal ful sodenly synk into grounde,   910
And þe grounde of Gomorre gorde into helle,
And vche a koste of þis kythe clater vpon hepes.'
Þen laled Loth: 'Lorde, what is best?
If I me fele vpon fote þat I fle moʒt,
Hov schulde I huyde me fro Hym þat hatz His hate kynned   915
In þe brath of His breth þat brennez alle þinkez?
To crepe fro my Creatour I know not wheder,
Ne wheþer His fooschip me folʒez bifore oþer bihynde.'
Þe freke sayde: 'No foschip oure Fader hatz þe schewed,
Bot hiʒly heuened þi hele fro hem þat arn combred.   920
Nov wale þe a wonnyng þat þe warisch myʒt,
And He schal saue hit for þy sake þat hatz vus sende hider,
For þou art oddely þyn one out of þis fylþe,
And als Abraham þyn eme hit at Himself asked.'
'Lorde, loued He worþe,' quoþ Loth, 'vpon erþe!   925
Þer is a cité herbisyde þat Segor hit hatte—
Here vtter on a rounde hil hit houez hit one.
I wolde, if His wylle wore, to þat won scape.'
'Þenn fare forth,' quoþ þat fre, 'and fyne þou neuer,
With þose ilk þat þow wylt þat þrenge þe after,   930
And ay goande on your gate, wythouten agayn-tote,
For alle þis londe schal be lorne longe er þe sonne rise.'
Þe wyʒe wakened his wyf and his wlonk deʒteres,
And oþer two myri men þo maydenez schulde wedde;
And þay token hit as tayt and tented hit lyttel;   935
Þaʒ fast laþed hem Loth, þay leʒen ful stylle.
Þe aungelez hasted þise oþer and aʒly hem þratten,
And enforsed alle fawre forth at þe ʒatez:
Þo wern Loth and his lef, his luflyche deʒter;
Þer soʒt no mo to sauement of cities aþel fyue.   940

All the blackness was broken abruptly. Dawn came.
Very early those angels were up, and they woke   895
Their host on behalf of God hastily then.
He awoke very willingly, worried with fear.
To gather his goods those men gave him the word:
"With your soon-to-be sons-in-law, sir, your wife,
And your daughters, depart from here! Death is at hand!   900
You must leave now, Sir Lot, before losing your life!
Take your family, friend, till you find a far hill.
You must make your way swiftly and stare straight ahead;
Don't look back! Don't be bold and look back as you go!
Do not stall in your steps; no, keep steady your pace.   905
Do not rest till you reach a refuge ahead.
For we'll wreck this region and ruin this town.
For its wickedness we will wipe out this land.
Yes, this place with its people we'll put to an end.
Very suddenly Sodom shall sink underground;   910
Soon Gomorrah will move, crumbling down into hell.
Every lea of this land will be lashed out at once!"
Then Lot cried out loudly, "O Lord, what is best?
If I fled with my feet, if I flew from this town,
Could I hide out from Him Whose behest this must be?   915
With His breath He could beat down and burn all the world!
Should I run from His wrath, though it wrecks the whole earth?
In His wrath He could ruin me, run where I will!"
Said the fellow, "Our Father shows favor toward you.
You've not fallen to filth like these fellows in town.   920
Therefore seek out some shelter, a safe dwelling now.
For your sake He Who sent us will spare you from harm.
You are singled out, surely, from Sodom's demise.
Your uncle, Abraham, asked it himself."
Said Lot, "May the Lord be loved on the earth!   925
There's a city called Zoar, and its site is nearby.
On a round, rolling hill Zoar rises aloft.
If God wills it, I'll wander, yes, wend my way there."
"To that spot with unceasing, quick steps now escape!
With your family go forth; they will follow along.   930
Make quick steps, never stopping or staring behind;
For destruction shall strike down this site before dawn!"
The man woke his wife and his daughters as well;
And the men who would marry those maidens he woke.
But it seemed to them sport, so they showed no concern;   935
Although Lot urged them loudly, they lay very still.
The angels came urging with awful, dire threats.
The family of four they pushed forth to the gates.
There was Lot with his two lovely daughters and wife;
None escaped from those cities besides that one group.   940

Þise aungelez hade hem by hande out at þe ȝatez,
Prechande hem þe perile, and beden hem passe fast:
'Lest ȝe be taken in þe teche of tyrauntez here,
Loke ȝe bowe now bi bot; bowez fast hence!'
And þay kayre ne con, and kenely flowen.   945
Erly, er any heuen-glem, þay to a hil comen.
Þe grete God in His greme bygynnez on lofte
To waken wederez so wylde; þe wyndez He callez,
And þay wroþely vpwaste and wrastled togeder,
Fro fawre half of þe folde flytande loude.   950
Clowdez clustered bytwene kesten vp torres,
Þat þe þik þunder-þrast þirled hem ofte.
Þe rayn rueled adoun, ridlande þikke
Of felle flaunkes of fyr and flakes of soufre,
Al in smolderande smoke smachande ful ille,   955
Swe aboute Sodamas and hit sydez alle,
Gorde to Gomorra, þat þe grounde laused,
Abdama and Syboym, þise ceteis alle faure
Al birolled wyth þe rayn, rostted and brenned,
And ferly flayed þat folk þat in þose fees lenged.   960
For when þat þe Helle herde þe houndez of heuen,
He watz ferlyly fayn, vnfolded bylyue;
Þe grete barrez of þe abyme he barst vp at onez,
Þat alle þe regioun torof in riftes ful grete,
And clouen alle in lyttel cloutes þe clyffez aywhere,   965
As lauce leuez of þe boke þat lepes in twynne.
Þe brethe of þe brynston bi þat hit blende were,
Al þo citees and her sydes sunkken to helle.
Rydelles wern þo grete rowtes of renkkes withinne,
When þay wern war of þe wrake þat no wyȝe achaped;   970
Such a ȝomerly ȝarm of ȝellyng þer rysed,
Þerof clatered þe cloudes, þat Kryst myȝt haf rawþe.
Þe segge herde þat soun to Segor þat ȝede,
And þe wenches hym wyth þat by þe way folȝed;
Ferly ferde watz her flesch þat flowen ay ilyche,   975
Trynande ay a hyȝe trot, þat torne neuer dorsten.
Loth and þo luly-whit, his lefly two deȝter,
Ay folȝed here face, bifore her boþe yȝen;
Bot þe balleful burde, þat neuer bode keped,
Blusched byhynden her bak þat bale for to herkken.   980
Hit watz lusty Lothes wyf þat ouer her lyfte schulder
Ones ho bluschet to þe burȝe, bot bod ho no lenger
Þat ho nas stadde a stiffe ston, a stalworth image,
Al so salt as ani se—and so ho ȝet standez.
Þay slypped bi and syȝe hir not þat wern hir samen-feres,   985
Tyl þay in Segor wern sette, and sayned our Lorde;
Wyth lyȝt louez vplyfte þay loued Hym swyþe,

The angels escorted them all through the gates.
As they preached of the peril, they pushed them along.
"Lest you're wiped out as well as these wicked men here,
You must hurry from here; make haste while you can!"
So they sped away swiftly, not staring back once.   945
Before day ever dawned to a hillock they came.
Then God, in His anger, began in the sky
To awaken the wildest of winds with His call;
Those winds began whirling and wrestling at once.
They crashed as they came from the corners of the earth.   950
Then rose clouds, which were clustered and climbing in peaks,
From which thrusts of thunder came thrashing aloud.
In a rushing and roaring the rain thickly fell.
Sulfur, flaming and fuming, fire in sparks,
And the stench of a smoke that was smothering all   955
Came to Sodom and struck from all sides at that time.
Gomorrah's ground moved, opened menacingly.
In Zeboim and Admah the same then occurred;
Thus four cities were scorched by that searing, bright rain!
The folk were afraid as it fell from the sky.   960
For when Hell himself heard the hounds of heaven,
He was gladdened to glean such a grisly event.
The abyss's great bars he broke, so that all
Of the region was wrecked; in a rift it was sunk!
The cliffs and the crags were cloven apart,   965
Like a book that is broken, whose binding explodes.
When the black smoke of brimstone had bled everywhere,
Those four cities had sunk; yes, they'd slipped into hell!
Their inhabitants, helpless, were harrowed with fear
When they saw no escape from destruction and death.   970
They clamored and called with such crying laments
That the clouds were cloven, and Christ would have wept!
But Lot hied away, hearing that hideous sound;
The women who went on the way heard it, too.
As they fled they were filled in their flesh with dread.   975
They maintained a fast trot, never turning to look.
Neither Lot nor his lily-white ladies—that is,
His two daughters—once dared to dawdle, look back.
But that worthless, bad woman, his wife, ever bold,
Just to stare at destruction then stopped in her tracks.   980
For an instant she eyed all that awful event,
Saw the city of Sodom destroyed by that rain,
And was stopped just as still as a statue or rock.
As the sea she is salty, and stands to this day.
Her companions slipped past, not perceiving her then.   985
They went swiftly to Zoar and straightaway praised
The Lord; there they lauded Him, lifted their praise.

Þat so His seruauntes wolde see and saue of such woþe.
Al watz dampped and don and drowned by þenne;
Þe ledez of þat lyttel toun wern lopen out for drede   990
Into þat malscrande mere, marred bylyue,
Þat noȝt saued watz bot Segor, þat sat on a lawe.
Þe þre ledez þerin lent, Loth and his deȝter;
For his make watz myst, þat on þe mount lenged
In a stonen statue þat salt sauor habbes,   995
For two fautes þat þe fol watz founde in mistrauþe:
On, ho serued at þe soper salt bifore Dryȝtyn,
And syþen, ho blusched hir bihynde, þaȝ hir forboden were;
For on ho standes a ston, and salt for þat oþer,
And alle lyst on hir lik þat arn on launde bestes.   1000
Abraham ful erly watz vp on þe morne,
Þat alle naȝt much niye hade nomen in his hert,
Al in longing for Loth leyen in a wache;
Þer he lafte hade oure Lorde he is on lofte wonnen;
He sende toward Sodomas þe syȝt of his yȝen,   1005
Þat euer hade ben an erde of erþe þe swettest,
As aparaunt to paradis, þat plantted þe Dryȝtyn;
Nov is hit plunged in a pit like of pich fylled.
Suche a roþun of a reche ros fro þe blake,
Askez vpe in þe ayre and vsellez þer flowen,   1010
As a fornes ful of flot þat vpon fyr boyles
When bryȝt brennande brondez ar bet þeranvnder.
Þis watz a uengaunce violent þat voyded þise places,
Þat foundered hatz so fayr a folk and þe folde sonkken.
Þer þe fyue citées wern set nov is a see called,   1015
Þat ay is drouy and dym, and ded in hit kynde,
Blo, blubrande, and blak, vnblyþe to neȝe;
As a stynkande stanc þat stryed synne,
Þat euer of smelle and of smach smart is to fele.
Forþy þe derk Dede See hit is demed euermore,   1020
For hit dedez of deþe duren þere ȝet;
For hit is brod and boþemlez, and bitter as þe galle,
And noȝt may lenge in þat lake þat any lyf berez,
And alle þe costez of kynde hit combrez vchone.
For lay þeron a lump of led, and hit on loft fletez,   1025
And folde þeron a lyȝt fyþer, and hit to founs synkkez;
And þer water may walter to wete any erþe
Schal neuer grene þeron growe, gresse ne wod nawþer.
If any schalke to be schent wer schowued þerinne,
Þaȝ he bode in þat boþem broþely a monyth,   1030
He most ay lyue in þat loȝe in losyng euermore,
And neuer dryȝe no dethe to dayes of ende.
And as hit is corsed of kynde and hit coostez als,
Þe clay þat clenges þerby arn corsyes strong,

His servants He'd saved from destruction and death!
All the doomed were now damned; all were drowned by that time.
For in fear the folk had been felled in that town.   990
All those people had perished; they'd plunged in the sea!
Only Zoar had been saved—as it sat on the hill—
From that doom. Thus from death the two daughters and Lot
Had been spared; for Lot's spouse still stood on the hill;
As a statue of salt, just like stone she remained,   995
Since that fool two faults had unfaithfully shown.
First, a supper all salted she'd served before God;
And second, she stared back at Sodom. For these
She both stands like a stone and of salt is composed.
In that land the lowly beasts lick at her sides.   1000
Very early was Abraham up the next day.
Through the night a man never had known such fear;
Ever waking and waiting he'd worried for Lot.
Where he'd left our Lord in that land he returned.
He stared at Sodom with searching, keen eyes.   1005
It had been earth's most beauteous, bounteous spot,
As a province of paradise planted by God.
Like a pit full of pitch now it's plunged in debris,
And a reeking stench rises around the locale.
From it ashes and embers fly up to the sky,   1010
Just as fiery, fat-laden fumes will ascend
From a kettle whose kindling is kicked into blaze.
With violence a vengeance thus voided those spots.
With those places those people all perished at once.
There a sea now is set where those five cities were.   1015
It is deadened and dim, dreary and still;
It is bubbling, black, and bad to approach.
Those towns sank in a swirling, vast sink at that time,
And stink with the stench of such sin to this day.
Thus the Dead Sea it's dubbed, darkened and grim;   1020
The death that was done there endures evermore.
It is bottomless, broad, and as bitter as gall;
What has life never lives very long in that sea.
It corrupts nature's qualities, causing strange things.
If you lay a lump of lead on that sea   1025
It will float; but a feather will fall through its depths!
And wherever its waters will wash up on earth,
Nothing green there can grow: neither grass nor plants.
If a body were brought to be buried, it would
Never sink in that stagnant, vast sea for a month;   1030
It would lie on that lake for the longest of times,
Never drawn down to death in the deeps of that pit.
Since its coasts are corrupted and cursed by nature,
All its clinging, dark clays are corrosive and vile.

As alum and alkaran, þat angré arn boþe,   1035
Soufre sour and saundyuer, and oþer such mony;
And þer waltez of þat water in waxlokes grete
Þe spumande aspaltoun þat spyserez sellen;
And suche is alle þe soyle by þat se halues,
Þat fel fretes þe flesch and festres bones.   1040
And þer ar tres by þat terne of traytoures,
And þay borgounez and beres blomez ful fayre,
And þe fayrest fryt þat may on folde growe,
As orenge and oþer fryt and apple-garnade,
Also red and so ripe and rychely hwed   1045
As any dom myȝt deuice of dayntyez oute;
Bot quen hit is brused oþer broken, oþer byten in twynne,
No worldez goud hit wythinne, bot wyndowande askes.
Alle þyse ar teches and tokenes to trow vpon ȝet,
And wittnesse of þat wykked werk, and þe wrake after   1050
Þat oure Fader forþrede for fylþe of þose ledes.
Þenne vch wyȝe may wel wyt þat He þe wlonk louies;
And if He louyes clene layk þat is oure Lorde ryche,
And to be couþe in His courte þou coueytes þenne,
To se þat Semly in sete and His swete face,   1055
Clerrer counseyl con I non, bot þat þou clene worþe.
For Clopyngnel in þe compas of his clene *Rose*,
Þer he expounez a speche to hym þat spede wolde
Of a lady to be loued: 'Loke to hir sone
Of wich beryng þat ho be, and wych ho best louyes,   1060
And be ryȝt such in vch a borȝe of body and of dedes,
And folȝ þe fet of þat fere þat þou fre haldes;
And if þou wyrkkes on þis wyse, þaȝ ho wyk were,
Hir schal lyke þat layk þat lyknes hir tylle.'
If þou wyl dele drwrye wyth Dryȝtyn þenne,   1065
And lelly louy þy Lorde and His leef worþe,
Þenne confourme þe to Kryst, and þe clene make,
Þat euer is polyced als playn as þe perle seluen.
For, loke, fro fyrst þat He lyȝt withinne þe lel mayden,
By how comly a kest He watz clos þere,   1070
When venkkyst watz no vergynyté, ne vyolence maked,
Bot much clener watz hir corse, God kynned þerinne.
And efte when He borne watz in Beþelen þe ryche,
In wych puryté þay departed; þaȝ þay pouer were,
Watz neuer so blysful a bour as watz a bos þenne,   1075
Ne no schroude hous so schene as a schepon þare,
Ne non so glad vnder God as ho þat grone schulde.
For þer watz seknesse al sounde þat sarrest is halden,
And þer watz rose reflayr where rote hatz ben euer,
And þer watz solace and songe wher sorȝ hatz ay cryed;   1080

There is bitumen, bitter and black; alum too;   1035
There is sulfur and sandiver; several kinds there.
From that water, in waxen lumps, wash up great heaps
Of black asphalt that spice dealers sell. All the earth
By the sides of that sea is so sour that it
Ever festers the flesh, ever fiercely rots bones.   1040
By that tarn there are treacherous trees growing high.
On their boughs they bear beautiful blossoms, as well
As the fairest of fruits to be found on the earth.
There are oranges and other fruit, pomegranates, too,
Just as red, and ripe, and rich in their hues   1045
As a fellow would fancy a fruit could become.
But when broken or bruised, or when bitten, they prove
To be worthless within, filled with winnowing ash.
These are symbols and signs; and they signify well
The stark vengeance He visits on vile, sinful ways   1050
When our Father sees foulness, filth among men.
Therefore cleanness, it's clear, our Lord cares for and loves.
If our God is so given to good, sinless acts,
And you're craving to come to His court in the sky,
If at last you are longing to look on His face,   1055
Then be clean. Better counsel I cannot advise.
For as Clopinel claims in his courtly *Romance*
Of the Rose, any reader who's wrenched with desire
To be loved by a lady, must "look to her ways,
Must behold the habits she happens to use,   1060
And in everything imitate actions she takes."
He adds: "Look to that loved one to learn of her ways;
If you do this, no doubt, though disdainful at first,
She will love you at last. So be like her in all."
And if likewise you long for the love of our God,   1065
If you fain would befriend Him, then follow His lead.
In His cleanliness copy Christ's ways on earth—
As a pearl He's perfectly polished and clean.
Bear in mind He emerged from a maiden, was born
In a marvelous miracle, mighty and pure;   1070
For no virgin was violently vanquished that time,
But was better for being the bearer of God.
The Lord's birth in the beauteous Bethlehem then
Was perfect and pure. They were poor as could be,
But their byre proved a bower blissful and clean;   1075
Their manger a marvelous manor house seemed.
No woman was ever so wondrously glad,
For the groaning was gone in the giving of birth.
There was rose scent where reeking and rankness had been;
There was solace and singing where sorrow had come.   1080

For aungelles with instrumentes of organes and pypes,
And rial ryngande rotes and þe reken fyþel,
And alle hende þat honestly moȝt an hert glade,
Aboutte my lady watz lent quen ho delyuer were.
Þenne watz her blyþe Barne burnyst so clene   1085
Þat boþe þe ox and þe asse Hym hered at ones;
Þay knewe Hym by His clannes for Kyng of nature,
For non so clene of such a clos com neuer er þenne.
And ȝif clanly He þenne com, ful cortays þerafter,
Þat alle þat longed to luþer ful lodly He hated,   1090
By nobleye of His norture He nolde neuer towche
Oȝt þat watz vngoderly oþer ordure watz inne.
Ȝet comen lodly to þat Lede, as lazares monye,
Summe lepre, summe lome, and lomerande blynde,
Poysened, and parlatyk, and pyned in fyres,   1095
Drye folk and ydropike, and dede at þe laste,
Alle called on þat Cortayse and claymed His grace.
He heled hem wyth hynde speche of þat þay ask after,
For whatso He towched also tyd tourned to hele,
Wel clanner þen any crafte cowþe devyse.   1100
So hende watz His hondelyng vche ordure hit schonied,
And þe gropyng so goud of God and Man boþe,
Þat for fetys of His fyngeres fonded He neuer
Nauþer to cout ne to kerue with knyf ne wyth egge;
Forþy brek He þe bred blades wythouten,   1105
For hit ferde freloker in fete in His fayre honde,
Displayed more pryuyly when He hit part schulde,
Þenne alle þe toles of Tolowse moȝt tyȝt hit to kerue.
Þus is He kyryous and clene þat þou His cort askes:
Hov schulde þou com to His kyth bot if þou clene were?   1110
Nov ar we sore and synful and sovly vchone;
How schulde we se, þen may we say, þat Syre vpon throne?
Ȝis, þat Mayster is mercyable, þaȝ þou be man fenny,
And al tomarred in myre whyle þou on molde lyuyes;
Þou may schyne þurȝ schryfte, þaȝ þou haf schome serued,   1115
And pure þe with penaunce tyl þou a perle worþe.
Perle praysed is prys þer perré is schewed,
Þaȝ hyt not derrest be demed to dele for penies.
Quat may þe cause be called bot for hir clene hwes,
Þat wynnes worschyp abof alle whyte stones?   1120
For ho schynes so schyr þat is of schap rounde,
Wythouten faut oþer fylþe ȝif ho fyn were,
And wax euer in þe worlde in weryng so olde,
Ȝet þe perle payres not whyle ho in pryse lasttes;
And if hit cheue þe chaunce vncheryst ho worþe,   1125
Þat ho blyndes of ble in bour þer ho lygges,
Nobot wasch hir wyth wourchyp in wyn as ho askes,

Many angels with instruments—organs and pipes,
Sweet viols and violins, vivid and pure—
And a group of good people, to gladden the heart,
Were along with my lady, who lay giving birth.
So perfect and pure was the precious new Child   1085
That the ox and the ass at once honored Him as
Nature's King. This His cleanness had caused them to know.
None so cleanly had come to that cow shed before.
And if clean was His coming, He was courteous in life;
For He hated most heartily heinous, vile acts.   1090
He was noble by nature and never would touch
What was evil or inwardly oozing with filth.
Yet repulsive, vile people approached our clean Lord,
Such as lepers, the lame, paralytics, the blind,
The poisoned, those pained with unpitying burns,   1095
And the dropsied—indeed, even dead ones at last.
They called on His courtesy, claimed from Him grace.
He with highness and holiness healed every one.
What He touched became truly untinctured and pure
Much more quickly and cleanly than craft could devise.   1100
Our Lord cast out uncleanness, caused it to fly.
He was gracious and great, both as God and as man.
And because of His capable, cleanly hands,
He never used knives when He needed to carve.
For He broke without blades any bread that He ate;   1105
His hands parted more perfectly pieces of bread,
And sundered more smoothly and smartly the loaf,
Than tools of Toulouse, if one tried, ever could.
He is clean, thus, Whose court you are craving to gain.
Could you come to that kingdom unclean in yourself?   1110
We are sinful, sickly, and soiled, one and all.
Can uncleanness come to His kingdom at last?
Yes, that Master is merciful! Mired though you be,
Indeed marred with such muck as you move through your life,
You may shine through confession, though shameworthy once,   1115
Be a pearl through penance, be purified still!
And the pearl's appraised the most priceless of gems,
Though not counted in coins the most costly of all.
For what reason? She's robed in the richest, clean hues,
And as such she's esteemed above shining white gems.   1120
She so shimmers and shines, and her shape is so round,
So faultless and fine, without filth anywhere,
That she wins all the world. And though worn until old,
Unimpaired is the pearl, and prized above all.
If uncherished by chance, if in chest she remains,   1125
Till, neglected, forgotten, her glow starts to dim,
She but wants to be washed in some wine and, behold,

Ho by kynde schal becom clerer þen are.
So if folk be defowled by vnfre chaunce,
Þat he be sulped in sawle, seche to schryfte,   1130
And he may polyce hym at þe prest, by penaunce taken,
Wel bryȝter þen þe beryl oþer browden perles.
Bot war þe wel, if þou be waschen wyth water of schryfte,
And polysed als playn as parchmen schauen,
Sulp no more þenne in synne þy saule þerafter,   1135
For þenne þou Dryȝtyn dyspleses with dedes ful sore,
And entyses Hym to tene more trayþly þen euer,
And wel hatter to hate þen hade þou not waschen.
For when a sawele is saȝtled and sakred to Dryȝtyn,
He holly haldes hit His and haue hit He wolde;   1140
Þenne efte lastes hit likkes, He loses hit ille,
As hit were rafte wyth vnryȝt and robbed wyth þewes.
War þe þenne for þe wrake: His wrath is achaufed
For þat þat ones watz His schulde efte be vnclene,
Þaȝ hit be bot a bassyn, a bolle oþer a scole,   1145
A dysche oþer a dobler, þat Dryȝtyn onez serued.
To defowle hit euer vpon folde fast He forbedes,
So is He scoymus of scaþe þat scylful is euer.
And þat watz bared in Babyloyn in Baltazar tyme,
Hov harde vnhap þer hym hent and hastyly sone,   1150
For he þe vesselles avyled þat vayled in þe temple
In seruyse of þe Souerayn sumtyme byfore.
Ȝif ȝe wolde tyȝt me a tom telle hit I wolde,
Hov charged more watz his chaunce þat hem cherych nolde
Þen his fader forloyne þat feched hem wyth strenþe,   1155
And robbed þe relygioun of relykes alle.
Danyel in his dialokez devysed sumtyme,
As ȝet is proued expresse in his profecies,
Hov þe gentryse of Juise and Jherusalem þe ryche
Watz disstryed wyth distres, and drawen to þe erþe.   1160
For þat folke in her fayth watz founden vntrwe,
Þat haden hyȝt þe hyȝe God to halde of Hym euer;
And He hem halȝed for His and help at her nede
In mukel meschefes mony, þat meruayl is to here.
And þay forloyne her fayth and folȝed oþer goddes,   1165
And þat wakned His wrath and wrast hit so hyȝe
Þat He fylsened þe faythful in þe falce lawe
To forfare þe falce in þe faythe trwe.
Hit watz sen in þat syþe þat Zedechyas rengned
In Juda, þat justised þe Juyne kynges.   1170
He sete on Salamones solie on solemne wyse,
Bot of leauté he watz lat to his Lorde hende:
He vsed abominaciones of idolatrye,
And lette lyȝt bi þe lawe þat he watz lege tylle.

She is naturally newer and nicer at once!
Thus if folk are defiled by filthy, black deeds,
Are stained in their souls, then for shrift they should look,   1130
And through priest-given penance be more purified than
The brightest of beryls or embroidered pearl-lace.
But beware! If you're washed with the water of shrift
And polished as plain as a parchment, do not
Ever sully your soul with sin afterwards.   1135
For, indeed, God disdains such misdeeds and will strike
At such foulness with fury more fierce than if you
From the first had stayed foul, unconfessed, in your sins.
If a soul has been shriven, made sacred to God,
Then He holds it His wholly, and have it He will!   1140
He is loathe if He loses it later, chagrined,
For it seems to be sinfully stolen by thieves.
So look out for His ire! His anger's aroused
When what once He had won makes its way back to filth.
Though it be but a basin, a bowl, or a cup,   1145
Or a saucer for soup; if it once served the Lord,
Then He firmly forbids its defilement on earth.
He is squeamish of sin Who establishes right!
This was borne out in brazen, bold Babylon once
When Belshazzar was suddenly seized with great woe.   1150
He used vainly and vilely the vessels that once
In God's temple had truly been treated with awe.
If you've time, I will tell you the tale in full.
You will see how the son came to suffer much more
Than his father who filched them by force before that,   1155
When he robbed of its rich, gleaming relics the church.
In his dialogues Daniel has dutifully told—
And his prophesies proved to be perfectly true—
How the Jewish gentry and Jerusalem once
Were besieged, destroyed, and struck to the ground.   1160
God had found those folk to be faithless, untrue.
Though they'd pledged to be pious and ply His decrees,
Though He'd hailed them as His and helped them as well
Through their trials and troubles—all truly profound—
Yet they fell from their faith and followed false gods.   1165
This aroused the Lord's wrath. It was raised to such heights
That He favored those faithful to false gods, so that
He might fell the false in the faith that was true.
Zedechiah was king when this came to unfold
(Then the Jews ruled Judah). As judge and king,   1170
He sat solemnly on Solomon's throne;
He was lax with the Lord in his loyalty, though,
Had taken to treasuring treacherous gods
And left off his love of the laws that are true.

Forþi oure Fader vpon folde a foman hym wakned: 1175
Nabigodenozar nuyed hym swyþe.
He pursued into Palastyn with proude men mony,
And þer he wast wyth werre þe wones of þorpes;
He herȝed vp alle Israel and hent of þe beste,
And þe gentylest of Judée in Jerusalem biseged,   1180
Vmbewalt alle þe walles wyth wyȝes ful stronge,
At vche a dor a doȝty duk, and dutte hem wythinne;
For þe borȝ watz so bygge batayled alofte,
And stoffed wythinne with stout men to stalle hem þeroute.
Þenne watz þe sege sette þe ceté aboute,   1185
Skete skarmoch skelt, much skaþe lached;
At vch brugge a berfray on basteles wyse
Þat seuen syþe vch a day asayled þe ȝates;
Trwe tulkkes in toures teueled wythinne,
In bigge brutage of borde bulde on þe walles;   1190
Þay feȝt and þay fende of, and fylter togeder
Til two ȝer ouertorned, ȝet tok þay hit neuer.
At þe laste, vpon longe, þo ledes wythinne,
Faste fayled hem þe fode, enfamined monie;
Þe hote hunger wythinne hert hem wel sarre   1195
Þen any dunt of þat douthe þat dowelled þeroute.
Þenne wern þo rowtes redles in þo ryche wones;
Fro þat mete watz myst, megre þay wexen,
And þay stoken so strayt þat þay ne stray myȝt
A fote fro þat forselet to forray no goudes.   1200
Þenne þe kyng of þe kyth a counsayl hym takes
Wyth þe best of his burnes, a blench for to make;
Þay stel out on a stylle nyȝt er any steuen rysed,
And harde hurles þurȝ þe oste er enmies hit wyste.
Bot er þay atwappe ne moȝt þe wach wythoute   1205
Hiȝe skelt watz þe askry þe skewes anvnder.
Loude alarom vpon launde lulted watz þenne;
Ryche, ruþed of her rest, ran to here wedes,
Hard hattes þay hent and on hors lepes;
Cler claryoun crak cryed on lofte.   1210
By þat watz alle on a hepe hurlande swyþee,
Folȝande þat oþer flote, and fonde hem bilyue,
Ouertok hem as tyd, tult hem of sadeles,
Tyl vche prynce hade his per put to þe grounde.
And þer watz þe kyng kaȝt wyth Caldé prynces,   1215
And alle hise gentyle forjusted on Jerico playnes,
And presented wern as presoneres to þe prynce rychest,
Nabigodenozar, noble in his chayer;
And he þe faynest freke þat he his fo hade,
And speke spitously hem to, and spylt þerafter.   1220
Þe kynges sunnes in his syȝt he slow euerych one,

So our Father fashioned a foe for that man;   1175
For the nonce it was Nebuchadnezzar who came
And pressed into Palestine proudly with men.
With war he laid waste the wide-ranging towns
And razed all of Israel, robbing the folk.
Jerusalem's gentry in Judea he fought.   1180
In a siege he surrounded that city with men;
At each door he set dukes. Thus a dungeon of sorts
The town seemed; though inside were the stoutest of men,
All prepared to repel the powerful siege.
But the siege that ensued on that city was grim!   1185
All the fighting was furious! Fierce were the wounds!
On wheels of wood there were war-towers built,
Which were turned on that town seven times every day.
But inside the soldiers and citizens fought.
They had raised up a rampart and rallied defense.   1190
Those folk fiercely fought off the foe in its siege.
Two years passed, yet that place was not pierced by the foe.
But at last those who lingered so long in that town
Began failing with fasting. Their food had run out!
What they suffered from starving then served them much worse   1195
Than the blows from the battle that battered their walls.
So those people, once powerful, pined away fast.
When the food began failing, they fell to disease.
Yet they found themselves fenced in and forced to stay put.
Not a step could they stray forth to search for food.   1200
Their king then called for a council at once;
All agreed they could gain on the grievous foe.
They would steal out and strike in the stillness of night;
Before that foe was informed, they'd attack.
But the siege's sentry sensed it and raised   1205
A clamoring cry to the clouds. He gave vent
To a loud, bold alarm through the land on that night.
Thus awakened, the warriors went for their gear;
On their heads they donned helmets, on horseback they leapt,
While that clamoring cry cut through the air.   1210
All were grouped together and gaining upon
Those folk, whom they fought when they found. Each man was
In no time overtaken and tossed from his horse;
Every prince's opponent was pushed to the ground.
On that day the Chaldeans thus downed the king,   1215
Outjousting his gentry on Jericho's plains.
To the prince all were proffered as prisoners then,
To that noble one, Nebuchadnezzar on throne.
He was pleased to see placed there those prisoners thus,
And spoke to them spitefully, spilling their blood.   1220
In his sight he slew the sons of the king,

And holkked out his auen yȝen heterly boþe,
And bede þe burne to be broȝt to Babyloyn þe ryche,
And þere in dongoun be don to dreȝe þer his wyrdes.
Now se, so þe Souerayn set hatz His wrake: 1225
Nas hit not for Nabugo ne his noblé nauþer
Þat oþer depryued watz of pryde with paynes stronge,
Bot for his beryng so badde agayn his blyþe Lorde;
For hade þe Fader ben his frende, þat hym bifore keped,
Ne neuer trespast to Him in teche of mysseleue,   1230
To colde wer alle Caldé and kythes of Ynde,
Ȝet take Torkye hem wyth—her tene hade ben little.
Ȝet nolde neuer Nabugo þis ilke note leue
Er he hade tyrued þis toun and torne hit to grounde.
He joyned vnto Jerusalem a gentyle duc þenne—   1235
His name watz Nabuzardan—to noye þe Jues;
He watz mayster of his men and myȝty himseluen,
Þe chef of his cheualrye his chekkes to make;
He brek þe bareres as bylyue, and þe burȝ after,
And enteres in ful ernestly, in yre of his hert.   1240
What! þe maysterry watz mene: þe men wern away,
Þe best boȝed wyth þe burne þat þe borȝ ȝemed,
And þo þat byden wer so biten with þe bale hunger
Þat on wyf hade ben worþe þe welgest fourre.
Nabizardan noȝt forþy nolde not spare,   1245
Bot bede al to þe bronde vnder bare egge;
Þay slowen of swettest semlych burdes,
Baþed barnes in blod and her brayn spylled;
Prestes and prelates þay presed to deþe,
Wyues and wenches her wombes tocoruen,   1250
Þat her boweles outborst aboute þe diches,
And al watz carfully kylde þat þay cach myȝt.
And alle þat swypped, vnswolȝed of þe sworde kene,
Þay wer cagged and kaȝt on capeles al bare,
Festned fettres to her fete vnder fole wombes,   1255
And broþely broȝt to Babyloyn þer bale to suffer,
To sytte in seruage and syte, þat sumtyme wer gentyle.
Now ar chaunged to chorles and charged wyth werkkes,
Boþe to cayre at þe kart and þe kuy mylke,
Þat sumtyme sete in her sale syres and burdes.   1260
And ȝet Nabuzardan nyl neuer stynt
Er he to þe temppple tee wyth his tulkkes alle;
Betes on þe barers, brestes vp þe ȝates,
Slouen alle at a slyp þat serued þerinne,
Pulden prestes bi þe polle and plat of her hedes,   1265
Diȝten dekenes to deþe, dungen doun clerkkes,
And alle þe maydenes of þe munster maȝtyly hokyllen
Wyth þe swayf of þe sworde þat swolȝed hem alle.

And grimly and gruesomely gouged out his eyes.
He bade him be brought into Babylon then,
To endure there in dungeon the darkest of fates.
Now observe how the Sovereign will seek His revenge! 1225
It was not for King Nebuchadnezzar at all
That King Zedechiah was cast down so low,
But because of his coarse, ugly conduct with God.
Had the Father stayed friend, as before; had that man
Never trespassed as traitor the truth of the Lord; 1230
All the armies of India, all of the Turks,
And Chaldeans could deal no destruction at all.
King Nebuchadnezzar would never retreat
Till he'd taken the town, seen it torn to the ground.
He arranged as Jerusalem's ruler a duke, 1235
Nebuzaradan, zealous to strike at the Jews.
Of his men he was master; and, mighty himself,
He was chief of his champions when charging in war.
So he broke down the bulwark and barriers, too,
And eagerly entered with ire in his heart. 1240
The defenders had fled! The defeat thus was less.
For the best when he broke in had bolted long since.
And, besides, those who stayed were so starved that it seemed
Even one of the women was worth four men.
Thus disaster with zeal Nebuzaradan wrought; 1245
In his ire he put all to the edge of the sword.
So they slew there the sweetest and seemliest maids,
And bashed out the brains of the babies they found.
Any prelate or priest was pressed to his death.
The wombs of wenches and wives were ripped out, 1250
So their bowels about the byways were strewn.
Whom they captured they cruelly killed on the spot.
Those allowed to live through the length of the siege
Were stripped, set astride marching steeds on that day.
They fettered their feet at the flanks of horses, 1255
And brought them to bale in Babylon then,
There to suffer in servitude stinging defeat.
The high were thus hurled into hard, churlish work;
Once-great lords and good ladies, who lounged in fine halls,
Now pulled carts and milked cows, now carried vast loads. 1260
Nebuzaradan's zeal went unceasing until
He had taken his troops to the temple at last.
He beat down its barriers, broke in the gates,
And slew at a stroke all who served in that place.
With haste they beheaded the highest of priests. 1265
They did deacons to death, dashed down the clerks,
And murdered that minster's fair maidens at once;
With a stroke of the sword they were swept to their deaths.

Þenne ran þay to þe relykes as robbors wylde,
And pyled alle þe apparement þat pented to þe kyrke—   1270
Þe pure pyleres of bras pourtrayd in golde,
And þe chef chaundeler charged with þe ly3t,
Þat ber þe lamp vpon lofte þat lemed euermore
Bifore þe *sancta sanctorum* þer selcouth watz ofte.
Þay ca3t away þat condelstik, and þe crowne als   1275
Þat þe auter hade vpon, of aþel golde ryche,
Þe gredirne and þe goblotes garnyst of syluer,
Þe bases of þe bry3t postes and bassynes so schyre,
Dere disches of golde and dubleres fayre,
Þe vyoles and þe vesselment of vertuous stones.   1280
Now hatz Nabuzardan nomen alle þyse noble þynges,
And pyled þat precious place and pakked þose godes;
Þe golde of þe gazafylace to swyþe gret noumbre,
Wyth alle þe vrnmentes of þat hous, he hamppred togeder;
Alle he spoyled spitously in a sped whyle   1285
Þat Salomon so mony a sadde 3er so3t to make.
Wyth alle þe coyntyse þat he cowþe clene to wyrke,
Deuised he þe vesselment, þe vestures clene;
Wyth sly3t of his ciences, his Souerayn to loue,
Þe hous and þe anournementes he hy3tled togedere.   1290
Now hatz Nabuzardan nummen hit al samen,
And syþen bet doun þe bur3 and brend hit in askes.
Þenne wyth legiounes of ledes ouer londes he rydes,
Her3ez of Israel þe hyrnez aboute;
Wyth charged chariotes þe cheftayn he fyndez,   1295
Bikennes þe catel to þe kyng, þat he ca3t hade;
Presented him þe prisoneres in pray þat þay token—
Moni a worþly wy3e whil her worlde laste,
Moni semly syre soun, and swyþe rych maydenes,
Þe pruddest of þe prouince, and prophetes childer,   1300
As Ananie, and Azarie, and als Mizael,
And dere Daniel also, þat watz deuine noble,
With moni a modey moder-chylde mo þen innoghe.
And Nabugodenozar makes much joye,
Nov he þe kyng hatz conquest and þe kyth wunnen,   1305
And dreped alle þe do3tyest and derrest in armes,
And þe lederes of her lawe layd to þe grounde,
And þe pryce of þe profecie prisoners maked.
Bot þe joy of þe juelrye so gentyle and ryche,
When hit watz schewed hym so schene, scharp watz his wonder;   1310
Of such vessel auayed, þat vayled so huge,
Neuer 3et nas Nabugodenozar er þenne.
He sesed hem with solemneté, þe Souerayn he praysed
Þat watz aþel ouer alle, Israel Dry3tyn;
Such god, such gounes, such gay vesselles,   1315

Like robbers they ran to the relics and seized
The liturgical treasures attached to that church.   1270
The brass pillars, painted with pure gold, they took.
And the lone candelabrum whose lamp ever glowed,
Ever shone on the sancta sanctorum below—
Where miracles, marvels, had many times come—
They stole. They seized, too, the sumptuous crown   1275
Made of glittering gold as it glowed on the altar.
All the goblets, the gridiron of glistening hue,
All the bright pillar bases, the bowls and cups,
All the platters and plates made of precious gold,
All the vials and vessels of virtuous stones: 1280
Nebuzaradan zealously seized every one.
All that place he had pillaged. He packed it all up,
From the vast, bulging vault, seizing valuable gold.
That temple's treasures he took on that day.
Out of spite with swiftness he sacked the whole place   1285
Which King Solomon solemnly sought to erect.
For the sagely King Solomon, certain years past,
Had devised those vessels and vestments for God.
For our Sovereign, King Solomon skillfully wrought
That temple and, too, all the treasures within.   1290
These in zeal Nebuzaradan seized on that day;
Then he burned the whole borough to brand and to ash.
Through lands with his legions that leader then rides,
And all Israel's areas eagerly takes.
With his chariots charging, its chieftains he finds;   1295
To his king he carries the captured at once.
They're presented as prisoners, prizes of war:
Many once-renowned worthies and once-noble folk;
Many mighty young men and maidens most high;
All the mightiest men; also Michael himself;   1300
Ananias, Azariah (the offspring of seers);
Good Daniel the dream-reader; dreary, vast throngs
Of the mightiest mothers' sons, more than enough!
Therefore Nebuchadnezzar was now overjoyed.
He had conquered that king, and that country he'd seized.   1305
He'd destroyed the strongest, slain one and all
Of the leaders of law; they were laid to the ground.
The prominent prophets were prisoners now.
When the temple's treasures were taken to him,
He was joyous and jocund, more jubilant still,   1310
Because Nebuchadnezzar had never been told
Of the truth of the temple's great treasures before.
He solemnly seized them. The Sovereign he praised,
Who of all was the Author, great Israel's God.
Vast possessions and spoils and sumptuous goods   1315

Comen neuer out of kyth to Caldée reames.
He trussed hem in his tresorye in a tryed place,
Rekenly, wyth reuerens, as he ryȝt hade;
And þer he wroȝt as þe wyse, as ȝe may wyt hereafter,
For hade he let of hem lyȝt, hym moȝt haf lumpen worse.   1320
Þat ryche in gret rialté rengned his lyue,
As conquerour of vche a cost he cayser watz hatte,
Emperour of alle þe erþe and also þe saudan,
And als þe god of þe grounde watz grauen his name.
And al þurȝ dome of Daniel, fro he deuised hade   1325
Þat alle goudes com of God, and gef hit hym bi samples,
Þat he ful clanly bicnv his carp bi þe laste,
And ofte hit mekned his mynde, his maysterful werkkes.
Bot al drawes to dyȝe with doel vpon ende:
Bi a haþel neuer so hyȝe, he heldes to grounde.   1330
And so Nabugodenozar, as he nedes moste,
For alle his empire so hiȝe in erþe is he grauen.
Bot þenn þe bolde Baltazar, þat watz his barn aldest,
He watz stalled in his stud, and stabled þe rengne
In þe burȝ of Babiloyne, þe biggest he trawed,   1335
Þat nauþer in heuen ne on erþe hade no pere;
For he bigan in alle þe glori þat hym þe gome lafte,
Nabugodenozar, þat watz his noble fader.
So kene a kyng in Caldée com neuer er þenne;
Bot honoured he not Hym þat in heuen wonies.   1340
Bot fals fantummes of fendes, formed with handes,
Wyth tool out of harde tre, and telded on lofte,
And of stokkes and stones, he stoute goddes callz,
When þay ar gilde al with golde and gered wyth syluer;
And þere he kneles and callez and clepes after help.   1345
And þay reden him ryȝt rewarde he hem hetes,
And if þay gruchen him his grace, to gremen his hert,
He cleches to a gret klubbe and knokkes hem to peces.
Þus in pryde and olipraunce his empyre he haldes,
In lust and in lecherye and loþelych werkkes,   1350
And hade a wyf for to welde, a worþelych quene,
And mony a lemman, neuer þe later, þat ladis wer called.
In þe clernes of his concubines and curious wedez,
In notyng of nwe metes and of nice gettes,
Al watz þe mynde of þat man on misschapen þinges,   1355
Til þe Lorde of þe lyfte liste hit abate.
Thenne þis bolde Baltazar biþenkkes hym ones
To vouche on avayment of his vayneglorie;
Hit is not innoghe to þe nice al noȝty þink vse
Bot if alle þe worlde wyt his wykked dedes.   1360
Baltazar þurȝ Babiloyn his banne gart crye,
And þurȝ þe cuntré of Caldée his callyng con spryng,

On that day to Chaldea were driven with speed.
To his treasury taking those trinkets at once,
He arranged such riches with reverent care.
He was right to revere them! You'll realize soon
He'd have had severe harm if he'd handled them ill.   1320
He in riches and royalty reigned all his life,
Conquered all coasts, and was called Caesar there.
Of the earth he was emperor, everyone's king;
And as "god of the ground" men engraved his name.
This was done because Daniel had deigned to advise   1325
That all goods are given by God. This he proved,
So that Nebuchadnezzar could know of its truth,
And be made therefore meek both in mind and in deed.
But, alas, all that lives must at length meet its death;
Every lord is brought low, be he lofty or meek.   1330
Thus Nebuchadnezzar, inevitably,
In the end, although awesome, in earth is interred.
His first son, though, Belshazzar, succeeded in line;
In his stead he established himself on the throne
As the best and the boldest in Babylon then,   1335
Without equal on earth, without equal on high.
At first all his father's vast fortune was his:
All that Nebuchadnezzar had nobly controlled.
Such a king had not come to Chaldea before!
But he didn't adore the Dweller on high;   1340
No, he followed false gods, fiends made by men,
Carved from trees with keen tools, set toweringly high,
Made of stumps and of stones. These Belshazzar adores
When they're gilded with glistening gold for the nonce;
There he prays and implores as he prostrates himself.   1345
If they presaged him aptly, he'd promise rewards;
If their grace was not granted, he'd grab a big club,
And bash them to bits with the bitterest wrath!
So with pride, pomp, and pleasures as well,
He with loathsome, dark lust and lechery reigns.   1350
For his wants he'd a worthy, fair wife as his queen;
But he kept many concubines, calling them all
His good "ladies." He lusted for ludicrous things,
For concubines, clothing, and cooking as well;
For the mind of that man dwelt on misshapen things.   1355
Thus he reigned till the Ruler of realms changed events,
When Belshazzar decided to show off his wealth,
To reveal his vanity, vainglory, and pride.
It is never enough for the noxious to sin;
They must publish with pride their pitiful deeds!   1360
So he caused this decree to be called through the town
(Indeed, all Chaldea then dinned with the news):

Þat alle þe grete vpon grounde schulde geder hem samen
And assemble at a set day at þe saudans fest.
Such a mangerie to make þe man watz auised,   1365
Þat vche a kythyn kyng schuld com þider,
Vche duk wyth his duthe, and oþer dere lordes,
Schulde com to his court to kyþe hym for lege,
And to reche hym reuerens, and his reuel herkken,
To loke on his lemanes and ladis hem calle.   1370
To rose hym in his rialty rych men soȝtten,
And mony a baroun ful bolde, to Babyloyn þe noble.
Þer bowed toward Babiloyn burnes so mony,
Kynges, cayseres ful kene, to þe court wonnen,
Mony ludisch lordes þat ladies broȝten,   1375
Þat to neuen þe noumbre to much nye were.
For þe bourȝ watz so brod and so bigge alce,
Stalled in þe fayrest stud þe sterrez anvnder,
Prudly on a plat playn, plek alþer-fayrest,
Vmbesweyed on vch a syde with seuen grete wateres,   1380
With a wonder wroȝt walle wruxeled ful hiȝe,
With koynt carneles aboue, coruen ful clene,
Troched toures bitwene, twenty spere lenþe,
And þiker þrowen vmbeþour with ouerþwert palle.
Þe place þat plyed þe pursaunt wythinne   1385
Watz longe and ful large and euer ilych sware,
And vch a syde vpon soyle helde seuen myle,
And þe saudans sete sette in þe myddes.
Þat watz a palayce of pryde passande alle oþer,
Boþe of werk and of wunder, and walled al aboute;   1390
Heȝe houses withinne, þe halle to hit med,
So brod bilde in a bay þat blonkkes myȝt renne.
When þe terme of þe tyde watz towched of þe feste,
Dere droȝen þerto and vpon des metten,
And Baltazar vpon bench was busked to sete,   1395
Stepe stayred stones of his stoute throne.
Þenne watz alle þe halle flor hiled with knyȝtes,
And barounes at þe sidebordes bounet aywhere,
For non watz dressed vpon dece bot þe dere seluen,
And his clere concubynes in cloþes ful bryȝt.   1400
When alle segges were þer set þen seruyse bygynnes,
Sturne trumpen strake steuen in halle,
Aywhere by þe wowes wrasten krakkes,
And brode baneres þerbi blusnande of gold,
Burnes berande þe bredes vpon brode skeles   1405
Þat were of sylueren syȝt, and served þerwyth,
Lyfte logges þerouer and on lofte coruen,
Pared out of paper and poynted of golde,
Broþe baboynes abof, besttes anvnder,

All the gentry should join with him, just as he wished,
On a set day assemble. That sultan thus asked
That his servants and stewards assemble a feast,   1365
For the kings of great countries would come on that day.
To Chaldea each duke out of duty and awe
Would thus come to his court and call him his lord.
As he reveled in riot he'd reverence the king,
And would label as "ladies" those lecherous whores.   1370
Thus to Babylon both great barons and dukes
Went in royalty. Richly they reverenced that king.
In that place there appeared such a plenteous crowd—
From courts and castles came kings, and from towns
In all lands came great lords with their ladies as well— 1375
That one never could name them and not take much time.
For that borough was broad! It was big and it sat
In the fairest of spots one could find beneath stars.
On a plain it sat proudly. And, pouring nearby,
There were seven pure streams sailing softly along.   1380
It had wondrous walls, which were wide and high,
Above which were battlements, built very well,
With towers and turrets at twenty spears' length,
And platforms and palisades, placed aptly there.
That city was square. All four sides of that town   1385
Were both straight and strong. They stretched very far;
Seven miles those mighty walls measured in length.
And the seat of the sultan was set in their midst:
A palace surpassing in pride all the rest
For the wonder its work and its walls could inspire.   1390
There a hall and the highest of houses were built
Through whose grandiose gates one could gallop on horse!
When the hour for all to assemble approached,
Nobles dutifully drew toward the dais within.
Then Belshazzar ascended the steps to his throne,   1395
Where he sat in state at the center of all.
Then the finest knights filled the floor of that hall,
And on benches the boldest of barons took seats;
For the dais that day had been duly reserved
For the king and his concubines, clothed in the best.   1400
All are seen to their seats as the service begins.
Bugles with banners of bright, brilliant gold
Begin fabulous fanfares that float through the hall,
And bounce and rebound off the beauteous walls.
Roast is borne to that banquet on broad platters next;   1405
It is served up, it seems, atop silver tureens,
Which are covered with canopies cut, for the nonce,
Out of paper plated and pointed with gold,
Showing baboons above and beasts all around,

Foles in foler flakerande bitwene,   1410
And al in asure and ynde enaumayld ryche;
And al on blonkken bak bere hit on honde.
And ay þe nakeryn noyse, notes of pipes,
Tymbres and tabornes, tulket among,
Symbales and sonetez sware þe noyse,   1415
And bougounz busch batered so þikke.
So watz serued fele syþe þe sale alle aboute,
With solace at þe sere course, bifore þe self lorde,
Þer þe lede and alle his loue lenged at þe table;
So faste þay weȝed to him wyne hit warmed his hert   1420
And breyþed vppe into his brayn and blemyst his mynde,
And al waykned his wyt, and welneȝe he foles;
For he waytez on wyde, his wenches he byholdes,
And his bolde baronage aboute bi þe woȝes.
Þenne a dotage ful depe drof to his hert,   1425
And a caytif counsayl he caȝt bi hymseluen;
Maynly his marschal þe mayster vpon calles,
And comaundes hym cofly coferes to lauce,
And fech forþ þe vessel þat his fader broȝt,
Nabugodenozar, noble in his strenþe,   1430
Conquerd with his knyȝtes and of kyrk rafte
In Judé, in Jerusalem, in gentyle wyse:
'Bryng hem now to my borde, of beuerage hem fylles,
Let þise ladyes of hem lape—I luf hem in hert;
Þat schal I cortaysly kyþe, and þay schin knawe sone,   1435
Þer is no bounté in burne lyk Baltazar þewes.'
Þenne towched to þe tresour þis tale watz sone,
And he with keyes vncloses kystes ful mony;
Mony burþen ful bryȝt watz broȝt into halle,
And couered mony a cupborde with cloþes ful quite.   1440
Þe júeles out of Jerusalem with gemmes ful bryȝt
Bi þe syde of þe sale were semely arayed;
Þe aþel auter of brasse watz hade into place,
Þe gay coroun of golde gered on lofte.
Þat hade ben blessed bifore wyth bischopes hondes   1445
And wyth besten blod busily anoynted,
In þe solempne sacrefyce þat goud sauor hade
Bifore þe Lorde of þe lyfte in louyng Hymseluen,
Now is sette, for to serue Satanas þe blake,
Bifore þe bolde Baltazar wyth bost and wyth pryde;   1450
Houen vpon þis auter watz aþel vessel
Þat wyth so curious a crafte coruen watz wyly.
Salamon sete him seuen ȝere and a syþe more,
With alle þe syence þat hym sende þe souerayn Lorde,
For to compas and kest to haf hem clene wroȝt.   1455
For þer wer bassynes ful bryȝt of brende golde clere,

Birds flying in fluttering foliage, too,   1410
All enameled in azure and indigo tints,
All held up on horses' backs, handily served!
There are kettledrums' clatter and clamoring pipes.
There are timbrels and tabors, well tuned, playing there.
To them sonorous cymbals are sounding replies;   1415
Drumsticks on drums make a dint in the air.
Again and again every guest was thus served
A course in that court as the king had ordained,
While that man with his many loose mistresses sat.
His servants swiftly served him good wine;   1420
To his brain it went boldly and broke all his sense.
Yes, it weakened his wit as it went to his head.
So he stupidly stared at his strumpets and gazed
At those barons on benches, all banqueting well.
There came to that king an uncomely idea;   1425
An obnoxious, unnatural notion occurred!
So that master commanded his marshal to come,
And told him to turn to the treasury then,
To fetch what his father had formerly won:
Vessels Nebuchadnezzar in noble display   1430
With his barons had borne from the bounteous church
In Judea, in Jerusalem, jousting in war.
"These you'll bring to my board! To the brim they'll be filled!
For these ladies I love will lap from those cups!
I will grant them gladly such graciousness here,   1435
And show them Belshazzar's outshone by no man!"
His instructions were told to the treasurer next,
Who with keys unclosed the great closets from which
Many burdens of bounty were brought to the hall.
Many cloths, white and comely, on cupboards were draped.   1440
From Jerusalem jewels and gems then appeared
And were lovingly lined up along that great hall.
The excellent altar was also arranged.
In that hall they hoisted on high the gold crown,
Which had often been blessed by bishops' pure hands,   1445
And as often anointed with animals' blood
In the sacrifice, savory, solemn, and pure,
Done to lift up lauds to the Lord of the sky
(It's set now in service of Satan the fiend).
Displayed to Belshazzar with show and with pomp,   1450
On that altar more excellent vessels were raised;
They'd been shaped with a skill that had seldom been matched.
More than seven years Solomon spent, and he used
Every skill that the Sovereign had sent him to make
Each one faultless and free from filth for the nonce.   1455
There were basins burnished with bright, gleaming gold,

Enaumaylde with azer, and eweres of sute,
Couered cowpes foul clene, as casteles arayed,
Enbaned vnder batelment with bantelles quoynt,
And fyled out of fygures of ferlylé schappes.   1460
Þe coperounes of þe couacles þat on þe cuppe reres
Wer fetysely formed out in fylyoles longe;
Pinacles pyʒt þer apert þat profert bitwene,
And al bolled abof with braunches and leues,
Pyes and papejayes purtrayed withinne,   1465
As þay prudly hade piked of pomgarnades;
For alle þe blomes of þe boʒes wer blyknande perles,
And alle þe fruyt in þo formes of flaumbeande gemmes,
Ande safyres, and sardiners, and semely topace,
Alabaundarynes, and amaraunz, and amaffised stones,   1470
Casydoynes, and crysolytes, and clere rubies,
Penitotes, and pynkardines, ay perles bitwene;
So trayled and tryfled atrauerce wer alle,
Bi vche bekyr ande bolle, þe brurdes al vmbe;
Þe gobelotes of golde grauen aboute,   1475
And fyoles fretted with flores and fleez of golde;
Vpon þat avter watz al aliche dresset.
Þe candelstik bi a cost watz cayred þider sone,
Vpon þe pyleres apyked, þat praysed hit mony,
Vpon hit basez of brasse þat ber vp þe werkes,   1480
Þe boʒes bryʒt þerabof, brayden of golde,
Braunches bredande þeron, and bryddes þer seten
Of mony koynt kyndes, of fele kyn hues,
As þay with wynge vpon wynde hade waged her fyþeres.
Inmong þe leues of þe lyndes lampes wer grayþed,   1485
And oþer louflych lyʒt þat lemed ful fayre,
As mony morteres of wax merkked withoute
With mony a borlych best al of brende golde.
Hit watz not wonte in þat wone to wast no serges,
Bot in temple of þe trauþe trwly to stonde   1490
Bifore þe *sancta sanctorum*, þer soþefast Dryʒtyn
Expouned His speche spiritually to special prophetes.
Leue þou wel þat þe Lorde þat þe lyfte ʒemes
Displesed much at þat play in þat plyt stronge,
Þat His jueles so gent wyth jaueles wer fouled,   1495
Þat presyous in His presens wer proued sumwhyle.
Soberly in His sacrafyce summe wer anoynted,
Þurʒ þe somones of Himselfe þat syttes so hyʒe;
Now a boster on benche bibbes þerof
Tyl he be dronkken as þe deuel, and dotes þer he syttes.   1500
So þe Worcher of þis worlde wlates þerwyth
Þat in þe poynt of her play He poruayes a mynde;
Bot er harme hem He wolde in haste of His yre,

All enameled with azure, and ewers to match.
There were castlelike cups with covers as lids.
As on castles, good courses were carved in their sides;
There were formed on them figures in fanciful shapes.   1460
And towers, attached to the tops of those cups,
Were made with what must have been marvelous skill.
There were pure, rising pinnacles placed here and there,
And above were embossed many branches and leaves.
Tiny magpies and parrots were perched upon boughs   1465
As if pecking proudly on pomegranates;
And the blossoms that bent down those boughs were of pearl.
All the fruit that was formed there was fashioned of gems;
There were sards, sapphires, and topaz as well,
Almandines, emeralds, amethysts bright,   1470
Chalcedonies, chrysolites, clear rubies red,
Peridots, pynkardines, and pearls everywhere.
To the brim every beaker and bowl was thus
Finely traced in with trailing, bright trefoils throughout.
All the goblets of gold were engraved everywhere,   1475
And the bowls had butterflies, blossoms of gold.
On that altar everything was amply arrayed.
On a cart servants carried the candlestick in;
It was borne on a base of brass to the hall.
The people praised its pillars at once   1480
And the boughs that above it were braided with gold.
Lovely birds in those boughs' many branches were perched;
Many species were shown, in a spectrum of hues.
They seemed wavering, wings in the wind, as they sat
In the lamps' glowing leaves. All was lovely and fine.   1485
Other lovely, bright lamps were lit up the hall.
And outside of the altar were still other lamps
With beasts carved with care. But that candlestick there
Was not wont to be wastefully, wickedly used;
In the towering temple of truth it had stood   1490
Near the holy of holies where high, mighty God
Would expound to His pious prophets His words.
You'll believe, then, the Lord felt great loathing and was
Much displeased with that sport! For He saw on that day
All His precious things, previously piously used,   1495
Being fouled by fellows unfaithful and low.
In His sacrifice such had been solemnly used,
As He'd sought through His summons while sitting on high.
Now those boasters on benches imbibe with those cups
Till they're drunk as the devil, and driveling too!   1500
The Creator of earth is so utterly wroth
He prepares a great plan while they're playing their games.
He'd not harm them in haste, though, in heat of His wrath;

He wayned hem a warnyng þat wonder hem þoȝt.
Nov is alle þis guere geten glotounes to serue, 1505
Stad in a ryche stal, and stared ful bryȝte;
Baltazar in a brayd: 'Bede vus þerof!
Weȝe wyn in þis won! Wassayl!' he cryes.
Swyfte swaynes ful swyþe swepen þertylle,
Kyppe kowpes in honde kyngez to serue; 1510
In bryȝt bollez ful bayn birlen þise oþer,
And vche mon for his mayster machches alone.
Þer watz rynging, on ryȝt, of ryche metalles,
Quen renkkes in þat ryche rok rennen hit to cache;
Clatering of couaclez þat kesten þo burdes 1515
As sonet out of sauteray songe als myry.
Þen þe dotel on dece drank þat he myȝt;
And þenne derfly arn dressed dukez and prynces,
Concubines and knyȝtes, bi cause of þat merthe;
As vchon hade hym inhelde he haled of þe cuppe. 1520
So long likked þise lordes þise lykores swete,
And gloryed on her falce goddes, and her grace calles,
Þat were of stokkes and stones, stille euermore—
Neuer steuen hem astel, so stoken is hor tonge.
Alle þe goude golden goddes þe gaulez ȝet neuenen, 1525
Belfagor and Belyal, and Belssabub als,
Heyred hem as hyȝly as heuen wer þayres,
Bot Hym þat alle goudes giues, þat God þay forȝeten.
Forþy a ferly bifel þat fele folk seȝen;
Fyrst knew hit þe kyng and alle þe cort after: 1530
In þe palays pryncipale, vpon þe playn wowe,
In contrary of þe candelstik, þer clerest hit schyned,
Þer apered a paume, with poyntel in fyngres,
Þat watz grysly and gret, and grymly he wrytes;
Non oþer forme bot a fust faylande þe wryste 1535
Pared on þe parget, purtrayed lettres.
When þat bolde Baltazar blusched to þat neue,
Such a dasande drede dusched to his hert
Þat al falewed his face and fayled þe chere;
Þe stronge strok of þe stonde strayned his joyntes, 1540
His cnes cachches toclose, and cluchches his hommes,
And he with plattyng his paumes dispyses his leres,
And romyes as a rad ryth þat rorez for drede,
Ay biholdand þe honde til hit hade al grauen
And rasped on þe roȝ woȝe runisch sauez. 1545
When hit þe scrypture hade scraped wyth a scrof penne,
As a coltour in clay cerues þe forȝes,
Þenne hit vanist verayly and voyded of syȝt,
Bot þe lettres bileued ful large vpon plaster.
Sone so þe kynge for his care carping myȝt wynne, 1550

He would send them a strange, moving sign before that.
To serve gluttons that gear is thus gathered and used;   1505
It is splendidly set up and shines very bright.
Belshazzar says suddenly, "Serve us therein!
We'll have wine here at once!" He cries, "Wassail, my friends!"
So the servants suddenly start through the hall;
They catch up the cups that the kings may imbibe.   1510
Those on benches with bright, lovely bowls are served.
(Every man serves his master, not minding the rest.)
There was clinking of cups in that court, to be sure,
When the servants would scurry to serve up the wine.
From the lids which those ladies would lift came a sound   1515
Just as sweet as a song from a psaltery then.
On the dais that dolt deeply drank without stop,
And in pleasure joined plenty of princes and dukes.
All carousing and carefree were concubines, knights;
Each one drank to the dregs every drink that was served.   1520
For a long time these lords imbibed liquor this way.
To false gods they gave glory; they groveled in prayer
Before stones and mere stocks that stayed still evermore.
Not a sound those gods sent them, so still were their tongues!
To those graven gold gods they gave glory and praise,   1525
To Belial, Beelzebub, Belfagor too,
And honors most high, as if heaven were theirs.
They forgot, though, that God Who all good confers,
And Who made there a miracle many would see.
First the king, then the crowd in that court, saw it there.   1530
In the principal palace, upon the bare wall,
By the candlestick casting its clear, burning light,
With a pointed pencil, appeared a great hand!
It was hideous, horrible, huge! And it wrote!
Just a fist with its fingers was formed in the air!   1535
In a place on the plaster it penned letters then.
Belshazzar stared at that strange, floating hand
And was stupefied, seized with such sharp, rushing fear
That his features fell, and his face became pale.
The strength of that stroke started straining his joints.   1540
His knees started knocking, as if near to collapse.
He ripped into rags his rich robes from fear.
Like a bull he bawled out; he bellowed aloud
When beholding the hand that was hovering there,
As it scratched on the surface those strange, runic words.   1545
It rasped as it wrote on the rough, empty wall,
As a coulter will carve within clay many rows;
Then with speed disappeared from their sight in thin air!
But the letters were left, written large on that wall.
The king spoke, though sorely distressed and afraid,   1550

He bede his burnes boʒ to þat were bok-lered,
To wayte þe wryt þat hit wolde, and wyter hym to say—
'For al hit frayes my flesche, þe fyngres so grymme.'
Scoleres skelten þeratte þe skyl for to fynde,
Bot þer watz neuer on so wyse couþe on worde rede,   1555
Ne what ledisch lore ne langage nauþer,
What typyng ne tale tokened þo draʒtes.
Þenne þe bolde Baltazar bred ner wode,
And bede þe ceté to seche segges þurʒout
Þat wer wyse of wychecrafte, and warlaʒes oþer   1560
Þat con dele wyth demerlayk and deuine lettres.
'Calle hem alle to my cort, þo Caldé clerkkes,
Vnfolde hem alle þis ferly þat is bifallen here,
And calle wyth a hiʒe cry: "He þat þe kyng wysses,
In expounyng of speche þat spredes in þise lettres,   1565
And makes þe mater to malt my mynde wythinne,
Þat I may wyterly wyt what þat wryt menes,
He schal be gered ful gaye in gounes of porpre,
And a coler of cler golde clos vmbe his þrote;
He schal be prymate and prynce of pure clergye,   1570
And of my þreuenest lordez þe þrydde he schal,
And of my reme þe rychest to ryde wyth myseluen,
Outtaken bare two, and þenne he þe þrydde."'
Þis cry watz vpcaste, and þer comen mony
Clerkes out of Caldye þat kennest wer knauen,   1575
As þe sage sathrapas þat sorsory couþe,
Wychez and walkyries wonnen to þat sale,
Deuinores of demorlaykes þat dremes cowþe rede,
Sorsers of exorsismus and fele such clerkes;
And alle þat loked on þat letter as lewed þay were   1580
As þay had loked in þe leþer of my lyft bote.
Þenne cryes þe kyng and kerues his wedes.
What! he corsed his clerkes and calde hem chorles;
To henge þe harlotes he heʒed ful ofte:
So watz þe wyʒe wytles he wed wel ner.   1585
Ho herde hym chyde to þe chambre þat watz þe chef quene.
When ho watz wytered bi wyʒes what watz þe cause—
Suche a chaungande chaunce in þe chef halle—
Þe lady, to lauce þat los þat þe lorde hade,
Glydes doun by þe grece and gos to þe kyng.   1590
Ho kneles on þe colde erþe and carpes to hymseluen
Wordes of worchyp wyth a wys speche.
'Kene kyng,' quoþ þe quene, 'kayser of vrþe,
Euer laste þy lyf in lenþe of dayes!
Why hatz þou rended þy robe for redles hereinne,   1595
Þaʒ þose ledes ben lewed lettres to rede,
And hatz a haþel in þy holde, as I haf herde ofte,

And bade that the book-learned be beckoned at once,
There correctly to read what the writing could mean:
"For they frighten my flesh, those fingers so grim!"
Soon the scholars all scrambled in, studied the wall;
What those words meant not one of those wise men could say,   1555
What lore or what language those letters comprised,
Nor what tale or tidings those tokens portrayed.
King Belshazzar then shook with a shivering fright,
And sent men to search through the city for all
Who were wizards in witchcraft or wise in such lore,   1560
Or who made use of magic and meanings discerned.
"Call to my court all the clerks of Chaldea.
In detail tell them of this terrible thing.
Say that the sage who deciphers those words,
Who untangles, interprets, those tokens above,   1565
And who guides me to grasp those engravings so that
I may learn through his lore what those letters convey,
He shall gaily be geared. Purple gowns he will wear;
A gold collar shall closely be clasped at his throat.
He'll be primate, most pure, of the priesthood as well.   1570
Near my throne he shall thrive as the third highest up.
In my realm as the richest, he'll ride with myself;
There will be thus above him in bounty but two!"
His men bore the message, and many arrived:
The most dexterous in dark arts Chaldea could boast,   1575
Wily sages and sorcerers, soothsayers, too,
Knowing witches and wizards, both wise and adept.
There arrived, too, the readers of riddling dreams,
And scholars and exorcists, steeped in their arts.
All who looked on those letters, though, learned just as much   1580
As they'd learn if they'd looked on my left leather boot.
The king begins clutching his clothes, as he screams.
What! He cursed his clerks and he called them all slaves!
All those scoundrels, he shouted, would surely be hung!
His fear mounted. That man went near mad at that time.   1585
From her chamber this chiding the chief of the queens
Could discern. When her servants expounded the cause,
When they told her how tidings had turned in the hall,
That lady, to lessen her lord's great despair,
Descended the stairs and went straight to the king.   1590
At his feet on the floor she fell to her knees.
Thus she went; and with wise, knowing words she implored.
"Valiant king," said that queen, "the earth's conqueror, brave!
May your life ever last in the length of its days!
Why rent thus your robe, as though robbed of advice,   1595
Just because these clerks can't make clear these signs?
There's a man in your minions, I've many times heard,

Þat hatz þe gost of God þat gyes alle soþes?
His sawle is ful of syence, saȝes to schawe,
To open vch a hide þyng of aunteres vncowþe.   1600
Þat is he þat ful ofte hatz heuened þy fader
Of mony anger ful hote with his holy speche.
When Nabugodenozar watz nyed in stoundes,
He devysed his dremes to þe dere trawþe;
He keuered hym with his counsayl of caytyf wyrdes;   1605
Alle þat he spured hym, in space he expowned clene,
Þurȝ þe sped of þe spyryt, þat sprad hym withinne,
Of þe godeliest goddez þat gaynes aywhere.
For his depe diuinité and his dere sawes,
Þy bolde fader Baltazar bede by his name,   1610
Þat now is demed Danyel, of derne coninges,
Þat caȝt watz in þe captyuidé in cuntré of Jues;
Nabuzardan hym nome, and now is he here,
A prophete of þat prouince and pryce of þe worlde.
Sende into þe ceté to seche hym bylyue,   1615
And wynne hym with þe worchyp to wayne þe bote;
And þaȝ þe mater be merk þat merked is ȝender,
He schal declar hit also cler as hit on clay stande.'
Þat gode counseyl at þe quene watz cached as swyþe;
Þe burne byfore Baltazar watz broȝt in a whyle.   1620
When he com bifore þe kyng and clanly had halsed,
Baltazar vmbebrayde hym, and 'Beue sir,' he sayde,
'Hit is tolde me bi tulkes þat þou trwe were
Profete of þat prouynce þat prayed my fader,
Ande þat þou hatz in þy hert holy connyng,   1625
Of sapyence þi sawle ful, soþes to schawe;
Goddes gost is þe geuen þat gyes alle þynges,
And þou vnhyles vch hidde þat Heuen-Kyng myntes.
And here is a ferly byfallen, and I fayn wolde
Wyt þe wytte of þe wryt þat on þe wowe clyues,   1630
For alle Caldé clerkes han cowwardely fayled.
If þou with quayntyse con quere hit, I quyte þe þy mede:
For if þou redes hit by ryȝt and hit to resoun brynges,
Fyrst telle me þe tyxte of þe tede lettres,
And syþen þe mater of þe mode mene me þerafter,   1635
And I schal halde þe þe hest þat I þe hyȝt haue,
Apyke þe in porpre cloþe, palle alþer-fynest,
And þe byȝe of bryȝt golde abowte þyn nekke,
And þe þryd þryuenest þat þrynges me after,
Þou schal be baroun vpon benche, bede I þe no lasse.'   1640
Derfly þenne Danyel deles þyse wordes:
'Ryche kyng of þis rengne, rede þe oure Lorde!
Hit is surely soth þe Souerayn of heuen
Fylsened euer þy fader and vpon folde cheryched,

Who to God—He Who governs all good—is contrite.
Though obscure, to his soul such sayings are clear;
He discerns in the strangest of signs their purport.   1600
He's the same who with speeches would soothe from his wrath
Your father when frequently fanned into ire.
For when Nebuchadnezzar was noisome, disturbed,
He'd erase his wrath just by reading his dreams.
With his sayings he saved him from suffering ill   1605
And answered whatever was asked by that king,
For his soul is sustained and his spirit is touched
By the goodliest God of all gods that men praise.
For his knowledge bold Nebuchadnezzar called him
A seer who sears with a shining, bright light.   1610
But he's deemed now wise Daniel, in dark knowledge steeped.
He was caught when we captured the country of Jews
Under Nebuchadnezzar. Thus now he is here:
From that province a prominent prophet, most wise.
So send word through our city to seek him at once;   1615
Beg him to bring to this business some light.
Though the matter here marked seems murky, obscure,
He'll interpret it truly and tell you what's meant."
In that court the queen's counsel was carefully heard.
And that seer was shown to Belshazzar's great hall.   1620
He came to the king and courteously bowed.
Belshazzar said, "Sir," when he saw him approach,
"I am told that you truly some time ago were,
In the province we plundered, a prophet of truth,
That you harbor in heart magic holy and pure,   1625
And the knowledge to know and prognosticate truths.
You are gifted by God—He Who guides all—and thus
Comprehend what the high King of heaven intends.
Among us a moving, strange miracle's been;
I'd like to learn what those letters might mean,   1630
But this city's wise scholars are stumped, one and all.
I'll reward you if wisely you work out the truth.
If you read this writing correctly to us,
If you tell me the truth of the text on that wall,
And to me you can make what it means very clear,   1635
What I pledged in my promise you'll presently have.
You will gaily be geared. Purple gowns will you wear;
A gold collar shall closely be clasped at your throat.
Near my throne you will thrive as the third highest up.
On my bench you'll be baron; you'll bide here in wealth."   1640
Daniel spoke in response to Belshazzar at once:
"Noble lord of this land, may our Lord be your guide!
It is certain the Sovereign, Whose seat is above,
Always favored your father before other kings.

Gart hym grattest to be of gouernores alle,   1645
And alle þe worlde in his wylle welde as hym lyked.
Whoso wolde wel do, wel hym bityde,
And quos deth so he dezyre, he dreped als fast;
Whoso hym lyked to lyft, on lofte watz he sone,
And quoso hym lyked to lay watz loȝed bylyue.   1650
So watz noted þe note of Nabugodenozar,
Styfly stabled þe rengne bi þe stronge Dryȝtyn,
For of þe Hyȝest he hade a hope in his hert,
Þat vche pouer past out of þat Prynce euen.
And whyle þat counsayl watz cleȝt clos in his hert   1655
Þere watz no mon vpon molde of myȝt as hymseluen;
Til hit bitide on a tyme towched hym pryde
For his lordeschyp so large and his lyf ryche;
He hade so huge an insyȝt to his aune dedes
Þat þe power of þe hyȝe Prynce he purely forȝetes.   1660
Þenne blynnes he not of blasfemy on to blame þe Dryȝtyn;
His myȝt mete to Goddes he made with his wordes:
"I am god of þe grounde, to gye as me lykes.
As He þat hyȝe is in heuen, His aungeles þat weldes.
If He hatz formed þe folde and folk þervpone,   1665
I haf bigged Babiloyne, burȝ alþer-rychest,
Stabled þerinne vche a ston in strenkþe of myn armes;
Moȝt neuer myȝt bot myn make such anoþer."
Watz not þis ilke worde wonnen of his mowþe
Er þenne þe Souerayn saȝe souned in his eres: 1670
"Now Nabugodenozar innoȝe hatz spoken,
Now is alle þy pryncipalté past at ones,
And þou, remued fro monnes sunes, on mor most abide
And in wasturne walk and wyth þe wylde dowelle,
As best, byte on þe bent of braken and erbes,   1675
With wroþe wolfes to won and wyth wylde asses."
Inmydde þe poynt of his pryde departed he þere
Fro þe soly of his solempneté; his solace he leues,
And carfully is outkast to contré vnknawen,
Fer into a fyr fryth þere frekes neuer comen.   1680
His hert heldet vnhole; he hoped non oþer
Bot a best þat he be, a bol oþer an oxe.
He fares forth on alle faure, fogge watz his mete,
And ete ay as a horce when erbes were fallen;
þus he countes hym a kow þat watz a kyng ryche,   1685
Quyle seuen syþez were ouerseyed, someres I trawe.
By þat mony þik fytherez þryȝt vmbe his lyre,
Þat alle watz dubbed and dyȝt in þe dew of heuen;
Faxe, fyltered and felt, floȝed hym vmbe,
Þat schad fro his schulderes to his schere-wykes,   1690
And twenty-folde twynande hit to his tos raȝt,

Through His grace he was greatest of governors once.   1645
All the world his will and his wishes obeyed.
Whom he wished to do well would be wealthy indeed;
And whose death he desired would die at his whim.
Whom he liked to see lofty was lifted at once;
Whom he cared to discredit was cast into ruin.   1650
Thus King Nebuchadnezzar was known. His reign
Was established in strength by the Sovereign on high.
His belief in the Lord was loyal and deep;
For the Lord, he believed, had delivered the earth.
Just as long as was locked that belief in his heart,   1655
Not one person could pry him from power on earth,
Till one time he was touched by the tincture of pride,
Which he learned from his luxury, lordship, and wealth.
Then he haughtily held up so highly his deeds
That the Prince's sheer power he promptly forgot.   1660
He broke into blasphemies, blaming our God,
Imagined he'd matched our Lord's might, and declared:
'I am god of the ground, and I govern at whim,
Just as He Who in heaven on high rules all.
As He fashioned all folk after forming the earth,   1665
So I've built mighty Babylon, best of all towns!
I established each stone with the strength of my arms;
There's no might except mine that could match such a deed.'
But this statement had scarcely escaped from his lips,
When the speech of the Sovereign he suddenly heard: 1670
'Now, King Nebuchadnezzar, enough of these words!
All your power and princedom have passed as of now!
And, removed from men, on a moor you shall live,
In the wilderness walk with the wildest of beasts.
You shall feed in the fields from ferns and from herbs.   1675
With the wolf you shall walk, with the wild, braying ass.'
He was hurled from the height of his haughtiness then;
From his solemn, high seat, and his solace was thrown,
Cast, full of care, to a country of bogs,
To a forest of fir trees where few ever go.   1680
His reason was rattled; he reckoned himself
A bellowing beast, a bull or an ox.
On all fours he would forage and feed on green grass.
He ate hay like a horse when he hadn't fresh herbs.
Once a king, he became but a cow in his mind!   1685
He stayed thus for seven long summers, I think.
By that time he had tufts on his torso of hair,
Which were dressed and adorned with the dew of the sky.
His hair, thick and hempen, hung everywhere;
It sprouted and spread from shoulders to groin.   1690
Twenty times it entwined him and touched his feet,

Þer mony clyuy as clyde hit clyȝt togeder.
His berde ibrad alle his brest to þe bare vrþe,
His browes bresed as breres aboute his brode chekes;
Holȝe were his yȝen and vnder campe hores,   1695
And al watz gray as þe glede, with ful grymme clawres
Þat were croked and kene as þe kyte paune;
Erne-hwed he watz and al ouerbrawden,
Til he wyst ful wel who wroȝt alle myȝtes,
And cowþe vche kyndam tokerue and keuer when Hym lyked.   1700
Þenne He wayned hym his wyt, þat hade wo soffered,
Þat he com to knawlach and kenned hymseluen;
Þenne he loued þat Lorde and leued in trawþe
Hit watz non oþer þen He þat hade al in honde.
Þenne sone watz he sende agayn, his sete restored;   1705
His barounes boȝed hym to, blyþe of his come,
Haȝerly in his aune hwef his heued watz couered,
And so ȝeply watz ȝarked and ȝolden his state.
Bot þou, Baltazar, his barne and his bolde ayre,
Seȝ þese syngnes with syȝt and set hem at lyttel,   1710
Bot ay hatz hofen þy hert agaynes þe hyȝe Dryȝtyn,
With bobaunce and with blasfamye bost at Hym kest,
And now His vessayles avyled in vanyté vnclene,
Þat in His hows Hym to honour were heuened of fyrst;
Bifore þe barounz hatz hom broȝt, and byrled þerinne   1715
Wale wyne to þy wenches in waryed stoundes;
Bifore þy borde hatz þou broȝt beuerage in þ'edé,
Þat blyþely were fyrst blest with bischopes hondes,
Louande þeron lese goddez þat lyf haden neuer,
Made of stokkes and stonez þat neuer styry moȝt.   1720
And for þat froþande fylþe, þe Fader of heuen
Hatz sende into þis sale þise syȝtes vncowþe,
Þe fyste with þe fyngeres þat flayed þi hert,
Þat rasped renyschly þe woȝe with þe roȝ penne.
Þise ar þe wordes here wryten, withoute werk more,   1725
By vch fygure, as I fynde, as oure Fader lykes:
Mane, Techal, Phares: merked in þrynne,
Þat þretes þe of þyn vnþryfte vpon þre wyse.
Now expowne þe þis speche spedly I þenk:
Mane menes als much as "Maynful Gode   1730
Hatz counted þy kyndam bi a clene noumbre,
And fulfylled hit in fayth to þe fyrre ende".
To teche þe of *Techal*, þat terme þus menes:
"Þy wale rengne is walt in weȝtes to heng,
And is funde ful fewe of hit fayth-dedes."   1735
And *Phares* folȝes for þose fawtes, to frayst þe trawþe;
In *Phares* fynde I forsoþe þise felle saȝes:
"Departed is þy pryncipalté, depryued þou worþes,

Where it snarled and stuck to itself as with mire.
Down his breast grew his beard to the bare forest floor.
His brows were like bristles of briars on his cheeks;
He had, under hairs, sunken hollows of eyes.   1695
Soon he grew just as gray as a great, soaring kite,
With claws that were crooked and keen to behold.
He was hued like a hawk. He was wholly transformed,
Till he recognized rightly Who wrought every strength
And Who conquered or cast away kingdoms at whim!   1700
God restored to his senses that sufferer then,
So that Nebuchadnezzar could know things aright.
He believed in and loved the Lord after that,
Because He in His hand ever holds all the world.
Soon he was sent back; his seat was restored.   1705
His barons all bowed to him, blithe that he'd come.
And, correctly, the crown on that king was replaced.
So his kingdom he quickly recovered at last.
Then, Belshazzar, his son, you succeeded as heir.
All these signs you have seen but set them at naught.   1710
You sinfully set up yourself against God,
Bombard Him with blasphemies, boasts, and taunts,
Using vainly and vilely the vessels which were
In His temple intended as treasures to Him.
To these barons you've brought them; they're brimming, indeed,   1715
With the same wine your wicked, low wenches are served.
To your board you have brought, filled with beverage unfit,
Cups that bishops once blessed! In your blasphemies here,
You have lifted your lauds up to lifeless, false gods
Made of stocks and of stones, though they're still and can't move!   1720
For such foulness and filth, the great Father above
All these strange, awesome sights has sent to this hall,
Sent the fist with its fingers, which flayed so your heart,
And rasped, as it wrote, with its ragged-edged pen.
As for what these strange words on the wall spell out,   1725
Here I find that our Father has fashioned them thus:
Mene's told there, and *tekel*, and *peres* as well.
These words in three ways serve to warn you for filth.
In their turn I intend to interpret them each.
First is *mene*, which means: 'The almighty, high God—   1730
After counting your kingdom, forecasting its days—
Has determined truly its terminal date.'
I'd interpret the term that reads *tekel* this way:
'Now your sovereignty's set in the scales in which
It is weighed and found wanting in worthy deeds.'   1735
For your faults *peres* follows there, formed on the wall;
And in faith in those figures I find this conveyed:
'You're deprived of your power. To Persia will fall

Þy rengne rafte is þe fro, and raȝt is þe Perses;
Þe Medes schal be maysteres here, and þou of menske schowued." '   1740
Þe kyng comaunded anon to clepe þat wyse
In frokkes of fyn cloþ, as forward hit asked;
Þenne sone watz Danyel dubbed in ful dere porpor,
And a coler of cler golde kest vmbe his swyre.
Þen watz demed a decre bi þe duk seluen: 1745
Bolde Baltazar bed þat hym bowe schulde
Þe comynes al of Caldé þat to þe kyng longed,
As to þe prynce pryuyest preued þe þrydde,
Heȝest of alle oþer saf onelych tweyne,
To boȝ after Baltazar in borȝe and in felde.   1750
Þys watz cryed and knawen in cort als fast,
And alle þe folk þerof fayn þat folȝed hym tylle.
Bot howso Danyel watz dyȝt, þat day ouerȝede;
Nyȝt neȝed ryȝt now with nyes fol mony,
For daȝed neuer anoþer day, þat ilk derk after,   1755
Er dalt were þat ilk dome þat Danyel deuysed.
Þe solace of þe solempneté in þat sale dured
Of þat farand fest, tyl fayled þe sunne;
Þenne blykned þe ble of þe bryȝt skwes,
Mourkenes þe mery weder, and þe myst dryues   1760
Þorȝ þe lyst of þe lyfte, bi þe loȝ medoes.
Vche haþel to his home hyȝes ful fast,
Seten at her soper and songen þerafter;
Þen foundez vch a felaȝschyp fyrre at forþ naȝtes.
Baltazar to his bedd with blysse watz caryed;   1765
Reche þe rest as hym lyst: he ros neuer þerafter.
For his foes in þe felde in flokkes ful grete,
Þat longe hade layted þat lede his londes to strye,
Now ar þay sodenly assembled at þe self tyme.
Of hem wyst no wyȝe þat in þat won dowelled.   1770
Hit watz þe dere Daryus, þe duk of þise Medes,
Þe prowde prynce of Perce, and Porros of Ynde,
With mony a legioun ful large, with ledes of armes,
Þat now hatz spyed a space to spoyle Caldéez.
Þay þrongen þeder in þe þester on þrawen hepes,   1775
Asscaped ouer þe skyre watteres and scayled þe walles,
Lyfte laddres ful longe and vpon lofte wonen,
Stelen stylly þe toun er any steuen rysed.
Withinne an oure of þe niyȝt an entré þay hade,
Ȝet afrayed þay no freke. Fyrre þay passen,   1780
And to þe palays pryncipal þay aproched ful stylle,
Þenne ran þay in on a res on rowtes ful grete;
Blastes out of bryȝt brasse brestes so hyȝe,
Ascry scarred on þe scue, þat scomfyted mony.
Segges slepande were slayne er þay slyppe myȝt;   1785

All your state when it's suddenly seized from your grasp;
For the Medes will be made here the masters at once.' "   1740
Then the king had him clothed in fine cloth, as he'd pledged;
He had Daniel adorned with a dear, purple coat.
As agreed, he was given the gayest of robes;
And a clear, golden collar was clasped on his neck.
A decree was proclaimed by the king after that;   1745
Bold Belshazzar insisted each subject—each man
Who was deemed a Chaldean—to Daniel should bow.
All should pay him respect as a prince, third in strength
Of Belshazzar's true subjects in city and field;
For but two in that township now topped him in rank.   1750
In that court this was cried out, proclaimed in effect.
In that place the people praised that decree.
After Daniel was dressed up, that day reached its end.
The fiercest misfortune then fell with the night,
Because day would not dawn when that dark night was through   1755
Till the doom was delivered that Daniel foretold.
Till the sun slowly sank on that sumptuous feast,
There was pleasure and pomp in that palace's hall.
Then the day became deepened with darkening clouds;
Thick mists, making murky the mild, pleasant day,   1760
Moved along the land from the low, distant fields.
In haste to his home each man hurries along,
Where he sits at his supper, and sings later on,
Therefore finding more fellowship far into night.
Belshazzar was shown to his sumptuous bed.   1765
Let him reach there his rest; he'll not rise from that sleep!
For in flocks his foes to the fields have come;
All who long to lay low his lands and estates
Are assembled now suddenly, set to wage war.
But of such not a soul in the city's aware.   1770
It was Darius, duke of the dangerous Medes,
The proud prince of Persia, and Porus—who had
With an awesome, vast army from India come—
Who were destined that day Chaldea to seize.
In the darkness they drove forth, a dense, crowded mass,   1775
And waded the waters. The walls they approached,
Where they lifted great ladders that led to their top.
All was seized before sentries could sound an alarm.
For not even an hour was eaten away
By the time they had taken that town. They with stealth   1780
To the principal palace approached, rousing none.
When they reached it they ran in a rushing crowd.
Then bugles began blasting and blaring within;
And the sound, as it soared to the sky, frightened men.
Before stirring from sleep, men were slaughtered that night.   1785

Vche hous heyred watz withinne a hondewhyle.
Baltazar in his bed watz beten to deþe,
Þat boþe his blod and his brayn blende on þe cloþes;
The kyng in his cortyn watz kaȝt bi þe heles,
Feryed out bi þe fete and fowle dispysed.   1790
Þat watz so doȝty þat day and drank of þe vessayl
Now is a dogge also dere þat in a dych lygges.
For þe mayster of þyse Medes on þe morne ryses,
Dere Daryous þat day dyȝt vpon trone,
Þat ceté seses ful sounde, and saȝtlyng makes   1795
Wyth alle þe barounz þeraboute, þat bowed hym after.
And þus watz þat londe lost for þe lordes synne,
And þe fylþe of þe freke þat defowled hade
Þe ornementes of Goddez hous þat holy were maked.
He watz corsed for his vnclannes, and cached þerinne,   1800
Done doun of his dyngneté for dedez vnfayre,
And of þyse worldes worchyp wrast out for euer,
And ȝet of lykynges on lofte letted, I trowe:
To loke on oure lofly Lorde late bitydes.
Þus vpon þrynne wyses I haf yow þro schewed   1805
Þat vnclannes tocleues in corage dere
Of þat wynnelych Lorde þat wonyes in heuen,
Entyses Hym to be tene, teldes vp His wrake;
Ande clannes is His comfort, and coyntyse He louyes,
And þose þat seme arn and swete schyn se His face.   1810
Þat we gon gay in oure gere þat grace He vus sende,
Þat we may serue in His syȝt, þer solace neuer blynnez.

                                                    Amen.

In haste every hovel and house was seized.
As he slept King Belshazzar was slain with fierce clubs;
Both his blood and his brains were thus blent on the sheets.
He was hastily hung by his heels and thus
Dragged about to be blasphemed, abused, and disgraced.   1790
Now a dog in a ditch is as dear as that man
Who was vile and vainly those vessels abused!
In the morning the master of Medes became king;
On that day noble Darius donned the crown,
To the seat of the city acceded, made peace   1795
With the barons abroad, who obeyed his decree.
Thus that land became lost for its lord's ugly sin,
For the filth of that fellow who defiled the things
That were held in God's house to be holy and pure.
He was cursed for uncleanness and caught in the act,   1800
For his deeds hurled down from his dignified place.
He was ousted forever from honor on earth
And deprived of the pleasure of peace in the sky;
I believe he'll not look on the Lord of all things.
Thus with three telling themes I have thoroughly shown   1805
That uncleanness cuts to the core of the heart
Of that lofty, great Lord Who is living on high;
It arouses His anger and ire at once,
While courteous cleanness comforts His heart.
Who are seemly and sweet, they shall see the Lord's face.   1810
May He grant us the grace to be gaily attired,
And unceasingly serve in His sight, knowing bliss!

                                   Amen

Patience

The facing-page text is reproduced from *The Poems of the Pearl Manuscript: Pearl, Cleanness, Patience, Sir Gawain and the Green Knight,* ed. Malcolm Andrew and Ronald Waldron (rev. ed. University of Exeter, 1987).

Pacience is a poynt, þaȝ hit displese ofte.
When heuy herttes ben hurt wyth heþyng oþer elles,
Suffraunce may aswagen hem and þe swelme leþe,
For ho quelles vche a qued and quenches malyce;
For quoso suffer cowþe syt, sele wolde folȝe,   5
And quo for þro may noȝt þole, þe þikker he sufferes.
Þen is better to abyde þe bur vmbestoundes
Þen ay þrow forth my þro, þaȝ me þynk ylle.
I herde on a halyday, at a hyȝe masse,
How Mathew melede þat his Mayster His meyny con teche.   10
Aȝt happes He hem hyȝt and vcheon a mede,
Sunderlupes, for hit dissert, vpon a ser wyse:
Thay arn happen þat han in hert pouerté,
For hores is þe heuen-ryche to holde for euer;
Þay ar happen also þat haunte mekenesse,   15
For þay schal welde þis worlde and alle her wylle haue;
Thay ar happen also þat for her harme wepes,
For þay schal comfort encroche in kythes ful mony;
Þay ar happen also þat hungeres after ryȝt,
For þay schal frely be refete ful of alle gode;   20
Thay ar happen also þat han in hert rauþe,
For mercy in alle maneres her mede schal worþe;
Þay ar happen also þat arn of hert clene,
For þay her Sauyour in sete schal se with her yȝen;
Thay ar happen also þat halden her pese,   25
For þay þe gracious Godes sunes schal godly be called;
Þay ar happen also þat con her hert stere,
For hores is þe heuen-ryche, as I er sayde.
These arn þe happes alle aȝt þat vus bihyȝt weren,
If we þyse ladyes wolde lof in lyknyng of þewes: 30
Dame Pouert, Dame Pitée, Dame Penaunce þe þrydde,
Dame Mekenesse, Dame Mercy, and miry Clannesse,
And þenne Dame Pes, and Pacyence put in þerafter.
He were happen þat hade one; alle were þe better.
Bot syn I am put to a poynt þat pouerté hatte,   35
I schal me poruay pacyence and play me with boþe,
For in þe tyxte þere þyse two arn in teme layde,
Hit arn fettled in on forme, þe forme and þe laste,
And by quest of her quoyntyse enquylen on mede.
And als, in myn vpynyoun, hit arn of on kynde: 40
For þeras pouert hir proferes ho nyl be put vtter,
Bot lenge wheresoeuer hir lyst, lyke oþer greme;
And þereas pouert enpresses, þaȝ mon pyne þynk,
Much, maugré his mun, he mot nede suffer;
Thus pouerté and pacyence arn nedes playferes.   45
Syþen I am sette with hem samen, suffer me byhoues;
Þenne is me lyȝtloker hit lyke and her lotes prayse,

Patience, though displeasing, is proof of goodwill.
For when hearts are made heavy with hurting or scorn,
Those who suffer such stings will be soothed in the end;
For all meanness she mends, and all malice undoes.
Who endures an indignity duly knows joy;   5
Who through spite is resentful just suffers the more.
Thus to bear what is bitter is better for me
Than to gripe or begrudge, though I'm grieved to the heart.
At a high Mass I heard on a holiday once
How Saint Matthew thus mimed what his Master had taught: 10
Of the eight, pure Beatitudes, each is repaid
What is due; although differently doled is the gift.
They are blessed who have borne in their breast being poor;
For high heaven they'll have, to hold without end.
Though bent down by burdens, they're blessed who are meek;   15
For they'll wield their will in this world at last.
And, as well, those who weep for their worldly sins
Will encounter great comfort in countries abroad.
They are blessed who have borne in their breast love of right;
For they fully will feel the force of the good.   20
They are blessed in whose breasts pity broadens and grows;
For all manners of mercy will match their goodwill.
They are blessed, too, whose breasts are unburdened and pure;
For the shining, bright Savior they'll see with their eyes.
They are blessed whose burden is bringing the peace;   25
For "the sons of the Savior" they'll surely be called.
They are blessed whose breasts can be brought to restraint;
Because high, mighty heaven they'll hold, as I said.
Thus we're bound to be brought to eight blessings at last,
If we love these eight ladies, are like them in all: 30
Good Dames Poverty, Pity, and Penance the third,
Dames Meekness and Mercy the fourth and the fifth,
And Dames Purity, Peace, with Dame Patience the last.
Each will bring a man bliss; one would best have them all!
Since I'm personally placed by Dame Poverty's side,   35
I must ply to Dame Patience, and play with them both.
For these two in the text as a team are portrayed,
In one formula fixed as the first and the last.
One can win their reward if their wisdom one seeks.
In life they are linked and alike, I am sure.   40
For where Poverty's present, it pleases her well
To linger at length, if we like it or not.
When Poverty pinches, complain all you like,
Willy-nilly you'll know of her nevertheless;
For playmates Dame Patience and Poverty are.   45
I must suffer their sting, since I'm stuck with the two!
For to love those two ladies and lavish them praise

Þenne wyþer wyth and be wroth and þe wers haue.
Ȝif me be dyȝt a destyné due to haue,
What dowes me þe dedayn, oþer dispit make?   50
Oþer ȝif my lege lorde lyst on lyue me to bidde
Oþer to ryde oþer to renne to Rome in his ernde,
What grayþed me þe grychchyng bot grame more seche?
Much ȝif he me ne made, maugref my chekes,
And þenne þrat moste I þole and vnþonk to mede,   55
Þe had bowed to his bode bongré my hyure.
Did not Jonas in Judé suche jape sumwhyle?
To sette hym to sewrté, vnsounde he hym feches.
Wyl ȝe tary a lyttel tyne and tent me a whyle,
I schal wysse yow þerwyth as holy wryt telles.   60
Hit bitydde sumtyme in þe termes of Judé,
Jonas joyned watz þerinne Jentyle prophete;
Goddes glam to hym glod þat hym vnglad made,
With a roghlych rurd rowned in his ere:
'Rys radly,' He says, 'and rayke forth euen;   65
Nym þe way to Nynyue wythouten oþer speche,
And in þat ceté My saȝes soghe alle aboute,
Þat in þat place, at þe poynt, I put in þi hert.
For iwysse hit arn so wykke þat in þat won dowellez
And her malys is so much, I may not abide,   70
Bot venge Me on her vilanye and venym bilyue;
Now sweȝe Me þider swyftly and say Me þis arende.'
When þat steuen watz stynt þat stowned his mynde,
Al he wrathed in his wyt, and wyþerly he þoȝt:
'If I bowe to His bode and bryng hem þis tale,   75
And I be nummen in Nuniue, my nyes begynes:
He telles me þose traytoures arn typped schrewes;
I com wyth þose typynges, þay ta me bylyue,
Pynez me in a prysoun, put me in stokkes,
Wryþe me in a warlok, wrast out myn yȝen.   80
Þis is a meruayl message a man for to preche
Amonge enmyes so mony and mansed fendes,
Bot if my gaynlych God such gref to me wolde,
For desert of sum sake þat I slayn were.
At alle peryles,' quoþ þe prophete, 'I aproche hit no nerre.   85
I wyl me sum oþer waye þat He ne wayte after;
I schal tee into Tarce and tary þere a whyle,
And lyȝtly when I am lest He letes me alone.'
Þenne he ryses radly and raykes bilyue,
Jonas toward port Japh, ay janglande for tene   90
Þat he nolde þole for noþyng non of þose pynes,
Þaȝ þe Fader þat hym formed were fale of his hele.
'Oure Syre syttes,' he says, 'on sege so hyȝe
In His glowande glorye, and gloumbes ful lyttel

Is far better than blaming them both, which brings grief.
If my destiny deems them, disdain is for naught;
For what good is it, grudging and grieving? What use?
If my lord, as he likes, on a lark sends me off,   50
Sends me riding or running to Rome on a chore,
What would grumbling get me but grief for my pains?
He would surely insist, though I squabbled and writhed;
And I'd suffer for sure, when I should have complied   55
Without fighting so fiercely the fate of my lot.
In Judea once Jonah pulled just such a stunt:
To escape things unsafe he sought out more grief!
If you linger a little while longer with me,
I'll recite the whole story as Scripture reports.   60
God picked him, appointed him prophet one day
Of the Gentiles in Judea; thus Jonah was called.
He was gloomy when God, with His great, sounding voice,
Came to speak to him. Sternly God said in his ear:
"Do not linger, delaying or letting time pass;   65
Go to Nineveh now. Not a noise from your lips!
In the streets of that city you'll spread My words,
Which I'll put—in that place at that point—in your heart.
For that city's so sinful, so set against good,
And so wickedly willed, I can't wait anymore,   70
But must vanquish their venom and villainy now!
Go now, speed to that city and spread there My words."
When that speech—which astonished him—stopped, he became
Afraid and confused; and he foolishly thought:
"If I bow to His bidding and bring them His words,   75
And those townspeople take me, my troubles would start!
He Himself just now said they are sinful, each one;
If I tender such tidings, they'll take me at once,
Put me in prison, place me in stocks,
Confine me in fetters, and fling out my eyes!   80
Here's a marvelous message to meet them all with!
These are fine words to fling amongst foes in that town!
But my gracious God wants to grieve me, no doubt;
For some sin He is seeking to slay me right now!
Despite God, I'll not go near the gates of that town.   85
No, I'll wander some way where He won't seek me out.
I will take off to Tarshish and tarry, unseen;
I will linger there, lost, and He'll leave me alone."
So he readily rises and right away goes
To Port Joppa. While journeying, Jonah insists   90
He'd not suffer such stings as were sent to him then,
Though the Father Who formed him should find him at last.
"Our Lord sits," the man says, "on a seat so high up,
So aglow in His glory, He'd grieve not at all

[Handwritten margin notes:]
no use to gripe.
poverty is enforced patience
make best of it what have
good will come

God picks Jonah to spread His word in Nineveh

Nineveh is a wicked city that must be converted

Jonah afraid for life if tries to convert violent sinner
decides to run away + hide

Þaȝ I be nummen in Nunniue and naked dispoyled,   95
On rode rwly torent with rybaudes mony.'
Þus he passes to þat port his passage to seche,
Fyndes he a fayr schyp to þe fare redy,
Maches hym with þe maryneres, makes her paye
For to towe hym into Tarce as tyd as þay myȝt.   100
Then he tron on þo tres, and þay her tramme ruchen,
Cachen vp þe crossayl, cables þay fasten,
Wiȝt at þe wyndas weȝen her ankres,
Spende spak to þe sprete þe spare bawelyne,
Gederen to þe gyde-ropes, þe grete cloþ falles,   105
Þay layden in on laddeborde, and þe lofe wynnes,
Þe blyþe breþe at her bak þe bosum he fyndes;
He swenges me þys swete schip swefte fro þe hauen.
Watz neuer so joyful a Jue as Jonas watz þenne,
Þat þe daunger of Dryȝtyn so derfly ascaped;   110
He wende wel þat þat Wyȝ þat al þe world planted
Hade no maȝt in þat mere no man for to greue.
Lo, þe wytles wrechche! For he wolde noȝt suffer,
Now hatz he put hym in plyt of peril wel more.
Hit watz a wenyng vnwar þat welt in his mynde,   115
Þaȝ he were soȝt fro Samarye, þat God seȝ no fyrre.
Ȝise, He blusched ful brode: þat burde hym by sure;
Þat ofte kyd hym þe carpe þat kyng sayde,
Dyngne Dauid on des þat demed þis speche
In a psalme þat he set þe sauter withinne: 120
'O folez in folk, felez oþerwhyle
And vnderstondes vmbestounde, þaȝ ȝe be stapen in folé:
Hope ȝe þat He heres not þat eres alle made?
Hit may not be þat He is blynde þat bigged vche yȝe.'
Bot he dredes no dynt þat dotes for elde.   125
For he watz fer in þe flod foundande to Tarce,
Bot I trow ful tyd ouertan þat he were,
So þat schomely to schort he schote of his ame.
For þe Welder of wyt þat wot alle þynges,
Þat ay wakes and waytes, at wylle hatz He slyȝtes.   130
He calde on þat ilk crafte He carf with His hondes;
Þay wakened wel þe wroþeloker for wroþely He cleped:
'Ewrus and Aquiloun þat on est sittes
Blowes boþe at My bode vpon blo watteres.'
Þenne watz no tom þer bytwene His tale and her dede,   135
So bayn wer þay boþe two His bone for to wyrk.
Anon out of þe norþ-est þe noys bigynes,
When boþe breþes con blowe vpon blo watteres.
Roȝ rakkes þer ros with rudnyng anvnder;
Þe see souȝed ful sore, gret selly to here;   140
Þe wyndes on þe wonne water so wrastel togeder

If in Nineveh knaves stripped me naked, and if
On a cross I were crucified cruelly by thieves!"
To that port Jonah passes, and passage he seeks.
When he sees there a ship that is set to depart,
Jonah casts to the crew goodly coins; they agree
Not to tarry, but take him to Tarshish with speed.
Therefore Jonah jumps aboard just as they hoist
The cross-sail with cables they've caught from below.
At the windlass they weigh every anchor with care.
To the bowsprit the bowline is bound and secured.
They gather the guy-ropes. The great cloth unfurls.
Oars are laid to the larboard; the luff is thus gained.
The breeze at their back fills their billowing sail,
Swiftly sending the ship from the port of Joppa.
Of all Jews the most joyous was Jonah himself,
Who'd eluded the law of the Lord on that day.
He believed that the Lord, Who all lands had ordained,
Had no strength on that sea to bring suffering, woe!
Thus behold him—who wholly had hoped to elude,
To escape his sorrows—soon stricken with woe!
For that man was quite mad when his mind came to doubt
That God sees, though one seek far Samaria's lands.
Yes, God saw him. He should have been certain of that;
Many times he'd been told in the true words the king—
Worthy David on dais—had deemed wise to write
In a psalm. In the Psalter he set down these words:
"O you simpletons, stop and show sense if you can!
Although slow, indeed stupid, still strain all your wit!
Cannot He Who made ears Himself hear every sound?
It can't be that He's blind Who has blessed us with eyes!"
An old dotard, he dreaded no dint from the Lord;
For to Tarshish he'd timidly taken his way.
But I trust that it took little time; before long
He was shown to have shot very short of his aim.
For the Wielder of wisdom—aware of all things,
Always watchful, awake—has His ways to insist.
So those forces He'd fashioned at first He invoked;
What He'd formed woke fully and fiercely when told:
"From the east, come, Aquilon; come, Eurus, you winds!
At My bidding now blow on the black, rolling seas!"
When those winds heard these words, neither wasted its time;
They were both to God's bidding obedient, true.
Thus anon from the northeast the noises began;
The winds bellowed and blew on the billowing seas.
Rough clouds arose over red, flashing light.
The sea began swaying with sounds strange to hear,
And the winds on the water so wondrously churned

95
100
105
110
115
120
125
130
135
140

Þat þe wawes ful wode waltered so hiȝe
And efte busched to þe abyme, þat breed fysches
Durst nowhere for roȝ arest at þe bothem.
When þe breth and þe brok and þe bote metten,   145
Hit watz a joyles gyn þat Jonas watz inne,
For hit reled on roun vpon þe roȝe yþes.
Þe bur ber to hit baft, þat braste alle her gere,
Þen hurled on a hepe þe helme and þe sterne;
Furst tomurte mony rop and þe mast after;   150
Þe sayl sweyed on þe see, þenne suppe bihoued
Þe coge of þe colde water, and þenne þe cry ryses.
Ȝet coruen þay þe cordes and kest al þeroute;
Mony ladde þer forth lep to laue and to kest—
Scopen out þe scaþel water þat fayn scape wolde—   155
For be monnes lode neuer so luþer, þe lyf is ay swete.
Þer watz busy ouer borde bale to kest,
Her bagges and her feþer-beddes and her bryȝt wedes,
Her kysttes and her coferes, her caraldes alle,
And al to lyȝten þat lome, ȝif leþe wolde schape.   160
Bot euer watz ilyche loud þe lot of þe wyndes,
And euer wroþer þe water and wodder þe stremes.
Þen þo wery forwroȝt wyst no bote,
Bot vchon glewed on his god þat gayned hym beste:
Summe to Vernagu þer vouched avowes solemne,   165
Summe to Diana deuout and derf Neptune,
To Mahoun and to Mergot, þe mone and þe sunne,
And vche lede as he loued and layde had his hert.
Þenne bispeke þe spakest, dispayred wel nere:
'I leue here be sum losynger, sum lawles wrech,   170
Þat hatz greued his god and gotz here amonge vus.
Lo, al synkes in his synne and for his sake marres.
I lovue þat we lay lotes on ledes vchone,
And whoso lympes þe losse, lay hym þeroute;
And quen þe gulty is gon, what may gome trawe   175
Bot He þat rules þe rak may rwe on þose oþer?'
Þis watz sette in asent, and sembled þay were,
Herȝed out of vche hyrne to hent þat falles.
A lodesmon lyȝtly lep vnder hachches,
For to layte mo ledes and hem to lote bryng.   180
Bot hym fayled no freke þat he fynde myȝt,
Saf Jonas þe Jwe, þat jowked in derne.
He watz flowen for ferde of þe flode lotes
Into þe boþem of þe bot, and on a brede lyggede,
Onhelde by þe hurrok, for þe heuen wrache,   185
Slypped vpon a sloumbe-selepe, and sloberande he routes.
Þe freke hym frunt with his fot and bede hym ferk vp:
Þer Ragnel in his rakentes hym rere of his dremes!

That the water in waves became wild and rose
Before dashing down, diving to depths. In that sea
The fishes were frightened and fled from the deep.
When the sky, the sea, and the ship met, the boat 145
On which Jonah sailed jostled, was joyless and grim,
For it rolled around on the rough, swelling waves.
The rigging and rudder were wrecked by the winds;
With the helm, they were hurled in a heap by the storm.
First the raging wind ripped up the ropes; then the mast 150
With its sail was sent to the sea. The ship drank
So much sea that the sailors were screaming in fear.
They cut free the cords, which they cast overboard.
Many fellows sprang forth in that fast-flooding ship;
Those who sought to escape madly scooped out the waves— 155
For though life may be loathsome, that life is still sweet.
Overboard they were busily bailing their things:
All their bags and their beds and their bright, shining clothes.
Then they cast off their coffers, their casks, and their chests;
All to lighten their load should a letup occur. 160
But loud winds went on wailing and whipping about,
At once the waves on the water increased.
Then those sailors, despairing of saving themselves,   FALSE GODS
Called on gods whom they guessed would best gain them respite;
To Vernagu or Neptune some now made their vows. 165
To Diana some others, awestruck, now prayed,
To Mahomet and Margot, the moon and the sun;
Thus each person there prayed as he practiced his faith.
Then the wisest there walked up, though wild with despair.
"I believe that a lawless, low, wretched man, 170
Who's brought grief to his god right now goes here," he said.
"For the sake of his sins we are sinking here now.
Let us lay out fair lots; he who loses the draw
By the crew will be caught up and cast to the sea.
When the guilty one's gone, the god of this storm 175
Will be pacified, pleased, and take pity on us."
Those assembled said they would see to the deed.
From each corner they caught up all crew members then;
Under hatches the helmsman hied to seek out
And carry up crew for the casting of lots. 180
No fellow he found down there failed to come forth,
Except Jonah the Jew who, unjostled, still slept.
He had fled out of fear from the foaming, wild storm.
On a bench in the boat's bulging bottom he lay.
There he huddled and hid; during heaven's great storm 185
He had slipped into sleep, and he slobbered and snored!
The man cursed and kicked him and caused him to rise.
May chained Ragnel arouse him from reverie thus!

Bi þe haspede hater he hentes hym þenne,
And broȝt hym vp by þe brest and vpon borde sette,   190
Arayned hym ful runyschly what raysoun he hade
In such slaȝtes of sorȝe to slepe so faste.
Sone haf þay her sortes sette and serelych deled,
And ay þe lote vpon laste lymped on Jonas.
Þenne ascryed þay hym sckete and asked ful loude: 195
'What þe deuel hatz þou don, doted wrech?
What seches þou on see, synful schrewe,
With þy lastes so luþer to lose vus vchone?
Hatz þou, gome, no gouernour ne god on to calle,
Þat þou þus slydes on slepe when þou slayn worþes?   200
Of what londe art þou lent, what laytes þou here,
Whyder in worlde þat þou wylt, and what is þyn arnde?
Lo, þy dom is þe dyȝt, for þy dedes ille.
Do gyf glory to þy godde, er þou glyde hens.'
'I am an Ebru,' quoþ he, 'of Israyl borne;   205
Þat Wyȝe I worchyp, iwysse, þat wroȝt alle þynges,
Alle þe worlde with þe welkyn, þe wynde and þe sternes,
And alle þat wonez þer withinne, at a worde one.
Alle þis meschef for me is made at þys tyme,
For I haf greued my God and gulty am founden;   210
Forþy berez me to þe borde and baþes me þeroute,
Er gete ȝe no happe, I hope forsoþe.'
He ossed hym by vnnynges þat þay vndernomen
Þat he watz flawen fro þe face of frelych Dryȝtyn;
Þenne such a ferde on hem fel and flayed hem withinne   215
Þat þay ruyt hym to rowwe, and letten þe rynk one.
Haþeles hyȝed in haste with ores ful longe,
Syn her sayl watz hem aslypped, on sydez to rowe,
Hef and hale vpon hyȝt to helpen hymseluen,
Bot al watz nedles note: þat nolde not bityde.   220
In bluber of þe blo flod bursten her ores.
Þenne hade þay noȝt in her honde þat hem help myȝt;
Þenne nas no coumfort to keuer, ne counsel non oþer,
Bot Jonas into his juis jugge bylyue.
Fyrst þay prayen to þe Prynce þat prophetes seruen   225
Þat He gef hem þe grace to greuen Hym neuer,
Þat þay in balelez blod þer blenden her handez,
Þaȝ þat haþel wer His þat þay here quelled.
Tyd by top and bi to þay token hym synne;
Into þat lodlych loȝe þay luche hym sone.   230
He watz no tytter outtulde þat tempest ne sessed:
Þe se saȝtled þerwith as sone as ho moȝt.
Þenne þaȝ her takel were torne þat totered on yþes,
Styffe stremes and streȝt hem strayned a whyle,
Þat drof hem dryȝlych adoun þe depe to serue,   235

The man seized him, snatching his shirt with his fist.
To the deck he thus dragged up the dotard at once,
Where he gruelingly grilled him to get him to tell
How he slept there so soundly while storms raged above.   190
When the lots were allotted, <u>the lone one soon fell</u>
Upon Jonah the Jew. Therefore judging him cause
Of the storm, all the seamen shouted aloud:
"What the devil you did we demand now to know!   195
What you sinfully seek on the sea we would learn!
For what cause would you kill us all, caught with you here?
Do you go without glorious gods, without faith,
That you slip into sleep before slain far from home?
What's the land that you left? Why you left it we'd know.   200
Just where in the world are you wandering now?
For your deeds your doom is ordained by the lots;
To your god, man, give glory. Then go to the sea!"
Jonah answered thus: "I am from Israel's land.   205
I worship the One Who the world once made,
He Who set all the stars in the sky, and the winds,
And made every man, all that moves, with a word!
This storm that is surging was sent after me;
I brought <u>grief to my God, and am guilty thereof.</u>   210
I believe you'll be luckless unless you act now;
Therefore catch me up, carry me, cast me adrift!"
Then by signs that he showed, they saw without doubt
That he'd fled from the face of the fair, noble Lord.
Such a fear befell them all, flayed them within,   215
That they left him alone; they lined up and rowed
From the sides of the ship with the stoutest of oars
(For the storm-broken sails had slid to the waves).
To escape the fierce storm, they stroked with those oars;
But they vied thus in vain. It availed them naught;   220
For the stormy, dark sea quickly splintered their oars,
And they hadn't on hand what might help them escape.
Neither comfort from cares nor counsel had they
But to judge at once Jonah the Jew, send him doom.
First they pray to the Prince Whom the prophets obey   225
That He grant them the grace not to grieve Him if now
In that boat with his blood they should blemish their hands,
Though they harmed one once hailed as His in that way.
By the head and the heels they hoist Jonah up;
He is quickly cast to that cold, raging sea.   230
In truth when they tossed him, the tempest withdrew!
The sea desisted as soon as she could.
Though their tackle was torn by the tempest and lost,
Though streams that moved swiftly constrained them awhile,
And, indeed, though the deeps kept on driving them back,   235

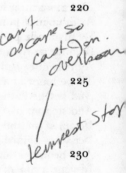

Tyl a swetter ful swyþe hem sweȝed to bonk.
Þer watz louyng on lofte, when þay þe londe wonnen,
To oure mercyable God, on Moyses wyse,
With sacrafyse vpset, and solempne vowes,
And graunted Hym on to be God and graythly non oþer.   240
Þaȝ þay be jolef for joye, Jonas ȝet dredes;
Þaȝ he nolde suffer no sore, his seele is on anter;
For whatso worþed of þat wyȝe fro he in water dipped,
Hit were a wonder to wene, ȝif holy wryt nere.
Now is Jonas þe Jwe jugged to drowne;   245
Of þat schended schyp men schowued hym sone.
A wylde walterande whal, as Wyrde þen schaped,
Þat watz beten fro þe abyme, bi þat bot flotte,
And watz war of þat wyȝe þat þe water soȝte,
And swyftely swenged hym to swepe, and his swolȝ opened;   250
Þe folk ȝet haldande his fete, þe fysch hym tyd hentes;
Withouten towche of any tothe he tult in his þrote.
Thenne he swengez and swayues to þe se boþem,
Bi mony rokkez ful roȝe and rydelande strondes,
Wyth þe mon in his mawe malskred in drede,   255
As lyttel wonder hit watz, ȝif he wo dreȝed,
For nade þe hyȝe Heuen-Kyng, þurȝ His honde myȝt,
Warded þis wrech man in warlowes guttez,
What lede moȝt leue bi lawe of any kynde,
Þat any lyf myȝt be lent so longe hym withinne?   260
Bot he watz sokored by þat Syre þat syttes so hiȝe,
Þaȝ were wanlez of wele in wombe of þat fissche,
And also dryuen þurȝ þe depe and in derk walterez.
Lorde, colde watz his cumfort, and his care huge,
For he knew vche a cace and kark þat hym lymped,   265
How fro þe bot into þe blober watz with a best lachched,
And þrwe in at hit þrote withouten þret more,
As mote in at a munster dor, so mukel wern his chawlez.
He glydes in by þe giles þurȝ glaym ande glette,
Relande in by a rop, a rode þat hym þoȝt,   270
Ay hele ouer hed hourlande aboute,
Til he blunt in a blok as brod as a halle;
And þer he festnes þe fete and fathmez aboute,
And stod vp in his stomak þat stank as þe deuel.
Þer in saym and in sorȝe þat sauoured as helle,   275
Þer watz bylded his bour þat wyl no bale suffer.
And þenne he lurkkes and laytes where watz le best,
In vche a nok of his nauel, bot nowhere he fyndez
No rest ne recouerer, bot ramel ande myre,
In wych gut so euer he gotz, bot euer is God swete;   280
And þer he lenged at þe last, and to þe Lede called:
'Now, Prynce, of Þy prophete pité Þou haue.

A light stream moved them swiftly to shore in the end.
When they landed they lifted their lauds and their hymns.
In the manner of Moses, to merciful God
They set up a sacrifice, solemnly vowed,
Quit false gods, and granted that God alone reigned.   240
They are joyous and jolly, but Jonah still fears;
Though he sought out his safety, he's suffering now!
For what happened to him would be hard to believe
If we hadn't had Holy Writ here to concur.
Now was Jonah the Jew therefore judged and condemned.   245
From that ship he was shoved very soon by those men;
And a wild, rolling whale from the watery deeps
Astir in that storm had just swum, as fate willed;
Aware of that one and awaiting his fall,
The fish moved by the man with his mouth opened wide.   250
As those folk held his feet that fish took him in;
Never touched by a tooth, Jonah tumbled inside.
The fish swung back and swam to the sea's raging depths
Along rough, jagged rocks, over rolling, white sands,
With that fellow, near fainting with fear, in his gut.   255
That the man was amazed was no marvel at all!
Had the high King of heaven not helped Jonah then—
Who lay deep in the dark of that devil's foul gut—
Who'd believe nature's laws would allow him to stay
And live for so long in that loathsome, black gut?   260
But the Sire Who sits in the sky succored him,
Who had held out no hope in that horrible fish.
As he drove through the deeps in the dark, Jonah churned.
O Lord, cold were his comfort and cares because he
Was aware—all too well—of the woes brought to him: 265
How he'd been by the beast from the boat roughly snatched,
How, unforced, he'd been flung to the fish's dark gut
Through its maw like a mote through a minster's wide door!
First he glides near the gills through the glistening slime;
Then he goes down the gullet, whose girth he thinks vast,   270
Always head over heel, always hurtling about,
Till he breaches the belly, as big as a hall.
To glean where he's gone, Jonah gropes in the dark.
So he stood in the stomach, which stank like hell.
In the fat and the festering filthiness there   275
Stood the household of him whom no harm would undo!
Then he slides about, seeking a shelter somewhere
In that cavern's dark corners, but cannot there find
Either respite or rest; only rankness and filth
Does he glean in those guts. Yet our God, He is kind!   280
So in grief Jonah gave in. To God he cried:
"O Prince of Your prophet, have pity on me!

[handwritten annotations:]
once outcasted Jonah, reached rest of people safety

Sailors praise God when come safely ashore Convert

Jon swallon by whale

Better chance than he really deserved

Whale catch / allegory / sliding thru / The whale's belly

doesn't sound like he wanted to
Jonah cries out to God in the whale

Jonah punished, but not destroyed for pity

Jonah cries

Þaȝ I be fol and fykel and falce of my hert,
Dewoyde now Þy vengaunce, þurȝ vertu of rauthe;
Thaȝ I be gulty of gyle, as gaule of prophetes,   285
Þou art God, and alle gowdez ar grayþely Þyn owen.
Haf now mercy of Þy man and his mysdedes,
And preue Þe lyȝtly a Lorde in londe and in water.'
With þat he hitte to a hyrne and helde hym þerinne,
Þer no defoule of no fylþe watz fest hym abute;   290
Þer he sete also sounde, saf for merk one,
As in þe bulk of þe bote þer he byfore sleped.
So in a bouel of þat best he bidez on lyue,
Þre dayes and þre nyȝt, ay þenkande on Dryȝtyn,
His myȝt and His merci, His mesure þenne.   295
Now he knawez Hym in care þat couþe not in sele.
Ande euer walteres þis whal bi wyldren depe,
Þurȝ mony a regioun ful roȝe, þurȝ ronk of his wylle;
For þat mote in his mawe mad hym, I trowe,
Þaȝ hit lyttel were hym wyth, to wamel at his hert;   300
Ande as sayled þe segge, ay sykerly he herde
Þe bygge borne on his bak and bete on his sydes.
Þen a prayer ful prest þe prophete þer maked;
On þis wyse, as I wene, his wordez were mony:
'Lorde, to Þe haf I cleped in carez ful stronge;   305
Out of þe hole Þou me herde of hellen wombe;
I calde, and Þou knew myn vncler steuen.
Þou diptez me of þe depe se into þe dymme hert,
Þe grete flem of Þy flod folded me vmbe;
Alle þe gotez of Þy guferes and groundelez powlez,   310
And Þy stryuande stremez of stryndez so mony,
In on daschande dam dryuez me ouer.
And ȝet I sayde as I seet in þe se boþem:
"Careful am I, kest out fro Þy cler yȝen
And deseuered fro Þy syȝt; ȝet surely I hope   315
Efte to trede on Þy temple and teme to Þyseluen."
I am wrapped in water to my wo stoundez;
Þe abyme byndes þe body þat I byde inne;
Þe pure poplande hourle playes on my heued;
To laste mere of vche a mount, Man, am I fallen;   320
Þe barrez of vche a bonk ful bigly me haldes,
Þat I may lachche no lont, and Þou my lyf weldes.
Þou schal releue me, Renk, whil Þy ryȝt slepez,
Þurȝ myȝt of Þy mercy þat mukel is to tryste.
For when þ'acces of anguych watz hid in my sawle,   325
Þenne I remembred me ryȝt of my rych Lorde,
Prayande Him for peté His prophete to here,
Þat into His holy hous myn orisoun moȝt entre.
I haf meled with Þy maystres mony longe day,

Though I'm foolish, fickle, and false in my heart,
Yet to me, Lord, be merciful; mitigate wrath!
Though I'm pitiful, puling, of prophets the worst,
You are God, and all goodness and grace are Your own!
On Your man have mercy, though he's mired in sin;
Prove You're Lord through the length of the land and the sea!"
Jonah crawled to a corner and crouched there, so that
No defilement or filth could fasten on him.
He stayed there, safe, although steeped in the dark;
As he'd slept in the ship, Jonah slept in that whale.   290
In the beast's giant belly he bides. Of the Lord
And His deeds Jonah dreams for three days and nights,
Of His mercy and might. Thus the man, who in health   295
Fled from God, now in grief prays that God will approach!
The whale in the water's wilderness swims,
Through the roughest of regions, enraged in his pride;
For that mote in his maw quickly made him—I think—
As it stuck in his side very sick in his heart.   300
Jonah had to have heard, as they hurried along,
The waves beating on the back of the boisterous, mad whale.
Then the prophet said promptly this prayer (I have heard
That the plenteous pleadings he proffered went thus):
"In my cares, Lord, I cried out. I called on Your name   305
From the hole of hell; and You heard me at once.
Though my voice was vague, yet You vouchsafed to hear!
In the dark, ocean deeps I was drenched at Your will;
In the flowing, high flood I was folded at once,
And was whipped in Your waters' fierce whirlpools and spouts. 310
In one course Your deep currents and cold, flowing streams—
Up and down ever dashing—now drive over me!
Yet I said as I sat in the sea's raging depths:
'Full of care am I cast from Your clear, shining eyes!
From Your sight am I severed; yet surely I hope   315
To be taken in time to Your temple on high!'
To my woe I'm awash in this water right now.
The abyss, Lord, is binding this body of mine;
It boldly bubbles above my poor head!
As a mere, earthly mortal, down mountains I fell!   320
Now each barrier binds me, each beach, and each shore.
Far from land am I lost, yet my life You have spared!
Justice sleeps while You save such a sinner, O Knight;
Through the might of Your mercy Your man has been spared!
When the excess of anguish first entered my soul   325
I remembered in moments my merciful God;
I prayed that He'd pity His prophet at last,
That my hymn to His holy, high household would reach.
With Your learned theologians I've long sought the truth;

Bot now I wot wyterly þat þose vnwyse ledes   330
Þat affyen hym in vanyté and in vayne þynges
For þink þat mountes to noȝt her mercy forsaken;
Bot I dewoutly awowe, þat verray betz halden,
Soberly to do þe sacrafyse when I schal saue worþe,
And offer Þe for my hele a ful hol gyfte,   335
And halde goud þat Þou me hetes: haf here my trauthe.'
Thenne oure Fader to þe fysch ferslych biddez
Þat he hym sput spakly vpon spare drye.
Þe whal wendez at His wylle and a warþe fyndez,
And þer he brakez vp þe buyrne as bede hym oure Lorde.   340
Þenne he swepe to þe sonde in sluchched cloþes:
Hit may wel be þat mester were his mantyle to wasche.
Þe bonk þat he blosched to and bode hym bisyde
Wern of þe regiounes ryȝt þat he renayed hade.
Þenne a wynde of Goddez worde efte þe wyȝe bruxlez: 345
'Nylt þou neuer to Nuniue bi no kynnez wayez?'
'Ȝisse, Lorde,' quoþ þe lede, 'lene me Þy grace
For to go at Þi gre: me gaynez non oþer.'
'Ris, aproche þen to prech, lo, þe place here.
Lo, My lore is in þe loke, lauce hit þerinne.'   350
Þenne þe renk radly ros as he myȝt,
And to Niniue þat naȝt he neȝed ful euen;
Hit watz a ceté ful syde and selly of brede;
On to þrenge þerþurȝe watz þre dayes dede.
Þat on journay ful joynt Jonas hym ȝede,   355
Er euer he warpped any worde to wyȝe þat he mette,
And þenne he cryed so cler þat kenne myȝt alle
Þe trwe tenor of his teme; he tolde on þis wyse:
'Ȝet schal forty dayez fully fare to an ende,
And þenne schal Niniue be nomen and to noȝt worþe;   360
Truly þis ilk toun schal tylte to grounde;
Vp-so-doun schal ȝe dumpe depe to þe abyme,
To be swolȝed swyftly wyth þe swart erþe,
And alle þat lyuyes hereinne lose þe swete.'
Þis speche sprang in þat space and spradde alle aboute,   365
To borges and to bacheleres þat in þat burȝ lenged;
Such a hidor hem hent and a hatel drede,
Þat al chaunged her chere and chylled at þe hert.
Þe segge sesed not ȝet, bot sayde euer ilyche:
'Þe verray vengaunce of God schal voyde þis place!'   370
Þenne þe peple pitosly pleyned ful stylle,
And for þe drede of Dryȝtyn doured in hert;
Heter hayrez þay hent þat asperly bited,
And þose þay bounden to her bak and to her bare sydez,
Dropped dust on her hede, and dymly bisoȝten   375
Þat þat penaunce plesed Him þat playnez on her wronge.

Yet never till now did I know that those fools   330
Who love vanity, vices, and vain, empty things
That are meaningless, mortal, Your mercy forsake.
Now I solemnly swear I will sacrifice all!
Once redeemed I will do what You deign; Your command
Be my guide! I'll give You a gift for my sake.   335
I will go where You guide me, I give You my word!"
To that fish our Father fiercely commands
That he cough him up quickly, cast him ashore.
The Lord's will the whale, without waiting, obeys;
Thus he swims to a strand where he spews out the man,   340
Who is swept to that shore in his stained, soiled clothes.
What he wore needed washing—no wonder at that!
The land that he looked on, along that wide shore,
Was the same that he'd sought from the start to avoid!
Then God's word in a wailing, low wind comes to chide: 345
"Will you not go to Nineveh now? By no road?"
"Yes, dear God, if You grant me Your grace!" said the man:
"By obeying Your bidding I'll bring myself good!"
"Then approach and prepare now to preach. Here's the town.
My learning is lodged in you. Let it be known!"   350
Therefore readied, he rapidly rose up and walked,
And by night he had neared mighty Nineveh's gates.
Now, the span of that city was certainly wide;
For it took just to travel that town three full days.
Thus Jonah the Jew came to journey one day   355
On his trek without talking to townspeople there.
Then he cried out so clearly the whole crowd could hear;
In that town his theme's tenor he told in this way:
"After forty days finally and fully have passed—
Be it known—then to nothing shall Nineveh fall!   360
For this town shall be taken and torn to the ground;
Upside down you'll be dumped, and deep in the black,
Broken soil you'll swiftly be swallowed at once.
Then will lifeblood be lost from those living herein!"
When this speech was spoken it spread everywhere: 365
To the bachelors, burghers, the best of that town.
Such a terror took those townspeople there
That they changed, became cheerless, were chilled to the heart.
To those men Jonah made his message clear:
"The Lord's vengeance will verily void all this town!"   370
The people were piteously pained at these words;
Fear of God at once gripped them. They grieved in their minds
And hearts. They took harsh, biting hair shirts at once;
To their backs and their bellies they bound that attire.
In dread they dropped piles of dust on their heads,   375
That their penance would please Who complained of their wrongs.

And ay he cryes in þat kyth tyl þe kyng herde,
And he radly vpros and ran fro his chayer,
His ryche robe he torof of his rigge naked,
And of a hep of askes he hitte in þe myddez.   380
He askez heterly a hayre and hasped hym vmbe,
Sewed a sekke þerabof, and syked ful colde;
Þer he dased in þat duste, with droppande teres,
Wepande ful wonderly alle his wrange dedes.
Þenne sayde he to his serjauntes: 'Samnes yow bilyue;   385
Do dryue out a decre, demed of myseluen,
Þat alle þe bodyes þat ben withinne þis borȝ quyk,
Boþe burnes and bestes, burdez and childer,
Vch prynce, vche prest, and prelates alle,
Alle faste frely for her falce werkes;   390
Sesez childer of her sok, soghe hem so neuer,
Ne best bite on no brom, ne no bent nauþer,
Passe to no pasture, ne pike non erbes,
Ne non oxe to no hay, ne no horse to water.
Al schal crye, forclemmed, with alle oure clere strenþe;   395
Þe rurd schal ryse to Hym þat rawþe schal haue;
What wote oþer wyte may ȝif þe Wyȝe lykes,
Þat is hende in þe hyȝt of His gentryse?
I wot His myȝt is so much, þaȝ He be myssepayed,
Þat in His mylde amesyng He mercy may fynde.   400
And if we leuen þe layk of oure layth synnes,
And stylle steppen in þe styȝe He styȝtlez Hymseluen,
He wyl wende of His wodschip and His wrath leue,
And forgif vus þis gult, ȝif we Hym God leuen.'
Þenne al leued on His lawe and laften her synnes,   405
Parformed alle þe penaunce þat þe prynce radde;
And God þurȝ His godnesse forgef as He sayde;
Þaȝ He oþer bihyȝt, withhelde His vengaunce.
Muche sorȝe þenne satteled vpon segge Jonas;
He wex as wroth as þe wynde towarde oure Lorde.   410
So hatz anger onhit his hert, he callez
A prayer to þe hyȝe Prynce, for pyne, on þys wyse:
'I biseche Þe, Syre, now Þou self jugge;
Watz not þis ilk my worde þat worþen is nouþe,
Þat I kest in my cuntré, when Þou Þy carp sendez   415
Þat I schulde tee to þys toun Þi talent to preche?
Wel knew I Þi cortaysye, Þy quoynt soffraunce,
Þy bounté of debonerté and Þy bene grace,
Þy longe abydyng wyth lur, Þy late vengaunce;
And ay Þy mercy is mete, be mysse neuer so huge.   420
I wyst wel, when I hade worded quatsoeuer I cowþe
To manace alle þise mody men þat in þis mote dowellez,
Wyth a prayer and a pyne þay myȝt her pese gete,

Jonah called out and cried till the king finally heard.
The king rose up quickly; he quit his high throne,
And, right away ripping his robe from his back,
Fell amidst a mound that was made out of ash. 380
A harsh, biting hair shirt he hastily donned;
He sewed on a sackcloth, sighed in his grief,
And with trickling tears tossed in the dust.
Thus he wondrously wept for his wicked misdeeds,
And said to his servants: "Assemble at once! 385
First disperse and spread through the city my will
That all bodies that bide in this borough with life—
All the animals, adults, and all that are young,
Every prince, every priest, every prelate as well—
Shall fast as is fit for their false, evil deeds. 390
Take each babe from the breast, though he bawls out and cries.
Take each beast from the broom sage; he'll bite on no grass,
Nor will pass to a pasture with plants there. And from
Water holes keep the horse, and from hay keep the ox.
We shall howl in the height of our hunger at once; 395
Thus by Him will be heard every howl of pain!
For who knows or can know if He'll not forgive all
With His heart, Who in heaven on high has His throne?
For I'm sure He's so strong that, though stricken with wrath,
Yet He might change His mind and show mercy at last. 400
If we cease our sickening sins and repent,
If we walk in the way that He wants us to take,
He will ease in His anger. If all now believe
That He's God, He'll forgive us our guilty misdeeds."
All believed in His law and so left off their sins, 405
And performed the penance their prince had decreed.
Therefore God in His goodness forgave the whole town.
Though He'd promised to punish, He put off His wrath!
Jonah certainly sank into sorrows. To God
He waxed as the wailing, cold wind in his wrath. 410
He was gripped by such grinding, sharp grief that he cried,
And prayed in his pain to the Prince in this way:
"I beseech You, Sir! Be Yourself final judge!
What's befallen I forecast at first, did I not,
When You told me to travel here, telling Your words, 415
When You told me to take to this town Your behest?
I knew well of Your ways, knew Your wisdom and truth,
Knew how gracious and great is Your goodness, O Lord,
Knew Your patience when placed before pitiful sin;
I gleaned You'd forgive the most grievous misdeed! 420
I said—once I'd spread through this city Your word,
And told to this town what You'd taught me to say—
That they'd pray and make penance and peace thus obtain.

And þerfore I wolde haf flowen fer into Tarce.
Now, Lorde, lach out my lyf, hit lastes to longe.   425
Bed me bilyue my bale-stour and bryng me on ende,
For me were swetter to swelt as swyþe, as me þynk,
Þen lede lenger Þi lore þat þus me les makez.'
Þe soun of oure Souerayn þen swey in his ere,
Þat vpbraydes þis burne vpon a breme wyse: 430
'Herk, renk, is þis ryȝt so ronkly to wrath
For any dede þat I haf don oþer demed þe ȝet?'
Jonas al joyles and janglande vpryses,
And haldez out on est half of þe hyȝe place,
And farandely on a felde he fetteľez hym to bide,   435
For to wayte on þat won what schulde worþe after.
Þer he busked hym a bour, þe best þat he myȝt,
Of hay and of euer-ferne and erbez a fewe,
For hit watz playn in þat place for plyande greuez,
For to schylde fro þe schene oþer any schade keste.   440
He bowed vnder his lyttel boþe, his bak to þe sunne,
And þer he swowed and slept sadly al nyȝt,
Þe whyle God of His grace ded growe of þat soyle
Þe fayrest bynde hym abof þat euer burne wyste.
When þe dawande day Dryȝtyn con sende,   445
Þenne wakened þe wyȝ vnder wodbynde,
Loked alofte on þe lef þat lylled grene;
Such a lefsel of lof neuer lede hade,
For hit watz brod at þe boþem, boȝted on lofte,
Happed vpon ayþer half, a hous as hit were,   450
A nos on þe norþ syde and nowhere non ellez,
Bot al schet in a schaȝe þat schaded ful cole.
Þe gome glyȝt on þe grene graciouse leues,
Þat euer wayued a wynde so wyþe and so cole;
Þe schyre sunne hit vmbeschon, þaȝ no schafte myȝt   455
Þe mountaunce of a lyttel mote vpon þat man schyne.
Þenne watz þe gome so glad of his gay logge,
Lys loltrande þerinne lokande to toune;
So blyþe of his wodbynde he balteres þervnder,
Þat of no diete þat day þe deuel haf he roȝt.   460
And euer he laȝed as he loked þe loge alle aboute,
And wysched hit were in his kyth þer he wony schulde,
On heȝe vpon Effraym oþer Ermonnes hillez:
'Iwysse, a worþloker won to welde I neuer keped.'
And quen hit neȝed to naȝt nappe hym bihoued;   465
He slydez on a sloumbe-slep sloghe vnder leues,
Whil God wayned a worme þat wrot vpe þe rote,
And wyddered watz þe wodbynde bi þat þe wyȝe wakned;
And syþen He warnez þe west to waken ful softe,
And sayez vnte Zeferus þat he syfle warme,   470

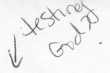

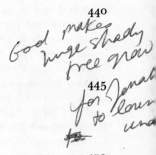

So I took off to Tarshish, or tried to, at least.
Therefore, Lord, take my life! It has lasted too long; 425
Drive me to death! Undo me right now!
I'd prefer to perish than preach in this town
To these people Your prophesies, proving me false."
Then the Sovereign responded; He spoke in his ear
To recriminate, chasten, and chide him at once: 430
"Is it right that you rise up in wrath and object
To a deed I have done or ordained as I wished?"
With that, Jonah the Jew very joylessly rose
And stalked to that city's east side, walking out.
In a far, rising field he fixed himself next, 435
There to wait in that way and to watch what would come.
He built up a bower, the best that he could:
From the ground Jonah gathered tall grasses and ferns;
For that plain was exposed, without patches of groves,
Without shade trees to shield from the sun as it blazed. 440
Jonah sat in this shady, grass shelter at once.
There he swooned and he slept very soundly all night.
And our God in His grace caused to grow from that soil
A wonderful, wide, thick-leaved woodbine that night.
When the day finally dawned, as ordained by the Lord, 445
Jonah woke by that winding and wondrous, high vine,
And looked on its leaves, shining lovely and green.
None had seen such a sumptuous sight before that;
For that bower was broad at the bottom, and high.
It had sides that were solid and seemed like a house. 450
That dwelling was decked with a door to the north.
It was shaded; no sunlight was shining within.
Jonah glanced at the green, brightly glistening leaves,
As they wondrously waved in the wafting, cool breeze.
The sun beat down brightly; no beam, though, no ray 455
Of the simmering sunlight could shine on that man.
Then the prophet was pleased with his pleasant abode.
He lounged there, lolling, and looked on the town.
So happy was he with his hut in the shade
That he dawdled all day—to the devil with food! 460
He laughed as he looked at the lodgings, and wished
That he'd found on Ephraim so fine an abode,
Or on Hermon's high hills, where his homelands lay.
"None could long for a lovelier lodge," Jonah said.
At the setting of sun Jonah sought out his rest. 465
When he slid into slothful, deep sleep, the Lord
Sent a worm to lay waste to the woodbine, so that
When he woke up the woodbine was withered and gone!
God then warned the west wind to waken at once,
And to Zephyrus said he should swiftly blow warmth 470

Þat þer quikken no cloude bifore þe cler sunne,
And ho schal busch vp ful brode and brenne as a candel.
Þen wakened þe wyʒe of his wyl dremes,
And blusched to his wodbynde þat broþely watz marred,
Al welwed and wasted þo worþelych leues;   475
Þe schyre sunne hade hem schent er euer þe schalk wyst.
And þen hef vp þe hete and heterly brenned;
Þe warm wynde of þe weste, wertes he swyþez.
Þe man marred on þe molde þat moʒt hym not hyde;
His wodbynde watz away, he weped for sorʒe;   480
With hatel anger and hot, heterly he callez:
'A, Þou Maker of man, what maystery Þe þynkez
Þus Þy freke to forfare forbi alle oþer?
With alle meschef þat Þou may, neuer Þou me sparez;
I keuered me a cumfort þat now is caʒt fro me,   485
My wodbynde so wlonk þat wered my heued.
Bot now I se Þou art sette my solace to reue;
Why ne dyʒttez Þou me to diʒe? I dure to longe.'
Ʒet oure Lorde to þe lede laused a speche:
'Is þis ryʒtwys, þou renk, alle þy ronk noyse,   490
So wroth for a wodbynde to wax so sone?
Why art þou so waymot, wyʒe, for so lyttel?'
'Hit is not lyttel,' quoþ þe lede, 'bot lykker to ryʒt;
I wolde I were of þis worlde wrapped in moldez.'
'Þenne byþenk þe, mon, if þe forþynk sore,   495
If I wolde help My hondewerk, haf þou no wonder;
Þou art waxen so wroth for þy wodbynde,
And trauayledez neuer to tent hit þe tyme of an howre,
Bot at a wap hit here wax and away at anoþer,
And ʒet lykez þe so luþer, þi lyf woldez þou tyne.   500
Þenne wyte not Me for þe werk, þat I hit wolde help,
And rwe on þo redles þat remen for synne;
Fyrst I made hem Myself of materes Myn one,
And syþen I loked hem ful longe and hem on lode hade.
And if I My trauayl schulde tyne of termes so longe,   505
And type doun ʒonder toun when hit turned were,
Þe sor of such a swete place burde synk to My hert,
So mony malicious mon as mournez þerinne.
And of þat soumme ʒet arn summe, such sottez formadde,
Bitwene þe stele and þe stayre disserne noʒt cunen,   510
What rule renes in roun bitwene þe ryʒt hande
And his lyfte, þaʒ his lyf schulde lost be þerfor;
As lyttel barnez on barme þat neuer bale wroʒt,
And wymmen vnwytté þat wale ne couþe
Þat on hande fro þat oþer, for alle þis hyʒe worlde.   515
And als þer ben doumbe bestez in þe burʒ mony,
Þat may not synne in no syt hemseluen to greue.'

That no cloud could quicken and cover the sun,
Which would blazingly break out and burn like a torch.
Jonah woke then from wild and wondrous deep dreams,
Saw the woodbine was withered and wasted, and saw—
Also withered and wasted—its worthy, thick leaves.
They'd been scorched by the sun as he slumbered away!
The beams from above began blazing down heat,
And the warm, western wind fiercely withered the plants.
So, exposed to the sun, Jonah suffered the heat;
Since his woodbine had withered, he wept in his grief,
And called out in his anger and anguish these words:
"O You Maker of man, is it mighty for You
Thus to punish Your prophet so pitilessly
With Your striking, great strength? Won't You spare me at last?
The one comfort I culled is now cast from my side;
My fair woodbine is withered that once kept me cool.
Now I see You are set on unseating my joy.
Why not deal me my death? I've endured here too long!"
Once again, then, our God to that grumbling man spoke:
"Is it righteous thus rashly to rail in grief,
Or to wax, when a woodbine is withered, with rage?
Why thus lash out so loud for so little a thing?"
"It is justice," raged Jonah the Jew, "that I seek,
Not some whim! Oh, I would that I were under earth!"
"Why so sore? Do you see it as strange, do you chafe
That I help now to heal what My hand wrought at first?
Since your woodbine has withered you wax in your rage,
Though to tend it you took not the time of an hour.
It was made in a moment, unmade in the next;
Yet you'd lose your life, such a load is your grief!
Don't reproach Me for pitying people I made,
Showing mercy to men who are moved to repent!
First I made them Myself—primal matter I used—
And led them and looked on them long as their guide.
If I lost all My labor at last and destroyed
At this time the whole town when it turned to Me now,
For that city the sorrow would sink to My heart;
For its many bad men have now mourned for their sins.
And that city has some who, stupid or mad,
Can't discern ladders' steps from their sides, and who can't
Just intuit the truths that distinguish the right
From the left, though what lay on the line were their death.
There are babies, still breast-feeding, blameless and mild;
There are withered old women too witless to tell—
For the region's vast riches—their right from their left.
There are beasts that abound in that borough as well;
They're certainly spotless, unsinning, and pure.

475

480

485

490

495

500

505

510

515

Why schulde I wrath wyth hem, syþen wyȝez wyl torne,
And cum and cnawe Me for Kyng and My carpe leue?
Wer I as hastif as þou heere, were harme lumpen;   520
Couþe I not þole bot as þou, þer þryued ful fewe.
I may not be so malicious and mylde be halden,
For malyse is noȝt to mayntyne boute mercy withinne.'
Be noȝt so gryndel, godman, bot go forth þy wayes,
Be preue and be pacient in payne and in joye: 525
For he þat is to rakel to renden his cloþez
Mot efte sitte with more vnsounde to sewe hem togeder.
Forþy when pouerté me enprecez and paynez innoȝe
Ful softly with suffraunce saȝttel me bihouez;
Forþy penaunce and payne topreue hit in syȝt   530
Þat pacience is a nobel poynt, þaȝ hit displese ofte.
                                                        Amen.

Should I punish a people repentant at last,
Who have come now to call Me their King and their Lord?
There'd be harm were I hasty and harsh as yourself;   520
Few would live if I lashed out as loosely as you!
I can hardly be harsh and be held to be mild,
Because mercy and mildness mitigate wrath."
Therefore, fight not so fiercely, sir! Follow your path,
And be proven patient in pain and in joy!   525
Because he who in haste very heatedly tears
At his shirt must in sorrow just sew it again.
When oppressed, then, by poverty, pains, and ill health,
I should suffer in silence what sadness I'm due.
Thus appears, through one's pains and one's penance, the fact: 530
Though displeasing, fair patience is proof of goodwill.

Amen

Sir Gawain
and the Green Knight

The facing-page text is reproduced from *The Poems of the Pearl Manuscript: Pearl, Cleanness, Patience, Sir Gawain and the Green Knight*, ed. Malcolm Andrew and Ronald Waldron (rev. ed. University of Exeter, 1987).

I

Siþen þe sege and þe assaut watz sesed at Troye,
Þe borȝ brittened and brent to brondez and askez,
Þe tulk þat þe trammes of tresoun þer wroȝt
Watz tried for his tricherie, þe trewest on erthe.
Hit watz Ennias þe athel and his highe kynde,   5
Þat siþen depreced prouinces, and patrounes bicome
Welneȝe of al þe wele in þe west iles.
Fro riche Romulus to Rome ricchis hym swyþe,
With gret bobbaunce þat burȝe he biges vpon fyrst
And neuenes hit his aune nome, as hit now hat;   10
Ticius to Tuskan and teldes bigynnes,
Langaberde in Lumbardie lyftes vp homes,
And fer ouer þe French flod, Felix Brutus
On mony bonkkes ful brode Bretayn he settez
        Wyth wynne,   15
    Where werre and wrake and wonder
    Bi syþez hatz wont þerinne
    And oft boþe blysse and blunder
    Ful skete hatz skyfted synne.

Ande quen þis Bretayn watz bigged bi þis burn rych   20
Bolde bredden þerinne, baret þat lofden,
In mony turned tyme tene þat wroȝten.
Mo ferlyes on þis folde han fallen here oft
Þen in any oþer þat I wot, syn þat ilk tyme.
Bot of alle þat here bult of Bretaygne kynges   25
Ay watz Arthur þe hendest, as I haf herde telle.
Forþi an aunter in erde I attle to schawe,
Þat a selly in siȝt summe men hit holden
And an outtrage awenture of Arthurez wonderez.
If ȝe wyl lysten þis laye bot on littel quile,   30
I schal telle hit astit, as I in toun herde,
        With tonge.
    As hit is stad and stoken
    In stori stif and stronge,
    With lel letteres loken,   35
    In londe so hatz ben longe.

Þis kyng lay at Camylot vpon Krystmasse
With mony luflych lorde, ledez of þe best—
Rekenly of þe Rounde Table alle þo rich breþer—
With rych reuel oryȝt and rechles merþes.   40
Þer tournayed tulkes by tymez ful mony,
Justed ful jolilé þise gentyle kniȝtes,
Syþen kayred to þe court, caroles to make;
For þer þe fest watz ilyche ful fiften dayes,

I

Since the siege and assault were ceased before Troy,
Which had broken and burned it to brand and to ash;
Since that trust-breaking traitor wrought treachery there,
And was tried for his treasons, his trickery deep;
Then the noble Aeneas and his knightly kin   5
Conquered far countries and crowned themselves kings
Of well-nigh all the West. Its wealth they made theirs.
For to Rome noble Romulus rapidly went,
Where he saw to that city's construction with pride,
Gave the new site his name; it is known for him still.   10
Having traveled to Tuscany, Ticius built homes;
In Lombardy, Langaberd left great estates.
Felix Brutus fared forth, far across the French sea
To the broad slopes of Britain to build there his realm
     So dear.   15
      As well as wonders, woe
      Has wavered year to year.
      And there, tossed to and fro,
      Have been both bane and cheer.

Since Britain was built by Brutus at first,   20
Bold men have been born there, betrothed to strife,
Who have frequently fanned hot the furnace of war.
More marvels have moved hearts of men in this place
Than all lands that I've learned of while listening to tales.
But of all the bold kings who in Britain have reigned,   25
King Arthur was kindest, most courteous and fair.
Thus a tale of those times I intend to recount,
Which some men still maintain is a marvel most strange,
Of Arthur's adventures the most awesome and rare.
Listen, then, to this lay if a little it please;   30
As they told it in town I'll retell it right now
     To you.
      Most masterfully made,
      This tale so tried and true,
      With letters well inlaid,   35
      Was recited hitherto.

In Camelot this king through the Christmastide stayed,
With the boldest, the best, and the bravest of men.
Around the Round Table these rich brethren came
For feasting, festivities, fitting and gay.   40
Many men for merriment made their way there.
To make joy many gentle knights joined in that place;
They had come to the court to make carols with cheer.
Thus for fifteen days feasts and festivities reigned,

With alle þe mete and þe mirþe þat men couþe avyse: 45
Such glaum ande gle glorious to here,
Dere dyn vpon day, daunsyng on nyȝtes—
Al watz hap vpon heȝe in hallez and chambrez
With lordez and ladies, as leuest him þoȝt.
With all þe wele of þe worlde þay woned þer samen,   50
Þe most kyd knyȝtez vnder Krystes Seluen
And þe louelokkest ladies þat euer lif haden,
And he þe comlokest kyng, þat þe court haldes;
For al watz þis fayre folk in her first age,
    On sille,   55
      Þe hapnest vnder heuen,
      Kyng hyȝest mon of wylle—
      Hit were now gret nye to neuen
      So hardy a here on hille.

Wyle Nw Ȝer watz so ȝep þat hit watz nwe cummen,   60
Þat day doubble on þe dece watz þe douth serued.
Fro þe kyng watz cummen with knyȝtes into þe halle,
Þe chauntré of þe chapel cheued to an ende,
Loude crye watz þer kest of clerkez and oþer,
Nowel nayted onewe, neuened ful ofte.   65
And syþen riche forth runnen to reche hondeselle,
Ȝeȝed "Ȝeres ȝiftes!" on hiȝ, ȝelde hem bi hond,
Debated busyly aboute þo giftes;
Ladies laȝed ful loude þoȝ þay lost haden
And he þat wan watz not wrothe—þat may ȝe wel trawe.   70
Alle þis mirþe þay maden to þe mete tyme.
When þay had waschen worþyly, þay wenten to sete,
Þe best burne ay abof, as hit best semed;
Whene Guenore ful gay grayþed in þe myddes,
Dressed on þe dere des, dubbed al aboute: 75
Smal sendal bisides, a selure hir ouer
Of tryed tolouse, of tars tapites innoghe
Þat were enbrawded and beten wyth þe best gemmes
Þat myȝt be preued of prys wyth penyes to bye
    In daye.   80
      Þe comlokest to discrye
      Þer glent with yȝen gray;
      A semloker þat euer he syȝe
      Soth moȝt no mon say.

Bot Arthure wolde not ete til al were serued;   85
He watz so joly of his joyfnes, and sumquat childgered.
His lif liked hym lyȝt; he louied þe lasse
Auþer to longe lye or to longe sitte,
So bisied him his ȝonge blod and his brayn wylde.

As merry and mirthful as men could devise.   45
Glorious, gladsome, and gleeful to hear,
Every day music dinned. There was dancing at night.
Thus happiness hovered in hall and in room.
All the lords and ladies were living in pomp.
With rich joy they rightfully reveled away: 50
In all Christendom the kindest, most courteous knights,
The loveliest ladies who've lived on the earth,
And the comeliest king of that court the true head,
In the fairest and finest and freshest of youth
      Each guest.   55
    With fortune fine and fair
    That court's kind king was blessed.
    To find so rich and rare
    A host were hard at best!

New Year's Day had dawned; it had duly arrived.   60
On a doubly heaped dais they dined, every guest.
When the king with his company came to the hall—
The chaste, lovely chants in the chapel now done—
There both laymen and clerics their loud cries exchanged,
And "Noel!" was renewed, named again and again.   65
For the giving of gifts then there gathered the lords;
"Here are prizes!" they pealed, as they passed them around;
And all wondered a while about the worth of each gift.
The ladies laughed loudly, though some lost the game:
He who won was not wroth, as you well may believe.   70
This mirth was thus made till the meal was due.
The guests washed themselves worthily, went to their seats;
Seated first were the finest, as fitting it seemed.
And Guinevere, gay, in this gathering's midst,
On a dais most dearly adorned, was arrayed   75
Very handsomely. High overhead there were draped
Fine Toulousian and Tharsian tapestries, wrought
With the finest and fairest of fabulous gems
That pennies, each precious, could purchase on earth
      Anywhere.   80
    No man has ever seen
    A gray-eyed gem so rare
    As looked that lovely queen;
    So fine she was and fair!

But King Arthur'd not eat until all had been served;   85
He was boisterous and bold, a bit boyish at times.
He liked to be lively; the less then he cared
To be seated too long or lie lounging about,
For his blood and his brain were too boisterous for that.

And also anoþer maner meued him eke,   90
Þat he þurȝ nobelay had nomen: he wolde neuer ete
Vpon such a dere day, er hym deuised were
Of sum auenturus þyng, an vncouþe tale
Of sum mayn meruayle þat he myȝt trawe,
Of alderes, of armes, of oþer auenturus;   95
Oþer sum segg hym bisoȝt of sum siker knyȝt
To joyne wyth hym in justyng, in jopardé to lay,
Lede, lif for lyf, leue vchon oþer,
As fortune wolde fulsun hom, þe fayrer to haue.
Þis watz kynges countenaunce where he in court were,   100
At vch farand fest among his fre meny
        In halle.
        Þerfore of face so fere
        He stiȝtlez stif in stalle;
        Ful ȝep in þat Nw ȝere,   105
        Much mirthe he mas with alle.

Thus þer stondes in stale þe stif kyng hisseluen,
Talkkande bifore þe hyȝe table of trifles ful hende.
There gode Gawan watz grayþed Gwenore bisyde,
And Agrauayn a la Dure Mayn on þat oþer syde sittes—   110
Boþe þe kynges sister-sunes and ful siker kniȝtes;
Bischop Bawdewyn abof biginez þe table,
And Ywan, Vryn son, ette with hymseluen.
Þise were diȝt on þe des and derworþly serued,
And siþen mony siker segge at þe sidbordez.   115
Þen þe first cors come with crakkyng of trumpes
Wyth mony baner ful bryȝt, þat þerbi henged;
Nwe nakryn noyse with þe noble pipes,
Wylde werbles and wyȝt wakned lote,
Þat mony hert ful hiȝe hef at her towches.   120
Dayntés dryuen þerwyth of ful dere metes,
Foysoun of þe fresche, and on so fele disches
Þat pine to fynde þe place þe peple biforne
For to sette þe sylueren þat sere sewes halden
        On clothe.   125
        Iche lede as he loued hymselue
        Þer laght withouten loþe;
        Ay two had disches twelue,
        Good ber and bryȝt wyn boþe.

Now wyl I of hor seruise say yow no more,   130
For vch wyȝe may wel wit no wont þat þer were.
Anoþer noyse ful newe neȝed biliue,
Þat þe lude myȝt haf leue liflode to cach;
For vneþe watz þe noyce not a whyle sesed,

So the king was thus keeping a custom intact: 90
On a holiday high as was this he would eat
Of his food not the first bite before he had heard
Some adventurous story, both strange and well told,
Miraculous, marvelous, moving, yet true:
Of nobility, boldness, betrothal, a tale. 95
Or a man there should move forth, a mighty opponent,
And there join him in jousting, in jeopardy place
A true life for a life, while allowing his foe
The favor of fate should that foe win the day.
Such was King Arthur's custom when keeping his court, 100
When he feasted his freemen, his fine knights, within
    The hall.
     Full proud does he appear;
     He stands both strong and tall.
     And young as the New Year, 105
     He makes much mirth with all.

Therefore standing in state was the strong king himself;
Of trifles he talked at the table of honor.
There sat Gawain, the good knight, by Guinevere's side;
Agravain a la Dure Main to dine was the next; 110
The king's nephews, each noble, with knights formed a row;
By Baldwin, the bishop, the best place was filled.
Next in row was arranged Urien's son, Ywain—
There to dine on the dais, be dutifully served.
To be served there were seated at side tables others. 115
The course was served finely with fanfares of horns
Which, with brightly hued banners, blared a sweet sound.
The new noise of drums and nimbly played pipes,
Sang out sonorous sounds, each so stately and pure
That the hearts in that hall could not help but heave sighs. 120
Then the dainties came duly, the dearest of treats:
The freshest of foods in the finest of ways,
All carefully crowded on cloth-covered plates.
With the finest and fairest of foods every guest
    Was fed. 125
     Each one takes what he wishes
     From that splendid spread.
     Each two thus take twelve dishes
     And beer and wine bright red.

Of that sumptuous service I'll say no more now, 130
For everyone knows that no want would be there.
Now a new noise was heard, drawing near of a sudden,
That would leave the lord the leisure to dine.
The music was mute for a moment or two,

And þe fyrst cource in þe court kyndely serued,   135
Þer hales in at þe halle dor an aghlich mayster,
On þe most on þe molde on mesure hyghe;
Fro þe swyre to þe swange so sware and so þik,
And his lyndes and his lymes so longe and so grete,
Half-etayn in erde I hope þat he were,   140
Bot mon most I algate mynn hym to bene,
And þat þe myriest in his muckel þat myȝt ride;
For of bak and of brest al were his bodi sturne,
Both his wombe and his wast were worthily smale,
And alle his fetures folȝande in forme, þat he hade,   145
        Ful clene.
    For wonder of his hwe men hade,
    Set in his semblaunt sene;
    He ferde as freke were fade,
    And oueral enker grene.   150

Ande al grayþed in grene þis gome and his wedes:
A strayt cote ful streȝt þat stek on his sides,
A meré mantile abof, mensked withinne
With pelure pured apert, þe pane ful clene
With blyþe blaunner ful bryȝt, and his hod boþe,   155
Þat watz laȝt fro his lokkez and layde on his schulderes;
Heme wel-haled hose of þat same grene,
Þat spenet on his sparlyr, and clene spures vnder
Of bryȝt golde, vpon silk bordes barred ful ryche,
And scholes vnder schankes þere þe schalk rides.   160
And alle his vesture uerayly watz clene verdure,
Boþe þe barres of his belt and oþer blyþe stones
Þat were richely rayled in his aray clene
Aboutte hymself and his sadel, vpon silk werkez;
Þat were to tor for to telle of tryfles þe halue   165
Þat were enbrauded abof, wyth bryddes and flyȝes,
With gay gaudi of grene, þe golde ay inmyddes.
Þe pendauntes of his payttrure, þe proude cropure,
His molaynes and alle þe metail anamayld was þenne,
Þe steropes þat he stod on stayned of þe same,   170
And his arsounz al after, and his aþel scurtes,
Þat euer glemered and glent al of grene stones.
Þe fole þat he ferkkes on fyn of þat ilke,
        Sertayn:
    A grene hors gret and þikke,   175
    A stede ful stif to strayne,
    In brawden brydel quik;
    To þe gome he watz ful gayn.

Wel gay watz þis gome gered in grene

And the court's first course served with care to the guests,   135
When in haste to the hall came a haughty, bold man,
In his stature the stoutest who stood on the earth.
From his neck to his waist he was wondrously strong;
His loins and limbs were both lengthy and great.
I might hold him a half-giant, haughty on earth,   140
But maintain he's a man, though mighty and large,
And assured: for his size the most sure on a horse.
Both the back and the breast of his body were strong.
He was wondrously wide; though his waist was quite thin.
Every feature was fair, every form was both pure   145
    And keen.
      It was a wondrous sight,
      That high man's hues to glean;
      His body, boldly bright,
      There shone in shades of green!   150

All of green was the garb that was gathered about him:
A coat, closely cut, nobly clung to his sides;
His mantle was marvelously made; it was trimmed
With the finest of fur one could find on the earth.
Of this fur, too, was fashioned a fine winter hood,   155
Which held back from his head and was hung on his shoulders.
His hose were held high, and their hue was bright green;
They clung to his calves. Arranged keenly below
There were beautiful bangles and bright, golden spurs
Which shimmered and shone. Quite shoeless he was.   160
All glistened and glowed with the greenest of hues:
The bars on his belt; the bright, gleaming gems
Which were richly and rightly arranged on his clothes;
And his saddle, which sported a silken design.
To portray each detail would be trying indeed: 165
The embroidered sweet birds, the butterflies there,
The green beads, and gold spinning gaily about.
The man's horse's harness, the haughty, good crupper,
The bosses and bit of the bridle were all,
Like the stirrups and saddlebows, strikingly bright,   170
Well enameled in metal, marvelously fine
And aglow with the glints of the greenest of stones.
And the haughty, high horse was itself like the rest
    In tint:
      A green steed, great and wild,   175
      A horse as hard as flint,
      But in the bridle mild,
      To man obedient.

Thus this rare man was richly arrayed in bright green.

And þe here of his hed of his hors swete: 180
Fayre fannand fax vmbefoldes his schulderes.
A much berd as a busk ouer his brest henges,
Þat wyth his hiʒlich here þat of his hed reches
Watz euesed al vmbetorne abof his elbowes,
Þat half his armes þervnder were halched in þe wyse   185
Of a kyngez capados þat closes his swyre;
Þe mane of þat mayn hors much to hit lyke,
Wel cresped and cemmed, wyth knottes ful mony
Folden in wyth fildore aboute þe fayre grene,
Ay a herle of þe here, anoþer of golde;   190
Þe tayl and his toppyng twynnen of a sute
And bounden boþe wyth a bande of a bryʒt grene
Dubbed wyth ful dere stonez, as þe dok lasted,
Syþen þrawen wyth a þwong; a þwarle knot alofte,
Þer mony bellez ful bryʒt of brende golde rungen.   195
Such a fole vpon folde, ne freke þat hym rydes,
Watz neuer sene in þat sale wyth syʒt er þat tyme
              With yʒe.
          He loked as layt so lyʒt—
          So sayd al þat hym syʒe.   200
          Hit semed as no mon myʒt
          Vnder his dynttez dryʒe.

Wheþer, hade he no helme ne hawbergh nauþeı
Ne no pysan ne no plate þat pented to armes
Ne no schafte ne no schelde to schwue ne to smyte;   205
Bot in his on honde he hade a holyn bobbe
(Þat is grattest in grene when greuez ar bare)
And an ax in his oþer, a hoge and vnmete,
A spetos sparþe to expoun in spelle quoso myʒt.
Þe hede of an elnʒerde þe large lenkþe hade,   210
Þe grayn al of grene stele and of golde hewen
Þe bit burnyst bryʒt, with a brod egge
As wel schapen to schere as scharp rasores.
Þe stele of a stif staf þe sturne hit bi grypte,
Þat watz wounden wyth yrn to þe wandez ende   215
And al bigrauen with grene in gracios werkes;
A lace lapped aboute þat louked at þe hede
And so after þe halme halched ful ofte,
Wyth tryed tasselez þerto tacched innoghe
On botounz of þe bryʒt grene brayden ful ryche.   220
Þis haþel heldez hym in and þe halle entres,
Driuande to þe heʒe dece—dut he no woþe.
Haylsed he neuer one bot heʒe he ouerloked.
Þe fyrst word þat he warp, 'Wher is,' he sayd,
'Þe gouernour of þis gyng? Gladly I wolde   225

Like his horse's, the hair on his head was green, too,   180
As it fanned down fully and fell on his shoulders.
A great beard like a bush on his breast, together
With his head's wavy hair hanging down, fell about
His thick torso in tangles, almost touching his elbows,
So that shrouded from sight were his strong upper arms   185
As if covered with a king's cape enclosing his neck.
The mane of his mighty steed, much like his hair,
Was carefully curled and combed. Entwined
With the green were graceful golden threads; for with each
And every fine hair could be found a gold strand.   190
Its forelock and tail were twisted with gold;
Both were bound with a band painted bright, glowing green,
Which was studded with stones that were stunningly lit
And tied with a thong knotted tightly, to which
Many burnished gold bells, each one bright, were attached.   195
Such a high, haughty hero, such a horse as he rode,
Such a strange, striking sight had been seen never once
    In that hall.
    He looked, as lightning, bright,
    And so swore one and all.   200
    Before his full-fledged might
    A foe would surely fall!

Yet he had neither helmet nor hauberk; was quite
Without ordinary armor at all; no breastplate
Did he sport, nor thick shield, nor spear for the kill.   205
With one hand he held out a fresh holly bob branch,
Which grows the most green when the groves are bare.
But an ax in the other he awesomely held;
It was deadly by any description, and cruel:
A full meter or more was its menacing blade;   210
The spike was green steel, speckled with gold.
It was burnished most brightly. The blade's cruel edge
Was shaped as the sheerest and sharpest of razors.
In his grip the man grimly was grasping that ax,
Which was well wrought and woven with wide bands of iron,   215
Engraved with green and graceful details.
From the ax's keen end was an able thong strung,
Which was looped along the length of its haft.
To it tassels were tied, far too many to count,
With embroidered green buttons, bounteous and rich.   220
In the hall thus this horseman haughtily burst.
Up he rode to the rich dais, royally set.
No greeting he gave, as he glared at them all.
His first word was not wasted; for, "Where," he asked, "is
The king of this company? Keenly would I   225

Se þat segg in syȝt and with hymself speke
   Raysoun.'
     To knyȝtez he kest his yȝe
     And reled hym vp and doun.
     He stemmed and con studie   230
     Quo walt þer most renoun.

Ther watz lokyng on lenþe þe lude to beholde,
For vch mon had meruayle quat hit mene myȝt
Þat a haþel and a horse myȝt such a hwe lach
As growe grene as þe gres and grener hit semed,   235
Þen grene aumayl on golde glowande bryȝter.
Al studied þat þer stod and stalked hym nerre
Wyth al þe wonder of þe worlde what he worch schulde.
For fele sellyez had þay sen bot such neuer are;
Forþi for fantoum and fayryȝe þe folk þere hit demed.   240
Þerfore to answare watz arȝe mony aþel freke
And al stouned at his steuen and ston-stil seten
In a swoghe sylence þurȝ þe sale riche.
As al were slypped vpon slepe so slaked hor lotez
     In hyȝe—   245
     I deme hit not al for doute
     Bot sum for cortaysye—
     Bot let hym þat al schulde loute
     Cast vnto þat wyȝe.

Þenn Arþour, bifore þe hiȝ dece, þat auenture byholdez   250
And rekenly hym reuerenced, for rad was he neuer,
And sayde, 'Wyȝe, welcum iwys to þis place.
Þe hede of þis ostel, Arthour I hat.
Liȝt luflych adoun and lenge, I þe praye,
And quatso þy wylle is we schal wyt after.'   255
'Nay, as help me,' quoþ þe haþel, 'He þat on hyȝe syttes,
To wone any quyle in þis won hit watz not myn ernde;
Bot for þe los of þe, lede, is lyft vp so hyȝe
And þy burȝ and þy burnes best ar holden,
Stifest vnder stel-gere on stedes to ryde,   260
Þe wyȝtest and þe worþyest of þe worldes kynde,
Preue for to play wyth in oþer pure laykez,
And here is kydde cortaysye, as I haf herd carp—
And þat hatz wayned me hider, iwyis, at þis tyme.
Ȝe may be seker bi þis braunch þat I bere here   265
Þat I passe as in pes and no plyȝt seche;
For had I founded in fere, in feȝtyng wyse,
I haue a hauberghe at home and a helme boþe,
A schelde and a scharp spere, schinande bryȝt,
Ande oþer weppenes to welde, I wene wel, als;   270

Now discourse with that king who this company rules
    With crown."
      He casts his keen, bright eye,
      Searching up and down,
      Distinctly to descry   230
      Who'd there reached most renown.

All looked for the longest of times on that man;
What was meant by this marvel each man wondered there.
Such a hue for a horse and its haughty master!
Both were green as the grass; even greener, perhaps,   235
Than bright green when it glints on gold, enameled.
All studied him, stunned—some stepped forward, dazed—
And they wondered the while just what he would do.
Many sights had they seen, but not something like this!
The throng therefore thought it a thing supernatural.   240
The many good men could not muster the courage
To speak, and sat silent as stones, truly awed.
In the hall thus there hovered a harrowing quiet.
It seemed as if sleep had just silenced each voice
    At night.   245
      A kind of courtliness—
      And not, I feel, sheer fright—
      Moved men to acquiesce;
      To reply was Arthur's right.

When the king of the court saw that curious sight,   250
Unafraid, in a form that was fitting, he spoke.
He said to him, "Sir, you're certainly welcome!
Of this house I am head and am hailed as Arthur.
Alight, and linger here long, if you please;
We would honor your will, sir, whatever it is."   255
But he quickly said, "No, I will not here remain.
By the Lord, not to linger in leisure I've come,
But rather because your renown is raised high.
For courtesy, courage, this castle's true knights
Are famous: for fearlessly fighting on horse.   260
They are known as the noblest of knights in their strength,
As the worthiest ones that the world has seen,
In great tournaments tested and tried many times.
Thus I come to this court on this Christmastide day.
By this branch that I bear, you may be assured   265
That in peace I approach this place of renown.
Had I meant here to march, militarily bent,
I'd have worn heavy helmet and hauberk as well,
I'd have shouldered a shield and spear for the nonce,
And I would have wielded stout weapons indeed.   270

Bot for I wolde no were, my wedez ar softer.
Bot if þou be so bold as alle burnez tellen,
Þou wyl grant me godly þe gomen þat I ask
  Bi ryȝt.'
  Arthour con onsware   275
  And sayd, 'Sir cortays knyȝt,
  If þou craue batayl bare,
  Here faylez þou not to fyȝt.'

'Nay, frayst I no fyȝt, in fayth I þe telle;
Hit arn aboute on þis bench bot berdlez chylder.   280
If I were hasped in armes on a heȝe stede,
Here is no mon me to mach, for myȝtez so wayke.
Forþy I craue in þis court a Crystemas gomen,
For hit is Ȝol and Nwe Ȝer, and here ar ȝep mony.
If any so hardy in þis hous holdez hymseluen,   285
Be so bolde in his blod, brayn in hys hede,
Þat dar stifly strike a strok for anoþer,
I schal gif hym of my gyft þys giserne ryche,
Þis ax, þat is heué innogh, to hondele as hym lykes,
And I schal bide þe fyrst bur as bare as I sitte.   290
If any freke be so felle to fonde þat I telle,
Lepe lyȝtly me to and lach þis weppen—
I quit-clayme hit for euer, kepe hit as his auen—
And I schal stonde hym a strok, stif on þis flet,
Ellez þou wyl diȝt me þe dom to dele hym anoþer   295
   Barlay,
  And ȝet gif hym respite
  A twelmonyth and a day.
  Now hyȝe, and let se tite
  Dar any herinne oȝt say.'   300

If he hem stowned vpon fyrst, stiller were þanne
Alle þe heredmen in halle, þe hyȝ and þe loȝe.
Þe renk on his rouncé hym ruched in his sadel
And runischly his rede yȝen he reled aboute,
Bende his bresed broȝez, blycande grene,   305
Wayued his berde for to wayte quoso wolde ryse.
When non wolde kepe hym with carp he coȝed ful hyȝe
Ande rimed hym ful richly and ryȝt hym to speke.
'What, is þis Arþures hous,' quoþ þe haþel þenne,
'Þat al þe rous rennes of þurȝ ryalmes so mony?   310
Where is now your sourquydrye and your conquestes,
Your gryndellayk and your greme and your grete wordes?
Now is þe reuel and þe renoun of þe Rounde Table
Ouerwalt wyth a worde of on wyȝes speche,
For al dares for drede withoute dynt schewed!'   315

But my garments are gentle, not given to war.
If you're as courteous a king as men claim you to be,
You will graciously grant me a game that I ask
    By right."
        "Good sir, both bold and brave,"   275
        Said Arthur now, "fine knight,
        If combat's what you crave,
        We'll find for you a fight."

"Not to find here a fight, in faith, have I come;
All about on these benches sit unbearded youth!   280
Were I wielding weapons, warlike on steed,
Not one man here could match me, though mighty and sure.
No! I come to this court for a Christmastide game.
It is Yule, the New Year, and your young men are brave.
Is there here one who holds himself haughty enough—   285
One so bold in his blood, in his brain so unsound—
That he'll stoutly exchange now one stroke for another?
As a gift I will give him my great, well-wrought ax;
It is his; he may handle it here as he pleases.
I'll sustain the first stroke of this sharply edged blade.   290
If there's one here who's willing this weapon to take,
Let him step forward, show himself, accept my proposal;
I will give him this great ax, so grievously sharp,
And endure the deadly stroke he deals me at once.
In return, mine's the right to requite the fierce blow   295
    Dealt here.
        So he'll sustain the same
        On this same day next year.
        The ground rules of the game
        Are these. Who'll answer here?"   300

Though the men had been moved by that marvel at first,
They were held now in harrowing awe, high and low.
In his saddle that stranger stirred about,
As he rolled his red eyes around that wide hall.
His eyebrows arched, which were awesomely green,   305
As he swung his head side to side, seeing who'd rise.
When not one knight in that noble house spoke,
He poised himself ponderously, preparing to speak,
And cried: "Is this the court for its courage renowned,
Whose repute is rung through all realms of the land?   310
Where's your nobleness now, or your knightly, high fame?
The bravery, boldness, the bellicose words,
The righteous renown of the Round Table here:
By a wanderer's words, all is withered to naught!
In this crowd all cower; no counter is offered!"   315

Wyth þis he laʒes so loude þat þe lorde greued;
Þe blod schot for scham into his schyre face
    And lere;
      He wex as wroth as wynde;
      So did alle þat þer were.   320
      Þe kyng, as kene bi kynde,
      Þen stod þat stif mon nere,

Ande sayde, 'Haþel, by heuen þyn askyng is nys,
And as þou foly hatz frayst, fynde þe behoues.
I know no gome þat is gast of þy grete wordes.   325
Gif me now þy geserne, vpon Godez halue,
And I schal bayþen þy bone þat þou boden habbes.'
Lyʒtly lepez he hym to and laʒt hit at his honde.
Þen feersly þat oþer freke vpon fote lyʒtis.
Now hatz Arthure his axe and þe halme grypez   330
And sturnely sturez hit aboute, þat stryke wyth hit þoʒt.
Þe stif mon hym bifore stod vpon hyʒt,
Herre þen ani in þe hous by þe hede and more.
Wyth sturne schere þer he stod he stroked his berde
And wyth a countenaunce dryʒe he droʒ doun his cote,   335
No more mate ne dismayd for hys mayn dintez
Þen any burne vpon bench hade broʒt hym to drynk
    Of wyne.
      Gawan, þat sate bi þe quene,
      To þe kyng he can enclyne,   340
      'I beseche now with saʒez sene
      Þis melly mot be myne.'

'Wolde ʒe, worþilych lorde,' quoþ Wawan to þe kyng,
'Bid me boʒe fro þis benche and stonde by yow þere,
Þat I wythoute vylanye myʒt voyde þis table,   345
And þat my legge lady lyked not ille,
I wolde com to your counseyl bifore your cort ryche.
For me þink hit not semly—as hit is soþ knawen—
Þer such an askyng is heuened so hyʒe in your sale,
Þaʒ ʒe ʒourself be talenttyf, to take hit to yourseluen,   350
Whil mony so bolde yow aboute vpon bench sytten
Þat vnder heuen I hope non haʒerer of wylle
Ne better bodyes on bent þer baret is rered.
I am þe wakkest, I wot, and of wyt feblest,
And lest lur of my lyf, quo laytes þe soþe.   355
Bot for as much as ʒe ar myn em I am only to prayse;
No bounté but your blod I in my bodé knowe.
And syþen þis note is so nys þat noʒt hit yow falles,
And I haue frayned hit at yow fyrst, foldez hit to me.

Then he laughed out so loudly the lord was offended;
Arthur blushed at his bombast, his boasting, his pride,
   And gall.
     As wroth as reckless wind,
     The knights were, one and all.   320
     That court's great king, chagrined,
     Stood haughtily in hall.

[handwritten annotation: enraged / acting out of shame / immature kind of response]

"What you say," Arthur said then, "is spoken amiss;
If you found here great folly it would be fitting indeed!
Not one fine man's afraid of your foolish, bold vaunts.   325
But, by God, if you give me that great ax right now,
I will play the part you propose with great cheer."
He sprang forward swiftly and seized that ax.
That man dismounted his mighty, green horse.
Arthur hovered there, holding the handle with strength,   330
Brandishing it about, ready boldly to strike.
The stranger stood very still before all;
In that hall by a head he was higher than any.
He stood there sternly, while stroking his beard.
With a face fully fixed he unfastened his coat;   335
He remained no more moved by the words of the king
Than he'd be if a boy had just brought him a cup
   Of wine.
     Sir Gawain, who by Guinevere
     Had sat that day to dine,   340
     Said, "Sir, I ask you here
     To make this matter mine.

"If you graciously grant me," Sir Gawain said,
"The right now to rise from this Round Table here,
And permit me to move, make my way to your side   345
(If the queen acquiesces, of course, and agrees),
In this court I would come to your counsel at once.
For it strikes me unseemly that a stranger's challenge
Should be met by a man who's as mighty as you—
Although clearly as king you are keen to respond—   350
When about you on benches such bold men are seated,
Under heaven no hardier in the whole of the realm,
In battle the boldest and bravest of men.
I'm the weakest, least worthy, in this wide hall today;
Thus the loss of my life would be little enough.   355
I am known as your nephew, for nothing else famed;
What my lineage left me is all that I claim.
Since it's surely unseemly for you to respond,
I request that this task be transferred to me.

[handwritten annotation: humble]

And if I carp not comlyly let alle þis cort rych   360
    Bout blame.'
        Ryche togeder con roun;
        And syþen þay redden alle same
        To ryd þe kyng wyth croun
        And gif Gawan þe game.   365

Þen comaunded þe kyng þe knyȝt for to ryse;
And he ful radly vpros and ruchched hym fayre,
Kneled doun bifore þe kyng and cachez þat weppen.
And he luflyly hit hym laft and lyfte vp his honde
And gef hym Goddez blessyng, and gladly hym biddes   370
Þat his hert and his honde schulde hardi be boþe.
'Kepe þe, cosyn,' quoþ þe kyng, 'þat þou on kyrf sette,
And if þou redez hym ryȝt, redly I trowe
Þat þou schal byden þe bur þat he schal bede after.'
Gawan gotz to þe gome with giserne in honde   375
And he baldly hym bydez—he bayst neuer þe helder.
Þen carppez to Sir Gawan þe knyȝt in þe grene,
'Refourme we oure forwardes, er we fyrre passe.
Fyrst I eþe þe, haþel, how þat þou hattes
Þat þou me telle truly, as I tryst may.'   380
'In god fayth,' quoþ þe goode knyȝt, 'Gawan I hatte
Þat bede þe þis buffet (quatso bifallez after)
And at þis tyme twelmonyth take at þe anoþer
Wyth what weppen so þou wylt—and wyth no wyȝ ellez
    On lyue.'   385
        Þat oþer onswarez agayn,
        'Sir Gawan, so mot I þryue
        As I am ferly fayn
        Þis dint þat þou schal dryue.'

'Bigog,' quoþ þe grene knyȝt, 'Sir Gawan, me lykes   390
Þat I schal fange at þy fust þat I haf frayst here.
And þou hatz redily rehersed, bi resoun ful trwe,
Clanly al þe couenaunt þat I þe kynge asked,
Saf þat þou schal siker me, segge, bi þi trawþe,
Þat þou schal seche me þiself, whereso þou hopes   395
I may be funde vpon folde, and foch þe such wages
As þou deles me today bifore þis douþe ryche.'
'Where schulde I wale þe?' quoþ Gauan. 'Where is þy place?
I wot neuer where þou wonyes, bi Hym þat me wroȝt,
Ne I know not þe, knyȝt, þy cort ne þi name.   400
Bot teche me truly þerto and telle me howe þou hattes,
And I schal ware alle my wyt to wynne me þeder—
And þat I swere þe for soþe and by my seker traweþ.'
'Þat is innogh in Nwe Ȝer—hit nedes no more,'

If my plan is both proper and pleasing, let all   360
    Declaim."
      That court considered his plea,
      Suggested, soon, the same:
      Relieved their lord should be,
      And Gawain given the game.   365

So the king commanded his kinsman to rise.
Gawain properly, promptly, prepared himself well,
As he kneeled most nobly before his good king,
Who graciously granted all, gave him the ax.
Arthur gave to Sir Gawain God's blessing and prayed   370
That his heart and his hand should be hardy and sure.
"Take good care, my fair cousin," the king said, "and give
One stroke dealt strongly; for certainly then
You'll endure the dread blow he will deal in turn!"
So Sir Gawain goes to that green man, well armed,   375
Where he boldly abides—not abashing him though.
The Green Knight to Gawain these great words addressed:
"Once again the agreement let's go over well.
Of the name you are known by I now wish to learn;
I trust that in truth you will tell me that much."   380
"In God's name," said the good knight, "Gawain I'm called.
A blow with this blade will I boldly give you;
In return, twelve months from today you yourself
Will requite; and you'll wield what weapon that you
    Decide."   385
      "Sir Gawain," the Green Knight spoke,
      "That, on this Christmastide,
      It's you who'll serve the stroke
      Provides me pleasure, pride.

"Yes, Sir Gawain, by Gog," said the Green Knight, "I'm pleased   390
That I'll have at your hand what I here have just sought,
That you've readily, rightly, rehearsed all the terms
Of the covenant cast to the king of this hall.
But I also insist you assure with a pledge
That wherever I am you'll eventually find—   395
I'll be found near or far—and you'll fetch there the wage
That you deal me today, as this dear court will see."
"But what way shall I wander, and where find your place?
I can't guess," said Sir Gawain, "by God high above.
Of your name I've no knowledge, sir, nor of your court.   400
By what name are you known? In what nook do you dwell?
I will work all my wit to wend my way there.
This I promise and pledge with the purest of hearts."
"That's enough, on the New Year—no more will be due,"

Quoþ þe gome in þe grene to Gawan þe hende. 405
'Ʒif I þe telle trwly quen I þe tape haue
And þou me smoþely hatz smyten, smartly I þe teche
Of my hous and my home and myn owen nome,
Þen may þou frayst my fare and forwardez holde;
And if I spende no speche þenne spedez þou þe better, 410
For þou may leng in þy londe and layt no fyrre.
　　Bot slokes!
　　Ta now þy grymme tole to þe
　　And let se how þou cnokez.'
　　'Gladly, sir, forsoþe,' 415
　　Quoþ Gawan; his ax he strokes.

The grene knyʒt vpon grounde grayþely hym dresses;
A littel lut with þe hede, þe lere he discouerez;
His longe louelych lokkez he layd ouer his croun,
Let þe naked nec to þe note schewe. 420
Gauan gripped to his ax and gederes hit on hyʒt;
Þe kay fot on þe folde he before sette,
Let hit doun lyʒtly lyʒt on þe naked,
Þat þe scharp of þe schalk schyndered þe bones
And schrank þurʒ þe schyire grece and schade hit in twynne, 425
Þat þe bit of þe broun stel bot on þe grounde.
Þe fayre hede fro þe halce hit to þe erþe,
Þat fele hit foyned wyth her fete þere hit forth roled;
Þe blod brayd fro þe body, þat blykked on þe grene.
And nawþer faltered ne fel þe freke neuer þe helder 430
Bot styþly he start forth vpon styf schonkes
And runyschly he raʒt out þereas renkkez stoden,
Laʒt to his lufly hed and lyft hit vp sone,
And syþen boʒez to his blonk, þe brydel he cachchez,
Steppez into stel-bawe and strydez alofte, 435
And his hede by þe here in his honde haldez;
And as sadly þe segge hym in his sadel sette
As non vnhap had hym ayled, þaʒ hedlez nowe
　　In stedde.
　　He brayde his bluk aboute, 440
　　Þat vgly bodi þat bledde.
　　Moni on of hym had doute,
　　Bi þat his resounz were redde.

For þe hede in his honde he haldez vp euen,
Toward þe derrest on þe dece he dressez þe face 445
And hit lyfte vp þe yʒe-lyddez and loked ful brode
And meled þus much with his muthe as ʒe may now here:
'Loke, Gawan, þou be grayþe to go as þou hettez
And layte as lelly til þou me, lude, fynde

Said the Green Knight to gracious Sir Gawain, adding,   405
"If you deftly and duly deal me the stroke,
I will tell you in truth, once I've taken the blow;
Of my house and my homeland you'll hear, and my name.
You may come there to keep our true covenant then.
The less speech I expend, you will speed all the better;   410
For you must here remain and not move out in search
        Of me.
        Now deal! Do not defer!
        Your stroke shall all here see."
        Says Gawain, "Gladly, sir!"   415
        He tests the blade truly.

To the ground the Green Knight graciously kneels.
As he leans forth a little, he lays his neck bare;
His long, lovely locks he lays over his head,
So the nape of the naked, green neck is exposed.   420
Then, gripping the great ax, Sir Gawain lifts it—
On the floor his left foot pushed forward a bit—
And swings it down swiftly; it strikes the thick neck;
In a single, bold stroke, the ax shatters the bone,
As it sinks through the skin, which it severs in two.   425
The bright edge of the blade bites into the ground,
And the fair head falls to the floor, tumbling down,
Where it's bounced back and forth by the boots of the guests.
The blood quickly bursts out, shines bright on the green.
But his form neither falls down nor falters a bit;
It stoutly strides forth on the strongest of legs.
And, reaching out roughly where the retainers stood,   430
He heaves his head high; yes, he holds it aloft!
He strides to his steed, seizes the bridle,
Steps in the stirrup, and straightaway mounts.   435
His own head by the hair he holds in his grip,
As he steadily sits in the saddle on high,
Not stunned from the stroke, though he sits there with
        No head.
        He moved his trunk with might.   440
        His body briskly bled.
        That hall was held in fright
        When he his say had said.

For the head in his hand he holds out to all,
To the dais directs it, to dear nobles there;   445
It lifts up its lids and looks about,
And, not waiting, says wonderful words, as you'll hear:
"Be prepared to perform as you've promised, Gawain.
You must ferret with faith till you find me at last,

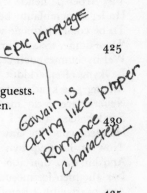

epic language

Gawain is acting like proper Romance character

As þou hatz hette in þis halle, herande þise knyȝtes.   45c
To þe Grene Chapel þou chose, I charge þe, to sotte
Such a dunt as þou hatz dalt—disserued þou habbez—
To be ȝederly ȝolden on Nw ȝeres morn.
Þe Knyȝt of þe Grene Chapel men knowen me mony;
Forþi me for to fynde, if þou fraystez, faylez þou neuer.   455
Þerfore com, oþer recreaunt be calde þe behoues.'
With a runisch rout þe raynez he tornez,
Halled out at þe hal dor, his hed in his hande,
Þat þe fyr of þe flynt flaȝe fro fole houes.
To quat kyth he becom knwe non þere,   460
Neuer more þen þay wyste from queþen he watz wonnen.
        What þenne?
        Þe kyng and Gawen þare
        At þat grene þay laȝe and grenne,
        Ȝet breued watz hit ful bare   465
        A meruayl among þo menne.

Þaȝ Arþer þe hende kyng at hert hade wonder,
He let no semblaunt be sene bot sayde ful hyȝe
To þe comlych quene wyth cortays speche,
'Dere dame, today demay yow neuer.   470
Wel bycommes such craft vpon Cristmasse—
Laykyng of enterludez, to laȝe and to syng—
Among þise kynde caroles of knyȝtez and ladyez.
Neuerþelece to my mete I may me wel dres,
For I haf sen a selly I may not forsake.'   475
He glent vpon Sir Gawen and gaynly he sayde,
'Now sir, heng vp þyn ax, þat hatz innogh hewen.'
And hit watz don abof þe dece on doser to henge,
Þer alle men for meruayl myȝt on hit loke
And bi trwe tytel þerof to telle þe wonder.   480
Þenne þay boȝed to a borde þise burnes togeder,
Þe kyng and þe gode knyȝt, and kene men hem serued
Of alle dayntyez double, as derrest myȝt falle,
Wyth alle maner of mete and mynstralcie boþe.
Wyth wele walt þay þat day, til worþed an ende   485
        In londe.
        Now þenk wel, Sir Gawan,
        For woþe þat þou ne wonde
        Þis auenture for to frayn
        Þat þou hatz tan on honde.   490

II

This hanselle hatz Arthur of auenturus on fyrst
In ȝonge ȝer for he ȝerned ȝelpyng to here.
Thaȝ hym wordez were wane when þay to sete wenten,

Just as here in this hall all have heard you now pledge.   450
To the Green Chapel's chambers I charge you to go.
Such a stroke as you've struck you'll receive in return.
You'll accept it yourself, good sir, New Year's morn.
I am known far and wide as the Knight of the Green Chapel,
Whom you'll find if you faithfully ferret me out.   455
Therefore come, or be called a most recreant knight!"
Then, ripping the reins, he reels about,
Quits the hall with his head in his hand in such rush
That fierce sparks start to shoot from his steed's mighty hooves.
To what region he rode no retainer there knew;   460
Nor from whence he had wandered could anyone guess.
        What then?
     The king and Gawain both
     At the Green Knight laugh and grin.
     But they think it, in truth,   465
     A marvel among all men.

Though Arthur thought this a wonder indeed,
He showed no semblance of shock. Soon he turned
To the comely queen with courteous speech:
"Dear lady, do not be dismayed by all this: 470
For such cunning becomes the Christmastide well,
As do masques, festive mirth, music, and such
Interluding light carols of ladies and knights.
To our feast, in faith, it is fitting we turn,
Although all here, if asked, would admit this a marvel."   475
Then, graciously glancing on Gawain, he said:
"Hang that ax high; it has hewn quite enough!"
On a beautiful broadcloth above the dais
It was mounted: a marvel all men might behold,
To the tale to be told of it testament sure.   480
So the two returned to the table to feast;
The good king and Gawain were graciously then
With doubly heaped dainties dutifully served,
With marvelous meats and with minstrelsy, too.
Thus they dallied all day till darkness came on   485
        The land.
     Bold Gawain, best beware,
     Lest fear leave you unmanned;
     Consider, knight, with care
     What now you hold in hand!   490

II

Thus was good Arthur given a gift of the New Year.
He had longed to listen to lofty, high tales;
At that banquet such boasting was absent at first.

Now ar þay stoken of sturne werk, staf-ful her hond.
Gawan watz glad to begynne þose gomnez in halle   495
Bot þaȝ þe ende be heuy haf ȝe no wonder:
For þaȝ men ben mery in mynde quen þay han mayn drynk,
A ȝere ȝernes ful ȝerne and ȝeldez neuer lyke;
Þe forme to þe fynisment foldez ful selden.
Forþi þis Ȝol ouerȝede, and þe ȝere after,   500
And vche sesoun serlepes sued after oþer:
After Crystenmasse com þe crabbed Lentoun,
Þat fraystez flesch wyth þe fysche and fode more symple,
Bot þenne þe weder of þe worlde wyth wynter hit þrepez,
Colde clengez adoun, cloudez vplyften,   505
Schyre schedez þe rayn in schowrez ful warme,
Fallez vpon fayre flat, flowrez þere schewen,
Boþe groundez and þe greuez grene ar her wedez,
Bryddez busken to bylde and bremlych syngen
For solace of þe softe somer þat sues þerafter   510
    Bi bonk,
    And blossumez bolne to blowe
    Bi rawez rych and ronk,
    Þen notez noble innoȝe
    Ar herde in wod so wlonk.   515

After þe sesoun of somer wyth þe soft wyndez,
Quen Zeferus syflez hymself on sedez and erbez,
Wela wynne is þe wort þat waxes þeroute,
When þe donkande dewe dropez of þe leuez,
To bide a blysful blusch of þe bryȝt sunne.   520
Bot þen hyȝes Heruest and hardenes hym sone,
Warnez hym for þe wynter to wax ful rype;
He dryues wyth droȝt þe dust for to ryse,
Fro þe face of þe folde to flyȝe ful hyȝe;
Wroþe wynde of þe welkyn wrastelez with þe sunne,   525
Þe leuez laucen fro þe lynde and lyȝten on þe grounde,
And al grayes þe gres þat grene watz ere;
Þenne al rypez and rotez þat ros vpon fyrst,
And þus ȝirnez þe ȝere in ȝisterdayez mony
And wynter wyndez aȝayn, as þe worlde askez,   530
    No fage,
    Til Meȝelmas mone
    Watz cumen wyth wynter wage.
    Þen þenkkez Gawan ful sone
    Of his anious uyage.   535

Ȝet quyl Al Hal Day with Arþer he lenges;
And he made a fare on þat fest for þe frekez sake,
With much reuel and ryche of þe Rounde Table.

Now they'd marvelous matter, much more than they'd planned.
Sir Gawain was glad to start games in the hall.   495
If this story ends sadly, though, suffer no shock;
For with many drinks men are made merry and light,
Although charging time changes, unchecked, all it touches;
And the last things are less like the first than we wish.
Thus that Yule and next year quickly yield to time.   500
The seasons in sequence succeed one another.
After Christmastime comes on the coldest of Lents,
Famishing the flesh with food much more drab.
The weather with winter is warring all month,
So the dank cold descends and the dark clouds arise.   505
The sparkling rain sprinkles down, sprightly and warm;
When it falls on the fields, bright flowers spring up;
Then both wide ways and woods are wearing bright green.
On each branch, perched to build nests and brightly to sing
For the solace of summer that soon would arrive,   510
    Is a bird.
  The buds soon bulged and bloomed.
  A while the woods whispered.
  And soon songs, sweetly tuned,
  In holt and heath were heard.   515

But the season of summer comes suddenly on,
When Zephyrus strokes every seedling and herb.
Fully pleased is the plant that can play in such wind;
After dawn, when the dew finally drops from his leaves,
He bathes in the beams of the bright summer sun.   520
But Harvest comes hurriedly, hastening him on,
Reminding him to ripen before arrival of winter.
With his droughts he drives the dust from the ground;
He fans that dust free from the face of the earth.
The wild, rising wind starts wrestling the sun.   525
The leaves from the linden alight on the earth.
The grass that was green turns to gray in the field;
All ripens and rots that had risen that spring.
Thus the year all its yesterdays yields in the end.
The whirling, cold wind of the winter then starts   530
    To din.
  But not before the moon
  Of Michaelmas moves in
  Does Gawain glean how soon
  His bold quest must begin.   535

With his dear lord he dwells till the Day of All Saints. Nov 1
On that high holiday there was held in his honor
A revel most rich at the Round Table, where

Kny3tez ful cortays and comlych ladies
Al for luf of þat lede in longynge þay were;   540
Bot neuer þe lece ne þe later þay neuened bot merþe.
Mony joylez for þat jentyle japez þer maden.
For aftter mete with mournyng he melez to his eme
And spekez of his passage, and pertly he sayde,
'Now, lege lorde of my lyf, leue I yow ask.   545
3e knowe þe cost of þis cace; kepe I no more
To telle yow tenez þerof – neuer bot trifel –
Bot I am boun to þe bur barely tomorne
To sech þe gome of þe grene, as God wyl me wysse.'
Þenne þe best of þe bur3 bo3ed togeder,   550
Aywan and Errik and oþer ful mony –
Sir Doddinaual de Sauage, þe Duk of Clarence,
Launcelot, and Lyonel, and Lucan þe gode,
Sir Boos and Sir Byduer, big men boþe,
And mony oþer menskful, with Mador de la Port.   555
Alle þis compayny of court com þe kyng nerre
For to counseyl þe kny3t, with care at her hert.
Þere watz much derue doel driuen in þe sale
Þat so worthé as Wawan schulde wende on þat ernde
To dry3e a delful dynt and dele no more   560
        Wyth bronde.
    Þe kny3t mad ay god chere
    And sayde, 'Quat schuld I wonde?
    Of Destinés derf and dere
    What may mon do bot fonde?'   565

He dowellez þer al þat day and dressez on þe morn,
Askez erly hys armez and alle were þay bro3t.
Fyrst a tulé tapit ty3t ouer þe flet,
And miche watz þe gyld gere þat glent þeralofte.
Þe stif mon steppez þeron and þe stel hondelez,   570
Dubbed in a dublet of a dere tars,
And syþen a crafty capados, closed aloft,
Þat wyth a bry3t blaunner was bounden withinne.
Þenne set þay þe sabatounz vpon þe segge fotez,
His legez lapped in stel with luflych greuez,   575
With polaynez piched þerto, policed ful clene,
Aboute his knez knaged wyth knotez of golde;
Queme quyssewes þen, þat coyntlych closed
His thik þrawen þy3ez, with þwonges to tachched;
And syþen þe brawden bryné of bry3t stel ryngez   580
Vmbeweued þat wy3, vpon wlonk stuffe,
And wel bornyst brace vpon his boþe armes,
With gode cowters and gay and glouez of plate,

Comely ladies came, and courteous knights,
In grief for Sir Gawain, and great, heartfelt love.   540
All sanguinely spoke that day solely of mirth;
Many joyless ones joked for that gentle knight's sake.
After the meal, mournfully reminding his uncle
Of his impending and perilous passage, he said:
"Liege lord of my life, for your leave I must ask.   545
I am bound and obliged in a bond, as you know;
But to tell of its trials would be trifling and idle.
So suffice it to say I must start off tomorrow,
As God gives me guidance, the Green Knight to seek."
There gathered together the greatest of the city: 550
There arrived both Eric and courageous Ywain;
Huntsman Dodinal; Duke of Clarence, his kin.
There was Lancelot; Lyonel; Lucan the Good;
Sir Bors; Sir Bedivere; bold, hearty knights;
And many good men, with Mador de la Porte.   555
Thus this courtly company comes forth to Arthur
Their companion to counsel, with care in their hearts.
For though hidden, a heaviness hung in the court;
That so worthy a one in the world as Gawain
Should thus suffer a sojourn so savage, all were   560
    Distressed.
    "Why pule, complain, or pout?"
    Said Gawain, showing zest,
    "What destiny deals out
    A man must put to test."   565

Gawain dwelt there all day and dressed on the next.
He asked early for arms; each and all were brought.
First a rich, red carpet was unrolled on the floor;
Armor, glistening and gilded, was gloriously brought.
The strong man stepped up, the steel to inspect.   570
He duly was dressed in a doublet from Tharsia.
A cape was clasped closely about him;
It was lined with a white and wonderful fur.
Two shoes made of steel were set on his feet.
On his legs servants lapped and tied lovely, bright greaves.   575
Polished knee-pieces, both perfectly made,
Were girded to the gear and with gold knots secured.
Cuisses, cunningly clasped, were placed
With new thongs on his thighs, which were thick and strong.
All was covered keenly with a coat of bright mail,   580
Which was wrapped around the rich cloth that he wore.
Then came braces, well burnished, on both of his arms,
And glorious, glistening gloves on his hands.

And alle þe godlych gere þat hym gayn schulde
    Þat tyde;   585
      Wyth ryche cote-armure,
      His gold sporez spend with pryde,
      Gurde wyth a bront ful sure
      With silk sayn vmbe his syde.

When he watz hasped in armes his harnays watz ryche: 590
Þe lest lachet oþer loupe lemed of golde.
So harnayst as he watz he herknez his masse
Offred and honoured at þe heȝe auter.
Syþen he comez to þe kyng and to his cort-ferez,
Lachez lufly his leue at lordez and ladyez,   595
And þay hym kyst and conueyed, bikende hym to Kryst.
Bi þat watz Gryngolet grayth and gurde with a sadel
Þat glemed ful gayly with mony golde frenges,
Ayquere naylet ful nwe, for þat note ryched,
Þe brydel barred aboute, with bryȝt golde bounden.   600
Þe apparayl of þe payttrure and of þe proude skyrtez,
Þe cropore, and þe couertor, acorded wyth þe arsounez.
And al watz, rayled on red, ryche golde naylez,
Þat al glytered and glent as glem of þe sunne.
Þenne hentes he þe helme and hastily hit kysses,   605
Þat watz stapled stifly and stoffed wythinne.
Hit watz hyȝe on his hede, hasped bihynde,
Wyth a lyȝtly vrysoun ouer þe auentayle,
Enbrawden and bounden wyth þe best gemmez
On brode sylkyn borde, and bryddez on semez,   610
As papjayez paynted peruyng bitwene,
Tortors and trulofez entayled so þyk
As mony burde þeraboute had ben seuen wynter
    In toune.
      Þe cercle watz more o prys   615
      Þat vmbeclypped hys croun,
      Of diamauntez a deuys
      Þat boþe were bryȝt and broun.

Then þay schewed hym þe schelde, þat was of schyr goulez
Wyth þe pentangel depaynt of pure golde hwez;   620
He braydez hit by þe bauderyk, aboute þe hals kestes.
Þat bisemed þe segge semlyly fayre
And quy þe pentangel apendez to þat prynce noble
I am in tent yow to telle, þof tary hyt me schulde.
Hit is a syngne þat Salamon set sumquyle   625
In bytoknyng of trawþe, bi tytle þat hit habbez;
For hit is a figure þat haldez fyue poyntez
And vche lyne vmbelappez and loukez in oþer

Thus he wore wondrous gear for whatever might then
    Betide.   585
      The coat of arms came last;
      And spurs with skill supplied;
      And broadsword, fastened fast
      In sword-sheath at his side.

Gawain's glorious gear was glistening and fine;   590
With a glinting, rich gold, each clasp glowed in the light.
Thus well dressed, he devoutly and duly heard Mass
Properly and piously performed at the altar.
To the king and the court's companions he went;
Of the ladies and lords took his leave graciously.   595
They kissed him, commended him to Christ, saw him off.
Then was Gringolet girded with a great, stately saddle,
Aglow with the glints of a good, golden fringe.
For the nonce studded newly with nails everywhere,
The rich bridle was barred with the brightest of gold.   600
The shimmering skirts and the shining poitrel
Were accorded with the caparison, crupper, and saddlebows—
All in red well arrayed, and with rich, golden studs
That would glisten and glint like the gleams of the sun.
Gawain held in his hand and hastily kissed   605
His helmet, most handily hewn and well lined.
It stood high on his head and was hasped at the back.
A cloth, placed carefully, covered the visor,
Embroidered and bound with the best, glowing gems
On the broad, silken border, and with birds on the seams,   610
In periwinkles parrots, portrayed with great skill.
There turtledoves, truelove knots, truly appeared,
As if sewn up by seamstresses seven long winters
    In town.
      And now on that fine knight   615
      Was placed a kind of crown,
      Arranged, both rich and right,
      With diamonds up and down.

They showed forth the shield that shone with bright red,
With its pentangle depicted in pure, golden hues.   620
Close about his broad neck, by its baldric, he swung it;
It suited him certainly, showed his grace.
Why that prince's pentangle is proper, indeed,
I intend now to tell, though I tarry a bit.
That pure star is a sign that King Solomon used   625
To betoken the truth that by title it holds.
It's a figure enfolded, with five outward points;
Each line is well linked with two lines at an angle,

And ayquere hit is endelez (and Englych hit callen
Oueral, as I here, 'þe endeles knot').   630
Forþy hit acordez to þis knyȝt and to his cler armez,
For ay faythful in fyue and sere fyue syþez,
Gawan watz for gode knawen and, as golde pured,
Voyded of vche vylany, wyth vertuez ennourned
        In mote.   635
    Forþy þe pentangel nwe
    He ber in schelde and cote,
    As tulk of tale most trwe
    And gentylest knyȝt of lote

Fyrst he watz funden fautlez in his fyue wyttez.   640
And efte fayled neuer þe freke in his fyue fyngres.
And alle his afyaunce vpon folde watz in þe fyue woundez
Þat Cryst kaȝt on þe croys, as þe Crede tellez.
And queresoeuer þys mon in melly watz stad,
His þro þoȝt watz in þat, þurȝ alle oþer þyngez,   645
Þat alle his forsnes he fong at þe fyue joyez
Þat þe hende Heuen Quene had of hir Chylde.
(At þis cause þe knyȝt comlyche hade
In þe inore half of his schelde hir ymage depaynted,
Þat quen he blusched þerto his belde neuer payred.)   650
Þe fyft fyue þat I finde þat þe frek vsed
Watz fraunchyse and felaȝschyp forbe al þyng,
His clannes and his cortaysye croked were neuer,
And pité, þat passez alle poyntez – þyse pure fyue
Were harder happed on þat haþel þen on any oþer.   655
Now alle þese fyue syþez forsoþe were fetled on þis knyȝt
And vchone halched in oþer, þat non ende hade,
And fyched vpon fyue poyntez þat fayld neuer,
Ne samned neuer in no syde, ne sundred nouþer,
Withouten ende at any noke I oquere fynde,   660
Whereeuer þe gomen bygan or glod to an ende.
Þerfore on his schene schelde schapen watz þe knot,
Ryally wyth red golde vpon rede gowlez,
Þat is þe pure 'pentaungel' wyth þe peple called
        With lore.   665
    Now grayþed is Gawan gay
    And laȝt his launce ryȝt þore
    And gef hem alle goud day –
    He wende for euermore.

He sperred þe sted with þe spurez and sprong on his way   670
So stif þat þe ston-fyr stroke out þerafter.
Al þat seȝ þat semly syked in hert
And sayde soþly al same segges til oþer,

Passing over and under two others. It's called
In English everywhere—as I've heard—"endless knot."   630
To that prince thus the pentangle's proper; for he
Was in fivefold ways faithful to five points of truth.
For Sir Gawain was as good as pure gold, unalloyed;
For his virtue without villainy that valiant knight
    Was known.   635
    That pentangle, painted new,
    On shield and coat thus shone.
    Untainted, trusted, true,
    Good Gawain stood alone.

He was, first, without fault in the five fleshly senses;   640
His five dexterous fingers never failed when employed;
And his faith was well founded in the five awful wounds
That our Christ on the cross, as the Creed says, received.
Whenever in war Gawain worthily fought,
On this thought, through all things, he was thoroughly fixed: 645
That his fortitude from the Five Joys was derived,
Which the high Queen of Heaven had had from her Child;
Appropriately pious, that prince always had
Inside his shield her face clearly drawn;
When he saw it, he stood always stalwart in war.   650
For the fifth of the five fives, I find that knight showed
To fellowmen, friendship; a free hand to all;
A kind-hearted courtesy; continence ever;
And surpassing piety fifth. These pure five,
As I know, in that noblest of knights were supreme: 655
Five pentads, each precious and pure; each joined
To another, never alone, never ending;
And finally affixed to the four other points;
Neither crowded too closely nor cloven asunder;
Without end at any angle that I can discover—   660
Where you started or stopped on the star was the same.
On his shield thus shaped was that shining, bright knot
In the richest of red-gold on royal red gules.
This precious and perfect pentangle learned men
    Revered.   665
    His lance he lifted high.
    That prince to all appeared.
    "Good friends," he said, "good-bye"
    (His last farewell, he feared).

As he spurred his steed and sprang on his way,   670
Sparks of fire flew forth as from flint struck by steel.
All who saw that grave scene were sorrowed at heart.
With woeful, deep whisperings, one to another,

Carande for þat comly, 'Bi Kryst, hit is scaþe
Þat þou, leude, schal be lost, þat art of lyf noble!   675
To fynde hys fere vpon folde, in fayth, is not eþe.
Warloker to haf wroȝt had more wyt bene
And haf dyȝt ȝonder dere a duk to haue worþed.
A lowande leder of ledez in londe hym wel semez,
And so had better haf ben þen britned to noȝt,   680
Hadet wyth an aluisch mon, for angardez pryde.
Who knew euer any kyng such counsel to take
As knyȝtez in cauelaciounz on Crystmasse gomnez?'
Wel much watz þe warme water þat waltered of yȝen
When þat semly syre soȝt fro þo wonez   685
          Þad daye.
        He made non abode
        Bot wyȝtly went hys way.
        Mony wylsum way he rode,
        Þe bok as I herde say.   690

Now ridez þis renk þurȝ þe ryalme of Logres,
Sir Gauan, on Godez halue, þaȝ hym no gomen þoȝt –
Oft leudlez alone he lengez on nyȝtez
Þer he fonde noȝt hym byfore þe fare þat he lyked;
Hade he no fere bot his fole bi frythez and dounez,   695
Ne no gome bot God bi gate wyth to karp –
Til þat he neȝed ful neghe into þe Norþe Walez.
Alle þe iles of Anglesay on lyft half he haldez
And farez ouer þe fordez by þe forlondez;
Ouer at þe Holy Hede, til he hade eft bonk   700
In þe wyldrenesse of Wyrale. Wonde þer bot lyte
Þat auþer God oþer gome wyth goud hert louied.
And ay he frayned, as he ferde, at frekez þat he met
If þay hade herde any karp of a knyȝt grene,
In any grounde þeraboute, of þe Grene Chapel.   705
And al nykked hym wyth 'Nay!'—þat neuer in her lyue
Þay seȝe neuer no segge þat watz of suche hwez
          Of grene.
        Þe knyȝt tok gates straunge
        In mony a bonk vnbene.   710
        His cher ful oft con chaunge,
        Þat chapel er he myȝt sene.

Mony klyf he ouerclambe in contrayez straunge.
Fer floten fro his frendez, fremedly he rydez.
At vche warþe oþer water þer þe wyȝe passed   715
He fonde a foo hym byfore, bot ferly hit were,
And þat so foule and so felle þat feȝt hym byhode.
So mony meruayl bi mount þer þe mon fyndez

"By Christ, it's a crime!" the court sadly said.
"That lord will be lost, whose life is so dear.   675
No peer could replace that prince in our time.
If with caution he'd chosen a course less final,
Without doubt a great duke that dear knight would become,
In the land a fine leader, a lord of renown.
That would be for the best. He'll be butchered, though, now,   680
By a spirit-man slaughtered; all solely for pride!
Has a king to such counsel consented before,
That such contest should count as a Christmastide game?"
Profusely tears flowed down the faces of all
When they watched that most worthy of knights riding off   685
    That day.
      He didn't stay. Instead,
      He went without delay—
      So tells the text I read—
      His wild and weary way.   690

Now this righteous knight rides through the realm of Logres.
He goes forth for God, but no game does it seem.
All alone does he lie through the long, winter nights.
What food he can find he must feed on to live.
In the forests he's friendless but for his horse;   695
Through the gorges no good friend but God is beside him.
Yet he rides till he reaches the realm of North Wales;
All along on his left are the Anglesey isles.
Alone, through the lowlands that lie by the sea,
Gawain hastens to Holy Head, hard by the shore,   700
Up to Wirral's bleak wilderness where few men lived
Who cared for a covenant with Christ or man.
All he asks there of each and of any he meets
Is for news of a knight who is known there to be
Tinted green, or of grounds of a Green Chapel nigh.   705
But none knows of that knight; none can name him at all;
None has seen such a sight nor assists Sir Gawain
    In his quest.
      Rough roads and roaring streams
      That precious prince rides past,   710
      And now despairs, now dreams,
      He'll see that site at last.

So he climbed many cliffs in that country for days,
Riding far from his friends in a foreign realm.
Whenever he wended his way over fords   715
There he found himself faced with a foe, which each time
Was so foul and fierce he must fight it or die.
In the mountains the marvels were many; indeed,

Hit were to tore for to telle of þe tenþe dole.
Sumwhyle wyth wormez he werrez and with wolues als,   720
Sumwhyle wyth wodwos þat woned in þe knarrez,
Boþe wyth bullez and berez, and borez oþerquyle,
And etaynez þat hym anelede of þe heȝe felle.
Nade he ben duȝty and dryȝe and Dryȝtyn had serued,
Douteles he hade ben ded and dreped ful ofte.   725
For werre wrathed hym not so much þat wynter nas wors,
When þe colde cler water fro þe cloudez schadde
And fres er hit falle myȝt to þe fale erþe.
Ner slayn wyth þe slete he sleped in his yrnes
Mo nyȝtez þen innoghe, in naked rokkez   730
Þeras claterande fro þe crest þe colde borne rennez
And henged heȝe ouer his hede in hard iisseikkles.
Þus in peryl and payne and plytes ful harde
Bi contray caryez þis knyȝt tyl Krystmasse Euen,
        Alone.   735
    Þe knyȝt wel þat tyde
    To Mary made his mone
    Þat ho hym red to ryde
    And wysse hym to sum wone.

Bi a mounte on þe morne meryly he rydes   740
Into a forest ful dep, þat ferly watz wylde,
Hiȝe hillez on vche a halue and holtwodez vnder
Of hore okez ful hoge, a hundreth togeder.
Þe hasel and þe haȝþorne were harled al samen,
With roȝe raged mosse rayled aywhere,   745
With mony bryddez vnblyþe vpon bare twyges,
Þat pitosly þer piped for pyne of þe colde.
Þe gome vpon Gryngolet glydez hem vnder
Þurȝ mony misy and myre, mon al hym one,
Carande for his costes, lest he ne keuer schulde   750
To se þe seruyse of þat Syre þat on þat self nyȝt
Of a burde watz borne oure baret to quelle.
And þerfore sykyng he sayde, 'I beseche Þe, Lorde,
And Mary, þat is myldest moder so dere,
Of sum herber þer heȝly I myȝt here masse   755
Ande Þy matynez tomorne, mekely I ask,
And þerto prestly I pray my Pater and Aue
        And Crede.'
    He rode in his prayere
    And cryed for his mysdede.   760
    He sayned hym in syþes sere
    And sayde, 'Cros Kryst me spede.'

Nade he sayned hymself, segge, bot þrye

To portray a tenth part is impossible here.
For with fierce wolves he fought; with ferocious dragons; 720
With crafty wood-creatures who crawled from the rocks;
With bulls and fierce bears; with boars and, as well,
Bold giants that jumped from the jagged ravines.
Had Christ never cared for, nor courage served, him,
He'd have died many deaths, without doubt, in that land. 725
Yet the winter was worse than those wearisome battles;
For a freezing rain fell from a frosty, gray sky,
And lay on the land and the lanes that he took.
Almost slain with such sleet, Gawain slept in his armor;
This noble spent night after night in the steeps. 730
Small waterfalls wandered their way through the rocks,
Where they hung in hard icicles high over Gawain.
Thus in peril and pain, that patient knight searches
Through rough country and creeks until Christmas Eve on
     His quest. 735
        That prince sent up his prayer,
        To Mary made request,
        That she should show him where
        He'd reach a place to rest.

By a mountain next morning that mighty knight rides 740
To a wide stretch of wood, both wild and dark—
On each side of it soars up a steep, rising hill—
Made of hundreds of huge, hoary oaks all about.
There the hazel and hawthorn are held twisted together,
And rough, ragged moss is arrayed everywhere. 745
There are birds on the bare, wintry boughs of the trees;
Each pipes its song piteously, pining with cold.
Sir Gawain on Gringolet glides underneath,
Moving through the marshes and mires alone.
He fears that finally he'll fail to attend 750
The service of our Savior Who that same evening was,
Every soul to save, to a sweet maiden born.
He says with a sigh, "I beseech you, O Lord,
And Mary, our mother so mild. Direct me
To a haven. With glad heart I would hear there the Mass; 755
Your matins tomorrow I meekly request.
Thus promptly I pray my Pater and Ave
     And Creed."
        That prince repents his sins
        And, solemn on his steed, 760
        Crossing himself, petitions:
        "Lord Christ, my cause now speed!"

When he'd signed himself thrice with the sign of the cross,

[handwritten marginal note:] highly unemphasized & nature is stressed as foe

Er he watz war in þe wod of a won in a mote,
Abof a launde, on a lawe, loken vnder boȝez   765
Of mony borelych bole aboute bi þe diches,
A castel þe comlokest þat euer knyȝt aȝte,
Pyched on a prayere, a park al aboute,
With a pyked palays pyned ful þik,
Þat vmbeteȝe mony tre mo þen two myle.   770
Þat holde þat on syde þe haþel auysed,
As hit schemered and schon þurȝ þe schyre okez.
Þenne hatz he hendly of his helme and heȝly he þonkez
Jesus and Sayn Gilyan, þat gentyle ar boþe,
Þat cortaysly hade hym kydde and his cry herkened.   775
'Now bone hostel,' coþe þe burne, 'I beseche yow ȝette!'
Þenne gederez he to Gryngolet with þe gilt helez
And he ful chauncely hatz chosen to þe chef gate,
Þat broȝt bremly þe burne to þe bryge ende
      In haste.   780
      Þe bryge watz breme vpbrayde,
      Þe ȝatez wer stoken faste,
      Þe wallez were wel arayed –
      Hit dut no wyndez blaste.

Þe burne bode on bonk, þat on blonk houed,   785
Of þe depe double dich þat drof to þe place.
Þe walle wod in þe water wonderly depe,
Ande eft a ful huge heȝt hit haled vpon lofte,
Of harde hewen ston vp to þe tablez,
Enbaned vnder þe abataylment, in þe best lawe;   790
And syþen garytez ful gaye gered bitwene,
Wyth mony luflych loupe þat louked ful clene;
A better barbican þat burne blusched vpon neuer.
And innermore he behelde þat halle ful hyȝe,
Towres telded bytwene, trochet ful þik,   795
Fayre fylyolez þat fyȝed, and ferlyly long,
With coruon coprounes, craftyly sleȝe.
Chalk-whyt chymnées þer ches he innoȝe,
Vpon bastel rouez þat blenked ful quyte.
So mony pynakle payntet watz poudred ayquere   800
Among þe castel carnelez, clambred so þik,
Þat pared out of papure purely hit semed.
Þe fre freke on þe fole hit fayr innoghe þoȝt
If he myȝt keuer to com þe cloyster wythinne,
To herber in þat hostel whyl halyday lested,   805
      Auinant.
      He calde, and sone þer com
      A porter pure plesaunt;
      On þe wal his ernd he nome
      And haylsed þe knyȝt erraunt.   810

He discovered a castle, enclosed in a moat,
Framed by boughs, high above a broad plain, on a hill.   765
There the tallest of trees were towering high.
A comelier castle could never exist!
It was built on good grounds. A green park lay about,
For protection palisaded with pikes in a row
That tied in two miles of trees, perhaps more.   770
Sir Gawain gazed on that great castle there,
As it shimmered and shone through the forest of oaks.
Devoutly he doffed his dear helmet, gave thanks
To Jesus and Julian—gentle are both.
In his grief, passing grave, they had granted his prayer!   775
"Now grant me," said Gawain, "a good lodging here."
He goaded on Gringolet with gilded, sharp spurs,
Who moved forward, fortuitously finding the road
That in due time drew to the drawbridge ahead
      That knight.   780
    But, barred and bolted fast,
    That bridge was raised upright.
    No blustering winter's blast
    Could bring that castle blight.

That horseman then halted and hung on the bank   785
Of the deep, double ditch that defended the place.
The wide castle walls in the water stood tall;
They rose to the rarest of rooftops above,
Climbing high to the cornices, keen and sublime.
In the best style, bold courses were built on those walls,   790
Great towers and turrets teeming above
With loopholes for looking, launching arrows in war.
A barbican better that bold knight hadn't seen.
He beheld the house; it was high and fine.
It too had its towers, topped with high spires   795
And pinnacles, precious and pointed at the top
With crowns that were crafted and carved with skill.
The chalky, strong chimneys were chiseled with care,
Like the towers and turrets, tall and pure white.
There were pinnacles painted and placed everywhere   800
About the broad battlements so boldly it seemed
That the castle was cut out of cardboard or paper.
On his horse Sir Gawain thought it grand and fine;
He wished that he were in that wide, lovely bailey
Well harbored in that hostel till holidays there   805
      Should end.
    He hailed. At his behest,
    A guardian, gracious, grand,
    Arrived, took his request,
    And found him a fine friend.   810

'Gode sir,' quoþ Gawan, 'woldez þou go myn ernde
To þe heȝ lorde of þis hous, herber to craue?'
'Ȝe, Peter!' quoþ þe porter, 'and purely I trowee
Þat ȝe be, wyȝe, welcum to won quyle yow lykez.'
Þen ȝede þe wyȝe ȝerne and com aȝayn swyþe   815
And folke frely hym wyth to fonge þe knyȝt.
Þay let doun þe grete draȝt and derely out ȝeden
And kneled doun on her knes vpon þe colde erþe
To welcum þis ilk wyȝ as worþy hom þoȝt.
Þay ȝolden hym þe brode ȝate, ȝarked vp wyde,   820
And he hem raysed rekenly and rod ouer þe brygge.
Sere seggez hym sesed by sadel quel he lyȝt
And syþen stabeled his stede stif men innoȝe.
Knyȝtez and swyerez comen doun þenne
For to bryng þis buurne wyth blys into halle.   825
Quen he hef vp his helme þer hiȝed innoghe
For to hent hit at his honde, þe hende to seruen;
His bronde and his blasoun boþe þay token.
Þen haylsed he ful hendly þo haþelez vchone
And mony proud mon þer presed þat prynce to honour.   830
Alle hasped in his heȝ wede to halle þay hym wonnen,
Þer fayre fyre vpon flet fersly brenned.
Þenne þe lorde of þe lede loutez fro his chambre
For to mete wyth menske þe mon on þe flor.
He sayde, 'Ȝe ar welcum to welde, as yow lykez,   835
Þat here is; al is yowre awen to haue at yowre wylle
        And welde.'
    'Graunt mercy,' quoþ Gawayn;
    'Þer Kryst hit yow forȝelde.'
    As frekez þat semed fayn   840
    Ayþer oþer in armez con felde.

Gawayn glyȝt on þe gome þat godly hym gret,
And þuȝt hit a bolde burne þat þe burȝ aȝte,
A hoge haþel for þe nonez and of hyghe eldee.
Brode, bryȝt watz his berde and al beuer-hwed,   845
Sturne, stif on þe stryþþe on stalworth schonkez,
Felle face as þe fyre, and fre of hys speche;
And wel hym semed forsoþe, as þe segge þuȝt,
To lede a lortschyp in lee of leudez ful gode.
Þe lorde hym charred to a chambre and chesly cumaundez   850
To delyuer hym a leude hym loȝly to serue;
And þere were boun at his bode burnez innoȝe
Þat broȝt hym to a bryȝt boure þer beddyng watz noble:
Of cortynes of clene sylk wyth cler golde hemmez
And couertorez ful curious with comlych panez   855
Of bryȝt blaunmer aboue, enbrawded bisydez,

"Good sir," said Gawain. "Would you go to your lord?
I am seeking a shelter, a safe place to stay."
Said the porter, "By Peter, I pray and believe
That you'll win here a welcome as warm as you'd like!"
In no time he retreated, returning in moments.   815
A crowd had courteously come to greet him.
They let down the drawbridge and duly came out.
Next they kneeled on the numbing, cold ground
To welcome this wayfarer as worthy of honor.
For Sir Gawain the great, wooden gates were raised.   820
He requested they rise; then he rode on the bridge.
As he stepped down, his saddle by servants was held,
And his steed to the stables with sure hands was taken.
Then the squires descended, and stalwart, true knights,
To welcome the warrior with warmth to the hall.   825
Gawain held out his helmet and handed it forth.
They sent it to servants, who received it with care,
And received, too, his sword and his shield, both bright.
Sir Gawain graciously greeted those knights;
All those proud men pressed near to pay their respects.   830
They escorted him courteously to the court in his armor.
There the fire was flaming fiercely in the hearth.
The host of that house in haste issued forth
Where he met that man in a mannerly way.
"Good sir," he said, "you certainly are   835
And will be most welcome to whatever you desire in
        This place."
            Then Gawain says, "Good Mercy!
            May Christ give you such grace
            As you, sir, show to me."   840
            As brothers they embrace.

Gawain looked on that lord whose largess he enjoyed:
The head of that house was a high prince, indeed,
A man bold and mighty, of middling age.
His thick beard was beaver-hued, bright and wide;   845
He stood on two sturdy and stalwart legs.
Though his face was as fierce as bright fire, his speech
Was judicious and gentle. Gawain judged him a great,
Noble leader and lord of a large, worthy house.
He was led by that lord to a large, sumptuous chamber   850
And assigned there a servant to see to his needs.
Many well-mannered men quickly moved up to him.
To a bedroom they brought him, abundant and fair:
It was crowded with clean, silken curtains, gold-hemmed,
And the comeliest coverlet, keen with designs,   855
Edged with wondrous, wide borders of white shining fur;

Rudelez rennande on ropez, red golde ryngez,
Tapytez tyȝt to þe woȝe, of tuly and tars,
And vnder fete, on þe flet, of folȝande sute.
Þer he watz dispoyled, wyth spechez of myerþe,   860
Þe burn of his bruny and of his bryȝt wedez;
Ryche robes ful rad renkkez hem broȝten
For to charge and to chaunge and chose of þe best.
Sone as he on hent and happed þerinne,
Þat sete on hym semly, wyth saylande skyrtez,   865
Þe ver by his uisage verayly hit semed
Welneȝ to vche haþel, alle on hwes,
Lowande and lufly alle his lymmez vnder;
Þat a comloker knyȝt neuer Kryst made,
         Hem þoȝt.   870
     Wheþen in worlde he were,
     Hit semed as he moȝt
     Be prynce withouten pere
     In felde þer felle men foȝt.

A cheyer byfore þe chemné, þer charcole brenned,   875
Watz grayþed for Sir Gawan grayþely with cloþez:
Whyssynes vpon queldepoyntes, þat koynt wer boþe;
And þenne a meré mantyle watz on þat mon cast,
Of a broun bleeaunt, enbrauded ful ryche
And fayre furred wythinne with fellez of þe best,   880
Alle of ermyn in erde, his hode of þe same.
And he sete in þat settel semlych ryche
And achaufed hym chefly, and þenne his cher mended.
Sone watz telded vp a tabil on trestez ful fayre,
Clad wyth a clene cloþe þat cler quyt schewed,   885
Sanap and salure and syluerin sponez.
Þe wyȝe wesche at his wylle and went to his mete.
Seggez hym serued semly innoȝe
Wyth sere sewes and sete, sesounde of þe best,
Doublefelde, as hit fallez, and fele kyn fischez—   890
Summe baken in bred, summe brad on þe gledez,
Summe soþen, summe in sewe sauered with spyces—
And ay sawses so sleȝe þat þe segge lyked.
Þe freke calde hit a fest ful frely and ofte
Ful hendely, quen alle þe haþeles rehayted hym at onez   895
         As hende,
     'Þis penaunce now ȝe take
     And eft hit schal amende.'
     Þat mon much merþe con make,
     For wyn in his hed þat wende.   900

Þenne watz spyed and spured vpon spare wyse,

On strong ropes curtains ran, with rings of red gold;
Toulousian and Tharsian tapestries, too,
Were on wondrous, bright walls and, as well, underfoot.
The attendants talked as they took off his things: 860
Both his marvelous mail and his mighty, bold armor.
Then rich robes arrived, which they wrapped him in well;
And with goodly, fresh garments was Gawain attired.
Just as soon as he'd slung on his shoulders the cloth—
For it folded and flowed on his form beauteously—   865
His limbs looked to all both so lovely and bright
That it seemed as if spring had just suddenly come
And was gleaming and glowing in glorious hues!
Jesus Christ had created no comelier prince,
    They thought.   870
    No one could find a knight,
    However hard he sought,
    To match this man's great might
    In field where fierce men fought!

Near a fire that flamed there was furnished a chair   875
That was covered with cloth, and carefully spread
With quilted, fine cushions, each craftily made.
That man in a marvelous mantle was dressed.
It was bright silk, embroidered beauteously,
And fur lined most fairly, fashioned within   880
With a wide fur, wondrous and white, of ermine.
He sat in that seat, which was seemly and rich,
And grew glad within at the glare of the fire.
A table on trestles was brought to the room—
It was clad in a cloth that was clean and fair—   885
With a silver saltcellar and spoons and napkin.
Gawain washed as he wished and went to his meal,
Which was served with skill by the servants at hand.
There were sumptuously seasoned thick stews and broths.
Of the fish that were furnished in fine, double helpings, 890
Some were baked in bread crumbs, and some broiled on coals,
Some were boiled, some with broth had been basted all day.
The dishes were dainty and dear to Gawain.
He found it a feast fully worthy of praise.
The servants were seeking Sir Gawain's approval   895
    And said:
    "As penance, precious prince,
    Accept this simple spread.
    You'll later feast!" He assents.
    Red wine had reached his head.   900

They requested their questions and queries he answer;

Bi preué poyntez of þat prynce put to hymseluen,
Þat he beknew cortaysly of þe court þat he were
Þat aþel Arthure þe hende haldez hym one,
Þat is þe ryche ryal kyng of þe Rounde Table,   905
And hit watz Wawen hymself þat in þat won syttez,
Comen to þat Krystmasse, as case hym þen lymped.
When þe lorde hade lerned þat he þe leude hade,
Loude laȝed he þerat, so lef hit hym þoȝt,
And alle þe men in þat mote maden much joye   910
To apere in his presense prestly þat tyme
Þat alle prys and prowes and pured þewes
Apendes to hys persoun and praysed is euer,
Byfore alle men vpon molde his mensk is þe most.
Vch segge ful softly sayde to his fere,   915
'Now schal we semlych se sleȝtez of þewez
And þe teccheles termes of talkyng noble.
Wich spede is in speche vnspurd may we lerne,
Syn we haf fonged þat fyne fader of nurture.
God hatz geuen vus His grace godly forsoþe,   920
Þat such a gest as Gawan grauntez vus to haue
When burnez blyþe of His burþe schal sitte
        And synge.
    In menyng of manerez mere
    Þis burne now schal vus bryng.   925
    I hope þat may hym here
    Schal lerne of luf-talkyng.'

Bi þat þe diner watz done and þe dere vp
Hit watz neȝ at þe niyȝt neȝed þe tyme.
Chaplaynez to þe chapeles chosen þe gate,   930
Rungen ful rychely, ryȝt as þay schulden,
To þe hersum euensong of þe hyȝe tyde.
Þe lorde loutes þerto and þe lady als;
Into a cumly closet coyntly ho entrez.
Gawan glydez ful gay and gos þeder sone.   935
Þe lorde laches hym by þe lappe and ledez hym to sytte
And couþly hym knowez and callez hym his nome
And sayde he watz þe welcomest wyȝe of þe worlde.
And he hym þonkked þroly; and ayþer halched oþer
And seten soberly samen þe seruise quyle.   940
Þenne lyst þe lady to loke on þe knyȝt;
Þenne com ho of hir closet with mony cler burdez.
Ho watz þe fayrest in felle, of flesche and of lyre
And of compas and colour and costes, of alle oþer,
And wener þen Wenore, as þe wyȝe þoȝt.   945
Ho ches þurȝ þe chaunsel to cheryche þat hende.
Anoþer lady hir lad bi þe lyft honde

To that prince they politely put personal words.
Of the court that he'd come from he courteously told:
He had hailed from the high, famous house of King Arthur,
From the royal Round Table, renowned far and wide.   905
Their guest is Sir Gawain, whom they'd gallantly welcomed
When he came, as it chanced, to their Christmastide feast.
When the lord there had learned whom he'd let in his door,
He let out a laugh, loud and long; he was pleased.
The courtiers cried in that castle for joy   910
And promptly appeared in the presence of Gawain.
For his prowess that prince was reputed, for his worth.
His person was praised as perfectly noble.
"This bold knight is the best; he's the bravest on earth,"
Each man said, as he stood aside, to his neighbor.   915
"Now we'll certainly see both the seemliest manners
And the phrases and figures of faultless discourse.
We will hear one handy in the high art of speech,
Since the paragon of politeness has paid us a visit.
We've been graced by the goodness of God, to be sure,   920
For a guest such as Gawain He has granted us all.
When we sit and sing, when we celebrate Christ
        Above,
    We'll learn to be polite;
    Our polish will improve,   925
    When we hear this high knight
    Discourse on courtly love."

When the dinner was done and that dear knight had risen,
The dark night had drawn nigh; it had nearly arrived.
To the choicest of chapels the chaplains together   930
Repaired to ring bells, as was right and pious,
For the solemn evensong of that season so high.
The lord with his lady led the way there.
With a gait very graceful she walked to her pew.
Sir Gawain with gladness and gaiety followed,   935
As the lord slowly led him along by the sleeve;
Called the knight by his name, as if known to him well.
While he welcomed him warmly with words in earnest,
Gawain thoroughly thanked him. Throughout they embraced.
Through the service they sat; both were solemn and pious.   940
The lady, though, liked much to look upon Gawain.
With her mild, lovely maidens, she moved from the pew,
In her face far the fairest and finest of all,
In her body and bearing the best on the earth.
She was goodlier than Guinevere, Gawain believed.   945
To greet that great lady Sir Gawain walked forth.
By the left hand a lady was leading her then.

Þat watz alder þen ho, an auncian hit semed,
And heȝly honowred with haþelez aboute.
Bot vnlyke on to loke þo ladyes were: 950
For if þe ȝonge watz ȝep, ȝolȝe watz þat oþer;
Riche red on þat on rayled ayquere,
Rugh ronkled chekez þat oþer on rolled;
Kerchofes of þat on wyth mony cler perlez;
Hir brest and hir bryȝt þrote, bare displayed,   955
Schon schyrer þen snawe þat schedes on hillez;
Þat oþer wyth a gorger watz gered ouer þe swyre,
Chymbled ouer hir blake chyn with chalk-quyte vayles,
Hir frount folden in sylk, enfoubled ayquere,
Toret and treleted with tryflez aboute,   960
Þat noȝt watz bare of þat burde bot þe blake broȝes,
Þe tweyne yȝen and þe nase, þe naked lyppez,
And þose were soure to se and sellyly blered,
A mensk lady on molde mon may hir calle,
    For Gode!   965
    Hir body watz schort and þik,
    Hir buttokez balȝ and brode;
    More lykkerwys on to lyk
    Watz þat scho hade on lode.

When Gawayn glyȝt on þat gay þat graciously loked,   970
Wyth leue laȝt of þe lorde, he lent hem aȝaynes.
Þe alder he haylses, heldande ful lowe,
Þe loueloker he lappez a lyttel in armez.
He kysses hir comlyly and knyȝtly he melez.
Þay kallen hym of aquoyntaunce and he hit quyk askez   975
To be her seruaunt sothly, if hemself lyked.
Þay tan hym bytwene hem, wyth talkyng hym leden
To chambre, to chemné, and chefly þay asken
Spycez, þat vnsparely men speded hom to bryng,
And þe wynnelych wyne þerwith vche tyme.   980
Þe lorde luflych aloft lepez ful ofte,
Mynned merthe to be made vpon mony syþez,
Hent heȝly of his hode and on a spere henged
And wayned hom to wynne þe worchip þerof
Þat most myrþe myȝt meue þat Crystenmas whyle.   985
'And I schal fonde, bi my fayth, to fylter wyth þe best,
Er me wont þe wede, with help of my frendez.'
Þus wyth laȝande lotez þe lorde hit tayt makez
For to glade Sir Gawayn with gomnez in halle
    Þat nyȝt,   990
    Til þat hit watz tyme
    Þe lord comaundet lyȝt.
    Sir Gawen his leue con nyme
    And to his bed hym diȝt.

She'd lived many more years than her younger companion
And was held in honor by the high courtiers.
But two ladies less like, one would look hard to find; 950
For if one was quite withered, most winsome was the other.
The young beauty seemed blushing and bathed in pink light,
While the roughest of wrinkles were riddling the other.
The one had a headdress, hung with fine pearls,
And her beauteous breast and bare neck were exposed, 955
Where they shone like the snow as it shimmers on hills.
As a covering, a coarse neckerchief wore the other;
It bedecked her black chin and was boldly milk white.
Silk fabrics enfolded her forehead closely,
That were trellised and turreted, tightly embroidered; 960
So the black brows were bared, like the blistered, old lips.
Nothing else was naked but the nose and the eyes,
Unsightly to see and exceedingly old.
A more dignified dame for that day no one could
      Provide. 965
    Her frame was heavy, hooked;
    Her buttocks big and wide.
    So much more lovely looked
    The beauty by her side!

Sir Gawain then gazed on that gracious, young lady. 970
With the leave of the lord, he politely went over;
Approaching the elder, he earnestly bowed;
And the lovelier lady he lightly embraced,
Courteously kissed, and true compliments gave.
When they welcomed him warmly, his wishes he stated 975
To follow them, faithful, their fond servant ever.
They led that lord—talking lightly the while—
To a room that was richly arrayed for the nonce.
There they sent for spice, which was speedily brought,
Along with red wine for the warming of hearts. 980
Then leaping up lightly, the lord of that house
Reminded the men to be merry that night.
He hung his hood on the haft of a spear:
Who made the most mirth that merry Christmas
Would win that award, the lord warmly declared. 985
"And I too will contend here to take this hood;
I'll compete for that prize before parting with it!"
Thus that lord gaily laughed to lighten the hall,
And to gladden with games Sir Gawain, his friend
      And guest. 990
    Lights blazed without abate
    (The royal lord's request).
    And mirth was made till late,
    When Gawain retired for rest.

On þe morne, as vch mon mynez þat tyme   995
Þat Dryȝtyn for oure destyné to deȝe watz borne,
Wele waxez in vche a won in worlde for His sake.
So did hit þere on þat day, þurȝ dayntés mony:
Boþe at mes and at mele messes ful quaynt
Derf men vpon dece drest of þe best.   1000
Þe olde auncian wyf heȝest ho syttez;
Þe lorde lufly her by lent as I trowe.
Gawan and þe gay burde togeder þay seten
Euen inmyddez, as þe messe metely come,
And syþen þurȝ al þe sale, as hem best semed,   1005
Bi vche grome at his degré grayþely watz serued.
Þer watz mete, þer watz myrþe, þer watz much joye,
Þat for to telle þerof hit me tene were,
And to poynte hit ȝet I pyned me parauenture.
Bot ȝet I wot þat Wawen and þe wale burde   1010
Such comfort of her compaynye caȝten togeder
Þurȝ her dere dalyaunce of her derne wordez,
Wyth clene cortays carp closed fro fylþe,
Þat hor play watz passande vche prynce gomen,
        In vayres.   1015
    Trumpez and nakerys,
    Much pypyng þer repayres.
    Vche mon tented hys
    And þay two tented þayres.

Much dut watz þer dryuen þat day and þat oþer,   1020
And þe þryd as þro þronge in þerafter—
Þe joye of Sayn Jonez day watz gentyle to here
And watz þe last of þe layk leudez þer þoȝten.
Þer wer gestes to go vpon þe gray morne;
Forþy wonderly þay woke and þe wyn dronken,   1025
Daunsed ful dreȝly wyth dere carolez.
At þe last, when hit watz late, þay lachen her leue,
Vchon to wende on his way þat watz wyȝe stronge.
Gawan gef hym god day; þe godmon hym lachchez,
Ledes hym to his awen chambre, þe chymné bysyde,   1030
And þere he draȝez hym on dryȝe and derely hym þonkkez
Of þe wynne worschip þat he hym wayned hade
As to honour his hous on þat hyȝe tyde
And enbelyse his burȝ with his bele chere.
'Iwysse, sir, quyl I leue me worþez þe better   1035
Þat Gawayn hatz ben my gest at Goddez awen fest.'
'Grant merci, sir,' quoþ Gawayn, 'in god fayth hit is yowrez,
Al þe honour is your awen—þe heȝe Kyng yow ȝelde—
And I am, wyȝe, at your wylle to worch youre hest,
As I am halden þerto in hyȝe and in loȝe   1040

On the morning when men are mindful that God ___ warrior-like 995
To be slain for the sake of our souls was born,
Great happiness hovers in houses on earth.
Likewise those lodgings knew lightness and joy.
At the meals there was merriment, mirth in between;
On the dais the daintiest dishes were served. 1000
In the chief, honored chair, the ancient wife sat.
By her side, I believe, was the bounteous lord.
By the gracious and gay lady Gawain was seated
At midtable. The meal was marvelously brought;
At that feast the finest were first richly served, 1005
Then down by degree the dear guests as well.
There was meat and merriness, mirth, and deep joy;
To describe the resplendence would surely elude me,
In truth, if I tried to portray it at all.
But I know that Sir Gawain was next to the lady. 1010
Such company, comely, brought comfort to both;
For their dainty dalliance was dear to each other.
It was perfectly proper, pure and chaste.
Their skill in the sport of speaking all must
     Commend.
    Fine trumpets fill the air 1015
    With sounds that softly blend.
    Each man makes much mirth there;
    Those two each other tend.

Thus much mirth was made that day and the next; 1020
No less gamesome, good-humored, and gay was the third;
Of Saint John's Day, the joy was both gentle and full,
The last, thought the ladies and lords, of the feast.
So that party, prepared to depart in the morning,
With wassails and wine stayed awake late that night. 1025
All dallied and danced to the dearest of songs.
It was late when the last there had left that bright hall,
Each one went to wend his own way, as was fit.
Sir Gawain then gave his good-byes. But the host
To his chamber with charm—he so cherished that guest— 1030
Led Sir Gawain and gratefully gave him to know
He'd been graciously granted the greatest of honors:
To be holiday host to the highest of knights,
Who had deigned to adorn his dwelling as guest.
"While I live, my lord, I believe I shall thrive, 1035
Since Gawain was my guest at our God's holy feast!"
Said Sir Gawain, "May God in His goodness reward you!
All the honor's your own, I assure you, good sir.
At your service I stand. I'll succumb to your will.
I'm beholden, good host; your behest I will do 1040

Bi riȝt.'
Þe lorde fast can hym payne
To holde lenger þe knyȝt;
To hym answrez Gawayn
Bi non way þat he myȝt.   1045

Then frayned þe freke ful fayre at himseluen
Quat derue dede had hym dryuen at þat dere tyme
So kenly fro þe kyngez kourt to kayre al his one,
Er þe halidayez holly were halet out of toun.
'Forsoþe, sir,' quoþ þe segge, 'ȝe sayn bot þe trawþe.   1050
A heȝe ernde and a hasty me hade fro þo wonez,
For I am sumned myselfe to sech to a place
I not in worlde whederwarde to wende hit to fynde.
I nolde bot if I hit negh myȝt on Nw Ȝeres morne
For alle þe londe inwyth Logres, so me oure Lorde help!   1055
Forþy, sir, þis enquest I require yow here:
Þat ȝe me telle with trawþe, if euer ȝe tale herde
Of þe Grene Chapel, quere hit on grounde stondez,
And of þe knyȝt þat hit kepes, of colour of grene.
Þer watz stabled bi statut a steuen vus bytwene   1060
To mete þat mon at þat mere, ȝif I myȝt last;
And of þat ilk Nw Ȝere bot neked now wontez,
And I wolde loke on þat lede, if God me let wolde,
Gladloker, bi Goddez Sun, þen any god welde!
Forþi, iwysse, bi ȝowre wylle, wende me bihoues;   1065
Naf I now to busy bot bare þre dayez,
And me als fayn to falle feye as fayly of myyn ernde.'
Þenne laȝande quoþ þe lorde, 'Now leng þe byhoues,
For I schal teche yow to þat terme bi þe tymez ende.
Þe Grene Chapayle vpon grounde greue yow no more   1070
Bot ȝe schal be in yowre bed, burne, at þyn ese
Quyle forth dayez and ferk on þe fyrst of þe ȝere
And cum to þat merk at mydmorn, to make quat yow likez
          In spenne.
      Dowellez whyle New Ȝeres daye   1075
      And rys and raykez þenne.
      Mon schal yow sette in waye;
      Hit is not two myle henne.'

Þenne watz Gawan ful glad and gomenly he laȝed:
'Now I þonk yow þryuandely þurȝ alle oþer þynge.   1080
Now acheued is my chaunce, I schal at your wylle
Dowelle and ellez do quat ȝe demen.'
Þenne sesed hym þe syre and set hym bysyde,
Let þe ladiez be fette to lyke hem þe better.
Þer watz seme solace by hemself stille;   1085

From this day."
He asked him if, perchance,
He longer might delay.
"Alas," replied that prince.
"At court I cannot stay."   1045

That leader and lord politely inquired
What great quest from his court had thus called him away,
What had caused him to quit his own king, all to ride
On the highest of holidays halls could observe.
Said Gawain the good knight, "You've guessed at the truth.   1050
I am called from my court on a quest, high and urgent.
I've been summoned to seek a mysterious place,
But must wend unaware of its whereabouts now;
I'd prefer, sir, to find it before New Year's morn
Than to hold all of Logres, may the Lord be my guide!   1055
Therefore, prince, I am pleading, appealing to you;
Will you tell me in truth if you've tales ever heard
Of the ground or the grove where the Green Chapel stands,
Of that chapel's bold keeper, who's colored all green?
For a bargain most binding, with bold oaths, we've struck: 1060
I'm to meet that same man on the morning, this New Year
Nigh approaching. That place we've appointed before.
I would look on that lord, if allowed by our God,
Much more gladly, by God's Son, than gain endless wealth!
I must start on my search, therefore, should you agree;   1065
For to locate that lord I have less than three days.
I'd prefer to fall dead than to fail in my quest."
The lord began laughing: "Then linger a while!
I will certainly show you that site in due time,
Yes, the ground of the Green Chapel. Grow easy, then!   1070
You may bask in your bed, you may be at your ease
Before you go forth on the first of the year,
And by midmorning make it. Good man, until then
        Please stay.
    Thus bask about, brave knight.   1075
    Here dwell till New Year's Day.
    Be sure you'll see that site.
    It's not two miles away!"

Sir Gawain was gladdened and gave out a laugh:
"My host, you have my wholehearted thanks!   1080
As my goal has been gained, I will gladly accept;
I shall dwell here and do what you deem is the best."
By his side the lord seated Sir Gawain, and had
The ladies let in, delightful and pure.
Those two men joy and merriment made. The lord   1085

Þe lorde let for luf lotez so myry
As wyȝ þat wolde of his wyte, ne wyst quat he myȝt.
Þenne he carped to þe knyȝt, criande loude,
'Ȝe han demed to do þe dede þat I bidde—
Wyl ȝe halde þis hes here at þys onez?'   1090
'Ȝe, sir, forsoþe,' sayd þe segge trwe,
'Whyl I byde in yowre borȝe be bayn to ȝowre hest.'
'For ȝe haf trauaylet,' quoþ þe tulk, 'towen fro ferre,
And syþen waked me wyth, ȝe arn not wel waryst
Nauþer of sostnaunce ne of slepe, soþly I knowe.   1095
Ȝe schal lenge in your lofte and lyȝe in your ese
Tomorn quyle þe messequyle and to mete wende
When ȝe wyl wyth my wyf, þat wyth yow schal sitte
And comfort yow with compayny til I to cort torne.
      Ȝe lende   1100
   And I schal erly ryse;
   On huntyng wyl I wende.'
   Gauayn grantez alle þyse,
   Hym heldande, as þe hende.

'Ȝet firre,' quoþ þe freke, 'a forwarde we make: 1105
Quatsoeuer I wynne in þe wod hit worþez to yourez
And quat chek so ȝe acheue chaunge me þerforne.
Swete, swap we so: sware with trawþe,
Queþer leude so lymp lere oþer better.'
'Bi God,' quoþ Gawayn þe gode, 'I grant þertylle;   1110
And þat yow lyst for to layke lef hit me þynkes.'
'Who bryngez vus þis beuerage, þis bargayn is maked,'
So sayde þe lorde of þat lede; þay laȝed vchone.
Þay dronken and daylyeden and dalten vntyȝtel,
Þise lordez and ladyez, quyle þat hem lyked,   1115
And syþen with frenkysch fare and fele fayre lotez
Þay stoden and stemed and stylly speken,
Kysten ful comlyly and kaȝten her leue.
With mony leude ful lyȝt and lemande torches
Vche burne to his bed watz broȝt at þe laste   1120
      Ful softe.
   To bed ȝet er þay ȝede,
   Recorded couenauntez ofte;
   Þe olde lorde of þat leude
   Cowþe wel halde layk alofte.   1125

III

Ful erly bifore þe day þe folk vprysen.
Gestes þat go wolde hor gromez þay calden
And þay busken vp bilyue blonkkez to sadel,

Was with Gawain so gleeful and giddy, he seemed
Like a man almost mad: he was mirthful and gay.
He spoke most unsparingly, saying aloud:
"Dearest prince, you have pledged to perform what I ask.
Will you act as agreed, will you honor your vow?"   1090
"Good sir," Gawain said, "Yes, I certainly will.
I'll obey your behest as I bide in your court."
"You have traveled far, toiled, are tired," he said.
"No rest you've received since you've reveled with us.
I am sure you lack sleep and sustenance now.   1095
Thus you'll lie until late. Yes, you'll linger in bed
Until Mass comes tomorrow. Then your meal will be served
As you wish. If you will, my wife will attend,
Your company keep in the court till I'm back.
    Abide!   1100
  But early I'll be woken.
  On horse to hunt I'll ride
  For sport." With what he'd spoken
  That precious prince complied.

"But we'll cast," he continued, "a covenant first: 1105
What I win in the woods or the wilds will be yours;
What you gain you will give, bad or good, in exchange.
So now swear to it; seal this swap with an oath:
What we gain we will give, whether great or else poor."
Said Gawain, "By God, I'll agree to your terms!   1110
I am glad you are given to games, to be sure."
"If a servant will serve us, we'll seal this with drink,"
Said the lord. Both men laughed aloud at their game.
Then the lords and ladies talked lightly and drank,
All lingered as late as they liked, giddily.   1115
With kindness and courtesy, customs of France,
They stood; then softly they said their good nights,
And together kissed tenderly, taking their leave.
Then by good servants, guiding with glowing, bright lamps,
They were brought to their bounteous beds, where they took 1120
    Their rest.
  By then they had their vow
  Repeatedly expressed.
  That happy host knew how
  To give games to a guest!   1125

III

The dear guests before dawn the next day arose.
Those guests who would go had to gather their servants,
Who hurried to harness the horses with saddles,

Tyffen her takles, trussen her males;
Richen hem þe rychest, to ryde alle arayde,   1130
Lepen vp ly3tly, lachen her brydeles,
Vche wy3e on his way þer hym wel lyked.
Þe leue lorde of þe londe watz not þe last
Arayed for þe rydyng with renkkez ful mony;
Ete a sop hastyly, when he hade herde masse,   1135
With bugle to bent-felde he buskez bylyue.
By þat any dayly3t lemed vpon erþe,
He with his haþeles on hy3e horsses weren.
Þenne þise cacheres þat couþe cowpled hor houndez,
Vnclosed þe kenel dore and calde hem þeroute,   1140
Blwe bygly in buglez þre bare mote.
Braches bayed þerfore and breme noyse maked;
And þay chastysed and charred on chasyng þat went,
A hundreth of hunteres, as I haf herde telle,
    Of þe best.   1145
  To trystors vewters 3od,
  Couples huntes of kest;
  Þer ros for blastez gode
  Gret rurd in þat forest.

At þe fyrst quethe of þe quest quaked þe wylde.   1150
Der drof in þe dale, doted for drede,
Hi3ed to þe hy3e, bot heterly þay were
Restayed with þe stablye, þat stoutly ascryed.
Þay let þe herttez haf þe gate, with þe hy3e hedes,
Þe breme bukkez also, with hor brode paumez;   1155
For þe fre lorde hade defende in fermysoun tyme
Þat þer schulde no mon meue to þe male dere.
Þe hindez were halden in with 'Hay!' and 'War!'
Þe does dryuen with gret dyn to þe depe sladez.
Þer my3t mon se, as þay slypte, slentyng of arwes;   1160
At vche wende vnder wande wapped a flone,
Þat bigly bote on þe broun with ful brode hedez.
What! þay brayen and bleden, bi bonkkez þay de3en,
And ay rachches in a res radly hem fol3es,
Hunterez wyth hy3e horne hasted hem after   1165
Wyth such a crakkande kry as klyffes haden brusten.
What wylde so atwaped wy3es þat schotten
Watz al toraced and rent at þe resayt,
Bi þay were tened at þe hy3e and taysed to þe wattrez,
Þe ledez were so lerned at þe lo3e trysteres;   1170
And þe grehoundez so grete þat geten hem bylyue
And hem tofylched as fast as frekez my3t loke
    Þer ry3t.
  Þe lorde, for blys abloy,

To take care of the tackles, and tend to the bags.
With their riding gear richly arrayed, those who left   1130
With skill mounted steeds and took softly the reins;
Each one took his way to his wonted estate.
The lord of that land no later rose up:
With his retinue ready for riding he sat
And that morning heard Mass. Then he meagerly ate.   1135
To the high fields he hurried with hunting horn then.
Just as daylight was dawning—it dimly arose—
That host was up high on his horse, with his men.
The helpers harnessed their hounds in matched pairs,
And unlocked the gates, unloosing those dogs   1140
By the blowing of bugles: three bold, single notes.
Those dogs raised a din not diminished until
They were scolded, restrained by the shouts of the men:
A hundred brave hunters, I've heard, every one
          renowned.   1145
     The servants, staying still,
     At last unleashed each hound.
     From bugles, sharp and shrill,
     The forest filled with sound.

All at once in those woods, the wild beasts quaked.   1150
Through the dale, the deer began dashing in fright;
Ascending for safety, they sped for high ground,
But the beaters sent them back with blows and loud shouts,
Though the high-antlered harts and the haughty, strong bucks—
With their long, branching antlers—were allowed to slip past.   1155
For that high lord prohibited hunting male deer;
None would capture nor kill them at close-season's term.
But the hinds were herded with *Heys!* and loud *Whoas!*
And the does with the din were thus driven to fields
Where the air was with arrows' arcs everywhere filled.   1160
At the tiniest movement an arrow was shot;
Its broad head would bite in the brown flesh at once.
How they brayed while they bled on the banks where they died!
Always harried by hounds, they were hotly pursued
By the hunters with high horns and hastened along.   1165
The sound of it seemed like the splitting of rocks!
Any doe that had dashed from a deathblow was then
Hunted down to the dales and driven to streams,
Was received, hotly seized, and slaughtered with knives.
They were skillful and swift at the stations below;   1170
The hounds were so huge that they hauled down the deer
With their fangs in a flash; they were faster by much
          Than sight.
     And gladdened, gleeful, gay,

Ful oft con launce and ly3t,   1175
And drof þat day wyth joy
Thus to þe derk ny3t.

Þus laykez þis lorde by lynde-wodez euez
And Gawayn þe god mon in gay bed lygez,
Lurkkez quyl þe dayly3t lemed on þe wowes,   1180
Vnder couertour ful clere, cortyned aboute.
And as in slomeryng he slode, sle3ly he herde
A littel dyn at his dor and derfly vpon;
And he heuez vp his hed out of þe cloþes,
A corner of þe cortyn he ca3t vp a lyttel,   1185
And waytez warly þiderwarde quat hit be my3t.
Hit watz þe ladi, loflyest to beholde,
Þat dro3 þe dor after hir ful dernly and stylle
And bo3ed towarde þe bed; and þe burne schamed
And layde hym doun lystyly and let as he slepte.   1190
And ho stepped stilly and stel to his bedde,
Kest vp þe cortyn and creped withinne
And set hir ful softly on þe bed-syde
And lenged þere selly longe to loke quen he wakened.
Þe lede lay lurked a ful longe quyle,   1195
Compast in his concience to quat þat cace my3t
Meue oþer amount. To meruayle hym þo3t;
Bot 3et he sayde in hymself, 'More semly hit were
To aspye wyth my spelle in space quat ho wolde.'
Þen he wakenede and wroth and to hir warde torned   1200
And vnlouked his y3e-lyddez and let as hym wondered
And sayned hym, as bi his sa3e þe sauer to worthe,
        With hande.
    Wyth chynne and cheke ful swete,
    Boþe quit and red in blande,   1205
    Ful lufly con ho lete
    Wyth lyppez smal la3ande:

'God moroun, Sir Gawayn,' sayde þat gay lady,
'3e ar a sleper vnsly3e, þat mon may slyde hider.
Now ar 3e tan astyt! Bot true vus may schape,   1210
I schal bynde yow in your bedde—þat be 3e trayst.'
Al la3ande þe lady lauced þo bourdez.
'Goud moroun, gay,' quoþ Gawayn þe blyþe,
'Me schal worþe at your wille and þat me wel lykez,
For I 3elde me 3ederly and 3e3e after grace;   1215
And þat is þe best, be my dome, for me byhouez nede!'
(And þus he bourded a3ayn with mony a blyþe la3ter.)
'Bot wolde 3e, lady louely, þen, leue me grante
And deprece your prysoun and pray hym to ryse,

> That lord would ride, alight,   1175
> Again and again, all day,
> Until the dark of night.

Thus the lord by the linden trees laughs in his sport,
While the good man, Sir Gawain, in gay bedsheets lies.
There he lingers till light has lit up the walls   1180
And the canopy covered with curtains about him.
Then half-sleeping, half-waking, he hears the soft sound
Of the door as it's deftly, deliberately breached.
He holds up his head from the heavy bedclothes
And, catching a corner of the curtain, lifts it up.   1185
Gawain gingerly glances to glean what it is.
It's the lady there, lovely and lingering as she
Slowly draws closed the door with a deft, quiet touch!
She steps noiselessly near. Now that knight is ashamed;
He turns, lightly tossing, pretending to sleep.   1190
She steps up with stealth to the side of the bed
And, catching the curtain, creeps fully within.
After seating herself on the side of the bed,
She lingers there long, as she looks on Sir Gawain,
Who is still feigning sleep, breathing softly and deep.   1195
All the while he is wondering what this might mean;
It's amazing, amounts to a marvel, he thinks.
But he says to himself, "I should surely inquire,
Through discourse discover her desire in good time."
So he stretches and stirs, to show he is waking,   1200
Looks surprised to see her thus sitting nearby,
And signs himself swiftly as if his salvation
> He seeks.
> Her face was fine and fair;
> Both pink and pure her cheeks.   1205
> With goodly, gracious air
> And sparkling smile, she speaks.

"Dear Sir Gawain, good morning," she graciously said,
"You must sleep quite unsafely; I've slipped in with ease.
In a trice you are taken! A truce you should make,   1210
Or I'll bind you in bed here, yes, be sure of that!"
The lady laughed right aloud at this game.
Said Gawain, "My lady, good morning to you.
I will work what you will; I am well content
To surrender myself and to sue for your mercy.   1215
What behooves me I'll heed; I'm beholden to you."
Thus he joined in the jest, and he jovially laughed.
"By your grace," said Sir Gawain, "if you gave me your leave,
If you pleased to permit your poor prisoner to rise,

I wolde boȝe of þis bed and busk me better;   1220
I schulde keuer þe more comfort to karp yow wyth.'
'Nay forsoþe, beau sir,' sayd þat swete,
'Ȝe schal not rise of your bedde.
I rych yow better:
I schal happe yow here þat oþer half als
And syþen karp wyth my knyȝt þat I kaȝt haue.   1225
For I wene wel, iwysse, Sir Wowen ȝe are,
Þat alle þe worlde worchipez; quereso ȝe ride,
Your honour, your hendelayk is hendely praysed
With lordez, wyth ladyes, with alle þat lyf bere.
And now ȝe ar here, iwysse, and we bot oure one;   1230
My lorde and his ledez ar on lenþe faren,
Oþer burnez in her bedde, and my burdez als,
Þe dor drawen and dit with a derf haspe;
And syþen I haue in þis hous hym þat al lykez,
I schal ware my whyle wel, quyl hit lastez,   1235
        With tale.
    Ȝe ar welcum to my cors,
    Yowre awen won to wale,
    Me behouez of fyne force
    Your seruaunt be, and schale.'   1240

'In god fayth,' quoþ Gawayn, 'gayn hit me þynkkez.
Þaȝ I be not now he þat ȝe of speken—
To reche to such reuerence as ȝe reherce here
I am wyȝe vnworþy, I wot wel myseluen—
Bi God, I were glad and yow god þoȝt   1245
At saȝe oþer at seruyce þat I sette myȝt
To þe plesaunce of your prys; hit were a pure joye.'
'In god fayth, Sir Gawayn,' quoþ þe gay lady,
'Þe prys and þe prowes þat plesez al oþer,
If I hit lakked oþer set at lyȝt, hit were littel daynté.   1250
Bot hit ar ladyes innoȝe þat leuer wer nowþe
Haf þe, hende, in hor holde, as I þe habbe here,
To daly with derely your daynté wordez
Keuer hem comfort and colen her carez,
Þen much of þe garysoun oþer golde þat þay hauen.   1255
Bot I louue þat ilk Lorde þat þe lyfte haldez
I haf hit holly in my honde þat al desyres,
        Þurȝe grace.'
    Scho made hym so gret chere,
    Þat watz so fayr of face.   1260
    Þe knyȝt with speches skere
    Answared to vche a cace.

'Madame,' quoþ þe myry mon, 'Mary yow ȝelde,
For I haf founden, in god fayth, yowre fraunchis nobele;

I would dutifully do so, don now my clothes,   1220
And, clad in more comfort, converse with you here."
But that lady replied, "I allow no such thing!
You'll not budge from your bed. I've a better idea.
I'll imprison you, pin you down pitilessly here,
And talk with the true knight I've taken here captive.   1225
For I know you're the knight whose name is Gawain,
Who is famous for fortitude far and near,
For bright courtesy, courage, and kind honor known
By ladies and lords, and by all living men.
Now he is right here! And we're happily alone,   1230
Both my lord and his liege men a long way from us;
Those here in the household still heavily sleep.
And this door I have drawn shut; it's doubly locked tight.
Since I have here this high knight beholden to me,
I will take my time now to talk, to enjoy   1235
          Repartee.
      My body's yours to use.
      I give it gleefully!
      Do with me what you choose:
      Your servant I shall be."   1240

Said Gawain, "In good faith, you've given me praise!
But I'm hardly that high knight of whom you have spoken.
To live up to the lauds that you've lavished on me
I'm incapable quite! You're too kind in your praise!
But by God, I'd be glad should you grant me the right, 1245
By some speech or some service to serve one so good.
I'd be proud; and to please you would please me as well."
"If I begrudged, Sir Gawain, your well-deserved fame,
I'd be graceless, ungrateful," that good lady said.
"Your repute for sheer prowess pleases the world.   1250
There's no lack of fine ladies who'd love nothing more
Than to have you to hold—as I have—in their arms,
And to dally in dainty discourse with yourself.
If you'd solace their sorrows, assuage their desires,
All their gold they would give; all their goods they would spurn. 1255
To the Holder of heaven, my humblest of thanks!
For I hold in my hand what the whole world wants
          Through grace."
      Thus plied, without pretense,
      That lady with lovely face.   1260
      Her moving arguments
      He answered in each case.

Said that man, "May Mary, our mother, reward you!
I have found you, in faith, beneficent and good.

And oþer ful much of oþer folk fongen hor dedez;   1265
Bot þe daynté þat þay delen for my disert nys euer—
Hit is þe worchyp of yourself, þat noȝt bot wel connez.'
'Bi Mary,' quoþ þe menskful, 'me þynk hit an oþer;
For were I worth al þe wone of wymmen alyue,
And al þe wele of þe worlde were in my honde,   1270
And I schulde chepen and chose to cheue me a lorde,
For þe costes þat I haf knowen vpon þe, knyȝt, here
Of bewté and debonerté and blyþe semblaunt—
And þat I haf er herkkened and halde hit here trwee—
Þer schulde no freke vpon folde bifore yow be chosen.'   1275
'Iwysse, worþy,' quoþ þe wyȝe, 'ȝe haf waled wel better;
Bot I am proude of þe prys þat ȝe put on me
And, soberly your seruaunt, my souerayn I holde yow
And yowre knyȝt I becom, and Kryst yow forȝelde.'
Þus þay meled of muchquat til mydmorn paste   1280
And ay þe lady let lyk a hym loued mych.
Þe freke ferde with defence and feted ful fayre;
Þaȝ ho were burde bryȝtest þe burne in mynde hade,
Þe lasse luf in his lode for lur þat he soȝt
　　Boute hone—   1285
　　　Þe dunte þat schulde hym deue,
　　　And nedez hit most be done.
　　　Þe lady þenn spek of leue;
　　　He granted hir ful sone.

Þenne ho gef hym god day and wyth a glent laȝed;   1290
And as ho stod ho stonyed hym wyth ful stor wordez:
'Now He þat spedez vche spech þis disport ȝelde yow,
Bot þat ȝe be Gawan hit gotz in mynde!'
'Querfore?' quoþ þe freke, and freschly he askez,
Ferde lest he hade fayled in fourme of his castes.   1295
Bot þe burde hym blessed and 'Bi þis skyl' sayde:
'So god as Gawayn gaynly is halden,
And cortaysye is closed so clene in hymseluen,
Couth not lyȝtly haf lenged so long wyth a lady
Bot he had craued a cosse bi his courtaysye,   1300
Bi sum towch of summe tryfle at sum talez ende.'
Þen quoþ Wowen: 'Iwysse, worþe as yow lykez;
I schal kysse at your comaundement, as a knyȝt fallez,
And fire lest he displese yow; so plede hit no more.'
Ho comes nerre with þat and cachez hym in armez,   1305
Loutez luflych adoun and þe leude kyssez.
Þay comly bykennen to Kryst ayþer oþer;
Ho dos hir forth at þe dore withouten dyn more,
And he ryches hym to ryse and rapes hym sone,
Clepes to his chamberlayn, choses his wede,   1310

Although men will admire and imitate peers,   1265
I don't merit being made others' model at all!
This esteem is your tribute. For, truly, you prize
And admire fellowmen." "By Mary, that's false!
Were I equal to any on earth, sir, or if
All the wealth of the world I wielded in hand,   1270
And decided to search to discover a man,
Your courtesy, kindness, and comely appearance,
Your manners, demeanor, and mildness are such—
I had heard them all hailed, and here can concur—
That by heaven I'd have you as husband of choice!"   1275
"But you're bound to a bolder, a far better, man;
Though I'm proud of the praise you have put to me here.
As your servant, I say you're my sovereign, in truth.
Starting now I'm your knight, in the name of Christ."
Till the middle of morning, such matter they shared.   1280
The lady still lavished her love on the knight;
And Sir Gawain, though gracious, still guarded himself.
For though were she the most wondrous of women on earth,
Occupied was that prince with the price that he soon
        Would pay.   1285
    For the beheading blow
    Determined was the day.
    The lady's leave to go
    He allowed without delay.

She glanced at him, gave him good day, as she laughed;   1290
And, while standing, with stern words astonished the knight:
"He Who sanctions all speech for this sport repay you!
For you're not the same knight who is named Sir Gawain."
"But how so?" Gawain said, of a sudden alarmed,
Most afraid he had failed in the forms of his speech.   1295
But she bountifully blessed that bold man and said,
"Such a good knight as Gawain is granted to be—
For his courtesy called in all courts the best man—
Could not linger so long with a lady nearby,
Without claiming a kiss, as is courteous and right,   1300
By some subtle suggestion when speeches are through."
"As you like," said that lord. "I allow this at once!
We will courteously kiss. This becomes one who fears
To displease one so pleasant. So plead, then, no more."
So she lovingly leaned toward that lord then and there;   1305
And, embracing him boldly, kissed him at once.
To Christ each kindly commended the other.
Thus she left that lord, did not linger for words.
He made rapidly ready to rise up at last,
Called for his chamberlain, chose his attire,   1310

Boȝez forth, quen he watz boun, blyþely to masse;
And þenne he meued to his mete, þat menskly hym keped,
And made myry al day til þe mone rysed,
    With game.
    Watz neuer freke fayrer fonge   1315
    Bitwene two so dyngne dame,
    Þe alder and þe ȝonge;
    Much solace set þay same.

And ay þe lorde of þe londe is lent on his gamnez,
To hunt in holtez and heþe at hyndez barayne;   1320
Such a sowme he þer slowe bi þat þe sunne heldet,
Of dos and of oþer dere, to deme were wonder.
Þenne fersly þay flokked in, folk, at þe laste,
And quykly of þe quelled dere a querré þay maked.
Þe best boȝed þerto with burnez innoghe,   1325
Gedered þe grattest of gres þat þer were
And didden hem derely vndo as þe dede askez.
Serched hem at þe asay summe þat þer were;
Two fyngeres þay fonde of þe fowlest of alle.
Syþen þay slyt þe slot, sesed þe erber,   1330
Schaued wyth a scharp knyf, and þe schyre knitten.
Syþen rytte þay þe foure lymmes and rent of þe hyde;
Þen brek þay þe balé, þe bowelez out token,
Lystily for laucyng þe lere of þe knot.
Þay gryped to þe gargulun and grayþely departed   1335
Þe wesaunt fro þe wynt-hole and walt out þe guttez.
Þen scher þay out þe schulderez with her scharp knyuez,
Haled hem by a lyttel hole to haue hole sydes;
Siþen britned þay þe brest and brayden hit in twynne.
And eft at þe gargulun bigynez on þenne,   1340
Ryuez hit vp radly ryȝt to þe byȝt,
Voydez out þe avanters and verayly þerafter
Alle þe rymez by þe rybbez radly þay lauce;
So ryde þay of by resoun bi þe rygge bonez
Euenden to þe haunche, þat henged alle samen,   1345
And heuen hit vp al hole and hwen hit of þere—
And þat þay neme for þe 'noumbles' bi nome, as I trowe,
    Bi kynde.
    Bi þe byȝt al of þe þyȝes
    Þe lappez þay lauce bihynde;   1350
    To hewe hit in two þay hyȝes,
    Bi þe bakbon to vnbynde.

Boþe þe hede and þe hals þay hwen of þenne
And syþen sunder þay þe sydez swyft fro þe chyne
And þe corbeles fee þay kest in a greue.   1355

Hurried forth happily, heard the Mass,
And afterwards went to his well-prepared meal.
He made mirth till the moon had made its complete
    Ascent.
      A knight has never known   1315
      Such sweet and sheer content;
      With lady and with crone
      He made much merriment.

All along, the lord of the land was at sport,
On the heaths kept up hunting the hind and the doe.   1320
By the setting of sun, he had slain many deer—
It's impossible plainly to picture the toll!
The hunters huddled, the hunt finally done.
The killed deer they quickly collected together.
With their helpers the huntsmen hastened right up,   1325
And gathered together those greatest with fat,
Had them cut up according to custom with skill.
At the test the deer turned out to be truly worth praise:
For two fingers' breadth of fat was found on the leanest.
They slit the throat's hollow, seizing the gullet,   1330
Which they scraped and sewed up with skill and finesse.
The legs were lopped off, the skin loosened and stripped.
The belly they broke, drew the bowels out with care,
Lest with lancing they loosen the ligature of the knot.
With a thrash the throat, although thick, was cut   1335
From the gullet. The guts were grabbed and tossed out.
The shoulders were severed with sharp, steely knives,
Which were held through small holes so the hide stayed intact.
The breast was breached; it was broken in two.
Anew with their knives at the neck they began;   1340
To the crotch of the carcass they cut and removed
All the offal they found in the flanks of the deer.
To the haunch of the hind those good hunters removed
From the bones of the back the bloody offal
As a whole—it was handled so handily there!   1345
Then they lifted it lightly and lopped it off whole.
It is known by the name of the "numbles"; such is
    My view.
      They saw with all their strength:
      With hasty hacks they hew   1350
      Along the backbone's length,
      The carcass cut in two.

They hewed off the head and the heavy, thick neck,
And they sundered the sides from the spine with their knives.
To the ground went the gristle for gathering crows.   1355

Þenn þurled þay ayþer þik side þur3 bi þe rybbe
And henged þenne ayþer bi ho3ez of þe fourchez,
Vche freke for his fee as fallez for to haue.
Vpon a felle of þe fayre best fede þay þayr houndes
Wyth þe lyuer and þe ly3tez, þe leþer of þe paunchez,   1360
And bred baþed in blod blende þeramongez.
Baldely þay blw prys, bayed þayr rachchez,
Syþen fonge þay her flesche, folden to home,
Strakande ful stoutly mony stif motez.
Bi þat þe dayly3t watz done þe douthe watz al wonen   1365
Into þe comly castel, þer þe kny3t bidez
        Ful stille,
    Wyth blys and bry3t fyr bette.
    Þe lorde is comen þertylle:
    When Gawayn wyth hym mette   1370
    Þer watz bot wele at wylle.

Thenne comaunded þe lorde in þat sale to samen alle þe meny,
Boþe þe ladyes on loghe to ly3t with her burdes.
Bifore alle þe folk on þe flette frekez he beddez
Verayly his venysoun to fech hym byforne;   1375
And al godly in gomen Gawayn he called,
Techez hym to þe tayles of ful tayt bestes,
Schewez hym þe schyree grece schorne vpon rybbes:
'How payez yow þis play? Haf I prys wonnen?
Haue I þryuandely þonk þur3 my craft serued?'   1380
'3e iwysse,' quoþ þat oþer wy3e, 'here is wayth fayrest
Þat I se3 þis seuen 3ere in sesoun of wynter.'
'And al I gif yow, Gawayn,' quoþ þe gome þenne,
'For by acorde of couenaunt 3e craue hit as your awen.'
'Þis is soth,' quoþ þe segge, 'I say yow þat ilke: 1385
Þat I haf worthyly wonnen þis wonez wythinne
Iwysse with as god wylle hit worþez to 3ourez.'
He hasppez his fayre hals his armez wythinne
And kysses hym as comlyly as he couþe awyse:
'Tas yow þere my cheuicaunce; I cheued no more.   1390
I wowche hit saf fynly, þa3 feler hit were.'
'Hit is god,' quoþ þe godmon, 'grant mercy þerfore.
Hit may be such hit is þe better, and 3e me breue wolde
Where 3e wan þis ilk wele bi wytte of yorseluen.'
'Þat watz not forward,' quoþ he; 'frayst me no more,   1395
For 3e haf tan þat yow tydez; trawe 3e non oþer
        3e mowe.'
    Þay la3ed and made hem blyþe
    Wyth lotez þat were to lowe.
    To soper þay 3ede asswyþe,   1400
    Wyth dayntés nwe innowe.

They ripped through the ribs with their razor-sharp hooks;
By the hocks of the haunches they hung up the beast.
His fee, as befits him, each fine hunter claimed.
The hounds with the hide of a hind were fed
On the lungs, the leathery lining of gut,   1360
And on bread bathed in blood—all was blended together.
When men blew on horns boldly, the barking commenced.
With their meat those men began making for home,
While blowing boldly on bright hunting horns.
When the dusk had descended, those dear men had come   1365
To the gates of the castle where Gawain awaited
      That crew.
   For its host the hall was set.
   The lord veered into view.
   Then he and Gawain met   1370
   With bliss between the two.

In behest of the host, the hall was then grouped;
The ladies alighted along with their maids.
Before all the folk there, that fine host had men
Next unveil to their view all the venison gained.   1375
He called Gawain gaily—the game was now on—
And the bountiful booty he boldly displayed.
He showed him the shining fat, shorn from the ribs.
"Are you pleased by this prize? Do you praise such sport?
My guest, with this game have I gained your full thanks?"   1380
Gawain said, "Certainly! Spoils such as these
I've not seen in these seven last seasons at least!"
The good host said, "Gawain, I give this to you,
As accords with our covenant. Call this your own."
"That is so," Gawain said, "and the same I declare.   1385
What I've worthily won in the walls of your house,
As agreed in our game, I give you, my lord."
Gawain boldly embraced his bounteous host
And kissed him both kindly and courteously.
"To these winnings you're welcome; I won here no more.   1390
Were they greater I gladly would give all to you."
"Now this game proves good! I gladly accept.
It would be, perhaps, best, if you boldly told all
Right now where in these walls you have won this gift."
"We agreed to give gifts," said Sir Gawain, "no more.   1395
You've secured what our covenant decreed. Ask no more
      Of me."
   At last they laughed, observed
   Much mutual amity.
   The supper soon was served,   1400
   A feast both fresh and free.

And syþen by þe chymné in chamber þay seten,
Wyȝez þe walle wyn weȝed to hem oft,
And efte in her bourdyng þay bayþen in þe morn
To fylle þe same forwardez þat þay byfore maden: 1405
Wat chaunce so bytydez hor cheuysaunce to chaunge,
What nwez so þay nome, at naȝt quen þay metten.
Þay acorded of þe couenauntez byfore þe court alle —
Þe beuerage watz broȝt forth in bourde at þat tyme —
Þenne þay louelych leȝten leue at þe last;   1410
Vche burne to his bedde busked bylyue.
Bi þat þe coke hade crowen and cakled bot þryse,
Þe lorde watz lopen of his bedde, þe leudez vchone,
So þat þe mete and þe masse watz metely delyuered,
Þe douthe dressed to þe wod, er any day sprenged,   1415
        To chace.
        Heȝ with hunte and hornez,
        Þurȝ playnez þay passe in space,
        Vncoupled among þo þornez
        Rachez þat ran on race.   1420

Sone þay calle of a quest in a ker syde;
Þe hunt rehayted þe houndez þat hit fyrst mynged,
Wylde wordez hym warp wyth a wrast noyce.
Þe howndez þat hit herde hastid þider swyþe
And fellen as fast to þe fuyt, fourty at ones.   1425
Þenne such a glauer ande glam of gedered rachchez
Ros þat þe rocherez rungen aboute.
Hunterez hem hardened with horne and wyth muthe;
Þen al in a semblé sweyed togeder
Bitwene a flosche in þat fryth and a foo cragge.   1430
In a knot bi a clyffe at þe kerre syde,
Þeras þe rogh rocher vnrydely watz fallen,
Þay ferden to þe fyndyng, and frekez hem after.
Þay vmbekesten þe knarre and þe knot boþe,
Wyȝez, whyl þay wysten wel wythinne hem hit were   1435
Þe best þat þer breued watz wyth þe blodhoundez.
Þenne þay beten on þe buskez and bede hym vpryse;
And he vnsoundyly out soȝt, seggez ouerþwert.
On þe sellokest swyn swenged out þere,
Long sythen fro þe sounder þat soȝt for olde,   1440
For he watz borelych and brode, bor alþer-grattest,
Ful grymme quen he gronyed; þenne greued mony,
For þre at þe fyrst þrast he þryȝt to þe erþe
And sparred forth good sped boute spyt more.
Þise oþer halowed 'Hyghe!' ful hyȝe, and 'Hay! Hay!' cryed,   1445
Haden hornez to mouþe, heterly rechated.
Mony watz þe miyry mouthe of men and of houndez

By the chamber's great chimney they chatted awhile,
As around them retainers served rich, flowing wine.
In their jesting and joy those two gentlemen said
They'd rekindle the covenant they'd come to before: 1405
To exchange—whether chances should change things or not—
Any wages they'd won when they met the next night.
In the court they concluded the covenant then;
Beverage was brought their new bargain to seal.
In time each retired in turn from that hall;   1410
Every gleeful guest went with graces to bed.
When the crow of the cock at last called loudly thrice,
The lord and his liege men leapt from their beds,
Ate their meal and heard Mass in the morningtime dark.
In the half-light they hastened; those hunters were on   1415
    The chase.
      The huntsmen blew their horns
      And passed through plains apace.
      And, threading through the thorns,
      Hounds ran a rapid race.   1420

They soon had a scent, which they signaled with barks.
So the chase was encouraged by cheers that the men
Quickly hurled to hasten the hounds on their way.
Those hounds hurried on as they heard the shrill calls;
Over forty then fell to the fast, urgent chase.   1425
Such a baying broke out from those bloodhounds at once,
That the rocks around fairly rang with the noise.
When the huntsmen blew horns, when they holloed them on,
The hounds grouped in together and glided between
A fen in the forest and forbidding crags   1430
To a mound by a marsh near a marvelous cliff,
Where a ridge of rough rock had recently dropped.
They pursued in a pack, and the pacing men followed
Till they met at the mound and the menacing crag.
All were well made aware that awaiting within   1435
Was the beast that the bloodhounds' loud baying announced.
When they beat on the bushes and bade him to stir,
He made his way, menacing men as he sprang;
The best of boars then burst out at them
(He'd abandoned the boar herd because of old age).   1440
He was grim and grisly, the greatest of all.
His groans were ghastly. He grieved everyone
When down to the dirt he dashed three in a stroke
And sprang off with speed, unscathed, on his way.
But the huntsmen holloed with, "Hey! Now gather!"   1445
They blew their horns boldly to beckon the hounds.
The huntsmen and hounds, with their heartiest cries,

Þat buskkez after þis bor with bost and wyth noyse,
    To quelle.
      Ful oft he bydez þe baye   1450
      And maymez þe mute innmelle.
      He hurtez of þe houndez, and þay
      Ful ȝomerly ȝaule and ȝelle.

Schalkez to schote at hym schowen to þenne,
Haled to hym of her arewez, hitten hym oft;   1455
Bot þe poyntez payred at þe pyth, þat pyȝt in his scheldez,
And þe barbez of his browe bite non wolde;
Þaȝ þe schauen schaft schyndered in pecez,
Þe hede hypped aȝayn weresoeuer hit hitte.
Bot quen þe dyntez hym dered of her dryȝe strokez,   1460
Þen, braynwod for bate, on burnez he rasez,
Hurtez hem ful heterly þer he forth hyȝez;
And mony arȝed þerat and on lyte droȝen.
Bot þe lorde on a lyȝt horce launces hym after,
As burne bolde vpon bent his bugle he blowez,   1465
He rechated, and rode þurȝ ronez ful þyk,
Suande þis wylde swyn til þe sunne schafted.
Þis day wyth þis ilk dede þay dryuen on þis wyse,
Whyle oure luflych lede lys in his bedde,
Gawayn, grayþely at home in gerez ful ryche   1470
    Of hewe.
      Þe lady noȝt forȝate
      To com hym to salue;
      Ful erly ho watz hym ate,
      His mode for to remwe.   1475

Ho commes to þe cortyn and at þe knyȝt totes.
Sir Wawen her welcumed worþy on fyrst,
And ho hym ȝeldez aȝayn ful ȝerne of hir wordez,
Settez hir sofly by his syde and swyþely ho laȝez
And wyth a luflych loke ho layde hym þyse wordez: 1480
'Sir, ȝif ȝe be Wawen, wonder me þynkkez,
Wyȝe þat is so wel wrast alway to god
And connez not of compaynye þe costez vndertake,
And if mon kennes yow hom to knowe, ȝe kest hom of your mynde:
Þou hatz forȝeten ȝederly þat ȝisterday I taȝt te   1485
Bi alder-truest token of talk þat I cowþe.'
'What is þat?' quoþ þe wyghe. 'Iwysse I wot neuer.
If hit be sothe þat ȝe breue, þe blame is myn awen.'
'ȝet I kende yow of kyssyng,' quoþ þe clere þenne,
'Quereso countenaunce is couþe, quikly to clayme;   1490
Þat bicumes vche a knyȝt þat cortaysy vses.'
'Do way,' quoþ þat derf mon, 'my dere, þat speche,

At the boar quickly bounded, raced boldly through dale
    And dell.
      The boar now baits at bay,   1450
      Now prongs the pack, pell-mell.
      The hounds he hurts now bray,
      Now yowl and yelp and yell!

To aim their keen arrows the archers advanced,
Shot them forth with fierceness and found the mark often;   1455
But the points didn't pierce the prey's leathery hide,
For his brows' thickened bristles would brush them away.
Though the force was so fierce that the shafts were split,
Arrowheads were hindered, though hitting their mark.
When the boar had been baited and battered by arrows,   1460
He made for the men in the madness of rage
And gored those he gained on, with ghastly abandon.
Many feared his fierceness and finally withdrew.
But the lord on his light horse lunged at the beast;
As on battlefield, boldly he blew his loud horn;   1465
Thus he gathered the great hounds to go through the brush.
Till the sun had descended they sought out the beast;
Until dusk to this deed they devoted themselves,
While the graceful Sir Gawain in his goodly, warm bed
At ease lay until late. In fine linen his morning   1470
    Was spent.
      The lovely lady right
      To gracious Gawain went.
      She planned to ply the knight,
      Persuade him to consent.   1475

So she lurked near the lovely bed, looking on him,
And was welcomed at once by the worthy Sir Gawain.
When she'd sat at his side very sweetly awhile
And had laughed aloud while lingering there,
With looks that were loving, she delivered these words: 1480
"I'm aghast if you're Gawain, the good knight, indeed!
For that man is well mannered and merry by birth,
While kindness and courtesy you can't understand!
You forget to be gracious, though given good lessons;
Though I've taught you the truest of teachings by now,   1485
Still you cast all that kindness and courtesy off."
"But pray tell," he said, troubled, "in truth, where I failed!
If I've blundered bitterly, blame me at once!"
"In the court-art of kissing I counseled you well:
If that favor is offered, refusing's unkind.   1490
But to kiss is becoming a courteous knight."
"Oh, please cease," Gawain said, "this speech right away!

For þat durst I not do, lest I deuayed were.
If I were werned, I were wrang, iwysse, ȝif I profered.'
'Ma fay,' quoþ þe meré wyf, 'ȝe may not be werned;   1495
Ȝe ar stif innoghe to constrayne wyth strenkþe, ȝif yow lykez,
Ȝif any were so vilanous þat yow devaye wolde.'
'Ȝe, be God,' quoþ Gawayn, 'good is your speche;
Bot þrete is vnþryuande in þede þer I lende,
And vche gift þat is geuen not with goud wylle.   1500
I am at your comaundement, to kysse quen yow lykez;
Ȝe may lach quen yow lyst and leue quen yow þynkkez,
      In space.'
          Þe lady loutez adoun
          And comlyly kysses his face.   1505
          Much speche þay þer expoun
          Of druryes greme and grace.

'I woled wyt at yow, wyȝe,' þat worþy þer sayde,
'And yow wrathed not þerwyth, what were þe skylle
Þat so ȝong and so ȝepe as ȝe at þis tyme,   1510
So cortayse, so knyȝtyly, as ȝe ar knowen oute—
And of alle cheualry to chose, þe chef þyng alosed
Is þe lel layk of luf, þe lettrure of armes;
For to telle of þis teuelyng of þis trwe knyȝtez,
Hit is þe tytelet token and tyxt of her werkkez   1515
How ledez for her lele luf hor lyuez han auntered,
Endured for her drury dulful stoundez,
And after wenged with her walour and voyded her care
And broȝt blysse into boure with bountées hor awen—
And ȝe ar knyȝt comlokest kyd of your elde,   1520
Your worde and your worchip walkez ayquere,
And I haf seten by yourself here sere twyes,
Ȝet herde I neuer of your hed helde no wordez
Þat euer longed to luf, lasse ne more.
And ȝe, þat ar so cortays and coynt of your hetes,   1525
Oghe to a ȝonke þynk ȝern to schewe
And teche sum tokenez of trweluf craftes.
Why! ar ȝe lewed, þat alle þe los weldez,
Oþer elles ȝe demen me to dille your dalyaunce to herken?
      For schame!   1530
          I com hider sengel and sitte
          To lerne at yow sum game;
          Dos techez me of your wytte,
          Whil my lorde is fro hame.'

'In goud fayþe,' quoþ Gawayn, 'God yow forȝelde!   1535
Gret is þe gode gle, and gomen to me huge,
Þat so worþy as ȝe wolde wynne hidere

For I dared not to do that; denial I feared.
If I tried and was turned down, I'd truly be rude."
"I know, sir, that none would deny you a kiss!   1495
Besides, your great strength could constrain any maid,
Any fool who'd refuse thus the finest on earth."
Said Gawain, "Both gracious and good are your words;
But forcefulness finds little favor in my land,
Nor do gifts when not given with goodwill at heart.   1500
But command, and I'll kiss you, as courtesy asks.
I'll allow your love if you like," Sir Gawain
     Explains.
       Then cheerfully his cheek
       She kisses. She remains;   1505
       And long of love they speak,
       Its pleasures and its pains.

"My lord, I would learn," that lady then said,
"If it does not displease or distress you, the reason
That a man of such mettle, such marvelous youth,   1510
So courteous and kind as you're considered to be
(For, of course, in the code of courts' chivalry
The most precious and praised of all practice is love;
When they tell of the trials of true knights, indeed,
Every tale—both the title and text of the work—   1515
Will relate how for love of their lady those knights
Always lay down their lives, always live in distress,
And with valor take vengeance on vicious, mean foes—
All to please and impress the true prize of their hearts!),
I would know why that knight, who is known for his grace,   1520
Whose far-reaching fame has traveled the world,
Whom I've sat beside on two separate mornings,
I would know, my knight, why never one word
In the language of love has yet leapt from your mouth.
If you're keenly accomplished in the casting of vows,   1525
You'll allow a young lady to learn at firsthand
Of courtesy's code and the craft of true love.
Is the glorious Gawain too ignorant? Fie!
Do you deem me too dull lovers' dalliance to learn?
     For shame!   1530
       Kind sir, to cultivate
       Love's courtly ways I came.
       My lord's away; I wait
       To learn the lovers' game."

Said Sir Gawain, "May God in His goodness reward you!   1535
I am glad that one goodly and gracious as you—
One so courteous and kind—would thus come here to me,

And pyne yow with so pouer a mon, as play wyth your knyʒt
With anyskynnez countenaunce; hit keuerez me ese.
Bot to take þe toruayle to myself to trwluf expoun   1540
And towche þe temez of tyxt and talez of armez
To yow, þat (I wot wel) weldez more slyʒt
Of þat art, bi þe half, or a hundreth of seche
As I am, oþer euer schal in erde þer I leue,
Hit were a folé felefolde, my fre, by my trawþe.   1545
I wolde yowre wylnyng worche at my myʒt,
As I am hyʒly bihalden, and euermore wylle
Be seruaunt to yourseluen, so saue me Dryʒtyn!'
Þus hym frayned þat fre and fondet hym ofte,
For to haf wonnen hym to woʒe, whatso scho þoʒt ellez;   1550
Bot he defended hym so fayr þat no faut semed,
Ne non euel on nawþer halue, nawþer þay wysten
       Bot blysse.
     Þay laʒed and layked longe;
      At þe last scho con hym kysse,   1555
     Hir leue fayre con scho fonge,
     And went hir waye, iwysse.

Then ruþes hym þe renk and ryses to þe masse,
And siþen hor diner watz dyʒt and derely serued.
Þe lede with þe ladyez layked alle day   1560
Bot þe lorde ouer þe londez launced ful ofte,
Swez his vncely swyn, þat swyngez bi þe bonkkez
And bote þe best of his brachez þe bakkez in sunder
Þer he bodˆ in his bay, tel bawemen hit breken
And madee hym mawgref his hed for to mwe vtter,   1565
So felle flonez þer flete when þe folk gedered.
Bot ʒet þe styffest to start bi stoundez he made,
Til at þe last he watz so mat he myʒt no more renne
Bot in þe hast þat he myʒt he to a hole wynnez
Of a rasse, bi a rokk þer rennez þe boerne.   1570
He gete þe bonk at his bak, bigynez to scrape—
Þe froþe femed at his mouth vnfayre bi þe wykez—
Whettez his whyte tuschez. With hym þen irked
Alle þe burnez so bolde þat hym by stoden
To nye hym onferum, bot neʒe hym non durst   1575
       For woþe;
     He hade hurt so mony byforne
     Þat al þuʒt þenne ful loþe
     Be more wyth his tusches torne,
     Þat breme watz and braynwod bothe.   1580

Til þe knyʒt com hymself, kachande his blonk,
Syʒ hym byde at þe bay, his burnez bysyde.

And take pains to make pastimes with so poor a man;
For the graces you've given I'm grateful, indeed.
Should I try, though, to teach you of true love's ways   1540
And to tell of the text, giving tales of knights
To a lady whose learning and lore in the craft
Is so deep, and who doubtless has double the skill
Than a score or more such as myself could display;
I'd be foolish, in faith, and my folly would show!   1545
What you please I'll perform, though, provided I can;
I am highly beholden; your behest I'll obey
As a servant a sovereign's, so save me my God."
Then she tempted him, testing and trying to bring
Him to sin. (Who can say what she sought in her heart?)   1550
But with graciousness Gawain still guarded himself
Without fault. Both felt not unfriendly at all
       But gay.
     Both bathed in blithe delight
     And laughed at lengthy play.   1555
     She kissed her comely knight
     And, waving, went away.

Sir Gawain got up; he would go to hear Mass.
A marvelous meal was made for the knight.
All day long that lord and the ladies made cheer,   1560
While lunging through leas was the lord of the house.
For the boar through the bushes was bursting away,
Or was biting and breaking the backs of the hounds.
He would bide, stand at bay, although battered with arrows;
He'd run out of reach of the rallying men.   1565
Overwhelmed by the welter of weapons at last,
He was forced, although fierce, to flinch once or twice.
In the end, exhausted, unable to run,
With a strength now unsteady he sped to a hole
In a ridge of bright rock that arose from a stream.   1570
With the bank at his back, there he bristled in rage.
There the froth freely foamed at his fiercely taut mouth.
He wetted his white tusks. And weary like him
Are the hunters who hover, harassing the boar
From afar; for in fear of the fierce beast all there   1575
       Agree.
     He'd maimed so many men
     No one there wished to be
     Torn up by tusks again.
     That beast bayed angrily!   1580

But the host by himself on his horse came right up,
Saw the bold men at bay and the boar in its wrath.

He ly3tes luflych adoun, leuez his corsour,
Braydez out a bry3t bront and bigly forth strydez,
Foundez fast þur3 þe forth þer þe felle bydez.   1585
Þe wylde watz war of þe wy3e with weppen in honde,
Hef hy3ly þe here; so hetterly he fnast
Þat fele ferde for þe freke, lest felle hym þe worre.
Þe swyn settez hym out on þe segge euen,
Þat þe burne and þe bor were boþe vpon hepez   1590
In þe wy3test of þe water. Þe worre hade þat oþer,
For þe mon merkkez hym wel, as þay mette fyrst,
Set sadly þe scharp in þe slot euen,
Hit hym vp to þe hult, þat þe hert schyndered
And he 3arrande hym 3elde and 3edoun þe water   1595
        Ful tyt.
    A hundreth houndez hym hent,
    Þat bremely con hym bite;
    Burnez him bro3t to bent
    And doggez to dethe endite.   1600

There watz blawyng of prys in mony breme horne,
He3e halowing on hi3e with haþelez þat my3t;
Brachetes bayed þat best, as bidden þe maysterez,
Of þat chargeaunt chace þat were chef huntes.
Þenne a wy3e þat watz wys vpon wodcraftez   1605
To vnlace þis bor lufly bigynnez.
Fyrst he hewes of his hed and on hi3e settez,
And syþen rendez him al roghe bi þe rygge after,
Braydez out þe boweles, brennez hom on glede,
With bred blent þerwith his braches rewardez.   1610
Syþen he britnez out þe brawen in bry3t brode cheldez,
And hatz out þe hastlettez, as hi3tly bisemez,
And 3et hem halchez al hole þe haluez togeder
And syþen on a stif stange stoutly hem henges.
Now with þis ilk swyn þay swengen to home.   1615
Þe bores hed watz borne bifore þe burnes seluen
Þat him forferde in þe forþe þur3 forse of his honde
        So stronge.
    Til he se3 Sir Gawayne
    In halle, hym þo3t ful longe;   1620
    He calde, and he com gayn,
    His feez þer for to fonge.

Þe lorde ful lowde with lote and la3ter myry,
When he se3e Sir Gawayn, with solace he spekez.
Þe goude ladyez were geten, and gedered þe meyny;   1625
He schewez hem þe scheldez and schapes hem þe tale
Of þe largesse and þe lenþe, þe liþernez alse

That brave lord then alighted from his lofty horse.
He brought out his bright sword and boldly advanced.
He strode through the stream to the spot where the boar—   1585
Quite aware of the warrior, weapon in hand—
Madly snorted and stamped, madly stuck out his bristles.
Many feared that the host would fall to his death.
The rugged boar ran for him, rushing along,
Till they tangled together. They twisted and raged   1590
In the white, whirling water. But worse was the boar;
For the lord finally lunged forth his long blade with skill,
Thrust it home in the hollow of the hoary boar's breast
To the hilt. Thus his heart was heavily burst.
Snarling he sank through the stream. That boar's death   1595
    Was grim.
    The hounds, before he sank,
    All lifted him by limb.
    Men brought him by the bank.
    To death the dogs did him.   1600

The bugles blared; they blew their horns loudly.
When the huntsmen holloed and hailed with pride,
Emboldened, there barked and bayed younger dogs,
As the chiefs of the chase had commanded them all.
One crafty in cutlery comes up with speed,   1605
And begins on the boar, at first breaching the throat.
Soon he hews off the head and he hangs it aloft.
He rends him with rough weapons, right down the spine,
Disembowels the beast, and broils the entrails,
Which he hurls to the hounds who hungrily eat.   1610
He breaches the brawn, as he breaks off great slabs,
Carves from the carcass, as custom insists,
The offal, and fastens firmly together
The two sides. On a spar he suspends them aloft.
With the carcass thus cut, they carry it home,   1615
With the boar's head borne up before the same man
Whose stoutness and strength had thus slain it within
    The brook.
    For Gawain, his guest and friend,
    The host in hall did look.   1620
    Gawain got there in the end;
    His gift he gladly took.

The lord, gaily laughing, called loudly in the hall
When he gleaned Sir Gawain, his guest, waiting there.
All the lords and their ladies alighted at once.   1625
As he showed them the slabs, the host started to tell
Of the size and the strength of the surly, wild boar,

Of þe were, of þe wylde swyn in wod þer he fled.
Þat oþer knyȝt ful comly comended his dedez
And praysed hit as gret prys þat he proued hade,   1630
For suche a brawne of a best, þe bolde burne sayde,
Ne such sydes of a swyn segh he neuer are.
Þenne hondeled þay þe hoge hed; þe hende mon hit praysed
And let lodly þerat, þe lorde for to here.
'Now, Gawayn,' quoþ þe godmon, 'þis gomen is your awen   1635
Bi fyn forwarde and faste, faythely ȝe knowe.'
'Hit is sothe,' quoþ þe segge, 'and as siker trwe,
Alle my get I schal yow gif agayn, bi my trawþe.'
He hent þe haþel aboute þe halse and hendely hym kysses
And eftersones of þe same he serued hym þere.   1640
'Now ar we euen,' quoþ þe haþel, 'in þis euentide,
Of alle þe couenauntes þat we knyt syþen I com hider,
    Bi lawe.'
        Þe lorde sayde, 'Bi Saynt Gile,
        Ȝe ar þe best þat I knowe!   1645
        Ȝe ben ryche in a whyle,
        Such chaffer and ȝe drowe.'

Þenne þay teldet tablez trestes alofte,
Kesten cloþez vpon; clere lyȝt þenne
Wakned bi woȝez, waxen torches   1650
Seggez sette, and serued in sale al aboute.
Much glam and gle glent vp þerinne
Aboute þe fyre vpon flet; and on fele wyse
At þe soper and after, mony aþel songez,
As coundutes of Krystmasse and carolez newe,   1655
With alle þe manerly merþe þat mon may of telle.
And euer oure luflych knyȝt þe lady bisyde;
Such semblaunt to þat segge semly ho made,
Wyth stille stollen countenaunce, þat stalworth to plese,
Þat al forwondered watz þe wyȝe and wroth with hymseluen,   1660
Bot he nolde not for his nurture nurne hir aȝaynez
Bot dalt with hir al in daynté, how-se-euer þe dede turned
        Towrast.
        Quen þay hade played in halle
        As longe as hor wylle hom last,   1665
        To chambre he con hym calle
        And to þe chemné þay past.

Ande þer þay dronken and dalten and demed eft nwe
To norne on þe same note on Nwe Ȝerez Euen;
Bot þe knyȝt craued leue to kayre on þe morn,   1670
For hit watz neȝ at þe terme þat he to schulde.
Þe lorde hym letted of þat, to lenge hym resteyed,

Of the fight in the forest they fiercely had waged.
Then, commending such mighty, such manly, brave deeds,
Gawain praised the host's prowess as precious indeed.   1630
For a beast near so bold, near so brawny and huge,
Gawain said he'd not seen; this he swore before all.
When the huge head was handled, he heartily praised it,
And—to please the proud host—appeared horrified.
"Now, my guest," said the good man, "this game is your own,   1635
As was fixed by our firm and final agreement."
He responded, "Good sir, that is certainly true.
What I've gained I will gladly now give in return."
Gawain boldly embraced him, bestowed him a kiss,
And served him a second time similarly.   1640
"Now the score's even, sir; and the slate is wiped clean.
For the covenant we came to is kept as of this
        Good date."
    "Saint Giles!" he said in glee.
    "You're gracious, Gawain, great!   1645
    You'll prosper, prince; you'll be
    Soon rich at this rare rate!"

On trestles great tables together were placed,
And covered with cloth. The court grew bright.
When in wide wall-holders waxen torches were lit,   1650
The servants skillfully served up the feast.
The guests were gleeful and gladdened with mirth
As they sat by the fireside, supping together.
They sang songs splendidly, straight through the evening—
The carols of Christmas and courtly part-songs—   1655
With more marvelous mirth than a man could describe.
Our noble, bold knight sported next to the lady.
But she showed him such soft and such sweet, loving looks,
Such attentions, such tender and touching gestures,
That our prince was surprised and displeased with himself;   1660
But he couldn't be uncourtly; decorum forbade it.
So he mustered fine manners, though they might be ill
        Construed.
    The guests play games in the hall,
    As meets their merry mood.   1665
    At evening's end, they all
    The spectacle conclude.

But the host by the hearth in the hall stays with Gawain,
And suggests that they game once again New Year's Eve.
Though Sir Gawain asks good leave to go in the morning—   1670
For the time of his tryst is but two days away—
The lord says he longs he would linger a bit.

And sayde, 'As I am trwe segge, I siker my trawþe
Þou schal cheue to þe Grene Chapel þy charres to make,
Leude, on Nw Ʒerez lyʒt, longe bifore pryme.   1675
Forþy þow lye in þy loft and lach þyn ese
And I schal hunt in þis holt and halde þe towchez,
Chaunge wyth þe cheuisaunce bi þat I charre hider.
For I haf fraysted þe twys and faythful I fynde þe.
Now "Þrid tyme, þrowe best" þenk on þe morne;   1680
Make we mery quyl we may and mynne vpon joye,
For þe lur may mon lach whenso mon lykez.'
Þis watz grayþely graunted and Gawayn is lenged;
Bliþe broʒt watz hym drynk and þay to bedde ʒeden
        With liʒt.   1685
    Sir Gawayn lis and slepes
    Ful stille and softe al niʒt;
    Þe lorde, þat his craftez kepes,
    Ful erly he watz diʒt.

After messe, a morsel he and his men token.   1690
Miry watz þe mornyng; his mounture he askes.
Alle þe haþeles þat on horse schulde helden hym after
Were boun busked on hor blonkkez bifore þe halle ʒatez.
Ferly fayre watz þe folde, for þe forst clenged;
In rede rudede vpon rak rises þe sunne   1695
And ful clere castez þe clowdes of þe welkyn.
Hunteres vnhardeled bi a holt syde;
Rocheres roungen bi rys for rurde of her hornes.
Summe fel in þe fute þer þe fox bade,
Traylez ofte atraueres bi traunt of her wyles.   1700
A kenet kryes þerof; þe hunt on hym calles;
His felaʒes fallen hym to, þat fnasted ful þike,
Runnen forth in a rabel in his ryʒt fare,
And he fyskez hem byfore; þay founden hym sone.
And quen þay seghe hym with syʒt þay sued hym fast,   1705
Wreʒande hym ful weterly with a wroth noyse,
And he trantes and tornayeez þurʒ mony tene greue,
Hauilounez and herkenez bi heggez ful ofte.
At þe last bi a littel dich he lepez ouer a spenné,
Stelez out ful stilly bi a strothe rande,   1710
Went haf wylt of þe wode, with wylez, fro þe houndes.
Þenne watz he went, er he wyst, to a wale tryster,
Þer þre þro at a þrich þrat hym at ones,
        Al graye.
    He blenched aʒayn bilyue   1715
    And stifly start onstray.
    With alle þe wo on lyue
    To þe wod he went away.

"I swear," he says, "be assured by my oath;
You will come to that chapel to keep there your vow
Before dawn New Year's Day, a great deal before prime.   1675
But until then, in truth, you will take ease in bed,
While I hunt in the holt. We will hold to our terms;
I'll return and we'll trade what we've taken that day.
I have tested you twice, and both times you've been faithful;
But the third's the best throw! You should think upon that.   1680
While we may, let's be merry, on mirth set our thoughts;
Because grief man may get when he goes out to find it."
This is graciously granted by Gawain. They drink
With gaiety, glee, and go off, led by
  A light.   1685
  To rest Gawain repaired,
  Serenely slept all night.
  The host, for hunt prepared,
  Was dressed before daylight.

That man and his men after Mass ate a bit.   1690
The morning was merry. His mount had arrived.
Those who'd hunt with the host on that high, winter day
Were already arrayed at the rich gates on horse.
The forest was fair, for the frost lingered still.
When through red clouds arose the radiant sun.   1695
They dispersed, and the sky was suffused with light.
By the holt the hunters their hounds then unleashed,
And the rocks began ringing with rich notes from horns.
When at first a few found where the fox was ahead,
They craftily closed in, so clear was the scent.   1700
Then a small hound who smelled fox was sent in pursuit,
While his fellows followed as fast as they could;
They went leaping and lunging along the right track.
They found soon the fox as before them he ran;
At that sight they pursued him, straight on the chase.   1705
As they ran they roared out with rough barks and bays.
But he dodged them adroitly and doubled back well—
He'd hang by thick hedges to hear all the dogs—
And at last by a little ditch leapt a high hedge.
Though he stole forth stealthily, skirting the brush   1710
To escape through such stealth the pursuing, fierce hounds,
Unawares he was waylaid, for he went to a hunt-station
Where three greyhounds—most grim and grisly—attacked
  Their prey.
  The fox, though filled with fear,   1715
  In dreary disarray,
  Drew back. To disappear
  In woods he went his way.

Thenne watz hit list vpon lif to lyþen þe houndez,
When alle þe mute hade hym met, menged togeder: 1720
Suche a sorȝe at þat syȝt þay sette on his hede
As alle þe clamberande clyffes hade clatered on hepes.
Here he watz halawed when haþelez hym metten,
Loude he watz ȝayned with ȝarande speche;
Þer he watz þreted and ofte 'þef' called,   1725
And ay þe titlerez at his tayl, þat tary he ne myȝt.
Ofte he watz runnen at when he out rayked,
And ofte reled in aȝayn, so Reniarde watz wylé.
And ȝe! he lad hem bi lagmon, þe lorde and his meyny,
On þis maner bi þe mountes quyle myd ouer vnder,   1730
Whyle þe hende knyȝt at home holsumly slepes
Withinne þe comly cortynes, on þe colde morne.
Bot þe lady, for luf, let not to slepe,
Ne þe purpose to payre þat pyȝt in hir hert,
But ros hir vp radly, rayked hir þeder   1735
In a mery mantyle, mete to þe erþe,
Þat watz furred ful fyne with fellez wel pured;
No hwef goud on hir hede, bot þe haȝer stones
Trased aboute hir tressour be twenty in clusteres;
Hir þryuen face and hir þrote þrowen al naked,   1740
Hir brest bare bifore, and bihinde eke.
Ho comez withinne þe chambre dore and closes hit hir after,
Wayuez vp a wyndow and on þe wyȝe callez
And radly þus rehayted hym with hir riche wordes,
    With chere: 1745
'A! mon, how may þou slepe?
Þis morning is so clere.'
He watz in drowping depe,
Bot þenne he con hir here.

In dreȝ droupyng of dreme draueled þat noble,   1750
As mon þat watz in mornyng of mony þro þoȝtes,
How þat Destiné schulde þat day dele hym his wyrde
At þe Grene Chapel when he þe gome metes
And bihoues his buffet abide withoute debate more.
Bot quen þat comly com he keuered his wyttes,   1755
Swenges out of þe sweuenes and swarez with hast.
Þe lady luflych com, laȝande swete,
Felle ouer his fayre face and fetly hym kyssed.
He welcumez hir worþily with a wale chere;
He seȝ hir so glorious and gayly atyred,   1760
So fautles of hir fetures and of so fyne hewes,
Wiȝt wallande joye warmed his hert.
With smoþe smylyng and smolt þay smeten into merþe,

Just to hear those hounds was a heartening thing!
They met, voices mingled, and made for the fox.   1720
On his head they were hurling their howls so loudly
That it seemed as if sharp cliffs had shattered in heaps.
When the hunters beheld him they holloed aloud,
And snarling dogs assailed and set after him.
The men threw at him threats, yelling "Thief!" as they rode.   1725
Fresh hounds leapt from the relays and lunged at the fox.
But again and again would he gain open fields,
Just to run to the rough; yes, that Reynard was wily!
Thus he led both the lord and his liege men astray.
In this manner he moved until midafternoon;   1730
While at court—asleep, calm—was the courteous knight.
It was cold, but the curtains were keeping him warm.
But the lady, longing to woo, lay awake.
To pursue her purpose, to pressure Sir Gawain,
She arose and arrived at his room very early,   1735
In a dear, full-length dress, which was dainty and gay,
And a fine, flowing fur; she was fashioned quite well!
She'd no coif as a cover; just clusters of pearls,
Which hung in her hair in a highly wrought fret.
Her face was fair, her fine throat exposed;   1740
Her breast and her back were both bared very low.
She came to the chamber and, closing the door,
Opened wide the bay window. To wake him she spoke,
To rally with rich words, to rouse him, and bring
    Him cheer: 1745
      "I've slipped in. Still you sleep!
      This morning's merry, clear!"
     Though he was drowsing deep,
     He could not help but hear.

In the deepest of dreams, Gawain drowsily spoke—   1750
As a man who's in mourning, with many sad thoughts—
Of the day that his destiny deigned that he must
At the Green Chapel greet the fierce Green Knight and take
A heavy blow from his hand; he was held to it, pledged!
But he quickly recovered. She came toward him then.   1755
Gawain, shaking off sleep, responded with skill.
That lovely fair lady, while laughing, approached,
Took his face in her fine hands and freely kissed him.
The knight welcomed her worthily, wished her good cheer.
When he gleaned her so gaily, so gloriously fine—   1760
For her features were faultless and fair was her skin—
A gladness then grew in him, glowed in his heart.
They both smiled sweetly and shared in their mirth.

Þat al watz blis and bonchef þat breke hem bitwene,
    And wynne.   1765
      Þay lauced wordes gode,
      Much wele þen watz þerinne.
      Gret perile bitwene hem stod,
      Nif Maré of hir knyȝt mynne.

For þat prynces of pris depresed hym so þikke,   1770
Nurned hym so neȝe þe þred, þat nede hym bihoued
Oþer lach þer hir luf oþer lodly refuse.
He cared for his cortaysye, lest craþayn he were,
And more for his meschef ȝif he schulde make synne
And be traytor to þat tolke þat þat telde aȝt.   1775
'God schylde!' quoþ þe schalk. 'Þat schal not befalle!'
With luf-laȝyng a lyt he layd hym bysyde
Alle þe spechez of specialté þat sprange of her mouthe.
Quoþ þat burde to þe burne, 'Blame ȝe disserue
ȝif ȝe luf not þat lyf þat ȝe lye nexte,   1780
Bifore alle þe wyȝez in þe worlde wounded in hert,
Bot if ȝe haf a lemman, a leuer, þat yow lykez better,
And folden fayth to þat fre, festned so harde
Þat yow lausen ne lyst—and þat I leue nouþe!
And þat ȝe telle me þat now trwly I pray yow;   1785
For alle þe lufez vpon lyue, layne not þe soþe
    For gile.'
      Þe knyȝt sayde, 'Be Sayn Jon'
      (And smeþely con he smyle)
      'In fayth I welde riȝt non,   1790
      Ne non wil welde þe quile.'

'Þat is a worde,' quoþ þat wyȝt, 'þat worst is of alle;
Bot I am swared forsoþe—þat sore me þinkkez.
Kysse me now, comly, and I schal cach heþen;
I may bot mourne vpon molde, as may þat much louyes.'   1795
Sykande ho sweȝe doun and semly hym kyssed,
And siþen ho seueres hym fro and says as ho stondes,
'Now, dere, at þis departyng do me þis ese:
Gif me sumquat of þy gifte, þi gloue if hit were,
Þat I may mynne on þe, mon, my mournyng to lassen.'   1800
'Now iwysse,' quoþ þat wyȝe, 'I wolde I hade here
Þe leuest þing, for þy luf, þat I in londe welde,
For ȝe haf deserued, forsoþe, sellyly ofte
More rewarde bi resoun þen I reche myȝt.
Bot to dele yow, for drurye, þat dawed bot neked!—   1805
Hit is not your honour to haf at þis tyme
A gloue for a garysoun of Gawaynez giftez.
And I am here an erande in erdez vncouþe

Between them was true joy and touchingly sweet
> Delight.   1765
> In sport their time they spend.
> They laugh aloud, both light.
> Yet perils there impend,
> Unless Mary mind her knight!

For that peerless princess pressed him so hard   1770
And so eagerly urged him that either he must
Take her favors or refuse her offensively then.
He was sorely concerned should his chivalry fail,
But he feared more his fate if he falsely should sin
As a traitor to his true host who'd treated him well.   1775
"God me shield!" he said, "No, that shall not occur!"
So with love-talk he laughed and eluded each one
Of the fond words of favor that fell from her lips.
But she sharply said, "You deserve to be blamed
If you love not the lady who lies here by you,   1780
In the world the most wounded of women from love!
For unless you've a lover you're linked to with vows,
Whom you've sworn to serve with unswerving devotion,
And would loathe to leave, you are less than polite!
If that's true, I entreat you to tell me at once;   1785
For the sake of your soul, do not sully the truth
> With guile."
> He said, "Now, by Saint John!"
> And started then to smile.
> "By heaven, have I none,   1790
> And won't for quite a while."

"Then your words," said the woman, "are the worst they could be!
Your reply, though it pains me, is perfectly honest.
If you kindly now kiss me, I'll quickly depart,
I'll be lovelorn for life; yes, lost to my grief."   1795
She stooped down and sighed, softly kissing the knight,
And said as she stood again, lingering there,
"As I go, fair Sir Gawain, please grant me one favor:
Just a gift from your goodness, a glove perhaps. Thus
I'd remember my man, and my mourning would ease."   1800
"For the world, I wish that I had with me here
A present both precious and pure for your sake!
You deserve—I will swear, for it's certainly true—
By your graces more gifts than I've got to bring forth.
As for leaving a love-token, little of worth,   1805
Your dignity's due more, I dare say, in truth,
Than a glove humbly given by Gawain in parting.
On an errand I am, in an unknown, far land,

And haue no men wyth no malez with menskful þingez
(Þat mislykez me, ladé) for luf, at þis tyme;   1810
Iche tolke mon do as he is tan—tas to non ille
    Ne pine.'
     'Nay, hende of hyȝe honours,'
     Quoþ þat lufsum vnder lyne,
     'Þaȝ I nade oȝt of yourez,   1815
     Ȝet schulde ȝe haue of myne.'

Ho raȝt hym a riche rynk of red golde werkez,
Wyth a starande ston stondande alofte,
Þat bere blusschande bemez as þe bryȝt sunne;
Wyt ȝe wel, hit watz worth wele ful hoge.   1820
Bot þe renk hit renayed and redyly he sayde,
'I wil no giftez, for Gode, my gay, at þis tyme;
I haf none yow to norne ne noȝt wyl I take.'
Ho bede hit hym ful bysily and he hir bode wernes
And swere swyfte by his sothe þat he hit sese nolde;   1825
And ho soré þat he forsoke and sayde þerafter,
'If ȝe renay my rynk, to ryche for hit semez,
Ȝe wolde not so hyȝly halden be to me,
I schal gif yow my girdel, þat gaynes yow lasse.'
Ho laȝt a lace lyȝtly þat leke vmbe hir sydez,   1830
Knit vpon hir kyrtel, vnder þe clere mantyle;
Gered hit watz with grene sylke and with golde schaped,
Noȝt bot arounde brayden, beten with fyngrez.
And þat ho bede to þe burne and blyþely bisoȝt,
Þaȝ hit vnworþi were, þat he hit take wolde;   1835
And he nay þat he nolde neghe in no wyse
Nauþer golde ne garysoun, er God hym grace sende
To acheue to þe chaunce þat he hade chosen þere.
'And þerfore I pray yow displese yow noȝt
And lettez be your bisinesse, for I bayþe hit yow neuer   1840
    To graunte.
     I am derely to yow biholde
     Bicause of your sembelaunt,
     And euer in hot and colde
     To be your trwe seruaunt.'   1845

'Now forsake ȝe þis silke,' sayde þe burde þenne,
For hit is symple in hitself? And so hit wel semez:
Lo! so hit is littel and lasse hit is worþy.
Bot whoso knew þe costes þat knit ar þerinne,
He wolde hit prayse at more prys, parauenture;   1850
For quat gome so is gorde with þis grene lace,
While he hit hade hemely halched aboute
Þer is no haþel vnder heuen tohewe hym þat myȝt,

Without train or retainers or treasures to give.
This galls me grievously, gracious lady.   1810
A man gets what he gets; don't be grieved, don't be sad,
    I plea."
        "Oh, no, my knight most true,
        Good sir!" she said shortly.
        "Though I get no gift from you,   1815
        You'll get a gift from me!"

Then she raised up a ring of the richest of gold:
A stone in it stood out, strikingly large;
From it beams seemed to burst, just as bright as the sun.
It was wondrously worthy, you well may believe!   1820
But he frankly refused it at first, and he said:
"By our God, you're too gracious! No gifts at this time!
Having nothing so nice, I can nothing receive."
Though she pressingly proffered, her pleas he refused;
As his soul he wished saved, Gawain said he'd not take it.   1825
His forsaking it sorrowed her; she could but add:
"If my ring as too rich and too rare you refuse,
As a thing that you think you would thanklessly hold,
Then I'll give you my girdle, a gift much less dear."
She unbuckled a belt from her body at once—   1830
From her mantle she moved it and made it appear.
It was girded with gold, out of green silk well made.
Embroidery bounded its borders with grace.
To accept it she earnestly asked Sir Gawain,
Though it showed, as she said, but the slightest of worth.   1835
But he said he'd receive neither soothing treasure
Nor gold before God sent him grace to achieve
His grave task undertaken with true oaths and vows.
"So please cease," he said, "nor be sorrowed or hurt.
Though you're noble and nice, I will never consent   1840
        To you.
        Yet, madam, I'll remain
        Your servant through and through.
        I'll ride through rough and rain,
        In truth, your champion true."   1845

"Do you spurn, then, this silk," she responded at once,
"Since it seems to be slight? Well, so it appears!
As its length is quite little, then little it's worth.
But the knight who knew what was knit in this belt
Would prize it as praiseworthy, precious, and fine!   1850
For if girdled, if graced with this green sash's length,
While it's tightly attached to his torso, a man
Can't be hewn under heaven by heroes, though fierce;

For he my3t not be slayn for sly3t vpon erþe.'
Þen kest þe kny3t, and hit come to his hert   1855
Hit were a juel for þe jopardé þat hym jugged were:
When he acheued to þe chapel his chek for to fech,
My3t he haf slypped to be vnslayn þe sle3t were noble.
Þenne he þulged with hir þrepe and þoled hir to speke.
And ho bere on hym þe belt and bede hit hym swyþe   1860
(And he granted and hym gafe with a goud wylle)
And biso3t hym for hir sake disceuer hit neuer
Bot to lelly layne fro hir lorde; þe leude hym acordez
Þat neuer wy3e schulde hit wyt, iwysse, bot þay twayne,
     For no3te.   1865
          He þonkked hir oft ful swyþe,
          Ful þro with hert and þo3t;
          Bi þat on þrynne syþe
          Ho hatz kyst þe kny3t so to3t.

Thenne lachchez ho hir leue and leuez hym þere,   1870
For more myrþe of þat mon mo3t ho not gete.
When ho watz gon, Sir Gawayn gerez hym sone,
Rises and riches hym in araye noble,
Lays vp þe luf-lace þe lady hym ra3t,
Hid hit ful holdely þer he hit eft fonde.   1875
Syþen cheuely to þe chapel choses he þe waye,
Preuély aproched to a prest and prayed hym þere
Þat he wolde lyste his lyf and lern hym better
How his sawle schulde be saued when he schuld seye heþen.
Þere he schrof hym schyrly and schewed his mysdedez,   1880
Of þe more and þe mynne, and merci besechez,
And of absolucioun he on þe segge calles;
And he asoyled hym surely and sette hym so clene
As domezday schulde haf ben di3t on þe morn.
And syþen he mace hym as mery among þe fre ladyes,   1885
With comlych caroles and alle kynnes joye,
As neuer he did bot þat daye, to þe derk ny3t,
     With blys.
          Vche mon hade daynté þare
          Of hym, and sayde, 'Iwysse,   1890
          Þus myry he watz neuer are,
          Syn he com hider, er þis.'

Now hym lenge in þat lee, þer luf hym bityde!
3et is þe lorde on þe launde ledande his gomnes.
He hatz forfaren þis fox þat he fol3ed longe;   1895
As he sprent ouer a spenné to spye þe schrewe,
Þeras he herd þe howndes þat hasted hym swyþe,
Renaud com richchande þur3 a ro3e greue,

No, he cannot be killed, not by cunning on earth."
Then that lord there thought long and allowed that it was   1855
For his great, grueling task a godsend indeed.
Could he value his vow and survive nonetheless,
Take his thrust and yet thrive, it would thoroughly please!
So in silence he suffered her speaking once more.
Again to Sir Gawain the girdle she offered.   1860
When he granted, she gladly gave him that belt.
For her sake, she beseeched he conceal the gift
From her lord. He allowed it at last; he agreed
To be loyal to the lady; his lips would remain
       Sealed tight.   1865
    Gawain, again and again,
    Thanks showered, showed delight.
    That loving lady then
    A good kiss gave her knight.

The lady took leave of the loyal Gawain,   1870
For more mirth with that man then she might not enjoy.
Thus she'd gone. Good Sir Gawain got quickly dressed;
He arrayed himself royally, richly in clothes
And laid by the love-lace the lady had left;
To return to that treasure, he tucked it away.   1875
He went on his way to the wide chapel next,
Where in private he approached the priest to inquire
If he'd help him by hearing his heart now confess,
Help to save his soul when he should pass away.
He confessed his sins and was shriven at once. → forgiven   1880
For his major and minor sins, mercy he asked.
When he prayed of the priest to be piously cleansed,
He absolved Gawain certainly; safely he'd face,
Though it dawned the next day, dreaded doomsday itself.
Then he made more mirth with those merry ladies,   1885
Sang more kinds of carols and caught there more joy,
Than he'd done before. Day thus to dark, brooding night
       Drew near.
    He gave each guest a grin.
    All said, "He shows such cheer!   1890
    So happy he's not been
    Since welcomed with us here."

But now let him there linger with love and with mirth.
For the lord is out leading his liege men in hunt.
He has felled the spry fox whom he'd followed all day: 1895
When he heard the hounds bark, the host quickly jumped
With his horse a thick hedge that grew high. He saw
Swift Reynard who ran from the roughest of thickets

And alle þe rabel in a res ryȝt at his helez.
Þe wyȝe watz war of þe wylde and warly abides,   1900
And braydez out þe bryȝt bronde and at þe best castez.
And he schunt for þe scharp and schulde haf arered;
A rach rapes hym to, ryȝt er he myȝt,
And ryȝt bifore þe hors fete þay fel on hym alle
And woried me þis wyly wyth a wroth noyse.   1905
Þe lorde lyȝtez bilyue and lachez hym sone,
Rased hym ful radly out of þe rach mouþes,
Haldez heȝe ouer his hede, halowez faste,
And þer bayen hym mony braþ houndez.
Huntes hyȝed hem þeder with hornez ful mony,   1910
Ay rechatande aryȝt til þay þe renk seȝen.
Bi þat watz comen his compeyny noble,
Alle þat euer ber bugle blowed at ones
And alle þise oþer halowed, þat hade no hornes;
Hit watz þe myriest mute þat euer mon herde,   1915
Þe rich rurd þat þer watz raysed for Renaude saule
      With lote.
      Hor houndez þay þer rewarde,
      Her hedez þay fawne and frote,
      And syþen þay tan Reynarde   1920
      And tyruen of his cote.

And þenne þay helden to home, for hit watz nieȝ nyȝt,
Strakande ful stoutly in hor store hornez.
Þe lorde is lyȝt at þe laste at hys lef home,
Fyndez fire vpon flet, þe freke þerbyside,   1925
Sir Gawayn þe gode, þat glad watz with alle—
Among þe ladies for luf he ladde much joye.
He were a bleaunt of blwe, þat bradde to þe erþe,
His surkot semed hym wel, þat softe watz forred,
And his hode of þat ilke henged on his schulder;   1930
Blande al of blaunner were boþe al aboute.
He metez me þis godmon inmyddez þe flore
And al with gomen he hym gret and goudly he sayde,
'I schal fylle vpon fyrst oure forwardez nouþe,
Þat we spedly han spoken, þer spared watz no drynk.'   1935
Þen acoles he þe knyȝt and kysses hym þryes
As sauerly and sadly as he hem sette couþe.
'Bi Kryst,' quoþ þat oþer knyȝt, 'ȝe cach much sele
In cheuisaunce of þis chaffer, ȝif ȝe hade goud chepez.'
'Ȝe, of þe chepe no charg,' quoþ chefly þat oþer,   1940
'As is pertly payed þe porchas þat I aȝte.'
'Mary,' quoþ þat oþer mon, 'myn is bihynde,
For I haf hunted al þis day and noȝt haf I geten
Bot þis foule fox felle—þe Fende haf þe godez!—

With the hounds at his heels, harassing that fox.
He awaited the wily fox warily then,   1900
And swung down his sword with a swift, deadly blow.
Reynard shrank from the stroke, but a stout hound at once
By his shank seized him swiftly and shook him to earth.
The hounds fell on the fox at the feet of the horse
And burst out with bays that were bold and loud.   1905
The lord alighted and lifted the fox;
From the hounds' jaws he hoisted him high in the air.
As he held him thus high, the host holloed aloud;
Those hounds of the hunt then heartily bayed.
The huntsmen there hied, blowing horns as they raced;   1910
While raising the recall, they reached the lord there.
When that courage-filled company came to his side,
Those who bore bugles blew them and bellowed at once;
Those who had there no horns loudly holloed for joy.
The merriest sound men could make on the earth   1915
Was the rich cry they raised up for Reynard. It filled
        The air!
    Rewards come, rich and grand;
    Each dog is dealt his share.
    Reynard they rend with hand;   1920
    They skin him then and there.

The huntsmen made haste for the hall, evening near,
Where they holloed and hailed with their horns as they wished.
At last the great lord alighted at home.
A warm fire was flaming. He found there at once—   1925
Feeling good and gay—Sir Gawain awaiting,
Delighting in the ladies with laughter and glee,
In a robe, blue and rich, which reached to the floor,
And a softly furred surcoat, fashioned quite well.
On his shoulder there shone of the same hue a hood   1930
Which with beauteous, bright fur was bordered in style.
When he met this man in the midst of the hall,
Sir Gawain, both gamesome and gay, said to him:
"Sir, permit me to meet the commitment we reached,
Which we swore to observe and sealed with oaths."   1935
He thrice kissed the host kindly and courteously then,
Just as heartily, handily, as ever he could.
The fine host held forth, "You have fared well, by Christ,
In your purchases, prince, if the prices were low!"
"Have no care for the costs," said the courteous Gawain.   1940
"Since I've publicly paid all the profit I earned."
"Alas, mine, by sweet Mary, is much less than this;
For I've hunted the whole day and haven't a thing
But this foul pelt of fox; let the fiend himself have it!

And þat is ful pore for to pay for suche prys þinges   1945
As ȝe haf þryȝt me here þro, suche þre cosses
    So gode.'
    'Inoȝ,' quoþ Sir Gawayn,
    I þonk yow, bi þe Rode,'
    And how þe fox watz slayn   1950
    He tolde hym as þay stode.

With merþe and mynstralsye, wyth metez at hor wylle,
Þay maden as mery as any men moȝten,
With laȝyng of ladies, with lotez of bordes,
(Gawayn and þe godemon so glad were þay boþe),   1955
Bot if þe douthe had doted oþer dronken ben oþer.
Boþe þe mon and þe meyny maden mony japez,
Til þe sesoun watz seȝen þat þay seuer moste;
Burnez to hor bedde behoued at þe laste.
Þenne loȝly his leue at þe lorde fyrst   1960
Fochchez þis fre mon and fayre he hym þonkkez
'Of such a selly sojorne as I haf hade here.
Your honour at þis hyȝe fest þe Hyȝe Kyng yow ȝelde!
I ȝef yow me for on of yourez, if yowreself lykez,
For I mot nedes, as ȝe wot, meue tomorne,   1965
And ȝe me take sum tolke to teche, as ȝe hyȝt,
Þe gate to þe Grene Chapel, as God wyl me suffer
To dele on Nw Ȝerez Day þe dome of my wyrdes.'
'In god fayþe,' quoþ þe godmon, 'wyth a goud wylle
Al þat euer I yow hyȝt halde schal I redé.'   1970
Þer asyngnes he a seruaunt to sett hym in þe waye
And coundue hym by þe downez, þat he no drechch had,
For to ferk þurȝ þe fryth and fare at þe gaynest
    Bi greue.
    Þe lorde Gawayn con þonk   1975
    Such worchip he wolde hym weue.
    Þen at þo ladyez wlonk
    Þe knyȝt hatz tan his leue.

With care and wyth kyssyng he carppez hem tille
And fele þryuande þonkkez he þrat hom to haue;   1980
And þay ȝelden hym aȝayn ȝeply þat ilk.
Þay bikende hym to Kryst with ful colde sykyngez;
Syþen fro þe meyny he menskly departes.
Vche mon þat he mette he made hem a þonke
For his seruyse and his solace and his sere pyne   1985
Þat þay wyth busynes had ben aboute hym to serue;
And vche segge as soré to seuer with hym þere
As þay hade wonde worþyly with þat wlonk euer.
Þen with ledes and lyȝt he watz ladde to his chambre

It's a poor price to pay for such precious things   1945
As you've given me, Gawain, as gifts: three kisses,"
     He sighed.
       "Enough! I thank you now,
       By cross of Christ!" he cried.
       The host then told him how   1950
       That fox was felled, and died.

With minstrelsy, mirth, and a marvelous feast,
All made there as merry as men ever could;
For the ladies laughed at the lively, sweet jests,
And the good lord and Gawain were glad as could be   1955
(Though obnoxious was neither, and neither was drunk).
The host of that household made hearty, sweet jokes
Till the time to retire, of leave-taking, arrived.
The guests of that good host went gleeful to bed.
Gawain humbly then hailed the host to take leave,   1960
Was the first there to furnish "Farewell!" For he said:
"May the King of kings for your kindness reward you,
For the stay you have shown me here since I arrived!
As your man I'll commit myself now if you wish;
For tomorrow I must make my way, as you know.   1965
Therefore grant me the guide whom you graciously pledged.
I must go to the Green Chapel. God, as He wishes,
New Year's Day will there deal me what doom He sees fit."
Said the host, "This I happily, heartily grant;
I'll provide what I promised; my pledge I'll fulfill!"   1970
He assigned him a servant to show him the way,
To help through the hillsides the hearty Sir Gawain,
And to lead him along the lanes until he
     Was nigh.
       He thanks his host in hall   1975
       With honors, heartfelt, high;
       He turns, then, and to all
       The ladies bids good-bye.

With care and with kissing, he courteously leaves;
When he thanks the whole throng there, thoroughly all   1980
Repay him in princely thanks plenteously,
And to Christ they commend him with keen, heartfelt sighs.
Gawain leaves in a lordly and loving way then,
Not forgetting to give to each guest his true thanks
For so serving him, showing solicitude (each   1985
Had bustled about to be busy to help).
All are saddened to see Gawain sallying forth
As if they'd lived all their lives with that lord before then.
With lanterns men lead him aloft to his cell;

And blyþely broȝt to his bedde to be at his rest.   1990
Ȝif he ne slepe soundyly say ne dar I,
For he hade much on þe morn to mynne, ȝif he wolde,
          In þoȝt.
     Let hym lyȝe þere stille;
     He hatz nere þat he soȝt.   1995
     And ȝe wyl a whyle be stylle,
     I schal telle yow how þay wroȝt.

IV

Now neȝez þe Nw Ȝere and þe nyȝt passez,
Þe day dryuez to þe derk, as Dryȝtyn biddez.
Bot wylde wederez of þe worlde wakned þeroute;   2000
Clowdes kesten kenly þe colde to þe erþe,
Wyth nyȝe innoghe of þe norþe þe naked to tene.
Þe snawe snitered ful snart, þat snayped þe wylde;
Þe werbelande wynde wapped fro þe hyȝe
And drof vche dale ful of dryftes ful grete.   2005
Þe leude lystened ful wel, þat leȝ in his bedde—
Þaȝ he lowkez his liddez ful lyttel he slepes;
Bi vch kok þat crue he knwe wel þe steuen.
Deliuerly he dressed vp er þe day sprenged,
For þere watz lyȝt of a laumpe þat lemed in his chambre.   2010
He called to his chamberlayn, þat cofly hym swared,
And bede hym bryng hym his bruny and his blonk sadel.
Þat oþer ferkez hym vp and fechez hym his wedez
And grayþez me Sir Gawayn vpon a grett wyse.
Fyrst he clad hym in his cloþez, þe colde for to were,   2015
And syþen his oþer harnays, þat holdely watz keped:
Boþe his paunce and his platez piked ful clene,
Þe ryngez rokked of þe roust of his riche bruny,
And al watz fresch as vpon fyrst, and he watz fayn þenne
          To þonk.   2020
     He hade vpon vche pece,
     Wypped ful wel and wlonk;
     Þe gayest into Grece
     Þe burne bede bryng his blonk.

Whyle þe wlonkest wedes he warp on hymseluen—   2025
His cote wyth þe conysaunce of þe clere werkez
Ennurned vpon veluet, vertuus stonez
Aboute beten and bounden, enbrauded semez,
And fayre furred withinne wyth fayre pelures—
Ȝet laft he not þe lace, þe ladiez gifte;   2030
Þat forgat not Gawayn, for gode of hymseluen.
Bi he hade belted þe bronde vpon his balȝe haunchez,
Þenn dressed he his drurye double hym aboute,

He is brought to his bed, there to be at his ease. 1990
Then that man has much on his mind; but whether
He is sleepless or sleeping soundly I can't guess
      Or tell.
    Now let that lord there lie
    In stillness in his cell. 1995
    Be patient; by and by
    I'll say what soon befell.

IV

Night passes now, and the New Year arrives;
The day fully dawns, as our dear Lord ordains.
Winter winds are warring, the one with the next, 2000
And the clouds drive the cold air down keenly to earth.
There is north wind enough to numb the flesh;
Snow is shooting down sharply and stinging each beast.
Howling wind comes whistling and wailing from high
As it drives through the dales vast drifts of new snow. 2005
Gawain listened to lashing winds, lying in bed.
Though his lids were kept lowered, he little found sleep.
With each crow of the cock he could count passing time.
Before daylight had dawned, he had dressed himself well
By the light of a lamp that was lit in his room. 2010
He called to the chamberlain, "Come!" He arrived.
Gawain bid him to bring his bright coat of mail.
When the servant had done so, and saddled his horse,
Sir Gawain was geared in the greatest of ways:
He was clad in thick clothing—so cold was the day— 2015
And his armor, well made, had been marvelously wrought.
The knight's breastplate was bright, seemed to beam and glow;
And the rings had been rocked free of rust. Gawain looked
Just as fresh as at first; and that fellow he thanked
      With heed. 2020
    He looked, when duly dressed,
    A noble knight indeed:
    From Britain to Greece the best.
    He sent for his stout steed.

Thus he put on his princely apparel: his surcoat 2025
With its sign of pure spotlessness, set on velvet,
And embroidered with beauteous, bountiful gems
That shimmered and sparkled and shone in the light.
The finest of fur lined the fair coat he wore.
And he didn't forget—for the good it would bring— 2030
The girdle of green which the good lady left;
When he belted his broadsword about his smooth hips,
Gawain twisted that love-token twice on his waist,

Swyþe sweþled vmbe his swange, swetely, þat knyȝt;
Þe gordel of þe grene silke þat gay wel bisemed,   2035
Vpon þat ryol red cloþe, þat ryche watz to schewe.
Bot wered not þis ilk wyȝe for wele þis gordel,
For pryde of þe pendauntez, þaȝ polyst þay were,
And þaȝ þe glyterande golde glent vpon endez,
Bot for to sauen hymself when suffer hym byhoued,   2040
To byde bale withoute dabate, of bronde hym to were
        Oþer knyffe.
    Bi þat þe bolde mon boun
    Wynnez þeroute bilyue,
    Alle þe meyny of renoun   2045
    He þonkkez ofte ful ryue.

Thenne watz Gryngolet grayþe, þat gret watz and huge,
And hade ben sojourned sauerly and in a siker wyse:
Hym lyst prik for poynt, þat proude hors þenne.
Þe wyȝe wynnez hym to and wytez on his lyre   2050
And sayde soberly hymself and by his soth swerez,
'Here is a meyny in þis mote þat on menske þenkkez.
Þe mon hem maynteines, joy mot he haue;
Þe leue lady, on lyue luf hir bityde!
Ȝif þay for charyté cherysen a gest   2055
And halden honour in her honde, þe Haþel hem ȝelde
Þat haldez þe heuen vpon hyȝe, and also yow alle!
And ȝif I myȝt lyf vpon londe lede any quyle,
I schuld rech yow sum rewarde redyly, if I myȝt.'
Þenn steppez he into stirop and strydez alofte;   2060
His schalk schewed hym his schelde, on schulder he hit laȝt,
Gordez to Gryngolet with his gilt helez,
And he startez on þe ston, stod he no lenger
        To praunce.
    His haþel on hors watz þenne,   2065
    Þat bere his spere and launce.
    'Þis kastel to Kryst I kenne,'
    He gef hit ay god chaunce.

The brygge watz brayde doun, and þe brode ȝatez
Vnbarred and born open vpon boþe halue.   2070
Þe burne blessed hym bilyue and þe bredez passed,
Prayses þe porter bifore þe prynce kneled—
Gef hym God and goud day, þat Gawayn He saue—
And went on his way with his wyȝe one,
Þat schulde teche hym to tourne to þat tene place   2075
Þer þe ruful race he schulde resayue.
Þay boȝen bi bonkkez þer boȝez ar bare;
Þay clomben bi clyffez þer clengez þe colde.

Thereby wrapping the rich silk around himself well.
On Sir Gawain that girdle of green appeared fine! 2035
It looked rich on that red cloth, and rightly adorned.
But it wasn't for wealth that he wore the green silk,
Nor through pride in the polished, fine pendants it bore—
Which glittered and glinted with gold in the light—
But to save his own skin when he'd suffer, that day, 2040
To receive the death stroke, not stopping what might
    Befall.
      And, finally finished then,
      Gawain goes to the hall.
      He's met by all the men 2045
      And thanks them, one and all.

Then is Gringolet, Gawain's horse, greatly prepared.
He'd been stabled and exercised since he arrived,
Was prepared now to prance with both power and zest.
When Sir Gawain gazed on his glistening coat, 2050
He said to himself, "Now I swear, by my truth,
In this castle great courtesy's keenly observed.
The man who maintains this place, may he have joy!
May the lady know love all her life, for her part!
Unchurlish in charity, cherishing guests, 2055
They give help in this hostel. May He Who above
Rules the world reward these worthy folk well!
Could I linger in this land any longer, I would,
And with wealth I'd reward all you worthy men!"
When he stepped in the stirrup and swung on his horse, 2060
His shining, bright shield from his servant he took,
And with gilded spurs goaded on Gringolet well,
Who streaked over stones, did not stay any longer
    To prance.
      One man with him sufficed 2065
      With spear and lofty lance.
      "O keep this castle, Christ,
      All free from foul mischance!"

When the drawbridge went down, the dark, wooden gates
Were unbarred and swung back along both of their hinges. 2070
Gawain cantered forth, carefully crossing himself,
And plenteously praised the porter (who'd kneeled,
And said "Good day!" to Gawain. "May God keep you safe!").
Gawain went on his way with the one who was guide
To the perilous place where that prince, that same day, 2075
Would receive—it was certain—the swift, deadly blow.
By boughs that were bare and by banks they rode forth.
They climbed up sharp cliffs where the cold bit the flesh,

Þe heuen watz vphalt, bot vgly þervnder.
Mist muged on þe mor, malt on þe mountez;   2080
Vch hille hade a hatte, a myst-hakel huge.
Brokez byled and breke bi bonkkez aboute,
Schyre schaterande on schorez, þer þay doun schowued.
Wela wylle watz þe way þer þay bi wod schulden,
Til hit watz sone sesoun þat þe sunne ryses   2085
        Þat tyde.
    Þay were on a hille ful hyȝe;
    Þe quyte snaw lay bisyde.
    Þe burne þat rod hym by
    Bede his mayster abide.   2090

'For I haf wonnen yow hider, wyȝe, at þis tyme,
And now nar ȝe not fer fro þat note place
Þat ȝe han spied and spuryed so specially after.
Bot I schal say yow for soþe, syþen I yow knowe
And ȝe ar a lede vpon lyue þat I wel louy: 2095
Wolde ȝe worch bi my wytte, ȝe worþed þe better.
Þe place þat ȝe prece to ful perelous is halden:
Þer wonez a wyȝe in þat waste, þe worst vpon erþe,
For he is stiffe and sturne and to strike louies,
And more he is þen any mon vpon myddelerde,   2100
And his body bigger þen þe best fowre
Þat ar in Arþurez hous, Hestor, oþer oþer.
He cheuez þat chaunce at þe Chapel Grene,
Þer passes non bi þat place so proude in his armes
Þat he ne dyngez hym to deþe with dynt of his honde;   2105
For he is a mon methles and mercy non vses.
For be hit chorle oþer chaplayn þat bi þe chapel rydes,
Monk oþer masseprest, oþer any mon elles,
Hym þynk as queme hym to quelle as quyk go hymseluen.
Forþy I say þe: as soþe as ȝe in sadel sitte,   2110
Com ȝe þere, ȝe be kylled, may þe knyȝt rede,—
Trawe ȝe me þat trwely—þaȝ ȝe had twenty lyues
        To spende.
    He hatz wonyd here ful ȝore,
    On bent much baret bende;   2115
    Aȝayn his dyntez sore
    Ȝe may not yow defende.

'Forþy, goude Sir Gawayn, let þe gome one
And gotz away sum oþer gate, vpon Goddez halue!
Cayrez bi sum oþer kyth, þer Kryst mot yow spede!   2120
And I schal hyȝ me hom aȝayn; and hete yow fyrre
Þat I schal swere "Bi God and alle His gode halȝez",
"As help me God and þe halydam", and oþez innoghe,

Where they hung beneath high clouds in a heavy drizzle,
In a mist; on the moor and the mountains it fell. 2080
Thus each hill had a hat and a huge, misty coat.
From their banks, swelling brooks in bursts tumbled down;
With loud roaring and raging, they rushed from the peaks.
Thus the way the men went was both wild and rough.
Till the sun had ascended, those slopes in the cold 2085
    They plied.
      They rode till they had reached
      The heights where snow lay wide.
      The guide then stopped, beseeched
      Bold Gawain to abide. 2090

"Sir Gawain," said the guide, "to this ground I've brought you.
You are near, my knight. Now the noted locale
That you've earnestly, eagerly, asked for is nigh.
I will certainly say to you, since you should know,
You're a lord whom I love with my life. I declare, 2095
You would fare well, my fine knight, to follow my words.
For the place you pursue is a peril indeed.
In that waste there is waiting the worst man on earth.
He is stern and strong, and to strike blows he loves.
He's a man who is mightier by much than any, 2100
With a body as big as the best four together
In the household of Hector or high Arthur's court.
He rules chance without check in the chapel of green.
No one passes that place, in the pride of his arms,
But he deals him a dint, a strong deathblow, at once. 2105
An immoderate man, he is merciless, grim.
Whether chaplain or churl by his chapel should pass,
Whether monk or Mass-priest, that man is as glad
There to cut him down coldly as keep life himself.
Just as sure as you sit in your saddle, good knight, 2110
If you go there you'll get the grimmest of deaths—
You may trust in my truth—though you'd twenty-odd lives
    To spend!
      Many a man there met
      A grim and grisly end. 2115
      Against his ghastly threat
      Yourself you can't defend.

"Therefore, Gawain, my good knight, give up your quest;
Right now leave this grim land for the love of our God,
And in safer realms sojourn, assured of Christ's care.
I shall head back home; in that hall, be assured, 2120
I shall swear by the saints, by my soul, and by God,
With my right hand on relics, as I relish my life,

Þat I schal lelly yow layne and lauce neuer tale
Þat euer ȝe fondet to fle for freke þat I wyst.'   2125
'Grant merci,' quoþ Gawayn, and gruchyng he sayde,
'Wel worth þe, wyȝe, þat woldez my gode,
And þat lelly me layne I leue wel þou woldez;
Bot helde þou hit neuer so holde, and I here passed,
Founded for ferde for to fle, in fourme þat þou tellez,   2130
I were a knyȝt kowarde, I myȝt not be excused.
Bot I wyl to þe chapel, for chaunce þat may falle,
And talk wyth þat ilk tulk þe tale þat me lyste,
Worþe hit wele oþer wo, as þe Wyrde lykez
        Hit hafe.   2135
        Paȝe he be a sturn knape
        To stiȝtel, and stad with staue,
        Ful wel con Dryȝtyn schape
        His seruauntez for to saue.

'Mary!' quoþ þat oþer mon, 'now þou so much spellez   2140
Þat þou wylt þyn awen nye nyme to þyseluen
And þe lyst lese þy lyf, þe lette I ne kepe.
Haf here þi helme on þy hede, þi spere in þi honde,
And ryde me doun þis ilk rake, bi ȝon rokke syde,
Til þou be broȝt to þe boþem of þe brem valay.   2145
Þenne loke a littel on þe launde, on þi lyfte honde,
And þou schal se in þat slade þe self chapel
And þe borelych burne on bent þat hit kepez.
Now farez wel, on Godez half, Gawayn þe noble!
For alle þe golde vpon grounde I nolde go wyth þe,   2150
Ne bere þe felaȝschip þurȝ þis fryth on fote fyrre.'
Bi þat þe wyȝe in þe wod wendez his brydel,
Hit þe hors with þe helez as harde as he myȝt,
Lepez hym ouer þe launde, and leuez þe knyȝt þere
        Alone.   2155
        'Bi Goddez Self,' quoþ Gawayn,
        'I wyl nauþer grete ne grone;
        To Goddez wylle I am ful bayn
        And to Hym I haf me tone.'

Thenne gyrdez he to Gryngolet and gederez þe rake,   2160
Schowuez in bi a schore at a schaȝe syde,
Ridez þurȝ þe roȝe bonk ryȝt to þe dale.
And þenne he wayted hym aboute, and wylde hit hym þoȝt,
And seȝe no syngne of resette bisydez nowhere,
Bot hyȝe bonkkez and brent vpon boþe halue   2165
And ruȝe knokled knarrez with knorned stonez;
Þe skwez of þe scowtes skayned hym þoȝt.
Þenne he houed and wythhylde his hors at þat tyde

LIE FOR YOU

I'll conceal your escape, never speak all my days
Of the fact that you fled from that fatal, grim tryst."   2125
Said Gawain, "Dear God, mercy grant to this man!
Reward him who wishes me well! I don't doubt
That you'd truly not tell of my retreat. But although
It would stay concealed, unspoken, unknown,
If I fled out of fear in the fashion you suggest,   2130
I'd become inexcusable, a cowardly knight.
I'll face chance at the chapel; I'll exchange speeches there
That I find are fit with that fierce, dangerous man,
Whether weal or woe be what providence there
      Allow.   2135
    Though that man metes out strife,
    Is vicious, as you vow;
    To save a servant's life
    High heaven's King knows how."

That man said, "By Mary! You might as well say   2140
You're determined to be dealt your own death. Very well;
If you long so to lose your own life, I'll assist!
On your head don your helmet; in hand take your spear.
There's a road down these rocks which you'll ride along
Till you reach a rough valley, rambling and strange.   2145
If you look on your left, you'll see lying right there
That same chapel you seek—for its site you'll have gained—
And you'll meet there the man who is master. Farewell,
Good Sir Gawain, may God be your guide! I would not
For all gold in the ground agree to join you,   2150
Or proceed one more step through this strange wood." He turned
His bridle about and broke for the hall,
Spurred his horse with his heels just as hard as he could.
He leapt right along, thereby leaving that knight
      Alone.   2155
    "By God," Sir Gawain swore,
    "I'll neither gripe nor groan,
    Nor pledge with God ignore;
    His will I won't postpone!"

So Sir Gawain guided Gringolet on   2160
A wild bank, rough and broken, beside a thick wood.
As he rode that rough bank he arrived at a dale
Where he waited a while. It was wild, Gawain thought.
There no sign could be seen of a shelter for miles.
But the banks of the broad dale on both sides were high   2165
And steep. They were strewn with huge stones everywhere.
To Sir Gawain those great crags seemed grazed by the clouds.
When he halted, withholding his horse at that time,

And ofte chaunged his cher þe chapel to seche.
He seȝ non suche in no syde—and selly hym þoȝt—   2170
Saue, a lyttel on a launde, a lawe as hit were,
A balȝ berȝ bi a bonke þe brymme bysyde,
Bi a forȝ of a flode þat ferked þare;
Þe borne blubred þerinne as hit boyled hade.
Þe knyȝt kachez his caple and com to þe lawe,   2175
Liȝtez doun luflyly and at a lynde tachez
Þe rayne of his riche, with a roȝe braunche.
Þenne he boȝez to þe berȝe, aboute hit he walkez,
Debatande with hymself quat hit be myȝt.
Hit hade a hole on þe ende and on ayþer syde,   2180
And ouergrowen with gresse in glodes aywhere,
And al watz holȝ inwith, nobot an olde caue
Or a creuisse of an olde cragge—he couþe hit noȝt deme
      With spelle.
    'We! Lorde,' quoþ þe gentyle knyȝt,   2185
    'Wheþer þis be þe Grene Chapelle?
    Here myȝt aboute mydnyȝt
    Þe Dele his matynnes telle!'

'Now iwysse,' quoþ Wowayn, 'wysty is here;
Þis oritore is vgly, with erbez ouergrowen.   2190
Wel bisemez þe wyȝe wruxled in grene
Dele here his deuocioun on þe Deuelez wyse;
Now I fele hit is þe Fende, in my fyue wyttez,
Þat hatz stoken me þis steuen to strye me here.
Þis is a chapel of meschaunce, þat chekke hit bytyde!   2195
Hit is þe corsedest kyrk þat euer I com inne!'
With heȝe helme on his hede, his launce in his honde,
He romez vp to þe roffe of þo roȝ wonez.
Þene herde he of þat hyȝe hil, in a harde roche
Biȝonde þe broke, in a bonk, a wonder breme noyse.   2200
Quat! hit clatered in þe clyff as hit cleue schulde,
As one vpon a gryndelston hade grounden a syþe.
What! hit wharred and whette as water at a mulne;
What! hit rusched and ronge, rawþe to here.
Þenne 'Bi Godde,' quoþ Gawayn, 'þat gere, as I trowe,   2205
Is ryched at þe reuerence me renk to mete
      Bi rote.
    Let God worche! "We loo!"
    Hit helppez me not a mote.
    My lif þaȝ I forgoo,   2210
    Drede dotz me no lote.'

Thenne þe knyȝt con calle ful hyȝe,
'Who stiȝtlez in þis sted, me steuen to holde?

Gawain searched on all sides to discern a chapel.
But he saw no such site. It was strange without doubt!   2170
He discerned, though, what seemed a sort of a mound
Or a barrow above the low banks of a stream
That was swirling and surging strangely along:
From its banks it would bubble up, boiling and wild.
Sir Gawain on Gringolet goes to the mound;   2175
Off his horse he hastens, and hitches the reins
To the branch of a bough that is bent down and gnarled.
He makes for the mound and moves over it,
Seeking to discern what that site there might be.
There are strange holes exposed on each side and in front.   2180
Tall grass is there growing in great, scattered patches.
In its midst that mysterious mound has a cave
Or a kind of a crevice; he cannot quite name
    The thing.
      "Alas, is this the site,   2185
    O Lord, I've long been seeking?
    Here may, around midnight,
    The devil his matins sing!

"Dear God, I declare it is desolate here!
Overgrown with dry grass is this grim oratory.   2190
It is fitting the fellow whose form is green
Should here do his devotions in devilish ways.
My five wits feel it's the fiend himself
Who to kill me has cast me in covenant now.
Let ill fortune befall this foul chapel of doom,   2195
An accursed, bleak church for a Christian to use!"
On his head was his helmet, in hand was his lance;
Thus he reached the wide roof of the rough barrow there
When he heard from that hill a hideous sound
From beyond the wide bank of the brook flowing near.   2200
As though cleaving the cliffs that noise clattered. It seemed
That a grindstone was grinding a great, awful scythe.
Loud as water it whirred at the wheel of a mill.
That ferocious, full sound was fearsome to hear.
Said Gawain, "By God, that grinding's for me!   2205
It's a fanfare for feats all too fatal; my doom
    Is near!
      God's will be done! To bray
    'Alas' won't help me here.
    Though I lose life, I'll stay;   2210
    A noise I'll never fear."

Then he started to shout; in a shrill voice he asked:
"Who's in power in this place? An appointment we have,

For now is gode Gawayn goande ry3t here.
If any wy3e o3t wyl, wynne hider fast,   2215
Oþer now oþer neuer, his nedez to spede.'
'Abyde!' quoþ on on þe bonke abouen ouer his hede,
'And þou schal haf al in hast þat I þe hy3t ones.'
3et he rusched on þat rurde rapely a þrowe
And wyth quettyng awharf, er he wolde ly3t;   2220
And syþen he keuerez bi a cragge and comez of a hole,
Whyrlande out of a wro wyth a felle weppen:
A denez ax, nwe dy3t, þe dynt with to 3elde,
With a borelych bytte bende by þe halme,
Fyled in a fylor, fowre fote large—   2225
Hit watz no lasse, bi þat lace þat lemed ful bry3t!—
And þe gome in þe grene gered as fyrst,
Boþe þe lyre and þe leggez, lokkez and berde,
Saue þat fayre on his fote he foundez on þe erþe,
Sette þe stele to þe stone and stalked bysyde.   2230
When he wan to þe watter, þer he wade nolde,
He hypped ouer on hys ax and orpedly strydez,
Bremly broþe on a bent þat brode watz aboute,
        On snawe.
    Sir Gawayn þe kny3t con mete;   2235
    He ne lutte hym noþyng lowe.
    Þat oþer sayde, 'Now, sir swete,
    Of steuen mon may þe trowe.'

'Gawayn,' quoþ þat grene gome, 'God þe mot loke!
Iwysse þou art welcom, wy3e, to my place,   2240
And þou hatz tymed þi trauayl as truee mon schulde;
And þou knowez þe couenauntez kest vus bytwene:
At þis tyme twelmonyth þou toke þat þe falled
And I schulde at þis Nwe 3ere 3eply þe quyte.
And we ar in þis valay verayly oure one;   2245
Here ar no renkes vs to rydde, rele as vus likez.
Haf þy helme of þy hede and haf here þy pay.
Busk no more debate þen I þe bede þenne
When þou wypped of my hede at a wap one.'
'Nay, bi God,' quoþ Gawayn, 'þat me gost lante,   2250
I schal gruch þe no grwe, for grem þat fallez;
Bot sty3tel þe vpon on strok and I schal stonde stylle
And warp þe no wernyng to worch as þe lykez
        Nowhare.'
    He lened with þe nek and lutte   2255
    And schewed þat schyre al bare,
    And lette as he no3t dutte;
    For drede he wolde not dare.

For the good Sir Gawain at this ground has arrived.
If anyone here has wishes or wants, let him come 2215
Either now or else never his needs to fulfill."
From above, on a bank, a voice bellowed: "Now stay!
In haste you will have what I heartily promised."
He resumed, with that screeching noise, sharpening then;
The man went on with whetting and working the grindstone. 2220
He climbed down a crag and soon came from a hole
And walked from a wide nook with weapon in hand:
A Danish ax, deadly, to deal Gawain's fate,
With a burnished, keen blade that was bent in a curve;
It was filed most finely—four feet was its arc, 2225
Nothing less, as the length of its lash would attest.
That great man was garbed in green as before:
His legs and his locks and his long, bright green beard.
But he was without horse; that knight walked on the ground.
He came toward Gawain, tapping that true ax on the ground, 2230
Going straight to the stream which with skill he vaulted
With the haft of his hearty ax. Haughtily then
The knight fiercely strode forth on a field all white
  With snow.
   Though Gawain greets him there, 2235
   He never once bows low.
   That green man says, "I swear,
   You honor debts you owe!"

The Green Knight said, "Gawain, may God protect you!
Let me welcome you warmly, with wide open arms. 2240
You have timed your long travel as true men should do;
Our contract, our covenant, you carry out well.
For you dealt me a deathblow this day twelve months back;
In turn now, at this New Year, I'll nicely repay.
We have met at this mound: we are two men alone, 2245
Without judges to jump between, joust as we like.
From your head take your helmet and have now your pay.
Do not moan any more than I moaned myself when
With a blow you beheaded me briskly last year."
"Now by God," said Sir Gawain, "Who gave me good life, 2250
Any harm that I have I'll not hold against you,
I will stay quite still. Take one stroke, only one!
I will acquiesce coolly, not coming to my
  Own aid."
   He bared his naked neck 2255
   Most boldly to the blade.
   To keep his cares in check
   He acted unafraid.

Then þe gome in þe grene grayþed hym swyþe,
Gederez vp hys grymme tole, Gawayn to smyte;   2260
With alle þe bur in his body he ber hit on lofte,
Munt as maȝtyly as marre hym he wolde.
Hade hit dryuen adoun as dreȝ as he atled,
Þer hade ben ded of his dynt þat doȝty watz euer.
Bot Gawayn on þat giserne glyfte hym bysyde,   2265
As hit com glydande adoun on glode hym to schende,
And schranke a lytel with þe schulderes for þe scharp yrne.
Þat oþer schalk wyth a schunt þe schene wythhaldez
And þenne repreued he þe prynce with mony prowde wordez:
'Þou art not Gawayn,' quoþ þe gome, 'þat is so goud halden,   2270
Þat neuer arȝed for no here by hylle ne be vale,
And now þou fles for ferde er þou fele harmez!
Such cowardise of þat knyȝt cowþe I neuer here.
Nawþer fyked I ne flaȝe, freke, quen þou myntest,
Ne kest no kauelacion in kyngez hous Arthor.   2275
My hede flaȝ to my fote and ȝet flaȝ I neuer;
And þou, er any harme hent, arȝez in hert.
Wherfore þe better burne me burde be called
        Þerfore.'
            Quoþ Gawayn, 'I schunt onez   2280
            And so wyl I no more;
            Bot þaȝ my hede falle on þe stonez
            I con not hit restore.

'Bot busk, burne, bi þi fayth, and bryng me to þe poynt—
Dele to me my destiné and do hit out of honde.   2285
For I schal stonde þe a strok and start no more
Til þyn ax haue me hitte—haf here my trawþe.'
'Haf at þe þenne!' quoþ þat oþer, and heuez hit alofte
And waytez as wroþely as he wode were.
He myntez at hym maȝtyly bot not þe mon rynez,   2290
Withhelde heterly his honde er hit hurt myȝt.
Gawayn grayþely hit bydez and glent with no membre
Bot stode stylle as þe ston oþer a stubbe auþer
Þat raþeled is in roché grounde with rotez a hundreth.
Þen muryly efte con he mele, þe mon in þe grene: 2295
'So, now þou hatz þi hert holle hitte me bihous.
Halde þe now þe hyȝe hode þat Arþur þe raȝt
And kepe þy kanel at þis kest, ȝif hit keuer may!'
Gawayn ful gryndelly with greme þenne sayde:
'Wy, þresch on, þou þro mon! Þou þretez to longe.   2300
I hope þat þi hert arȝe wyth þyn awen seluen.'
'Forsoþe,' quoþ þat oþer freke, 'so felly þou spekez,
I wyl no lenger on lyte lette þin ernde
            Riȝt nowe.'

So the Green Knight got ready, gripping the ax;
With marvelous might the man took his hold,   2260
And lifted the long blade to lower the blow.
Next he steadied the steel for the stroke to be fierce.
Had the stroke that he struck been as strong as he threatened
Gawain no doubt would have dismally died from the blow.
But Gawain once glanced at that grievous, sharp ax   2265
As it arced through the air to arrive at its mark,
And his shoulders shrank from the sharp, falling blade.
The other balked; he jerked back at the blade at once,
And reproved the prince with these proud, haughty words:
"You're not Gawain whose good fame has gone through the land,   2270
Who from fear never flinched on a field or a hill;
For you cringe, before cut, like a coward or worse!
Gawain never was known as ignoble or scared.
When you struck me I stooped there, both steady and quiet,
Nor caviled like a coward in King Arthur's hall.   2275
My head flew to my feet, but fixed I remained.
Yet untouched here you tremble and take to quailing.
I'd be known as the nobler true knight of us two,
    I say!"
        "From second stroke," he said,   2280
    "I shall not shrink away.
    But if you hew *my* head,
    Asunder it will stay.

"But by God above, go ahead; get on with it!
Now my destiny deal through the dint of that ax.   2285
I will stand for the stroke and not start back again,
Till I'm hit with the heavy ax here—on my word!"
"Then get ready!" he roared, as he raised the ax high.
He stared down, stern, as if stricken with rage.
He started the stroke; but he stopped all at once.   2290
He held back on the blade before bringing it down.
Staying firm and unflinching, as fixed as a rock,
Gawain stayed just as still as a stump in the earth
That is gripping the ground with its great, hundred roots.
The Green Knight was gladdened. To Gawain he said: 2295
"So your courage rekindled! I'll cut at you now!
Let the order of Arthur now answer for you,
Let it save you from certain death served by the ax!"
In a rush of rage he replied with this speech:
"No more words! Strike away; for I weary of threats!   2300
For it seems you've been stricken, unstrung, with great fear."
"Your reply is rash; you are raging," he said.
"I will finish you fiercely, nor further mere talk
    Allow."

Þenne tas he hym stryþe to stryke   2305
And frounsez boþe lyppe and browe.
No meruayle þaȝ hym myslyke
Þat hoped of no rescowe.

He lyftes lyȝtly his lome and let hit doun fayre
With þe barbe of þe bitte bi þe bare nek.   2310
Þaȝ he homered heterly, hurt hym no more
Bot snyrt hym on þat on syde, þat seuered þe hyde.
Þe scharp schrank to þe flesche þurȝ þe schyre grece,
Þat þe schene blod ouer his schulderes schot to þe erþe.
And quen þe burne seȝ þe blode blenk on þe snawe,   2315
He sprit forth spenne-fote more þen a spere lenþe,
Hent heterly his helme and on his hed cast,
Schot with his schulderez his fayre schelde vnder,
Braydez out a bryȝt sworde and bremely he spekez—
Neuer syn þat he watz barne borne of his moder   2320
Watz he neuer in þis worlde wyȝe half so blyþe—
'Blynne, burne, of þy bur! Bede me no mo!
I haf a stroke in þis sted withoute stryf hent
And if þow rechez me any mo I redyly schal quyte
And ȝelde ȝederly aȝayn—and þerto ȝe tryst—   2325
      And foo.
   Bot on stroke here me fallez—
   Þe couenaunt schop ryȝt so,
   Festned in Arþurez hallez—
   And þerfore, hende, now hoo!'   2330

The haþel heldet hym fro and on his ax rested,
Sette þe schaft vpon schore and to þe scharp lened
And loked to þe leude þat on þe launde ȝede,
How þat doȝty, dredles, deruely þer stondez,
Armed ful aȝlez; in hert hit hym lykez.   2335
Þenn he melez muryly wyth a much steuen
And, wyth a rynkande rurde, he to þe renk sayde,
'Bolde burne, on þis bent be not so gryndel.
No mon here vnmanerly þe mysboden habbez,
Ne kyd bot as couenaunde at kyngez kort schaped.   2340
I hyȝt þe a strok and þou hit hatz—halde þe wel payed.
I relece þe of þe remnaunt of ryȝtes alle oþer.
Iif I deliuer had bene, a boffet paraunter
I couþe wroþeloker haf waret, to þe haf wroȝt anger.
Fyrst I mansed þe muryly with a mynt one   2345
And roue þe wyth no rof-sore. With ryȝt I þe profered
For þe forwarde þat we fest in þe fyrst nyȝt;
And þou trystyly þe trawþe and trwly me haldez:
Al þe gayne þow me gef, as god mon schulde.

He stands to strike at him,   2305
With brittle lip and brow.
Sir Gawain's grieved and grim:
He'll not be rescued now!

He lifted the long ax and let it down hard;
He brought down the blade on the bare, exposed neck.   2310
Though he lunged with the long ax, he left not much more
Than a nick on the neck of that knight. The blade's edge
Only severed the skin; and it sent forth some blood.
From Gawain's shoulders blood sprang, as it spurted in drops.
He beheld his red blood shining bright on the snow,   2315
And sprang forth a spear-length suddenly then.
On his head he hefted his helmet and jerked
Forth his shield, which he'd slung on his shoulder before.
He brandished his bright sword and boldly spoke out
(Since the bright day, years back, of his birth, he had not 2320
Been so grateful or glad or so gleeful as now):
"Now desist your striking and swing not once more!
For a stroke I've withstood without stirring at all.
Blow for blow I'll give back if you boldly keep on.
If you fight I'll defend myself fiercely; I'll even   2325
       The score.
     You've given back the blow,
     As we agreed before.
     I've given what I owe.
     Enough's enough; no more!"   2330

That lordly man lightly then leaned on his ax,
Set its haft, as he held it in hand, on the ground,
And gazed on Sir Gawain, that good knight, in thought.
When he found Gawain fearless and feisty withal,
He was pleased and impressed, and proceeded to speak   2335
Words which boomed in a bold and bellowing voice
And roared out richly, went ringing about:
"Be less bellicose, bold man, nobody has erred;
No one here has behaved in a hostile, bad way.
What our covenant called for I've carried out here.   2340
You've been paid what I promised; that's perfectly fair.
I release you at last from all lingering debts.
I'd have wielded woe, were I adroit,
And have done you some damage with the dint of my blade.
When I first merely feinted to fell you, good knight,   2345
But spared you instead, well then, such was my right:
Such accords with the covenant we cast at the start.
You then honestly honored the oaths that we made
When you gave me your gift, as a good man should do.

Þat oþer munt for þe morne, mon, I þe profered: 2350
Þou kyssedes my clere wyf, þe cossez me raʒtez.
For boþe two here I þe bede bot two bare myntes
    Boute scaþe.
   Trwe mon trwe restore;
   Þenne þar mon drede no waþe.   2355
   At þe þrid þou fayled þore,
   And þerfor þat tappe ta þe.

For hit is my wede þat þou werez, þat ilke wouen girdel.
Myn owen wyf hit þe weued, I wot wel forsoþe.
Now know I wel þy cosses and þy costes als,   2360
And þe wowyng of my wyf. I wroʒt hit myseluen;
I sende hir to asay þe, and sothly me þynkkez
On þe fautlest freke þat euer on fote ʒede.
As perle bi þe quite pese is of prys more,
So is Gawayn, in god fayth, bi oþer gay knyʒtez.   2365
Bot here yow lakked a lyttel, sir, and lewté yow wonted;
Bot þat watz for no wylyde werke, ne wowyng nauþer,
Bot for ʒe lufed your lyf—þe lasse I yow blame.'
Þat oþer stif mon in study stod a gret whyle,
So agreued for greme he gryed withinne;   2370
Alle þe blode of his brest blende in his face,
Þat al he schrank for schome þat þe schalk talked.
Þe forme worde vpon folde þat þe freke meled:
'Corsed worth cowarddyse and couetyse boþe!
In yow is vylany and vyse, þat vertue disstryez.'   2375
Þenne he kaʒt to þe knot and þe kest lawsez,
Brayde broþely þe belt to þe burne seluen:
'Lo! þer þe falssyng—foule mot hit falle!
For care of þy knokke, cowardyse me taʒt
To acorde me with couetyse, my kynde to forsake: 2380
Þat is larges and lewté, þat longez to knyʒtez.
Now am I fawty and falce, and ferde haf ben euer
Of trecherye and vntrawþe—boþe bityde sorʒe
    And care!
   I biknowe yow, knyʒt, here stylle,   2385
   Al fawty is my fare.
   Letez me ouertake your wylle
   And efte I schal be ware.'

Thenn loʒe þat oþer leude and luflyly sayde,
'I halde hit hardily hole, þe harme þat I hade.   2390
Þou art confessed so clene, beknowen of þy mysses,
And hatz þe penaunce apert of þe poynt of myn egge,
I halde þe polysed of þat plyʒt and pured as clene
As þou hadez neuer forfeted syþen þou watz fyrst borne.

The feint that followed was for the next day   2350
When you kissed my wife kindly, and kisses gave me.
In turn for those two days I turned back the fine
    Sharp blade.
      The true, you see, are spared,
      And need not be afraid.   2355
      The third day, though, you erred,
      And with that prick were paid.

"For that girdle of green that you go with is mine;
I'm aware that my wife was the one who gave it.
Of your kisses and conduct I'm quite well informed,   2360
For I worked out my wife's plan of wooing you, sir,
All to test and to try you; and, truly, you seem
The most perfect of princes who walk upon earth!
As pearls are more precious than peas, when compared,
So much greater is Gawain, I glean, than all knights!   2365
But you lapsed just a little; your loyalty flagged.
Since the cause was not courtship or covetousness,
But the love of your life, so much less do I blame."
Sir Gawain stood gazing a great while, stunned.
In his anger and awe he was openly moved,   2370
And the blood from his breast began brightening his face.
At that speech he had shrunk out of shame and dismay.
The first words he formed on that field were these:
"Be accursed, gross cowardice, coveting life!
You are villainous vices that virtue destroy!"   2375
He grasped the green girdle, its great knot untied;
And with fierceness it flew at the feet of that knight.
"Evil fortune befall that false, wicked belt!
I succumbed here to cowardice, cared for my life,
And, becoming most covetous, keenly fell short   2380
Of the loyalty, largess, belonging to knights.
Now I'm faulty and false, afraid for my life.
May all forms of foul falseness fare poorly, as
    They should!
      Profound's my perfidy.   2385
      But if I ever could
      Regain your grace, I'd be
      Most grateful, ever good."

Laughing both loudly and long, the man said:
"Any harm I have had is hereby amended;   2390
As you've fully confessed, you are fully absolved.
All your penance you paid at the point of my blade;
You're as free of your faults as you'd find yourself if
Since your birth you had been unbendingly pure.

And I gif þe, sir, þe gurdel þat is golde-hemmed;   2395
For hit is grene as my goune, Sir Gawayn, ȝe maye
Þenk vpon þis ilke þrepe þer þou forth þryngez
Among prynces of prys, and þis a pure token
Of þe chaunce of þe Grene Chapel at cheualrous knyȝtez.
And ȝe schal in þis Nwe ȝer aȝayn to my wonez   2400
And we schyn reuel þe remnaunt of þis ryche fest
    Ful bene.'
      Þer laþed hym fast þe lorde
      And sayde, 'With my wyf, I wene,
      We schal yow wel acorde,   2405
      Þat watz your enmy kene.'

'Nay forsoþe,' quoþ þe segge, and sesed hys helme
And hatz hit of hendely and þe haþel þonkkez,
'I haf sojorned sadly—sele yow bytyde,
And He ȝelde hit yow ȝare þat ȝarkkez al menskes!   2410
And comaundez me to þat cortays, your comlych fere,
Boþe þat on and þat oþer, myn honoured ladyez,
Þat þus hor knyȝt wyth hor kest han koyntly bigyled.
Bot hit is no ferly þaȝ a fole madde
And þurȝ wyles of wymmen be wonen to sorȝe;   2415
For so watz Adam in erde with one bygyled,
And Salamon with fele sere, and Samson, eftsonez—
Dalyda dalt hym hys wyrde—and Dauyth, þerafter,
Watz blended with Barsabe, þat much bale þoled.
Now þese were wrathed wyth her wyles, hit were a wynne huge   2420
To luf hom wel and leue hem not, a leude þat couþe.
For þes wer forne þe freest, þat folȝed alle þe sele
Exellently, of alle þyse oþer vnder heuen-ryche
    Þat mused;
      And alle þay were biwyled   2425
      With wymmen þat þay vsed.
      Þaȝ I be now bigyled,
      Me þink me burde be excused.

'Bot your gordel,' quoþ Gawayn, '—God yow forȝelde!—
Þat wyl I welde wyth guod wylle, not for þe wynne golde,   2430
Ne þe saynt, ne þe sylk, ne þe syde pendaundes,
For wele ne for worchyp, ne for þe wlonk werkkez;
Bot in syngne of my surfet I schal se hit ofte,
When I ride in renoun remorde to myseluen
Þe faut and þe fayntyse of þe flesche crabbed,   2435
How tender hit is to entyse teches of fylþe.
And þus, quen pryde schal me pryk for prowes of armes,
Þe loke to þis luf-lace schal leþe my hert.
Bot on I wolde yow pray, displeses yow neuer:

I give you this golden-hemmed girdle to keep   2395
Since it's green as my gown, Sir Gawain, perhaps
You'll remember our meeting when making your way
Among praiseworthy princes. This pure sign will stand
For the game at the Green Chapel good knights once played.
But for now let's renew our New Year's delights;   2400
We will feast, my friend, and be festive with pomp
    And show.
      A little longer dwell.
      And with my wife, I know,
      We'll reconcile you well—   2405
      Though she was once your foe."

"I cannot," said the knight. And he nobly gave thanks.
From his head Gawain hefted his helmet at once.
"I have lingered too long. But good luck go with you;
May you have high honors at the hands of the Lord!   2410
Also give my regards to your gracious wife,
And as well to that wizened, old woman: ladies
Who beguiled their guest with their grievous wiles.
It's no feat when a fool's great folly's exposed
By the wiles of women, and woe thus ensues.   2415
For by one wily woman was Adam beguiled;
By several was Solomon; Samson, as well,
Was undone by Delilah; and David himself
By Bathsheba was shown both sorrow and woe.
Now if such men have suffered, we'd surely do well   2420
If we loved them, but little believed what they said.
And I've named but the noblest, most noteworthy men
Who, though favored by fortune, have fallen to women's
    Misuse.
      Since these most mighty men   2425
      Have suffered such abuse,
      If I've been taken in,
      I might have some excuse.

"But by God," said Gawain, "your girdle I'll keep;
I will go with it gladly for goodwill, not pride   2430
In the sash or the silk or the swinging pendants,
Nor for wealth, nor to win thus a wide-ranging fame.
But instead it shall serve as a sign of my fault;
When I ride through the realm I'll recall, to my shame,
Both the falseness and frailty of flesh, how it tends   2435
To invite the most vicious, the vilest, of sins.
Thus when pricked onto pride through my prowess of arms,
I will look on this love-lace to lay that pride low.
But I'd ask you in earnest, unless it displease:

Syn ʒe be lorde of þe ʒonder londe þat I haf lent inne   2440
Wyth yow wyth worschyp—þe Wyʒe hit yow ʒelde
Þat vphaldez þe heuen and on hyʒ sittez—
How norne ʒe yowre ryʒt nome, and þenne no more?'
'Þat schal I telle þe trwly,' quoþ þat oþer þenne:
'Bertilak de Hautdesert I hat in þis londe.   2445
Þurʒ myʒt of Morgne la Faye, þat in my hous lenges,
And koyntyse of clergye, bi craftes wel lerned—
Þe maystrés of Merlyn mony ho hatz taken,
For ho hatz dalt drwry ful dere sumtyme
With þat conable klerk; þat knowes alle your knyʒtez   2450
      At hame.
        Morgne þe goddes
        Þerfore hit is hir name;
        Weldez non so hyʒe hawtesse
        Þat ho ne con make ful tame—   2455

'Ho wayned me vpon þis wyse to your wynne halle
For to assay þe surquidré, ʒif hit soth were
Þat rennes of þe grete renoun of þe Rounde Table;
Ho wayned me þis wonder your wyttez to reue,
For to haf greued Gaynour and gart hir to dyʒe   2460
With glopnyng of þat ilke gome þat gostlych speked
With his hede in his honde bifore þe hyʒe table.
Þat is ho þat is at home, þe auncian lady;
Ho is euen þyn aunt, Arþurez half-suster,
Þe duches doʒter of Tyntagelle, þat dere Vter after   2465
Hade Arþur vpon, þat aþel is nowþe.
Þerfore I eþe þe, haþel, to com to þyn aunt.
Make myry in my hous: my meny þe louies
And I wol þe as wel, wyʒe, bi my faythe,
As any gome vnder God, for þy grete trauþe.'   2470
And he nikked hym 'Naye!'—he nolde bi no wayes.
Þay acolen and kyssen and kennen ayþer oþer
To þe Prynce of paradise, and parten ryʒt þere
      On coolde.
        Gawayn on blonk ful bene   2475
        To þe kynges burʒ buskez bolde,
        And þe knyʒt in þe enker grene
        Whiderwarde-soeuer he wolde.

Wylde wayez in þe worlde Wowen now rydez
On Gryngolet, þat þe grace hade geten of his lyue;   2480
Ofte he herbered in house and ofte al þeroute,
And mony a venture in vale he venquyst ofte
Þat I ne tyʒt at þis tyme in tale to remene.
Þe hurt watz hole þat he hade hent in his nek
And þe blykkande belt he bere þeraboute,   2485

As the lord of the land I have lingered within   2440
And to which I've been welcomed—the One Who above
Sits on high and upholds all of heaven bless you!—
By what name are you known? There is no more I'd ask."
"I will tell you that truly," returned that knight.
"I am called in this countryside Bertilak de Hautdesert,   2445
Through the might in my manor of Morgan le Fay.
My demesne by the might of her magic is held;
For the magic of Merlin she mastered herself
When she lingered in love a long time ago
With that sage. Now their story has spread; they enjoy   2450
    Wide fame.
    The 'Goddess Morgan' thus
    Became her well-known name.
    The proud and prosperous
    She'll dominate and tame.   2455

"In this shape Morgan sent me to seek out your hall,
For the purpose of putting its pride to the test,
And arraigning the Round Table's richly famed knights.
She bewitched me this way to bewilder you all,
And to goad Guinevere to a grievous death—   2460
From her shock at the sight of a strange, bright green man
As he hailed the hall with his head in his grip.
She's that crone in my court whom you courteously met;
She's your aunt and King Arthur's own half-sister, too,
And the daughter, indeed, of the Duchess of Tintagel,   2465
Who bore Arthur to Uther—now Arthur holds sway.
Thus I earnestly ask, to your aunt now return,
In my mansion make merry; my men there all love you.
I pray, for my part, that you prosper indeed
For your truth and integrity, tested and proved!"   2470
But that knight answered, "No." He could not remain.
So they kissed; and each kindly commended his friend
To the Prince of paradise, parting where cold
    Wind blows.
    In haste to Arthur's hall   2475
    The good Sir Gawain goes.
    The Green Knight did not stall,
    But wandered where he chose.

Now Gawain on Gringolet goes through the wilds.
By the grace of God, he'd been granted his life.   2480
He slept in shelters and sometimes outside.
In adventures in vales he vanquished his foes—
At this time in our tale I won't tell of them all.
The hurt quickly healed that he'd had on his neck.
On his breast Gawain bore the green belt made of silk;   2485

Abelef, as a bauderyk, bounden bi his syde,
Loken vnder his lyfte arme, þe lace, with a knot,
In tokenyng he watz tane in tech of a faute.
And þus he commes to þe court, knyȝt al in sounde.
Þer wakned wele in þat wone when wyst þe grete   2490
Þat gode Gawayn watz commen; gayn hit hym þoȝt.
Þe kyng kyssez þe knyȝt and þe whene alce,
And syþen mony syker knyȝt þat soȝt hym to haylce,
Of his fare þat hym frayned; and ferlyly he telles,
Biknowez alle þe costes of care þat he hade,   2495
Þe chaunce of þe chapel, þe chere of þe knyȝt,
Þe luf of þe ladi, þe lace at þe last.
Þe nirt in þe nek he naked hem schewed
Þat he laȝt for his vnleuté at þe leudes hondes
          For blame.   2500
    He tened quen he schulde telle;
    He groned for gref and grame.
    Þe blod in his face con melle,
    When he hit schulde schewe, for schame.

'Lo! lorde,' quoþ þe leude, and þe lace hondeled,   2505
'Þis is þe bende of þis blame I bere in my nek.
Þis is þe laþe and þe losse þat I laȝt haue
Of couardise and couetyse, þat I haf caȝt þare;
Þis is þe token of vntrawþe þat I am tan inne.
And I mot nedez hit were wyle I may last;   2510
For mon may hyden his harme bot vnhap ne may hit,
For þer hit onez is tachched twynne wil hit neuer.'
Þe kyng comfortez þe knyȝt, and alle þe court als
Laȝen loude þerat and luflyly acorden
Þat lordes and ledes þat longed to þe Table,   2515
Vche burne of þe broþerhede, a bauderyk schulde haue,
A bende abelef hym aboute, of a bryȝt grene,
And þat, for sake of þat segge, in swete to were.
For þat watz acorded þe renoun of þe Rounde Table
And he honoured þat hit hade, euermore after,   2520
As hit is breued in þe best boke of romaunce.
Þus in Arthurus day þis aunter bitidde—
Þe Brutus bokez þerof beres wyttenesse.
Syþen Brutus, þe bolde burne, boȝed hider fyrst,
After þe segge and þe asaute watz sesed at Troye,   2525
          Iwysse,
    Mony aunterez herebiforne
    Haf fallen suche er þis.
    Now þat bere þe croun of þorne,
    He bryng vus to His blysse!   2530
               Amen

HONY SOYT QUI MAL PENCE.

As a baldric he'd bound it about his right shoulder
And looped it below his left arm with a knot, — *like pentangle*
As a sign of the stain he'd sustained through his fault.
Thus he came to the court, unscathed from his trials.
When the nobles all knew that their knight had returned,   2490
They were gleeful and glad at the good they'd received.
The king and the queen in turn kissed that fair knight,
And each guest came to greet Sir Gawain as well.
Of his quest they inquired; of his quandaries he told.
He confessed what befell him: his faults and mistakes,   2495
What had chanced at the chapel, the cheer of the knight,
The love of the lady, and, lastly, the belt.
To those nobles the nick on his neck he then showed,
All along his lapse and disloyalty he'd
     Proclaim.   2500
    He grieved to tell the tale
    Behind that badge of blame,
    But, blushing, did unveil
    His scar, that sign of shame.

pendures b/c ashamed

"My lord, look!" he said, lifting the lace in his hand.   2505
"Here's the badge of the blame that I bear on my neck.
It's a sign of the shame I deserved in my tryst;
It incarnates my cowardice, coveting life.
This token of treachery, untrustworthiness,
Just as long as I live I'll keep lashed to my breast,   2510
For one's sins when concealed are one's sins nonetheless;
When a trust is mistreated, it's tainted forever."
The king and the court brought comfort to him.
They laughed right out loud, and at last all agreed—
Every lady and lord who belonged to the Table—   2515
That a baldric be borne by the brotherhood's men,
A silk band wrapped about of bright, glowing green
For the sake of that shining knight, showing respect.
Thus that token the Table took as a sign
Of renown; and that knight ever knew honor—   2520
In our richest romance this is written down well.
These deeds were thus done in the days of King Arthur
(As the books about Brutus will bear witness to),
Since Brutus came boldly to Britain's fair shore
When the siege and assault had been ceased before Troy.   2525
    Since this,
    There've been in dale and down
    Adventures various.
    May Christ Who bore the crown
    Of thorns bring us His bliss!   2530
       Amen

odd exchange

he doesn't see as a gain

HONY SOYT QUI MAL PENCE.

Saint Erkenwald

The facing-page text is reprinted from *Saint Erkenwald*, ed. Clifford Peterson
(Philadelphia: University of Pennyslvania Press, 1977).

At London in Englonde no3t fulle longe sythen—
Sythen Crist suffride on crosse and Cristendome stablyde—
Ther was a byschop in þat burghe, blessyd and sacryd:
Saynt Erkenwolde as I hope þat holy mon hatte.
In his tyme in þat toun þe temple alder-grattyst   5
Was drawen doun, þat one dole, to dedifie new,
For hit hethen had bene in Hengyst dawes
Þat þe Saxones vnsa3t haden sende hyder.
Þai bete oute þe Bretons and bro3t hom into Wales
And peruertyd alle þe pepul þat in þat place dwellide.   10
Þen wos this reame renaide mony ronke 3eres
Til Saynt Austyn into Sandewiche was sende fro þe pope;
Þen prechyd he here þe pure faythe and plantyd þe trouthe
And conuertyd alle þe communnates to Cristendame newe.
He turnyd temples þat tyme þat temyd to þe deuelle   15
And clansyd hom in Cristes nome and kyrkes hom callid;
He hurlyd owt hor ydols and hade hym in sayntes
And chaungit cheuely hor nomes and chargit hom better:
Þat ere was of Appolyn is now of Saynt Petre,
Mahoun to Saynt Margrete oþir to Maudelayne;   20
Þe synagoge of þe Sonne was sett to oure Lady,
Jubiter and Jono to Jhesus oþir to James.
So he hom dedifiet and dyght alle to dere halowes
Þat ere wos sett of Sathanas in Saxones tyme.
Now þat London is neuenyd—hatte þe New Troie—   25
Þe metropol and þe mayster-toun hit euermore has bene.
Þe mecul mynster þerinne a maghty deuel aght
And þe title of þe temple bitan was his name,
For he was dryghtyn, derrest of ydols praysid,
And þe solempnest of his sacrifices in Saxon londes.   30
Þe thrid temple hit wos tolde of Triapolitanes,
By alle Bretaynes bonkes were bot othire twayne.

Now of þis Augustynes art is Erkenwolde bischop
At loue London toun and the laghe teches,
Syttes semely in þe sege of Saynt Paule mynster   35
Þat was þe temple Triapolitan as I tolde are.
Þen was hit abatyd and beten doun and buggyd efte new—
A noble note for þe nones and New Werke hit hatte.
Mony a mery mason was made þer to wyrke,
Harde stones for to hewe wyt eggit toles,   40
Mony grubber in grete þe grounde for to seche
Þat þe fundement on fyrst shuld þe fote halde.
And as þai makkyde and mynyde a meruayle þai founden
As 3et in crafty cronecles is kydde þe memorie,
For as þai dy3t and dalfe so depe into þe erthe   45
Þai founden fourmyt on a flore a ferly faire toumbe.

Once in London, not long since our Lord, Jesus Christ,
Was cruelly crucified—Christendom since
Had been built—lived a bishop most blessed and pure.
I have heard he was hailed as Saint Erkenwald there.
At that time in that town was a temple of old, 5
Which to rubble was razed to erect a new church.
It was held once by heathens in Hengist's time
(For that Saxon was sent there to share Britain's wars,
But he soon beat the Britons far back into Wales).
In that place all the people, apostate and bad, 10
Came to love false beliefs many long, sinful years,
Till Saint Augustine answered an order from Rome;
He was sent into Sandwich to set them aright,
Reconvert them to value the virtue of Christ.
At that time all the temples he turned from false gods, 15
And he cleansed them as churches in Christ's mighty name.
Therefore Augustine ousted the idols therein
And chiefly rechristened each church under God.
Where Apollo was prayed to, now Peter got lauds;
Where Mahomet once, Magdalen, Margaret, now reigned; 20
What was set to the Sun now was seized for our Lady;
What was Jupiter's, Juno's, turned Jesus', James's.
What was pagan, impious, he pledged to the Lord
Or assigned to His saints, whom the Saxons had shunned.
New Troy at the time was retitled itself; 25
Now it's lauded as London, the land's finest town.
In that township the tallest of temples of all
Had been deemed the devil's own dark, evil house
(For the greatest of gods he was granted to be);
To him Saxons would solemnly sacrifice in 30
What was thought to be third of the three pagan sees.
(There were only two others in England's whole realm.)

Now Saint Erkenwald's bishop of Augustine's see;
In London the law of the land he upholds
And sits in the seat of the see of Saint Paul, 35
In its temple, now turned in that town to a church.
Then that temple was torn down and turned to new ends,
Became known as the New Work, both noble and good.
On that minster were many masons employed.
Many hacked and hewed at the hardest of stones; 40
Many gripped at the gravel on the ground with their picks;
All to dig a foundation of depth for the church.
As they made their way, mining, a marvel they found,
As the chronicles clearly record to this day.
When they'd dug to the depths of the dark, hardened earth, 45
The men found on a floor at their feet a great tomb.

Hit was a throghe of thykke ston thryuandly hewen,
Wyt gargeles garnysht aboute alle of gray marbre.
The sperle of þe spelunke þat sparde hit o-lofte
Was metely made of þe marbre and menskefully planede,   50
And þe bordure enbelicit wyt bry3t golde lettres,
Bot roynyshe were þe resones þat þer on row stoden.
Fulle verray were þe vigures þer auisyde hom mony,
Bot alle muset hit to mouthe and quat hit mene shulde:
Mony clerkes in þat clos wyt crownes ful brode   55
Per besiet hom a-boute no3t to brynge hom in wordes.
Quen tithynges token to þe toun of þe toumbe wonder
Mony hundrid hende men highide þider sone.
Burgeys boghit þerto, bedels ande othire,
And mony a mesters mon of maners diuerse.   60
Laddes laften hor werke and lepen þiderwardes,
Ronnen radly in route wyt ryngande noyce.
Per commen þider of alle kynnes so kenely mony
Pat as alle þe worlde were þider walon wytin a honde-quile.
Quen þe maire wyt his meynye þat meruaile aspied   65
By assent of þe sextene þe sayntuaré þai kepten,
Bede vnlouke þe lidde and lay hit byside;
Pai wolde loke on þat lome quat lengyd wytinne.
Wy3t werke-men wyt þat wenten þer-tille,
Putten prises þerto, pinchid one vnder,   70
Kaghten by þe corners wyt crowes of yrne,
And were þe lydde neuer so large þai laide hit by sone.
Bot þen wos wonder to wale on wehes þat stoden,
That my3t not come to knowe a quontyse strange.
So was þe glode wyt-in gay, al wyt golde payntyde   75
And a blisfulle body opon þe bothum lyggid
Araide on a riche wise in rialle wedes.
Al wyt glisnande golde his gowne wos hemmyd,
Wyt mony a precious perle picchit þer-on,
And a gurdille of golde bigripide his mydelle,   80
A meche mantel on-lofte wyt menyuer furrit
(Pe clothe of camelyn ful clene wyt cumly bordures),
And on his coyfe wos kest a coron ful riche
And a semely septure sett in his honde.
Als wemles were his wedes wyt-outen any tecche   85
Oþir of moulynge oþir of motes oþir moght-freten,
And als bry3t of hor blee in blysnande hewes
As þai hade 3epely in þat 3orde bene 3isturday shapen.
And als freshe hym þe face and the fleshe nakyde
Bi his eres and bi his hondes þat openly shewid   90
Wyt ronke rode, as þe rose, and two rede lippes
As he in sounde sodanly were slippide opon slepe.
Per was spedeles space to spyr vch on oþir

Its four sides were of stone very skillfully carved.
In the gray marble, gargoyles grimaced and crouched.
The lid, which was locked with a long, bolted spar,
Was masterfully made out of marble of gray,
With a border embellished with bright, golden words,   50
Which were runelike, unreadable, rare, and obscure.
What they meant—although masterfully made and intact—
No one knew; they could never pronounce them aloud.
At length many learned men looked on those words,   55
But they failed to find out what those figures meant.
When word of the wonder had wafted through town,
There came numerous nobles from near and far;
From the borough's ends burghers and beadles approached.
From manors came masters in multitudes then.   60
Lads left off their labor and came leaping to see;
In a rout they rapidly ran, making noise.
Every sort came so swiftly, it seemed all the world
At that site in a second assembled to watch.
Then the mayor and his men, once they'd made their way there,   65
With the sexton's assent, had the site cordoned off,
Bid the lid be unlocked and laid to the side:
They would look on what lay in that long-buried tomb.
Then strong workmen came wielding thick wedges and bars,
Which as levers they laid at the lid of the tomb;   70
And with crowbars they clawed at its corners so that,
Though the top weighed a ton, they'd have taken it off.
Then all standing there saw an unsettling thing,
Just as much of a marvel as man could withstand!
There were golden sides, glistening, gleaming within;   75
At the bottom a beautiful body reposed,
All arrayed in the richest, most royal attire!
With glistening gold was his gown filigreed.
Many precious pearls appeared on his robe.
A girdle, all golden, was girt round his waist.   80
A mantle, well made, trimmed with miniver, hung
From his shoulders—it shone with a shimmering cloth!
On his coif stood a crown which was costly and fine,
And a sumptuous scepter was set in his hand.
All his clothes were clean; on them clung no spot.   85
Neither mold nor moth holes had marred what he wore.
All the colors had kept uncorrupted and bright,
As though done by the dyer the day before last!
And his features were fresh and as fine as could be;
For the flesh of his face and his fine, opened hands   90
Was as ruddy and red as a rose. The man seemed
To have suddenly slipped into sleep in full health!
Then all asked without answer the others around

Quat body hit my3t be þat buried wos ther.
How longe had he þer layne his lere so vnchaungit   95
And al his wede vnwemmyd þus ylka weghe askyd:
"Hit my3t not be bot suche a mon in mynde stode longe;
He has ben kynge of þis kithe as couthely hit semes.
He lyes doluen þus depe hit is a derfe wonder
Bot summe segge couthe say þat he hym sene hade."   100
Bot þat ilke note wos noght for nourne none couthe,
Noþir by title ne token ne by tale noþir
Þat euer wos breuyt in burghe ne in boke notyde,
Þat euer mynnyd suche a mon, more ne lasse.
Þe bodeworde to þe byschop was broght on a quile   105
Of þat buriede body, al þe bolde wonder.
Þe primate wyt his prelacie was partyd fro home;
In Esex was Ser Erkenwolde an abbay to visite.
Tulkes tolden hym þe tale wyt troubulle in þe pepul
And suche a cry aboute a cors, crakit euer-more.   110
The bischop sende hit to blynne by bedels and lettres
Ande buskyd þiderwarde by-tyme on his blonke after.
By þat he come to þe kyrke kydde of Saynt Paule;
Mony hym metten on þat meere þe meruayle to telle:
He passyd in-to his palais and pes he comaundit,   115
And deuoydit fro þe dede and ditte þe durre after.
Þe derke ny3t ouerdrofe and day-belle ronge
And Ser Erkenwolde was vp in þe vghten ere þen,
Þat welneghe al þe ny3t hade naityd his houres
To biseche his souerayn of his swete grace   120
To vouche safe to reuele hym hit by a visioun or elles.
"Þaghe I be vnworthi," al wepande he sayde
Thurghe his deere debonerté, "digne hit my Lorde
In confirmynge þi Cristen faithe, fulsen me to kenne
Þe mysterie of þis meruaile þat men opon wondres."   125
And so longe he grette after grace þat he graunte hade
An ansuare of þe Holy Goste and afterwarde hit dawid.
Mynster dores were makyd opon quen matens were songen;
Þe byschop hym shope solemply to synge þe heghe masse;
Þe prelate in pontificals was prestly atyride.   130
Manerly wyt his ministres þe masse he begynnes,
Of *Spiritus Domini* for His spede on sutile wise,
Wyt queme questis of þe quere wyt ful quaynt notes.
Mony a gay grete lorde was gedrid to herken hit
(As þe rekenest of þe reame repairen þider ofte),   135
Tille cessyd was þe seruice and sayde þe later ende.
Þen heldyt fro þe autere alle þe heghe gynge—
Þe prelate passide on þe playn, þer plied to hym lordes;
As riche reuestid as he was he rayked to þe toumbe,
Men vnclosid hym þe cloyster wyt clustrede keies,   140

Just whose body there buried they'd brought to the light.
How long had he lain there, his limbs thus intact, 95
With his clothes thus so clean and unclotted with dirt?
"Such a man must remain within memory's grasp;
He was clearly once king of this kingdom!" they said.
"It can't be that nobody who bides in this town
Ever saw him. There's someone who's seen this great king!" 100
But their protests were pointless; no person was found
Who could tell them in truth what those tokens there meant,
Or could tell them his tale. Nor could tomes be brought forth
In that city that spoke of the stranger they'd found.
To that borough's high bishop was broken the news 105
Of the buried man's body, unblemished and fresh.
With his prelates that primate was presently gone
To an abbey in Essex. Sir Erkenwald thus
Was soon told the tale of disturbances there,
Of the clamoring crowd and the corpse it had seen. 110
Then the bishop sent beadles to bring about calm,
And set out himself to that city on horse,
Till he came to the cherished, famed church of Saint Paul,
Where the many who met him the marvel explained.
Then he passed to his palace. There peace he decreed 115
(He'd not been to the body) and bolted the door.
Darkness drew down till the day bells were heard;
But Sir Erkenwald, up almost all of the night,
Had again and again humbly given out prayers,
Had beseeched his great Sovereign to send down His grace, 120
To vouchsafe a vision and advise him at last.
"Though I'm weak and unworthy," he weepingly said,
"In Your goodness yet grant me the grace to do right.
In confirming Christ's faith, unfold to me, Lord,
What this marvelous mystery means in Your plan!" 125
The Holy Ghost heard his behest and his prayers;
Before day finally dawned he'd been deigned his request!
At matins the minster's doors moved to reveal
The saint there, inside, set to sing the High Mass.
There the prelate appeared in his priestly attire. 130
By that man, as is mannerly, Mass is begun;
The service—the *Spiritus Domini*—starts
With the song of the singers who sit in the choir.
Many lords and their ladies were listening there
(For the best of the borough's nobility came), 135
Till the service and singing were ceased at the end,
And the Mass's high ministers moved from the font.
When the prelate approached, all the people then bowed.
In rich, sumptuous robes, he arrived at the tomb.
Men unclosed the great cloister with keys on long chains. 140

Bot pyne wos wyt þe grete prece þat passyd hym after.
The byschop come to þe burynes him barones besyde,
Þe maire wyt mony maȝti men and macers before hym.
Þe dene of þe dere place deuysit al on fyrst
Þe fyndynge of þat ferly, wyt fynger he mynte.   145
"Lo, lordes," quoþ þat lede, "suche a lyche here is
Has layn loken here on loghe how longe is vnknawen,
And ȝet his colour and his clothe has caȝt no defaute,
Ne his lire ne þe lome þat he is layde inne,
Þer is no lede opon lyfe of so longe age   150
Þat may mene in his mynde þat suche a mon regnyd
Ne noþir his nome ne his note nourne of one speche.
Queþer mony porer in þis place is putte into grave
Þat merkid is in oure martilage his mynde for euer,
And we haue oure librarie laitid þes longe seuen dayes   155
Bot one cronicle of þis kynge con we neuer fynde.
He has non layne here so longe, to loke hit by kynde,
To malte so out of memorie bot meruayle hit were."
"Þu says soþe," quoþ þe segge þat sacrid was byschop,
"Hit is meruaile to men þat mountes to litelle   160
Towarde þe prouidens of þe prince þat paradis weldes,
Quen Hym luste to vnlouke þe leste of His myȝtes.
Bot quen matyd is monnes myȝt and his mynde passyde,
And al his resons are to-rent and redeles he stondes,
Þen lettes hit Hym ful litelle to louse wyt a fynger   165
Þat alle þe hondes vnder heuen halde myȝt neuer.
Þere-as creatures crafte of counselle oute swarues,
Þe comforthe of þe creatore byhoues þe cure take.
And so do we now oure dede, deuyne we no fyrre;
To seche þe sothe at oure selfe ȝee se þer no bote,   170
Bot glow we alle opon Godde and His grace aske
Þat careles is of counselle and comforthe to sende,
And þat in fastynge of ȝour faithe and of fyne bileue.
I shal auay ȝow so verrayly of vertues His
Þat ȝe may leue vpon longe þat He is Lord myȝty,   175
And fayne ȝour talent to fulfille if ȝe Hym frende leues."

Then he turnes to þe toumbe and talkes to þe corce,
Lyftande vp his eghe-lyddes he loused suche wordes:
"Now lykhame þat þer lies, layne þou no lenger;
Sythen Jhesus has iuggit to-day His ioy to be schewyde,   180
Be þou bone to His bode, I bydde in His behalue.
As He was bende on a beme quen He His blode schedde,
As þou hit wost wyterly and we hit wele leuen,
Ansuare here to my sawe, councele no trouthe.
Sithen we wot not qwo þou art witere vs þiselwen   185
In worlde quat weghe þou was and quy þow þus ligges,

He approached, and the press of the people felt awe.
Then the bishop, with barons, the buried man neared, *only religious figure*
With the mayor, his men, and the mace-bearers next.
When they came to the coffin, the canon retold
Of the marvelous miracle men had unearthed: 145
"Lords and ladies, now look! Here is lying a corpse.
It has lain here, locked up—how long is unknown.
Yet his color and clothes haven't come, through the years,
To decay; and his coffin is comely and new!
But no man here among us remembers his reign;   150
None has lived here a long enough life to recall!
There is nothing announcing the name of this man,
Yet our long, well-kept lists of those laid to their rest
Record many a man who was much less than he!
Though we've seven days scoured our scrolls and our books,   155
Not one mention is made of this man, this great king!
From his looks, he's not lain very long in this grave;
It's a marvel he'd melt out of memory thus!"
Then the saint very solemnly said, "Though that's true,
What to men is a marvel amounts to a trifle   160
When compared with the power the Prince can unlock
When He wishes to wield His wonders on earth.
When the might and minds of mere men are undone,
When their faculties fail, and they find themselves lost,
Then the Lord can unloose with a light finger's touch   165
What all hands under heaven can't hold up in place!
When a creature's wise counseling comes thus to naught
It behooves him to heed then the high, mighty Lord.
Let us work the Lord's will, then, and wonder no more!
All alone, we are lost, cannot locate the truth.   170
Let us pray to the Prince, plead for His grace;
For He comforts our cares and sends counsel to men
By confirming their faltering faith in the truth.
I'll unveil all His various virtues to you;
And at length you'll believe He's the Lord of the sky;   175
If you've faith, He's your friend and fulfills all your needs!"

Then he turns to the tomb and talks to the corpse,
While he leans down to lift up the lids of its eyes:
"In this sepulcher stay in your silence no more!   *bids corpse to talk*
Our Lord destined this day to display His deep joy;   180
And you're bound to abide Jesus' bidding at once.
On a cross He was crucified cruelly for us,
As you know, and we heartily, wholly believe.
Thus respond to my speech! Don't conceal the truth!
We would learn of your life; therefore, let us all know.   185
In this world what were you? We wish now to learn

How longe þou has layne here and quat laghe þou vsyt
Queþer art þou ioyned to ioy oþir iuggid to pyne."
Quen þe segge hade þus sayde and syked þer-after,
Þe bryȝt body in þe burynes brayed a litelle   190
And wyt a drery dreme he dryues owte wordes,
Þurghe sum Goste lant lyfe of hym þat al redes.
"Bisshop," quoþ þis ilke body, "þi bode is me dere.
I may not bot boghe to þi bone for bothe myn eghen;
To þe name þat þou neuenyd has and nournet me after   195
Al heuen and helle heldes to and erthe bitwene.
Fyrst to say the þe sothe quo my selfe were—:
One þe vnhapnest hathel þat euer on erthe ȝode.
Neuer kynge ne cayser ne ȝet no knyȝt nothyre,
Bot a lede of þe laghe þat þen þis londe vsit.   200
I was committid and made a mayster-mon here
To sytte vpon sayd causes, þis cité I ȝemyd
Vnder a prince of parage of paynymes laghe,
And vche segge þat him sewide þe same faythe trowid.
Þe lengthe of my lyinge here, þat is a lewid date,   205
Hit is to meche to any mon to make of a nommbre:
After þat Brutus þis burghe had buggid on fyrste,
Noȝt bot fife hundred ȝere þer aghtene wontyd
Before þat kynned ȝour Criste by Cristen acounte
A þousande ȝere and þritty mo and yet threnen aght.   210
I was of heire and of oyer in þe New Troie
In þe regne of þe riche kynge þat rewlit vs þen,
The bolde Breton Ser Belyn, Ser Berynge was his brothire.
Mony one was þe busmare boden hom bitwene
For hor wrakeful werre quil hor wrathe lastyd.   215
Þen was I iuge here enioynyd in gentil lawe."
Quil he in spelunke þus spake þer sprange in þe pepulle
In al þis worlde no worde, ne wakenyd no noice
Bot al as stille as þe ston stoden and listonde
Wyt meche wonder forwrast, and wepid ful mony.   220
The bisshop biddes þat body, "Biknowe þe cause,
Sithen þou was kidde for no kynge, quy þou þe croun weres,
Quy haldes þou so heghe in honde þe septre
And hades no londe of lege men ne life ne lym aghtes?"
"Dere Ser," quoþ þe dede body, "deuyse þe I thenke.   225
Al was hit neuer my wille þat wroght þus hit were;
I wos deputate and domesmon vnder a duke noble
And in my power þis place was putte al to-geder.
I iustifiet þis ioly toun on gentil wise
And euer in fourme of gode faithe more þen fourty wynter.   230
Þe folke was felonse and fals and frowarde to reule,
I hent harmes ful ofte to holde hom to riȝt.
Bot for wothe ne wele ne wrathe ne drede

Your beliefs and how long you have lain in this spot.
Are you headed for heaven or hell? Tell us now!"
This was said by the saint, and he sighed at the end.
Then the man through a miracle moved in his tomb! 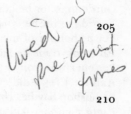 190
And with sounds that were solemn, he spoke before all,
For some great, holy ghost then granted him help.
The body said, "Bishop, your bidding is dear!
I must bow to this bidding and bend to His will.
For the name that just now you have named is supreme; 195
His behest all of heaven and hell must obey!
First what life I have lived, I will let you all know.
The least fortunate fellow who fared on the earth,
I was neither a knight nor a nobly born king;
I was merely a man who administered law, 200
Who was made here a master of men in their suits.
In the city's disputes I presided as judge;
For the prince of the pagans appointed me thus
(All his subjects then swore to the same pagan faith).
But how long I have lain here none living can know; 205
It's too much for a mortal to make out the years!
After Brutus built this borough at first,
I lived four hundred, fourscore, and fully two years
Before Christ, by Christian accounts, was born
(I mean fifty plus four plus a thousand years ago). 210
In the oyer and eyre courts I everywhere judged
In the reign of the rich king who ruled this place,
The bold Breton, Sir Belin. Sir Brennin, who was
The king's brother, with Belin would bitterly feud.
Those brothers' fierce battles were bloody and long! 215
I was judge, then, enjoined to bring justice and law."
As he talked from his tomb, the townspeople stood
Fully silent, solemn, and stricken with awe;
Each one stayed just as still as a stone in the earth.
Many wondered at what they had witnessed, and cried. 220
But the bishop just bids the body: "Say next,
Since no king, why you carry a crown on your head,
Why you hold up the scepter so high in your hand,
If no lands and no liege men as lord you controlled?"
He replied, "Gentle preiate, I plan to respond. 225
Never once were my wishes to wear such a crown!
Through the duke I was deputy, destined to serve;
This place in my power was put by decree.
When I judged here I jealously justice upheld,
And followed good faith over forty years' time. 230
Though the folk were felonious, false to the laws,
My task many times was to teach them the good.
Not for profit, power, pleasure, or gain,

Ne for maystrie ne for mede ne for no monnes aghe,
I remewit neuer fro þe riȝt by reson myn awen   235
For to dresse a wrange dome, no day of my lyue.
Declynet neuer my consciens for couetise on erthe,
In no gynful iugement no iapes to make
Were a renke neuer so riche for reuerens sake.
Ne for no monnes manas ne meschefe ne routhe   240
Non gete me fro þe heghe gate to glent out of ryȝt,
Als ferforthe as my faithe confourmyd my hert.
Þaghe had been my fader bone, I bede hym no wranges,
Ne fals fauour to my fader, þaghe felle hym be hongyt.
And for I was ryȝtwis and reken and redy of þe laghe   245
Quen I deghed for dul denyed alle Troye.
Alle menyd my dethe, þe more and the lasse
And þus to bounty my body þai buriet in golde,
Cladden me for þe curtest þat courte couthe þen holde,
In mantel for þe mekest and monlokest on benche,   250
Gurden me for þe gouernour and graythist of Troie,
Furrid me for þe fynest of faithe me wytinne.
For þe honour of myn honesté of heghest enprise
Þai coronyd me þe kidde kynge of kene iustises
Þer euer wos tronyd in Troye, oþir trowid euer shulde,   255
And for I rewardid euer riȝt þai raght me the septre."
Þe bisshop baythes hym ȝet wyt bale at his hert,
Þaghe men menskid him so, how hit myȝt worthe
Þat his clothes were so clene: "In cloutes me thynkes
Hom burde haue rotid and bene rent in rattes longe sythen.   260
Þi body may be enbawmyd, hit bashis me noght
Þat hit thar ryue ne rote ne no ronke wormes,
Bot þi coloure ne þi clothe—I know in no wise
How hit myȝt lye, by monnes lore, and last so longe."
"Nay bisshop," quoþ þat body, "enbawmyd wos I neuer   265
Ne no monnes counselle my clothe has kepyd vnweɯmyd
Bot þe riche kynge of reson þat riȝt euer alowes
And loues al þe lawes lely þat longen to trouthe.
And moste he menskes men for mynnynge of riȝtes
Þen for al þe meritorie medes þat men on molde vsen;   270
And if renkes for riȝt þus me arayed has
He has lant me to last þat loues ryȝt best."
"Ȝea bot sayes þou of þi saule," þen sayd þe bisshop,
"Quere is ho stablid and stadde if þou so streȝt wroghtes?
He þat rewardes vche a renke as he has riȝt seruyd   275
Myȝt euel forgo the to gyfe of His grace summe brawnche,
For as He says in His sothe psalmyde writtes:
'Þe skilfulle and þe vnskathely skelton ay to me'.
Forþi say me of þi soule in sele quere ho wonnes
And of þe riche restorment þat raȝt hyr oure Lorde."   280

Nor for mastery, money, or malice's sake,
Would I turn from the truth or to taking of bribes.   235
All my judgments were just, never jealously made.
My conscience was clear, without covetousness;
Never once did I win any wealth from a case,
Or show bias for barons, men born with great wealth,
Or submit to a menacing man, hurling threats.   240
Never once did I wander from what I thought right,
As confirmed by the faith that I felt in my heart.
Though my father'd been felled, I'd be fair at the trial;
I'd be fair though my father were facing his death.
As a judge I was just in each judgment I made.   245
On the day of my death all were doleful in Troy;
Every man started mourning, both mighty and poor;
In bounty they buried my body in gold,
And clad me in clothes that were courtly to praise.
The most merciful, moderate man on the bench.   250
Thus they gave me this governor's garb from respect.
For my faith they put fine, courtly fur in my coat.
And to honor my honesty, equaled by none,
They crowned me as king, in the courts the most fair,
The most honest of arbiters ever to judge.   255
This scepter you see here, they set in my hand."
Then the anguished Sir Erkenwald asks him to tell
How, though cast in a cold, buried coffin for years,
All his clothes are so clean: "From decay, I'd have thought,
They'd be torn; they'd be tattered and turned into rot!   260
If your body's embalmed, it abashes me not
That it's run not to rot or to rank, gnawing worms;
But your color and clothes! I am quite at a loss!
By what learning or lore have they lasted so long?"
Then the body said, "Bishop, embalmed I was not.   265
My clothes remain clean by the craft of no man.
No, the Ruler of right was responsible here,
For He loves every law that belongs to the truth!
He honors whomever is upright and just,
As He values those virtuous, valiant, and true.   270
If men for my merits have made thus my grave,
For my love of the law He has left me intact."
Then the saint said, "Yet speak of your soul to us now.
As you acted with honor, I ask, where is she?
He who pays every person who's pious and true   275
Couldn't grudge you the gift of His grace and joy!
That is certain! He says in His psalm in these words:
'All the righteous will reap their reward by My side.'
Therefore say where your soul is residing in bliss;
Of the grace she's been granted by God let us know."   280

Þen hummyd he þat þer lay and his hedde waggyd,
And gefe a gronyng*e* ful grete and to Godde sayde,
"Ma3ty maker of men, thi myghtes are grete—
How my3t þi mercy to me amounte any tyme?
Nas I a paynym vnpreste þat neuer thi plite knewe,   285
Ne þe mesure of þi mercy ne þi mecul vertue,
Bot ay a freke faitheles þat faylid þi laghes
Þat euer þou Lord wos louyd in?—Allas þe harde stoundes!
I was non of þe nommbre þat þou wyt noy boghtes,
Wyt þe blode of thi body vpon þe blo rode;   290
Quen þou hergh*e*des helle-hole and hentes hom þeroute,
Þi loffynge oute of limbo, þou laftes me þer.
And þer sittes my soule þat se may no fyrre,
Dwynande in þe derke deth*e* þat dy3t vs oure fader,
Adam oure alder þat ete of þat appull*e*   295
Þat mony a ply3tles pepul has poysned for euer.
3e were entouchid wyt his tethe and toke in þe glotte
Bot mendyd wyt a medecyn 3e are made for to lyuye
Þat is, fulloght in fonte wyt faitheful bileue,
And þat han we myste alle merciles, myselfe and my soule.   300
Quat wan we wyt oure wele-dede þat wroghtyn ay ri3t,
Quen we are dampnyd dulfully into þe depe lake
And exilid fro þat soper so, þat solempne fest
Þer richely hit arne refetyd þat after right hungride?
My soule may sitte þer in sorow and sike ful colde,   305
Dymly in þat derke dethe þer dawes neuer morowen,
Hungrie in-wyt helle-hole, and herken after meeles
Longe er ho þat soper se oþir segge hyr to lathe."
Þus dulfully þis dede body deuisyt hit sorowe
Þat alle wepyd for woo þe wordes þat herden,   310
And þe bysshop balefully bere doun his eghen
Þat hade no space to speke so spakly he 3oskyd,
Til he toke hym a tome and to þe toumbe lokyd,
To þe liche þer hit lay, wyt lauande teres.
"Oure Lord lene," quoþ þat lede, "þat þou lyfe hades,   315
By Goddes leue, as longe as I my3t lacche water
And cast vpon þi faire cors and carpe þes wordes,
'I folwe þe in þe Fader nome and His fre Childes,
And of þe gracious Holy Goste' and not one grue lenger;
Þen þof þou droppyd doun dede hit daungerde me lasse."   320

Wyt þat worde þat he warpyd þe wete of eghen
And teres trillyd adoun and on þe toumbe lighten,
And one felle on his face and þe freke syked.
Þen sayd he wyt a sadde soun, "Our Sauyoure be louyd;
Now herid be þou hegh*e* God, and þi hende moder,   325
And blissid be þat blisful houre þat ho The bere in,

The corpse in the coffin then cast up his eyes,
Gave out a groan, and to God said these words:
"Awesome Maker of men, You are mighty and great!
Could Your mild, endless mercy to me now descend?
Unexposed to Your plan, as a pagan I died;   285
I lived without learning Your loving, mild ways,
Without gleaning the grace that You give to the soul,
Nor the law You are loved for! Alas, the hard times!
I was separate from souls You saved when You died,
When the bounteous blood of Your body was spilled.   290
When You harrowed hell, I was held back from grace.
Souls in limbo You led off but left me to stay!
There my soul still sits, without sight of Your grace;
There she dwells, ever doomed to the death Adam brought,
Our forefather who first ate the fruit, bringing woe.   295
Our first parent poisoned his progeny thus.
Though you, too, were touched with his teeth's poisoned slime,
You were mended with medicine, made as if new,
And to baptism's bounty were brought, and belief;
While myself and my soul haven't seen the Lord's grace.   300
Therefore, what did we win with the good works we performed,
When we're damned thus to drown in the deep, burning lake,
Shut out from that supper, both solemn and glad,
Where who sought the Lord's sweetness are served in the end?
Here my soul can but sigh in her sorrow and pine   305
In a dark, chilly death where the dawn never comes.
Pine in hell, ever hungry for heaven's great feast
Before seeing the supper the saved all enjoy!"
Thus he spoke of his sufferings, sorrows, and pains.
And all wept out of woe at the words of the corpse.   310
First Saint Erkenwald's eyes at the edges grew wet;
He was speechless, sighing and sobbing aloud,
As he paused at that place till composure returned.
Toward the body he bowed, then, and bathed it in tears,
As he let out: "O Lord, sustain life in this man!   315
For this corpse I would quickly acquire Your pure,
Holy water, with which I would wet him, and say:
'You are born again, baptized, and brought to new life
By the Trinity's truth; although truant, you're cleansed!'
Though he dropped into death, I'd have done thus Your will!" 320

All the while he'd wept, as he worded his prayer,
His tears to the tomb had been tumbling in streams.
When one fell on its face, the corpse faintly sighed,
And solemnly said: "O great Savior of all,
With Your mother, the maiden, for mercy be praised!   325
Let us praise, too, Your precious, unparalleled birth!

And also be þou, bysshop, þe bote of my sorowe
And þe relefe of þe lodely lures þat my soule has leuyd in.
For þe wordes þat þou werpe and þe water þat þou sheddes—
Þe bryȝt bourne of þin eghen—my bapteme is worthyn;   330
Þe fyrst slent þat on me slode slekkyd al my tene.
Ryȝt now to soper my soule is sette at þe table,
For wyt þe wordes and þe water þat weshe vs of payne
Liȝtly lasshit þer a leme, loghe in þe abyme,
Þat spakly sprent my spyrit wyt vnsparid murthe   335
Into þe cenacle solemply þer soupen alle trew;
And þer a marcialle hyr mette wyt menske alder-grattest
And wyt reuerence a rowme he raȝt hyr for euer.
I heere þerof my heghe God and also þe bysshop,
Fro bale has broȝt vs to blis; blessid þou worthe."   340
Wyt this cessyd his sowne, sayd he no more.
Bot sodenly his swete chere swyndid and faylide
And alle the blee of his body wos blakke as þe moldes,
As roten as þe rottok þat rises in powdere.
For as sone as þe soule was sesyd in blisse   345
Corrupt was þat oþir crafte þat couert þe bones,
For þe ay-lastande life þat lethe shalle neuer
Deuoydes vche a vayne-glorie þat vayles so litelle.
Þen wos louynge oure Lorde wyt loues vp-halden,
Meche mournynge and myrthe was mellyd to-geder;   350
Þai passyd forthe in processioun and alle þe pepulle folowid
And alle þe belles in þe burghe beryd at ones.

Good bishop, you've blessed me and brought me from gloom,
Have saved thus my soul from suffering death!
Through the water you wept and the words that you used,
You have bathed me in baptism, brought me new life;   330
For your tears thus have touched me and tendered relief.
At that supper my soul is seated right now!
With the words and the water that wash away sin
You have lit up a lamp in the lightless abyss!
In a second my spirit was stricken with joy,   335
And went forth to the feast where the faithful are served!
By a guard she was greeted and guided along
To a stall set aside, where she'll stay evermore!.
For your gift and the goodness of God I give thanks;
For the bliss you have brought me, be blessed in turn!"   340
Then he slipped into silence; no sound could be heard.
Of his visage all vestiges vanished at once.
His body turned black as the blistering dirt,
Just as dry as the dust when it's driven in swirls.
For as soon as his soul had settled in peace,   345
Then the corpse that had clothed her decayed, and was gone.
For the life everlasting, that lives beyond time,
Leaves behind every hindrance that held it to earth.
All who looked on gave lauds to our Lord, feeling awe;
There was mourning mixed with mirth and praise!
When the laymen and laity left on that day,   350
All the bells in the borough beckoned and rang.

Notes

With the exception of those for *Saint Erkenwald*, the notes for the poems—set in quotation marks and attributed—are in large part from Andrew and Waldron's original edition, and the reader is urged to refer to this indispensable work. Here, however, they are radically modified. Many of Andrew and Waldron's exhaustive notes have been dropped altogether; their abbreviations have been spelled out; ellipses have intervened in their text; spelling has been Americanized; and so on. All of this has been performed, moreover, silently. In addition, here and there I have modified their notes—sometimes enhancing a point, sometimes commenting on the decisions of the translation—and sometimes I have provided new notes altogether. These latter modifications are not rendered silently.

In citing these and other editors' comments, I have generally omitted page locations; most of the references are drawn from the notes of the various editions and thus are keyed to the line numbers of the poems.

PEARL

1. "A large, decorated initial marks the beginning of each group of stanzas (misplaced in line 961—see note)" (Andrew and Waldron, 52).

1–2. "The first line of the poem is echoed in the last, by which stage the *prynce*, here an earthly ruler, has come to signify Christ. The opening echoes a formula common in medieval verse lapidaries. This suggests the earthly appreciation of the pearl as an object of value—a view which, like the significance of *prynce*, is to be transformed during the course of the poem" (Andrew and Waldron).

3–4. "The emphatic use of the first-person pronoun sets a pattern, maintained throughout the poem, of ideas presented through the experience and reflections of a created and fully realized *persona*" (Andrew and Waldron).

5–6. "These lines clearly anticipate the identification of the pearl with the Maiden (see 190, 241ff., 411–12, and notes). The poet draws on stock epithets used in courtly literature to describe beautiful women (cf., for instance, Chaucer *Troilus* 3:1248)" (Andrew and Waldron).

8. Whereas in the original a feminine pronoun is used here, a neuter pronoun is used in 10. "The feminine pronouns (cf. 6, 8, 9, etc.) prepare us for the later identification of the pearl with the Maiden, while the neuter

341

pronouns of 10, 13, etc., keep in mind the symbol-object" (Andrew and Waldron).

9.   I've translated *erbere* as "garden." "The word is derived from Old French *erbier* ('garden,' and also 'grass plot' and 'vegetation'), and in the late fourteenth century had a range of meaning which could have included 'garden,' 'herb garden,' 'pleasure garden,' and 'grass plot.' In medieval literature, gardens are usually associated with seclusion and delight, sacred (as in the terrestrial paradise) or profane (as in the gardens of love in romance). This tradition, both verbal and iconographic, shows the absorption of the classical idea of the *locus amoenus* ('delightful place'). In its sacred applications, the garden is associated with the *hortus conclusus* ('enclosed [pleasure-] garden') from the Song of Songs 4:12: this was variously interpreted as allegorically representing the Virgin Mary, Christ's human nature, Christ's resurrection, and the Church (see Hamilton). At this point, however, the garden is primarily to be understood literally, the sacred and symbolic associations emerging in the transfigured landscape of the vision" (Andrew and Waldron).

11.   "*Luf-daungere* may be the poet's own compound, but the word *daungere* ('feudal power') signifies the power of a mistress over her suitor, specifically her power to keep him at a distance, and is so personified in the *Roman de la Rose* (cf. also the usage in 250). *Luf-daungere* is here used metaphorically to suggest longing for, and separation from, any love object" (Andrew and Waldron).

12–60.   "In this section, the concatenation word *spot(e)* is used in two senses, 'blemish' and 'place,' between which wordplay is maintained throughout, one sense occurring in the last line of each stanza, the other in the first line of each stanza. The words *withouten spot* (12, 24, etc.) translate the Vulgate *sine macula*, a phrase applied to the Brides of the Lamb in Revelation 14:5—thus suggesting some anticipation of the heavenly vision near the end of the poem" (Andrew and Waldron).

19–22.   The translation of these lines, like that of many lines in *Pearl*, is very loose. Andrew and Waldron translate more literally: "Never yet did a song seem to me to have such sweetness as a moment of peace let steal over me. In truth there used to come many (such moments)."

22–23.   "The description of the burial of the pearl suggests human burial (a theme returned to in 320, 857, and 957–58), and is retrospectively identified with the burial of the Maiden. Since there was a traditional belief that the pearl survived untarnished its burial in mire, the Dreamer is here unconsciously betraying his earthbound view (cf. *Cleanness* 1111–48n)" (Andrew and Waldron). Cf. *Erkenwald*, where the issue of a corpse surviving untarnished its burial is crucial.

31–32.   "Cf. John 12:24–5, I Corinthians 15:35–8. This is a familiar Christian formula of *solacium* ('consolation, solace') for the inevitable fact of death" (Andrew and Waldron).

39–40.   "Various identifications for the original's *hyȝ seysoun* have been suggested: Transfiguration of Christ (Madeleva), the Assumption of the Virgin (Osgood), and Lammas (Gollancz [1891] and Gordon). Of these, the Feast of

Lammas (August 1), with its associations of harvest, seems the most appropriate. Harvesting is represented as the occupation of the month for August (and/or July) in medieval calendars (e.g., in the Très Riches Heures of the Duc de Berri, and the Peterborough Psalter)—and this is reflected in encyclopedic literature (see, e.g., Trevisa IX.16), and ecclesiastical carving (e.g., in the schemes at Chartres, Amiens, and Paris), as well as in poetry. The tradition of the occupations of the months is discussed by Tuve, 122–70, and Pearsall and Salter, 128–60. In the light of the reminiscences of St. John and St. Paul (see note to 31–32) the harvesting imagery clearly symbolizes the possibility of resurrection, which the Dreamer does not yet understand. The St. John text is used to make the same point in *Piers Plowman* C 13.179ff." (Andrew and Waldron).

51–56. "The contrast between the responses prompted by reason and those prompted by passion anticipates the theme of the central debate between the Dreamer and the Maiden, through which he is brought by reason to an understanding of Christian doctrine and acceptance of God's will" (Andrew and Waldron).

57–60. "Hamilton points out that a special perfume associated with divine grace occurs frequently in such works as Grail legends and Saints' Lives" (Andrew and Waldron). The *odour* of 57 is unfortunately lost in my translation.

61–120. "The concatenation word *adubbement(e)* ['wonderment, wondrous'] focuses attention on the supernatural splendor of the terrestrial paradise, which is presented as a transformed garden, the concept of artifice being used metaphorically to set off the transitoriness of the natural world" (Andrew and Waldron).

65ff. "The original of line 65 may be idiomatic ('I had no idea at all where I was'); alternatively, it may allude to the medieval notion of the actual existence of paradise in a remote part of the world. Pearsall and Salter quote Honorius of Autun's *Elucidarium: Quid est paradisus? . . . locus amoenissimus in Oriente* ('What is paradise? . . . a most delightful place in the Orient'). On the presentation of the paradisal garden in medieval literature, see 9n and Patch" (Andrew and Waldron).

71. "The later Middle Ages produced particularly splendid tapestries. Cf. 91–92, 749ff.: the other world can only be described through earthly comparisons, but the poet keeps the ultimate inadequacy of such images before us" (Andrew and Waldron).

77–80. As always, Andrew and Waldron's translation is skillfully literal: " 'the leaves, which quivered densely on every branch, slid over each other like burnished silver. When the gleam from clear patches of sky glided over them, they shone most brightly with a lovely shimmering.' (The sense seems to be that the clear patches of sky seem to be moving because of the movement of the clouds.)"

97–100. "Though at this stage the Dreamer thinks he is led by haphazard fortune (*Fortwne* 98), retrospectively the power guiding him is seen to be divinely ordained: cf. 129, 249n" (Andrew and Waldron).

106. The river becomes a crucial element of the poem's entire mise-en-

scène. Cf. 907 and note. "As Gordon points out, this is identified with the river of the water of life, which flows from beneath the throne of God, as is described later (in 974 and 1055–60). Cf. Revelation 22:1–2" (Andrew and Waldron).

113–16.   "The exotic river with jewels on its bed is found frequently in medieval literature—not only in mystical visions (see Dante *Paradiso* 30.61–9), but also in travel books like Mandeville, and romances such as *Floire et Blancheflor*: for further references see Patch, Kean 1967, 105–8, and Pearsall and Salter, 58" (Andrew and Waldron).

114.   Glass, presumably stained glass, is an important metaphor for the poet. Cf. *Pearl* 990, 1018, 1106.

121–80.   The concatenation words of this section, *more and more*, mark a climax in tension leading to the recognition of the Maiden.

129–32.   Andrew and Waldron argue that "the overall sense of the passage is that a man in the position of the Dreamer, who is achieving his desire, will wish for more and more." But if we accept the *her* in line 131 (which Andrew and Waldron have emended to *his*), the *wylle* becomes Fortune's, and the overall meaning of the passage is that when Fortune brings good or ill to men, they receive it in abundance.

133–36.   "This theme, of the inadequacy of the human body and mind to perceive and comprehend paradisal and heavenly experience, has already been touched on (99–100) and is picked up later in the poem, e.g., at 223–26 and 1189ff." (Andrew and Waldron).

139–40.   Compare Andrew and Waldron's more exact translation: " 'I supposed that the water was a division between pleasure-gardens laid out beside pools.' The Dreamer assumes that such an ordered estate must be that of a great house; thus the emphasis of 141–42" (Andrew and Waldron).

141.   I translate *mote* as "city," but might have used "castle." (It may also mean "spot, stain.") This is the first notion of the New Jerusalem, or at any rate the periphery of the New Jerusalem, as urban. The appearance of a "city" here, called "paradise" a few lines earlier, is a bit surprising. Until now, we have been given a pastoral setting and have had pastoral experiences. Still, we must not insist on discovering anything like the modern opposition between city and country in the fourteenth century.

149–54.   "The Dreamer's state of mind is that of a social inferior trespassing in the grounds of a castle. Later the Maiden finds him *vncortoyse* (303) and criticizes his manners (313ff.); the same metaphor of social class (cf. 264n) is implicit in many of the exchanges of Dreamer and Maiden (e.g., 381–82, 389–94, 489–92)" (Andrew and Waldron).

160–94.   "It has been suggested that this passage may show the influence of Dante, in particular his account of the meeting with Beatrice in *Purgatorio* 30.31–99" (Andrew and Waldron).

163.   "Cf. Revelation 19:8" (Andrew and Waldron).

178.   "Similar comparisons occur in the Harley Lyric 'A Wayle whyt ase whalles bon' 1, and Chaucer, *The Book of the Duchess* 946" (Andrew and Waldron).

181–240.   "The concatenation gives emphasis to the connection between the newly discovered Maiden and pearls, both as objects and symbols" (Andrew and Waldron). The concatenation of this group of stanzas is interesting. At its minimum, the rule seems to be that while the last line of every stanza in the section must contain the words *perle(z)* and *pyȝt*, the first line of every section must contain the word *pyȝt*. But in four of the five stanzas, the last line also contains the word *precios* (enough to make it part of the pattern of concatenation). And in three of the five stanzas (including stanza 21), the word *perle(z)* occurs in the first line. Cf. 481–540n.

185. Andrew and Waldron gloss *porpose* as "aim, quarry," suggesting that the poet is continuing "the hunting metaphor implicit from 183" (Andrew and Waldron). "Provident" is an unfortunate translation for *gostly* ("spiritual"). At any rate, the otherworldly is suggested.

190. "The striking echo of 6 reinforces the growing sense of the identification of the pearl Maiden with the lost pearl described at the beginning of the poem—though it is not made explicit until 241–52" (Andrew and Waldron).

193–96. " 'There by good fortune one might see pearls of royal worth set, when that (one) fresh as fleur-de-lis directly came down the slope' " (Andrew and Waldron).

195. Cf. 753.

197. "Cf. Revelation 19:8" (Andrew and Waldron).

197–228. "This passage provides a detailed picture of the Maiden's costume, which is essentially that of an aristocratic young woman in the second half of the fourteenth century. The long sleeves (201) fashionable during the period are also mentioned in *Winner and Waster* 410–12. Gordon points out that while maidens and brides wore their hair unbound (as in 213–14), matrons wore theirs coiffed. Cf. *Gawain* 1738n" (Andrew and Waldron).

199–200. "By returning to the theme of judging gems, the poet reinforces the connection between this passage and the beginning of the poem (cf. 7–8, 190n)" (Andrew and Waldron).

221–22. "The Maiden later (729–44) associates this great pearl with the Pearl of Price (Matthew 13:45–6), and also refers to it as a symbol of salvation. This latter significance is reinforced in the vision of the New Jerusalem, when the Dreamer observes that similar pearls are worn by all the saved (1103–4)" (Andrew and Waldron).

223–26. "Cf. 133–36n. The magnitude of the pearl symbolizes its value and significance. Cf. *Cleanness* 117n" (Andrew and Waldron).

231–32. "Cf. the similar idiom in *Gawain* 2023" (Andrew and Waldron).

233. "On the basis of this line many critics have seen the relationship between the Dreamer and the Maiden as that of father and daughter, and this view is indeed consistent with the varying tone of their speeches to each other. However, it is probably significant that an explicit statement of their relationship is not made; the reader is thereby encouraged to see the theme of loss in a more general light" (Andrew and Waldron).

235. The translation elides the fact that the original calls the Maiden a "special spice." "Spice is a traditional metaphor for an admired woman, probably as a reminiscence of the Song of Songs 4:12:16" (Andrew and Waldron).

237–38. "The removal of the crown should probably be seen as a gesture of humility—as in *The Awntyrs off Arthure* 626—signifying the Maiden's willingness to set aside her heavenly authority and meet the Dreamer as an equal. It is striking that in 255 she replaces her crown before rebuking him for his erroneous views" (Andrew and Waldron).

241–300.   "The concatenation word *jueler(e)* is rich in potential significance. In 7 the Dreamer has presented himself as a judge of gems; the varied use of the word in the present section, however, draws attention to the contrast between earthly and heavenly values—a distinction which he has yet to learn. The use of the word in 730 and 734 further identifies the true 'jeweler' with the merchant of the parable of the Pearl of Price (Matthew 13:45–6)" (Andrew and Waldron).

241–52.   "With its echoes of the beginning of the poem, the first part of this speech identifies the Maiden with the lost pearl (cf. 190n). The injured, self-pitying tone of the second half establishes the Dreamer's partial blindness at this stage of his experience and complicates the reader's sympathy for him" (Andrew and Waldron).

246–50.   Cf. 333–36, 1187.

249.   *Wyrde* is, "from the Dreamer's point of view, random fate, but from that of the Maiden, which comes increasingly to dominate the poem, it suggests rather the power of Providence. Cf. 97–98, 129, 273, and notes; cf. also *Patience* 248n and *Gawain* 2134" (Andrew and Waldron).

254.   "Heroines of medieval romances often have gray eyes: cf. *Gawain* 82, and (e.g.) Chaucer, 'General Prologue' *Canterbury Tales* 1.152, and *The Awntyrs off Arthure* 599. It is, however, possible that the Middle English *gray(e)* (and Old French *vaire*) when applied to eyes designated a color which we would call blue, or that it referred to brilliance rather than hue, and hence meant 'bright, shining' " (Andrew and Waldron).

255.   "Cf. 237–38n" (Andrew and Waldron).

257–60.   I've translated *cofer* ("coffer") as "bed." "Piehler (145) points out the rich ambiguity between the senses 'treasure chest' and 'coffin'; in *Cleanness*, *cofer* is employed metaphorically to describe the ark (310 etc.)" (Andrew and Waldron).

264.   "*Gentyl*: 'courteous, noble.' The courtly term is used to imply metaphorically the equivalent spiritual value: see note to 421–80. *Kynde* (276) belongs to the same metaphorical system by virtue of its use in the sense 'proper, courtly' (e.g., in *Gawain* 473)" (Andrew and Waldron).

269.   "An ancient tradition associates the rose with mutable beauty. In courtly poetry, it is frequently used to symbolize the woman as an object of love, most strikingly as the central image of the *Roman de la Rose*, while in religious writings it becomes the *rosa caritatis* ('rose of divine love')—a transformation which takes place between the two occurrences of the symbol in *Pearl*: cf. 906" (Andrew and Waldron).

274–75.   "The Maiden's point is usually understood to be that God has made the Dreamer something eternal out of something ephemeral—the pearl out of the rose" (Andrew and Waldron).

277.   *Geste*, whether it means "guest" or "visitor," is curious in this context, in which the Dreamer seems to be the guest, and the Maiden the hostess.

277–88.   "The stanza functions ironically, since the Dreamer's blithe optimism is based on a misunderstanding of the true import of the Maiden's *gentyl sawez*" (Andrew and Waldron).

301–60.   "The different meanings of the concatenating word *deme* (variously 'allow,' 'consider,' 'judge,' 'condemn,' 'ordain') draw attention to the gap between the Dreamer's fallible will and judgment and the power of God to ordain what will be" (Andrew and Waldron).

301–8.   "Cf. the ironical use made by Chaucer of this argument in *The Legend of Good Women*, Prologue 1–16" (Andrew and Waldron).

307–12.   "Some interplay between courtly and Christian ethical vocabulary is evident in phrases like *poynt o sorquydryȝe* (309)—cf. *Gawain* 311, 2457" (Andrew and Waldron).

318–24.   "As in the best of the religious lyrics, these physical details reinforce the hope of immortality" (Andrew and Waldron).

326.   "Cf. 11" (Andrew and Waldron).

333–34.   Cf. 246–50, 1187. "This may contain an allusion to the theme of exile, common in Old English poetry, and associated in Middle English poetry with unrequited love" (Andrew and Waldron).

336.   Andrew and Waldron translate the line literally: " 'what can one expect but lasting sorrow?' Cf. the tone of Jonah's outbursts against God in *Patience* 425ff., 482ff., and 493ff." (Andrew and Waldron). But see also, in *Patience* at 46ff., the poet's presumably more enlightened tone.

339–40.   "Excessive indulgence in mourning an earthly loss can lead to sin, which may reduce a man's chances of salvation" (Andrew and Waldron).

345ff.   "Cf. the earlier use of a hunting metaphor: see 185n. These lines are very close to the moral of *Patience* (specifically, cf. 342 with *Patience* 525, and 344 with *Patience* 5–8)" (Andrew and Waldron).

356.   "*Mercy* is a quasi-personification: cf. *Patience* 31–33n" (Andrew and Waldron).

361–420.   "The concatenation phrase emphasizes the central concern of section VII: the understanding of the difference between true and false felicity. This is the theme of Boethius's *De Consolatione Philosophiae*" (Andrew and Waldron).

365.   "Cf. Psalms 21:15 (Vulgate), 22:14 (Authorized Version). This simile, here used of uncontrolled human emotion bursting forth, later recurs as an image of God's limitless bounty (607–8), thus conforming to the pattern of transformation from earthly to heavenly values" (Andrew and Waldron).

380–81.   Classic British understatement.

388.   The sorrow here is described as *hate*, "burning." "In Old English poetry the pangs of suffering are often described as hot, as in *The Seafarer* 11, *Beowulf* 282" (Andrew and Waldron).

411–12.   "The Maiden herself here echoes the usage of the opening stanzas, where the pearl is a symbol for the dead child: see 241–52n" (Andrew and Waldron).

413.   "*Godhede*: 'godhead, divinity.' The form is also current in the fourteenth century in the sense 'goodness': possibly both meanings are intended here" (Andrew and Waldron).

417–18. "Kean 1967, 187–88, points out that the language has legal associations, *sesed in* meaning 'to possess legally,' and *herytage* 'something given or received as a legal possession.' These lines thus anticipate the distinction between the innocent who are saved by right and those who, stained by the sin inevitably attendant upon living in the world, need the mercy of God: see section XII" (Andrew and Waldron).

421–44. Cf. the initial exchange between Gawain and the lady in *Gawain* 1263ff.

421–80. "The poet's use of the concatenation word *cortaysye* and the terminology of an earthly court is typical of his willingness to use courtly language metaphorically to express the values and relationships of heaven. Thus *cortaysye*, a word which suggests the attributes of courtly graciousness, comes to suggest those of divine grace when applied to the Virgin Mary (432, etc.). Cf. *Cleanness* 1069ff." (Andrew and Waldron).

430. "It is more common for the phoenix to symbolize Christ than the Virgin. However, Fletcher points out that in Albertus Magnus's treatise *De Laudibus Beatae Mariae* ('In praise of the blessed Mary'), V.1.1, VII.3.1, the Virgin's uniqueness is related to that of the phoenix. Chaucer uses the comparison in a secular context to praise the uniqueness of Blanche in *The Book of the Duchess* 982" (Andrew and Waldron).

449–52. Andrew and Waldron provide a more literal translation: " 'and yet one shall never dispossess another, but each one (be) glad of the others' possession, and wish their crowns were five times as precious, if any improvement of them were possible.' The use of the figure five in such phrases is idiomatic."

459–66. "This argument is derived from I Corinthians 12:14ff.; cf. its use in John of Salisbury, *Policratus* 6.24, and in Shakespeare, *Coriolanus* I.1.94ff." (Andrew and Waldron).

469–92. "The debate between the Maiden and the Dreamer centers upon the confrontation between the Old Law of justification by works and the New Law of grace (see Hamilton)" (Andrew and Waldron).

472. This line is missing from the manuscript. A number of editors have supplied their own lines (along with arguments for them), but I have chosen to leave it out (cheating a little, since lines 471–74 of the translation—unlike the original—read as a continuous, uninterrupted sentence).

481–540. "*Date*, the concatenation word of this section [translated as 'due'], is used by the poet with great dexterity to suggest a range of meanings associated with time, measurement, and degree. The Dreamer's scale of values is thus kept in mind, as the central agent of its modification—the telling of the parable of the vineyard, with its teaching about heavenly rewards—is introduced" (Andrew and Waldron). One might note that the concatenation pattern seems also loosely to include the word *dere* (present in the last line of two of the five stanzas in the section) and *day* (present in the last line of three of the five stanzas and in the first line of three stanzas). Cf. 181–240n.

481–82. "Cf. Jonah's complaint about God's prodigal 'courtesy' in *Patience* 417ff." (Andrew and Waldron).

484–86. "The Pater and Creed were the first prayers a child would have learned" (Andrew and Waldron).

493–98. "In her exposition of the nature of heavenly reward, the Maiden uses the same sermon technique as is used by the narrator of *Patience* (cf. especially *Patience* 57–60)—a moral statement supported by scriptural illustration. As in *Patience* 9 and *Cleanness* 51, the biblical text is seen from a layman's point of view, in the context of the *messe* (which appears to be used in *Cleanness* 51 as a synonym of *gospel*)" (Andrew and Waldron). According to Moorman 1977, the Mass referred to "is that of the Septuagesima where the parable of the vineyard is read as gospel."

501ff. Here (500 in the translation) Christ is being quoted by the Maiden.

501–72. "The parable of the vineyard is based on Matthew 20:1–16" (Andrew and Waldron).

541–600. "This section concentrates on the question of the quantitative evaluation of reward—emphasized by the concatenation word *more*—and ends, at the poem's halfway point, with a direct confrontation between earthly and heavenly values" (Andrew and Waldron).

565–66. Cf. *Gawain* 2346.

569–88. "Here it is stated explicitly that the penny symbolizes salvation, and that the Maiden has received her 'penny' (cf. 614). The identification between the penny in this parable and salvation is traditional: see Ackerman and *Glossa Ordinaria* in Migne" (Andrew and Waldron).

579–80. Andrew and Waldron translate: " 'than all the people in the world could win if they were to ask for a reward according to justice.' This is the central theme of section XII."

581–88. "This interpretation of the parable has been much discussed. The laborers in the vineyard are traditionally seen as virtuous Christians, and their varying times of entry as the different times of life at which they were converted (see St. Augustine, Sermon 87 [Migne 58:530–39]). In the poet's interpretation, entry into the vineyard at the eleventh hour is taken to represent the death of a baptized Christian in childhood. Many critics have felt that this is at odds with the traditional reading. However, Robertson (1950a) points out that there were variations on the Augustinian view which did not actually contradict it" (Andrew and Waldron).

593–96. "The reference is to Psalms 61:12–13 (Authorized Version 62:11–12)" (Andrew and Waldron).

600. "The line is more emphatic than logical. St. Augustine provides the answer to the Dreamer's point: *Non murmuret ergo qui post multum tempus accepit, contra eum qui post modicum tempus accepit* 'therefore let him who has received (the reward) after a long time not complain against him who has received it after a short time,' Migne 38:533" (Andrew and Waldron).

601–4. "It is standard Christian doctrine that the reward of heavenly life will be given to all the saved, but that there will be variations in the degree and kind of the joys in heaven" (Andrew and Waldron).

609–12. Andrew and Waldron translate these difficult lines: "His (God's) generosity is great (*or* abundant): those who at any time in their lives submitted to Him who rescues sinners—from them no bliss will be withheld, for the grace of God is great enough."

613–14. "Emerson (1927) proposed that *now* (613) be emended to *inow* (a form of *inoghe*) for the sake of concatenation. However, *now* makes better sense; moreover, this may be a case of punning concatenation, as in 732–33, 756–57, and 865; see also 913–72n" (Andrew and Waldron). But since the *noghe* of *inoghe* and *now* no longer sound alike, and the pun is therefore lost, I have used *enough* in 613 of the translation.

625–27.   "Cf. *Cleanness* 163–64" (Andrew and Waldron).

637–48.   Cf. *Cleanness* 235–48 and *Erkenwald* 295–99. "The Maiden expounds the central Christian doctrine of atonement, with particular emphasis on innocence and baptism" (Andrew and Waldron).

649–56.   Unfortunately, my translation omits the *glayue so grymly grounde* ("spear so cruelly sharpened") in 654 of the original. "St. John's Gospel (19:34) describes how a soldier (not named in St. John, but called Longinus in the apocryphal Gospel of Nicodemus) pierces the side of the crucified Christ with a spear, and how blood and water pour forth. The poet draws on the traditional symbolic identification of this outpouring of blood and water with the grace made available to man through Christ's sacrifice. This motif is also linked with the image of the well or fountain of grace (649; cf. 607–8, 1058–59)" (Andrew and Waldron).

655–56.   Christ *washed* away the sins in which we were *drowned*; in this delightfully mixed metaphor, liquid is used to bring both death and life.

661–720.   "In this section a whole line is used for concatenation, with only slight variation. The theme, the right of the innocent to salvation, is of central significance both dramatically (because the Maiden is one of the innocent) and thematically (because the point is essential to her exposition of Christian doctrine)" (Andrew and Waldron).

661–64.   "The poems share a general concern with penance; see, for instance, *Cleanness* 1111ff., *Patience* 305ff., and *Gawain* 2385ff." (Andrew and Waldron).

665–66.   "God is here portrayed as a quasi-personification of reason" (Andrew and Waldron).

671–72.   "The Maiden is here applying the logic of 665–66" (Andrew and Waldron).

674.   Moorman 1977 has it that "the two men whom God will save are the righteous man (675 ['penitent' in the translation]) and the guiltless (676 ['innocents' in the translation])."

675–84.   "The passage echoes the Beatitudes (also used in *Patience* 13–28 and *Cleanness* 23–8): see Matthew 5:3–10. Cf. also Revelation 22:4, I Corinthians 13:12, and 677n" (Andrew and Waldron).

677.   "The reference is probably to Psalms 14 (Authorized Version 15):1–3 or Psalms 23 (Authorized Version 24):3:6" (Andrew and Waldron).

689–94.   "This passage is based partly on Wisd. 10:10: *Haec profugam irae fratris iustum deduxit per vias rectas, et ostendit illi regnum Dei dedit illi scientiam sanctorum, honestavit illum in laboris et complevit labores illius* 'She [Wisdom] conducted the just, when he fled from his brother's wrath, through the right ways, and showed him the kingdom of God, and gave him the knowledge of the holy things, and made him honorable in his labors, and accomplished his labors.' The poet changes the gender of the personification *Wisdom* (*He* [in the original; *Wisdom* in the translation] 691) possibly to conform to the common medieval identification of Wisdom with Christ (an association best illustrated in late medieval literature by the morality play *Wisdom*: cf. *Patience* 37ff and note)" (Andrew and Waldron).

697–700. "Cf. Psalms 142 (Authorized Version 143):2" (Andrew and Waldron).

701–2. "The Maiden is, of course, speaking of the Last Judgment" (Andrew and Waldron).

703–4. Andrew and Waldron translate: " 'if you plead right you may be refuted in argument by this same speech that I have noticed': i.e., that no man can claim salvation by right. The use of legal terminology is discussed by Everett and Hurnard."

711–24. "This passage is mainly based on Luke 18:15–17, but also reflects the influence of the accounts of Matthew (19:13–15) and Mark (10:13–16)" (Andrew and Waldron).

721–80. "In the thirteenth section, the concatenation is supplied by *mascellez* (or *makellez*) *perle*. There is some play between the similar but distinct meanings of *mascellez* 'spotless' and *makellez* 'matchless': a distinction picked up by the Maiden in 781–84. In the final line of the section the two words are used together" (Andrew and Waldron).

721–33. Line 721 in the manuscript does not contain the word *Ryʒt*, which is supplied by Andrew and Waldron, who remind us that this marks "the only break in the pattern of concatenation, where one would expect the line to start with *ryʒt*. Emerson (1927) suggests adding *Ryʒt* before MS *Jesus*, but this is unacceptable both syntactically and metrically. The conviction seems unavoidable, in view of the formal regularity of the poem, that the poet wrote *Ryʒt con calle*, personifying Jesus as 'Justice,' and that MS *Jesus* is a scribal substitution for the sake of greater explicitness. Similar personifications, in which the deity is equated with a single virtue, have occurred at 665 (*Resoun*) and 690 (*Koyntise*, most editions). Moreover, the name *Jesus* has been used twice in the preceding stanza; the poet could therefore reasonably expect the reader to make the identification" (Andrew and Waldron). This personification may well be correct, but it is certainly a bold intrusion into the text we have inherited. It is just as possible, after all, that the poet, rather than the scribe, is responsible for the break in the concatenation and that such emendation is overly scrupulous. In the translation, at any rate, I have cheated by including both *right* and *Christ*.

725–26. "The idea of sin soiling the purity of the soul recurs throughout the poems: see 1060, *Patience* 342, *Cleanness* 12, 134, 169–76, 1111ff., *Gawain* 2436, and notes" (Andrew and Waldron).

730–39. "The Maiden associates the great pearl she wears with that in the parable of the Pearl of Price (Matthew 13:45–46)—an association already suggested in 221–22. She interprets the pearl of the parable as signifying salvation, and thus heaven. In this she does not depart from the accepted medieval exegetical viewpoint (though there are considerable differences in emphasis between the various commentators: see Osgood's note to 735–43, and Robertson 1950b)" (Andrew and Waldron).

736. The original for "world's Wielder" is *Fader of folde and flode* ("Father of earth and water"). This is one of numerous periphrases for God found

throughout the oeuvre. Cf. *Cleanness* 5 (and note), 280, 552, 1528; *Patience* 111, 206–7, 261, 398; *Gawain* 256, 1292, 2441–42.

738.   "*Endelez rounde*: The pearl's shape is thus seen to symbolize the perfection and infiniteness of heaven. It may be argued that the poem itself, with its meticulously proportioned construction, imitates this formal perfection. In particular, the end of *Pearl* echoes its beginning, thus providing the sense of circular form. This is a characteristic shared, in varying degrees, by *Cleanness*, *Patience*, and *Gawain*" (Andrew and Waldron).

749–52.   "The usual view, that in this passage the poet is drawing directly on the *Roman de la Rose* (Chaucerian version, 3205–16), is questioned by Pilch, who argues that the comparison is traditional" (Andrew and Waldron).

750–52.   Andrew and Waldron translate: " 'Pygmalion never painted your face, nor did Aristotle through his learning speak of the nature of these special virtues.' "

763.   My translation tries to capture the sexual language of the original, in which Christ addresses the Maiden in terms of courtly romance. 763–64 are "based on the Song of Songs (4:7–8)—from which the metaphor of the mystical marriage is derived" (Andrew and Waldron). Cf. 796, 805, 829.

766–67.   "The clothes symbolize the state of the soul: cf. *Patience* 342, and *Cleanness* 12, 134, and 169–76, and notes" (Andrew and Waldron).

768.   "The soul is represented in scripture as a bride adorned with jewels: see Isaiah 61:10" (Andrew and Waldron).

773–80.   "The Dreamer's incredulity is similar to that in 421–32, where the claims of the Maiden appear to him to challenge the position of the Virgin Mary" (Andrew and Waldron).

775–80.   "For extensions of this type of construction, see 166, 1100" (Andrew and Waldron).

781–840.   "Once again concatenation is thematically significant. *Jerusalem* emphasizes that the Maiden is speaking from the viewpoint of an inmate of the City of God; its association with the earthly Jerusalem continues the contrast and juxtaposition of earthly and heavenly counterparts; and the references to the Apocalypse remind us that the knowledge expounded here was shown to John (see 788n) in a mystical vision and made available to man through scripture. This discussion of John's vision also anticipates the Dreamer's (977–78), and perhaps reminds us of the dream vision medium through which the Dreamer is instructed, and the poem presented to the audience" (Andrew and Waldron).

785ff.   Here, heaven is described as a kind of harem or collective bridal chamber that Christ shares with his wives just as concretely as it is articulated as a banquet in *Erkenwald* 336ff.

788.   "The author of Revelation was usually identified with the apostle St. John" (Andrew and Waldron).

790.   "*Gostly drem*: Medieval writers commonly divided mystical visions into three categories—corporeal, spiritual, and intellectual. In the first, a man physically sees an object invisible to others; in the second, a man in sleep or prayer sees images through divine revelation; in the third, the soul is 'ravished' inwardly. As the poet's terminology suggests, John's Apocalyptic vision was

normally assigned to the second category. See Knowles, 125" (Andrew and Waldron).

790–91. "See Revelation 19:7–8, 21–22" (Andrew and Waldron).

795. "*Juelle*: The use of this word to designate Christ gains force and meaning from the cumulative associations surrounding the ideas of pearls and jewels on the one hand and the role of the 'jeweler' or judge of gems on the other" (Andrew and Waldron).

796. *Lemman fre* ("fair beloved") is a construction that reiterates the metaphor of the Maiden's salvation as a ritual of courtly love. Cf. 763, 805, 829.

797–801. "The reference is to Isaiah 53, a key Messianic prophecy in the Christian interpretation of the Old Testament" (Andrew and Waldron).

803. "Christ's silence is prophesied in Isaiah 53:7, and dramatized with great effectiveness in some of the mystery plays (e.g., York No. 35)" (Andrew and Waldron).

805. In the original the Maiden calls Christ her *Lemman* ("lover") in the language of secular love. Cf. 763, 796, 829.

805–16. "Osgood justly points out that the language of these lines is similar to that used in some meditations on the Passion" (Andrew and Waldron).

806. My reading here is that the *boyez bolde* are the two thieves with whom Christ was crucified. Andrew and Waldron, however, read them as the Roman soldiers: "The uncouthness as well as the ruthlessness of those responsible for putting Christ on the Cross becomes a commonplace in the Middle Ages; this is illustrated in the mystery plays (e.g., York No. 35 and Chester No. 16). There is also an interesting parallel in *Patience* 95–96: when Jonah expresses his fear of possible crucifixion, he characterizes his imagined persecutors as merciless ruffians."

809–10. "Cf. Matthew 26:67, Mark 14:65, and Luke 22:64" (Andrew and Waldron).

817–18. "In the Gospels John is described as baptizing in Jordan (see Matthew 3:13, Mark 1:4–9, Luke 3:3, John 1:28), and some of these accounts imply proximity to Jerusalem. Various explanations for the inclusion of *Galalye* have been offered—Osgood that it is through association of Herod being Tetrarch of Galilee, Gordon that it indicates a lack of familiarity with the geography of the region, and Gollancz [1891] that it is the result of a particular interpretation of John 1:28" (Andrew and Waldron).

819–24. "The Maiden cites the words of John the Baptist from John 1:29 as a direct allusion to the prophecy of Isaiah 53" (Andrew and Waldron).

823–26. "Cf. Isaiah 53:6, 9, 11" (Andrew and Waldron).

827–28. "Cf. Isaiah 53:8" (Andrew and Waldron).

829–1152. "The Book of Revelation is the main source for this part of the poem" (Andrew and Waldron).

833–34. The third iteration of the point is in the Book of the Apocalypse. "Cf. Revelation 5:6" (Andrew and Waldron).

835–40. "Cf. Revelation 5:1, 3, 6–8, 13" (Andrew and Waldron).

837–39. "The poet visualizes the scroll of Revelation as a book" (Andrew and Waldron).

841–912. "This section is unique in that it contains six stanzas instead of the usual five. Osgood (xlvi) argues that a stanza probably should be rejected—his candidate for expulsion is the second (853–64). Gollancz [1891] is in partial agreement, saying that *if* a stanza should be rejected it is this, while Gordon (88) suggests that 901–12 is otiose. Against their arguments should be weighed the interesting fact that (*including* this extra stanza) *Pearl* contains 101 stanzas, the same number as *Gawain*—a parallel hard to credit as coincidence. [Also of note is the fact that this extra stanza (leaving aside the problem of 472—see note) brings the total number of lines to 1212 (twelve twelves?).] The concatenation words *neuer þe les(se)* emphasize the limitless quality of heavenly bounty" (Andrew and Waldron).

847–50. "The Maiden provides a final answer to the Dreamer's earlier objection that her elevation involved the displacement of other candidates for the marriage (733–80)" (Andrew and Waldron).

853–64. "See note to 841–912" (Andrew and Waldron).

857–58. "Cf. 320 and note to 318–24" (Andrew and Waldron).

860. "The death [in line 859 of the translation] is, of course, that of Christ, through which salvation is made possible. Cf. Hebrews 10:14" (Andrew and Waldron).

866–900. "This account is based on Revelation 14:1–5" (Andrew and Waldron).

869. I have translated *maydennez* as "virgins." "This word is probably intended to include both men and women (it could be used in Middle English without reference to gender). In the Homilies on the Apocalypse attributed to St. Augustine it is emphasized that the 144,000 are those, regardless of their sex, who were pure Christians and thus made themselves fit to be brides of Christ: see Robertson, 1950b" (Andrew and Waldron).

886–87. "Cf. Ezekiel 1:10 and Revelation 4:4, 6–8. As Hillmann [1961] points out, the *aldermen* are the four and twenty elders, identified by commentators with the holy men of the Old and New Testaments, and the *fowre bestez* represent the four orders of nature—man, cattle, birds, and wild animals. It is worth adding that it was from this account of the four orders of nature that the symbols of the Evangelists, so familiar in medieval iconography, developed—the man standing for Matthew, the lion for Mark, the ox for Luke, and the eagle for John" (Andrew and Waldron).

894. "The harvest metaphor, which at the beginning of the poem (25ff.) conveys predominantly the sense of loss, is here introduced in more overt reference to the hope of resurrection" (Andrew and Waldron).

901ff. The Dreamer here poses his questions to the Maiden reluctantly and hesitatingly. Cf. the way in which Abraham timidly forces the issue of the destruction of the cities with God in *Cleanness* 735ff. "Here the Dreamer speaks for the first time since 780; it is apparent that, in the interim, the transformation of his frame of mind from rebellious pride to obedient humility has been completed" (Andrew and Waldron).

903–5. Andrew and Waldron translate more concretely: " 'I should not so presumptuously test the wisdom of you who are chosen for Christ's bridal chamber.' "

905. In the original, the Dreamer calls himself, more vividly, "filth and dust mingled together."

905–8. "The Dreamer's words are reminiscent of his earlier statement in 381–82, and of Abraham's similarly self-deprecatory attitude in *Cleanness* 736. The significance of the rose image (906) has been transformed from that of a mutable earthly beauty to that of heavenly perfection: see note to 269" (Andrew and Waldron).

907. Here, again, we are reminded of the poem's setting, through the middle of which runs the river. For an account of a visionary experience, the poem is surprisingly *located* in a particular space. Cf. 107 and note.

913. I have translated *cler* ("beautiful one") as "lady."

913–18. "As Gordon observes, the Dreamer visualizes the heavenly city in terms of a medieval town, with a castle and houses within a perimeter wall. Cf. the presentation of Babylon in *Cleanness* 1385ff." (Andrew and Waldron).

913–73. "Spot," the translation's substitute for the original's concatenation word *mote*, is less than felicitous. Among other problems, the original does not, as the translation here suggests, return to the concatenation word of the first section. "In this section the concatenation form *mote* (sometimes *motelez*) involves play between two words, meaning 'blemish' and 'city,' and thus continues the juxtaposition of earthly and heavenly values" (Andrew and Waldron).

917–18. Appropriately for the period, the Dreamer assumes the Maiden is of aristocratic status. My translation of *haf* as "own" is slightly anachronistic: "hold" would be better.

918ff. Cf. *Gawain* 398ff., where Gawain wonders about the home of the Green Knight.

921. Clearly, the Dreamer continues to confuse the earthly (here the earthly Jerusalem) with the heavenly.

923. The word "moon" here anticipates its use as a part of the concatenation pattern in 1033–93.

942. The original, interestingly rendered in the passive voice, does not mention "the Son"; it says, instead, that the "old guilt was ended."

947–48. "The emphatic wordplay [not captured in the translation] is similar to that between *Lombe* and *lompe* in 1045ff. There would have been no impropriety for a contemporary audience, despite the solemnity of the subject" (Andrew and Waldron).

948. The original has God's *mote* ("city") without a *moote* ("stain"). The subtle semantic play is significant, since the City of God and any earthly (stained) city are at once utterly different from one another and absolutely related.

952. "The first interpretation of the significance of *Jerusalem* is based on Hebrews 12:22 and Revelation 3:12, while the second is found frequently in medieval literature, from Cynewulf's *Christ* onwards" (Andrew and Waldron).

957–58. Cf. *Erkenwald* 345–48.

961. "In the MS *Motelez* is given a decorated initial. Presumably the scribe mistook this for the beginning of a new section as a result of the extra stanza in section XV (see note to 841–912)" (Andrew and Waldron).

962. The translation relocates 962 to 964.

966.   I have taken *tor* ("tower") and relocated it as "height" in 963.

973–1032.   "In section XVII the concatenation words *apostel John* (see note to 788) serve to emphasize the scriptural authority for the vision. The major source is Revelation 21:10–21. Kean 1967, 207–9, compares the vision in *Purgatorio* 29.4–18" (Andrew and Waldron). See also *Paradiso* 31.

982.   In the original, the city is *schyrrer* ("brighter") than the sun.

984ff.   The vision—by definition an unmediated form of seeing—of the New Jerusalem turns out paradoxically to be mediated by the textual authority and precedent of John (see 973–1032n). There is a deep and abiding tradition in English mystical literature whereby supposedly unmediated visions, in which the veil of fallen consciousness is seemingly lifted, nevertheless betray a mediated status. See Finch 1987.

985ff.   This long passage marks an interesting inversion of the usual medieval claim to authority. Conventionally, a medieval writer claims that his assertions are borne out and verified in a respectable (usually textual) precedent. Here, however, the visionary experience of the speaker seems to ground, and to give truth to, the biblical precedent. The difference is nuanced, but it is worth noting.

990.   Cf. 115, 1018, 1106.

999.   "This is not the same as modern jasper. *OED* states that in Middle English this name is applied to any chalcedony except carnelian, but particularly to green stones" (Andrew and Waldron).

1003.   "It is clear enough that by *calsydoyne* the poet here intends 'a crypto-crystalline sub-species of quartz having a lustre nearly of wax, and being either transparent or translucent' (*OED*)" (Andrew and Waldron).

1006.   "*Sardonyse*: 'A variety of onyx or stratified chalcedony having white layers alternating with one or more strata of sard' (*OED*)" (Andrew and Waldron).

1007.   "*Rybé*: In the Vulgate the gem is *sardinus* or *sardius* (Revelation 21: 20). Gollancz [1891] therefore emends to *sarde*, suggesting that *rybé* is the result of scribal interference, motivated by the desire to differentiate this gem from the preceding *sardonyse*. Gordon's argument, that *rybé* is probably what the poet intended, as *sardius* in Exodus 28:17 is sometimes interpreted as 'ruby,' is more convincing, particularly in view of the allusion to the Exodus text in 1041" (Andrew and Waldron).

1018.   The original uses a simile comparing jasper to glistening glass. Cf. 115, 990, 1106.

1030.   "The biblical account has 12,000 furlongs (Revelation 21:16), and it is not clear why the poet altered this figure" (Andrew and Waldron).

1033–92.   "The concatenation word (*mone*) again serves as a focus for the contrast between heaven and earth. The section draws heavily on Revelation 21 and 22" (Andrew and Waldron).

1039–42.   Andrew and Waldron translate more exactly: " 'To each [gate] in written characters was joined a name of the children of Israel, following their dates, that is to say, according to their dates of birth.' These lines draw on the description of the High Priest's ephod in Exodus 28 as well as on Revelation

ऀीीीीीीीीीीीी

ीीीीीीी

ीीीीीीीीीीीीीीीी

ीीी

ीी

21. As Gordon observes, these two texts were often related in Christian commentary."

1043. In the original it is not the city as a whole but the streets that are said to gleam with light.

1046–47. The original contains dense wordplay. God is called their *lombe-ly3t* ("lamplight"), while the *Lombe* ("Lamb") is called their *lantyrne* ("lantern").

1049–50. Cf. *Gawain* 794ff. and note.

1055–56. "The river symbolizes the outpouring of the holy spirit: cf. 605ff." (Andrew and Waldron).

1060. "This alludes to the familiar symbolic association of filth with sin: see note to 725–26" (Andrew and Waldron).

1065–68. "Cf. Revelation 21:27" (Andrew and Waldron).

1069–70. "The description derives relevance from the position of the sphere of the moon in medieval cosmology, in which it forms the border between the unchanging aetherial regions above and changeable nature below (hence 'sublunary'). See Lewis, 92ff., and Milton, *Paradise Lost*, 1.291" (Andrew and Waldron).

1077–80. "Cf. Revelation 22:2" (Andrew and Waldron).

1085. "Again the poet expresses the Dreamer's feelings of shock in terms of a hunting metaphor: cf. notes to 185 and 344ff." (Andrew and Waldron).

1093–1152. "The concatenation word *delyt*, with its overlapping senses of 'delight' and 'desire,' suggests the function of this section—to emphasize both the bliss of salvation and the Dreamer's growing desire to cross the water and joined the saved. Once more, the poet draws extensively on Revelation, particularly 5:6–13" (Andrew and Waldron).

1106. Cf. 115, 990, 1018. In the original, the gates are not inlaid. "Cf. Revelation 21:21" (Andrew and Waldron).

1107. "Cf. Revelation 5:11, 7:9" (Andrew and Waldron).

1109. Who had most cheer, that is, among the virgins.

1126. "*Vertues*: one of the nine orders of angels. A brief review of this subject is provided by Lewis, 71–74" (Andrew and Waldron). The dominions, thrones, cherubim, and seraphim ascend above the virtues, while the powers, principalities, archangels, and angels are ordered below them.

1135. "This is, of course, the wound inflicted at the Crucifixion. Cf. note to 649–56" (Andrew and Waldron).

1146. Though the original has no economic metaphor, I have chosen here to echo the language of the parable of the vineyard. "Cf. Matthew 19:29, John 10:10" (Andrew and Waldron).

1147ff. "A saved child appears as one of the 144,000 virgins also in Chaucer's 'The Parson's Tale' (*Canterbury Tales* VII.579–85). See Hart" (Andrew and Waldron).

1152. *Luf-longyng.* "Though the primary sense of the word is secular, it is used elsewhere with a religious meaning, as in the Harley Lyric on the Five Joys of the Virgin (16) and Julian of Norwich, *Revelations of Divine Love* (chapter 71). Cf. 11n for the similar compound *luf-daungere*" (Andrew and Waldron).

1153–1212. "The concatenation word in the last section is *paye* 'pleasure,' with the specific sense of the will of God (it is *Pryncez paye* in three of the five stanzas). Thus the concatenation emphasizes the Dreamer's progression from self-absorbed rebelliousness to obedience to God's will—a sense reinforced by the echoes of the beginning of the poem" (Andrew and Waldron).

1153–61.   "Implicit in this passage is the familiar metaphor drawn from secular love, of passion overcoming reason and the lover being smitten through the eyes. Cf. 1152n" (Andrew and Waldron).

1154.   The original may be translated more literally: "My human's mind to madness melted."

1163.   A more literal translation would be: "From that purpose I was called."

1167.   See 1163 and note.

1171ff.   "The physical setting is unaltered (cf. 9–60); the change which has taken place is in the Dreamer's spiritual state. His immediate response is again one of passionate sorrow, but this is now controlled by his recognition of the place of human loss in the new structure of values he has learned in the vision" (Andrew and Waldron).

1176.   The Dreamer speaks here and later, as does Gawain occasionally (Cf. *Gawain* 2056–57), *in petto*.

1186.   "Gordon and Hillmann [1961] interpret the *garlande gay* metaphorically to signify the heavenly procession, and refer to the parallel usage of *ghirlanda* in *Paradiso* 10.91–93 and 12.19–20. But, as Bishop points out (1957), the parallel is not precise, for Dante refers not to a procession but to a circle of the blessed. In view of the fact that the *corona* ('crown') was commonly understood to stand for the circle of the blessed, it is more likely that *garlande* here signifies the Maiden's crown (previously described in 205ff.) which itself symbolizes her heavenly setting" (Andrew and Waldron).

1187.   Cf. 246–50, 333–36.

1189–94.   "The speech is an acknowledgement of the Dreamer's lack of restraint in trying to cross the stream" (Andrew and Waldron).

1199–1200.   It is implied, then, that the Dreamer had turned not to the Creator but to the creation. "This statement would also serve as a summary of the moral of *Patience*: see *Patience* 1–60, 524–31" (Andrew and Waldron).

1201–2.   "The possibility of resolution derived from *resoun* is recognized in 52 [51 in the translation]; in 665, *Resoun* is transformed into a personification of God. Here, resolution is finally achieved through acceptance of God's will" (Andrew and Waldron).

1205.   I have translated *lote* ("chance") as "fortune."

1212.   "The last line echoes the first, and brings the poem full circle" (Andrew and Waldron).

CLEANNESS

1–4.   The first four lines are difficult. Andrew and Waldron translate: " 'Whoever were to commend cleanness fittingly, and reckon up all the arguments that she demands by right, lovely examples would he be able to find in advancing his discourse, and in the reverse enormous trouble and difficulty.' "

A large initial occurs at the beginning of this line (and 125, 193, 249, 345, 485, 557, 601, 689, 781, 893, 1157, and 1357) in the manuscript. These initials "are located unevenly and sometimes arbitrarily, apparently by scribal rather than authorial choice" (Andrew and Waldron, 52).

5. The poems "contain many such periphrases for God: cf. (for example) *Cleanness* [280], 552, 1528; *Gawain* 256, 1292, [2441–42]; *Patience* 111, [261], 397–98; and especially *Patience* 206, which is almost identical" (Andrew and Waldron). Cf. also *Pearl* 736.

10. I have adopted the gloss of Gollancz 1974 on *rechen*. But Andrew and Waldron argue persuasively that the word is *rychen*, probably meaning "arrange" or "prepare."

11. "The priests handle Christ's body and use it sacramentally in the celebration of the eucharist. The same idea occurs in *Everyman* 739" (Andrew and Waldron).

12. "Here [around 20 in the translation] begins the extended 'clothing' metaphor, which prepares the ground for the explicit parable of the wedding feast. The contrast is partly between a literal outward seemliness and inner turpitude (13–16), and partly between clean and unclean spiritual 'clothing' (33–35). The reference to priests and their possible defilement of God's *gere* (16) also broaches the theme of defilement of sacred vessels, which is explored in the story of Belshazzar" (Andrew and Waldron). For the poet's concern with clothing, cf. also the miraculously unstained clothes of the pagan judge in *Erkenwald* (85–88).

13–16. Menner 1920 reminds us that "this is the only passage in all the poet's works where he alludes to the vices of the clergy." Indeed, the *Pearl* poet is decidedly not a part of the anticlerical tradition that flourished in the fourteenth century.

21. The translation has lost the directness of the original, which Andrew and Waldron translate: "if He were not scrupulous and fastidious."

23. "Christ's *carp* is the Sermon on the Mount, in which the eight Beatitudes are specified (Matthew 5:1–11). This is alluded to in a similar, but fuller, way in *Patience* (9ff.)" (Andrew and Waldron).

27–30. This comparison of the blessed with the bad marks what Andrew and Waldron call an "inversion" that "foreshadows the method of the poem as a whole, for in it cleanness is celebrated mainly by means of a series of negative *exempla*—stories which describe the activities and downfalls of the unclean." As Menner 1920 has it, after paraphrasing in 27–28 Matthew 5:8 ("Beati mundo corde, quoniam ipsi Deum videbunt" [see *Patience* 23–24]), the text on which the poem is based, "the poet states the text conversely in 29–30, since he is to develop and illustrate his theme by contraries, and intends to set forth, not so much the joys that await the pure in heart, but the terrible doom that falls upon those who violate purity."

48. In this, the prelude to the parable of the wedding feast, the guest is punished even though he did no harm "in talle ne in tuch." He is punished, that is, for crimes of omission. Cleanness, then, is a virtue that must be actively exercised.

49. *Wordlych* ("worldly") is Andrew and Waldron's emendation of the

manuscript *worþlych* ("worthless"). The emendation "restores the contrast between the earthly ruler in this line and the king of heaven in the next." But the contrast might be rendered even more emphatic if the prince were worthless in comparison with the Prince of Heaven.

49–160.   "The poet's account of the parable of the wedding feast draws on the versions in both St. Luke (14:16–24) and St. Matthew (22:1–14)" (Andrew and Waldron). Gollancz 1974 rightly notices that the poet's use of the passage from Luke explains the omission of Matthew 22:6–7.

51.   *Masse* here is used as a synonym of *gospel*. Cf. *Pearl* 497–98n.

63.   Andrew and Waldron translate this line more literally—"One had bought himself an estate, he said, by his troth"—and rightly notice that this marks an instance of indirect speech. While this technique is dramatically evident, for instance, in the Prologue to the *Canterbury Tales*, overall it is quite rare this early in English literature. In fact, indirect speech is not fully developed until Jane Austen, after whom it becomes *the* crucial literary mode (see Finch and Bowen).

73ff.   "The similarity of this description to a number of accounts of God's reaction to human misdeeds in both *Patience* (e.g., 129–32, 429–32) and *Cleanness* (e.g., 249–92, 557–600) may serve to emphasize that the earthly lord here represents God allegorically" (Andrew and Waldron).

78.   It is hard to know what *ceté* connotes here: perhaps a baronial manor, perhaps an estate or a homestead in a rural setting (like the one purchased by the man invited to the feast, 63–64), but certainly nothing like the London, for instance, of *Erkenwald*.

80.   All classes are included, as they are in the crowd in *Erkenwald* 63–64.

112.   That is, some were bastards.

114–20.   Cf. *Gawain* 1005–6.

117–18.   The guests' clothing clearly indicates their social standing, from highest to lowest; but no one is filthy or raggedly dressed.

133ff.   "In biblical, devotional, and homiletic literature, foul or ragged clothes are often used to symbolize the soul stained by sin or neglected" (Andrew and Waldron).

139ff.   "The lord has specifically requested that people should wear their best clothes to his feast (53–54), and therefore considers that the ill-dressed man is treating him with disdain. Modern readers may find the lord's reaction extreme or not entirely just; but it does not appear to have caused anxiety to medieval commentators, perhaps because the wedding garment could so readily be allegorized as good works—as indeed it is in 169ff.—the lack of which was self-evidently reprehensible. It is also possible that at the literal level there was the understanding that wedding garments were available to all who chose to ask for them" (Andrew and Waldron).

157–60.   "The terms in which this punishment is described emphasize that it is an allegorical representation of the pains of hell" (Andrew and Waldron).

161ff.   "Here the poet makes clear in true homiletic fashion the *significacio* of the parable. St. Matthew's account of the parable of the wedding feast ends with the words *Multi enim sunt vocati, pauci vero electi* 'For many are called, but few are chosen' (22:14)" (Andrew and Waldron).

164. "The poet emphasizes the importance of baptism, which is also a central theme in *Pearl*" (Andrew and Waldron). And the problem of baptism, of course, is crucial to *Erkenwald*. Cf. also *Pearl* 625–28.

168ff. Such exegeses are quite rare in the *Pearl* poet.

169–76. "As a complement to the preceding account of the allegorical significance of foul clothes, the poet now states plainly (in a manner similar to that adopted in contemporary homiletic and devotional writings) that clean clothes stand for good works and virtuous living" (Andrew and Waldron).

175ff. It is not clear whether this list of errors (*fautez*) is ad hoc or has a specific tradition. Cf. the list of the five interlocking virtues of Gawain's pentangle, *Gawain* 640ff.

180. "Hell mouth was often represented by the mouth of a whale, dragon, or less specific monster. See the account of Jonah being swallowed by the whale in *Patience* (247ff.)" (Andrew and Waldron).

193ff. Citing one's authority in this way is a standard trope in medieval discourse, and it shows up often in the *Pearl* poet.

197ff. "The poet's habit of describing and explaining God's actions, motivations, and even feelings in human terms is well exemplified in this passage. His attitude is in striking contrast to that of most Christian commentators, who normally try to avoid any suggestion of God behaving like a man" (Andrew and Waldron).

203–4. The point here—indeed, it is much of the poem's point as a whole— is that when God punishes vice He generally mitigates His wrath. Even Satan's pride and man's first disobedience are punished moderately (see 215, 230, and 247). But uncleanness drives God over the edge. (But see 249–50n.)

211. *Tramountayne* is problematic (Gollancz 1974 calls this the earliest instance of the word recorded in English); but it probably once meant "beyond the Alps," i.e., from an Italian perspective, "north." "The devil is traditionally associated with the north, an idea probably based on Isaiah 14:12–13" (Andrew and Waldron).

217–23. "Despite the fiend's excessive pride in his bright beauty (217–18), once he and the rebel angels fall, they become *black* fiends (220). Their disadvantaged and discredited position is given further emphasis by the poet's techniques of comparing them in successive similes (222–23) to small and insignificant objects" (Andrew and Waldron). Notice, too, that the motif of clothing is thus extended.

235–46. Cf. *Pearl* 637–44.

235–48. "The poet moves from the fall of angels to the fall of man. He sees both as events in which the protagonist neglects to fulfill his obligations to God" (Andrew and Waldron).

237–48. Cf. *Pearl* 637–48; *Erkenwald* 295–99.

240. "The idea that man was to inherit the place of the fallen angels in heaven was a commonplace. In the Old English *Genesis* (356–441) the poet uses this idea to motivate Satan's envy of Adam and Eve and his plan to corrupt them" (Andrew and Waldron).

241–42. Menner 1920 rightly reminds us of "the strikingly similar phraseology of *Erkenwald* 294–96."

248.   Indeed, we will learn of this event in 1069ff. Menner 1920 calls our attention to *Erkenwald* 298.

249–50.   "The Flood is seen as the third vengeance, the first two being the fall of the angels (205–34) and the fall of man (235–48)" (Andrew and Waldron). Most critics of *Cleanness* point out that whereas the fall of Satan and man had earned God's *mitigated* punishment, this uncleanness inspires his unmeasured wrath. And surely this distinction was a part of the poet's intention. But— remembering God's chastisement of Jonah for immoderate behavior—we should remain sensitive to the ways in which even God's punishment of uncleanness is moderated with temperance. The Flood, for instance, is of course quite severe; but God nevertheless places certain limits on his destruction (see 327ff.) and later promises not to repeat it.

249–528.   "The account of the Flood is based on Genesis 6:1–9:1" (Andrew and Waldron).

257–61.   Gollancz's translation (1974) is more rigorous: "For they were the first progeny that the earth produced, / The sons of the noble ancestor that was called Adam, / To whom God had given all that might profit him, / And bliss without harm, that body might have; / And those were likest to him that lived next after."

285.   The *Pearl* poet's God is utterly anthropomorphic; here, and at 291, he regrets his creation of man. See 519, where he regrets even his punishment. For Menner 1920 "it is perhaps noteworthy that the poet expressly states that God grieved as man, since such an implication of human feeling was generally explained away by the commentators."

293.   Each of the poem's three major *negative* exempla of uncleanness contains *positive* exemplars of cleanness (in one form or another). Here, of course, it is Noah.

301–44.   "This passage is based on Genesis 6:13–22. Though the poet expands the biblical narrative and adds some extra touches, which contribute to the liveliness of the passage and help to define the feelings and motives of God and Noah, he does not alter the essential facts" (Andrew and Waldron).

306.   "The people's impurity is symbolized by physical filth and slime: cf. *Patience* 269–344, where the foulness of the whale's belly symbolizes Jonah's sinful state (see *Patience* 342n)" (Andrew and Waldron).

324.   There is the sense here that God is first systematically erasing the creation He had fashioned, after which He will establish it anew. See 521ff. and note.

347.   Noah responds to God as a vassal to his lord.

348–49.   "Noah's point is that the plans devised by God's infinite wisdom have been carried out by a man whose intellectual capacity, though God-given, is comparatively limited" (Andrew and Waldron).

355.   The poet—appropriately in a poem about uncleanness—thus interprets the Flood as a vast purification of filth.

357.   The motif of escape is crucial to the *Pearl* poet. Later in the poem Lot and his daughters escape the destruction of the cities. In *Patience*, Jonah escapes from the belly of the whale. The judge's soul escapes to heaven in *Erkenwald*.

And the Pearl Maiden, of course, has escaped her earthly grave to enter the New Jerusalem.

363ff.   The *Pearl* poet lingers lovingly over meteorological description. Consider the representation of seasonal change in *Gawain* (500ff.) or the depiction of the storm in *Patience* (135ff.).

371ff.   "The poet evokes considerable sympathy for the victims of the Flood" (Andrew and Waldron).

382–84.   "The poet visualizes the hills surrounding valleys transformed into shores of huge lakes" (Andrew and Waldron).

393ff.   "The idea seems to be that their cries for mercy, which are not answered, indicate that God is set on revenge" (Andrew and Waldron).

416ff.   The poet's love of the technology of ships and seamanship is evident here and in *Patience* 101ff.

415ff.   "The ark's lack of navigational gear, which is not mentioned in Genesis, is added by the poet to emphasize the total submission of Noah and his companions to the will of God. There are records of holy men in the early Celtic church going to sea in boats without rudders and oars specifically to demonstrate their willingness to be sent wherever God might wish" (Andrew and Waldron).

424.   "Cf. *Patience* 257ff., where Jonah's survival inside the whale is attributed to the protection of God" (Andrew and Waldron).

425–28.   Menner 1920 reminds us that "the date of the Flood, which is given at the beginning of the Biblical account (Genesis 7:10–11), is transferred by the poet to the end [of the account in *Cleanness*], and connected with the statement of the duration of the Flood in 429 (Genesis 7:24)."

448.   "Gollancz [1974] suggests that this is derived from the French Mandeville: 'Mes ly Iuys lappellant Thanez' (Warner, 195). He reports that, among the variant readings for *Thenez*, *Chano* is the closest to the word from which this name is derived, the Persian for *Ararat*, *Kuhi-Noh* 'Noah's mountain' " (Andrew and Waldron).

456.   "The raven proves *vntrwe* in that it fails to honor its obligation to Noah, and return to the ark with the news" (Andrew and Waldron). And see their Introduction, 24–29.

459–64.   "Though there is no scriptural authority for this account of the raven's being lured from its duty to Noah by the desire to gorge itself on carrion, it is a commonplace in the works of the commentators, encyclopedists, and homilists, and is also reflected in the mystery plays. The unworthiness of the raven's actions is given emphasis by the repulsive physical details of 461–62" (Andrew and Waldron).

468.   In the original, Noah curses *all* animals.

519.   God's words here sound regretful. The *Pearl* poet's God is capable of the very human emotions of rage followed by regret.

521ff.   God's words here, echoing as they do his words to Adam and Eve earlier in Genesis, indicate that a new beginning is to be made.

523–27.   This marks another instance of the theme—everywhere evident in the oeuvre—of the cyclical nature of the world. Cf. *Gawain* 16–19, 496–99.

545–56. "The story of the Flood concluded, the poet points out, in typical homiletic fashion, the moral lessons it may provide for the edification of his audience" (Andrew and Waldron).

554ff. "Jewels are used to symbolize spiritual cleanness throughout *Pearl*. The wording of 556 may be compared with *Pearl* 721–80, where a similar phrase is used in the concatenation; the brightness and purity of the beryl is also observed in *Pearl* 110 and 1011" (Andrew and Waldron).

557–600. "These lines provide moral generalization based on the preceding account of particular sin and retribution, and function as a transitional passage between the story of the Flood and that of Abraham. The attribution of human feelings to God is once more striking, particularly that of regret of the Flood, as this has no scriptural basis" (Andrew and Waldron).

576. "Thus the poet argues that those of *vnsounde hert* will miss the reward promised in the sixth Beatitude: *Beati mundo corde* 'Blessed are the clean of heart' (Matthew 5:8)" (Andrew and Waldron).

583–86. See *Patience* 123–24, where the same point is made.

592. "The poet is arguing that God has insight into man's most personal thoughts and wishes, including those concerning sexuality and emotions; one might translate: 'searching out the sexual and emotional longings of every man' " (Andrew and Waldron).

595. "The poet is speaking of the revelation of divine truth achieved by the righteous, and alluding once more to the Beatitude 'Blessed are the clean of heart; for they shall see God' " (Andrew and Waldron).

599. This is a God whom the Old Testament's J-writer might recognize.

600. "Thus the story of Abraham is introduced specifically as an *exemplum*: cf. *Patience* 57–60" (Andrew and Waldron).

601–1012. "This section of the poem is based on Genesis 18:1–19:28" (Andrew and Waldron).

603–5. Cf. the description of the miraculous woodbine in *Patience* 445–57.

607–8. The *Pearl* poet likes to tease his audience with hints (sometimes misleading) of the story's conclusion. Cf. *Gawain* 496–99.

611–780. "The poem alternates between singular and plural forms in referring to the divine presence. The point is that it is at once singular (God) and plural (three persons). A similar device occurs in the corresponding biblical narrative, Genesis 18—a text which was used by commentators to illustrate the nature of the Trinity" (Andrew and Waldron).

612ff. "Abraham's position as a servant of God is emphasized, specifically at 639. The relationship between an earthly lord and his servants is used as a metaphor for the relationship between God and man elsewhere in the poems, for instance in the parable of the wedding feast in *Cleanness*, and in *Pearl* 1189–1212" (Andrew and Waldron).

625ff. The poet is fairly obsessed with the details of meals and feasting. Consider the parable of the wedding feast and Belshazzar's feast here in *Cleanness*, the feast in heaven described at the end of *Erkenwald*, or the numerous feasts in *Gawain*.

633. "Abraham removes his hat as a mark of respect" (Andrew and Waldron). Cf. *Pearl* 237, where the Maiden removes her crown.

670. My translation has not captured the strikingly idiomatic tone of the original *bot let we hit one*, which might be rendered more faithfully: "But skip it!"

682ff. "Once again, God's response and motivation are seen in human terms" (Andrew and Waldron). 682–88 are an aside.

697–700. My translation has lost something of the original sense. Andrew and Waldron translate: " 'I devised a natural way for them and taught it to them secretly, and esteemed it in My ordinance singularly precious, and set love within it, intercourse sweetest of all, and I Myself devised the play of love.' "

697–708. "The emphatic statement of the value of sexual love is a startlingly unusual attitude to find in a medieval homiletic poem—particularly as the poet gives these words to God" (Andrew and Waldron).

711–12. "God states his intention to make examples of the inhabitants of Sodom and Gomorrah—an idea not derived from the account in Genesis. (The poet himself is, of course, using their story in precisely this way)" (Andrew and Waldron).

715–65. Two points should be made about this passage. First, the conversation between Abraham and God is comparable to a vigorous bargaining session in which a shrewd buyer and an equally shrewd seller negotiate a price. Second, whereas the dramatic force of the moment depends upon God's *lack* of omniscience, elsewhere in the poem (and in the oeuvre), of course, God's omniscience is emphatically asserted (cf., for instance, 583–86).

726ff. Abraham's quite sensible argument that the innocent should not be destroyed along with the wicked is, indeed, God's argument to Jonah in *Patience* 501ff.

735. Abraham forces the issue with God reluctantly and hesitantly. Cf. the Dreamer's self-effacing manner of questioning the Maiden in *Pearl* 421ff., 901ff.

749ff. "Abraham realizes that God's wisdom and mercy are not subject to human limitations—a point which Sarah has earlier failed to understand" (Andrew and Waldron).

763. "Presumably Abraham, asking God to pardon the sinful majority for the sake of the virtuous minority, is merely expressing the hope that God's patience would be rewarded by the sinners mending their ways" (Andrew and Waldron).

765ff. It is interesting to compare this moment to the one in which the Dreamer in *Pearl* unwittingly allows the Maiden to proceed ahead to the city of the New Jerusalem.

771–76. "The special plea of Abraham for Lot is not in the biblical account" (Andrew and Waldron).

773. Far from poor, "in terms of worldly possessions, Lot is rich (see 786n, 812, 878). The word *pouere* is probably here intended to suggest spiritual poverty, the quality celebrated in the first Beatitude (Matthew 5:3), and consisting in humble obedience to the will of God" (Andrew and Waldron).

786. "Lot's wealth was traditional" (Andrew and Waldron).

789ff. "In medieval portraits, both verbal and pictorial, angels are normally characterized by fair boyish beauty: see Villette" (Andrew and Waldron).

796ff. Lot's treatment of the angels is, of course, comparable to Abraham's of the divine presence. As Andrew and Waldron state, "Lot immediately recognizes the angels for what they are, and adopts the role and manner of a servant before his lord."

803. Cf. 618.

805. "Cf. *Gawain* 1836" (Andrew and Waldron).

817ff. "The episode in which Lot's wife puts salt into the food does not occur in the Bible, but the story and its thematic link with her ultimate fate (see 996–1000) are well known in Hebraic tradition" (Andrew and Waldron).

822ff. "The application by Lot's wife of the disrespectful term *vnsaueré hyne* ['disagreeable or unsavory fellows'] to the angels emphasizes the contrast between her attitude to divine authority and Lot's. [Perhaps, though, she does not recognize them as such.] Gollancz ([1974], p. xxvi) explains that 'the angels must not be offered leaven, which sets up fermentation, a form of corruption' " (Andrew and Waldron).

832. "Cf. *Gawain* 884, 1648" (Andrew and Waldron).

839. The translation of *clos* as "cottage" is imperfect. The original "should perhaps be translated 'enclosure': the poet probably has in mind a house and land enclosed by a perimeter wall" (Andrew and Waldron).

846–48. "Sin is often associated with foul smell: see the description of the belly of the whale in *Patience* (especially 274–75)" (Andrew and Waldron).

861–72. "Rabanus Maurus, in his *Commentary on Genesis* ([Migne] 107:555), suggests, as compensation for Lot's sin in offering to prostitute his daughters, his concern for his guests, his wish to avoid a greater wrong (the insult to the angels), and his perturbation of mind. Nevertheless, Rabanus gravely remarks that Lot's conduct *nullo modo imitanda est* ('is by no means to be imitated'). We need not suppose that, however sympathetically the poet presents Lot, he entirely endorses Lot's behavior in this respect" (Andrew and Waldron).

881. "Guests," i.e., the angels.

885–86. Andrew and Waldron's translation is more literal: " 'They (the angels) struck a blow among that cursed people, so that they strayed about, as blind as Bayard ever was.' The blindness of Bayard, supposedly Charlemagne's horse, was proverbial" (Andrew and Waldron).

891. "Shocked" is an imperfect translation of *wakned al wrank* ("woken quite awry"), which "appears to be a grimly humorous understatement" (Andrew and Waldron).

900. "Sir Loth" is addressed by the angels as a medieval knight.

910–13. "Compare Jonah's prophecy about Nineveh: *Patience* 361–64" (Andrew and Waldron).

913–18. "Unlike Jonah (*Patience* 83–88, 109–28), Lot realizes that it is impossible to hide from the wrath of God. It is a characteristic of the positive characters in the poem that they understand something of the nature of God, as does Abraham" (Andrew and Waldron).

935–36. "The two prospective sons-in-law refuse to leave (cf. Genesis 19:

14–16)" (Andrew and Waldron). They die, therefore, with the rest of the Sodomites.

938. "The only survivors are these three and Lot. The subsequent well-known story about Lot's incest with his daughters (Genesis 19:20–28) depends on their not having husbands" (Andrew and Waldron).

945ff. The escape of Lot and his family from the destruction of the cities is, of course, comparable to the escape of Noah and his family from the Flood.

947ff. "Cf. the description of the winds in *Patience* 131ff., and *Gawain* 525" (Andrew and Waldron).

961–62. "Hell is personified, as it is systematically in the Gospel of Nicodemus. Gollancz [1974] observes that the *houndez of heuen* may be related to the Northern tradition of the 'Gabriel hounds,' a mysterious pack whose appearance in the sky presaged disaster. One might also compare the Greyhound in Dante's *Inferno* I.100–111" (Andrew and Waldron).

966. As with the image of the fallen angels as strained meal rising in a small cloud from a sieve (226), here the poet concretizes the sublime, the nearly ineffable, in a tiny, quotidian simile. "The startling perspective of the image emphasizes man's feebleness in relation to God's enormous power; cf. *Patience* 268, which has a similar effect" (Andrew and Waldron).

979ff. Here the *Pearl* poet's antifeminism—here and there latent in his work and indeed traditional in the English fourteenth century—becomes explicit.

980. The poet's habit of providing psychological motivation for his characters is here evident in an interesting way: Lot's wife is what contemporary traffic reports call a rubbernecker.

986–88. "Their response to survival is similar to that of Noah and his companions: cf. 497" (Andrew and Waldron).

1006–7. "The comparison is from Genesis 13:10: *antequam subverteret Dominus Sodomam et Gomorrham, sicut paradisus Domini* 'before the Lord destroyed Sodom and Gomorrah, as the paradise of the Lord' " (Andrew and Waldron).

1013. "Cf. *Patience* 370: the destruction of the cities is of course very similar to the fate with which Jonah threatens the Ninevites" (Andrew and Waldron).

1015. *Fyue citées.* A problem, of course, exists, since we had thought that only four cities were destroyed. Indeed, in the manuscript itself, the original *fyue* ("five") has been erased and replaced with the word *faure* ("four") by a later hand. "The later scribe probably made his emendation for the sake of consistency with 956ff., where the poet names four cities which are to be destroyed. In 926 God undertakes to spare Zoar (which would have been the fifth), and in 992 the poet confirms that it was spared. According to tradition it was destroyed many years later" (Andrew and Waldron).

1025ff. "As the Dead Sea was brought about by sin—the perverse reversal of God's natural order—so it is characterized by these reversals of natural properties and functions. The poet's account draws from *Mandeville's Travels*" (Andrew and Waldron).

1037. *Waxlokes* refers, according to Gollancz 1974, to "curly spiral shapes, resembling convoluted sticks of wax." He continues: " 'Lok,' in this sense, recalls Chaucer's 'With lokkes crulle, as they were leyd in presse,' Prologue 81."

1043–48.   "The ultimate source of this description of the bitter [fruit] by the Dead Sea is Josephus (*Wars* IV.viii.4), but the idea had become a commonplace in medieval commentaries and encyclopedic writing. The poet emphasizes the contrast between the [fruits'] beautiful outer appearance and the bitterness of their inner substance: thus they are made a telling symbol of the false seeming of sin. This sense is supported by the way in which they bring to mind the apple in the Garden of Eden" (Andrew and Waldron).

1057–59.   Everywhere in the oeuvre, the *Pearl* poet proves himself sensitive to the codes of medieval romance. Indeed, he has a flair for the courtly forms of ideal behavior by which a man interacts dallyingly with "ladies." Consider Gawain's interaction with Bertilak's wife in *Gawain*, the persona's flirtation with Dame Poverty and Dame Patience in *Patience*, and Christ's treatment of the Maiden in *Pearl* as a lover. "*Clopyngnel* is Jean de Meun. This passage (1057–64) alludes to *Le Roman de la Rose* 7689–7764 (ed. F. Lecoy, Paris, 1970). Jean's account concerns romantic love; the poet deliberately transforms its significance to the plane of divine love" (Andrew and Waldron).

1068.   "A well-known tradition, going back ultimately to the parable of the Pearl of Price (Matthew 13:45–6), associates the pearl with heaven and salvation. This association is, of course, essential to *Pearl*" (Andrew and Waldron).

1069–88.   "Like the Dead Sea, the Virgin Birth is presented in terms of the breaking of the laws of nature—though in this case with a supernaturally creative instead of a supernaturally destructive effect. The uniqueness of the birth of Christ is given emphasis by the repeated assertions (1078ff.) of its difference from the expected norms of childbirth. This was a familiar theme in medieval Christian literature. In the mystery plays, for instance, emphasis is given to the painlessness of the birth and Mary's cleanness afterwards (e.g., York No. 17, 293–94, Ludus Coventriae No. 15, 203–4, 229ff., 302ff.). The freedom from pain produces a symbolic reversal, in that the pain of childbirth was a curse of the Fall (see, e.g., Chester No. 2, 313ff.). The Virgin Birth was also seen as one of the Five Joys of Mary—itself one of the symbolic 'fives' well known in the Middle Ages (cf. *Gawain* 631–65)" (Andrew and Waldron).

1069ff.   This passage expands on the point made earlier (248) about the birth of Christ.

1081–88.   "The singing of angels and the adoration of the ox and ass are traditional elements derived from apocryphal writings. Both are reflected, for instance, in the mystery plays and in contemporary religious art" (Andrew and Waldron).

1093–1108.   "Though Christ is characterized by a special, superhuman cleanness (1085–92), it is particularly fitting that the unclean should come to Him for help. The symbolic association of physical sickness and healing with spiritual sickness and healing is a strong and ancient tradition, in which the most significant influence is the New Testament portrayal of Christ as physical and spiritual healer. The diseases specified here include those normally regarded in the Middle Ages as resulting from unclean or incontinent living of one kind or another" (Andrew and Waldron).

1096.   The translation has left out the *drye folk*, those "with an excess of the dry humors—cholera and melancholia" (Andrew and Waldron).

1105–8.   "This idea developed around the account of the supper at Emmaus in Luke 24:35, where Christ is recognized by the disciples by means of the way he breaks bread. Toulouse was not normally associated with knives, and it is therefore probable (as Gollancz [1974] points out) that the poet intended Toledo, which was. A reference to the blades of Toledo is made in the *Chanson de Roland* 1611" (Andrew and Waldron).

1111–48.   "This passage of moral commentary between narratives tackles the question of how a man may apply the lessons illustrated in the stories to his own life: of how he may find salvation. Thus the penitential nature of the poem is made clear (particularly in 1113–16 and 1129–32). The use of mire to symbolize sin recurs throughout *Cleanness*. Here the poet also alludes to the traditional idea of the pearl surviving untarnished its burial in mire, which often represented allegorically the relationship between the soul and the body: see Kean 1967, 147ff., and *Pearl* 22–23. The symbolic identification of the pearl with the righteous soul and salvation is central to the symbolism, structure, and meaning of *Pearl*" (Andrew and Waldron). Cf. *Erkenwald*, where the issue of a corpse surviving untarnished its burial is crucial.

1117–18.   "The idea that the pearl is undervalued by the worldly, derived perhaps from commentary on the parable of not casting pearls before swine (Matthew 7:6), is a commonplace in medieval religious writings" (Andrew and Waldron).

1133ff.   One thinks of the very sticky issue of the hero's "sin" and confession in *Gawain*.

1134.   "The comparison is also found (in more extended form) in a twelfth-century sermon designed to appeal to illuminators of manuscripts: 'Let us consider how we may become scribes of the Lord. The parchment on which we write for him is a pure conscience, whereon all our good works are noted by the pen of memory, and make us acceptable to God. The knife wherewith it is scraped is the fear of God, which removes from our conscience by repentance all the roughness and unevenness of sin and vice. The pumice wherewith it is made smooth is the discipline of heavenly desires.' (see Mynors, 9)" (Andrew and Waldron).

1143–48.   "Here the poet makes the thematic transition from the subject of the uncleanness of men to the related subject of the desecration of the holy vessels. This passage is necessary in order to demonstrate the thematic relevance of the final narrative. The unifying factor is the symbol of the vessel dedicated to God, which may be both a vessel literally and represent man symbolically" (Andrew and Waldron).

1149.   Compare the opening into the narrative here with that in *Patience* 57.

1157–74.   "This account is based on 2 Chronicles 36:11–14" (Andrew and Waldron).

1175–1292.   "This narrative is based mainly on Jeremiah 52:4–19" (Andrew and Waldron).

1202ff.   In the Old Testament account, no such surprise attack is planned; the people merely attempt to escape the city by night.

1226.   The original for Nebuchadnezzar is *Nabugo*. Menner 1920 argues that "this curious abbreviation of Nebuchadnezzar's name, which occurs again at 1233, is due to the French manner of dividing the name—*Nabugo de Nozar* (so always in MS)."

1229–32. Thomas translates: "For if the Father had still been his friend and Zedekiah had not turned against him, neither Chaldea, nor India, nor even Turkey would have had the energy to attack him—their indignation would have been too slight."

1258–60. Here, of course, is the traditional trope of the wheel of fortune that brings the high low.

1261–92. "The passage is based on Jeremiah 52:13–19" (Andrew and Waldron).

1283. The *gazafylace* ("vault" in the translation) was, as Moorman 1977 tells us, the "box in which offerings to the Temple were received."

1286–87. "Solomon's temple project is described in 3 Kings (Authorized Version 1 Kings) 5–7 and 2 Chronicles 2–5" (Andrew and Waldron).

1292. "Cf. *Gawain* 2" (Andrew and Waldron).

1317–20. "Here the contrast between the way in which Nebuchadnezzar treats the holy vessels and the way in which Belshazzar will do so (the main subject of 1357–1804) is anticipated" (Andrew and Waldron).

1346–48. "The poet presents Belshazzar's conduct as not only sinful but also comic in its folly" (Andrew and Waldron). In this respect, Belshazzar is rather like Jonah in *Patience*.

1354. One should bear in mind here the *Pearl* poet's very special love for such things of this world as clothing, food, and, indeed, luxury. The poet, in fact—and in spite of his intention to condemn the feast as decadent—describes Belshazzar's feast in terms every bit as admiring as those he uses to describe Arthur's in *Gawain*.

1363ff. This might be compared with the invitation to the wedding feast sent out by the rich man earlier in the poem.

1377–1492. "This description is partially based on Mandeville (Warner, 105–7, 136)" (Andrew and Waldron).

1381ff. The city might be compared to (or contrasted with) the New Jerusalem in *Pearl*.

1385ff. "The poet turns from describing the outer walls of the *bourȝ* (Babylon conceived as a medieval castle or fortified town) to describing the palace (*place* in the sense of 'house, hall')" (Andrew and Waldron).

1392. As the Green Knight gallops on horseback through the entry and into the hall in *Gawain*.

1402–3. "The fanfare at Arthur's feast is similarly described in *Gawain* 116–20" (Andrew and Waldron).

1406. "Perhaps the point is that the dishes were so large that one would not expect them to be real silver, but nevertheless they looked as if they were" (Andrew and Waldron).

1407–12. "This describes a rather exotic version of the elaborate table decoration fashionable during the late Middle Ages" (Andrew and Waldron).

1408. "Cf. *Gawain* 802, where the castle momentarily looks like one of these table decorations" (Andrew and Waldron).

1417–1660.   "This passage is partly based on Daniel 5:1–20" (Andrew and Waldron).

1421.   "It was believed that the effect of wine on the mind was caused by vapors rising from the stomach into the brain" (Andrew and Waldron).

1444.   "Since no crown is mentioned among the vessels commissioned by Solomon for the Temple, the word *coroun* in 1444 (like *crowne*, 1275) appears to designate a gold cincture or moulding, such as surrounded the ark of the covenant and the incense-altar made by Bezalel for the Tabernacle of Moses (see Exodus 25:24–25, 37:1–3 and 25–27, where the Hebrew *zer* 'border, edge' is translated by *corona* 'crown' in the Vulgate). The link between Solomon's altar of brass and the altars of Bezalel may have been provided for the poet by 2 Chronicles 1:5, where it is stated that before building the Temple, Solomon offered sacrifices on the brazen sacrificial altar made for Moses by Bezalel" (Andrew and Waldron). But since the poet, who is hardly fastidious about his sources, seems really to provide the banquet with a crown, I have done so also.

1478–80.   "The poet follows Daniel 5:5 in alluding to only one candlestick (the accounts of the furnishing of the Temple of Solomon mention, in 2 Chronicles 4:7 and 3 Kings [Authorized Version 1 Kings] 7:49, ten candelabra). For the description of the candelabrum here, the poet turns again to the description of the construction of Moses's tabernacle and the account of the single candelabrum there (Exodus 25:31ff. and 37:17ff.)" (Andrew and Waldron).

1482–85.   It is interesting to compare this description of the artificial birds on artificial branches with that of the supernatural birds on supernatural branches in *Pearl* 89–96. See also *Gawain* 610ff.

1507.   I have followed Andrew and Waldron's recommendation in starting Belshazzar's speech at 1507. Other editors, however, have read the second half of this line not as a direct quotation but as an instance of indirect speech. See, for example, Anderson 1977.

1512.   "The idea," according to Anderson 1977, is that "the servants compete with each other in racing to seize the vessels and fill them with drink for their masters."

1515–16.   These lines describe a general clattering of the bowls and cups.

1523–25.   "Cf. the earlier description of Nebuchadnezzar's false gods, 1341–48" (Andrew and Waldron).

1526.   *Belfagor* is a false god associated with pride (see Numbers 25:3). *Belyal* means 'evil' in Hebrew, and becomes personified in biblical tradition (see 2 Cor. 6:15). *Belssabub* was traditionally chief of the false gods; his name means 'lord of the flies' in Hebrew (see Matthew 12:24)" (Andrew and Waldron).

1530–1740.   Cf. *Erkenwald* 51–56, where the mysterious words are never deciphered.

1532.   "By the candlestick" is the poet's translation of Daniel 5:5 *contra candelabrum*.

1541–42.   The precise meaning of these lines has eluded commentators. Andrew and Waldron, reading the MS *displayes his lers* as *dispyses his leres* ("cheeks") and more or less in agreement with Anderson 1977 translate: "his knees knock together and his thighs bend, and with the striking of his palms he treats his cheeks with scorn." I believe, however, that the MS needs no emendation and that *displayes his lers* is best translated by "exposes his limbs (by rending his clothes)." See also 1582, where the king (again, I think) tears at his clothes, and 1595, where the queen refers to his having rent his robes.

1545.   The alliteration of the original supplies a very vivid sense of the supernatural sound of the pen rasping on the wall.

1551ff.   This passage might be compared to that in *Erkenwald* (51–56), when the puzzling words are discovered in the tomb of the judge.

1559–60.   Lords having to send out a summons more than once is a recurring motif of the poem.

1577.   I have, very imperfectly, translated *walkyries* as "wizards." Moorman 1977 calls this an interesting, because very late, reference to the warrior maidens of Teutonic myth. As Gollancz 1974 points out, this "is the only instance of the word recorded later than the Anglo-Saxon period. It must be noted, however, that this remarkable word occurs in a poem marked by Scandinavian influence. The modern English 'valkyrie' was of course reintroduced into English by Gray and Percy from their studies of Northern antiquities."

1579.   For Anderson 1977, the exorcists are literally "sorcerers who have to do with exorcisms."

1580–81.   "The poet's unexpected use of this piece of colloquial humor does not only serve to amuse: it also suggests the emptiness of the sorcerers' pretensions to knowledge" (Andrew and Waldron).

1586.   Ironically, the queen is the poem's first "good woman" (in the medieval sense of the term).

1610.   "The poet follows the Vulgate in identifying the earlier name of Daniel with that of Belshazzar. The Authorized Version, in contrast, has Belteshazzar" (Andrew and Waldron).

1612–13.   "This event is described in 1293–1308" (Andrew and Waldron).

1635.   Anderson 1977 glosses *mode* as " 'thought, inner meaning.' Belshazzar differentiates between the interpretation of the outer form (*tyxte* [1634]) of the mysterious writing, and the inner meaning, as does Daniel when he comes to read the inscription (1725ff.)."

1657.   Nebuchadnezzar's story is not unlike the fiend's (205ff.).

1667.   Cf. Daniel 4:27: *"in robore fortitudinis meae."*

1675.   Cf. *Patience* 392.

1681ff.   The problem of madness arises now and again in the *Pearl* poet's work. In *Pearl*, for instance, the vision is often said to be of such intensity that it would put a mortal mind in jeopardy. In *Patience* 509ff., God is concerned for the stupid and mad.

1681.   There are significant parallels between Nebuchadnezzar's behavior in this story and Belshazzar's in the feast.

1684.   The meaning of the passage, according to Gollancz 1974, is clear: "when the herbs were decayed, i.e. in winter, and there was no more *fogge* ['grass'] for Nebuchadnezzar to eat, he was fed as a horse, probably with oats. The idea is evidently an elaboration of the passage in the Bible, where it is said that 'they fed him with grass like oxen,' Daniel 5:21."

1687. Quite persuasively, Andrew and Waldron translate this: "By that time many thick feathers crowded around his face." But I have stayed more or less with Menner 1920 here.

1687ff. Nebuchadnezzar's animalistic, indeed, almost vegetal, condition might be compared to that of the Green Knight in *Gawain* (18off.).

1689–98. "Compare the description of the giant in the alliterative *Morte Arthure* 1078–90" (Andrew and Waldron).

1701–2. "Like Jonah, Nebuchadnezzar learns through suffering: cf. *Patience* 296" (Andrew and Waldron). The *he* in 1701 of the original is ambiguous and has caused some editors, including Menner 1920 and Morris, to read Nebuchadnezzar as the antecedent. But I have followed Anderson 1977 and other commentators in reading it as God.

1707. "In the context of 1706–8 this is evidently a reference to the solemn reinstatement of Nebuchadnezzar (Vulgate *et in regno meo restitutus sum* 'and I was restored to my kingdom' [Daniel 4:33]), which is symbolized by a new coronation" (Andrew and Waldron).

1719–20. "These false gods have been described twice previously, in 1341–48 and 1523–25" (Andrew and Waldron).

1730–32. "The poet is rendering the mysterious message of Daniel 5:26" (Andrew and Waldron).

1730ff. Daniel's translation of the three words exhibits a yearning for technical accuracy comparable to that of the Maiden when she distinguishes between the Old and the New Jerusalem, *Pearl* 937ff.

1741ff. "Belshazzar gives Daniel the rewards promised in 1623–40" (Andrew and Waldron).

1762. For Anderson 1977, this signifies "not Belshazzar's guests, who would hardly be in need of a *soper*, but the ordinary people of the town who hurry home to escape the worsening weather, and whose simple pleasures contrast to the luxury of the palace."

1764. "The groups of feasters finally disperse to bed" (Andrew and Waldron).

1804. The translation is not literal. Andrew and Waldron translate more exactly: " 'to look on our lovely Lord will happen late (for him)': i.e., he will never do so."

1805. "The three stories alluded to are those of the Flood, the Destruction of the Cities, and Belshazzar's Feast" (Andrew and Waldron).

1810. "The line is reminiscent of the Beatitudes: see 23–28 and notes, and *Patience* 9–33" (Andrew and Waldron).

1811–12. "The bright clothes are again symbolic of purity, and thus of salvation" (Andrew and Waldron).

PATIENCE

1. As this first line of the poem is echoed in the last, the whole thus constitutes a kind of loop whose beginning and end are connected. In this it is like *Pearl*—the last line of which echoes the first—and *Gawain*, the closing

moments of which reiterate the mythical story of the founding of Britain by the Trojan Brutus told at the poem's beginning. What is more, the first word of three of the five poems in the oeuvre—*Clannesse, Perle,* and *Pacience*—announces the theme and, consequently, the title that editors have conferred upon them. A large initial occurs at the beginning of this line (and 61, 245, 305, and 409) in the manuscript. These initials "are located unevenly and sometimes arbitrarily, apparently by scribal rather than authorial choice" (Andrew and Waldron, 52).

3. The *Pearl* poet is, in a sense, a writer of Christian comedies who finds solace and redemption at the end of hardship and trial; good men are "soothed in the end," however great their suffering.

9. The *Pearl* poet is fond of citing his sources, assuring us that his stories are "received" and, therefore, authoritative. Throughout the oeuvre is a sense that the tales being told are very much a part of common lore and that, as an audience, we are participating in an ongoing tradition of transmission.

9ff. "Cf. *Piers Plowman* C.6.272–73. In the present Roman Missal the Beatitudes passage from St. Matthew is the Gospel for the Feast of All Saints (1 November) and its Octave, that of St. Boniface (5 June) and of certain other martyrs. This association with the Feast of St. Boniface, the eighth-century English apostle to Saxony, may have been in the poet's mind in prefacing it to the story of the unwilling prophet Jonah. For a briefer reference to St. Matthew and the Beatitudes, in somewhat similar wording, see *Cleanness* 23–28" (Andrew and Waldron).

10–28. Here we have the *Pearl* poet's most complete paraphrase of the eight Beatitudes as they are articulated in Matthew 5:3–10 of the Vulgate:

3 Beati pauperes spiritu: quoniam ipsorum est regnum coelorum. ("Blessed are the poor in spirit; for theirs is the kingdom of heaven.")

4 Beati mites: quoniam ipsi possidebunt terram. ("Blessed are the meek; for they shall possess the earth.")

5 Beati, qui lugent: quoniam ipsi consolabuntur. ("Blessed are those who mourn; for they shall be consoled.")

6 Beati, qui esuriunt et sitiunt justitiam: quoniam ipsi saturabuntur. ("Blessed are those who hunger and thirst for justice; for they shall be well fed.")

7 Beati misericordes: quoniam ipsi misericordiam consequentur. ("Blessed are the merciful; for they shall receive mercy in turn.")

8 Beati mundo corde: quoniam ipsi Deum videbunt. ("Blessed are the pure-hearted; for they shall see God.")

9 Beati pacifici: quoniam filii Dei vocabuntur. ("Blessed are the peaceful; for they shall be called God's children.")

10 Beati, qui persecutionem patiuntur propter justitiam: quoniam ipsorum est regnum coelorum. ("Blessed are those who suffer persecution for the sake of justice; for theirs is the kingdom of heaven.")

11–12. The theme of the payment of spiritual or worldly gifts is crucial to the poet. Consider, for instance, the issue of payment in the parable of the vineyard in *Pearl*, the exchanging of gifts in *Gawain*, or Saint Erkenwald's reference to God in his speech to the judge: " 'He who pays every person who's pious and true / Couldn't grudge you the gift of His grace and His joy!' " (*Erkenwald* 275–76).

17–18. *Harme* "could mean either 'injury (done to them)' or 'sin'—the Vulgate has simply *Beati qui lugent* 'Blessed are they that mourn'—but a common medieval gloss is *pro suis vel aliorum peccatis* ('for their own sins or those of others'). It is probable that the poet has this interpretation in mind, for the personification to which this Beatitude relates is called *Dame Penaunce* (31)" (Andrew and Waldron).

25. Andrew and Waldron are correct in literally translating: " 'they are blessed also who remain quiet.' Cf. Vulgate *Beati pacifici* 'Blessed are the peacemakers': as in 17, the English rendering is an interpretation rather than a direct translation. It also reflects the influence of the commentaries: the *Glossa Ordinaria* ([Migne] 114:90) cites the following (Augustinian) definition: *Pacifici sunt qui omnes motus animus componunt et rationi subjiciunt* ('The peaceful are those who quieten all motions of the soul and subdue them to reason')" (Andrew and Waldron). *Halden her pese*, however, may also suggest the original meaning, as here translated.

27. Andrew and Waldron compare the English with the Vulgate: *"qui persecutionem patiuntur propter justitiam* 'that suffer persecution for justice' sake.' This is the poet's only radical departure from the Vulgate text of the Beatitudes in St. Matthew. His alteration places emphasis on self-control and moderation— a theme of major relevance to the story of Jonah."

30–34. It is characteristic of the *Pearl* poet's pragmatic humor and his belated relation to the chivalric tradition that he here playfully personifies the Beatitudes as courtly ladies with whom one must flirt. The poet's penchant for drawing on the courtly language of love—often in a mildly ironic fashion—is evident throughout his works.

31–33. As Andrew and Waldron point out, "these figures personify the virtues celebrated in the Beatitudes." And they correspond respectively to the list of the eight Beatitudes.

34. The note struck here is indeed playfully sexual.

35. Critics have often read this moment as a reference to spiritual, rather than material, poverty. It's quite possible, though, that this line is frankly autobiographical and that the *Pearl* poet was, as he complains, rather poor.

36–37. One formula indeed serves both: Beati pauperes spiritu: quoniam ipsorum est regnum coelorum ("Blessed are the poor in spirit; for theirs is the kingdom of heaven," Matthew 5:3); Beati, qui persecutionem patiuntur propter justitiam: quoniam ipsorum est regnum coelorum ("Blessed are those who suffer persecution for the sake of justice; for theirs is the kingdom of heaven," Matthew 5:10). The linking of the first and the last, moreover, is a theme—as well as a structural principle—that appears in many of the poems.

37–39. "*Quoyntyse* ('wisdom' 39) suggests both the metaphorical beauty of the 'ladies' and the wisdom of the virtues they represent: cf. the metaphor of courtship in *Cleanness* 1057–64. This passage may also allude to the identification—often found in medieval commentaries, and made specifically in the morality play *Wisdom*—between Christ and wisdom (cf. 1 Corinthians 1:24). Thus 39 could be interpreted as suggesting the pursuit of Christ: cf. *Pearl* 689–94n" (Andrew and Waldron).

46–56.   This marks a paradigmatic instance of the poet's pragmatic, even playful, outlook. The words enjoin us emphatically to succumb to the will of God. But they imply at the same time a sophisticated and realistic attitude that is neither entirely uncynical nor absolutely solemn.

50ff.   Cf. *Gawain* 562–65 and 1811 for the same pragmatic spirit of resignation to what life doles out.

51–52.   This marks one of the many parallels between the narrator and Jonah that the poem emphasizes; for Jonah, too, is sent off on a chore.

52.   I have followed Andrew and Waldron's—and others'—suggestion that the city is meant here and not the verb *to roam*: "Thus the idea of going to Rome is used as a metaphor for any arduous journey. Possibly the preacher-narrator also implies the situation of a priest sent to Rome by his bishop. If so, this would serve to emphasize both the specific connection between Jonah and the narrator as men under an obligation to preach the Word of God, and (in more general terms) the universal relevance of the ensuing story of Jonah" (Andrew and Waldron).

57ff.   Here we are introduced to the story of Jonah, with which the poem is centrally occupied. (Compare the opening into the narrative here with that in *Cleanness* 1149.) As in *Cleanness*, the use of negative exempla to explain virtues is crucial to the poet's homiletic method. Andrew and Waldron gloss *jape* as "trick, device": "*Jape* anticipates the comic element in the poet's treatment of Jonah."

59–60.   Cf. a similar narrative moment in *Gawain* (30–32).

60.   "The story of Jonah is of course mainly based on the Old Testament Book of Jonah" (Andrew and Waldron). Layered on top of the original story are perhaps some figural typologies supplied by later Christian exegetes. See Friedman.

64.   "This line foreshadows the way in which God later works through the elements, in the storm and again in the episode of the woodbine" (Andrew and Waldron).

75–88.   From the characteristically laconic Vulgate translation of the Jonah story (1:3) we learn only that the prophet, after receiving God's injunction to bear His message to the Ninevites, flees instead to Tarshish: "Et surrexit Jonas, ut fugeret in Tharsis a facie Domini." ("And Jonah got up in order to take flight to Tarshish from the face of God.") In the *Pearl* poet's rendition, by contrast, we are given a monologue that reveals in elaborate detail the immediate and ongoing condition of Jonah's mind. This is characteristic. Jonah's attempts to evade the call of God, moreover, should be contrasted to Gawain's pious resignation to his fate, *Gawain* 545–49, 562–65.

83–88.   "Note the bitterness against God in Jonah's comments as he tries to justify his desire to shirk his duty. The futility of his plan to escape from God is demonstrated by the storm, and already suggested by 49ff." (Andrew and Waldron).

95–96.   "This description clearly suggests the Crucifixion (cf. *Pearl* 806), encouraging the reader to see Jonah's conduct in comparison to Christ's" (Andrew and Waldron).

101–8.   Concern for professional knowledge and language, for the technicalities of cooking, armor, falconry, military strategy, architecture, bookbinding, and, as here, sailing, is demonstrated throughout the poems. Cf., for instance, *Cleanness* 416ff.

102.   The cross-sail is presumably the ship's mainsail, hung from a horizontal mast.

103.   The windlass is a winch used to raise and lower a ship's anchor(s). To "weigh" an anchor is to heave it up preparatory to sailing.

104.   The bowsprit is a large spar projecting forward from the stem of a ship to carry the sail forward. Bowlines are fastened near the middle of the perpendicular edge of a square sail and used to keep the weather edge of the sail taut forward when the ship is close-hauled. But this particular bowline seems, for the time being, to serve no such purpose; it is merely secured to the bowsprit.

105.   Here the guy-ropes, which are used to reinforce and steady the masts, are tightened; they are not involved in unfurling the sail.

106.   The larboard is the left-hand side of the ship (to one on board facing the box [front]). The luff is "the advantage of the wind" (Andrew and Waldron).

121–24.   "This is translated from Psalms 93 (Authorized Version 94):8–9; cf. the similar use of this text in *Cleanness* 581ff." (Andrew and Waldron).

123–24.   See *Cleanness* 583–86, where the same point is made. Here begins a series of periphrases for God, a rhetorical device for which the *Pearl* poet is noted. These periphrases are not empty flourishes; they are crucial to the ongoing explanation of the nature of God.

125.   As Andrew and Waldron remind us, "there is no biblical support for this suggestion that Jonah's folly may result from senility; neither has any source been found among the Christian commentators." Interestingly, the comment foreshadows God's justification for taking mercy on the stupid, the mad, and the old (see 509–15).

131ff.   "These lines emphasize God's control over nature, which is a key factor in both the storm and the woodbine episodes. In classical terminology, Eurus is a wind from the east or south-east, and Aquilon from the north or north-north-east. Cf. Virgil *Aeneid* 1:52ff." (Andrew and Waldron).

135–36.   Unlike Jonah, the elements are immediately obedient to the will of God.

137ff.   "The description of the storm may be compared to the account of the Flood in *Cleanness* 363ff." (Andrew and Waldron).

157ff.   "The implied contempt for the trappings of civilization gives a subdued moral tone to the narrative. As Wilson, 61, points out, this passage echoes the conventional homiletic theme of the irrelevance of luxuries to the man facing imminent death" (Andrew and Waldron).

164–67.   "The names of these deities are not found in the Vulgate account, which says simply *clamaverunt viri ad deum suum* 'the men cried to their god' (1: 5). *Vernagu* (165): a giant who appears in the Charlemagne romances. *Diana deuout* (166): Diana is 'devout' in the special sense of being devoted to chastity.

Neptune (166): Gollancz [1924] suggests that MS *Nepturne* results from scribal confusion with the ending of *Saturne,* but does not emend. *Mahoun* (167): Mahomet, who was regarded as a false god by medieval Christians. In the mystery plays, evil characters (such as Herod) often swear by him and sometimes express allegiance to him. *Mergot* (167): Margot, a heathen god mentioned in the Charlemagne romances, and probably related to the biblical Magog (see Genesis 10:2, Ezekiel 38:2)" (Andrew and Waldron).

170ff. "The sailor's speech emphasizes the fact that Jonah, through his selfish desire to escape his duty, has endangered the lives of innocent people. Thus, once again, his conduct is in contrast to Christ's" (Andrew and Waldron).

186. "The description of Jonah is most uncomplimentary, and his sleep is probably intended to symbolize moral lassitude. Sleep is often used in medieval religious writings to signify lack of moral awareness" (Andrew and Waldron). But sleep can also have very different significations for the poet. Consider the treatment of sleep in the dream vision *Pearl;* in *Gawain* (244–45, 1182ff., 1209, 1746ff., 2007); in *Erkenwald* (91–92); and in *Cleanness* (1765ff.).

188. "*Ragnel:* the name of a devil" (Andrew and Waldron).

205–12. "It is significant that as soon as Jonah is challenged with his misdemeanors he accepts full responsibility for them and agrees that he should be thrown from the boat: the poet here introduces the positive side of Jonah's character" (Andrew and Waldron).

206–8. Jonah's extended periphrasis for God has the function here of distinguishing the true God, the actual creator, from the false gods worshipped by the seamen.

225–28. "The sailors, who have previously (164–68) addressed their supplications to a variety of heathen gods, now address the true God, and do so again later in thanks for their escape from the storm (237–40)" (Andrew and Waldron).

231–40. This marks an interesting dramatic moment, when the immediate narrative is temporarily suspended in order to ferry the sailors safely to land and to complete their conversion. Like the narrator, God has the ability to take time out from a larger plan to complete smaller tasks along the way.

242. "The poet emphasizes that Jonah's fate results from his lack of patience: cf. 6" (Andrew and Waldron).

244. "Once again we are reminded of the story's scriptural authority" (Andrew and Waldron).

247. "The Old English *wyrde* originally meant 'fate' but changed its meaning under the pressure of Christian philosophy. Here it clearly indicates providence controlled directly by God, rather than fate working in a random manner. The appearance of the whale at this juncture is an example of God's using, for a specific purpose, a component of divinely ordered nature—as similarly with the winds, the sun, the woodbine, and the worm" (Andrew and Waldron).

257ff. "Jonah's survival inside the whale, impossible according to the laws of nature, is brought about through the protection of God. Many commentators saw the fact that Jonah was not digested as miraculous" (Andrew and Waldron).

258. I've translated *warlowes* as "devil's," but in other contexts it might mean

"wizard's." "The symbolic connection between the whale and hell was a commonplace during the Middle Ages. Sea monsters' jaws were used to represent hell mouth in performances of the mystery cycles, and appear with the same significance in 'doom' paintings on church walls" (Andrew and Waldron).

268. "This fine image, with its striking perspective, emphasizes Jonah's insignificance in relation to the vastness of the whale, and thus suggests the futility of his struggle against God. Though the belly is associated with the devil and hell, the entrance is compared to a *munster* ('cathedral') *dor*" (Andrew and Waldron).

269–80. The vivid description of Jonah's plight in the whale marks a wonderful instance of the poet's love for special, often grisly, effects. Cf., for example, the description in *Cleanness* of the hand of God at Belshazzar's feast (1530ff.).

282–88. "Jonah has previously shown awareness of his misdeeds, when he accepts responsibility for them in the storm (205–12). Now we see that he is willing to ask God for forgiveness, and this brief speech is thus a prelude to his full confession in 305–36" (Andrew and Waldron).

292ff. "Jonah's spiritual state during his sleep in the boat, when he was ignoring his misdemeanors, is in sharp contrast to his state in this period inside the whale, during which he comes to a full awareness of his failings" (Andrew and Waldron).

294. "Commentators normally saw Jonah's three days in the belly as a type of Christ's three days in hell" (Andrew and Waldron).

305–36. "Cf. Psalms 68 (Authorized Version 69). In medieval psalters this psalm was often illustrated with a picture of Jonah, usually emerging from the whale" (Andrew and Waldron).

341–42. "One would expect Jonah's clothes to be dirty after he has spent three days and nights in the whale's belly, the foul and slimy nature of which the poet has emphasized; but it is clear that Jonah's soiled cloak also symbolizes the defilement of sin. Cf. *Piers Plowman* B.13.272ff., where Haukyn is advised to wash his sin-stained coat; interestingly, he is afterwards addressed by Patience on the subject of poverty. Cf. also the symbolic use of dirty clothes in the parable of the wedding feast (*Cleanness* 51ff.)" (Andrew and Waldron). See *Cleanness* 306 note. Cf. also the miraculously unstained clothes of the pagan judge in *Erkenwald* (85–88).

343–44. "These lines call attention to the utter futility of Jonah's attempt to avoid obeying God" (Andrew and Waldron).

359–64. "Jonah's prophecy may be compared with the description of the destruction of Sodom and the other cities in *Cleanness* (947ff.)" (Andrew and Waldron).

365–66. Cf. how the news of the tomb spreads rapidly through London in *Erkenwald* (57–59). Also note how crowds often operate in perfect unison in the works of the *Pearl* poet. In this at least, the pure souls of the New Jerusalem in *Pearl* and the lascivious citizens of Sodom in *Cleanness* are alike.

385–404. "The King here orders that the Ninevites should admit their guilt and appeal to God for mercy: just as Jonah has done from the belly of the whale" (Andrew and Waldron).

413–16. "The answer to Jonah's question is, of course, 'no': he made no such prediction. Note the excessive concern with reputation throughout this speech, especially in 427–28" (Andrew and Waldron).

431–32. God's rhetorical question, unlike Jonah's (413–16), is well taken.

433. My translation has lost the word *janglande* ("grumbling"), which "is used also in 90 to describe Jonah's state of angry rebellion against God" (Andrew and Waldron).

445–57. Cf. the description of the shady oak in *Cleanness* 604–5.

460. Andrew and Waldron rightly call the expression of the original "so idiomatic that it resists literal translation." Cf. *Gawain* 1944.

479. "Jonah's suffering is also mentioned in the Old Testament (4:8)" (Andrew and Waldron).

482–88. "Jonah forgets that God has mercifully spared him in the belly of the whale, and appears even to claim credit for the provision of the woodbine (485). For the second time, he invites God to end his life (cf. 425–28)" (Andrew and Waldron).

493. A more literal translation might be: " 'It is no trifle,' said the man, 'but more a matter of justice.' " "Jonah is claiming that it is the principle of the matter that is important" (Andrew and Waldron).

495ff. "In this speech God explains his motives in terms identifiable with human emotional response. Thus it is a good instance of the poet's tendency to 'humanize' God" (Andrew and Waldron).

496. "God emphasizes his role as creator: cf. 131. In the Old English poem *Genesis* B (455) Adam is referred to as *godes handgesceaft* 'God's handiwork' " (Andrew and Waldron).

501ff. God's argument that the innocent or repentant should not be destroyed echoes Abraham's in *Cleanness* 726ff. Consider also, in this context, the discussions in *Pearl* concerning the difference between the innocent and the righteous.

507–8. "The poet emphasizes that God's mercy is aroused by the repentance of the Ninevites, and we are reminded that he pardoned Jonah under similar circumstances. Cf. *Cleanness* 1699–1708" (Andrew and Waldron).

509–15. The syntax of the original is so distorted that it has caused some editors to suggest—and Andrew and Waldron to adopt—an emended line order. "In the MS 510–12 follow 513–25, producing a lack of continuity between 515 and 510 (numbering this edition). The sequence adopted here was suggested by Gollancz [1924] but not implemented by him. He believed that 510–12 are displaced, and that they were canceled by the poet and replaced by 513–15. In his text the lines are left as they stand in the MS, but 510–12 are enclosed in square brackets; in this he is followed by Anderson [1969]. But it is interesting that both these editors were influenced by their desire to maintain the quatrain arrangement, which is disrupted by the retention of 510–12. Whether the lines were canceled by the poet remains hypothetical, but the above sequence does give a rationally ordered series of innocent groups— idiots, children, foolish women, and dumb beasts (516–17)" (Andrew and Waldron). I have followed these suggestions in the translation.

524. "Opinions have differed as to precisely where in this passage God's

speech should end, and the voice of the narrator resume: Gollancz [1924] puts it at the end of 527; we have chosen, with Bateson and Anderson [1969] to put it at the end of 523. Both are legitimate interpretations. It can be argued on the one side that 524 sounds more like the tone of God speaking to Jonah than the narrator addressing his audience, and on the other side that the exhortation to patience in 525 picks up the concerns of the 'prologue,' and is thus more appropriate to the narrator than to God. A definitive argument either way is difficult to envisage. This passage (524–27) functions as a bridge between the voice of God speaking to Jonah and the voice of the narrator in the persona of a preacher, God's representative on earth, addressing an audience on the principles of Christian conduct. Thus a certain similarity between the two voices is fitting, and the precise point at which the speaker changes remains elusive" (Andrew and Waldron). It remains, in fact, a matter for either the reader or the oral interpreter of the poem to decide.

526–27. "This metaphor may be compared with that at the center of the parable of the wedding feast in *Cleanness* (51–192: see especially 144–45)" (Andrew and Waldron).

SIR GAWAIN AND THE GREEN KNIGHT

1. Cf. 2525. A large initial occurs at the beginning of this line (and 491, 619, 763, 1126, 1421, 1893, 1998, and 2259) in the manuscript. Except for lines 1, 491, 1126, and 1998—where "extra large and prominent initials" are located, and "which have traditionally been accepted by editors as marking the beginnings of four narrative fitts"—these initials "are located unevenly and sometimes arbitrarily, apparently by scribal rather than authorial choice" (Andrew and Waldron, 52).

3–4. The "trust-breaking traitor" is probably Antenor, or so Gollancz 1940 and Moorman 1977 agree. Andrew and Waldron, however, argue that "it seems likely that the poet is enunciating the motif of 'shame or success' (or *blysse and blunder*) which is dominant in the present adventure of Gawain, a descendant of Aeneas, and which can be discerned in the lives of other members of the *highe kynde*, Brutus and Arthur (see notes to 13, 2465–66.). The account in the *Laud Troy Book* (ca. 1400), which does not attempt to exonerate Aeneas, relates the trial and exile of Aeneas and Antenor with their kin, after the departure of the Greeks.".

11–12. "While Langaberde and Brutus are well known in medieval legend as eponymous founders of Lombardy and Britain respectively, the name of Ticius is not recorded elsewhere. Recognized 'founders' of Tuscany include a Tuscus and a Tirius" (Andrew and Waldron).

13. "*Felix* is unique as a praenomen of Brutus (great-grandson of Aeneas), though the epithet ('happy') is associated in Roman tradition with founders of cities, etc. It is appropriately used of Brutus, who is said to have been fated to early misfortune (his mother died giving birth to him and he later killed his father by accident) but upon exile from Italy successfully founded Britain" (Andrew and Waldron).

13–14.   Cf. 2524.

16–19.   The theme of the oscillating nature of things is crucial to the *Pearl* poet. Cf. 496–99; *Cleanness* 523–27.

24.   The poet habitually underscores the fact that his material is borrowed or carried across from older sources and authorities. See 31–36n.

30.   *Laye* is "an Old French word used by Marie de France (twelfth century) to designate the short Breton tales which she versified; originally 'a short narrative poem intended to be sung or recited,' it had come to mean simply 'poem' or 'song' by the fourteenth century, though perhaps with some 'Celtic' associations of magic and love; the present context suggests that it was still associated with minstrelsy" (Andrew and Waldron).

31–36.   I have blurred the original of 31–32, which Andrew and Waldron, rightly conveying the intended oral delivery of the poem, render: "I shall tell it at once, aloud, as I have heard it in the court [or town]." For Andrew and Waldron, "33–35 are evidently a reference to the text of the present poem, which the reciter would have in front of him." It is possible, however, that the poet is referring not to his own text but to the original *Sir Gawain and the Green Knight*, which he plans to transcribe or translate. Indeed, 35–36 seem to indicate that the story had long been written down in alliterative verse as a part of the lore of the land. But such statements could merely be rhetorical posturing; in the medieval period, writing conferred an authority not necessarily enjoyed by oral traditions. For Tolkien and Gordon, incidentally, this reference underscores the "continuity of the alliterative tradition" and thus discredits the notion that English alliterative poetry, waning after the Norman invasion, experienced a rejuvenation in the late medieval period.

37.   "According to French romance, Arthur held court five times a year on the great Christian festivals, Easter, Ascension, Whitsun, All Saints (cf. 536–37), and Christmas. In the *Livre de Carados*, possibly the poet's source for the story of the beheading game, the challenger enters Arthur's court at Carduel during Whitsuntide feast" (Andrew and Waldron).

51–55.   This passage constitutes a fine example of the medieval convention of the superlative; banquets are always the most luxurious, knights the finest, and ladies the most lovely. See 121–25, 131, 153ff.

54–55.   "Arthur and his courtiers were all in their youth (*first age*); by implication this was also the golden age of Arthur's court and reign, before the appearance of the treachery which brought about the downfall of the Round Table. The theme of the first stanza (the rise and fall of kingdoms) is heard faintly in the background" (Andrew and Waldron).

64.   Scholars do not agree upon the nature of these chants, but certainly one form or another of the Mass had been performed.

65.   "I.e., the festive spirit of Christmas Day was renewed on New Year's Day" (Andrew and Waldron).

66–70.   These lines describe a game played at Christmas in which, according to Andrew and Waldron, gifts are given to subordinates and to equals.

69.   This describes "a guessing game like Handy Dandy (cf. *bi hone* 67) with forfeits; if the lady fails to guess which hand the present is in, the knight wins a kiss (hence the somewhat arch comment of 69–70.)" (Andrew and Waldron).

81ff. "Guinevere is meant, of course, a jewel beyond price in comparison with those of 78–80" (Andrew and Waldron).

91–95. This marks an interestingly reflexive moment. Arthur calls for a story or entertainment, perhaps a tale in verse much like *Sir Gawain and the Green Knight*, a composition, after all, designed to be performed at just such an occasion of court. What he gets, ironically, is the real thing.

110. "Agravain [of the hard hand] and Gawain were sons of Lot [sometimes Loth], King of Orkney [sometimes Orkeney]; their mother was Arthur's half-sister, Anna (sometimes known as Belisent). Another half-sister of Arthur was Morgan, cf. 2463ff. Guinevere sits on Arthur's left, at the center of the table, Gawain and Agravain are to the left of her. On Arthur's right are Bishop Baldwin and Iwain" (Andrew and Waldron).

112. Baldwin literally " 'sits in the place of honor' (at the right of the host, cf. 1001). When the host sat at the end of the table the guest of honor would occupy the first place on his right at the 'top' of the long side. The poet does not introduce the Round Table, though he uses the phrase for the abstract 'Arthur's court'; in general the background details of the romance are drawn from contemporary aristocratic life" (Andrew and Waldron).

116. "A *cors* comprised a variety of dishes (enough to constitute a complete meal by any modern standard). A medieval banquet consisted of a number of these courses. Cf. 128" (Andrew and Waldron).

118. Stone 1959 tells us that the instrument here, the nakers, is a "double military drum slung on the body, which Crusaders brought back from the east. A picture in the National Gallery, London, the *Madonna with the Girdle* by Matteo di Giovanni, shows a musical angel playing nakers. Modern banjos are direct descendants of nakers."

121–28. See 51–55n.

132–33. Arthur will be able to eat because this new noise ushers in the adventure he had called for, before which he would not eat (see 90ff.). The joke is rather elaborate, since Arthur, of course, had in mind either a representation or a conventional joust and not an actual peril.

150. The fact of his greenness, his most striking characteristic, is delayed for dramatic effect. Moorman 1977 provides a thorough note on the Green Knight's color.

160. "I.e., he wore only stockings or soft socks—considered appropriate wear for peaceful pursuits (e.g., hunting) in the fourteenth century. Knights in armor, on the other hand, wore steel shoes (*sabatounz*, cf. 574); the expression 'shoeless,' therefore, accords with the assurance (203ff.) that the Green Knight had no piece of armor about him" (Andrew and Waldron).

168. I have inadequately translated *payttrure* ("poitrel") as the harness. For while the harness indicates the entire accoutrement (the breast collar, the britching, the belly straps, etc.), the poitrel is a very specific piece of armor (see 601n.). The crupper is a leather loop attached to the saddle and passed under the horse's tail to prevent the saddle from creeping forward.

169. The bosses are decorative studs placed at either end of the bit. The bit is placed at the back (the soft part) of the horse's mouth.

170. The feet are placed in the stirrups for steadiness and balance.

171.   *Arsounz* ("saddlebows") are the two separate, but interlocked, parts of the saddle. *Scurtes* ("skirts") refers to the leather that surrounds the saddle. Skirts were often elaborately decorated.

177.   The bridle is the gear that covers the head of the horse.

180ff.   Some of the Green Knight's unruly and animalistic physical characteristics might be usefully compared to those of Nebuchadnezzar in *Cleanness* 1687ff.

203.   "Note the dramatic nature of the description; the speculation that 'it seemed as if no man might survive his blows' (201–2) leads the observer (as it were) to look more closely for armor and weapons" (Andrew and Waldron).

206–7.   As Stone 1959 tells us, "the holly cluster or wassail bob (its living green leaves promising that spring would succeed dead midwinter) was a symbol of Christmas good luck, though its origin as such is pagan. The early Christians in Rome probably took it over from the Saturnalia, in which it figured prominently, Saturn's club being made of holly wood." "A branch carried in his hand was a sign of peace (cf. 265–66 and *Cleanness* 486–90). Messengers in the Middle Ages often carried an olive branch; it is entirely in keeping with the enigmatical humor of the Green Knight that he should carry a Christmas evergreen, like some wassailer wishing peace and joy to the house, while showing an enormous weapon of war in the other hand" (Andrew and Waldron).

210.   "Cf. the second ax, 2225. Both axes evidently had half-moon shaped blades measuring about four feet from upper to lower extremity. In addition, the poet appears to describe this one, at least, as having a spike (*grayn*) sticking out at the back of the blade" (Andrew and Waldron).

237.   Those who step forward are "presumably the servants, whose naïve curiosity is thus suitably differentiated from the stunned silence of the courtiers (241ff.)" (Andrew and Waldron).

254.   "As king, Arthur properly uses the singular pronoun to everyone except Guinevere; his general manner toward the Green Knight is courteous and hospitable in the extreme. The latter's use of *thou* to Arthur, however, is a mark of disrespect (contrast Gawain's manner of addressing the king in 343ff.)" (Andrew and Waldron).

274.   "I.e., 'by prerogative of the Christmas season' " (Andrew and Waldron).

280.   The phrase "unbearded youth," according to Moorman 1977, "—along with 354, 219–20 (the rod of initiation), the 'year and a day' of Gawain's pledge, the pentangle, the chastity test, the blow of initiation, Gawain's costume, and the wearing of the baldric—is brought forward by Cargill and Slauch as proof of a connection between the poem and the Order of the Garter."

288.   "The term *gisarm* [*giserne*] was usually applied to a battle-ax with a long blade in line with the shaft, sharpened on both ends and ending in a point, though the description in 209ff. appears to distinguish the *grayn* ('spike') from the blade" (Andrew and Waldron).

296.   My translation omits the word *barlay*, a term of truce, Gollancz (1940) reminds us, still operative in children's games.

298.   "In the present case, from 1 January 'a twelvemonth' would extend to 31 December, and the extra day is mentioned to make it clear that the term

expires on the following day, 1 January" (Andrew and Waldron). I have elided the construction in the translation.

309–10. "The scornful question, with its implication that they are failing to live up to their reputation, is a technique also adopted by the Lady of Hautdesert—see 1481ff. and cf. 1528" (Andrew and Waldron).

336. I take *dintez* (literally "blows") to be intended metaphorically to refer to Arthur's bold words to the Green Knight, which do not frighten him. (A number of critics have read the *dintez* as the equivalent of a baseball player's warm-up swings in the batter's box.) But, in the words of Moorman 1977, Baughan's literal interpretation of the *dintez* as earnest blows of the ax "has come to play a great part in modern theories of the theme of the poem, the issue being whether Arthur struck a number of ineffectual blows at the Green Knight's neck and had to be rescued from an embarrassing position by Gawain."

341–42. "These two lines are probably intended to be understood as a brief summary of Gawain's speech to the king, which is given in its full elaboration in the next stanza; for the same device (*transitio*), cf. 387–89, 734–39, 2185–88, 2237–38" (Andrew and Waldron).

343ff. "Gawain's *cortaysye* shows in this stanza as an elaborate politeness of manner and speech" (Andrew and Waldron).

356. Moorman 1977 notes how striking is the "close relationship of uncles and nephews in medieval literature—e.g. Mark-Tristan, Charlemagne-Roland, Mygelas-Beowulf—a motif which probably reflects the custom of younger sons of noble houses sending their sons to be trained at their elder brothers' courts."

360. Andrew and Waldron provide alternative translations: " 'and if I speak unfittingly let all this noble court (speak) without offense' "; or " 'let all this noble court be free from blame' "; or " 'let all this court decide without reproach whether I speak fittingly or not.' "

373–74. "In addition to the humorous implication 'because he'll be dead,' there may well be a pun on *byden*, which can mean 'endure' or 'wait for' " (Andrew and Waldron).

384. "If this means 'with no one else present' it was not included in the challenge, unless in the obscure *barlay*, though Gawain does meet the Green Knight alone (cf. especially 2149ff., 2242–46). However, the meaning is almost certainly 'at the hands of no other living person'; Gawain might be expected to insist on this point, which appears to give him a good chance of escaping the return blow (cf. 373–74, 410)" (Andrew and Waldron). I have tried to capture this sense with "you yourself" (383).

398ff. Cf. *Pearl* 918ff.

404. "The New Year is still a time for making solemn resolutions. The Green Knight discourages Gawain from taking a stronger oath" (Andrew and Waldron).

428. This kicking of the decapitated head is, as Stone 1959 argues, "no meretricious horror. In folklore, if an enchanter has his head chopped off and can be prevented from re-uniting head and body, he really dies. So the kicking is probably purposeful. This enchanter not only regains his head, but demonstrates superior power by riding off with his 'head in his hand.' "

429. Cf. 2315.

442–43. This is "a good instance of the poet's use of the *wheel* for surprise and suspense" (Andrew and Waldron).

463–77. For Stone 1959, "the king's laughter and explanation are the calculated actions of a good leader restoring normality and morale to the community after a terrifying and dangerous experience." But laughter in the poem has a deeper significance than critics have been able to unearth. Cf. the court's laughter at the poem's end, 2514.

472–73. "The term *enterludez* (Latin *interludium*, lit. 'between play') was possibly first used of short dramatic or mimic entertainments between courses at a banquet. Though by the late fourteenth century it seems to have designated simply 'plays' (sometimes 'miracle plays'), the word may have retained a derogatory association with minstrelsy and mumming. In contrasting what they have just seen with the courtiers' own *caroles*, King Arthur conveys an aristocratic disdain for professional entertainment and at the same time contrives to suggest that the beheading may have been no more than an illusionist's trick (cf. *craft*)" (Andrew and Waldron).

477. "Arthur aptly (*gaynly*) quotes a proverbial expression meaning 'cease from strife' " (Andrew and Waldron).

477–80. The court will similarly commemorate the girdle with which Gawain returns from his adventure (see 2516). In this world, adventures produce tokens; and the tokens, in turn, recall to mind the adventures.

487ff. This apostrophe to the protagonist is unusual in the *Pearl* poet, who is much more likely to apostrophize the reader/listener.

491–94. The exact tone here is elusive. Is the situation slightly comic, the king having received more than he bargained for when he first hoped for an adventure? Is it monitory, the king having been reckless?

496–99. The *Pearl* poet likes to tease his audience with hints (here strangely misleading) of the story's conclusion. Cf. *Cleanness* 607–8.

500ff. See Pearsall's comment (1955,131) on these lines as conventional.

504. The original has the weather literally at war with the winter. "The changing of the seasons was traditionally imagined as a battle between Summer and Winter which manifested itself particularly in the equinoctial storms (cf. 523ff.)" (Andrew and Waldron).

507–20. This is an exceptionally skillful, though standard, late medieval description of the advent of spring and summer. Cf. the famous beginning of Chaucer's Prologue to *The Canterbury Tales*.

518–22. Here we have a curious and exquisite micronarrative of a single personified plant experiencing the vicissitudes of the changing seasons.

521–24. Like the plant, Harvest is personified.

523. The antecedent of *his* and *he* is Harvest.

525. "The reference is to the equinoctial gales" (Andrew and Waldron).

529. "This use of 'yesterday' to suggest the mutability of earthly life is no doubt reminiscent of texts such as Job 8:9 and Psalms 89 (Authorized Version 90)" (Andrew and Waldron).

536. November 1.

542. The mirth here clearly intends to turn attention away from the sadness

of the situation. And this detail should be borne in mind when, at the end of the tale, the court makes a jest of Gawain's purported failure.

545–49; 562–65.   Gawain's resignation to duty is to be contrasted against Jonah's attempts to evade the call of God, *Patience* 75ff.

551ff.   "Some of the knights mentioned here (e.g,. Eric, Lancelot, Bedevere) play an important part in other Arthurian romances. Here their names are introduced (like those of 110ff.) in order to invest the story with authenticity for readers conversant with the Arthurian background" (Andrew and Waldron).

554.   As Stone 1959 reminds us, "Bedevere, who in Malory is the last survivor of Arthur's battle with Mordred, was the great friend of Kay. Together they went with Arthur to meet the giant of St. Michael's Mount, and later fought prodigiously in Arthur's great victory over the Romans. According to Geoffrey of Monmouth, both were slain in this battle."

562–65.   Cf. 1811 and *Patience* 50ff. for a different expression of the same pragmatic spirit of resignation.

568ff.   "A passage on the arming of the hero frequently occurs in the medieval romance and would seem to be inherited from the epic. Gawain's armor (see Tolkien and Gordon's note) is that of the late fourteenth century" (Moorman 1977).

571–72.   "The armor was put on over the knight's clothes (the doublet and capados); cf. 2015" (Andrew and Waldron). The doublet was a quilted undergarment reinforced by rings of mail and worn under the armor proper.

575.   Greaves were plates of armor that protected the knight's leg below the knee.

578.   Cuisses were plate armor for the front of the thighs.

583.   The braces were sometimes called "brassards"; they protected the knight's upper arms.

586.   This is "the knight's surcoat, or coat of arms, i.e., a cloth tunic worn over the armor and embroidered with his heraldic device (which hence itself receives the name 'coat-of-arms')" (Andrew and Waldron).

597.   In Chrétien de Troyes, too, Gawain's horse is called Gringolet. Stone 1959 argues that "the word probably derives from 'Gwyngalet,' meaning 'white-hard.' Later the name was assigned to the boat of the mythical hero Wade, the son of Wayland the Smith and Bodhilda, the King of Sweden's daughter."

600.   For bridle, see 177n.

601.   See the description of a horse's skirts in 171n. The poitrel was a hanging piece of armor designed to protect the breast of the horse.

602.   The caparison was the sweeping, ornamental drapery that hung ceremoniously from a horse's neck and backside. For crupper, see 168n. For saddlebows, see 171n.

610.   Cf. *Cleanness* 1410, 1482ff.

614.   The seamstresses ply their trade "in town" then, where the poet has heard the tale itself (see 31).

620.   For a summary of critical discussions of the pentangle, see Moorman 1977.

625.   "In the Middle Ages the idea developed that Solomon's magic seal bore a six-pointed star made of two interlaced triangles; in course of time this

became identified with the five-pointed star (*pentangle, pentacle, pentalpha,* or *pentagramma*) which was used by Pythagoreans and other sects as a symbol of health or perfection. In Christian eyes it was associated with black magic, but was sometimes made symbolic, instead, of the name Jesus or Maria (each of five letters), or of the five wounds of Christ" (Andrew and Waldron).

626. "The complex unity of the figure makes it a 'natural' symbol of moral integrity, in the manner expounded in the lines which follow" (Andrew and Waldron).

627. *Poyntez* is "a significant pun, in as much as the word can mean 'virtue, quality' in Middle English (cf. 657 and *Patience* 1n). Perhaps it is also to be understood after *ay faythful in fyue* in 632" (Andrew and Waldron).

628–29. "Each line of the pentangle passes over one, and under one, and joins the other two at its ends" (Andrew and Waldron).

630. "In fact, the phrase is not elsewhere recorded" (Andrew and Waldron).

632. "The five pentads of virtue are detailed in the next stanza" (Andrew and Waldron).

640ff. Cf. the list of vices in *Cleanness* 177ff.

641. See Green's discussion of the five fingers as virtues.

643. "The Apostle's Creed (*crucifixus, mortuus, et sepultus*)" (Andrew and Waldron).

646. "The Five Joys of Mary were the Annunciation, Nativity, Resurrection, Ascension, and Assumption; with the Five Wounds of Christ they form the subjects of popular devotions in the Middle Ages" (Andrew and Waldron).

649. "In Geoffrey of Monmouth it is Arthur who has the image of the virgin painted inside his shield" (Andrew and Waldron).

651–55. "The virtues of chivalry are to be seen as forming a single group on a par with the other pentads of 640, 641, 642, and 646" (Andrew and Waldron).

654. "*Pity* and *piety* are not completely differentiated in meaning at this date (both forms of the word go back, through Old French, to Latin *pietas*). Here, among the virtues of chivalry, the sense is primarily 'compassion' (cf. Chaucer's *For pitee renneth soone in gentil herte*), but 'devotion to duty' is also of obvious importance in Gawain's story (as in that of his ancestor Aeneas)" (Andrew and Waldron).

681. "The courtiers' underground criticism of Arthur, for his encouragement of the beheading bargain and for his acceptance of Gawain's obligation to keep his word, introduces into the poem a remarkably detached view of the ideals of chivalry. It also touches on a relation between games and morality, a theme which recurs throughout; cf. note to 1876–84" (Andrew and Waldron).

689. "A conventional reference to the romance-writer's source, real or imaginary" (Andrew and Waldron). Cf. 30–36.

691. *Logres* is "Geoffrey of Monmouth's name for Arthur's Britain" (Andrew and Waldron). See Speirs 231–32. Throughout Gawain's journey to the castle there is a sense that survives from the Anglo-Saxon period of the world as a vast expanse of dangerous and anarchic energy only occasionally punctuated by an outpost of Christian civilization.

698ff. "I.e., Anglesey itself and the neighboring small islands (including

Holy I. and Puffin I.). Gawain's journey takes him to Caernarvon and eastwards along the north coast of Wales. A fourteenth-century map in the Bodleian Library shows the usual route as passing through Bangor, Conway, Abergele, Rhuddlan, and Flint. With its geographical particularity, the description of this part of the journey contrasts with that of the beginning and end, which (appropriately enough) are clouded in romantic vagueness. The poet, writing in the north-west midlands, probably knew, and expected his original audience to know, this part of the journey" (Andrew and Waldron).

699. "Apparently a reference to his crossing of Conway and Clwyd. *Holy Hede* (700) may then be identifiable as Holywell, near Basingwerk Abbey, where the Roman road reaches the Dee. The lowest identifiable medieval fording place was at Shotwick, some eight miles up river, where the Dee is much narrower; the poet may have had a boat-crossing in mind here, however, as the phrase *hade eft bonk* suggests. The name has been much discussed; the only real certainty is that it does not refer to Holyhead in Anglesey (cf. 698)" (Andrew and Waldron).

701–2. "The forest of Wirral was a notorious refuge for outlaws in the fourteenth century" (Andrew and Waldron).

709ff. Gawain travels into Cumberland's Inglewood Forest, according to Madden.

721. The original is *wodwos*: "(Old English *wudu wasa* 'wood man'); hairy woodland monsters of medieval imagination, they were often portrayed in medieval art and civic pageantry, and seem to have appealed to alliterative writers" (Andrew and Waldron).

740. The next morning is "Christmas Eve (cf. 755–56.). The stanza amplifies the preceding wheel" (Andrew and Waldron).

756. "I.e., Matins of Christmas Day" (Andrew and Waldron).

769. "In the thirteenth-century French romance *La Mule Sans Frein*, in which a version of the beheading game occurs (as also in the German *Diu Krône*, apparently derived from it), Gawain arrives at a castle surrounded by a circle of stakes on each of which (with one exception!) is a human head. The *pyked palays* plays no such role in the English poem but its presence may be due to reminiscence of this version in the story" (Andrew and Waldron).

774. "St. Julian, the patron saint of travelers" (Andrew and Waldron).

787–93. "The description is of the outer fortification (barbican)" (Andrew and Waldron).

790. Courses, implied rather than explicitly named in the original, would be horizontal barriers intended to repel invaders seeking to scale the castle wall.

792. I have included an implied definition of loopholes in the translation.

794ff. The technology of Renaissance perspective changed verbal as well as visual representation. Here we confront a distinctly medieval use of multiple perspective; for Gawain, who is clearly quite close to the base of the castle's towering outer walls (within earshot, in fact, 811–14), is apparently able to see a great deal of the hall within. Cf. the description of both the outside and the inside of the New Jerusalem in *Pearl* 985–1152, especially 1049–50, where the dual perspective is justified by the transparency of the city's walls.

802.   "The castle is compared to the paper cut-outs which sometimes decorated food brought to table in fourteenth-century banquets. Cf. the description of Belshazzar's feast in *Cleanness* (especially 1408)" (Andrew and Waldron).

813.   As Peter is traditionally the gatekeeper of heaven, this is "an appropriate oath for a porter" (Andrew and Waldron).

833.   "The lord's chamber is to be imagined as a small room leading off a gallery, from which he comes down to greet Gawain in the hall" (Andrew and Waldron).

844.   "The portrait echoes, in muted tones, features of the description of the Green Knight (cf., e.g., 844 and 137ff., 845 and 182, 846 and 431)" (Andrew and Waldron).

847–48.   "Cf. 1031ff. and contrast the arrogance of the Green Knight in Fitt I" (Andrew and Waldron).

871–74.   Cf. 196–202.

884.   Cf. 1648, and *Cleanness* 832.

897–98.   "They modestly refer to the meal as a 'penance' (Christmas Eve being a day of abstinence) and promise him better fare later (i.e., on Christmas Day)" (Andrew and Waldron).

919.   "In many medieval romances Gawain is the *beau idéal* of courtesy, though not of chastity; from the thirteenth century onwards, however, his character tends to be denigrated by writers whose chief aim is to idealize other knights (e.g., Lancelot or Tristan). This development accounts for the contradiction in Malory's treatment of Gawain and for Tennyson's unsympathetic attitude toward him" (Andrew and Waldron).

930.   "The poet has in mind a large castle with several chapels, like Caernarvon" (Andrew and Waldron).

934.   "Her closed pew is evidently in the chancel; cf. 942–46" (Andrew and Waldron).

943–69.   "The contrast effectively sets off the lustrous beauty of the young lady against the wrinkled decrepitude of the old (identified in 2463 as Morgan le Fay), who is here described in terms reminiscent of religious lyrics of the 'Signs of Old Age' and 'Signs of Death' types. Obliquely, therefore, the portraits suggest the homiletic theme that old age is a mirror of the frailty of the flesh" (Andrew and Waldron).

970–76.   This is apparently some of that polite behavior the court had eagerly anticipated.

995–96.   "The two lines are a periphrasis for 'On Christmas Day' " (Andrew and Waldron).

1003.   According to Stone 1959, "the formal pairing at table of Gawain and his hostess would appear significant to listeners familiar with folk-tales and romances in which kings offered their wives to guests, usually to test them or gain power over them. Behind this tradition lies the primitive hospitality of wife-sharing with a guest." But recall that Gawain was seated next to Guinevere the year before without any such suggestion.

1005–6.   Cf. *Cleanness* 114–20.

1021ff.   "*þe þryd* (St. John's Day) is 27 December; but the hunting (which begins on the morning when the guests leave) occupies the last three days of December. So 28 December—Holy Innocents' Day—is unaccounted for. Perhaps, as Gollancz [1940] suggested, it was referred to in a line between 1022 and 1023, now lost" (Andrew and Waldron).

1027ff. "The guests who are leaving early next morning take their leave before going to bed (cf. 1120, 1126–27.). The situation is repeated in 1960ff." (Andrew and Waldron).

1029. Gawain appears prepared to leave the castle on the morning with the other departing guests.

1032ff. "Cf. *Cleanness* 785–86 and Lot's words in 799–801" (Andrew and Waldron).

1055. See 691n.

1087. "The last expression has an idiomatic appearance: cf. the Old English poem *Judith* 68–69, *swa he nyste ræda nanne / on gewitlocan*, of the drunken Holofernes (who appears to have been actually unconscious, however)" (Andrew and Waldron).

1106–7. "The antithetical *chek* ['booty,' 'gain'] is outwardly expressive of the host's courtly generosity (cf. *lere* ['worse'] 1109) but has sinister overtones; in chess it is 'check(mate)' (suggestive of the battle of wits in the bedroom episodes), and in hawking 'A false stoop, when a hawk forsakes her quarry for baser game' (*OED*), (suggesting Gawain's lapse from the pursuit of the highest ideals). The word has an unequivocally negative sense at 1857 and 2195" (Andrew and Waldron).

1112. "*Beuerage* became a technical term in this sense in Middle English and was also used for 'bargain' itself (cf. also 1409, 1684)" (Andrew and Waldron).

1133ff. As Moorman 1977 reminds us, "the description of the three hunts, almost certainly the work of the *Gawain*-poet, has been analyzed from a number of points of view. Perhaps the most famous theory regarding them is that of Savage 1956 who sees in the three hunts parallels to the three temptations of Gawain."

1141. According to Stone 1959, "the fourteenth-century hunting horn has only one note; a combination of shorts and longs was used for making different calls, which were transcribed as *mote, trut, trororout, tротototout*." Three single notes, according to Andrew and Waldron, were "the signal for unleashing the hounds."

1153. "The purpose of the ring beaters (*stablye*) which encircled the hunting area was to drive the quarry toward the arrows of the huntsmen (1160). Those which were not killed outright were pulled down by hounds at the receiving stations (1168)" (Andrew and Waldron).

1154–59. "The close-season (*fermysoun*) for the male deer, harts (*herttez*) and bucks (*bukkez*), was 14 September–24 June; these the beaters allow to pass. The females, the hinds and does, could be hunted during the winter, however, and were therefore prevented from escaping and driven back (1158–59)" (Andrew and Waldron).

1179ff. The abrupt contrast between the boisterous activity of the hunt and the peaceful, sleepy scene in Gawain's bedchamber will be modulated when the points of comparison between the two situations become clearer.

1208ff.   The lady playfully—and a bit lasciviously—deploys the language of individual combat between knights and their enemies or prisoners. It seems she has listened to the late medieval romances with enough attention to appreciate the complicity between the language of combat and the language of love.

1212.   I have translated *bourdez* ("jests") as "game." Much of the complex moral tension of the poem derives from the way it represents games, jests, and even half-drunken challenges as both frivolous and deadly earnest.

1233.   The lady has blocked Gawain's avenues of escape, even as the beaters (1153) have prevented the does and hinds from fleeing the hunters.

1237–38.   "The lady's declaration is not as unequivocal as it appears to the modern reader: *my cors* is used in Middle English as a periphrasis for 'me' (cf. *His body, Cleanness* 32, *his corse, Cleanness* 683, 'him'); the line can therefore be understood as 'I am pleased to have you here,' and this is how Gawain chooses to take it (cf. 1241). The bolder suggestion is, however, apparent in the next line: 'to take your own pleasure' " (Andrew and Waldron). Nor is the expression *my cors* ever entirely periphrastic, ever entirely free from a bodily emphasis (one thinks, e.g., of the Wife of Bath's "My joly body schal a tale telle"). Indeed, part of the subtle humor here involves the suggestion that the lady, while she may have familiarized herself with a number of romances, nevertheless personally applies their sexual politics crudely and unsophisticatedly.

1239–40.   "Basing her argument on Gawain's illustrious reputation as a courtier (borne out, she says, by his behavior in her house) the lady attempts to reverse the usual roles and become *his* 'servant' (cf. 1214–16)" (Andrew and Waldron).

1263ff.   Cf. the exchange between the Dreamer and the Maiden in *Pearl,* 421–44.

1265–68.   "The passage is somewhat elliptical, perhaps reflecting Gawain's tact; he wants to dismiss his reputation (especially among women—cf. 1249ff.) as mere tittle-tattle, without implying too strongly that *she* is over-credulous" (Andrew and Waldron).

1274.   "The lady is rebutting Gawain's modest denial at 1266" (Andrew and Waldron).

1276.   Gawain's rhetorical move is admirably economical; it expresses in a single gesture both a statement of his own (polite) humility and a reminder of her marital duties.

1278.   In this kind of chivalric love talk, clearly, the upper hand is *gained* by positioning oneself, paradoxically, as the other's servant. Thus, Gawain here tries to switch the positions first dramatically reversed by the lady in 1237–40.

1292.   Here one of the *Pearl* poet's characteristic periphrases for God is, interestingly, placed in the mouth of the lady.

1293–1301.   The lady chides Gawain for failing to live up to his reputation, even as the Green Knight had chided the Arthurian court (309–15).

1327.   "The breaking of only one deer is described but the description is evidently meant to be representative. [Cf. the description of the single, but synecdochic, plant, 523ff.] The breaking (or brittling) of the deer is a romance convention which reflects the importance attached to hunting skills as aristocratic accomplishments" (Andrew and Waldron). Cf. 1605–14.

1328. *Asay* ("test") is "a ceremonious testing of the quality of the game; the word was also used of the part of the breast where the cut was made (cf. *The Parlement of the Thre Ages*, 70)" (Andrew and Waldron).

1334. That is, the knot they had made in the gullet (1331).

1347. The "numbles," or, as Stone 1959 has it, "offal," derives "from the back and loins."

1355. The *corbeles fee* ("raven's fee") is, for Stone 1959, "a piece of gristle on the end of the breast-bone [which] was always flung to the ravens and crows which gathered at the hunt—to propitiate the gods."

1377. I have translated *tayles* (literally "tails") as "booty." The word "appears to contain a deliberate pun ('tails' and 'tallies'); the tails were left on the carcasses and would serve as tallies" (Andrew and Waldron).

1382. "I.e., 'for many a year.' For a parallel use of the figure five as a round number, cf. *Pearl* 449–52n" (Andrew and Waldron).

1396–97. "Gawain may be conscious that the kisses were Bertilak's by right of a husband as well as of the game" (Andrew and Waldron).

1419. "An indication that they are to hunt the boar, which lived among the thorns and thick bushes" (Andrew and Waldron).

1436. The bloodhounds are "larger hounds (resembling the modern blood-hound) used, especially in boar-hunting, to attack the game at close quarters" (Andrew and Waldron).

1440. I have translated *sounder* as "boar herd." "The technical term for a herd of wild pig" (Andrew and Waldron).

1443. Andrew and Waldron are probably correct in reading the "three" of the original as implying "three men."

1456–57. "The bristles of the brow," as Stone 1959 tells us, "grow more thickly when the boar has its winter coat. When at bay, with its flanks and rear protected, the boar could be fatally hit only with a shot between the eyes."

1474–75. The original is "no doubt deliberately ambiguous: 'Very early she visited him (or 'was pestering him') in order to bring about a change in his attitude' " (Andrew and Waldron).

1478–79. I have reversed the order of these lines.

1481ff. If on the first morning the lady sounded Gawain out (even as the beaters had done to the male deer), here her strategy is more aggressive; indeed, she seems to have him backed into a corner (where the hounds and hunters have the boar) from which he tries to extricate himself. Cf. 2270ff., where the Green Knight also accuses Gawain of failing to live up to his reputation.

1483. The original may be more literally translated: "and cannot understand the ways of *compaynye* ('polite society' or 'lovemaking')." "*Compaynye* already had some of the amorous connotation of the modern 'keep company,' as it has also in Chaucer's lines on the Wife of Bath: "Housbondes at chirche dore she hadde fyve, / Withouten oother compaignye in youthe (*Canterbury Tales* I:460–61.)" (Andrew and Waldron).

1499. "Gawain skillfully counters her argument on her own terms and once more politely declares his unwillingness to take the initiative" (Andrew and Waldron).

1508ff. "The syntax of the speech effectively suggests the informality of conversation (cf. 2446–58); after a long parenthesis (1512–19) giving the lady's views on the importance of love in the code of chivalry, the construction begun at 1509 is loosely resumed" (Andrew and Waldron).

1513. *Lettrure of armes* is " 'the (very) doctrine of knighthood'; as 1515–19 show, the rules of love are conceived as a set of guiding principles for active knighthood" (Andrew and Waldron).

1515–19. The joke here is that the lady, while clearly unfamiliar with the kind of romance *Sir Gawain and the Green Knight* represents, has nevertheless indulged her taste for more ordinary romances. The overall effect is rather like that in nineteenth-century novels when novel reading is condemned.

1548. Again and again, the upper hand paradoxically seems to lie in giving the "opponent" the upper hand by becoming his or her "servant."

1550. "Sin" is perhaps too strong; "wrong" or "grief" or even "harm" might suffice. Andrew and Waldron translate " 'in order to bring him to grief (wrong), whatever else she intended.' The poet appears to wish to exonerate the lady. Alternatively *woʒe* can be interpreted as a verb 'woo' and the second half-line would then imply 'though she had no genuine desire for his advances.' However, the closest syntactic parallel (831) leads one to expect a noun rather than a verb here; also the whole tone of the comment (cf. *fondet* 'tempted' 1549) favors the sense 'wrong, sin' (or perhaps 'harm,' in view of the possible consequences)" (Andrew and Waldron).

1571ff. "When at bay, the boar sharpens his lower tusks against his upper ones and scrapes the ground with his feet" (Andrew and Waldron).

1605–14. As in 1325–61, the cleaning and preparing of the prey is lovingly described.

1644. "Giles was a saint of the seventh century who lived as a hermit in a forest near Nîmes with a hind for companion. This association makes him perhaps an appropriate saint for the hunting day" (Andrew and Waldron). According to Stone 1959, there is a tradition "that during a hunt he was accidentally hit in the knee by an arrow shot by Childeric, a seventh-century king of France."

1647. "The knight means that Gawain has doubled his takings in one day" (Andrew and Waldron).

1648. Cf. 884; *Cleanness* 832.

1680. "From the game of dice: 'Third time lucky' " (Andrew and Waldron).

1699. "Although descriptions of the hunting of deer and boar are common in medieval romance, descriptions of fox-hunting are rare. It was certainly a less noble sport, and the host's attitude to his quarry (1944) accords with the general view of the fox as being little better than vermin" (Stone 1959).

1728. Reynard was a "popular medieval name for the fox" (Andrew and Waldron).

1729. Andrew and Waldron translate more literally: " 'led them in a string'; *lagmon* is a rare word, perhaps related to the noun *lag* 'last person in a race, etc.' " (Andrew and Waldron).

1738–39. "If Gollancz's suggestion [1940] is correct, that the MS *hwez* is a form of Old English *hufe* (Middle English *howve*) 'head-covering, coif,' the implication here is that it would have been a more seemly head-dress for a married woman. Cf. the Wife of Bath's paraphrase of I Tim. 2:9: ' "In habit maad with chastitee and shame / Ye wommen shul apparaille yow," quod he, / "And noght in tressed heer and gay peree (*precious stones*) / As perles, ne with gold, ne clothes riche." ' " (Andrew and Waldron). See *Pearl* 197–228 and note.

1768. Like Gawain, we readers had expected the perils to lie not in the bedchamber but in the Green Chapel. Here the poet seeks to trouble such complacency.

1776. "In Middle English the negative connotation of a prohibition is regularly repeated in the noun clause and (but for the indicative *schal*) Gawain's thought might be interpreted 'God forbid that that should happen,' and is usually so punctuated. The present punctuation (which is justified by *schal*, instead of *schulde*) makes the expression of his determination stronger" (Andrew and Waldron).

1777. Gawain's elusive maneuvers are implicitly equated with the fox's.

1788. "St. John the Apostle, by tradition supremely dedicated to celibacy" (Andrew and Waldron).

1791. In the original, Gawain is more forceful: "Nor none will I have at present."

1811. Cf. 562–66; *Patience* 5off.

1814. The original for "she"—*lufsum vnder lyne* ("lovely [one] under linen")—is an interesting example of the poet's use of periphrasis.

1815–16. Here the theme of the exchange of gifts is deeply complicated.

1825. Another instance of indirect speech. Cf. *Cleanness* 63n.

1835. "As in 1847–48, the lady is being modest—or pretending to be" (Andrew and Waldron).

1836ff. Interestingly, Gawain implies here that his arrangement with the Green Knight (one form of exchange) precludes his making other comparable arrangements; but, of course, he has already repeatedly entered into such an agreement with the host.

1853. The original word *tohewe* ("cut down," "cut to pieces") is "calculated to make Gawain think of his own plight, just as *slyȝt* ('skill, stratagem') in 1854 seems designed to suggest that the girdle may be a match for the Green Knight's magical powers (cf. 1858)" (Andrew and Waldron).

1864–65. According to Stone 1959, "although Gawain swears to conceal the gift of the girdle, it seems that when he dressed for his ordeal (2030–2036) it is visible, and it is a fair inference from line 2358 that the Green Knight can see it."

1876–84. "Gawain's confession has been much discussed by critics in the light of the fact that he evidently does not confess his concealment of the *luf-lace* and his incipient violation of the exchange agreement with the host. Probably the most satisfactory solution is that it is only in retrospect, when he sees its full significance, that the concealment becomes a grave moral fault for him. At the time, to violate the rules of a parlor game (note the element of jest in the descriptions in 1112–13, 1392–99, 1404, 1409, 1623, 1644–47, 1681–85 and 1932ff.) would hardly have seemed a sin at all" (Andrew and Waldron).

1881. "Contemporary penitential manuals classify the branches of sin minutely" (Andrew and Waldron).

1883–84. Cf. 2391–94.

1885–92. As Moorman 1977 notes, "the poet insists that both the confession (1880) and absolution (1883–84) bestowed by the priest were complete, and certainly Gawain's joy following his absolution is in marked contrast with his previous fearfulness."

1927. Andrew and Waldron gloss the original *for luf* " 'on account of friendship'; the phrase is little more than a tag, however, a conventional accompaniment of *lady* (as perhaps in 1733)."

1934. "On the two previous evenings the host has been first" (Andrew and Waldron). Perhaps Gawain is feeling nervous about the concealed gift.

1938–41. "Some of the wit of these lines stems from the ambiguity of *chepe* 'trade, bargain, market, price' " (Andrew and Waldron).

1944. Cf. *Patience* 460.

1975–76. My translation differs from Andrew and Waldron's sense that the giver of thanks here is the host. At any rate, the language of the original is ambiguous.

1987. Cf. 672ff.

1991–93. As Andrew and Waldron point out, the original language suggests that he slept badly if he slept at all.

1994. Cf. 1893.

1994ff. This marks yet another address by the poet to the reader.

1995. My translation takes liberties with the original, which might be glossed more literally: "He has near (him just) what he sought."

2000. "See 504n, and cf. *Cleanness* 948" (Andrew and Waldron).

2003. The original for "beast"—*wylde*—is glossed perhaps more strictly by Andrew and Waldron as 'the wild animals.'

2011–44. This donning of Gawain's armor structurally matches the earlier moment, 567–622.

2027–28. "Jewels were thought to have power against various evils and diseases" (Andrew and Waldron).

2036. The red cloth is "his surcoat, which forms a red background to the gold pentangle. The poet's emphatic (and ironic) reference to the juxtaposition of pentangle and girdle is suggestive, for in failing to hand over the latter to the host he has fallen short of the high virtues symbolized by the former" (Andrew and Waldron).

2043–46. "None of the household, except his servant, is present on this occasion, of course; he has, in fact, already said goodbye and thanked them individually the night before (1979–90). The quatrain is again an anticipatory summary of the following stanza (cf. 341–42.)" (Andrew and Waldron).

2057. "Addressed (*in petto*) to the whole household (cf. 2043–46n)" (Andrew and Waldron). Cf. also *Pearl* 1176.

2061. This is "the guide allotted to him, who acted as his squire. He hands over Gawain's helmet and lance at 2143" (Andrew and Waldron).

2073. I have changed indirect to direct speech here.

2081. Andrew and Waldron gloss *myst-hakel* as " 'cap-cloud' (lit. 'cape of mist'—a poetic compound of a type very common in Old English but less so in Middle English alliterative poetry)" (Andrew and Waldron).

2102. This is "either *Hector* (of Troy) or less probably a reference to the Arthurian knight Hector de la Mare" (Andrew and Waldron).

2123. A more literal translation of the original would be " 'As may God and the holy object help me'—a form of oath which originated in the practice of swearing on a sacred relic" (Andrew and Waldron).

2134. I've translated *Wyrde* as "providence," a crucial notion, e.g., in Old English literature. "Cf. 2138 and *Patience* 247n" (Andrew and Waldron).

2137. The original has the Green Knight " 'armed with a club.' Gawain echoes the guide's description of the guardian of the chapel as a wild man of the woods, though there is no apparent reason for him to conceal the fact that he knows the Green Knight; if it is not a slip on the poet's part, we may perhaps interpret it as wishful thinking: Gawain would no doubt prefer an encounter with ordinary *wodwos* (cf. 721) to another meeting with the Green Knight" (Andrew and Waldron).

2180ff. Stone 1959 notes that "as the poet described it, the Green Chapel is exactly like an entrance to the Celtic Other World. But Gawain as a Christian sees it as an entrance to Hell."

2187–88. "In monastic houses, matins, the first of the canonical hours, were sung before daybreak; however, midnight is probably mentioned here as an appropriate hour for the Devil's matins" (Andrew and Waldron).

2293. Here we see explicitly at work one of Gawain's pentangle qualities. For the *fyue wyttez* (640) that we learned of in the description of the pentangle here tell Gawain that he is encountering the *Fende*.

2201. Andrew and Waldron identify the *Quat!* of the original, like the Old English *Hwæt!*, as "an exclamation of surprise or a call for attention; here it may also be intended to echo the sound itself (cf. 1163—the sound of the arrow?)." Cf. also *Cleanness* 1545.

2208–11. "Cf. the Vernon poem *Deo Gracias* I, 45–8: 'Though I weore out of bonchef brought, / What help weore to me to seye "Allas!" / In the nome of God, whatever be wrought, / I schal seie, *"Deo Gracias"* ' " (Andrew and Waldron).

2221. "The Green Knight (who is standing on a hill on the opposite side of the stream from Gawain) appears to descend by some sort of hidden passage. From the allusive nature of the description it would appear that the poet had an actual site in mind. This has been variously identified, but most convincingly by Day [and Serjeantson] (in the introduction to Gollancz [1940], p. xx) as Wetton Mill, Staffs." (Andrew and Waldron).

2225–26. "In describing the earlier ax, the poet mentions a *lace* ('cord') which is wrapped about its handle (217–20); if a similar cord is alluded to here, however, it is difficult to see how it could play any part in an observer's assessment of the size of the blade. The best solution is that *bi þat lace þat lemed ful briȝt* is an oath on the green girdle (cf. the description at 2038), spoken *in petto* by Gawain; at the moment when he sees the ax, with its huge blade, it is understandable that his thoughts should fly to his magic charm" (Andrew and Waldron).

2253–54. My rendering strays from the original, which might be more literally translated: "And give you no resistance (while) you do what you like / Anywhere." "Gawain implies that the remoteness of the valley is immaterial, provided that the Green Knight intends to stick to the single blow of the agreement" (Andrew and Waldron).

2270ff. Cf. 1481ff.

2285. "The fact that [the original] *out of honde* is the earliest recorded instance of this phrase (*OED* and *MED*) reinforces the impression that the language of the speeches is often extremely up to date and colloquial" (Andrew and Waldron).

2297–98. "Although Gawain does not realize it at this point, the outcome of the beheading game is made dependent on his conduct during his last three days in the castle. The Green Knight is implying, 'Let us see if your knighthood enabled you to resist the temptations of the third day' " (Andrew and Waldron).

2315. Cf. 429.

2316. "Gawain's instinctive reaction is an unprepared standing-jump" (Andrew and Waldron). Cf. 2231–32.

2317–18. "Gawain is carrying his shield slung on his shoulder in readiness (cf. 2061, and contrast 621); the jerk is evidently a practiced movement to make it slide down the left arm while he draws his sword with the other hand" (Andrew and Waldron).

2320–21. Cf. 2393–94.

2322ff. "Gawain is saying that he will no longer consider himself bound by the rules of the game, but will fight" (Andrew and Waldron).

2330. "W. A. Davenport (*English Language Notes*, 11 [1973], 87–88.) points out that *hoo* 'stop' occurs elsewhere in the context of cnivalrous encounters; he suggests that, with *hende*, its overtones would remind the Green Knight of gentlemanly codes of conduct" (Andrew and Waldron).

2338. "Cf. *be not so gryndel* with *Patience* 524" (Andrew and Waldron).

2346. Cf. *Pearl* 565–66.

2347. In the phrase "the first night," the "host appears to conflate the evening *before* the first hunt, when the agreement was first made (*fest*), with the evening *of* the hunt, when it was carried out; the *morne* of 2350 is evidently the day of the second hunt" (Andrew and Waldron).

2367. "*Wylyde werke*: probably 'intricate (skilled) workmanship' (i.e., of the girdle); cf. 2430–32 and (for the author's statement of Gawain's motives) 2037–40" (Andrew and Waldron).

2387. "For both men the scene takes on the character of a chivalric 'confession'; cf. 2390ff., and notes to 1876–84 and 2445" (Andrew and Waldron).

2391–94. Cf. 1883–84, and 2320–21.

2396–99. "Note that it is Gawain (2433ff.) who stresses the humbling effect of the girdle" (Andrew and Waldron).

2400ff. "The Green Knight evidently has in mind a social scene, like that of 2513–21" (Andrew and Waldron).

2411ff. Gawain's bitter antifeminist diatribe, conventional as it is in the fourteenth century, nevertheless seems gratuitous and therefore diversionary here; he appeals to the antifeminist lore mechanically and automatically, as though his own faults might thereby be excused. Contemporary audiences were doubtless intended to discern this irony. Nevertheless, we read the poem anachronistically, or rather, we misread it altogether if we interpret, e.g., 2425–28, as the moment of Gawain's most grievous fault.

2445. "Since the Green Knight is here revealing his everyday name, *Haut-*

desert must be the name of his castle rather than another designation of the Green Chapel. Nevertheless, the introduction of the title ('of the high hermitage' [of great merit?]) at this point may remind us that the Green Knight performs some of the confessional functions of the hermits of the spiritualized French Arthurian *Quest del saint Graal*" (Andrew and Waldron).

2446. Morgan le Fay, wife of King Uryens, is the half-sister and enemy of Arthur. Moorman 1977 provides a note summarizing the discussions of Morgan's role in the poem.

2446ff. "The loose conversational structure of this speech is comparable to that of 1508ff. Sir Bertilak picks up on the thread in 2456, after the digression on the fame and history of Morgan" (Andrew and Waldron).

2454–55. Andrew and Waldron translate this more literally: " 'there is no one so exalted in pride (*hawtesse*) whom she cannot humble completely.' "

2465–66. The Duchess of Tintagel was Igerne. "The pointed contrast between Arthur's shameful origins (he was conceived out of wedlock) and present renown recalls one of the themes of the opening stanza of the poem (there in connection with Aeneas and Felix Brutus)" (Andrew and Waldron).

2481ff. Gawain's journey back is to be compared with his journey from Camelot to Bertilak's castle, 691–762.

2487. The word *knot* recalls the pentangle (cf. 662). By now the girdle has supplemented the pentangle in representing Gawain's character.

2506–9. "Gawain adopts the girdle as the ribbon of an 'order' of shame (contrast 2519–20). The very fact that he identifies the belt and the scar as twin tokens of his fault makes the passage difficult to construe" (Andrew and Waldron).

2515. Andrew and Waldron have adopted Burrow's emendation of *ladis* to *ledes* ("men") "on the grounds that the context is entirely masculine and that ladies would not belong to such a military brotherhood." But as such contexts in the poem have never been exclusively masculine, and as the MS clearly has *ladis* ("ladies"), I have restored the women to the scene.

2521. Cf. 689n.

2523. The original is *Brutus bokez*: " 'chronicles of Britain,' Brutus being the legendary founder; cf. 13, 2524" (Andrew and Waldron).

2525. Cf. 1.

HONY SOIT QUI MAL PENCE. "The Garter motto appears to have been added to the poem in order to associate it with that order (instituted by Edward III about 1348). Its color, however, is blue and it is doubtful whether the poet intended any such direct connection" (Andrew and Waldron).

SAINT ERKENWALD

1. Here and at line 177—and nowhere else in the manuscript—the first letter of the line is a bold, rubricated, two-line capital. Scribally at least, the poem is thus divided into two halves of 176 lines each. Whether or not the poem is structurally so divided remains a matter of conjecture.

1–3. Erkenwald became bishop of London ca. A.D. 675.

5–14. That is, the "temple of old" and, by extension, London itself, had been converted from heathen to Christian dominion only to relapse into pagan hands until the coming of Augustine of Canterbury (not Hippo), when it was finally restored as a great Christian site. We confront, then, another instance of the *Pearl* poet's fascination with the cycles of upheaval, with the fluctuations to which events on earth are inclined. One thinks, for example, of the passage in *Gawain* in which we learn that in Britain "As well as wonders, woe / Has wavered year to year. / And there, tossed to and fro, / Have been both bane and cheer" (16–19).

7–11. Around 449, Hengist marshaled the Saxons into Britain, ostensibly to aid the British king Vortigern in defending the realm against northern invaders. But, in Morse's words, once "Hengist's men were well established, they turned on Vortigern and invited other Saxon tribes to join them. The Britons were driven back into, among other places, Wales." According to the *Pearl* poet, Hengist, having successfully routed the Britons into Wales (9), let the realm return to pagan ways.

12–13. Bede (*Historia Ecclesiastica* I:25) is not alone in recounting the landing of Augustine of Canterbury in 597 on the Kentish coast for the purpose, ordained by Pope Gregory I, of converting Britain. In a letter dated 29 July 598, Gregory tells Eulogius of Alexandria that Augustine was received by King Ethelbert of Kent and on Christmas Day, 597, allowed to baptize "more than 10,000 Englishmen."

19. Gollancz 1932 reminds us, for instance, of John Flete's fifteenth-century *History of Westminster Abbey*, which refers to the conversion of a temple of Apollo into a church called Saint Peter's.

21. Gollancz 1932—identifying "what was set to the Sun" with the temple of Minerva at Bath in Wales, where the church of "St. Mary Stall" was said to have been established—implies that the poet here expands his description of the conversion of Britain beyond the temples in London. Peterson 1977, however, disagrees, arguing that the poet may simply "have had in mind the progenitive power of both the sun and the mother of God."

22. Here is yet another instance of the indeterminacy of the links between the heathen and Christian figures in this sequence. Gollancz 1932 discovered nothing other than alliterative felicity to join the names of Jupiter and Juno to those of Jesus and James. Savage 1926, on the other hand, finds a significant "mention of a temple dedicated to Jupiter in the city of London" in the 1807 edition of Holinshed's *Chronicle*. And Peterson 1977 suggests that "Juno as the goddess of childbirth is obviously parallel to 'oure Lady' [from line 21] and Jupiter as the supreme deity would be parallel to Jesus, as one of the persons of the one true god of Christianity."

25. According to legend, Brutus fled Troy after its destruction by the Greeks and founded Britain in general and "New Troy" (London) in particular. As in the opening of *Sir Gawain and the Green Knight*, where this story is mentioned, here the *Pearl* poet's paradoxical sense of history as change within continuity is emphasized.

28. For Savage 1926, the devil here is the Saxon god Woden. But such specificity is surely unnecessary.

31. *Triapolitanes*, which I've translated as "the three pagan sees," probably refers to a tripartite division of secular and religious power among London, York, and Caerusk or, perhaps, Canterbury, which was transferred from pagan to Christian rule during the conversion. According to Peterson 1977, "it is clear in any event that the poet is referring to a tripartite ecclesiastical division, and the poet's sense seems to be that this pagan division was adapted to the Christian church's administration." Again, therefore, we find the *Pearl* poet stressing continuity within radical change.

32–33. The line break here, and at 320–21, is editorially imposed. Peterson 1977 reminds us that "there seems to be a thematic break after the first 32 lines which, as Gollancz 1932 pointed out, appear to function as a historical prologue. It might also be said that the final 32 lines of the poem form an epilogue. With line 321 the dialogue between Erkenwald and the judge is ended, the bishop ceases to participate in the action, and the essential baptism has taken place, releasing the judge's soul from limbo, whence it immediately ascends to heaven. The first 32 lines are concerned with time past, before the main action of the poem, the last 32 with a spiritual state that transcends time as it is known by the participants in that action, who have wondered at the failure of what they know as time to have its effects on the judge's body. These two possible subdivisions in the poem have been set off from the rest of the text as given here by a slightly wider than usual spacing between lines 32 and 33, and 320 and 321. No such distinctions occur in the manuscript, and it must be emphasized that the division here is based on an editorial judgment of the poem's thematic structure."

34. Erkenwald is thus implicitly compared to the judge.

38. By *New Werke* the poet means the section of Saint Paul's that was renovated in the mid-thirteenth century. There, as Savage 1926 reminds us, "at the time at which the poet wrote, the tomb of St. Erkenwald was situated." Gollancz 1932, therefore, suggests that "the poet is obviously transferring to the time of Erkenwald" much more recent renovations.

46. This marks the first of four narrative events (the discovery of the tomb, the reanimation of the heathen judge [190–92], his baptism [314–24], and his salvation [324ff.]) that, for many critics, comprise the main plot of the poem.

51–56. These words might be compared to those written on the wall during Belshazzar's feast in *Cleanness* (1551ff.).

52. *Roynyshe*, as Savage 1926 states, has "puzzled all commentators." Savage rightly asserts, however, that "the meaning 'mysterious' fits exactly into the impression that the poet was endeavoring to convey, of a tomb whose origin and content are obscured, rather than revealed, by the hieroglyphics carved on its border." This is reminiscent of the depiction of Belshazzar's feast in *Cleanness* where the hand of God scratches on the wall the "strange, runic (*runisch*) words (1545)."

66. The sexton would have been the cathedral's caretaker and custodian. See Peterson 1977.

75–92. Morse points out that "the poet has reversed the usual order, from head to toe, of the topos of description of a person."

81. As Savage 1926 reminds us, "the presence of miniver upon the cape distinguished the robe or cloak of the justice from that of the sergeant-at-law."

83. The coif is a tight, hoodlike covering traditionally worn by justices of the law.

85ff. For the poet's concern with clothing (whether immaculate or filthy) see, for example, *Patience* 341–42 (and note), and *Cleanness* 49–192.

91–92. Sleep, metaphorical or otherwise, plays a significant role in each of the five poems of the *Pearl* poet. In *Patience*, the nap Jonah takes during the storm at sea is a sign of his moral lassitude: "On a bench in the boat's bulging bottom he lies. / There he huddles and hides; during heaven's great storm / He has slipped into sleep, and he slobbers and snores! (184–86)." In *Gawain*, we are given poignant descriptions of the knight's troubled sleep. The final scene of *Cleanness* depicts an assault on a sleeping city. And *Pearl*, of course, is a dream vision, a kind of record of sleep itself.

107. As Peterson 1977 points out, London boasted no primate in the sixth (see his notes for 31, 33, and 107), seventh, or fourteenth century. The term is used loosely here for the Bishop of London.

108. As editors have suggested from the beginning, this is doubtless the abbey at Barking in Essex, which Erkenwald established and whose abbess was Ethelburga, his sister. The primary source is Bede's *Historia Ecclesiastica* 4:6: "Hic sane priusquam episcopus factus esset duo praeclara monasteria, unum sibi, alterum sorori suae Ethelbergae, construxerat, quod utrumque regularibus disciplinis optime instituerat." ("Before becoming bishop, [Erkenwald] had founded two monasteries under the best and most regular discipline, one for himself, and the other for his sister, Ethelburga.") Note also the treatment of the saint as a medieval knight (*ser Erkenwolde*). Cf. *Cleanness* 900.

116. Erkenwald is thus implicitly contrasted with the crowds of the curious who come flocking to the tomb, seeking, like the Dreamer in *Pearl*, an earthly experience of the ineffable.

121. Savage 1926 argues that the "revelation by [a vision] for which St. Erkenwald prayed, must have been imparted in [ecstasy], a state of the [spiritual vision] in which the inabilities and imperfections natural to the mind are overcome by divine aid"; and that what Erkenwald recited "almost (but not quite) all night" were the canonical prayers. Morse, however, suggests that what the bishop experiences "corresponds with *visio*, a true prophetic dream, in medieval dream theory." Cf. *Pearl* 790n.

122–23. Here the *debonerte* of the original is perhaps Erkenwald's (in which case it means "humility") rather than God's (in which case it means "goodness" or "graciousness"). In the former instance, the lines would translate, " 'Although I am unworthy,' he said as he wept / In his pious humility, 'Yet vouchsafe it, my Lord!' " I have followed Gollancz 1932, however, in assuming that the *debonerte* is God's and that the quotation reopens at the beginning of the line. Cf. *Pearl* 798.

128–30. This passage might be compared with *Gawain* 566–67.

129. The High Mass here, as Peterson 1977 argues, "may be the mass for Whitsun Day (Pentecost)." As he suggests in his introduction, "if the tomb was discovered on the Saturday within the Ascension Octave, that would be the

third day after the Harrowing of Hell, a not insignificant lapse of time ('And on the third day He rose again . . .'). Seven days of searching the records, beginning on this Sunday, would end on the Vigil of Pentecost, the night in which (perhaps) Erkenwald closed himself away from the world and prayed for help from the Holy Ghost (122–27). The bishop would then be saying the mass of *Spiritus Domini* on Pentecost itself."

131.   The Sarum Missal provides three Masses whose offices begin with the invocation "Spiritus Domini." Peterson 1977 isolates the third, meant to be performed on Pentecost, as the pertinent Mass in this context. See his introduction, 45–50.

140.   The cloister here is merely the enclosed space in which the tomb is marked off. In Dugdale's seventeenth-century *History of St. Paul's*, as Savage 1926 tells us, a representation of the site is provided, "which shows an iron grating surrounding it." It is this grating, perhaps, that is unlocked. And the *clustrede keies* that unlock the grating are, for McAlindon, symbolic of the keys of the kingdom of heaven that Christ gave to Peter (Matthew 16:19), which denote the power that Christ passed on to his ministers "to remove 'the obstacle of sin' and to unlock the doors of Hell and of Heaven (489)" through baptism and penance.

141.   As Savage 1926 writes, "the moment was a tense one. The calm and determined Christian priest was going to deal with unknown forces of the spiritual world, and the populace awaited the outcome with deep anxiety."

143.   The mace-bearers, or *macers*, were legal functionaries.

144.   I have translated *dene* ("dean") as "canon."

146–58.   The dean's, or canon's, attitude toward the miraculous, which can be taken to reflect that of the populace in general, is comparable to the attitude the Dreamer reveals in *Pearl*. For the dean here betrays his allegiance to the earth and to culture for explanations of the extraordinary. As Peterson 1977 puts it, "the dean appears to be suggesting that the miracle is that human memory should fail, rather than that the body should have 'layne so longe' without appearing to have done so. If so, the dean would be displaying the unwarranted pride in the human mental faculties which the bishop seeks to correct in 163ff."

155.   At least a week, then, has passed since the exhumation.

160–66.   Cf. *Cleanness* 663.

167–68.   Gollancz 1932 translates these lines: " 'When the creature's craft swerves entirely from counsel, then it behooves the creature to accept the strengthening of the Creator.' " But Savage 1926 translates them: " 'Where the creature's power swerves away from wisdom, the Creator's strengthening must needs take the cure.' " And Peterson 1977 translates: " 'whereas creatures' intelligence swerves away from wisdom, the spiritual comfort and wellbeing of the creature behoves thee [the dean] take heed [of what I have to say].' " The precise meaning remains elusive.

177.   The first letter of the line is rubricated in a two-line capital, "the only manuscript evidence," as Peterson 1977 says, "of structural division in the poem." See 1n.

192.   The translation is an admittedly inadequate compromise in the face of

a debate among scholars over the finer points of the poem's soteriology. Peterson 1977 emends *lant* ["loaned, granted"] *goste lyfe* to *Goste lant lyfe*, thus offering a reading that reinforces his (quite persuasive) argument that the "Holy Spirit, when it 'lends life' to the judge, makes available to him the knowledge of Christianity, and through the baptism promised in Acts 1:5, baptism 'in þe Fader nome and His fre Childes, / And of þe Holy Goste' (ll. 318–19), lends him eternal life, the redemption of man promised fifty days earlier by the resurrection of Christ." William Quinn, however, has argued (equally persuasively) that *goste* does not refer specifically and exclusively to the Holy Ghost and that the "apparently deliberate mysteriousness of the 'ghost' in question should be maintained" (180). For Quinn, *goste* remains something inexplicable, a soul on loan, as it were, and as such an instance of God's power to alter his design in the name of mercy. My translation, accordingly, seeks to suggest both the Holy Ghost and at the same time a force, as Quinn has it, that is "(deliberately) obfuscated (190)" in order to underscore the limitlessness and malleability of God's mercy.

194.   My translation has lost some of the poet's characteristic concreteness. The original might be rendered more literally: "I must submit to your command for [the sake of] both of my eyes."

198.   The translation is hyperbolic. In the original, the judge calls himself simply "one of the unhappiest men that ever went on the earth."

201.   *Mayster mon* ("master of men") may be translated alternatively as "leader," "chief executive," or "officer."

205–16.   The judge's chronology presents a conundrum, labyrinthine and perhaps unsolvable. Most scholars and editors—adopting Schumacher's suggestion and working on the assumption that the poet sets Erkenwald's life correctly in the seventh rather than the sixth century—have emended line 208 to yield 782 (rather than 482) years. In this reading, the judge lived 782 years after Brutus founded London in 1136 B.C. (according to the Septuagint) or in 1116 B.C. (according to the Hebrew texts). Therefore, the judge's date is either 354 or 334 B.C. But we have no evidence to suggest that our knowledge that Erkenwald flourished in the seventh century was shared by the *Pearl* poet. On the contrary, by assuming that the poet has placed his protagonist in the *sixth* century, we eliminate a number of chronological and textual problems. In this way we can accept, for instance, Peterson's 1977 transcription of D. C. Fowler's rendition of lines 207–10: "Paraphrase: 'After Brutus built London (time unspecified), / [I lived] 482 years / before the birth of Christ, or in other words / 1054 years [ago]!' (assuming as date of exhumation AD 572)." According to Peterson, Fowler continues, "the poet's dates for Belinus and Brennius (482 BC) and for Erkenwald (AD 572) are about a century too early . . . but otherwise the statement seems straightforward and 'accurate.'" See Peterson 1977.

211.   I have here followed the recommendation of Peterson 1977 that "it seems safest to regard the judge as having two posts," one on the eyre court and one on the oyer court. This would account for the wide range of cases over which he seems to have presided. The eyre was essentially a circuit court that functioned in the name of the king and that traveled the countryside every seven years or so to hear whatever cases presented themselves in which one

group or individual sought arbitration for a grievance against another. The eyre was thus essentially concerned with what we today call "private" law; cases were brought before the eyre court, and its decisions involved compensations from one party to another. The oyer court, by contrast, concerned what we have come to call "public" law; it presided over criminal cases, high crimes, for instance, and treasons against the crown. The oyer court often raised its own charges, and the penalties it meted out tended to be physical punishments— including death—rather than compensations. Again, the sense conveyed by the judge seems to indicate that he oversaw both forms of legal action. However, entirely different possibilities also exist. Morse, for instance, suggests that the judge is merely calling himself an *heir*, or "child of wrath."

213–15.   Book 3 of Geoffrey of Monmouth's *Historia Regum Britanniae* is best consulted for the story of the enmity between Belinus and Brennius.

227.   The judge calls himself *deputate and domesmon*, that is, "deputy and principal judge."

240–41.   The sense of the original is richer than the translation conveys. It might be literally rendered: " 'Not because of the threats of any man, nor from [fear of] harm, nor out of unjustified pity / Did I [ever] stray from the high path to deviate from right.' "

242.   The "faith" the judge felt in his heart is, of course, not yet the faith in Christ. For Peterson 1977, "it is uncertain whether the line means that the judge's faith 'conformed,' i.e., regulated, the judge's heart, or means simply that heart and faith were compatible." At any rate, what is underscored is the *Pearl* poet's conviction about the *natural* human ability—independent of revealed law or an incarnate spirit—to sense the good.

246.   Troy, here, is "New Troy," that is, London. See 25n.

248.   In the original, the judge tells Erkenwald that his contemporaries buried him in gold "to bounty my body," which, according to Savage 1926, means to reward it.

255.   This line encapsulates in miniature the theological problem that is posed by the poem as a whole and that critics over the last century have tended to place at the center of their discussions. The question, bluntly, concerns whether salvation is possible for the unbaptized, non-Christian soul, however virtuous or righteous. For readings of *Saint Erkenwald* as an orthodox insistence on the soteriological cruciality of the sacraments in general and baptism in particular, see, for instance, Savage 1926, lxvii-lxxv; Faigley; and, above all, R. W. Chambers. For readings of the poem as an account of the inscrutability and flexibility of God's power, see, for example, both McAlindon and Reichardt 1971. And for readings of the poem as a Pelagian document that stresses the soteriological importance of good deeds, see especially McNamara, 78–82; Morse, 8, 47; and Stone 1971, 23–25.

257.   Here Erkenwald is referred to as *bisshop*, but I have taken advantage of the opportunity to call him "Sir Erkenwald," as he is called in lines 108 and 118 of the original, where the translation fails to provide this form.

277–78.   One is reminded of *Pearl* 674–83 and of Psalm 23 of the Vulgate (Authorized Version 24):3–4: "Quis ascendet in montem Domini? Aut quis stabit in loco sancto eius? Innocens manibus et mundo corde." ("Who will ascend the mountain of God? Or who will stand in His holy place? He whose hands were harmless and whose heart was pure.") However, although the poet mentions the Psalms, the line seems to allude more to the Beatitudes in general (Matthew 5:1–10) and to Matthew 5:8 in particular: "Beati mundo corde: quoniam ipsi Deum videbunt." ("Blessed are the pure hearted; for they shall see God.")

281–82.   The translation unfortunately fails to convey much of the creatural, almost macabre, aspect of the reanimated corpse here. It might be translated more literally: "Then he who lay there moaned, and his head wagged / And gave [out] a great groan and said to God . . ."

291–94.   This refers, of course, to the harrowing of hell, in which Christ, between the Crucifixion and the Resurrection, broke open hell and raised the Old Testament worthies from the *limbus patrum*. The tradition, officially accepted at the Fourth Lateran Council (1215), was based on a part of the apocryphal Gospel of Nicodemus. But these lines also suggest a second limbo for the unbaptized, in which the judge is left behind. See Dante's *Divine Comedy, Inferno*, Canto 4.

295–99.   Cf. *Pearl* 637–48 and *Cleanness* 237–48.

297.   The "you" here (and in 298) refers not only to Erkenwald but also to all the present London witnesses and, by extension, to all Christians.

315–23.   Savage 1926, following the guidelines of Aquinas (*Summa Theologica*, pars. 3, quaest. 66, arts. 1, 4, 5, 7), is satisfied that here, "the conditions required for the sacrament of baptism are all fulfilled in this novel case." But a great deal of debate has centered on the problematic nature of this baptism.

319.   Though the translation refers merely to the Trinity, the original ritualistically names all three Persons. See 315–23n.

320–21.   See 32–33n.

332–40.   The body remains momentarily intact in order to tell the story of its soul's ascendancy to the feast of heaven. The importance of the feast and the literalness with which it is described are interesting in light of the place of food and feasts in the entire oeuvre of the *Pearl* poet. Consider, for instance, the glorious feasts in *Gawain*; Jonah's rejection of food in *Patience*; and, in *Cleanness*, the parable of the wedding feast, 35–164, the meal Abraham supplies for God, and Belshazzar's feast.

336ff.   Heaven is presented as a banquet. Cf. *Pearl* 785, where heaven is depicted as a harem.

337.   I have translated *marcialle* as "guard." As Morse writes, the marshal's duty "is to escort [the judge] to his place, according to his rank." Everywhere in the works of the *Pearl* poet, heaven is imagined paradoxically as a hierarchy among equals. And the feast there is, as always, emphatically aristocratic.

345–48.   Cf. *Pearl* 957–58.

347.   The redundancy of the original is kept in the translation.

350.   A more literal translation would be: "Much mourning and mirth were spoken aloud together."

Glossary

The Glossary, reproduced from the edition of Malcolm Andrew and Ronald Waldron, "is intended as a practical aid to the reader in the interpretation of the text and should be used in conjunction with the notes. The aim has been to include all word-forms which may give difficulty to the modern reader; a word is omitted only if it has the same (or nearly the same) spelling in modern English and is used in the text in a sense which is still current. . . . When looking up a word, the reader should first look for the line-reference in question; if this is not separately recorded, one of the common meanings (which are entered without line-references, or with a few references followed by '*etc*.') may be assumed to apply. Normal alphabetical order is observed (ʒ follows *g*, þ follows *t*) and variations in spelling are fully cross-referenced" (Andrew and Waldron, p. 301).

a, aa! *interj.* ah!
a *see also* **ho**
abate *v.* end
abate *see also* **abyde**
abayst *pp.* abashed, confounded
Abdama *n.* Admah
abelef *adv.* diagonally
abide(n) *see* **abyde**
able *adj.* entitled, *Pe* 599
abloy *adj.* transported, carried away
abod *see* **abyde**
abode *n.* stay, delay, *G* 687
abof, aboue(n) *adv. & prep.* above; on top; in a higher place, *G* 73; in the place of honour, *G* 112
abominacion *n.* abominable practice
aboue(n) *see* **abof**
ab(o)ut(t)e, abowte *adv. & prep.* about, around, round about; on account of, *Pe* 268; engaged in, *G* 1986
Abraham, Habraham *n.* Abraham
abroched *pp.* given utterance, expressed
abyde, -i- *v.* (**abate, abod** *pa.t.*, **abiden** *pp.*) wait, stop, remain; await; endure, *Pe* 348, 1090, *Cl* 856, *Pat* 7, *G* 1754; delay, *Pat* 70
abydyng *n.* enduring, tolerance
abyme *n.* abyss
abyt *n.* clothing
acces *n.* accession, attack
achaped *pa.t.* escaped
achaufed *pa.t. & pp.* kindled, aroused, *Cl* 1143; warmed, *G* 883
acheue *v.* achieve, obtain, accomplish; **a. to** reach (*cf.* **cheue**)

acole *v.* embrace
acorde *n.* agreement; **of care and me made a.** made sorrow familiar to me, *Pe* 371
acorde *v.* agree; correspond, *Pe* 819; match, *G* 602, 631; reconcile, *G* 2380, 2405
acroche *v.* acquire
adaunt *v.* daunt
adoun *adv.* down
adreʒ *adv.* back. *See also* **dryʒ(e)**
(a)dubbement(e) adornment, splendour
adyte *v.* accuse, arraign
affray *n.* dismay
affyen *v.* trust
afrayed *pa.t.* frightened, disturbed
after *prep., adv. & conj.* after, afterwards, for; along, *Pe* 125, *G* 218, 1608; by, from, *Pe* 998; to match, *G* 171; over, *Pat* 86
afyaunce *n.* trust
agayn, aʒayn *adv.* in reply, in return, back (again); again, *Pe* 326
agayn(e), agaynes, agayn(e)z, aʒayn(ez) *prep.* against; contrary to; towards; **nurne a.** refuse, *G* 1661
agayntote *n.* looking back
aghlich *adj.* fearsome
aglyʒte *pa.t.* slipped away
Agrauayn *n.* Agravain
agrete *adv.* generally, without distinction, *Pe* 560
agreued *pp.* overcome (with), *G* 2370
aʒayn(ez) *see* **agayn(e)**
aʒlez *adj.* fearless
aʒly *adv.* terribly, menacingly
aʒt(e) *adj.* eight

aȝt(e) *see also* **oghe**
aȝtsum *adj.* one of eight
aȝtþe *adj.* eighth
al *see* **al(le)**
alabaundarynes *n.* alamandines (precious stones), *Cl* 1470
alarom *n.* alarm, alarum
alce *see* **als(e)**
alder *compar. adj.* older, elder
alderes *n.* princes, *G* 95
aldermen *n.* elders, senators, *Pe* 887, 1119
alder-truest *adj.* truest of all
aldest *superl. adj.* oldest, eldest
alegge *v.* plead
algate *adv.* anyway, at any rate
aliche *adv.* alike, in similar manner
alkaran *n.* mineral pitch
al(le) *adj., adv., pron. & conj.* all, everything, everybody; *adv.* everywhere, completely, quite; *conj.* even though, *G* 143; **of a. and sum** in full, *Pe* 584; **a. kynez** of all kinds; **Al Hal Day**, All Saints' Day
allyt *see* **lyte**
almyȝt(y) *adj.* almighty
aloft(e) *prep. & adv.* upon, up, at the top, above
aloȝ *adv.* softly
alone *adv.* alone; only, *Pe* 933
along(e) *prep. & adv.* along; throughout
alosed *pp.* famed, *Cl* 274; praised, *G* 1512
alow *v.* recognize, *Pe* 634
aloynte *pp.* far removed
als(e), also, alce *adv.* also, as well. *See also* **as** *adv.*
altogeder *adv.* entirely, wholly
alþaȝ *conj.* although
alþer-fayrest *adj.* fairest of all
alþer-fynest *adj.* finest of all
alþer-grattest *adj.* greatest of all
alþer-rychest *adj.* richest of all
alþer-swettest *adj.* sweetest of all
aluisch *adj.* other-worldly
alway *adv.* always
alyue *adj.* alive; living, *Pe* 445
amaffised *n.* amethyst
amarauntz *n.* emeralds; *cf.* **emerad(e)**
amatyst *n.* amethyst
ame *n.* aim, mark
amed *pa.t.* considered, esteemed
amende *v.* improve, *G* 898; *pp.* remedied, *Cl* 248
amesyng *n.* gentleness
amonestes *v.* admonishes, warns
among *prep.* among; *adv.* mingled together, *Pe* 905; at intervals, *Cl* 1414
amount *v.* amount (to), signify, *Cl* 395n, *G* 1197
anamayld *pp.* enamelled
Ananie *n.* Hananiah
and(e) *conj.* and; and yet, but, *Pe* 273, 931, *etc.* *Pat* 322; if, *Pe* 598, *Cl* 730, 739, *G* 1009, 1245, *etc.*
anelede *pa.t.* pursued
anende, onende *prep.* concerning, about, of, *Pe* 186, 697; against, near, *Pe* 1136; **-z** *prep.* opposite, *Pe* 975

angardez *n.* of arrogance (arrogant), *G* 681
angelez *see* **a(u)ngelez**
angel-hauyng *n.* angelic bearing
anger *n.* anger, resentment; harm, *G* 2344
angré *adj.* sharp, bitter
anguych *n.* anguish
anious *adj.* arduous
anjoynt *adj.* united
ankres, -z *n.* anchors
anon *adv.* at once, immediately after
anoþer *adj. & pron.* another, a second
anournementes *n.* ornaments, decoration
answ(a)r(e) *see* **onsware**
anvnder, onvunder *prep. & adv.* under; below, at the foot of, *Pe* 166; *adv.* underneath, *Pe* 991
anyskynnez *adj.* of any kind (at all)
aparaunt *n.* dependency
apassed *pp.* passed
apende *v.* appertain
apere *v.* appear
apert *adj. & adv.* open(ly); plain(ly); exposed, *G* 154
Apocalyp(p)ez, -(e)ce, Apokalypez, -ce *n.* Apocalypse, Revelation
apparayl(mente) *n.* adornment, ornamentation
apparement *n.* equipment, ornaments
apple-garnade *n.* pomegranate
appose *v.* interrogate
apyke *v.* adorn, array
aqoyntaunce *n.* acquaintance, company
aquyle *v.* lead, *Pe* 691; obtain permission, *Pe* 967
Ararach *n.* Ararat
aray(e) *n.* dress, array; setting, *Pe* 5; position, rank, *Pe* 491
aray(e)d, -de *pp.* dressed, prepared, adorned; constructed, *G* 783; **mad a.** in a state of frenzy, *Pe* 1166
araynced *pa.t.* questioned
arc *see* **ark**
are *adv.* before, *Cl* 438, 1128, *G* 239, 1632, 1891
ar(e)nde *see* **er(a)nd(e)**
arered *pp.* retreated, *G* 1902n.
arest *v.* stop; remain, *Pat* 144
areþede *n.* (people of old); old times, *Pe* 711
arewez, arwes *n.* arrows
arȝe *adj.* afraid, *G* 241
arȝe *v.* be afraid
ark, arc *n.* ark
Armene *adj.* Armenian
armes, -ez *n.* feats of arms, chivalry, *G* 95, 1513, *etc.*; armour (and weapons), *Cl* 1306, 1773, *G* 204, 281, *etc.*; coat-of-arms, *G* 631(?)
ar(n)(e), arnde *see* **be, er(a)nd(e)**
aros *pa.t.* arose
Arraby *n.* Arabia
arsoun(e)z *n.* saddle-bows
arwes *see* **arewez**
aryȝt, o- *adv.* in proper fashion; straight on, *Pe* 112
aryue *v.* arrive
as *conj.* as, while; according as, *Cl* 92; where, *G* 1004; as if, as though, *Cl* 82, *etc.*; **also ... a.** just as ... as, *Cl* 1618

as, als(o) *adv.* like, as, such as; according to, *Pe* 595; (intensive) **a. bare** as plainly as possible, *Pe* 836; **a. helde** quite probably, *Pe* 1193; **a. tyd, a. bylyue, a. fast** very quickly, *Cl* 64, 1239, *etc.*

asaute *see* **as(s)aut(e)**

asay *see* **as(s)ay**

asayled *pa. t.* assailed

ascaped, asscaped *pa.t.* escaped, *Cl* 569, *Pat* 110; crossed safely, *Cl* 1776

ascry, asscry, askry *n.* outcry, clamour, alarm

ascrye *v.* shout; cry to, *Pat* 195

asent(e) *n.* accord, harmony; **in a.** together, *Cl* 788; **sette in a.** agreed, *Pat* 177

aske *v.* ask (for); demand, require, *Cl* 1127, 1742, *G* 530, 1327; seek, *Cl* 1109

askes, -z *n.* ashes

askry *see* **ascry**

askyng *n.* request

aslypped *pp.* slipped away

asoyled *pa.t.* absolved

aspaltoun *n.* asphalt

asperly *adv.* sharply

as(s)aut(e) *n.* assault, attack

as(s)ay *n. & v.* test

asscaped, asscry *see* **ascaped, ascry**

assemblé *n.* union, *Pe* 760

as(s)pye *v.* see, catch sight of; discover, *Pe* 704, *G* 1199

as(s)tate *n.* condition, *Pe* 393; rank, *Pe* 490

asswype *adv.* immediately

as(s)yse *n.* manner, fashion, custom

astate *see* **as(s)tate**

astel *pa.t.* stole forth

astit, -y- *adv.* at once, in a moment, quickly, soon

astount *pp.adj.* amazed, stupified, *Pe* 179*n*

astraye *adv.* wildly, off course, *Pe* 1162

astyt *see* **astit**

asure, azer *n.* lapis lazuli

aswagen *v.* assuage

asyngne *v.* assign

asyse *see* **as(s)yse**

at *pron.* which; þat **a.** what, *Pe* 536

at(e) *prep. & adv.* at; in; to, *G* 929, 1671; of, *G* 359, *etc.*; from, *Cl* 1619, *G* 328, 391, *etc.*; for, *G* 648, 1320; with, *Pe* 287, *G* 1474, 2399; according to, *Pe* 199, 1164, *Cl* 348, *Pat* 134, 339, *etc.*, *G* 1006, 1546

athel, atle *see* **aþel, at(t)le**

atlyng *n.* purpose, intention

atrauerce, -res *adv.* from side to side

atslyke *v.* be spent

atteny *v.* reach

at(t)le *v.* intend, *G* 27; pretend, *G* 2263; *pp.* designed (to be), *Cl* 207

at(t)yred *pp.* attired

atwap(p)e *v.* escape

aþel, athel *adj.* noble, glorious

auayed *pp.* informed

aucly *adj.* untoward, perverse

Aue *n.* Ave Maria

auen *see* **aune**

auentayle *n.* neck-guard, *G* 608*n*

auenture, av-, aw-, a(u)nter *n.* strange happening, marvel, exploit; quest, *Pe* 64, *G* 489; **on a.** in peril, *Pat* 242

auenturus *adj.* daring

auinant *adj. or adv.* pleasant(ly), *G* 806

auise, auyse, avyse, awyse *v.* devise, *G* 45, 1389; contemplate, *G* 771; **watz auised** intended, *Cl* 1365

aumayl *n.* enamel

auncetere? *n.* ancestor's, *Cl* 258

auncian *adj.* aged, venerable; *as n.* *G* 948

aune, auen, awen, owen, owne *adj. & pron.* own

a(u)ngelez, aungel(l)(e)s *n.* angels

aunter *see* **auenture**

auntered *pa.t.* ventured, risked, *G* 1516

auter *n.* altar

auþer *see* **oþer**

auwhere *adv.* anywhere

auyse *see* **auise**

avanters *n.* offal near the neck, *G* 1342

avaunt *n.* promise, boast

avayment *n.* display

aventure *see* **auenture**

avow, avowe *v.* promise, affirm

avoy *interj.* shame on you!, *Cl* 863

avyled *pa.t. & pp.* defiled, profaned

avysyoun *n.* vision

away(e) *adv.* away; gone, absent, *Pe* 258, *Cl* 1241, *Pat* 480, 499; **here a.** hither, (to) here, *Cl* 647

awayed *pp.* taught, instructed, *Pe* 710

awayled *pa.t.* availed

awen, awenture *see* **aune, auenture**

awharf *pa.t.* turned aside

awhyle *adv.* for a time

awowe, awyse *see* **avow, auyse**

ay *adv.* always, ever; all the time, *Pe* 56, 132, *etc.*, *Cl* 132, *etc.*, *G* 562, *etc.*; in each case, *Cl* 114, *G* 128, 190; everywhere, *Pe* 44, *G* 167, *etc.*

ay *n.* hay, *Cl* 1684

ayled *pp.* troubled

ayquere *adv.* everywhere

ayre *n.[1]* air

ayre, hayre, here *n.[2]* heir

ayþer *adj. & pron.* each, both; **a. oþer, a. . . . oþer** each other

Aywan *n.* Iwain

aywhere *adv.* everywhere

Azarie *n.* Azariah

azer *see* **asure**

babel *adj. or adv.* foolish(ly), *Cl* 582

Babiloyn(e), Babyloyn *n.* Babylon

baboynes *n.* baboons

babtem *see* **baptem**

bachlerez, bacheleres *n.* young men

badde *adj.* bad, wicked

bade *see* **byde**

baft *adv.* abaft, astern

bagges *n.* bags

bak(bon) *n.* back(bone)

baken *pp.* baked

bald(e)ly *adv.* boldly, vigorously

bale *adj.* dire

bale n.¹ harm, pain, Pe 478, 651, Cl 276, Pat 276, 513; calamity, Cl 980, G 2041; sorrow, grief, Pe 18, 123, etc., Cl 1256, G 2419
bale n.² cargo, Pat 157
balé n. belly, G 1333
balelez adj. innocent
bale-stour n. death agony, Pat 426
baly(e) adj. smooth and rounded
balleful adj. wretched
balke n. (grave) mound, Pe 62
Baltazar n. Belshazzar; Belteshazzar, Cl 1610n
balterande adj. stumbling
balteres v. rolls around
baly n. stronghold, Pe 1083
bande see **bende**
baner n. banner
banne n. proclamation, order
banned pp. cursed
bantelez, bantel(le)s n. bantels; tiers, coursings (of a building), Pe 992, 1017, Cl 1459n
baptem, babtem n. baptism, Pe 627, 653
barayne adj. barren, Cl 659; not breeding, G 1320
barbe n. point, G 2310; pl. bristles, G 1457
barbican n. fortified gateway
bare adj. bare, naked; single, G 1141; clear, Pe 1025; without armour, G 277, 290; mere, G 2352; adv. plainly, Pe 836; openly, G 465; only, Cl 1573, G 1066; as n. bare skin, Cl 791; -ly positively, G 548
bared pp. disclosed, made apparent, Cl 1149
bare-heued adj. bare-headed
barer(e)s n. barriers, defences
baret n. battle, strife; enmity (with God), G 752
barlay see G 296n
barme n. breast
barnage n. childhood
barne n. child; a child, G 2320 (MS: **burne**)
baronage n. company of barons
baroun n. baron; **b. vpon benche** lord of the king's council, Cl 1640
barred pp. decorated with bars, G 159, 600
barrez, -s n. bars; barriers, Cl 963; decorative bars, G 162
Barsabe n. Bathsheba
barst see **breste**
bases, basez n. bases
basse n. (lowest) course, Pe 1000
bassyn n. basin, vessel
bastel n. tower; assault tower mounted on wheels, Cl 1187n; **b. roues** roofs of towers, G 799
basyng n. foundation, Pe 992
batayl n. (a) duel, G 277
batayled adj. fortified with battlements
bate n. baiting, persistent attacks, G 1461
batede pa.t. abated, ceased
batelment n. battlement
batered pa.t. clattered
baþe v. bathe; imperat. plunge, Pat 211
bauderyk n. baldric, belt, strap
baume v. comfort
bausenez n. badgers
Bawdewyn n. Baldwin
bawelyne n. bowline (a rope fastening the sail to the bow), Pat 104, Cl 417

bawemen n. archers
bay n.¹ a space between columns, Cl 1392
bay, baye n.² baying of hounds; defensive stance; **byde (at) þe b.** or **in his b.** stand at bay
Bayard n. a bay horse, Cl 886n
baye v. bay (at)
bayly n. dominion, Pe 442; realm, Pe 315
bayn adj. obedient; willing, Pe 807, Pat 136; adv. readily, Cl 1511
baysment n. confusion, Pe 174
bayst pa.t. was dismayed, G 376
bayted pp. fattened
baythe(n) v. agree (to), grant
be see **be(ne), bi**
beau, beue adj. beautiful, Pe 197; **b. sir** good sir, (lit. (my) handsome lord), Cl 1622, G 1222
beauté, bewté n. beauty
becom(e) see **bicum**
bed, bedd(e) n. bed
bed(de), bede(n)(e) see **bid(de)**
befalle, begyn(n)e see **bifalle, bygyn(n)e**
beholde, by- v. (**behelde** pa.t., **bihalden, biholde** pp.) behold, look (at); pp. obliged
behoue see **bihoue**
beke n. beak
beknew, beknowe(n) see **biknowe**
bekyr n. beaker, goblet
belde n. courage, G 650
bele adj. gracious, pleasant, G 1034
bele v. burn, Pe 18
Belfagor n. Baalpeor
Belssabub n. Beelzebub
Belyal n. Belial
bem(e) n. beam, ray; (wooden) beam, Pe 814
ben see **be(ne)**
bench(e) n. bench; see also **baroun**
bende, bande n. band; ribbon, G 2506, 2517
bende pa.t. (**bende, bent(e)** pp.) (bent); arched, G 305; fastened (**bi:** to), G 2224; fixed, set, Pe 1017; attached, Pe 664; submitted, Pe 1189; caused, G 2115
bene adj. & adv. pleasant(ly), beautiful(ly); gentle, Pat 418; happily, G 2475
be(ne), by v. (**was(se), watz, wace, wore, ware, wer(e)(n)** pa.t., **ben(e)** pp.) be
bent n. field, battlefield; grass, Pat 392; bank (of stream), G 1599; **burne on b.** warrior, G 1465, 2148; **bentfelde** hunting field, G 1136
ber n. beer, G 129
berde n. beard
berdles, -z adj. beardless
bere v. (**ber(e)** pa.t., **born(e), bore** pp.) bear, lift, wear; swing, G 2070; keep, G 2151; press, G 1860; have, possess, Pe 100, 756, Cl 333, 1023; **b. lyf** live; **b. þe face** make for, Pe 67; **b. to** strike, Pat 148
b(e)rest(e) see **breste**
berez n. bears, G 722
berfray n. a movable tower used in sieges
berȝ(e) n. barrow, mound
beryng n. bearing, behaviour
bes see **be(ne)**
best superl. adj. & adv. best (in various contex-

tual senses) *G* 78, 1216, *etc.*; perfect, *Pe* 863; noblest, *Pe* 1131; noble one, *Pe* 279; of highest rank, *Cl* 1202, *G* 73; nobles, *Cl* 1179, *G* 550, 1325; **of þe b.** from among the best, *G* 38, *etc.*; in the best manner, *G* 889, 1000

best(t)(e) *n.* beast, animal (**besten** *gen. pl.*, *or adj. Cl* 1446)

bete *v.*[1] (**bet(e)(n)** *pa.t.*, **beten** *pp.*) beat; *pp.* driven, *Pat* 248; inlaid, embroidered, *G* 78, 1833, 2028

bete *v.*[2] (**bet(te)** *pp.*) kindle, mend, make up (a fire), *Cl* 627, 1012, *G* 1368; amend, *Pe* 757

better *compar. adj. & adv.* better; rather, *Pe* 341

betydes *see* **bityde**

betz *see* **be(ne)**

Beþelen *n.* Bethlehem

beue *see* **beau**

beuerage *n.* drink

beuer-hwed *adj.* the colour of beaver

bewté *see* **beauté**

beyng *n.* nature, *Pe* 446

bi, be, by *prep.* by, beside, along, according to, from; through, *Pe* 684, 751; beside, *Pe* 140; against, *G* 2310; *for phrases see also the nouns* **contray, skyl, syþe(s),** *etc.; conj.* until, *G* 1006; by the time that, *Cl* 403, *G* 1169; when, *G* 2032; **b. þat** *adv.* by that time, *G* 597, 1868; then, *G* 2152; *conj.* by the time that, *Pat* 468, *G* 443, *etc.*; when, *G* 1678, 1912, 2043

bibbes *v.* drinks

bicnv *see* **biknowe**

bicum, bicome, be- by- *v.* (**becom, bicome, bycom** *pa.t.*) become; arrive (at), *G* 460

bid(de), bydde, bedde, bede *v.* (**bed(e)(n)** *pa.t.*, **bedene, boden** *pp.*) bid, command, ask; offer, *Cl* 1640, *G* 374, 382, 1824, *etc.*

bide(n) *see* **byde**

bifalle, be-, by- *v.* (**bifel** *pa.t.*, **bifallen** *pp.*) happen

bifore, byfore *adv. & prep.* before (*of time or place*); formerly; in front (of)

bigan *see* **bygyn(n)e**

big(ge), byg(g)(e) *adj. & adv.* (**bygger** *compar.*, **big(g)est** *superl.*) big, great; strong, *Cl* 1190, 1377, *G* 554, 2101; *adv.* strongly, *Cl* 1183

big(g)e *v.* build, make

bigyled, by- *pp.* beguiled

bigly, bygly *adv.* strongly, powerfully

bigog! *interj.* by God! *G* 390

bigonne(n) *see* **bygyn(n)e**

bigrauen *pp.* carved, *G* 216

biȝonde *see* **byȝonde**

bihalde(n), biholde *see* **beholde**

bihoue, be-, by- *v.impers.* (**bihous, bos, boz** *pres3s.*, **bihoued, byhod(e)** *pa.t.*) behove, be obliged, must

bihyȝt *pa.t. & pp.* promised

bihynde, byhynde(n) *prep. & adv.* behind; inferior, *G* 1942

bikenne, by- *v.* (**bikende** *pa.t.*) commend; deliver, *Cl* 1296

biknowe, be- *v.* (**beknew, bicnv** *pa.t.*, **benowen** *pp.*) confess, acknowledge

bilde *see* **bylde**

bileued *pa.t.* remained, *C* 1549

biliue *see* **bylyue**

bilooghe *adv.* below, *Cl* 116

bilyue *see* **bylyue**

birlen *v.* (**byrled** *pp.*) pour (out)

birolled *pp.* drenched, covered

bischop, bisshop *n.* bishop; *gen.pl.* bishops' *Cl* 1445

biseche, bysech(e) *v.* (**bisoȝt(en)** *pa.t.*) beseech, implore

biseged *pa.t.* besieged

biseme, by- *v.impers.* suit, become, befit

bisides, bisied *see* **bisyde, busy**

bisinesse, busynes *n.* importunity, *G* 1840; solicitude, *G* 1986

bisoȝt(en) *see* **biseche**

bispeke *pa.t.* spoke

bisshop *see* **bischop**

bisyde, by-, be- *prep. & adv.* beside, near; at his side, *G* 1083; alongside, *G* 1582(?), 2230; round about, *G* 2088; **þer (her) b.** nearby; *see also* **lay; bisides, bisydez,** *adv.* round about, *G* 76, 856, 2164

bitalt *pp.* shaken, *Pe* 1161

bite, byte *v.* (**bot(e), bited** *pa.t.*, **biten, byten** *pp.*) bite; torment, *Cl* 1243, *Pat* 373; penetrate, *Pe* 355, *G* 1457; **b. (on)** eat, *Pe* 640, *Cl* 1675, *Pat* 392

biteche *v.* (**bytaȝt(e)** *pa.t.*) commit, deliver

bitid(d)e *see* **bityde**

bit(te), bytte *n.* blade

bitwene *see* **bytwene**

bityde, bitide, be-, by- *v.* (**bitid(d)e, bityde** *pa.t.*) happen, befall

biþenkke *v.* (**biþoȝt** *pa.t.*) resolve, consider, reflect

biwyled *pp.* deceived, *G* 2425

biys *n.* fine linen (garment), *Pe* 197

blades *n.* knives, *Cl* 1105

blaȝt *adj.* pure white, *Pe* 212

blak(e) *adj.* black; *as n. Cl* 1009

blame *n.* blame, reproach, guilt; reproof, rebuke, *Pe* 715, *Cl* 43, *G* 2500, 2506

blame *v.* blame; disparage, *Cl* 1661

blande *n.* **in b.** together, *G* 1205. See also **inblande**

blande *pp.* trimmed, *G* 1931

blasfemy(e) *n.* blasphemy

blasoun *n.* shield, *G* 828

blastes, -z *n.* blasts

blaunmer, blaunner *n.* ermine, fur

blayke *adj.* white, pale, *Pe* 27

ble *n.* colour, complexion; **b. of Ynde** indigo, *Pe* 76

ble(e)aunt *n.* silk (garment), mantle

blemyst *pa.t.* impaired

blench *n.* trick, stratagem

blenched *pa.t.* dodged

blende *see* **blende(n), blynne**

blended *pp.* deluded (**with:** by), *G* 2419

blende(n), blent(e) *pa.t. & pp.* blended, mingled; *pa.subjunc.* (should) steep, *Pat* 227; *pp.* situated, *Pe* 385

blenk(e) *v.* shine

blent(e) *see* **blende(n)**

blesse *v.* bless; cross (oneself), *Pe* 341(?), *G*

2071; say 'God bless you (me)', *Pe* 341(?), *G* 1296*n*

bliþe *see* **blype**

blo *adj.* livid, dark

blober *see* **bluber**

blod(e) *n.* blood; descendant, *Cl* 686; **blody** *adj. Pe* 705

blok *n.* compartment

blom *n.* bloom, flower; *fig.* perfection, *Pe* 578

blonk *n.* (**blonkken** *gen.pl.*) horse

blosched *see* **blusche**

blot *n.* stain

blowe *v.*[1] blow, bloom, *G* 512

blowe *v.*[2] (**blw(e), blowed** *pa.t.*) blow

bluber, blober *n.* seething water

blubrande *presp.adj.* bubbling, surging

blubred *pa.t.* surged

bluk *n.* trunk, torso, *G* 440

blunder *n.* turmoil, strife

blunt *adj.* stunned, dazed, *Pe* 176

blunt *pa.t.* stopped

blusch *n.* gleam, *G* 520

blusche, -o- *v.* look, gaze, glance; **-ande** *presp. adj.* flashing, *G* 1819

blusnande *see* **blysned**

blustered *pa.t.* blundered about, strayed about, *Cl* 886

blwe *adj. & n.* blue

blw(e) *see* **blowe** *v.*[2]

blycande, blykkande *presp.* shining

blykke *v.* shine

blykned *pa.t.* grew pale; **blyknande** shining, *Cl* 1467 (*cf.* **blycande, blykke**)

blynde *adj.* blind; dim, *Pe* 83; as *n. Cl* 1094

blynde *v.* become dim

blynne *v.* (**blende** *pp., Cl* 967) cease (**of:** from)

blysful *adj.* blissful, full of bliss *or* blessing; joyful, happy; delightful; as *n. Pe* 421

blysned *pa.t.* shone, *Pe* 1048; **blysnande, blusn-** *presp.adj.* gleaming, shining

blysse *n.* bliss, joy

blype, -i- *adj. & adv.* glad, happy, joyful; gentle, kind, *Pe* 1131, *Cl* 1085, 1228; bright, lovely, *G* 155, 162; *adv.* happily, *G* 1684

blype *n.* mercy, *Pe* 354

blyp(e)ly *adv.* gladly, happily, joyously

bob(b)aunce *n.* arrogance, pomp, pride

bobbe *n.* bunch, clump

bode, bot *n.* bidding, command; offer, *G* 1824; **bi b.** according to command, *Cl* 944*n*

bod(e) *see also* **byde**

bodé, bodi *see* **body**

boden *see* **bid(de)**

bodworde *n.* message

body, bodi, bodé *n.* body; person

bodyly *adj.* bodily, physical, of (in) the body

bo(e)rne *n.* sea, flood, *Cl* 482, *Pat* 302; burn, stream, *G* 731, 1570, 2174

boffet *see* **buffet**

boȝe *n.* bough

boȝ(e)(d), boȝt *see* **bowe, by(y)e**

boȝted *pp.adj.* vaulted

bok(e) *n.* book

bok-lered *adj.* book-learned

bol, bul(l) *n.* bull

bold(e) *adj. & adv.* bold, valiant, daring;

noble, fine, *Cl* 789, 1333 *etc.*; as *n. Cl* 811, *G* 21; *adv.* valiantly, *G* 2476

bolle *n.*[1] bowl, *Cl* 1511

bol(l)e *n.*[2] trunk (of tree), *Pe* 76, *Cl* 622, *G* 766

bolled *pp.* embossed

bolne *v.* swell

bonchef *n.* happiness

bonde *adj. or n.* in a state of serfdom, serfs

bone *adj.* good; *see also* **(h)ostel**

bon(e) *n.*[1] bone

bone *n.*[2] request, prayer, *Pe* 912, 916, *G* 327; command, commandment, *Cl* 826, *Pat* 136; boon, favour, *Pe* 1090

boner *adj.* kind, compassionate

bonerté *n.* beatitude, *Pe* 762

bongré *prep.* in accordance with

bonk(k)(e) *n.* hill, hillside, ridge; bank (of stream), *Pe* 106, 1169, *G* 785; shore, *Pat* 236, *G* 700 *etc.*; bank of water, *Cl* 363

Boos *n.* Bors

bor *n.*[1] boar, *Cl* 55, *G* 722, *etc.*

bor *n.*[2] *see also* **bo(u)r(e)**

borde *n.*[1] board; table; wood, *Cl* 1190; side (of ship), *Pat* 211; **vpon b.** on deck, *Cl* 470, *Pat* 190; **bynne b.** on board (ship)

borde *n.*[2] band (of material), *G* 159, 610

borde *see also* **bo(u)rde**

bore *see* **bere**

bor(e)lych *adj.* massive, huge; noble, *Cl* 1488

borges *n.* citizens

borgoune *v.* bud

borȝ(e), borlych *see* **burȝ(e), bor(e)lych**

born(e) *see* **bere, bo(e)rne**

bornyst(e), burnyst, -ist *pp.* burnished, shining

boroȝt *see* **bryng**

bos *n.* cow-stall, *Cl* 1075

bos *see also* **bihoue**

bose *n.* coarse, awkward person, *Pe* 911

bosk(ed) *see* **busk(ke)**

boskenz *n.* divisions between stalls, *Cl* 322*n*

bost *n.* boasting; clamour, *G* 1448

boster *n.* boaster

bostwys, bu- *adj.* rough, crude

bosum *n.* swelling (of sail), *Pat* 107

bot *adv., conj. & prep.* but, except, only; quite, *G* 1230; but that, *Pat* 176; **b. (if)** unless, *Pe* 308, 428 *etc.*, *Cl* 1110, 1360, *Pat* 83, *G* 716, 1782 *etc.*; **b. þat** were it not that, *Cl* 881; **no more b.** only to the extent of, *G* 2312; **neuer b.** only, *G* 547; **noȝt b.** nothing but, *Cl* 209 *etc.*, only, *G* 1267, completely, *G* 1833

bot *v.* announce, proclaim, *Cl* 473

bot(e) *n.*[1] help, remedy

bote *n.*[2] boot, shoe

bot(e) *n.*[3] boat

bot(e) *see also* **bite, bode**

both(e), boþe *adj., pron. & adv.* both; each, *G* 2070, 2165; also, as well, *Cl* 11, 57, *G* 129, *etc.*

botounz *n.* buttons

boþe *n.* booth, arbour

boþe *see also* **both(e)**

boþem, bothem, boþom *n.* bottom; valley; deep place, *Cl* 1030

boþemlez *adj.* bottomless

bouel *n.* (**boweles, -z** *pl.*) bowel
bougounz *n. gen.pl.* of drumsticks, *Cl* 1416
boun *adj.* ready; setting off, *G* 548; arranged, *Pe* 534; fixed, fastened, *Pe* 992, 1103
bounden *see* **bynde**
bounet *pp.* ready, prepared, *Cl* 1398
bounté *n.* virtue, merit; liberality, *Cl* 1436
bo(u)rde *n. & v.* joke, jest; **bourdyng** *n.* jesting, *G* 1404
bo(u)r(e) *n.* bower, bedroom, private room; house, home, *Pe* 964; stall, *Cl* 322
boury, bourne *see* **burȝ(e), bu(u)rne**
bout(e) *prep.* without
bowe, boȝ(e) *v.* go, come; bow, submit, *Cl* 1746; stoop, *Pat* 441; **b. after** follow, *Cl* 1750; **b. to, bi** obey, comply with, *Cl* 944(1), *Pat* 56, 75
boweles, -ez *see* **bouel**
boy *n.* lout, ruffian
boyle *v.* boil
boz *see* **bihoue**
brace *n.* arm-pieces
brach(et)es, -ez *n.* hounds
brad *pp.* grilled, *G* 891
bradde *pa.t.* reached, *G* 1928
brade *see* **brod(e)**
brake *v.* spew, vomit, *Pat* 340
braken *n.* bracken
bras(se) *n.* brass; brass trumpets, *Cl* 1783
braste *see* **breste**
brath(þe) *n.* (**braþez** *pl.*) ferocity, *Cl* 916; impetuosity, *Pe* 1170; *pl.* agonies, *Pe* 346
braþ *see also* **broþe**
braunch(e), bronch *n.* branch
braundysch *v.* struggle
brawden *see* **brayde**
brawen, brawne *n.* boar's flesh, meat; **b. of a best** well-fleshed boar, *G* 1631
brayd(e) *n.* **at a b.** quickly, *Cl* 539; **in a b.** in a sudden impulse, suddenly, *Cl* 1507
brayde *v.* (**brayd(e)(n)** *pa.t.*, **brayden, brawden, browden** *pp.*) draw, pull; take, *G* 621; bring, *Pe* 712; jerk, *Pe* 1170; fling, *G* 2377; gush, *G* 429; *pp.* embroidered, woven, intertwined, linked, *Cl* 1132, 1481, *G* 177, 220, 580, 1833; **b. doun** let down, *G* 2069
brayn *adj.* mad, reckless, *G* 286
brayn *n.* brain, brains
braynwod *adj.* maddened
bred *n.* bread
brede *n.*[1] breadth, *Pe* 1031, *Cl* 316
brede *n.*[2] board, *Pat* 184, *G* 2071
brede *n.*[3] *pl.* roast meats, *Cl* 1405
brede *v.*[1] (**bred(den)** *pa.t.*) breed, *Cl* 257; grow, flourish, *Pe* 415, *Cl* 1482, *G* 21; become, *Cl* 1558
brede *v.*[2] stretch, *Pe* 814
bredful *adj.* brimful, *Pe* 126. (Cf. **brurdful**)
breed *adj.* terrified, *Pat* 143
bref *adj.* transitory, *Pe* 268
brek(e)(n) *pa.t.* (**broken** *pp.*) broke; opened, *G* 1333; burst forth, *G* 1764
brem(e) *adj. & adv.* fierce, wild, stern, loud; terrible, *Cl* 229; intense, *Pe* 863; firmly, *G* 781; **-ly(ch)** *adv.* loudly, fiercely; quickly, *G* 779

brenne *v.* (**bren(n)(e)d** *pa.t.*, **brent, brende,** *pp.*) burn; broil, *G* 1609; *pp.adj.* refined (by fire) *or* burnished, *Pe* 989, *Cl* 1456, 1488, *G* 195
brent *adj.* steep, *Pe* 106, *G* 2165; *superl. Cl* 379
brere-flour *n.* briar-rose
breres *n.* briars
bresed *pp.adj.* bristly
brest *n.* trespass, outrage, *Cl* 229
breste, bereste *n.* breast
breste *v.* (**barst, braste, bursten** *pa.t.*, **brusten** *pp.*) burst (out), break
Bretaygne, Bretayn *n.* Britain
breth(e), breþe *n.* breath, *Cl* 916; wind, *Pat* 107, 145; smoke, smell, *Cl* 509, 967
breþer *n.* brothers(-in-arms)
breue *v.* declare, tell; reveal, *G* 1436
breyþed *pa.t.* 'breathed', rose as a vapour, *Cl* 1421*n*
brit(t)en *v.* destroy, *G* 2, 680; cut open, *G* 1339; **b. out** cut up, *G* 1611
brod(e) *adj.* broad, wide, great; *of time* long; *adv.* broadly, widely; **ful b.** far and wide, *Pat* 117, with eyes wide open, *G* 446
broȝes, -z, broȝt(e)(n) *see* **browes, bryng(e)**
brok(e) *n.* brook; sea, *Pat* 145
brom *n.* broom
bronch *see* **braunch(e)**
bronde, bront *n.* sword; firebrand, *Cl* 1012; charred stick, *G* 2
broþe, braþ *adj.* angry, fierce
broþely *adv.* wretchedly, *Cl* 1030, 1256, *Pat* 474; violently, *G* 2377
broþelych *adj.* venomous, vile, *Cl* 848
broþer *n.* brother; kinsman, *Cl* 772
broun *adj.* brown; dark, *Pe* 537; burnished, bright, *Pe* 990, *G* 426
browden *see* **brayde**
browes, broȝes, -z *n.* eyebrows
brugge *see* **bryg(g)e**
brunt *n.* blow, shock
bruny, bryné *n.* coat of mail
brurdes *n.* rims, edges
brurdful *adj.* brimful, *Cl* 383. (*Cf.* **bredful**)
brused *pp.* bruised
brusten *see* **breste**
brutage *n.* wooden platforms, *Cl* 1190*n*
bruxle *v.* upbraid
brych *n.* sin, *fig.* vomit, *Cl* 848
bryd *n.* bride, *Pe* 769
brydale *n.* wedding-feast, *Cl* 142
bryddes, -z *n.* birds
brydel *n.* bridle
bryg(g)e, -u- *n.* drawbridge
bryȝt *adj. & adv.* bright(ly); shining; beautiful; *as n. Pe* 755, *Cl* 470; *superl.* the most beautiful, *G* 1283
brym(me) *n.* bank, (water's) edge, *Cl* 365, *Pe* 232, *G* 2172; surface, *Pe* 1074
bryné *see* **bruny**
bryng(e) *v.* (**broȝt(e)(n)** *pa.t.*, **b(o)roȝt** *pp.*) bring; **b. to resoun** explain, *Cl* 1633
brynkez *n.* brinks, edges
brynston *n.* brimstone
buffet, bo- *n.* blow
bukkez *n.* bucks

bulde, bult *see* **bylde**
bulk *n*. hold, *Pat* 292
bul(l)ez, bur *see* **bol, bur(re)**
burde *n*. maiden, lady, woman
burde *v.impers*. **me (þe,** *etc*.**) b.** I (you, *etc*.) ought (to)
burȝ(e), bo(u)rȝ(e), burghe *n*. city, castle; estate, *Cl* 63; **in vch a b.** everywhere, *Cl* 1061
burne, burnyst *see* **bu(u)rn(e), bornyst(e)**
bur(re) *n*. onslaught, blow; force, *G* 2261; shock, *Cl* 32; strong wind, *Pat* 148
bursten *see* **breste**
burþen *n*. load, *Cl* 1439
busch *n*. noise, beating, *Cl* 1416
busch *v*. dash, plunge, *Pat* 143; rise, shoot up, *Pat* 472
busily *see* **busyly**
busk *n*. bush, *G* 182, 1437
busk(ke), bosk *v*. prepare; go, hasten; dress, *Cl* 142, *G* 1220; bring, *Cl* 351, 1395
busmar *n*. scorn
bustwys *see* **bostwys**
busy *adj*. as *n*. hurry, *Pat* 157
busy *v*. (**bisied** *pa.t*.) stir, *G* 89; bestir oneself, *G* 1066; *reflex*. concern oneself, *Pe* 268
busyly, busily, bysily *adv*. earnestly; carefully, *Cl* 1446
busynes *see* **bisinesse**
bu(u)rn(e), bourne, buyrne *n*. man, warrior, knight; sir, *Pe* 397, *G* 1071, *etc*.
by *see* **bi, be(ne)**
bycalle *v*. (**bycalt** *pp*.) call upon, *Pe* 913; *pp*. summoned, *Pe* 1163
bycom, bydde *see* **bicum, bid(de)**
byde, bide *v*. (**bod(e), bade, byden** *pa.t*., **biden** *pp*.) remain, wait (for); stay, *Cl* 616; live, *Pat* 318; lie, *Pe* 75; endure, *Pe* 664, *Cl* 32, *G* 290 *etc*.; enjoy, *G* 520; **b. to** await, *Cl* 467
bydene *adv*. directly, *Pe* 196; continuously, *Cl* 659
Byduer *n*. Bedivere
bye, byfallen, byfore, byg(g)(e) *see* **by(y)e, bifalle, bifore, big(ge)**
byg(g)yng *n*. building, house, home
bygly *adj*. (habitable); pleasant, *Pe* 963. *See also* **bigly**
bygyled *see* **bigyled**
bygyn(n)e, be-, bi- *v*. (**bygan, bygonne** *pa.t*., **bygonne(n)** *pp*.) begin; found, *G* 11; **b. þe table** sit in the place of honour, *G* 112; **is bygonne** has its origin (in), *Pe* 33
bygynner *n*. originator, *Pe* 436
byȝe *n*. ring, bracelet, necklace
byȝonde, bi- *prep*. beyond, across
byȝt *n*. fork (of animal's legs), *G* 1341, 1349
byhod(e), byholde, byhoue, byhynde(n), bykenne *see* **bihoue, beholde, bihoue, bihynde, bikenne**
bylde *n*. dwelling, *Pe* 727, 963
bylde *v*. (**bylde, bult** *pa.t*., **bilde, bulde, bylded** *pp*.) build; live, dwell, *G* 25; build up, *Pe* 123
byled *pa.t*. boiled, bubbled, *G* 2082; **boyled** *pp*., *G* 2174

bylyue, bilyue, biliue, byliue *adv*. quickly, swiftly, immediately, soon; **as b.** as soon as possible, *Cl* 1239
bynde *n*. woodbine (climbing plant), *Pat* 444. *See also* **wodbynde**
bynde *v*. bind, tie; **bounden** *pp*. tied, fastened; lined, *G* 573; trimmed, adorned, *Pe* 198, *G* 600, 609, 2028
bynne *prep*. **b. borde** within board, on board ship
byrled *see* **birlen**
byrþ-whatez *n*. dates of birth
bysech(e), byseme, bysily *see* **biseche, biseme, busyly**
bysulpe *v*. defile
bysyde *see* **bisyde**
byswyke *v*. cheat, *Pe* 568
bytaȝt(e), byte(n) *see* **biteche, bite**
bytoknyng *n*. sign
bytte *see* **bitte**
bytterly *adv*. bitterly
bytwene, bi- *prep. & adv*. between; in between, here and there, at intervals; **b. hem** aside, by themselves, *G* 977
bytwyste *prep*. between
bytyde, byþenk *see* **bityde, biþenkke**
by(y)e *v*. (**boȝt** *pa.t. & pp*.) buy; redeem, *Pe* 651, 893

cable, k- *n*. cable
cace, cas(e) *n*. matter, affair, *Pe* 673, *G* 546, 1196; chance, *G* 907; **vche a c.** everything that turned up, *G* 1262, every misfortune, *Pat* 265
cach(ch)(e), kach *v*. (**cached, caȝt(e)(n), kaȝt(en)** *pa.t. & pp*.) catch, seize, take, snatch; knock, *Cl* 1541; **c. to** *Pe* 50, *G* 2376; receive, obtain, accept, *Cl* 1619, *G* 643, 1011, 1938; conceive, *Cl* 1426; become infected with, *G* 2508; urge on, spur, drive, *Cl* 16, *G* 1581, 2175; hasten, start, go, *Cl* 629, *G* 1794; **c. of** take off, *Pe* 237; **c. vp** lift, hoist, *Pat* 102, *G* 1185
cacheres *n*. hunters
cagge *v*. bind, tie up
caȝt(e)(n) *see* **cach(ch)(e)**
cal *n*. invitation
Caldé(e), Caldye *n*. Chaldea, Chaldean
Caldéez *n*. the Chaldeans
calder *see* **co(o)lde**
calle, k- *v*. call, call out, summon; entreat, *Cl* 1522; **c. of** beg for, ask for, *G* 975, 1882, signal, *Cl* 1421
callyng *n*. proclamation, summons
calsydoyne *n*. chalcedony
Cam *n*. Ham
cambe *n*. comb; **comly onvunder c.** (beautiful) lady, *Pe* 775
campe *adj*. shaggy
can *see* **con**
candel *n*. candle
candelstik, con- *n*. candlestick
capados *n*. hood, cape
cap(e)le *n*. horse
captyuidé *n*. captivity
caraldes *n*. casks**

carayne *n.* carrion
care, kare *n.* sorrow, distress, trouble; **c. of** concern for, *G* 2379
care *v.* be concerned
careful *adj.* sorrowful, anxious
carf *see* **kerue**
carfully *adv.* wretchedly, in suffering
carle, karle *n.* churl
carneles, -z *n.* battlements
carole *n.* courtly ring-dance with singing
carp(e) *n.* speech, discourse, conversation
carping *n.* speech, power of speech
carp(p)(e), karp *v.* speak, say, talk; **here c.** hear tell, *G* 263
carye *v.* carry, *Cl* 1765
carye *see also* **cayre**
case(e) *see* **cace**
cast, kest(e) *v.* (**cast, kest(en)** *pa.t.*, **cast(e), kast(e), kest(e)** *pp.*) cast (out), throw (out); convey, *Pe* 66; direct, aim, *G* 228, 1901; speak, utter, *Pat* 415, *G* 64, 249, 2275; arrange, *G* 2242; consider, *G* 1855; devise, *Cl* 1455
cast(e), kest *n.* intention, *Pe* 1163; speech, *G* 1295; stroke, *G* 2298; glance, *Cl* 768; fastening, *G* 2376; device, trick, *G* 2413; contrivance, *Cl* 1070
castel, k- *n.* castle; **castel-walle** *n.* castle wall, *Pe* 917n
casydoynes *n.* chalcedonies
catel *n.* property
caue *n.* cave
cauelaciounz *see* **kauelacion**
cause, cawse *n.* cause, reason; case, *Pe* 702
cayre, kayre, carye (*G* 734) *v.* go, ride; traverse, *Pe* 1031; pull, *Cl* 1259; bring, *Cl* 1478 (*cf.* **carye**)
cayser, kayser *n.* emperor
caytif, caytyf *adj.* evil, base, wretched
cemmed *pp.* combed
cercle *n.* circlet
certez *adv.* certainly
cerues *see* **kerue**
ceté, -y, cité, cyté, -y *n.* city
ceuer *see* **keuer**
chace *n.* the chase, *G* 1416; hunt, *G* 1604
chace *v.* drive, oust, *Pe* 443
chaffer *n.* trade, merchandise
chalk-whyt, -quyte *adj.* chalk-white
chambre *n.* room, private room, bedroom; bridal chamber, *Pe* 904
chapayle, chapel(le) *n.* chapel
charde *see* **charre**
charg *n.* importance; **no c.** no matter
charge *v.* charge, instruct, *Cl* 464, *G* 451; put on, *G* 863; load, burden, *Cl* 1258; *pp.* heavy, *Cl* 1154; laden, *Cl* 1295; **c. with** carrying, *Cl* 1272
chargeaunt *adj.* onerous, demanding
chariotes *n.* waggons, carts
charre *v.* (**charred, charde** *pa.t.*) turn aside (*reflex.*), *G* 850; turn back, *G* 1143; return, *G* 1678; fail, *Pe* 608
charres *n.* business affairs, *G* 1674
chast *v.* correct, restrain
chastyse *v.* chastise, punish; scold, *G* 1143

chaufen *v.* warm, excite
chaunce *n.* chance, fortune; **for c. þat** whatever, *G* 2132; adventure, exploit, *G* 1081 *etc.*; deed, *Cl* 1129
chauncely *adv.* fortuitously
chaundeler *n.* candlestick stand
chaunge *v.* change, exchange. *See also* **cher(e)**
chaunsel *n.* chancel
chauntré *n.* singing of mass, *G* 63
chawlez *n.* jaws
chayer(e), cheyer *n.* throne; chair, *G* 875
chef *adj.* chief, main; first, *Cl* 684
chef *n.* head, commander
chefly, cheuely *adv.* quickly, especially, first of all
cheftayn, cheue(n)tayn *n.* chieftain, ruler; captain, *Cl* 464
cheke *n.* cheek; **maugref my chekes** despite my objections, *Pat* 54
chek(ke) *n.* bad luck; doom, *G* 1857; onslaught, attack, *Cl* 1238
chelde, chemné *see* **(s)chelde, chymné**
chepe *n.* trade, bargain, market, price, *G* 1939, 1940n
chepen *v.* haggle
cher(e), schere *n.* face, expression; demeanour, manner, mood; cheerfulness, friendliness, welcome, *Cl* 641, *G* 562, 1259, *etc.*; **make god c.** make merry, *Cl* 641, behave cheerfully, *G* 562; **chaunge c.** look about, *G* 711n, 2169
cherych(e), -yse, -isch *v.* welcome, entertain; cherish, take care of, *Cl* 543, 1154, 1644
ches(e), chesly *see* **chose, chysly**
cheualrye *n.* body of knights; knighthood
cheue *v.* get, *G* 1271, 1390; come, *G* 63; **c. to** reach, *G* 1674; **c. þat (þe) chaunce** bring it about, *G* 2103, happen, *Cl* 1125
cheuely, cheue(n)tayn *see* **chefly, cheftayn**
cheuisaunce (-y-c-) *n.* winnings; acquisition, *G* 1939
childer, childgered *see* **chylde**
chorle *n.* serf; villain, *Cl* 1583
chose *v.* (**ches(e), chos(en)** *pa.t.*, **ichose, chosen** *pp.*) choose; perceive, *Pe* 187, *G* 798; make one's way, go, *G* 451, *etc.* (also **c. þe gate, waye**); devote oneself to, *G* 1838
chyche *n.* niggard, skinflint
chyde *v.* chide, scold; **for to c.** complaining, *Pe* 403
chylde *n.* (**chylder, childer** *pl.*, **chyldryn** *gen. pl.*) child; **childgered** *adj.* boyish, high-spirited, *G* 86
chylled *pa.t.* grew cold
chymbled *pp.* muffled up
chymné, chemné *n.* fireplace; chimney, *G* 798
chyne *n.* chine, backbone, *G* 1354
chyn(ne) *n.* chin
chysly, chesly *adv.* dearly, solicitously, *Cl* 543, *G* 850n
chyst, ciences, cité *see* **kyst(e), syence, ceté**
clad *pa.t. & pp.* dressed, covered
clam(be) *see* **clym**
clamberande *presp.*, **clambred** *pp.* clustering, crowding

clanly(ch) *adv.* purely, chastely, *Cl* 264, 1089; neatly, *Cl* 310; completely, wholly, *Cl* 1327, *G* 393; courteously. *Cl* 1621; radiantly *or* chastely, *Pe* 2

clanner *see* **clene**

clannes(se), Clannesse *n.* cleanness, purity; Purity (*personified*), *Pat* 32

claryoun *n.* clarion

clater *v.* clatter, rattle, crash; splash, echo, *G* 731

clawres *n.* claws

clay *n.* clay; clay wall, *Cl* 1618

clay-daubed *adj.* plastered with clay

clayme, clem *v.* claim

cleche *v.* (**cleȝt** *pa.t.*) obtain, *Cl* 12; hold, fasten, *Cl* 858; hold fast, *Cl* 1655; **c. to** seize. *See also* **clyȝt**

clef, cleȝt, clem *see* **cleue, cleche, clayme**

cleme *v.* plaster, daub, *Cl* 312

clene *adj. & adv.* (**clener, clanner** *compar.*) clean, pure, chaste; bright, fair, (*sometimes blended with pure*), *Pe* 227, 289, 737, *etc.*, *Cl* 792, *etc.*, *G* 158, 576, *etc.*; fine, *Cl* 119; exact, *Cl* 1731; *adv.* cleanly; neatly, skilfully, perfectly, *Cl* 1382, *G* 792; completely, *Pe* 754(?), *Cl* 1606, *G* 146, 161, 1298, *etc.*; righteously, *Cl* 1287; plainly, *Pe* 949; *compar. adv.* more perfectly, *Cl* 1100

clenge *v.* cling; shrink, *G* 505 (*cf.* **clynge**)

clente *pp.* (riveted); enclosed, *Pe* 259

clepe *v.* call

cler(e) *adj. & adv.* (**cler(r)er** *compar.*, **clerest** *superl.*) clear, bright; fair, lovely (*& as n.*); pure; plain, easily understood, *Cl* 26, 1056; *adv.* clearly

clergye *n.* learning

clerk(k), k- *n.* priest, scholar; physician, *Pe* 1091; choirman, *G* 64

clernes *n.* beauty, splendour

clerrer *see* **cler(e)**

clepe *v.* clothe, dress

cleue *v.* (**clef, cleuen** *pa.t.*, **clouen** *pp.*) split (asunder); rise sheer, *Pe* 66

clobbez, clomben *see* **klubbe, clym**

Clopyngnel *n.* Clopinel, i.e. Jean de Meun, *Cl* 1057n

clos(e) *adj. & adv.* close, fast; enclosed, *Cl* 12, 1070; closed, *Pe* 183; secret, *Cl* 512; tight, secure, *Pe* 512

clos *n.* enclosure, house

close *v.* enclose; contain, *Pe* 271, *G* 1298; encircle, *G* 186; close, fasten, *Pe* 803, *Cl* 1569, *G* 572, 1742; set, *Pe* 2; **closed fro** free from, *G* 1013

closet *n.* closed pew

clot *n.* clod, earth; mound, hill, *Pe* 789

cloþ(e) *n.* cloth; tablecloth; canvas, sail, *Pat* 105; *pl.* (table-)cloths, coverings; clothes, garments; bed-clothes, *Cl* 1788, *G* 1184

cloþed *pp.* dressed, clothed

cloude, clouen *see* **clowde, cleue**

cloutes, clowtez *n.* pieces, shreds

clowde, cloude *n.* cloud

cloyster, -or *n.* castle bailey, *G* 804; city, city wall, *Pe* 969

cluchche *v.* bend, *Cl* 1541n

clutte *adj.* patched

clyde *n.* plaster

clyff(e), klyf(f)e *n.* cliff, crag, hillside

clyȝt *pa.t.* held, *Cl* 1692. *See also* **cleche**

clyket *n.* latch

clym, klymbe *v.* (**clam(be), clomben** *pa.t.*) climb

clynge *v.* waste away, *Pe* 857

clyppe *v.* fasten

clypper *n.* shearer, *Pe* 802

clyue(n), clyuy *v.* stick, cling (together); pertain, belong, *Pe* 1196

cnawe *see* **knaw(e)**

cnawyng *n.* understanding

cnes *see* **kne**

cnoke, knokke *v.* knock, *Pe* 727; strike, *G* 414

cnowen *see* **knaw(e)**

cof *adj. & adv.* quick; quickly

coke, kok *n.* cock(erel)

cokrez *n.* leggings

colde *see* **co(o)lde**

cole *adj. & adv.* cool(ly)

cole *n.* coal, *Cl* 456

colen *v.* cool, assuage

coler *n.* collar

colored *pp.* coloured

colo(u)r *n.* colour; hue (whiteness), *Pe* 215; (white) complexion, *Pe* 22, 753, *G* 944

coltour *n.* coulter

colwarde *n.* malice

com *see* **com(me)**

comaund, cu- *v.* command; commend, *G* 2411

comaundement *n.* command

combraunce *n.* difficulty

combre *v.* destroy

come *n.* coming, *Pe* 1117; return, *Cl* 467, 1706

come(n) *see also* **com(me)**

comende *v.* commend

comfort(e), coum-, cum-, coumforde *n.* comfort, relief, consolation; pleasure, *Cl* 459, 512, *Pat* 264, 485, *G* 1011, 1221, 1254

comfort *v.* amuse, *G* 1099; console, *G* 2513

comly(ch), cumly *adj. & adv.* (**comloker, -est** *compar. & superl.*) comely, fair, fine; proper, *Cl* 512; *as n.* noble (fair) one, *Pe* 775, *G* 674, 1755, 1794; *adv.* beautifully, fairly; **comlyly, comly(che)** *adv.* fittingly, *G* 360, 648, *etc.*; courteously, *G* 1307, *etc.*

com(me), cum *v.* (**com(e)(n)** *pa.t.*, **com(m)en, cum(m)en** *pp.*) come, arrive, go

commune *adj.* belonging in common

comparisunez *v.* compares

compas *n.* circuit, path, *Pe* 1072; shape, figure, *G* 944; compass, limits, *Cl* 1057; measure, *Cl* 319

compas *v.* (**compast** *pa.t.*) devise, plan; ponder, *Cl* 1196

companyny(e), compeyny *n.* company

comynes *n.* common people

con, cunen *v.* (**cowþe, couth, couþe** *pa.t. & pp.*) be able, can, know how (to). *See also* **next**

con, can *auxil. v. (orig. fr. [be-]gan, confused w. prec.)* did, *Pe* 78n, 81, 88, *etc.*, *Cl* 301, 344, 363, *etc.*, *Pat* 10, 138, *etc.*, *G* 230, 275, 340, *etc.*; cowþe *pa.t. of* con *v. used in same way G* 2273; con + *inf. = pres. tense Pe* 271, 495, 509, *etc.*; conez *pres2s. Pe* 482, 909, 925

conable *adj.* excellent

conciens, -ce *n.* mind, *G* 1196; conviction, *Pe* 1089

condelstik *see* candelstik

conez *see* con *auxil. v.*

confourme *v.* conform; c. þe to model yourself upon, *Cl* 1067

connyng, coning *n.* learning; *pl.* branches of learning, *Cl* 1611

conquerd *pa.t.* won

conquest *pp.* conquered, *Cl* 1305

consayue *v.* conceive

constrayne *v.* force

conterfete *see* co(u)nterfete

contraré, -y *adj.* contrary; unnatural, *Cl* 266; as *n. Cl* 4; in c. of opposite, *Cl* 1532

contray, co(u)ntré, cuntré *n.* country, region; bi c. across country, *G* 734

controeued *pa.t.* contrived

contryssyon *n.* contrition

conueye(n) *v.* accompany, conduct; follow, *Cl* 768; escort to gate, *G* 596

conysaunce *n.* cognisance, badge

co(o)lde *adj.* (calder *compar.*, *Pe* 320) cold; lacking in zeal, *Cl* 1231; melancholy, *Pat* 264, *G* 1982; chilling, grievous, *Pe* 50, 808; as *n.* cold, *G* 505, *etc.*, (wintry) ground, *G* 2474; in hot and c. through thick and thin, *G* 1844; *adv.* sadly, *Pat* 382

coostez *see* cost(e)

cop(e)rounes *n.* tops, finials

corage *n.* heart

corbel, corbyal *n.* raven

cordes *n.* ropes

coro(u)nde *pa.t. & pp.* crowned

c(o)roun(e), crowne *n.* crown, diadem; top of head, *G* 419, 616; cincture, *Cl* 1275, 1444n

cors, cource, course *n.*[1] course, *Cl* 264; course (of a meal) *Cl* 1418 (*pl.*), *G* 116, 135

cors(e) *n.*[2] body; mi c., his c. me, him, *Cl* 683n, *G* 1237n

corsed *pa.t. & pp.* cursed

corsour *n.* horse, charger

corsyes *n.* corrosives

cort, court(e), kort *n.* court

cort(a)yn *n.* bed-curtain; cortyned *pp.* curtained, *G* 1181

cortays(e), cortez *adj.* courteous, gracious, fair; as *n.* gracious one, *Pe* 481, *Cl* 1097, *G* 2411; -ly *adv.* courteously, graciously

cortaysy(e), -sé *see* co(u)rtaysy(e)

cortel, kyrtel *n.* kirtle, gown

cortez *see* cortays(e)

cort-ferez *n.* fellow courtiers

cortyn *see* cort(a)yn

coruen, coruon *see* kerue

coruppte *adj.* corrupt

cosse *n.* kiss

cost *n.*[1] nature, *G* 546; contrivance, *Cl* 1478; *pl.*

qualities, *Cl* 1024, *G* 1272, 1849; manners, *G* 944, 1483; actions, *G* 2360; observances, *G* 750; c. of care hardships, *G* 2495

cost(e), koste *n.*[2] (costese, coostez *pl.*, *Cl* 460, 1033) coast; region; shore

costoum *n.* custom

cosyn *n.* cousin (nephew), *G* 372

cote *n.* coat, tunic; surcoat, *G* 637, 2026 (= cote-armure, *G* 586n)

coþe *pa.t.* quoth, said

couacles, couaclez *n.* covers (of cups)

couardise, cowardise, coward(d)yse *n.* cowardice

couenaunt, -aunde *n.* covenant, agreement, contract; *pl.* conditions

couered *pa.t. & pp.* covered

couerto(u)r *n.* caparison (ornamental cloth covering for horse's trappings) *G* 602; counterpane, *G* 855, 1181

couetyse *n.* avarice

coueyte *v.* covet, desire

coumforde, -fort *see* comfort(e)

coundue *v.* conduct

coundutes *n.* part-songs, *G* 1655n

counsayl, counse(y)l *n.* counsel, advice; plan, purpose

counte *v.* count; reckon, consider

countenance *n.* expression, *Cl* 792, *G* 335; custom, *G* 100; favour, approval, *G* 1490, 1539 *pl.* looks, *G* 1659

co(u)nterfete *v.* feign; imitate; dotz hem vus to c. liken them to us, *Pe* 556

countes *n.* countess, *Pe* 489

co(u)ntré *see* contray

couple, cupple *n.* couple, pair, *Cl* 333; leash, *G* 1147

course, cource *see* cors *n.*[1]

court(e) *see* cort

co(u)rtaysy(e), -sé *n.* courtesy, chivalry; *fig.* goodness, moral virtue, generosity, (divine) grace, *Pe* 432, 444, *etc.*, *Cl* 13, *Pat* 417

cout *v.* cut

couth *see* con

couþe *pp.adj.* known; manifest, *G* 1490

couþ(e) *see also* con

couþly *adv.* familiarly

covhous *n.* cow-shed

cowpes *see* cuppe

cowpled *pa.t.* leashed in pairs, *G* 1139

cowters *n.* elbow-pieces

cowþe(z) *see* con

cowwardely *adv.* basely, disgracefully

coynt, k-, qu-, quaynt *adj.* skilfully made; beautiful, *Cl* 871; skilful, *Pe* 889; wise, *Pat* 417; wise, fastidious, *Cl* 160, *G* 1525; -ly(ch) *adv.* gracefully, daintily; cleverly, *G* 2413

coyntyse, koynt-, quaynt-, quoynt-, -is(e) *n.* wisdom, skill; fine dress, *Cl* 54; Koyntyse (person.) Wisdom; *Pe* 690n

crabbed *adj.* harsh, *G* 502; perverse, *G* 2435

craft(e) *n.* artistry, (display of) skill; power, *Pat* 131; wisdom, *Cl* 13; practice, way, method, *Cl* 697, 865; *pl.* arts, powers; deeds, *Cl* 549; sports, *G* 1688

crafty *adj.* skilfully made

craftyly *adv.* skilfully
crag(g)e *n.* crag
crak, krak *n.* blast, blare
crakkande *presp.* ringing
crakkyng *n.* blaring
crapayn *n.* churl, boor
craue *v.* ask (for), beg (for); claim, *G* 1384
Creato(u)r *n.* Creator
Crede *n.* Apostle's Creed
crepe *v.* creep
cresped *pp.* curled
cresse *n.* cress; **not a c.** not a jot
creste *n.* mountain-top, *G* 731; crest, (heraldic) device, *Pe* 856
creuisse *n.* fissure
criande *see* **crye**
croked *adj.* hooked, curve, *Cl* 1697; crooked, out of true, *G* 653; dishonest, *Cl* 181
crokez *n.* sickles
cronez *n.* cranes
cropure, cropore *n.* crupper
Cros Kryst Christ's Cross
crossayl *n.* cross-sail, square-sail (a mainsail placed square across the ship)
croukez *v.* croaks
croun, crowne *see* **c(o)roun(e)**
croys *n.* cross
crue *pa.t.*, **crowen** *pp.* crowed
cruppelez *n.* cripples
cry(e), kry *n.* cry; proclamation, *Cl* 1574; blast, *G* 1166
crye, k- *v.* (**criande** *presp.*) cry (out), call; give tongue, *G* 1701; proclaim, *Cl* 1361, 1751; plead for, *Cl* 394; weep, *Cl* 1080, *G* 760; resound, *Cl* 1210
crysolyt *n.* chrysolite
crysopase *n.* chrysoprase
Cryst(es), Cryst(en)masse *see* **Kryst(e)**
cubit, cupyd *n.* cubit
cum, cum(m)en *see* **com(me)**
cumaundez, cumfort, cumly, cunen, cuntré *see* **comaund, comfort(e), comly(ch), con, contray**
cupborde *n.* sideboard
cuppe, cowpe, k- *n.* cup
cupple, cupydez *see* **couple, cubit**
cure *n.* care
curious, kyryous *adj.* rare, exquisite; skilful, *Cl* 1452; fastidious, *Cl* 1109
cyté, cyty *see* **ceté**

dabate *see* **debate**
dazed *pa.t.* dawned
dale *n.* dale, valley (bottom)
dalt(en), daly *see* **dele, daylye**
dalyaunce *n.* courtly conversation
Dalyda *n.* Delilah
dam *n.* (pool); stream, water, *Pe* 324; water, flood, *Cl* 416, *Pat* 312
dame, Dame *n.* lady, Lady; ladies, *G* 1316
dampned *pp.* condemned, *Pe* 641
dampped *pp.* **stifled**, *Cl* 989 (*cf. also* **dampned**)
damvsel(le) *n.* damsel, young lady
Danyel, Daniel *n.* Daniel
dar(e) *v.*[1] (**durst, dorst(e)(n)** *pa.t.*) dare

dare *v.*[2] shrink, cower, *G* 315, 2258; bow down, submit, *Pe* 609, 839
Dary(o)us *n.* Darius
dasande *presp.adj.* dazing, stupefying
daschande *adj.* dashing, rushing
dased *pa.t. & pp.* lay dazed, *Pat* 383; *pp.adj.* dazed, *Pe* 1085
date *n.* limit, *Pe* 493; (point of) time, *Pe* 504, 529, *Cl* 425; beginning, *Pe* 516, 517; end, *Pe* 528, 540, 541; date, *Pe* 1040; season, *Pe* 505; rank, *Pe* 492
daube *v.* daub, plaster
Dauid, -yth *n.* David
daunce, -se *v.* dance; leap, writhe, *Pe* 345
daunger *n.* danger; fear, *Cl* 342; power, *Pat* 110; coldness, insolence, *Cl* 71; (state of) deprivation, *Pe* 250
daunsyng *n.* dancing
dawande *adj.* dawning
dawed, dawez *see* **dowe, day**
day(e) *n.* (**dayez, dawez** *pl.*) day, daylight; **in d.** ever, *G* 80; (**vpon**) **dayez** (*gen.*) in the day, *G* 1072, by day, *Cl* 578; **out of dawez** out of existence, *Pe* 282 (*see* **do**); **dayez of ende** last days, days of Judgement, *Cl* 1032; **dayez** for the duration, *Cl* 520
day-glem *n.* light of day (i.e. sun), *Pe* 1094
daylye, daly *v.* converse, flirt; speak, *Pe* 313
daylyzt *n.* daylight
daynté, daynty(e) *n.* honour, courtesy; delight (in), *G* 1889; *pl.* luxuries, delicacies; *adj.* charming, *G* 1253
day-rawe *n.* dawn, first light of day
debate, da- *n.* resistance; contention, *Pe* 390
debonere *adj.* gracious in manner
debonerté *n.* courtesy, graciousness; meekness, *Pe* 798
dece, des(e) *n.* dais; throne, *Pat* 119
declar *v.* interpret
declyne *v.* fall (from prosperity), *Pe* 333; **d. into acorde** come to an agreement, *Pe* 509
decre *n.* decree
ded *see* **do, ded(e)**
dedayn *n.* indignation
ded(e) *adj.* dead; *as n. Cl* 1096; **D. See** Dead Sea
dede *n.* deed, act, activity, work; action, *Pe* 481
defence *n.* prohibition, *Cl* 243, 245; circumspection, *G* 1282
defende *v.* defend; forbid, *G* 1156
defoule *n.* defilement, *Pat* 290
defowle *v.* defile, pollute
degré *n.* rank; *pl.* steps, *Pe* 1022
deze, dize, dyze(n) *v.* die
dezt(t)er(e)(s) *see* **dozter**
dekenes *n.* deacons
dele *v.* (**dalt(en)** *pa.t.*, **dalt, deled** *pp.*) deal (out), mete out; bestow (on), *G* 1266, 1805; utter, deliver, *Cl* 344, 1641; perform, execute, *Cl* 1756, *G* 2192; associate, *Cl* 137; behave (towards), *G* 1662; converse, *G* 1668; partake of, *G* 1968; exchange, buy, *Cl* 1118; **d. drury wyth** exchange love with, have the love of; **d. vntyztel** behave freely, let oneself go
del(e) *see also* **doel, deuel**

delful, dulful *adj.* sorrowful, grievous; **-ly** *adv.* *Pe* 706

delit, delyt *n.* delight, joy, pleasure; desire; **la3t d.** conceived a wish, *Pe* 1128

deliuer, delyuer *adj.* quick, nimble, *G* 2243; delivered, *Cl* 1084; **-ly** *adv.* quickly, nimbly, *G* 2009

delyuer *v.* release, save; despatch, *G* 1414; destroy, *Cl* 286; assign, *G* 851

demay *reflex.v.* be perturbed, *G* 470

deme *v.* judge, consider, assess, think fit; expect, *Pe* 336; ordain, *Pe* 348; condemn, *Pe* 325; censure, *Pe* 349; agree, *G* 1089, 1668; allow, *Pe* 324; decree, declare, *Cl* 110, 1745, *Pat* 386, 432; utter, *Pat* 119; speak (of), say, *Pe* 337, 361, 1183, *G* 2183

demerlayk *n.* magic; **demorlaykes** *pl.* phantoms

demme *v.* be baffled, *Pe* 223; fill (with water), *Cl* 384

dene *n.* valley

denez ax *n.* Danish axe, battle-axe, *G* 2223 (*see G* 288*n*)

denned *pa.t.* lurked, lay deep, *Pe* 51

denounced *pp.* proclaimed, *Cl* 106*n*

departe *v.* depart, *Cl* 396, 1677; part, *G* 1983; separate, part, divide, *Pe* 378, *Cl* 1074, 1738, *G* 1335; **departyng** *n.* parting, *G* 1798

depaynt(ed) *pp.* painted, portrayed; adorned, *Pe* 1102

depe *adj. & adv.* deep(ly); great, profound, *Cl* 1425, 1609; intense (whiteness of complexion), *Pe* 215; *as n.* depths, *Pe* 109; sea, *Pat* 235, 263, *etc.*

deprece *v.*[1] release, *G* 1219

deprece, depres(e) *v.*[2] subjugate, *G* 6; press, *G* 1770; drive away, *Pe* 778

depryue *v.* take away, dispossess

dere *adj.*[1] (**derrest** *superl.*) dear, beloved, *Pe* 368, 758, 795, *Cl* 52, 814, *G* 470, 754; precious, *Pe* 1183, 1208, *Cl* 698, *etc.*, *G* 121, 193, *etc.*; private, privy, *Cl* 683; essential, *Cl* 1604; noble, worthy, splendid, *Pe* 72, 85, 97, 121, *etc.*; exalted, *Pe* 492; festal, *G* 92, 1047; pleasant, pleasing, *Pe* 400, 880, *G* 47, 564, *etc.*; intimate, *G* 2449; good, right, *Pe* 504; dear(ly), *Pe* 733; *as n.* noble one(s), *Pe* 777, *Cl* 1394, 1399, *G* 678, 928; *superl.* most precious, *Cl* 1118; noblest, *Cl* 115, 1306, *G* 445; **derrest** *adv.* most nobly, *G* 483

dere *adj.*[2] severe, harsh, *Cl* 214

der(e) *n.* deer

dere *v.* harm, hurt, *Pe* 1157, *Cl* 862, *G* 1460

derely *adv.* courteously, in courtly style; deeply, *G* 1842; splendidly, *Pe* 995; extremely, gloriously, *Cl* 270

derez *n.* injuries, hindrances; **did me d.** put obstacles in my way, *Pe* 102

derf, derue *adj.* bold, strong; loud, fierce, *Cl* 862; painful, *G* 558, 564; dreadful, *G* 1047; **-ly** *adv.* boldly, quickly; ?wickedly, *Cl* 1518

derk *adj.* dark; *as n.* darkness, *Pe* 629, *Cl* 1755, *Pat* 263

derne *adj.* secret, hidden; confidential, *G* 1012; profound; *Cl* 1611; *as n.* secret, *Pat* 182; *adv.* secretly, *Cl* 697; **-ly** *adv.* secretly

derrest *see* **dere** *adj.*[1]

derþe *n.* glory, splendour, *Pe* 99

derue(ly) *see* **derf**

derworth *adj.* splendid, *Pe* 109; **derworþly** *adv.* sumptuously, *G* 114

des(e) *see* **dece**

deseuered *pp.* separated, *Pat* 315

des(s)ert(e) *see* **dis(s)ert**

dessypelez *n.* disciples, *Pe* 715

destyné, destiné *n.* destiny, fate

desyre, dezyre *v.* desire

determynable *adj.* incontrovertible, *Pe* 594

deþe, deth(e) *n.* death

deuaye, -v- *v.* refuse

deue *v.* strike down

deuel, dele *n.* devil

deuely *adj.* desolating, *Pe* 51

deuice *see* **deuise**

deuine *n.* prophet, diviner

deuine *v.* interpret

deuinores *n.* diviners

deuise, -ce, deuyse, -v- *v.* contemplate, *Pe* 1129; conceive, *Cl* 1046; devise, *Cl* 1100, 1288; explain, expound, *Cl* 1157, 1325, *etc.*; describe, *Pe* 99, 984, 995, 1021; relate, *G* 92; order, *Cl* 110; appoint, *Cl* 238

deuocioun *n.* devotion

deuote, deuout *adj.* devoted, devout

deuoutly, dewoutly *adv.* devoutly, reverently

deuoyde, -v-, -w- *v.* dispel, *Pe* 15; destroy, annihilate, *Cl* 908; withdraw, forgo, *Pat* 284

deuys(e), n. division, *Pe* 139; **a d.** as fine as one could think, perfect, *G* 617; **at my d.** in my opinion, to my wish, *Pe* 199

deuyse *see* **deuise**

deuysement *n.* description

devaye *see* **deuaye**

devised, devyse(d) *see* **deuise**

devoyde *see* **deuoyde**

devoydynge *n.* destroying

dew(e) *n.* dew

dewoutly, dewoyde *see* **deuoutly, deuoyde**

dewyne, do- *v.* languish, pine away, *Pe* 11, 326

dezyre *see* **desyre**

dialokez *n.* discourses

diamauntez *n.* diamonds

dich(es) *see* **dych(e)**

did(en) *see* **do**

diete *n.* food

di3e *see* **de3e**

di3t, dy3t(t) *v.* (**di3t, dy3t** *pa.t.*, **dy3t(e)** *pp.*) ordain, appoint; dispose, *Pe* 360; dress, adorn, *Pe* 202, 987, *Cl* 1688, 1753; prepare, *Cl* 632, *G* 1559, 1689, 2223; serve, *Cl* 818; set, place, *Pe* 920, *Cl* 699, 1794, *G* 114; *reflex.* direct oneself, *G* 994; **d. to deþe** put to death, *Cl* 1266

dille, dylle *adj.* stupid, *G* 1529; slow, *Pe* 680

dint *see* **dynt**

diptez, dipped *pa.t.* dipped, plunged

disceuer, discouer, dys- *v.* reveal, disclose

discrye *v.* discern

dishes *see* **dysche**

dispayred *adj.* in despair

dispit, dyspyt *n.* resistance, defiance

displayed *pa.t.* *intrans.* separated, was exposed; *pp.* displayed, revealed
displese, dys- *v.* displease; be displeased, *Cl* 1494; *reflex.* be offended, *Pe* 422, *G* 1839, 2439
disport *n.* pleasure
dispoyled *pp.* stripped, *Pat* 95; divested, *G* 860
dispyse *v.* treat with scorn, abuse
disserne *v.* distinguish
dis(s)ert, des(s)ert(e) *n.* desert, merit; **for d. of** in recompense for, *Pat* 84
disserue *v.* deserve, *Cl* 613, *G* 452, 1779, 1803
distresed *pa.t.subjunc.* would have harassed, *Cl* 880
distres(se), disstrye *see* **dys(s)tresse, dys(s)trye**
ditte *v.* (**dutte** *pa.t.*, **dit** *pp.*) close, shut, fasten; **dutande** *presp.adj.* fitting
diuinité *n.* learning in divinity, *Cl* 1609
do *n.* doe, *Pe* 345
do *v.* (**dos, dotz** *pres.*, **ded, did(en), dyd, dyt** (*Pe* 681) *pa.t.*, **don(e)** *pp.*) do, make, cause; put, *Pe* 250, 282, 366, 1042, *Cl* 1224, 1801, *G* 478; give, pay, *Pe* 424; have, cause to (be), *Pat* 443, *G* 1327; *reflex.* go, *G* 1308; *pp.* finished, *G* 928, 1365; ruined, *Cl* 989; **d. (a)way** stop, put an end to, *Pe* 718, 823, *Cl* 286, 862, *G* 1492; **d. down of** put down from, *Cl* 1801; **d. out of dawez** annihilate, *Pe* 282; **d. pyne** take trouble, *Pe* 511
dobler *n.* large plate; **dubleres** *pl.*
doc *see* **duk**
do(e)l, del(e) *n.* sorrow, grief, lamentation
doel-doungoun *n.* dungeon of sorrow, *Pe* 1187
doel-dystresse sorrow of grief, grief-and-sorrow, *Pe* 337
dogge *n.* dog
doȝter *n.* (**deȝt(t)er(e)s, doȝterez** *pl.*) daughter
doȝty *see* **duȝty**
dok *n.* tuft (of tail and forelock), *G* 193
dol *see* **do(e)l**
dole *see* **dool(e)**
dom(e) *n.* judgement, decre; trial; doom, *Pat* 203; command, *Cl* 632; award, *Pe* 580; right, *G* 295; mind, *Pe* 157, *Cl* 1046; **domezday** *n.* doomsday
don(e) *see* **do** *v.*
donkande *presp.adj.* moistening
dool(e), dole *n.* part, *Pe* 136, *Cl* 216, *G* 719; intercourse, *Cl* 699
dor(e) *n.* door
dorst(e)(n) *see* **dar(e)** *v.*¹
dos *see* **do** *v.*
doser *n.* tapestry, backcloth
dotage *n.* folly, madness
dote *v.* be demented, behave foolishly; be astonished, *Cl* 852; **doted** *pp.adj.* foolish, demented, *Pat* 196, *G* 1956; frenzied, *G* 1151
dotel *n.* fool
dotz *see* **do** *v.*
doublefelde *adv.* in double helpings, *G* 890
doumbe *adj.* dumb
doun *adv. & prep.* down
doun, down *n.* hill
doungoun *n.* dungeon

doured *pa.t.* grieved
dousour *n.* sweetness, *Pe* 429
doute *n.* fear, *G* 246, 442; doubt, *Pe* 928; **douteles** *adj.* doubtless
d(o)uth(e), -þe *n.* company of men; host, *Pe* 839; **þe d.** men, mankind, *Cl* 270, 597
douue *see* **dowue**
dowe *v.* (**dawed, dowed** *pa.t.*) avail, *Pat* 50, *Cl* 374; *pa.t.subjunc.* would be worth, *G* 1805
d(o)welle *v.* dwell, remain
down *see* **doun**
dowrie *n.* dowry
dowue, douue *n.* dove
dowyne *see* **dewyne**
draȝe, draw(e), drowe *v.* (**droȝ(en)** *pa.t.* **drawen** *pp.*) draw, pull; bring, *Pe* 699, 1116, *Cl* 1160; shut, *G* 1188, 1233; carry on, bring home, *G* 1647; move, go, *Cl* 500, 1329, 1394; **d. on lyte (allyt), d. on dryȝe (adreȝ)** hold back, *Cl* 71, 599, *G* 1031, 1463
draȝt *n.* drawbridge, *G* 817; *pl.* **draȝtes** characters, marks, *Cl* 1557
draueled *pa.t.* muttered
draw(e)n *see* **draȝe**
drechch *n.* delay
dred(e) *n.* dread, fear; **wythouten d.** without doubt; **dredles** *adj.* fearless
drede *v.* (**dred** *pa.t.*) fear, be afraid
dreȝ(e)(d), dreȝly *see* **dryȝ(e), adj. & v.**
drem(e) *n.* dream(ing); vision, *Pe* 790
drepe *v.* slay, kill, destroy
dres(se) *v.* arrange, assign, position, place; serve, *Cl* 1518; ordain, *Pe* 495; derive, *Pe* 860; direct, *G* 445; proceed, *G* 474 (*reflex.*), 1415; get up, *G* 566, 2009; **vpon grounde hym dresses** takes his stand, *G* 417
dreue *v.* make one's way, *Pe* 323, 980
drink(ez) *see* **drynk**
driuen, drof *see* **dryue**
droȝ(en) *see* **draȝe**
droȝþe *n.* drought
dronk(k)en *adj.* drunk
drop(p)e *v.* drop; **droppande** *presp.adj.* flowing, *Pat* 383
drounde *see* **drowne**
droupyng, drowping *n.* slumber, heaviness
drouy *adj.* turbid
drowe *see* **draȝe**
drowne *v.* (**drowned, drounde** *pa.t.* **drowned** *pp.*) drown
drowping *see* **droupyng**
drury(e), drwry(e) *n.* love, love-making; love-token, *G* 1805, 2033
druye *see* **drye**
drwry *adj.* cruel, *Pe* 323
drwry(e) *see also* **drury(e)**
drye, druye, dryȝe *adj.* dry, *Cl* 385, 412, 460, 1096; *as n.* (dry) land, *Cl* 472, *Pat* 338
dryed *pp.* dried, *Cl* 496
dryf *see* **dryue**
dryftes *n.* snowdrifts
dryȝ(e), dreȝ *adj. & adv.* heavy, great, *Pe* 823, *Cl* 342; deep, *G* 1750; straight, unmoved, *G* 335; long-suffering, *G* 724; incessant, *G* 1460; **draȝe on d.** detain, *G* 1031; **-ly(ch)** *adv.* angrily, *Cl* 74; solemnly, *Cl* 344; incessantly,

continually, *Pe* 125, *Cl* 476, *G* 1026; relentlessly, *Pat* 235; utterly, *Pe* 223

dryȝe(e), dreȝe *v.* suffer, endure

dryȝe *see also* **drye**

Dryȝt(t)yn *n.* God, the Lord

drynk, drink *n.* drink

drynk *v.* (**drank** *pa.t.*) drink

dryue, dryf *v.* (**drof** *pa.t.*, **driuen, -y-** *pa.t. & pp.*) drive; hurtle, *Cl* 416, *G* 1151, 2263; pour (in), *Pe* 1153, *Pat* 312, *G* 121; fly, *Cl* 472; rise, *Cl* 692; strike, *G* 389; sink, *Pe* 30, 1094; pass (time), *G* 1176, 1468; make, *G* 558, 1020; *pp.* brought, *Pe* 1194; hammered, *Cl* 313; **d. out** proclaim, *Pat* 386; **d. to** press against, *G* 786, 1999; make for, *G* 222; come to, *Cl* 219; strike, *Cl* 1425

dubbed, -et *pp.* dressed, arrayed; adorned, decorated

dubbement(e), dubleres *see* **(a)dubbement(e), dobler**

dublet *n.* doublet, jacket

Duches *n.* Duchess

due *adj.* due, *Pe* 894; inevitable, *Pat* 49

duȝty, -o- *adj.* bold, brave; *as n.* *G* 2334

duk, doc *n.* duke, ruler

dulful, delful *adj.* sorrowful, grievous

dumpe *v.* plunge

dungen *see* **dyngez**

dunne *adj.* dun, *Pe* 30

dunt(e) *see* **dynt**

durande *presp.adj.* lasting, *Pe* 336

dure *v.* continue, last; live, survive, *Pat* 488

durst *see* **dar(e)** *v.*[1]

dusched *pa.t.* rushed

dust(e) *n.* dust

dut *n.* merriment, *G* 1020

dutande, duthe *see* **ditte, doupe**

dut(te) *pa.t.* feared

dutte *see also* **ditte**

dwellez *see* **d(o)welle**

dych(e), dich *n.* ditch

dyd, dyȝe(n) *see* **do** *v.*, **deȝe**

dyȝt(e), dyȝttez *see* **diȝt**

dylle *see* **dille**

dymly *adv.* gloomily

dym(me) *adj.* dark; dim, *Pe* 1076

dyn(e) *n.* noise; report, *Cl* 692; tumult, complaining, *Pe* 339, *Cl* 862; sound of revelry, *G* 47

dynge *v.* (**dungen** *pa.t.pl.*) strike

dyngne *adj.* noble, worthy

dyngneté *n.* high office

dynt, dint, dunt(e) *n.* blow

dysche *n.* dish; **disches** *pl.*

dyscouered *see* **disceuer**

dyscreuen *v.* see, discern, *Pe* 68

dysheriete *v.* disinherit

dysplese(s), dyspyt *see* **displese, dispit**

dyssente *v.* descend, *Pe* 627

dys(s)tresse, distres(se) *n.* sorrow, distress; constraint, *Pe* 898; force, violence, *Cl* 1160

dys(s)trye, disstrye *v.* destroy; end, *Pe* 124

dyt *see* **do** *v.*

Ebru *adj.* Hebrew

edé *adj.* (*as n.*) blessed, *Cl* 1717*n*

Effraim *n.* Ephraim

eft(e) *adv.* again, once more; later; back, *Pat* 143; next time, *G* 898, 2388; likewise, *Cl* 562, 1073, *G* 641

eftersones, eftsonez *adv.* again

egge *n.* edge; ridge, *Cl* 451; sword, blade, *Cl* 1104, 1246; blade, weapon, *G* 2392

eggyng *n.* egging, instigation

eke *adv.* also

elde(e) *n.* age; old age, *Cl* 657, *Pat* 125; generation, time, *G* 1520

ellez, elles *adv. & conj.* else; besides; otherwise, *Pe* 32, 724, *G* 1082; provided that, *Cl* 466, 705, *G* 295; *as n.* anything else, *Pat* 2

elngerde *n.* measuring-stick of 45 ins. (one ell)

em(e) *n.* uncle

emerad(e) *n.* emerald

emperise *n.* empress, *Pe* 441

emperour *n.* emperor

empyre, empire *n.* empire, imperial rule; control, *Cl* 540

enaumayld(e) *pp.* enamelled

enbaned *pp.adj.* fortified, *Cl* 1459, *G* 790*n*

embelyse *v.* adorn, grace

enbrauded, -aw-, -en *pp.adj.* embroidered

enchace *v.* urge on

enclose *v.* shut in, *Cl* 334; contain, *Pe* 909

enclyin *adj.* lying prostrate, *Pe* 1206

enclyne *v.* bow, *Pe* 236, *G* 340; sink, *Pe* 630; *pp.* inclined, *Cl* 518

encres *v.* increase

encroche *v.* obtain, *Pat* 18; bring, *Pe* 1117

ende *n.* end; **last e.** conclusion, outcome, *Cl* 608; (**vp)on e.** upright, *Cl* 423, at last *Cl* 1329, to death, *Pat* 426; **dayes of e.** last days, *Cl* 1032

ende *v.* end, die

endelez, -s *adj. or adv.* endless(ly), perfect(ly)

endent(e) *pp.* inlaid, set, *Pe* 1012; *fig. Pe* 629

endentur *n.* jointing

end(e)ure *v.* endure; have power (to), *Pe* 225

endite, endyte *v.* ?accuse, condemn, *G* 1600; utter (in song), *Pe* 1126

endored *pp.adj.* gold-adorned, *Pe* 368

ene *adv.* once; **at e.** at once, *Pe* 291; **mad at e.** settled, made certain, *Pe* 953

enfamined *pa.t.* starved

enforse *v.* drive

enfoubled *pp.adj.* swathed

engendered *pa.t.* begot

Englych *adj.* (*as n.*) the English, *G* 629

enherite *v.* inherit

enker *adj.* pure, intense

enlé *adv.* separately, *Pe* 849

enleuenpe *adj.* eleventh

enmy *n.* (**enmyes, enmies** *pl.*) enemy

Ennias *n.* Æneas

en(n)(o)urned *pp.* adorned; set

enourled *pp.* surrounded

enpoysened *pa.t.* poisoned

enpresses, enprecez *v.* oppresses

enpryse *n.* renown

enprysonment *n.* imprisonment

enquest *n.* question

enquylen *v.* obtain

ensens *n.* incense

entayled *pp.* embroidered
entent *n.* resolution
enterludez *n.* interludes, plays, *G* 472*n*
enurned *see* **en(n)(o)urned**
entre, enter *v.* enter
entré *n.* entry
entyse *v.* provoke, *Cl* 1137, 1808; attract, catch (infection), *G* 2436
er(a)nd(e), ar(e)nde *n.* errand, mission, business
erbes, erbez *n.* herbs, grass, plants
erber *n.*[1] gullet, *G* 1330
erber(e) *n.*[2] (herb) garden, *Pe* 9*n*, 38, 1171
erd(e) *n.* land, region; **on e.** on earth, *Cl* 892; *as intensive:* of old, *Cl* 601, *G* 2416, real-life, *G* 27, truly, *G* 140, the best on earth, *G* 881
ere *n.* ear
er(e) *prep., conj. & adv.* before, until; until then, *Pat* 212; first, *Pe* 319; **e. þis** until (before) now; **e. þenne** before
erigaut *n.* herigaut, cloak
erle *n.* earl
erly *adv.* early; **e. and late** all the time, *Pe* 392
Ermonnes *n.* (*gen.*) Hermon's, *Pat* 463
ermyn *n.* ermine
ernd(e) *see* **er(a)nd(e)**
erne-hwed *pp.adj.* eagle-coloured
ernestly *adv.* gravely, seriously, *Cl* 277; sternly, *Cl* 1240
erraunt *adj.* travelling, questing
Errik *n.* Eric
errour *n.* (in) error, *Pe* 422
erþe, vrþe *n.* earth, ground
erytage *see* **(h)erytage**
eschaped *pa.t.* eluded, *Pe* 187
ese *n.* ease, pleasure
est *n. & adj.* east, eastern
etayn *n.* giant
ete *v.* (**et(t)e** *pa.t.*) eat, dine
eþe *adj.* easy
eþe *v.* entreat
Eue *n.* Eve
euel *adj., adv. & n.* evil; *adv.* ill, *Pe* 310, 930; *as n.* sin, *Cl* 573, unpleasantness, *G* 1552
euen *adj. & adv.* even, quits, *G* 1641; *adv.* directly, exactly, straight, right; actually, *G* 2464
euen *n.* eve (*i.e.* day before), *G* 734, 1669
euen *v.* vie, *Pe* 1073
euenden *adv.* right down, *G* 1345
euentyde, -tide *n.* evening
euer(more) *adv.* (for) ever, always, all the time; *intensive:* **er e.** before ever; **e. þe lenger** the longer, *Pe* 180, by however much, *Pe* 600; **wych ... so e.** whichever
euer-ferne *n.* fern
euervch *adj.* every
euesed *pp.* clipped
euez *n.* edge, border, *G* 1178
eweres *n.* water pitchers
Ewrus *n.* Eurus
exellently *adv.* pre-eminently, *G* 2423
exorsismus *n.pl.* incantation, calling up spirits
expoun, expowne *v.* expound, set forth, explain; describe, *Pe* 37, *G* 209; utter, *G* 1506

expounyng *n.* explanation
expresse *adj. or adv.* explicit(ly), *Pe* 910; *adv.* plainly, clearly, *Cl* 1158

face *n.* face; surface, *G* 524. *See also* **bere**
fade *adj.* bold(?), *G* 149
fader *n.* father
fage *n.* deceit; **no f.** in truth, *G* 531
faȝt *see* **fyȝt**
falce, fals(e) *adj.* false; *as n.*, *Cl* 1168
fale *adj.*[1] brownish, dun, *G* 728
fale *adj.*[2] cheap; **f. of** indifferent about, *Pat* 92
falewed *pa.t.* grew pale
falle *v.* (**fel(le), fellen** *pa.t.*, **fallen** *pp.*) fall, sink; go, rush, *Cl* 399, 837, *G* 1425, 1702; die, perish, *Cl* 725, 1684; befall, happen, come, *Cl* 22, 494, *etc.*, *G* 23, 483, 2378, *etc.*; fall (to someone's lot), *Pat* 178, *G* 2243, 2327; befit, *G* 358, 890, 1303, 1358; **f. fro** spring from, *Cl* 685; **f. in** hit upon, *G* 1699; **is fallen forþwyth my face** has presented itself to me, *Cl* 304
fals(e) *see* **falce**
falssyng *n.* deception, *G* 2378
famacions *n.* defamations
famed *pp.* reputed
fande *see* **fynde**
fange, fonge *v.* (**feng** *pa.t.*, **fonge(d)** *pp.*) take, get, receive; welcome, *G*, 816 *etc.*; **f. in fere** sing together, *Pe* 884
fannand *presp.adj.* spreading out like a fan, *G* 181
fannez *v.* flaps, flutters
fantoum *n.* (**fantummes** *pl.*) illusion
farand(e) *adj.* handsome, *Cl* 607; splendid, *Cl* 1758, *G* 101; wonderful, *Pe* 865
farandely *adv.* pleasantly
fare *n.* journey; fortune; track, *G* 1703; behaviour, *Cl* 861, *G* 1116, 2386; bearing, *Pe* 832; food, *G* 694; celebration, *G* 537
fare *v.* (**ferde(n)** *pa.t.*, **faren** *pp.*) go, travel; behave, bear oneself; pass, *Cl* 403; fare, *Cl* 466; behave, happen, *Cl* 1106
Fasor *n.* Creator, *Pe* 431
fasoun *n.* form, *Pe* 983; manner, *Pe* 1101
faste *adj.* firm, binding, *G* 1636
fast(e), fest *adv.* swiftly, quickly; hard, earnestly, insistently, *Pe* 54, 150, *Cl* 936, *G* 1042, 2403; firmly, *Cl* 1147, *G* 782; fast (deeply), *Pat* 192; closely, *Pat* 290; almost, *Cl* 1194; **a(l)s f.** as quickly as possible, immediately
faste *v.* (*pres.subjunc.*) fast, *Pat* 390
fasten, festen *v.* fasten; establish, confirm, *Cl* 327, *G* 1783, 2329; make fast, *Pat* 273
fasure *n.* form
fat *adj.* fattened, *Cl* 627
fatez *v.* fades, *Pe* 1038
fatte *n.* vat, tub, *Cl* 802
fatted *pp.* fattened
faþmez *v.* gropes, *Pat* 273; **faþmed** *pa.t.* embraced, *Cl* 399
faunt *n.* child
fauo(u)r *n.* grace, noble quality, *Pe* 428; favour, *Pe* 968
faure *see* **fawre**

faurty, fo(u)rty *adj.* forty
faut(e), fawte *n.* fault, misdeed, sin; offence, *G* 1551; sinfulness, *G* 2435
fautles, -z *adj.* (**-lest** *superl.*) faultless, perfect
fauty, fawty *adj.* sinful, guilty
fawne *v.* fondle, *G* 1919
fawre, faure, four(r)e, fowre *adj.* four
fawte, fawty *see* **faut(e), fauty**
fax(e) *n.* hair
fay(e) *n.* faith; **in f.** indeed, truly, *Pe* 263; (**par**) **ma f.** by my faith, (on) my word, *Pe* 489, *G* 1495
fayl(y), fayle *v.* (**faylande** *presp.*) fail, fall short; be missing, lacking, *Cl* 737, 1535, *Pat* 181; miss, lack, *G* 278; sink, *Cl* 1758; finish, end, *Cl* 658; fail to be productive, *Pe* 34; grow pale, *Cl* 1539; wither, *Pe* 270; **f. of** miss, fail to obtain, *Pe* 317, *Cl* 889, *G* 1067
fayn *adj.* (**faynest** *superl.*) glad; **f. (of)** pleased to meet, *Cl* 642, *G* 840; *adv.* gladly, dearly, *Cl* 1629; **f. scape wolde** were anxious to escape, *Pat* 155
fayned *pp.adj.* false
fayntyse *n.* fallibility, deceitfulness, *G* 2435
fayr(e) *adj. & adv.* (**fayr(er), feier** *compar.*, **fayrest** *superl.*) *adj.* fair, lovely, fine; courteous, *Cl* 729, *G* 1116; *as n.* **þe fayrer** the upper hand, *G* 99; *adv.* fitly, well; humbly, courteously; precisely, neatly, *Pe* 1024, *Cl* 316, *G* 2309; delightfully, *Pe* 88; reverently, *Cl* 506
fayryȝe *n.* the supernatural, *G* 240
fayth-dedes *n.* deeds of faith
fayth(e), fayþ(e) *n.* belief, religion; (word of) honour, *G* 986, 1783, *etc.*; **in (god) f.** truly
faythful, fayþful *adj.* faithful, religious, *Cl* 1167; trustworthy, *G* 632, 1679
fayþely *adv.* truly, *G* 1636
feb(e)le *adj.* poor, mean; **feblest** *superl.* weakest, *G* 354
fech(e) *v.* (**feched** *pa.t.*, **fette** *pp.*) fetch, bring, receive; seize, *Cl* 1155; deal (a blow), *Pe* 1158; *reflex.* bring upon oneself, *Pat* 58
fedde *pp.adj.* fed (for killing), *Cl* 56
fede *v.* feed, *G* 1359
fede *adj.* faded, *Pe* 29
fee *n.* fee, payment; *pl.* domain, city, *Cl* 960
fe(e)rsley, ferslych *adv.* fiercely, brightly, *G* 832; proudly, haughtily, *G* 329; spiritedly, *G* 1323; sternly, *Pat* 337
feȝt(yng), feier *see* **fyȝt, fayr(e)**
fel *adv.* cruelly, *Cl* 1040
fel *see also* **falle**
felaȝes *n.* fellows, *G* 1702
felaȝschip, -schyp *n.* brotherly love, *G* 652; company, *Cl* 1764, *G* 2151; intercourse, *Cl* 271
felde *n.* field, country
felde *v.* fold, embrace, *G* 841
felde *see also next*
fele *v.*[1] (**felde** *pa.t.*, *Pe* 1087) feel, perceive; taste, *Cl* 107; smell, *Cl* 1019
fele *v.*[2] conceal; (*pa.subjunc.*) were to conceal, *Cl* 914
felle *adj.* fierce, stern, cruel; daring, *G* 291, 874; deadly, *Pe* 655; *as n.* fierce animal, *G* 1585

felle, fele *adj. & pron.* many; **feler** *comp.* more; **felefolde** many times over, *G* 1545
felle *n.*[1] fell, hill, *G* 723
felle *n.*[2] fur, skin
felle(n) *see* **falle**
felly *adv.* fiercely, cruelly
felonye *n.* crime, sin
feloun *n.* wretch
felt *pp.* matted, *Cl* 1689
femed *pa.t.* foamed, *G* 1572
femmalez *n.*(*gen.*) of a female, *Cl* 696
fende *n.* fiend, devil; (the) Devil; (*pl.*) sinners, *Pat* 82
fende *v.* **f. of** ward off, *Cl* 1191
fenden *adj. or n. g. pl.* fiendish, of fiends
feng *see* **fonge**
fenny *adj.* dirty; *fig.* vile, sinful, *Cl* 1113
Fenyx *n.* Phoenix, *Pe* 430
fer *see* **fer(re)**
ferde *pa.t.* feared, *G* 1588
ferd(e) *pp.* frightened, afraid; **for f.** in fear; *see also next*
ferde *n.* fear
ferde(n) *see also* **fare**
fere *adj.* proud, dignified, *G* 103
fere *n.*[1] (show, array); dignity, reward, *Pe* 616; martial array, *G* 267
fere *n.*[2] (company); **in f.** together
fere *n.*[3] companion; wife, *G* 2411; mistress, *Cl* 1062; equal, *G* 676
fereles *adj.* without equal, unique, *Pe* 431*n*
ferez *v.* conveys, takes, *Pe* 98; **feryed** *pp.* brought, carried
ferk(ke) *v.* go (quickly), ride, pass; **f. vp** jump up; **ferkez hym vp** bestirs himself, *G* 2013
ferly *adj.* wonderful; exceptional, *G* 716 (*or n.*); *n.* marvel; amazement, *Pe* 1086
ferlylé *adj.* marvellous, *Cl* 1460
ferly(ly) *adv.* wonderfully, exceedingly, greatly, terribly
fermysoun *n.* close-season, *G* 1156*n*
fer(re) *adv.* far; **fyr** *adj.* distant, *Cl* 1680; **ferre, fire, fyrre** *compar.* farther (*adj. Pe* 148), further, moreover; **f. þen** in excess of, *Pe* 563
fers, fyrce *adj.* proud, bold; fierce, vehement, *Pe* 54
fersly(ch), feryed *see* **fe(e)rsly, ferez**
fest *see also* **fast(e)**
fest(e) *n.* festival, feast; **ma f.** (*lit.* make a festival) rejoice, *Pe* 283
festen(ez) *see* **fasten**
festiual *adj.* befitting a feast, *Cl* 136
festned, -s *see* **fasten**
festres *v.* festers
fet(e) *see* **fot(e)**
fete *n.* (fact); ?deed(s), action(s), *Cl* 1062; **in f.** indeed, *Cl* 1106
feted *pa.t.* behaved, *G* 1282
fetled *see* **fettele**
fetly *adv.* gracefully, neatly
fet(t)e *v.* (**fette** *pp.*) fetch, bring
fette *see also* **fech, fot(e)**
fettele *v.* (**fettled** *pa.t.*, **fet(t)led** *pp.*) prepare; set, fix, *Cl* 585, *G* 656; arrange, *Pat* 38
fetterez, fettres *n.* fetters

fettled *see* **fettele**
fetures, -z *n.* features, parts (of body)
fetys(e) *adj.* well-proportioned, *Cl* 174; **for f.** through skill, *Cl* 1103
fetysely *adv.* skilfully, elegantly
feþer-beddes *n.* feather-beds
fewe *adj.* few; lacking (**of:** in), *Cl* 1735
feye *adj.* doomed, dead
fiften *see* **fyftene**
figure, fygure *n.* figure, form; (written) character, *Cl* 1726; image, *Pe* 1086
fildore, fyldor *n.* gold thread
fire *see* **fer(re), fyr**
fis(s)che(z) *see* **fysch(e)**
flaȝ(e) *see* **fle, flyȝe** *v.*[1]
flaȝt *n.* grass, turf, *Pe* 57
flake *n.* flake, *Cl* 954; blemish, *Pe* 947
flakerande *presp.* fluttering
flambe *v.* shine, *Pe* 769; **flaumb(e)ande** *presp. adj.* flaming, glowing
flat *n.* lowlands, *G* 507
flaumb(e)ande *see* **flambe**
flaunkes *n.* sparks
flauorez *n.* scents, perfumes, *Pe* 87
flawen *see* **fle**
flayed *pp.* terrified, *Cl* 960; *pa.t. Cl* 1723, *Pat* 215
flayn *see* **flyȝe** *v.*[2]
flayr *n.* scent
fle *v.* (**flaȝ(e), fled, flowen** *pa.t.,* **flawen, flowen** *pp.*) flee, *Cl* 377, 914, 945, 975, *Pat* 183, 214, 424, *G* 1628, 2125, 2130, 2272, 2274, 2276(2)*n*; escape, *Pe* 294
fleez *see* **flyȝes**
fleȝe *see* **flyȝe** *v.*[1]
flem *n.* flow
fleme *v.* drive (out), banish; **of f.** banish, *Pe* 358
flesch(e) *n.* flesh, body; living thing, *Cl* 303, 356, *etc.;* **-ly(ch)** *adv.*
flet *see* **flet(te)**
flete *v.* (**flet(t)e, flot(t)(e), fleten** *pa.t.,* **floten** *pp.*) float, drift; fly, *G* 1566; swim, *Cl* 432; flood, fill, *Cl* 685
flet(te) *n.* floor; city, *Pe* 1058; **vpon (on þis, þe) f.** in (this, the) hall
flod(e) *n.* water, *Cl* 531, 538, *etc.;* stream, *G* 2173; river, *Pe* 1058; sea, *Pe* 736, *Pat* 126, *etc.;* flood, *Cl* 369, 397; **f. lotes** the sea's roarings, *Pat* 183; **French f.** English Channel, *G* 13; **flodez fele** (*gen.*) of many waters, *Pe* 874
floȝed *see* **flowed**
flok *n.* (**flokkes, -z** *pl.*) flock, crowd, company
flokked *pa.t.* flocked; **f. in** assembled, *G* 1323
flokkes, flokkez *see* **flok**
flonc *pa.t.* rushed, *Pe* 1165
flone *n.* arrow
flor *n.* floor
flor-de-lys, flores *see* **flo(u)r-de-lys, flo(u)r**
flosche *n.* pool, swamp
flot *n.*[1] scum, *Cl* 1011
flot(e) *n.*[2] host, company
flot(en), flot(t)e *see also* **flete**
floty *adj.* stream-filled, *Pe* 127
flo(u)r, flowr *n.* flower; **vyrgyn f.** virginity, *Pe* 426

flo(u)r-de-lys *n.* fleur-de-lis (water iris), *Pe* 195, 753
floury *adj.* flowery, *Pe* 57
flowed, floȝed *pa.t.* flowed
flowen *see* **fle, flyȝe** *v.*[1]
flowr *see* **flo(u)r**
flowred *pa.t.* flowered
flurted *pp.* figured (with flowers), *Pe* 208
flwe *see* **next**
flyȝe *v.*[1] (**flaȝ(e), fleȝe, flwe, flowen** *pa.t.*) fly, *Pe* 89, 431, *Cl* 432, 1010, *G* 459, 524, 2276(1)*n*
flyȝe *v.*[2] (**flayn** *pp.*) flay, scourge, *Pe* 809, 813
flyȝes, fleez *n.* butterflies, flying insects, *G* 166, *Cl* 1476
flyȝt *n.* flight
flyt *n.* strife
flyte *v.* strive, wrangle
fnast(ed) *pa.t.* snorted, panted
fo *see* **fo(o)**
foch(che) *v.* take
fode *n.* food; **fodez** *pl.* people, *Cl* 466
fogge *n.* grass (of the second growth), *Cl* 1683
foȝt *see* **fyȝt**
fol *adj.* foolish
fol *see also* **fol(e)** *n.*[2], **ful**
folde *n.* earth; land, ground, *Cl* 477, 1014, *G* 23; **of f.** away, *Pe* 334; **(vp)on f.** on earth, living, *etc.;* **forme vpon f.** very first, *G* 2373
folde *v.* fold; bow, bend, *Pe* 813; pack up, *G* 1363; match, *G* 499; place, lay, *Cl* 1026; assign, *G* 359; enfold, *Pat* 309; **folde(n)** *pp.* wrapped, *G* 959; pledged, *G* 1783; **f. in** plaited, *G* 189; **f. vp** upturned, *Pe* 434
fole *n.*[1] horse; *gen.sg. G* 459; *gen.pl. Cl* 1255
fol(e) *n.*[2] fool
folé, foly *n.* folly
foler *n.* foliage, *Cl* 1410
foles *v.* goes mad, *Cl* 1422
foles *see also* **fole** *n.*[2], **fowle**
folez *see* **fol(e)** *n.*[2]
folȝe *v.* follow, pursue; accompany, *Cl* 677, 974; **f. tylle** serve, *Cl* 1752; **folȝande, fol(e)wande** *presp.* following; matching, *G* 859; in proportion (?) *G* 145*n*; in the order of, *Pe* 1040
folk(e) *n.* folk, people; *as pron.* anyone, *Cl* 1129; **folken** *gen.pl., Cl* 271
folmarde *n.* polecat
folwande, foly *see* **folȝe, folé**
folyly *adv.* foolishly, lewdly, *Cl* 696
foman *n.* foe, *Cl* 1175
fon *see* **fyne**
fonde *v.* try; tempt, *G* 1549; visit, *Pe* 939
fonde(n), fonge *see* **fynde, fange**
font *n.* font, *Cl* 164
fonte *see* **fynde**
foo *adj.* wicked, *G* 1430; *adv.* in hostility, *G* 2326
fo(o) *n.* foe, *G* 716
fooschip *see* **foschip**
for *conj.* (*also* **f. þat**) for, because; but(?), *G* 147*n*
for, fore, four (*Cl* 756) *prep.* for, because of, on account of, through, for the sake of, in exchange for; according to, *Pat* 12; as, *Pe* 830, *etc., Cl* 275, *etc., Pat* 519, *G* 240, *etc.;*

(enough) for, *Pe* 211; to, *Cl* 75, 143, *etc.*; with regard to, *Cl* 740, 867, *Pat* 439; in spite of, *Pe* 890, *Cl* 1332, 1550, *G* 1854, 2132, 2251; for fear of, *Cl* 1143, *G* 1334; before, *G* 965, 1822; **f. to** to; though (I), *Pe* 333; **þe ... f.** for which, *Pe* 734. *See also* **olde, ferde, fetys(e)**

forbe, forbi *prep.* beyond, more than

forbede *v.* (**forboden** *pp.*) forbid

forbi *see* **forbe**

forbrent *pp.* burned up

force, forse *n.* necessity, *G* 1239; strength, *G* 1617

forclemmed *pp.adj.* pinched with hunger

fordez *see* **forþe**

fordidden *pa.t.* destroyed, quelled, *Pe* 124

fordolked *pp.* grievously wounded, *Pe* 11

fore *see* **for** *prep.*

forfare *v.* (**fo(u)rferde** *pa.t.*) kill, destroy; perish, *Cl* 560

forfaren *pp.* headed off, *G* 1895

forferde *see* **forfare**

forfete *v.* forfeit, *Pe* 619, 639; transgress, *G* 2394; lose (their right), *Cl* 743

forgart *pa.t.* (**forgarte** *pp.*) forfeited, lost

forgat *see* **forȝete**

forged *pp.* made, constructed

forgif, forgyue *v.* (**forgef** *pa.t.*) forgive

forgo *v.* lose, give up

forgyue *see* **forgif**

forȝ *n.* furrow, *Cl* 1547; channel, *G* 2173

forȝelde *v.* recompense

forȝete *v.* (**forgat, forȝate, forȝet(e)(n)** *pa.t.*, **forȝeten** *pp.*) forget; forsake, *Cl* 203

forhedez *n.* foreheads, *Pe* 871

forjusted *pp.* overthrown in combat

forknowen *pp.* neglected

forlete *pa.t.* lost, *Pe* 327

forlondez *n.* headlands, *or* low-lying lands near the sea, *G* 699

forlonge *n.* furlong

forlotez *v.* (*imperat.*) omit, overlook, *Cl* 101

forloyne *v.* err, stray; forsake, *Cl* 1165; *pp.adj.* erring, *Cl* 1155

formadde *adj.* stupid

formast *superl. adj.* first (in time), *Cl* 494

forme *adj.* first, *Pe* 639, *Cl* 257, *Pat* 38(2), *G* 2373; *as n.* beginning, *G* 499

forme *v.* form, fashion, make

forme *see also* **fo(u)rme**

forne *adv.* of old, *G* 2422

fornes *n.* furnace, cauldron

forpayned *pp.* afflicted

forray *v.* plunder

forred, furred *adj.* lined (with fur)

forsake *v.* (**forsoke** *pa.t.* **forsaken** *pp.*) renounce; refuse, *Cl* 75, *G* 1826, 1846; deny, *G* 475

forse *see* **force**

forselet *n.* fortress

forser *n.* casket

forsettez *v.* (*imperat.*) beset, surround

forsnes *n.* courage, fortitude

forsoke *see* **forsake**

forsoþe *adv.* indeed, in truth, truly

forst *n.* frost

forth(e), forþ(e) *adv.* forth, forward, on, out;

at f. naȝtes late at night, *Cl* 1764*n*; **f. dayez** well on in the day, *G* 1072

forth *see also* **forþe**

fortune, fortwne *n.* fortune

forty *see* **faurty**

forþe, forth, ford(e) *n.* ford

forþ(e) *see also* **forth(e)**

forþer *v.* (**forþrede** *pa.t.*) carry out

forþering *n.* promoting, advancing

forþi *see* **forþy**

forþikke *adv.* very thickly

forþoȝt *see* **forþynkez**

forþrast *pp.* destroyed

forþwyth *prep.* before, in front of

forþy, forþi *conj.* therefore, and so

forþynkez *v.impers.* (**forþynk** *pres.subjunc.*, **forþoȝt** *pa.t.*) it grieves, displeases

forward(e) *n.* covenant, agreement; *pl.* terms

forwondered *pp.adj.* astonished

forwroȝt *pp.adj.* exhausted with toil

foschip, fooschip *n.* enmity

foster *n.* offspring

fot(e) *n.* (**fet, fet(t)e, fote(z)** *pl.*) foot; *pl.* footsteps, example, *Cl* 1062 (*see also* **fete** *n.*)

fotte *v.* receive, *G* 451

foul *see* **ful**

foule, fouled *see* **fowle, fowled**

founce, founs *n.* bottom

founde *v.* hasten, go, set out. *See also* **fynde**

foundementez, founde(n) *see* **fundament, fynde**

foundered *pp.* engulfed, *Cl* 1014

founs, foun *see* **founce, for**

fourchez *n.* legs, haunches

fourferde *see* **forfare**

fo(u)rme *n.* form, shape, figure; pattern, example, *Cl* 3; outward appearance, *G* 145*n*; formula, *Pat* 38; manner, *G* 1295, 2130

four(r)e, fourty *see* **fawre, faurty**

fowle, foule *adj.* foul, dirty, vile; ugly, *G* 717; poor, *G* 1329; *as n.* evil, *G* 2378; *adv.* shamefully

fowle, fo(u)le *n.* bird, fowl

fowled, fouled *pa.t. & pp.* defiled

fowre *see* **fawre**

foyned *pa.t.* struck at

foysoun *n.* abundance; *as adj.* copious, *Pe* 1058

fraunchis, fraunchyse *n.* liberality, generosity

frayes *v.* frightens

frayn *v.* ask; put to test, *G* 489, 1549; wish, *Pe* 129

frayst *v.* (**frayst(ed)** *pp.*) ask (for), seek; try, test, *G* 503, 1679; scrutinize, *Pe* 169

fre *adj.* (**freest** *superl.*) noble, honourable, gracious; liberal, *Pe* 481; *as n.* noble one, *Cl* 929, *G* 1545, *etc.*; *pl.* free men, *Cl* 88

frech, freest *see* **fre(s)ch(e), fre**

frek(e) *n.* warrior, man, knight

frelich, frely(ch) *adj.* noble, glorious; fair, beautiful, *Cl* 173; *as n.* gracious one, *Pe* 1155

frely *adv.* generously, *G* 894; plentifully, abundantly, *Pat* 20, *G* 816; willingly, *Pat* 390; **freloker** *compar.* more nobly, more perfectly, *Cl* 1106

426 Glossary

fremedly adv. as a stranger, G 714

frende n. friend

frenges n. fringes

frenkysch fare refined manners, G 1116

fres pa.t. froze, G 728

fre(s)ch(e) adj. fresh, bright, fair, unsullied, Pe 87, Cl 173, G 2019; as n. fair (one), Pe 195; **þe f.** fresh food, G 122; **freschly** adv. eagerly, G 1294

frete v. (**freten** pp.) eat, devour, corrode

frette v. (imperat.) supply, Cl 339; **fretted** pp. adorned

fro conj. (also **f. þat**) after, from the time that

fro prep. & adv. from, away from; **f. me warde** away from me, Pe 981; adv. **to me f.** neither this way nor that, Pe 347

frok(ke) n. garment

frote v. rub, stroke

froþande adj. foaming, defiling, Cl 1721

froþe n. froth

frounse v. crease, pucker

frount n. forehead

frunt pa.t. struck, kicked, Pat 187

frym adv. richly, in strength

fryst v. delay

fryt(e), fruyt n. fruit; fruit tree(?), Pe 87

fryth n. wood(land), forest

ful, fo(u)l adv. fully, entirely, very, quite, most, completely

ful see also **ful(le)**

fulfylle v. fulfil; complete, Cl 1732

fulȝed pp. baptized

ful(le) adj. full; as n. **to þe f.** fully. See also **ful** adv.

fulsun v. help

fundament n. foundation; **foundementez** layers of the foundation, Pe 993

funde(n), furred, furst see **fynde, forred, fyrst(e)**

furþe adj. fourth, Pe 1005

fust see **fyste**

fuyt, fute n. trail

fyched pp. or pa.t. fixed, established

fyf, fyue adj. & n. five

fyft, fyfþe adj. fifth

fyftene, fiften adj. fifteen

fyfty, fyfté adj. fifty

fygure see **figure**

fyȝed pa.t. joined exactly (to their towers), G 796

fyȝt, feȝt (faȝt, foȝt pa.t.) v. fight; contend, Pe 54

fyȝt, feȝt(yng) n. fighting

fyin see **fyn(e)**

fyked pa.t. flinched

fykel adj. fickle, unreliable

fyldor see **fildore**

fyled pp.[1] soiled, defiled, Cl 136

fyled pp.[2] (filed); sharpened, G 2225; **f. out** carved out (with a file), Cl 1460

fylle v. fill; carry out, G 1405, 1934

fylor n. grindstone

fylsened pa.t. aided

fylter v. struggle, engage; contend, G 986; cling together, Cl 224; mix, join together, Cl 696; pp. tangled, Cl 1689

fylþe n. filth, defilement, impurity

fylyoles, -z n. turrets, pinnacles

fynde v. (**fande, fonde, founden** pa.t., **fonde(n), fonte, f(o)unde(n)** pp.) find, discover; perceive, notice, Pe 170, 871, Cl 133; **fonde** pa.subjunc. would find, G 1875

fyndyng n. find, dislodgement (of game)

fyn(e), fyin adj. fine, perfect, choice, complete; good, Cl 721; pure, G 1239; precise, G 1636

fyn(e) adv. completely, perfectly, G 173, 1737; in full, Pe 635; **fynly** completely, G 1391

fyne v. (**fon, fyned** pa.t.) end, cease; die, Pe 328; come to an end, Pe 1030

fynisment n. end

fynger n. (**fyng(e)res, -z** pl.) finger

fynly see **fyn(e)** adv.

fynne n. fin

fyoles n. cups

fyr, fyre, fire n. fire, sparks; pl. inflammations, Cl 1095n

fyr see also **fer(re)**

fyrce see **fers**

fyrmament n. firmament, heaven

fyrre see **fer(re)**

fyrst(e), furst adj. & adv. first; at first, G 2227; **at þe f.** first; Pe 635; **of f.** from the beginning, Cl 1714; (**vp)on f.** first, in the beginning; as n. first day, G 1072

fysch(e), fis(s)che n. fish

fyskez v. scampers

fyste, fust n. fist, hand

fyþel n. fiddle

fyþer n. feather

fyue see **fyf**

gafe see **gif**

Galalyc n. Galilee

galle, gawle n.[1] gall, bile, Cl 1022; bitterness, Pe 463

galle, gaule n.[2] flaw, impurity, Pe 189, 915, 1060; scum, Pat 285; pl. wretches, Cl 1525

game, gamnez see **gomen**

gardyn n. garden

garez v. (**gart(en)** pa.t., **gart** pp.) causes, makes

gargulun n. throat

garlande n. garland, Pe 1186n

garnyst adj. adorned

gart(en) see **garez**

garysoun n. treasure; trophy, G 1807

garytez n. watch-towers

gast adj. afraid

gate n. way, road; street, Pe 1106; **hyȝe g.** highway, Pe 395; **bi g.** on the way, G 696; **haf þe g.** pass, G 1154. See also **chose**

Gaua(y)n, Gawa(y)n(e), Gawen, Wawan, Wawen, Wowayn, Wowen n. Gawain

gaudi n. beadwork(?), dye(?), G 167

gaue see **gif**

gaule, gawle see **galle** n.[1] & n.[2]

gay(e) adj. bright, lovely, beautiful, fine; merry, Cl 830; blissful, Pe 1186; as n. fair lady, fine knight

gay(e), gayly adv. finely, splendidly

gayn adj., adv. & prep. good, profitable; well-

suited, *G* 178; directly, *G* 1621; *prep.* nearby, *Pe* 138; **at þe gaynest** most directly; **-ly** *adv.* aptly, appropriately, *G* 476; rightly, *G* 1297
gayn(e) *v.* profit, help, serve, benefit; avail, *Cl* 1608
gaynly(ch) *adj.* gracious. *See also* **gayn**
Gaynour, Guenore, Gwenore, Wenore *n.* Guenever
gazafylace *n.* treasury, *Cl* 1283
geder *v.* gather, assemble; lift up, heave up, *G* 421, 2260; pick up (path), *G* 2160; **g. to** spur at, *G* 777, haul on, *Pat* 105
gef *see* **gif**
gele *v.* linger, stroll
gemme *n.* gem, jewel
gendered *pp.* begotten
gendrez *n.* kinds, species
generacyoun *n.* ancestry, *Pe* 827
gent(e) *adj.* noble, fair; courteous, kind, *Pe* 265, 1134
gentryse *n.* nobility
gentyl(e), jentyle *adj.*[1] noble, excellent, fine; reverent, *Cl* 1432; courteous, kindly, *Pe* 278, etc., *G* 774, etc.; as *n.* noble man, *G* 542; kindly being, *Pe* 602; *collect.* nobility, *Cl* 1216; *superl.* noblest (ones), *Cl* 1180
gentyl(e), jentyle *adj.*[2] gentile, heathen, pagan, *Cl* 76; **j. prophete** prophet to the gentiles, *Pat* 62
gentylmen *n.* gentlemen
gere, guere *n.* gear, *Pat* 148; armour, *G* 569, 584; clothes, *Cl* 1810; bedclothes, *G* 1470; utensil(s), instrument(s), *Cl* 16, 1505, *G* 2205
gere *v.* dress, clothe, *G* 1872
gered *pp.* arrayed, attired, adorned; made, *G* 1832
geserne *see* **giserne**
gesse *v.* discern, judge, *Pe* 499
gest(e) *n.* guest; visitor, visitant, *Pe* 277
get *n.* winning(s), *G* 1638
gete *v.* (**ȝat, gete(n)** *pa.t.*, **geten** pp.) get, fetch, capture; find, obtain
gettes *n.* fashions
geuen *see* **next**
gif, giue, gyf, gyue, gef, ȝef *v.* (**gef, gafe, gaue** *pa.t.*, **geuen, gyuen** *pp.*) give; allow, *Pe* 270; make known, reveal, *Cl* 1326, 1627; bestow upon, wish, *G* 370, 668, 1029 *etc.*; *reflex.* give in, *G* 1861
gift(e), gyft(e), ȝ- *n.* gift; giving, *Pe* 565; **of my** (*etc.*) **g.** as a gift from me (*etc.*)
gilde, gilt, gyld *pp.* gilded
Gile (Saynt) *n.* St Giles (Aegidius)
giles *n.* gills, *Pat* 269
gilofre *n.* gillyflower, clove-scented pink, *Pe* 43
gilt, girdel *see* **gilde, gordel**
Gilyan (Sayn) *n.* St Julian
giserne, geserne *n.* battle-axe
giue *see* **gif**
glace *v.* glide, *Pe* 171
glad *adj.* happy, merry; **-ly** *adv.* gladly, cheerfully; **-loker** *compar.* with greater pleasure, *G* 1064
glade *v.* (**gladande** *presp.*, **gladed** *pa.t.*) gladden, rejoice
gladnez *n.* gladness(es), joys, *Pe* 136

glam *see* **gla(u)m**
glas(se) *n.* glass
glauer *n.* babble, *G* 1426
glauerez *v.* deceives, *Pe* 688
gla(u)m *n.* din, noise; speech, *Cl* 830; voice, message, *Cl* 499, *Pat* 63
glaym *adj.* slime, *Pat* 269
glayre *n.* egg-white, *Pe* 1026
glayue *n.* spear, *Pe* 654
gle *n.* sound of revelry, music, *Pe* 95, 1123, *G* 46, 1652; joy, *G* 1536
glede *n.*[1] kite, *Cl* 1696
glede(z) *n.*[2] red-hot embers
glem *n.* radiance, brightness, *Cl* 218, *G* 604; beam, ray, *Pe* 79
glemande *presp.* gleaming, shining, *Pe* 70, 990; **glemed** *pa.t.* *G* 598
glemered *pa.t.* shone, glimmered
glene *v.* glean
glent(e) *n.* beam of light, *Pe* 114; glance, twinkle, *G* 1290; *pl.* glances, *Pe* 1144
glent(e) *pa.t.* shone, sparkled, glinted; sprang, *G* 1652; flinched, *G* 2292; glanced, *G* 476; turned aside (*or* looked?), *Pe* 671
glet(te) *n.* filth, slime
glewed *pa.t.* called, *Pat* 164
glod *see* **glyde**
glode *n.* clear patch of sky, *Pe* 79; bright patch, *G* 2181; **on g.** in a flash, *G* 2266
gloped *pa.t.* was shocked, *Cl* 849
glopnedly *adv.* fearfully, in alarm
glopnyng *n.* shock, terror, *G* 2461
glori, glory(e) *n.* glory; praise, *Pe* 1123; splendour, radiant beauty, *Pe* 70, 934, 959; exultation, *Pe* 171
glorious, gloryous *adj.* glorious
gloryed *pa.t.* gloried, exulted
glotounes *n.* gluttons
gloue *n.* glove
gloumbes *v.* frowns
glowed *pa.t.* shone, glowed, *Pe* 114; **glowande** *presp.* shining
glyde *v.* (**glod** *pa.t.*) glide, come, go
glyfte *pa.t.* looked, glanced, *Cl* 849, *G* 2265
glyȝt *pa.t.* looked; glinted, *Pe* 114
glymme *n.* radiance
glysnande *presp.adj.* glistening, shining
glyter *v.* glitter
gnede *adv.* in a niggardly manner
go, goande *see* **go(n)**
gob(e)lotes *n.* goblets
God(d)(e), god(de) *n.* God, god
goddes *n.* goddess, *G* 2452
god(e), godeliest *see* **go(u)d(e), godlych**
god(e)mon, godman, goodmon *n.* householder, landlord, host; sir, *Pat* 524
godhede *n.* divinity, (goodness?), *Pe* 413
godly *see* **go(u)d(e)**
godlych *adj.* (**godeliest** *superl.*) gracious, *Cl* 753, 1608; goodly, fine, *G* 584
godman *see* **god(e)mon**
godnesse *n.* goodness, generosity
gold(e) *n.* gold; **golde-hemmed** *adj.* hemmed with gold
golf *n.* deep source, *Pe* 608
gome *n.* man, knight; servant, *Cl* 77

gomen, game(n) *n.* (**gomnez, -s, gamnez** *pl.*) game, pleasure; merriment, *G* 1376, 1933; sport (hunting), *G* 1319, 1894; catch, *G* 1635; process, *G* 661; **gomenly** *adv.* happily, *G* 1079

Gomorre, Gomorra *n.* Gomorrah

go(n) *v.* (**gotz, gos, gon** *pres.*, **goande** *presp.*, **ʒod ʒede(n)** *pa.t.*, **gon** *pp.*) go, walk

good *see* **go(u)d(e)**

goodmon *see* **god(e)mon**

gorde, -y- *v.* (**gorde** *pa.t.*) strike; spur, *G* 2062, 2160; rush, *Cl* 911

gorde *see also* **gurde**

gordel, girdel, gurdel *n.* girdle

gore *n.* filth, foulness

gorger *n.* neckerchief, wimple

gorstez *n.* gorse-heaths

gos *see* **go(n)**

gost(e) *n.* spirit, soul; **g. of lyf**, breath of life, *Cl* 325

gostly *adj.* spiritual, *Pe* 185, 790

gostlych *adv.* in supernatural manner, *G* 2461

gote *n.* current, stream

gotz *see* **go(n)**

go(u)d(e), go(w)d, good *adj. & n.* good, righteous, worthy; *as n.* good, goodness, good thing, profit, benefit; *s. or pl.* goods, *Pe* 731, 734, *Cl* 1200, 1282, 1315, *G* 1064, 1944; **go(u)dly** *adv.* graciously, generously; properly, *Pat* 26

gouernour *n.* (**gouernores** *pl.*) master, ruler

goulez, gowlez *n.* gules, heraldic red

goun(e) *n.* gown, robe, vestment

gowdez, gowlez *see* **go(u)d(e), goulez**

grace *n.* grace, mercy, salvation; good fortune, *Pe* 194; favour, prayer, *Cl* 1347

gracio(u)s(e) *adj.* gracious; beautiful, pleasing, pleasant; *as adv.* delightfully, *Pe* 260

gracyously, graciously *adv.* pleasingly, *Cl* 488; graciously, kindly, *G* 970

grame *n.* trouble, vexation

grante, grant merci, grattest *see* **gra(u)nte, gra(u)nt mercy, gret(e)**

grauayl *n.* gravel

grauen *pp.* engraved; buried, *Cl* 1332

graunt *n.* permission, *Pe* 317

gra(u)nte *v.* grant, consent, agree (to); acknowledge, *Pat* 240

gra(u)nt mercy, -i many (*lit.* great) thanks

gray(e) *adj.* grey; (of eyes) blue-grey, *Pe* 254n, *G* 82; *as n.* greyhounds, *G* 1714

grayes *v.* becomes grey, *G* 527

grayn *n.* spike, *G* 211

graynez *n.* seeds, *Pe* 31

graythly *see* **graythely**

grayþ(e) *adj.* ready

grayþe *v.* prepare, make ready; adorn, dress, *G* 151, 666, 2014; install, seat, *G* 74, 109; *pa. subjunc.* would avail, *Pat* 53

grayþely, graythly *adv.* promptly, readily, *Cl* 341, *G* 417, 1683; truly, properly, *Pat* 240, 286, *G* 1006, 1335, 2292; comfortably, *G* 876, 1470; aptly, *Pe* 499

gre *n.* pleasure

grece *n.*[1] steps, *Cl* 1590

grece, gres *n.*[2] fat, flesh; skin, *G* 2313

Grece *n.*[3] Greece

gredirne *n.* gridiron

gref(fe) *n.* suffering, grief

grehoundez *n.* greyhounds

grem(e) *n.* wrath, vexation; resentment, *Pe* 465; injury, *G* 2251

greme *v.* anger; annoy, *Pat* 42; become angry, *Cl* 138

grene *adj.* (**grener** *compar.*) green; *as n.* grassy place, *Cl* 634; vegetation, *Cl* 1028; **þat g.** the green man, *G* 464

grenne *v.* grin, smile, *G* 464

gres(se) *n.* grass; plant, shoot, *Pe* 31. *See also* **grece** *n.*[2]

gret *pa.t.* greeted, *G* 842, 1933

grete *v.* weep, *Pe* 331, *G* 2157

gret(e), grett *adj.* (**grattest** *superl.*) great, big; exalted, *Pe* 578; magnificent, *G* 2014; boastful, *G* 312, 325; *as n.* noble(s), *Cl* 1363, *G* 2490; **g. cloþ** main sail, *Pat* 105; **grattest of gres** fattest, *G* 1326; **grattest in grene** greenest, *G* 207; *adv.* in general, *Pe* 637 (*cf.* **agrete,** *Pe* 560)

gretyng *n.* weeping, *Cl* 159

greue *n.*[1] wood, thicket; **Paradys g.** grove of Paradise, *i.e.* the garden of Eden, *Pe* 321

greuez *n.*[2] greaves (armour), *G* 575

greue(n) *v.* trouble, distress, offend; harm, punish, *Cl* 138, *Pat* 112, 517; *intrans.* be troubled

greuing *n.* grieving

grewe(n) *see* **growe**

grome *n.* man, retainer

gromylyoun *n.* gromwell

grone *v.* groan

gronyed *pa.t.* snorted, *G* 1442

gropande *presp.* searching, testing

gropyng *n.* touch, handling

grouelyng *adv.* prostrate, *Pe* 1120

grounde *n.* ground, earth; foundation, basis, *Pe* 372, 384 *etc.*, *Cl* 591, 911; field, *G* 508; land, region, *G* 705; (**vp)on g.** on earth, on the ground

groundelez *adj.* bottomless

grounde(n) *see* **grynde**

growe *v.* (**grewe, grewen** *pa.t.*) grow, increase

gruch *v.* (**gruʒt** *pa.t.*) bear ill will, *G* 2251; be unwilling to grant, refuse, *Cl* 810, 1347

gruchyng *presp.* ill-humouredly, *G* 2126

grwe *n.* grain; **no g.** not a bit, *G* 2251

grychchyng *n.* grumbling

gryed *pa.t.* shuddered, *G* 2370

grymly *adv.* sternly, *Cl* 1534; cruelly, *Pe* 654

grym(me) *adj.* fierce, grim, ugly

grynde *v.* (**grounde(n)** *pp.*) make a grinding sound, *Pe* 81; *pp.* sharpened, *Pe* 654, *G* 2202n

gryndel *adj.* fierce, angry; **-ly** *adv.*

gryndellayk *n.* ferocity

gryndelston *n.* grindstone

Gryngolet *n.* (Gawain's horse)

grypez *v.* (**gripped, gryped, grypte** *pa.t.*) grips

grysly *adj.* horrible

gryspyng *n.* gnashing

gryste *n.* anger, spite

Guenore *see* **Gaynour**
guere *see* **gere**
guferes *n.* depths
gult(e), gylt *n.* guilt
gulty, gyltyf *adj.* guilty; *as n. Pe* 669, *Pat* 175
gurde, gorde *pp.* girt
gurdel *see* **gordel**
gut *n.* (**guttez** *pl.*) gut, intestine
Gwenore *see* **Gaynour**
gyde-ropes *n.* guy ropes
gye *v.* rule
gyf, gyft(e), gyld *see* **gif, gift(e), gilde**
gyle *n.* guile, deceit, treachery
gylt(ez), gyltyf *see* **gult(e), gulty**
gyltlez *adj. as n.* guiltless, innocent (one)
gyn *n.* craft
gyng *n.* company
gyngure *n.* ginger
gyrde *see* **gorde**
gyrle *n.* girl
gyse *n.* dress
gyternere *n.* cithern-player
gyue(n) *see* **gif**

ȝare *adv.* soon, *G* 2410; clearly, *Pe* 834
ȝark(k)(e) *v.* prepare, make ready, institute, set up; grant, *Cl* 758; **ȝ. vp** open, *G* 820
ȝarm *n.* outcry
ȝar(r)ande *presp.adj.* snarling
ȝat *see* **gete**
ȝate *n.* gate, outer door
ȝaule *v.* howl
ȝayned *pp.* greeted
ȝe *adv.* yea, yes, *Cl* 347, *G* 813, 1091, *etc.*
ȝe *pron.* (**ȝow,** *dat. & acc.*) you
ȝede *see* **go(n)**
ȝederly *adv.* promptly, quickly; entirely
ȝedoun *pa.t.* went down, *G* 1595*n*
ȝef *see* **gif**
ȝeȝe *v.* cry (out)
ȝelde *v.* (**ȝelde(n), ȝolden** *pa.t.,* **ȝolden** *pp.*) yield, give, deliver, (re)pay; restore, *Cl* 1708; reply, *G* 1478; *reflex.* yield, surrender, *G* 1215, 1595
ȝelle *v.* yell
ȝellyng *n.* yelling
ȝelpyng *n.* valiant boasting
ȝeme *v.* govern, rule
ȝemen *n.* labourers, *Pe* 535
ȝender, ȝonder *adj. & adv.* yonder, that
ȝep(e) *adj.* young, new, *G* 60; youthful, active, vigorous, *G* 881, *G* 105, 284, 1510; fresh, blooming, *G* 951; *as n.* alert man, *Cl* 796; **-ly** *adv.* promptly, quickly
ȝer(e) *n.* (**ȝer(e)** *pl.*) year; **on ȝ.** a (*i.e.* each) year, *Pe* 1079; **ȝeres ȝiftes** New Year's gifts, *G* 67
ȝern(e) *adj. & adv.* quick(ly), eager(ly), *G* 498, 1478, 1526
ȝerne *v.*[1] yearn (for), wish, desire
ȝerne, ȝirne *v.*[2] (**ȝornen** *pa.t.*) run, pass, *Cl* 881, *G* 498, 529
ȝestande *presp.adj.* frothing
ȝet(e), ȝette *adv.* yet, still, even; further, moreover; nevertheless; hitherto, *Cl* 197, 815, *etc., Pat* 432; again, *Pat* 489

ȝet(t)e *v.* grant, allow; **ȝ. out** yield, send out, *Cl* 842
ȝif, ȝyf, i(i)f *conj.* if, whether; in case, *Pat* 160, *G* 1774; *with force of* though, *Pe* 45, 147, *etc., Cl* 914, *etc.*; **bot if** unless; **if hit were** for example, *G* 1799
ȝiftes *see* **ȝer(e), gift(e)**
ȝirne *see* **ȝerne** *v.*[2]
ȝis(se), ȝise, ȝys *adv.* yes, truly, indeed
ȝisterday *n.* yesterday; *gen.* of yesterday, *Cl* 463
ȝod *see* **go(n)**
ȝokkez *n.* yokes
ȝol *n.* Yule
ȝolden *see* **ȝelde**
ȝolȝe *adj.* yellow, sallow
ȝolped *pa.t.* shouted
ȝomerly *adj. & adv.* miserable, miserably
ȝon *adj.* yonder, that
ȝonde *adj.* yonder, that
ȝonder *adj.* yonder, that
ȝong(e), ȝonke *adj.* young
ȝore *adv.* long since, a long time, *G* 2114; **for long ȝ.** for a long time, *Pe* 586
ȝorefader *n.* ancestor (i.e. Adam), *Pe* 322
ȝore-whyle *adv.* some time ago, *Cl* 842
ȝourez, ȝourself, ȝowre *see* **yourez, yourself, yo(u)r(e)**
ȝys *see* **ȝis(se)**

hab(b)es, habbe(z) *see* **haue**
Habraham *see* **Abraham**
hach *n.* hatch, deck; **vnder h.** on board ship, *Cl* 409; **vnder hachches** below deck, *Pat* 179
hadet *pp.* beheaded (**wyth:** by), *G* 681
haf(e) *see* **haue**
hafyng *n.* possession
haȝer *adj.* goodly, noble, *G* 1738*n; compar.* **-er** more skilful, handy, resourceful, *G* 352
haȝerly, hagherlych *adv.* fitly, fittingly
haȝþorne *n.* hawthorn
hal *see* **hal(le)**
halawed *see* **halowe**
halce, hals *n.* neck
halche, halse *v.* embrace, salute; enclose, *G* 185; loop around, *G* 218; fasten, *G* 1852, 1613; interlace, *G* 657
halde, holde *v.* (**helde** *pa.t.,* **halden holden** *pp.*) hold; possess, *Cl* 35, 652, *etc., Pat* 14, *G* 627; keep (to), *Cl* 244, 335, *etc., Pat* 333, *G* 698, 1043, 1090, *etc.; reflex.* keep oneself, remain, *Pe* 1191, *Pat* 289; govern, *G* 53, 904, *etc.*; contain, *Pe* 1029, *Cl* 1387, *G* 124; occupy, *Pe* 1002; consider, *Pe* 301, *Cl* 276, 1062, *etc., Pat* 522, *G* 28, 259, *etc.; pp.* bound, *G* 1040, beholden, *G* 1828; **h. alofte** keep up, *G* 1125; **halden her pese** remain quiet, *Pat* 25; **h. in honde** dispense, *G* 2056; **h. of** be faithful to, *Cl* 1162; **h. out** go out, *Pat* 434; **h. vtter** put outside, *Cl* 42
hale *v.* (**hal(l)ed** *pa.t.,* **halet** *pp.*) pull, draw, *Pat* 219, *G* 1338; shoot (arrow), *G* 1455; drink, drain, *Cl* 1520; hasten, rush, *Cl* 380, *G* 136, 458; pass, *G* 1049; sweep, *Cl* 458, *G* 788; flow, *Pe* 125

half, halue n., adj. & adv. half; side, Pe 230, Pat 434, 450, G 649, etc.; part, Cl 719; part, quarter, Cl 950; shore, Cl 1039; **(vp)on Godez h.** for God's sake, in God's name.

halȝed pa.t. hallowed, consecrated

halȝez n. saints

halidayez see **halyday**

halkez n. corners, recesses

hal(le) n. hall, dining hall, castle

halled see **hale**

halme n. handle

halowe, -awe v. shout (at)

halowing n. shouting

hals, halsed see **halce, halche**

halt adj. lame

halte n. stop, stand; **take me h.** offer obstruction to me, Pe 1158

halue(s) see **half**

halydam n. holy object, relic

halyday, -i- n. festival, holy day

hame see **home**

hamppred pa.t. packed

han, hande see **haue, hond(e)**

hande-helme n. helm, tiller

hanselle see **hondeselle**

hapenez v.impers. it befalls

hapnesse see **happen**

hap(pe) n. good fortune, happiness, blessing, Pe 16, 713, 1195, Pat 212, G 48; pl. blessings, blessed states, beatitudes, Cl 24, Pat 11, 29

happe v. cover, Cl 626; imprison, G 1224; pp. enclosed, Pat 450; fastened, G 655; wrapped, G 864

happen adj. (**hapnest** superl.) blessed, fortunate

hard(e)(e) adj. & adv. hard, difficult, severe; as n. what is hard, Pe 606, a hard fate (or adv. badly), Cl 424; adv. hard, severely, fiercely; violently, Cl 44; firmly, G 1783, 655 (compar.)

harden v. encourage

hardily adv. assuredly

hardy adj. bold

harez n. hares

harled pp. entwined

harlot, -lat n. villain, beggar

harlottrye n. obscenity

harme n. harm, injury, offence; evil, wrong, sin, Pe 681, Pat 17n (cf. G 2511); sorrow, Pe 388

harme v. harm

harmlez adj. guiltless, Pe 676, 725

harnays n. armour, accoutrements

harnayst pp. armed, accoutred

harpen v. harp

harporez n. harpers

hasel n. hazel

haspe n. hasp, latch, G 1233

hasp(p)e v. fasten, buckle; clasp, G 1388; pp. with a clasp, Pat 189n

hast(e) n. haste, speed; **in (with) h.** quickly or in haste

hasted pa.t. urged on, Cl 937, pressed hard upon, G 1897; hastened, G 1165, 1424

hastif, hasty adj. hasty, rash, Pat 520; urgent, G 1051

hasty(f)ly, hastily adv. quickly

hastlettez n. pig's offal

hat see **hat(te)**

hate n. hate, hatred

hate see also **hot(e)**

hatel adj. fierce; cruel, Pat 367; bitter, Pat 481; vile, Cl 227; **for h.** because of anger, Cl 200

hater n. clothing; pl. clothes

hatte n. hat; **hard h.** helmet, Cl 1209

hat(te) v. (**-s** pres2sg., **hyȝt** pa.t. (pres. Pe 950), **hatte** pp.) be called

hatter, hatz see **hot(e), haue**

haþel n. man; knight; Lord, G 2056

hauberghe, hawbergh n. tunic of mail

haue, haf(e) v. & auxil. (**hab(b)es, habbe(z), hatz, haue(z), hauen, haf, han** pres.) have; receive, Cl 461, accept, G 1980; keep, Cl 1140; take, Cl 349, 941, Pat 336, 460n, G 773, 1612, etc.; draw, G 1051; bring, Cl 1443; put, Cl 321, G 1446; reach, G 700; beget, G 2466; **h. in honde** control, Cl 1704; **haf at þe** take guard, G 2288

hauek, hawk n. hawk

hauen n. haven, harbour, Cl 420, Pat 108

hauilounez v. doubles back

haunte v. practise, Pat 15

hawbergh see **hauberghe**

hawtesse n. pride

hay exclam. hey!

hay, ay n. hay, Cl 1684, Pat 394, 438

haylse, haylce v. greet, salute

hayre n. hair shirt, Pat 373, 381

hayre see also **ayre**

he pron. (**him hym** dat. & acc.) he

hed(e), heued n. head; (of stream), Pe 974

hede v. observe, Pe 1051

hedlez adj. headless

hef see **heue**

hegge n. hedge

heȝe, heȝest see **hyȝ(e)** adj.

heȝed pa.t. vowed, Cl 1584n

heȝly see **hyȝly**

heȝt, heȝþe see **hyȝt**

helde adv. readily; **as h.** quite probably, Pe 1193; **helder** compar.: **neuer þe h.** none the more (for that), G 376, 430

helde v. turn, come, go (reflex. G 221); sink, fall, Cl 1330, G 1321; bow, G 972, 1104; fall, become (insane), Cl 1681

helde see also **halde**

hele n.¹ health, healing, Pe 713, Cl 1099; safety, Pat 92, 335; prosperity, Cl 920; well-being, Pe 16

hele n.² heel; pl. spurs, G 777, etc.

heled pa.t. healed

helle n. hell; gen. of hell, Pe 643. See also **hellen**

helle-hole n. the pit of hell

hellen adj. of hell

helme n.¹ helmet

helme n.² helm, tiller, Pat 149

help n. help

help(e) v. (**help** pa.t., Cl 1163) help

hem, him, hom, hym pron. (dat. & acc.) (to, for) them; themselves (reflex.), Pe 551, Cl 62 etc., Pat 216 etc., G 1130, etc.

hemself, hemseluen, hymseluen pron. themselves; (it pleased) them, G 976

heme adj. neat
hemely adv. closely
hemme n. hem; (edge), step, Pe 1001
hende, hynde adj. noble, gracious, courteous; meek, well-behaved, Pe 184; as n. gracious knight, lady, Pe 909, G 827, etc.; pl. gracious things, Cl 1083; **-ly** adv.
hendelayk n. courtesy
hend(e)ly see **hende**
heng(e) v. hang
henne adv. hence
hens, hence adv. hence
hent(e) v. (**hent** pa.t. & pp.) take, receive, seize; find, Pe 669; suffer, Pe 388, Cl 151, G 2277
hepe n. heap; **on a h.**, (**vp)on hepes, -z** in a heap/crowd
her, hir, hyr adj.[1] & pron. (acc. & dat.) her; reflex. herself, G 1193, 1735, etc.
her, here, hor adj.[2] their, Pe 92, 93, etc., Cl 24, 75, etc., Pat 16, 17, etc., G 54, 130, etc.
herande see **here** v.
herber n. lodging; v. lodge
herd(e) see **here** v.
her(e), heere adv. here; in this instance, Pat 520; in this respect, G 2366; **hereaway** hither, (to) here, Cl 647
here n.[1] warrior-band, G 59; army, G 2271; company, Cl 409, 902
here n.[2] hair, G 180, etc.
here v. (**herande** presp., **herd(e)** pa.t. & pp.) hear
here see also **ayre**
her(e)after adv. hereafter
hered, heyred pa.t. worshipped, Cl 1086, 1527. See also **herʒe**
herebiforne adv. before now
heredmen n. retainers
her(e)inne adv. herein, in this place; ?dressed in this, Cl 147; in this matter, Cl 1595
herʒe v. (**herʒed** pa.t., **herʒed, heyred** pp.) ravage, harry, Cl 1179, 1294, 1786; **h. out** rout out, Pat 178
heritage, (h)erytage n. heritage
herk, herk(k)en v. listen (to), hear
herle n. strand, G 190
hernez n.[1] eagles, Cl 537
hernez n.[2] brains, Pe 58
herre see **hyʒ(e)** adj.
hersum adj. glorious, festal
hert see **hurt**
hert(e), hertte n.[1] heart; mind; courage, G 2296; purpose, Cl 682
herttes, herttez n.[2] harts, stags, Cl 391, 535, G 1154
heruest n. harvest, autumn
hes n. promise
hest(e) n. command, bidding; promise, Cl 1636
Hestor n. Hector, G 2102
hete n. heat. See also **hetes**
hete v. (**hyʒt(e), hettez** pa.t., **hyʒt, hette** pp.) promise, assure; command, decree, Pat 11, 336. See also **heʒed**
heter adj. rough
heterly see **het(t)erly**

hetes n. promises, assurances, G 1525
hethe see **heþe**
het(t)erly adv. bitterly, fiercely; cruelly, Cl 1222; suddenly, quickly
hette(z) see **hete**
heþe, hethe n. heath
heþen adv. hence, away; **h. into Grece** from here to Greece, Pe 231
heþyng n. scorn, contempt, abuse
heué, heuy adj. heavy; serious, G 496; grievous, Pe 1180
heue, hef v. (**hef** pa.t., **houen, hofen** pp.) lift, raise; rise, G 120; mount, Pat 477; heave, Pat 219; address (words), Pe 314; pp. raised
heued see **hed(e)**
heuen n. (**heuen(e)z, heuenesse** pl.) heaven; attrib. of heaven, Pat 185, G 647; **heuenglem** light of dawn; **heuen-kyng** king of heaven; **heuen-ryche** (kingdom of) heaven
heuen v. raise, exalt; increase, Pe 16; extol, Cl 24
heuy see **heué**
h(e)we, huee n. hue, colour, complexion
h(e)we v. cut; **hewen** pp. made, cut
heyred see **hered, herʒe**
hid, hid(d)e see **hyde** v.
hider(e), hyder adv. hither, here
hidor n. terror
hiʒe see **hyʒ(e)**
hiʒlich adj. splendid, G 183
hiʒly see **hyʒly**
hiʒtly adv. fitly; **h. bisemez** is right and proper, G 1612
hiled pp. covered, Cl 1397
hil(le), hyl(le) n. hill; (castle-)mound; **on h.** in (any) castle (?), G 59 (but cf. G 2271)
him, hym pron. (dat. & acc.) him; them, Pe 635, etc., Cl 130, etc., Pat 213, etc., G 49, etc. (also **hem, hom**)
himself(e), himseluen see **hymself**
hir, hindez see **her, hyndez**
hirself pron. herself
his(e), hys(se) possess. pron. & adj. his; its, G 447
hisseluen see **hymself**
hit, hyt pron. (**his, hit** possess.) it; **h. ar(n)** (**wern**) they are (were), Pe 895, 1199, Cl 171, etc., Pat 38, etc., there are, G 280, 1251; **his** possess. its, G 447; **hit** possess. Pe 108, etc., Cl 264, etc., Pat 12, etc.
hitself, -seluen pron. itself
hit(te), -y- v. hit, strike; jump, fall, Pat 380, G 427; come down, Cl 479; **h. to** come upon, Pat 289; seek, wish, Pe 132
ho, a pron. (**her, hir, hyr** dat. & acc.) she; unstressed **a**, G 1281
ho-bestez n. female animals
hod(e) n.[1] hood
hode n.[2] order of knighthood, G 2297
hodlez adj. hoodless
hofen see **heue**
hoge, huge n. huge, great
hoʒez n. hocks, G 1357
hokyllen v. pres.pl. cut down, Cl 1267n
hol see **hol(l)(e)**

holde *n.* stronghold, *G* 771; grasp, *G* 1252; dominion, *Cl* 1597
holde(ly) *adv.* carefully, faithfully
holde(n) *see also* **halde**
hole *n.* hole
hole *see also* **hol(l)(e)**
hole-foted *adj.* web-footed
holȝ(e) *adj.* hollow
holkked *pa.t.* dug
hol(l)(e) *adj.* whole, sound; healed, *G* 2484; amended, *G* 2390; total, *Pe* 406; perfect, *Pat* 335; **þi hert h.** all your courage, *G* 2296
hol(l)y *adv.* wholly, completely
holsumly *adv.* restoratively, *G* 1731
holt *n.* wood
holt(e)wodez *n.* woods
holy *adj.* holy. *See also* **hol(l)ly**
holyn *n.* (*attrib.*) holly, *G* 206
hom *see* **hem**
home, hame *n.* home
homered *pa.t.* (hammered), struck, *G* 2311
homly *adj.* humble, obedient (*perh. also of* [God's] household), *Pe* 1211
hommes *n.* backs of the knees
hond(e), hande *n.* hand; **out of h.** at once; **halden in h.** dispense, *G* 2056; **me on h.** to my notice, *Pe* 155; **h. myȝt** power, *Pat* 257
hondel(e) *v.* handle
hondelyng *n.* handling, touch
hondelyngez *adv.* with the hands
hondeselle, hanselle *n.* (*collect.*) New Year's presents, gratuities, *G* 66; omen, present (*iron.*), *G* 491
hondewerk *n.* handiwork, creation
hondewhyle *n.* moment
hondred *see* **hundreth**
hone *n.* delay, *G* 1285
hone *v.* be situated, *Pe* 921
honest(e) *adj.* clean, pure, seemly
honestly *adv.* fittingly, properly
honour *n.* honour, dignity; favour (hospitality), *G* 1963, 2056
honour, honowr *v.* honour, worship; *pp.* celebrated, *G* 593
honysez *v.* condemns, ruins
hoo! *interj.* stop!, *G* 2330
hope *n.* expectation; belief, *Cl* 1653; hope, trust, *Pe* 860
hope *v.* think, suppose, believe; hope, *Cl* 860; **h. of** expect, *G* 2308
hor, horce *see* **her** *adj.²*, **hors(s)(e)**
hore *adj.* grey (with frost), *G* 743
hores *n.* hairs, *Cl* 1695
hores *possess. adj.* theirs, *Pat* 14, 28
horne *n.* horn
hors(s)(e), horce *n.* horse; horse's, *G* 180, 1904
hortyng *see* **hurt** *v.*
horwed *adj.* unclean
horyed *pa.t.* hurried
hose *n.* hose, tights, *G* 157
(h)ostel *n.* house; **bone h.** good lodging, *G* 776n
hot(e), hate *adj.* hot; angry, *Cl* 200; biting, *Cl* 1195, 1602, *Pat* 481; grievous, burning, *Pe* 388; *adv.* hotly; **hatter,** *compar. adv.*

houe *v.* pause, tarry; lie, be situated, *Cl* 927; rest, *Cl* 485
houen *see* **heue**
houes *n.* hoofs, *G* 459
houndes, -z, howndes, -z *n.* hounds
(h)oure, howre *n.* hour
hourlande *see* **hurle**
hourle *n.* sea, surge
hous-dore *n.* house-door
hous(e), hows *n.* house, building; hall, castle, church, temple, *etc.*
housholde *n.* household
hov, how(e) *adv.* how; **h. þat** how
howndes, -z *see* **houndes**
howre, hows *see* **(h)oure, hous(e)**
howso, how-se-euer *adv.* however
hue *n.* shout, cry, *Pe* 873
hue(e), huge *see* **h(e)we, hoge**
hult *n.* hilt
hundreth, -eþe, hundred, hondred *n.* hundred
hunt(e) *n.* huntsman
hurkele *v.* (**hurkled** *pa.t.*) cower, crouch, squat
hurle *v.* (**h(o)urlande** *presp.*) rush; *trans.* hurl, fling, *Cl* 44, 223, *Pat* 149; whirl, *Pat* 271
hurrok *n.* rudder-band, *Pat* 185n
hurt *n.* hurt, wound, *G* 2484
hurt *v.* (**hurt, hert** *pa.t.*, **hurt** *pp.*) hurt, pain; harm, injure; **hortyng** *vbl.n.* *Cl* 740
huyde *see* **hyde**
huyle, hyul, hylle *n.* clump of plants, gravemound, *Pe* 41, 1172, 1205
hwe *see* **h(e)we**
hwed *pp.* coloured, *Cl* 1045
hyde *n.* hide, skin
hyde, huyde *v.* (**hid** *pa.t.*, **hid, hid(d)e** *pp.*) hide; *pp.adj.* hidden; *as n.* secret thing, *Cl* 1628
hyder *see* **hider**
hyghe! *interj.* look out!, *G* 1445
hyȝ(e), hiȝ(e), heȝe *adj.* (**herre** *compar.*, **hyȝest, heȝest** *superl.*) high, tall, lofty, great; noble, excellent, great, supreme, *Pe* 596, 1051, *etc.*, *Cl* 35, 193, *etc.*, *Pat* 257, 412, *etc.*, *G* 5, 57, *etc.*; soemn, important, *Pe* 39 (**h. seysoun**: festival), *Pat* 9 (high mass), *G* 932, *etc.*; vigorous, *Cl* 976; mature, *G* 844 (*cf. Cl* 656 & *see* **out**); loud, *Cl* 1564, *etc.*, *G* 1165; *as n.* high ground, *Cl* 391, *G* 1152, *etc.*; **h. and loȝe** great and small; **on h.** on high, *Cl* 413, *Pat* 463, *G* 1607, 2057; **on (ful) h.** loudly, aloud, *G* 67, 307, 468, 1602; **ful h.** highest, supreme, *Pe* 454; **h. gate** highway, *Pe* 395; *adv.* high, loud(ly). *See also* **hyȝly**
hyȝe *n.¹* servant, *Cl* 67
hyȝe *n.²* haste; **in h.** suddenly, *G* 245
hyȝ(e), hiȝe *v.* hurry, hasten
hyȝly, heȝly, hiȝly *adv.* greatly, generously, solemnly; up on end, *G* 1587
hyȝt, heȝt, heȝþe *n.* height; **(vp)on h.** on high, *Pe* 501, aloft, *Cl* 458, *G* 421, towering, *G* 332, as strongly as possible, *Pat* 219
hyȝt(e) *see also* **hat(te), hete**
hyȝtled *pa.t.* adorned, ornamented
hyl-coppe *n.* hilltop, *Pe* 791

hyl(le) *see* **hil(le), huyle**
hym *see* **him**
hymself, hymselue(n), himself(e), himseluen, hisseluen *pron.* (*reflex. & emph.*) himself; him, *Cl* 924 *etc.*, *G* 113 (*i.e.* Baldwin), 226, *etc. See also* **hemself**
hyndez, hindez *n.* hinds (female deer)
hynde *see also* **hende**
hyne *n.pl.* labourers, *Pe* 505, 632; servants, *Pe* 1211; fellows, *Cl* 822. *Cf. also* **hyȝe** *n.*[1]
hypped *pa.t.* vaulted, *G* 2232; **h. aȝayn** bounced back, *G* 1459
hyr *see* **her**
hyre, hyure *n.* pay; (terms of) hire, *Pe* 534, *Pat* 56
hyre *v.* hire
hyrne *n.* corner, nook.
hys(se) *see* **his**
hyt, hyttez *see* **hit, hit(te)**
hyue *n.* hive
hyul, hyure *see* **huyle, hyre**

I *pron.* (**me** *dat. & acc.*, **me** *reflex.*) I
ibrad *pa.t.* spread over
iche, ichose *see* **vch(e), chose**
idolatrye *n.* idolatry
i(i)f *see* **ȝif**
iisseikkles *n.* icicles, *G* 732
iles *n.* islands, *G* 698; regions, *G* 7
ilk(e) *adj. & pron.* same, very; **þat i.** the same; **of þat i.** to match
ille, ylle *adj.* evil; *as n.* evil, sin; **ta(t)z to non i.** do not take (it) amiss
ille *adv.* ill, badly, amiss; with ill will, *Cl* 1141; wrongfully, *Pe* 681
ilych(e) *adv.* alike, in similar manner; equally; **ay i., euer i.** all the time, *Cl* 975, *Pat* 369 everywhere, absolutely, *Cl* 1386; **i. ful** kept up in full, *G* 44
image, ymage *n.* statute, *Cl* 983; image, *G* 649
in, inn(e) *prep. & adv.* in; on; into; within; for (*of time*), *Pe* 416; at, *Cl* 781, *G* 1096, *etc.*
inblande *prep.* among, *Cl* 885
inhelde *pp.* poured in
inlyche *adv.* alike, the same, *Pe* 546, 603
inmong(ez) *prep.* among
inmelle *see* **in(n)melle**
inmyddes, inmyd(d)ez *prep.* amongst, in the middle (of)
inn(e) *see* **in**
innermore *adv.* farther in, *G* 794
in(n)melle *adv. & prep.* in the midst (of them), *G* 1451; amongst, *Pe* 1127
innocens *n.* innocence
innocent, innos(s)ent, inoscente *adj.* innocent, *Pe* 672; *as n. Pe* 625 *etc.*
in(n)ogh(e), in(n)oȝ(e), innowe *adj. & adv.* enough, *Pe* 649, 661, *etc.*, *Cl* 669, 808, *etc.*, *G* 404, *etc.*; many, in plenty, *Cl* 116, *Pat* 528, *G* 77, 219, *etc.*; very, *G* 289, 803 (*iron.?*), 888; very well, *Pe* 637, *Cl* 297
innome, innowe *see* **nym(e), in(n)ogh(e)**
inobedyent *adj.* disobedient
inogh(e), inoȝ(e) *see* **in(n)ogh(e)**
inore *adj.* inner, *G* 649
innos(s)ent, inoscente *see* **innocent**

inspranc *pa.t.* sprang into
insyȝt *n.* opinion
into *prep.* into, to; (from here) to, *Pe* 231, *G* 2023; up to, *Cl* 660
inwyth, inwith *prep. & adv.* within
ire, yre *n.* wrath
irked *pa.t.* (*impers.*) it wearied, *G* 1573
Israel, Israyl *n.* Israel
iwys(s)(e), iwyis *adv.* indeed, certainly

jacynght *n.* jacinth
janglande *presp.* grumbling
jape *n.* trick, device; pastime, *Cl* 877; jest, joke, *Cl* 864(?), *G* 542, 1957
Japh *n.* Joppa
jasper, jasporye *n.* jasper
jaueles *n.* louts
jeauntez *n.* giants
jentyle *see* **gentyl(e)**
Jerico *n.* Jericho
Jerusalem, Jherusalem *n.* Jerusalem
John, Jon *n.* (**Jonez** *gen.*) John
joly(f), jolef *adj.* noble, worthy, *Cl* 300, 864; lively, happy, *Pat* 241, *G* 86; lovely, *Pe* 842, 929; *adv.* **jolilé** gallantly, *G* 42
Jonas *n.* Jonah
jopardé, joparde *n.* jeopardy; uncertainty, *Pe* 602
jostyse *n.* judge
journay *n.* day's journey, *Pat* 355
jowked *pa.t.* lay asleep
joy(e) *n.* joy
joyfnes *n.* youth, *G* 86
joyful, joyfol *adj.* joyful
joyles, -z *adj.* joyless
joyne *v.*[1] join, unite, *Cl* 434 (*& cf. next*), *G* 97; add, *Pe* 1009; **j. to** unite with, share in, *Cl* 726
joyne *v.*[2] enjoin, order, *Cl* 1235; appointed, *Cl* 877, *Pat* 62
joynt *adv.* continuously
joyntes *n.* joints
joyst *adj.* lodged
Juda *n.* Judah
Judé(e) Judy londe *n.* Judea
Jue, Jwe *n.* (**Jues, -z, Juise** *pl.* **Juyne** *gen. pl.*) Jew
jueler(e), joueler *n.* jeweller
juel(l)(e) *n.* jewel, treasure, *Pe* 23, 249, *etc.*, *Cl* 1441, *etc.*, *G* 1856
juelrye *n.* jewellery
jugge *v.* judge; try, *Pe* 804; condemn, *Pat* 224, 245; adjudge, assign, *G* 1856
juggement *n.* judgement
juis(e) *n.* judgement, doom
Juise *see* **Jue**
jumpred *pp. as n.* those jumbled together, *Cl* 491n
juste *v.* joust, *G* 42; **justyng** *n.* jousting
justyfyet *pp.* justified
justised *pa.t.* ruled
Juyne *see* **Jue**

kable *n.* cable
kach, kaȝt(en) *see* **cach(ch)(e)**
kakez *n.* cakes
kalle *see* **calle**

kanel *n.* neck
kare *see* **care**
kark *n.* trouble
karle, karp *see* **carle, carp**
kart *n.* cart
kast(e), kastel *see* **cast, castel**
kauelacion, cauelacioun *n.* argument, objection
kay *adj.* left
kayre *v.* lament, grieve, *Cl* 945
kayre *see also* **cayre**
kayser, kende *see* **cayser, kenne**
kene *adj.* (**kennest** *superl.*) bold, brave, great; zealous, *G* 482; bitter, *G* 2406; wise, *Cl* 1575; stout, *Cl* 839; sharp, *Pe* 40, *Cl* 1253, *etc.*; **ken-(e)ly** *adv.* quickly, eagerly, *Cl* 945, *G* 1048; keenly, bitterly, *G* 2001
kenet *n.* small hound
kenne *v.* (**kende, kenned** *pa.t.*) make known, teach, *Pe* 55, *Cl* 697, 865, *G* 1484, 1498; recognize, *Cl* 1702; understand, *Pat* 357; commend, *G* 2067, 2472
kennest *see* **kene**
kepe *v.* keep, hold, possess; obey, *Cl* 979; preserve, *Cl* 1229, *G* 2016, 2298; await, *G* 1312; entertain, *Cl* 89; take notice of, *Cl* 292; attend to, *G* 1688; behave, *Cl* 234; care, *G* 546, 2142; wish (for), *Cl* 508, *Pat* 464; *reflex.* take care, *G* 372
kerchofes *n.* kerchiefs
ker(re) *n.* wooded marsh
kerue, cerue *v.* (**carf, coruen** *pa.t.* **coruen, coruon** *pp.*) cut, carve; fashion, make; tear, rend, *Cl* 1582
kest(e)(n) *see* **cast, cast(e)**
keue *v.* sink, *Pe* 320; **keued** *pa.t. or pp.* fell away, *Pe* 981n
keuer, c- *v.* manage (to); recover, *G* 1755; restore, *Cl* 1605, 1700; find, obtain, *Pat* 223, 485, *G* 1221, 1254; give, *G* 1539; come, *G* 2221; **c. to** reach, *Pe* 319
keyes *n.* keys
klerk *see* **clerk(k)**
klubbe, clobbe *n.* club
klyf(f)e, klymbe *see* **clyff(e), clym**
knaged *pp.* fastened
knape *n.* fellow
knarre *n.* rock, ⌐ ̄͘
knaue *n.* servant, *Cl* 801; knave, *Cl* 855
knaw(e), know(e), cnawe *v.* (**kn(e)w(e)(n)** *pa.t.*, **knawen, knowen, knauen, cnowen** *pp.*) know, acknowledge; perceive, recognize, *Pe* 66, *etc.*, *Cl* 281, 373, *etc.*, *G* 1272
knawlach *n.* knowledge; **com to k.** recover one's senses, *Cl* 1702
kne, cne *n.* knee
knele *v.* (**knelande** *presp.*, **kneled** *pa.t. & pp.*) kneel
knew(e)(n), knit, knokkes *see* **knaw(e), knyt(ten), cnoke**
knokled *adj.* lumpy, knobbed
knorned *adj.* rugged
knot *n.* knot; group, *Pe* 788; wooded mound, *G* 1431, 1434
know(e)(n), knwe *see* **knaw(e)**
knyf(fe) *n.* knife

knyʒt, -i- *n.* knight
knyʒtly *adv.* in courtly manner, *G* 974
knyʒtyly *adj.* courtly, chivalrous, *G* 1511
knyt(ten), knit *pa.t. & pp.* tied, *G* 1331, 1831; established, agreed on, *Cl* 564, *G* 1642; *pp.* woven (*& fig.* bound up), *G* 1849
kok, kort, koste *see* **coke, cort, cost(e)**
kote *n.* cottage, *Cl* 801
kow *n.* (**kuy** *pl.*) cow
kowarde *adj.* cowardly, *G* 2131
kowpes *see* **cuppe**
koynt(yse), (-ise) *see* **coynt, coyntyse**
krakkes, kry(es) *see* **crak, cry(e)**
Kryst(e), Cryst, -i- *n.* Christ; **-mas(se), -enmasse** *n.* Christmas
Krysten, Krystyin *adj.* Christian
kuy, kyd(de) *see* **kow, kyþe**
kylle *v.* (**kylled, kylde** *pp.*) kill; strike, *Cl* 876
kyndam, kyndom *n.* kingdom
kyn *n.* (**kynnes, kyn(n)ez** *g. & pl.*) kind(s) (of); **what k. he be** what he is like, *Pe* 794
kynde *adj.* natural, lawful, *Cl* 697; proper, courtly, *Pe* 276, *G* 473
kynde *n.* nature; true character; quality, kind, *Pe* 74; species, sort, *Cl* 334, 336, *etc.*; race, offspring, *G* 5; **þe worldes k.** mankind, mortal men, *G* 261; **agayn k.** unnaturally, *Cl* 266; **by k.** properly, *G* 1348; **bi lawe of any k.** by any natural law, *Pat* 259
kynd(e)ly, *adv.* properly, fittingly; gently, courteously, *Pe* 369; exactly, *Cl* 319
kyndom *see* **kyndam**
kyng(e) *n.* king
kynnes, -z *see* **kyn**
kynned *pa.t. & pp.* was conceived, *Cl* 1072; engendered, aroused, *Cl* 915
kyppe *v.* seize
kyrf *n.* cut, blow, *G* 372
kyrk(e) *n.* church
kyrtel, kyryous *see* **cortel, curious**
kysse *v.* (**kyssed(es), kyst(en)** *pa.t.*, **kyst** *pp.*) kiss
kyssyng *n.* kissing
kyst(e), chyst *n.* coffer, chest, casket; vessel, ark, *Cl* 346, *etc.*
kyte *n.* (*gen.*) kite's, *Cl* 1697
kyth(e) *n.* country, region; **kythyn** *gen.pl. or adj.* of (all) lands, *Cl* 1366
kyþe *v.* (**kyd(de), kyþed** *pa.t.*, **kyd(de)** *pp.*) show, make known; speak of, declare, *Cl* 23, 851, *Pat* 118; behave (towards), *G* 775, 2340; acknowledge, *Cl* 1368; *pp.adj.* renowned, *G* 51, 263

labor *v.* work (in), *Pe* 504
lace *n.* cord, *G* 217; belt, *G* 1830, *etc.*
lach(ch)e *v.* (**laght, laʒt, leʒten** *pa.t.*, **lach(ch)ed** *pp.*) catch, seize, take; receive, *Cl* 166, 1186, *G* 2499, 2507, *etc.*; conceive, *Pe* 1128; reach, *Pat* 322; **laʒt** *pp.* drawn back, *Pe* 156; **l. leue** take leave; **þis lote I laʒte** this happened to me, *Pe* 1205n.
lachet *n.* loop
lad *see* **lede**
ladde *n.* fellow
laddeborde *n.* larboard side, port side

laddres *n.* ladders
lad(de) *see* **lede**
lade *pp.* laden, filled, *Pe* 1146
laden, ledden *n.* (*pl.*) voices, sounds, *Pe* 874, 878
lady, ladi, ladé *n.* (**ladi(e)s, ladiez, ladyes, ladyez** *pl.*) lady; **my l.** the Virgin Mary; **ladyly** *adv.* queenly, *Pe* 774
ladyschyp *n.* queenly rank, *Pe* 578
laft(e), laften *see* **leue** *v.*²
lagmon *n. G* 1729*n*
laght *see* **lach(ch)e**
laȝe *v.* (**laȝed, loȝe(n)** *pa.t.*) laugh
laȝt *see* **lach(ch)e**
laȝter *n.* laughter
lake, llak *n.* lake
lake-ryftes *n.* lakeside dens
lakked *pa.t.* sinned against, *Cl* 723; disparaged, *G* 1250; (*impers.*) **yow l.** you fell short, *G* 2366
laled *pa.t.* spoke, said
lamp, laumpe *n.* lamp
langage *n.* language
langour *n.* anguish, *Pe* 357
lante(z) *see* **lene**
lantyrne *n.* lantern, *Pe* 1047
lape *v.* drink, *Cl* 1434
lappe *n.* flap, fold; hanging sleeve, *Pe* 201
lappe *v.* embrace, *G* 973; *pp.* wrapped, *Cl* 175, *G* 217; enclosed, *G* 575
large *adj.* large, great, wide; *as n.* breadth, *Cl* 314
larges(se) *n.* width, *G* 1627; liberality, *G* 2381
lasched *pa.subjunc.* would blaze, burn, *Cl* 707
lasse, les(se) *compar. adj. & adv.* (**lest** *superl.*) smaller; less; lower, *Pe* 491; **þe l. in werke** those who have done less work, *Pe* 599, 600; **bryng ... lasse of** diminish, *Pe* 853; *adv.* **les** *Pe* 888 (*see also* **neuer, neuerþelese**)
lassen *v.* (**lasned** *pa.t.*) lessen, diminish, *G* 1800; subside, *Cl* 438, 441
last(e) *adj.* last; farthest, *Pat* 320; *as n.* **at, bi þe l., vpon l.** at last, finally
laste *pp.* laden, *Pe* 1146
lastes *n.* sins
last(t)(e) *v.* (**last(e), lasted, lested** *pa.t.*) last, endure; stretch, *Cl* 227
lat(e) *adj. & adv.* late; remiss; tardy
later *compar. adv.* **neuer þe l.** nevertheless
laþe *v.* invite, urge
laþe *see also* **loþe**
lauande *adj.* flowing, *Cl* 366
lauce(n), -us-, -ws- *v.* loosen, break, burst, undo; open, *Cl* 1428; relieve, *Cl* 1589; utter, speak, *Cl* 668, *Pat* 350, 489, *G* 1212, 1766, 2124
laucyng *n. as presp.* undoing, *G* 1334
laue *v.* bale out, *Pat* 154; pour out, *Pe* 607
laue *see also* **law(e)**
laumpe *n.* lamp
launce *n.* lance, spear: *pl.* boughs, *Pe* 978
launce *v.* shoot, gallop
launde *n.* glade, field, grassy plain
laused, lausen *see* **lauce(n)**
law(e), laue *n.*¹ law, religion; style, *G* 790; **bi l.** formally, *G* 1643

lawe *n.*² mound, hill
lawles *adj.* lawless
lawsez *see* **lauce(n)**
lay *v.* lay, lay down; abase, lay low, *Cl* 1307, 1650; bestow upon, *G* 1480; assign, set, *Cl* 425; deal out, *Pat* 173; put, *Pat* 106, 174; commit, *Pat* 168; **l. hym bysyde** turn aside, parry, *G* 1777, **l. vp** put away, *G* 1874; **in teme l.** discuss, *Pat* 37
laye *n.* poem, *G* 30*n.*
lay(e) *see also* **ly(ȝ)(e)**
layk *n.* game, sport, fun; holiday, *G* 1023; practice, *Cl* 274, *Pat* 401, *G* 1513; behaviour, *Cl* 1053, 1064
layke *v.* play, amuse oneself, *Cl* 872, *G* 1111, etc.
laykyng *n.* playing, *G* 472
layne *v.* conceal; **l. yow (me)** keep your (my) secret
layt *n.* lightning, *G* 199
layt(e) *v.* seek
layth *adj.* foul, *Pat* 401
lazares *n.* leprous beggars
le, leauté *see* **le(e), lewté**
lebardez *n.* leopards
led *n.* lead, *Cl* 1025
ledden *see* **laden**
led(e), leede, leude, lude *n.* man, knight, prince; sir, *Pe* 542, *G* 449, etc.; *collective* people, *Cl* 691, 772, *G* 833, 1113, 1124; **leudlez** *adj.* companionless
lede *v.* (**lad(de)** *pa.t.*, **lad** *pp.*) lead; pursue, *G* 1894; cultivate, *Pat* 428; live, experience, *G* 1927, 2058
leder *n.* leader; **-es** *pl.* leading men, *Cl* 1307
ledisch, ludisch, ludych *adj.* of the people, national, *Cl* 73, 1375, 1556
leede *see* **led(e)**
le(e) *n.* shelter, castle
lef, leef, leue *adj.* (**leuer** *compar.*, **leuest** *superl.*) beloved, dear; delightful, pleasant, *G* 49, 909, 1111; *as n.* dear one, beloved, *Cl* 939, 1066, *Pe* 418; **þat leuer wer** (*impers.*) who would rather, *G* 1251
lef *n.* (**leuez, leues** *pl.*) leaf; *collect.* foliage, *Pe* 77, *Pat* 447; *pl.* leaves of a book, *Pe* 837, *Cl* 966
lefly *adj.* dear, lovely, *Cl* 977
lefsel *n.* bower of leaves, *Pat* 448
leg(g) *n.* leg, *Pe* 459, *G* 575, 2228
leg(g)e *adj.* liege, sovereign, requiring allegiance; *as n.* lord, *Cl* 1368
leghe *see* **ly(ȝ)(e)**
legioun, legyoun *n.* legion
leȝ(en), leȝten, leke *see* **ly(ȝ)(e), lach(ch)e, louke**
leke *see* **lere-leke, louke**
lel(e) *adj.* loyal, faithful, true
lel(l)y *adv.* loyally, faithfully
leme *v.* shine, gleam
lem(m)an *n.* sweetheart, mistress, love, lover
len(c)þe, lenkþe *n.* length, duration (*space or time*); **on l.** along the length (of the table) *Cl* 116, afar, *G* 1231, for a long time, *G* 232
lende *v.* (**lent** *pa.t. & pp.*) remain, stay, dwell, *Cl* 993, *Pat* 260, *G* 1100, 1499, 2440; sit, *G* 1002: come, approach, go, *Pat* 201, *G* 971,

1319; **is lent** is away, *G* 1319; **watz lent** was present, *Cl* 1084

lene *v.* (**lante(z)** *pa.t.*, **lent** *pp.*) grant, give, *Cl* 256, 348, *Pat* 347, *G* 2250

lened *pa.t.* leant, reclined; **he l. with þe nek** he bent his neck, *G* 2255

leng(e) *v.* remain, stay, live; **hym l.** let him stay, *G* 1893; *pp.* persuaded to stay, *G* 1683

lenger, lengest *see* **long(e)**

lenghe *n.* duration, *Pe* 416; **on l.** for a long time, *Pe* 167

lenkþe *see* **len(c)þe**

lent *see* **lende, lene**

Lentoun *n.* Lent

lenþe *see* **len(c)þe**

lepe *v.* (**lep** *pa.t.*, **lopen** *pp.*) leap, run; gallop, *G* 2154 (*reflex.*); burst, *Cl* 966

lepre *adj.* leprous

lere *adj.* worse (?), *G* 1109 (*cf.* **lur**)

lere *n.*[1] ligature, *G* 1334

lere, lyre *n.*[2] cheek, face, *Cl* 1542, 1687, *G* 318, 943, 2228; flesh, *G* 418; coat, *G* 2050; **lere-leke** wimple, *Pe* 210n

lere *v.* teach, *Cl* 843

lerne *v.* learn; teach *G* 1878; *pp.adj.* well-instructed, skilful, *G* 1170, 2447

les *see* **lasse, les(e)**

lesande *presp.* opening, *Pe* 837

les(e) *adj.* false, *Cl* 1719, *Pat* 428, *Pe* 865

lese *v.* (**lest(e)** *pa.t.*, **lorne, lest** *pp.*) lose; destroy, *Cl* 932; fail, *Cl* 887

lesse *see* **lasse**

lest *conj.* lest, in case

lest(e) *see* **lasse, lese**

lested *see* **last(t)(e)**

lesyng *n.* lie, *Pe* 897

let(t)(e) *v.*[1] let, allow; leave, *Cl* 670; utter, speak, *G* 1086, 1206; behave, pretend, *G* 1190, *etc.*; have, cause, *G* 1084; **l. be** stop, *Pe* 715; **l. lyȝt bi, of** care little for, neglect, *Cl* 1174, 1320; **l. se** show, *G* 299, 414

lette *v.*[2] hinder, dissuade, *G* 1672, 2142, 2303; prevent, deprive, *Cl* 1803; obstruct, *Pe* 1050

letter, lettre *n.* letter (of the alphabet); inscription, *Cl* 1580

lettrure *n.* learning, doctrine, *Pe* 751, *G* 1513

lepe *n.* calm, *Pat* 160

lepe *v.* soften, humble, *G* 2438; be merciful (to), *Cl* 752; assuage, be assuaged, *Pe* 377, *Pat* 3; cease, *Cl* 648

leþer *n.* leather, *Cl* 1581; skin, *G* 1360

leude, leudlez *see* **lede**

leue *n.* leave, permission; leave-taking, *G* 1288; **take l.** depart, *G* 401

leue *v.*[1] (**laft, lafte(n)** *pa.t.*) leave; leave off, stop, *Cl* 1233, *G* 1502; leave out, *G* 2030; forsake, *Pe* 622; give up, *G* 369; allow, *G* 98

leue(n), *v.*[2] believe, *Pe* 69, 302, *etc.*; *Cl* 608, *etc.*; *Pat* 170, *etc.*; *G* 1784, 2421, *etc.*; **l. on** assent to, *Pat* 405

leue *see also* **lyue**

leued *pp.* leaved, *Pe* 978

leue(r), leuest *see* **lef** *adj.*

leues, leuez *see* **lef** *n.*

lewed *adj.* ignorant, uninstructed

lewté, leauté *n.* loyalty, good faith

leyen, lif, liflode, liȝt(e) *see* **ly(ȝ)(e), lyf, lyflode, lyȝt(e)**

liddez *n.* eyelids, *G* 2007

lik, lyk *v.* lick, *Cl* 1000; sip, drink, *Cl* 1521; taste (*metaph.*), *Cl* 1141, *G* 968

like(s), lis, list(e) *see* **lyke, ly(ȝ)e, lyst(e)**

littel, little *see* **lyt(t)el**

lipernez *n.* viciousness, *G* 1627

liuréz *n.* liveries, garments; *Pe* 1108

llak *see* **lake**

lode *n.* way of life, (?burden), *Pat* 156; **on l., in his l.** under guidance, *Pat* 504, with her (him), *G* 969, 1284

lodesmon, lodezmon *n.* pilot, steersman

lodly(ch), loþelych *adj.* loathsome, horrible; *as n.*, loathsome people, *Cl* 1093; *adv.* with loathing; with a show of repugnance, *G* 1634, 1772

lof *n.* praise, value; **of l.** fine, *Pat* 448

lof(den) *see also* **luf**

lofe *n.* luff, *Pat* 106n

lofly(est) *see* **luflych**

loft(e) *n.* upper room, *G* 1096, 1676; (**vp)on l.** aloft, on high, above, up

log(g)e *n.* small house, arbour

logge *v.* lodge, stay the night

logging *n.* house

loghe *see* **loȝ(e)**

Logres *n.* Britain, *G* 691n, 1055

loȝ(e), loghe, low(e) *adj. & adv.* (**lowest** *superl.*) low; **on l.** down, *G* 1373

loȝ(e), loghe *n.* flood, sea; stream, *Pe* 119

loȝe *see also* **laȝe**

loȝed *pp.* humbled, abased, *Cl* 1650

loȝen *see* **laȝe**

loȝly *adv.* humbly

loke *n.* look, glance, expression, *Pe* 1134, *G* 1480; (act of) looking, *G* 2438

loke *v.* look, watch, see; take care, *Cl* 317, 905, 944, *G* 448; consider, *Pe* 463; watch over, *Pat* 504, *G* 2239

loke(n) *see* **louke**

lokkez *n.* locks, hair

lokyng *n.* gazing, *G* 232; gaze, *Pe* 1049

loltrande *presp.* lounging, *Pat* 458

lombe, lomp(e), loumbe, lamb(e) *n.* lamb; *gen.* of the lamb, *Pe* 1141

lombe-lyȝt *n.* lamplight, *Pe* 1046n

lome *adj.* lame, *Cl* 1094

lome *n.* tool, weapon, *G* 2309; vessel, *Cl* 314, *etc.*, *Pat* 160

lomerande *adj.* stumbling, hobbling, *Cl* 1094

lomp(e) *see* **lombe**

londe, lont *n.* land; world; field, *G* 1561; **in l.** in the land, on earth. *Cf.* **launde**

lone *n.* lane, roadway, *Pe* 1066

long(e) *adj.* (**lenger** *compar.*, **lengest** *superl.*) long (*of space and time*); **vpon l.** at length, *Cl* 1193; *adv.* for a long time

longe *v.* (**longande** *presp.*, *Pe* 462) belong, pertain (to)

longe *v.* *impers. in* **me longed** I longed, had a longing, *Pe* 144

long(e)yng(e), longing *n.* anxiety; longing, *Pe* 244, 1180

lont, lopen *see* **londe, lepe**

lord(e) *n.* lord; God; landowner, master; husband, *Cl* 656, *G* 1231
lordeschyp, lort- *n.* dominion, command
lore *n.* teaching, *Pat* 350, 428; learning, *Cl* 1556, *G* 665*n*; manner, fashion, *Pe* 236
lorne *see* **lese**
los *n.*[1] renown, *G* 258, 1528
los, losse *n.*[2] loss; losing lot, *Pat* 174; injury, harm, *Cl* 1589, *G* 2507
lose *v.* (**losed, lost(e)** *pp.*) lose, forgo; destroy, end, *Cl* 909, *Pat* 198; perish, *Pe* 908
losyng *n.* perdition
losynger *n.* traitor
lot(e) *n.*[1] speech, word, sound; echoes, *G* 119; noise, clamour, *Pat* 161, *G* 1917; voice, *G* 244, 1623, *Pe* 238; *pl.* manners, *Pat* 47, *G* 1399 (?)
lot(e) *n.*[2] lot, *Pat* 194; casting of lots, *Pat* 180; chance, happening, *Pe* 1205; **lay lotes on** cast lots among, *Pat* 173
Loth, Lot, Loot *n.* Lot
loþe *adj.* hateful, *G* 1578
loþe, laþe *n.* injury, *G* 2507; grief, suffering, *Pe* 377; **withouten l.** without offence, ungrudged, *G* 127
loþelych *see* **lodly(ch)**
loud(e), lowde *adj. & adv.* loud(ly)
loue, louue, lovue, lowe *v.* praise, glorify, *Pe* 285, 342, 1124, 1127; *Cl* 497, 925, 987, 1289, 1703, 1719, *G* 1256; be praised, *G* 1399; advise, *Pat* 173
loue *see also* **luf**
loueloker, louelokkest, louely(ch) *see* **lufly(ch)(e)**
louez *n.* palms (of hands), *Cl* 987
louflych *see* **lufly(ch)(e)**
louke, lowke *v.* (**leke, louked** *pa.t.*, **loke(n)** *pp.*) shut, *G* 2007; *intrans.* fasten, *G* 217, 628, *etc.*; shrink, *Cl* 441; *pp.* enclosed, enshrined *or* linked, *G* 35; framed, *G* 765; locked, contained, *Pat* 350
loumbe *see* **lombe**
loupe *n.*[1] loop, *G* 591
loupe *n.*[2] loop-hole, *G* 792
loute *v.* (**lut(te)** *pa.t. & pp.*) bow, bend; come, go, *Pe* 933, *G* 833, 933; defer (to), *G* 248
louue, louy(e) *see* **loue, luf**
louyly *adj.* lawful, *Pe* 565
louyng *n.* praising, *Cl* 1448, *Pat* 237
lovue *see* **loue**
lowande *presp.* shining, brilliant
lowde, lowest, lowke *see* **loud(e), loȝ(e), louke**
low(e) *see* **loȝ(e), loue**
luche *v.* pitch, *Pat* 230
lude *see* **lede**
ludisch, ludych *see* **ledisch**
luf, lof, loue *n* love, affection, friendship; wooing, *G* 1733, 1810, 2497; lover, loved one, *Cl* 401: *collect.* paramours, *Cl* 1419
luf, loue, louy(e) *v.* (**lofden** *pa.t. pl.*) love, like
luf-daungere *n.* aloofness, distance of the beloved, *Pe* 11
luf-lace *n.* (belt as love token), *G* 1874, 2438
luf-laȝyng *n.* flirtatious wit, *G* 1777
luf-longyng *n.* love-longing, *Pe* 1152

luf-lowe *n.* flame of love, *Cl* 707
lufly(ch)(e), louely(ch), louflych, lofly *adj.* (**loueloker** *compar.*, **louelokkest, loflyest** *superl.*) lovely, gracious, courteous, beautiful, comely, *Pe* 693, 962, *Cl* 939, *G* 38, *etc.*; dear, *Cl* 1804; *also iron.*: *G* 433 (precious), *etc.*; **l. loke** look of love, *G* 1480; *adv.* (*also* **luflyly**) courteously, in a friendly manner, *Cl* 81, *G* 369, 595, 981, *etc.*; kindly, *G* 254; gladly, *G* 1606; beautifully, *Pe* 880, 978
lufs(o)um *adj. as n.* lovely (one)
luf-talkyng *n.* conversation about love, *G* 927
luged *pa.t.* moved heavily, laboured, *Cl* 443
lulted *pp.* sounded, *Cl* 1207
luly-whit *adj.* lily-white
lumpen *see* **lymp(e)**
lur *n.* loss; injury, *Pat* 419; penalty, *G* 1284, 1682; *pl.* losses, griefs, *Pe* 339, 358
lurk(k)e *v.* lurk, lie low, *Pat* 277; stay in bed, lie quiet, *G* 1180; *pp.* with eyes closed, *G* 1195; **l. by** pass under, *Pe* 978
lust *see* **lyste**
lusty *adj.* vigorous, *Cl* 981
lut(te) *see* **loute**
luþer, lyþer *adj. & adv.* wicked; vile, *Pat* 156; *as n.* evil, *Pe* 567, *Cl* 1090; *adv.* ill, *Pat* 500
lyf, lif, lyue *n.* life; soul, *Pe* 305, 687; being, person, *Pat* 260, *G* 1780; (**vp)on l.** alive, on earth (*or intensive:* indeed); **l. haue, bere** live *Cl* 308, *etc.*
lyfed *see* **lyue**
lyflode, liflode *n.* means of life, *Cl* 561; food, *G* 133
lyft(e) *adj.* left
lyfte *n.* heaven, sky, *Cl* 212, 366, *etc.*, *G* 1256
lyft(e) *v.* (**lyft(e)** *pa.t. & pp.*) lift, raise; decree, set up, *Cl* 717; **lyftande** *presp.adj.* heaving, *Cl* 443
lygges, lyg(g)ez, lyggede *see* **ly(ȝ)e**
lyȝe *n.* lie, *Pe* 304
ly(ȝ)(e) *v.* (**lyg(g)ez, lys, lis** *pres3sg.*, **lyȝe, lay(e), leȝ(en), leghe, lyggede** *pa.t.*, **leyen** *pp.*) lie; exist, *Pe* 602; be in residence, *G* 37; stay in bed, *G* 88; **l. þeroute** sleep out of doors, *Pe* 930; **l. in hym** be in his power, *Pe* 360
lyȝt *adj.*[1] light (in weight), *Cl* 1026; swift, *Cl* 987, *G* 199; active, energetic, *G* 87, 1119, 1464; joyful, *Pe* 238; **let l.** of care little for, *Cl* 1174, 1320; **set at l.** think lightly of, *G* 1250; **lyȝte** *adv.* lightly, *Pe* 214
lyȝt, lyȝte *adj.*[2] bright, *Pe* 500; pure, unsullied, *Pe* 682
lyȝt *n.* light; first light, dawn, *G* 1675
lyȝt(e), liȝt(e) *v.* (**lyȝt(e)** *pa.t. & pp.*) fall, alight, descend, come down; dismount, *G* 822, *etc.*; stop, *Cl* 800; *pp.* fallen, *Pe* 247
lyȝten *v.* lighten, *Pat* 160
lyȝtloker *compar. adj.* easier, better, *Pat* 47
lyȝtly *adj.* brilliant, dazzling, *G* 608
lyȝtly *adv.* quickly, readily; easily, *Pe* 358, *G* 1299; probably, *Pat* 88
lyk *see* **lik**
lyk(e) *adj.* (**lykker** *compar.*, **lykkest** *superl.*) like, similar (to); *as n.* the same, *G* 498; *conj.* as if, *Cl* 1008, *G* 1281

lyke, like *v.* like, be pleased, *Cl* 36, 73, *etc.*, *Pat* 47, *G* 694, 893; please, *Cl* 1064, *G* 87, *etc.*; *impers.* it pleases (him, me, *etc.*), *Pe* 566, *Cl* 717, *etc.*, *Pat* 397, *etc.*, *G* 289, *etc.*; **l. oþer greme** whether it please or annoy (anyone), i.e. whether you like it or not, *Pat* 42

lykkerwys *adj.* delicious, *G* 968

lykne *v.* compare, *Pe* 500; **l. tylle** resemble, *Cl* 1064

lyknyng *n.* imitation, *Pat* 30

lykores *n.* liquors, *Cl* 1521

lykyng *n.* pleasure; inclination, desire, *Cl* 172

lylled *pa.t.* quivered, *Pat* 447

lym, lym(m)e *n.* limb, member

lymp(e) *v.* (**lumpen** *pp.*) happen, befall; fall (on), *Pat* 174, 194

lynde *n.*[1] tree, *Cl* 1485, *G* 526, 2176

lyndes *n.*[2] loins, *G* 139

lynde-wod *n.* forest, *G* 1178 (*gen.*)

lyne *n.*[1] line; course of events, *Pe* 626

lyne, lynne *n.*[2] *& adj.* linen, *Pe* 731; **vnder l.** in linen, lady, *G* 1814*n*

lyppe *n.* lip

lyounez *n.* lions

lyre, lys *see* **lere, ly(ȝ)(e)**

lysoun *n.* glimpse, *Cl* 887

lyst *n.*[1] edge, *Cl* 1761

lyst *n.*[2] trick, practice, *Cl* 693

lyste, list, lust *n.*[3] desire, *Pe* 173, *Cl* 843; joy, delight, *Pe* 467, 908, *G* 1719; pleasure, (?lust), *Cl* 1350

lyst(e) *v.impers.* (**lyste, liste** *pa.t.*) it pleases, it pleased; I longed, *Pe* 146, 181; *pa.subjunc.* would see fit, *Pe* 1141

lyste *v.* hear, *G* 1878

lysten *n.* sense of hearing, *Cl* 586

lysten *v.* listen (to), *G* 30; hear, *Pe* 880, *G* 2006

lystyly *adv.* cunningly, cleverly

lyt(e) *adj. & adv.* little; *pl.* few, *G* 701

lyte *n.* *in* **on l., allyt** in delay, in hesitation, *Cl* 599, *G* 1463, 2303

lyth *n.* limb, *Pe* 398

lyt(t)el, littel, little *adj. & adv.* little; small, *Pe* 604; insignificant, *Pe* 574; *as n.* a little; **set at l.** considered of little importance, *Cl* 1710; **wyth l.** in a short time *or* to little effect, *Pe* 575

lyþe *v.* assuage, *Pe* 357

lyþen *v.* hear, *G* 1719

lyþer *see* **luþer**

lyþerly *adv.* meanly, wretchedly

lyue, lyuy(e), lyuie, leue (**lyued, lyfed** *pa.t.*) *v.* live

lyue(s), (-z) *see also* **lyf**

lyued *pp.* given life to, *Cl* 172

lyuer *n.* liver

ma *see* **make, par**

mace *see* **make**

mach *n.* mate, *Cl* 695; companion, *Cl* 124

mach(ch) *v.* equal, match, *G* 282; *reflex.* settle, agree, *Pat* 99; exert oneself, strive, *Cl* 1512

mad *see* **make**

mad(de) *adj.* mad. *See also* **arayde**

madde *v.* rave, *Pe* 359; behave stupidly, *G* 2414

maddyng *n.* madness, *Pe* 1154

made(n), maȝt *see* **make, myȝt(e)**

maȝty, myȝty *adj.* mighty, powerful

maȝtyly *adv.* forcefully; fiercely, *Cl* 1267

Mahoun *n.* Mohammed (*as a heathen deity*)

make *n.* wife, spouse; mate; equal, *Cl* 248*n*

make, ma *v.* (**makes, matz, mas, mace** *pres3sg.*, **man** *pres.pl.*, **mad(e)(n)** *pa.t.*, **mad(e), maked** *pp.*) make; create; cause, compel, *Pe* 176, *Cl* 1566, *Pat* 54, *G* 1567, *etc.*; do, perform, *Cl* 1238, *G* 43, 1073, *etc.*; tell, *Pe* 304; *see also* **acorde, cher(e), ene, fest(e), paye, rescoghe, somoun, toȝt**

makel(l)ez *adj.* matchless, peerless

male *n.*[1] male

males, -z *n.*[2] bags, *G* 1129, 1809

malicious *adj.* wicked, *Pat* 508; severe, *Pat* 522

malscrande *adj.* bewildering

malskred *pp.* dazed

malte *v.* (**malt(e)** *pa.t.*) melt; condense, trickle, *G* 2080; be resolved, *Cl* 1566; soften (*trans.*), *Cl* 776; dissolve (*trans.*), *Pe* 1154; **m. in** enter into, comprehend, *Pe* 224

malys, malyce *n.* wickedness, sin; anger, *Cl* 250; malice, resentment, *Pat* 4; severity, *Pat* 523

Mambre *n.* Mamre

man *see* **make, mon**

manace *v.* (**mansed** *pa.t.*) threaten

manayre *see* **maner**

mancioun *n.* dwelling place

Mane *n.* **Mene**

maner, manayre *n.*[1] (manor); house, *Pe* 918; city, *Pe* 1029

maner *n.*[2] custom; kind, *G* 484; way, *G* 1730; *pl.* manners, *Pe* 382, *G* 924; ways, *Pat* 22

manerly *adj.* polite, dignified, *G* 1656

manerly *adv.* properly, courteously, *Cl* 91

manez *see* **mon**

mangerye, -ie *n.* banquet, feast

mankyn *n.* mankind, *Pe* 637

mankynde, monkynde *n.* mankind

mannez *see* **mon**

mansed *pp.adj.* cursed. *See also* **manace**

mantyle, -ile *n.* mantle, cloak

marchal, mare *see* **marschal, more**

margyrye, margary, marjory, margeryeperle *n.* pearl, *Pe* 199, 206, 1037

marie *v.* (**maryed** *pp.*) marry

marked *n.* market, *Pe* 513

marre *v.*[1] destroy, *Cl* 991 (*pp.*), *G* 2262; corrupt, *Cl* 279; disfigure, *Pe* 23; *intrans.* perish, *Pat* 172, 474; suffer, *Pat* 479

marre *v.*[2] lament, *Pe* 359

marryng *n.* spoiling

mar(s)chal *n.* marshal, master of ceremonies

maryag(e) *n.* marriage

Mary(e) *n.* (the Virgin) Mary; marry!, *G* 1942, 2140

mas *see* **make**

mase *n.* confusion, damnation, *Cl* 395*n*

maskl(l)e, mascle *n.* spot

maskel(l)ez, -es, mascellez *adj.* spotless, flawless
mas(se), messe *n.* (service of) Mass; gospel read at Mass, *Cl* 51. *See also* **mes(se)**
masseprest *n.* ordained priest
mat(e) *adj.* frightened, subdued, *G* 336; exhausted, *G* 1568; dejected, *Pe* 386
mate *v.* shame, defeat, *Pe* 613
mater *n.* matter, substance; primal matter, *Pat* 503
matz *see* **make**
Maþew, Mathew *n.* (St) Matthew
maugré, maugref, mawgref *prep.* in spite of (**my chekes, his hed,** *etc.* myself, himself, *etc.*). *See Pat* 44*n*
mawe *n.* belly
mawgré *n.* displeasure, *Cl* 250
mawgref *see* **maugré**
may *n.* maiden, *Pe* 435, *etc.*; woman, *G* 1795(2)
mayden(n) *n.* maiden; virgin, *Pe* 869*n*; (the Virgin Mary), *Cl* 248, 1069
may(e) *v.* (**may, moun, mowe** *pres.pl.*, **my3t(ez), mo3t(e)(n)** *pa.t.*) can, may, will (*fut.*); **quat he m.** (*sc.* **do**) what he would do, *G* 1087
mayn *adj.* great, *G* 94, *etc.*; strong, *G* 497
maynful *adj.* mighty, powerful
maynly *adv.* loudly
maynteine, -tyne, menteene *v.* maintain (in argument), *Pe* 783; support (as lord), *G* 2053; exercise, *Pat* 523
mayntnaunce *n.* maintenance, supporting
mayny *see* **me(y)ny**
mayster *n.* lord, master; **maystres** *pl.* learned men, *Pat* 329
maysterful *adj.* arrogant, *Pe* 401, *Cl* 1328
mayster(r)y *n.* victory, triumph
maystrés *n.* miraculous powers, *G* 2448
maystres *see also* **mayster**
me *pron.* one, *Cl* 553. *See* **mon** *indef.pron.*
me *see also* **I**
med *see* **mete**
mede *n.* reward; **to m.** as a reward, *Pat* 55
medoes *n.* meadows
megre *adj.* thin
meke *adj.* meek, gentle, submissive; merciful, *Cl* 771; *as n.* humble servant, *Cl* 776
mekely *adv.* meekly
mekenesse, Mekenesse *n.* meekness; Meekness (*personified*), *Pat* 32
mekned *pa.t.* humbled
mele *n.*[1] meal, flour, *Cl* 226, 625
mele *n.*[2] meal, dinner, *G* 999
mel(l)e *v.*[1] speak, say, tell
melle *v.*[2] mingle, flow, *G* 2503
melly *n.* quarrel, *G* 342; battle, *G* 644
membre *n.* limb, member
men *see* **mon**
menddyng *n.* amendment, *Cl* 764; improvement, *Pe* 452
mended *pa.t.* improved, *G* 883
mendez *n.* recompense, *Pe* 351
mene *adj.* poor, *Cl* 1241
mene *v.* mean, signify, *Pe* 293, 951, *G* 233; refer to, *Pe* 937; say, *Cl* 1625

meng(e) *v.* mix, mingle; **menged** *pp.* mingled, *G* 1720
menscla3t *n.* manslaughter
mensk *adj.* charming, courteous, *G* 964
mensk(e) *n.* honour, courtesy, grace; **of m.** courteous, *Pe* 162, courteously, *Cl* 646
menske *v.* honour, *Cl* 118, 141; *pp.* adorned, *G* 153
menskful *adj.* fine, noble (*& as n.*)
menskly *adv.* fittingly, with honour
menteene, meny *see* **maynteine, me(y)ny**
menyng *n.* understanding, *G* 924
mercy, merci, Mercy, mersy *n.* mercy; Mercy (*personified*), *Pat* 32. *See also* **gra(u)nt mercy**
mercyable *adj.* merciful
mercyles *adj.* merciless
mere *adj.* noble, *G* 924
mere *n.*[1] sea, *Cl* 991, *Pat* 112; pool, water, *Pe* 140, 158, 1166
mere *n.*[2] boundary, *Cl* 778, *Pat* 320; rendezvous, *G* 1061
meré *see* **myry**
Mergot *n.* Margot, *Pat* 167*n*
merit *n.* reward
merk *adj.* dark, obscure
merk *n.*[1] darkness, *Cl* 894, *Pat* 291
merk *n.*[2] appointed place, rendezvous, *G* 1073
merk(k)e *v.* aim at, *G* 1592; set out, place, *Cl* 558, 637, 1487; write, *Cl* 1617, 1727; *pp.* situated, *Pe* 142
mersy *see* **mercy**
merþe, mirþe, my(e)rþe *n.* joy, pleasure, amusement; merriment, rejoicing; pleasant subjects, *Cl* 132, *G* 541, 1763; harmony, music, *Pe* 92; **make m.** rejoice, make merry. *See also* **myrþe** *v.*
meruayl(e), merwayle *n.* marvel, wonder, amazement; **had m.** wondered, *G* 233; *adj.* marvellous, *Pat* 81
meruelous *adj.* miraculous, *Pe* 1166
mery(ly), mes *see* **myry(ly), mes(se)**
meschaunce *n.* doom, disaster
meschef *n.* misfortune, trouble; plight, guilt, *G* 1774
mese *v.* moderate
message *n.* message; messenger, *Cl* 454
mes(se) *n.* meal, *Pe* 862; 'breakfast' (light meal), *G* 999(1); dish (of food), *Cl* 637, *G* 999(2), 1004. *See also* **mas(se)**
messequyle *n.* time of Mass, *G* 1097
mester *n.* need, *Pat* 342, *Cl* 67
mesurable *adj.* moderate, mild
mesure *n.* moderation; size, *Pe* 224; **on m. hyghe** in height, *G* 137
met *see* **met(e)** *adj.*
metail (metalles *pl.*) *n.* metal
mete, med *adj.* proper, fitting; equal, *Cl* 1662; proportionate, *Cl* 1391*n*; sufficient, *Pat* 420; reaching, *G* 1736; **is ... m.** agrees, *Pe* 833; **-ly** *adv.* properly
mete *n.* food; meal, feast
mete *v.*[1] meet; find, *Pe* 329; greet, *G* 834, 2206*n*, 2235
mete *v.*[2] measure, *G* 2206*n*; **meten** *pp.* measured, *Pe* 1032

meth *see* **meþe**

methles, meþelez *adj.* intemperate, immoderate

mettez *n.* measures

metz *n.* mildness, mercy

meþe, meth *n.* moderation, mildness, mercy

meþelez *see* **methles**

meue, mwe *v.* move, proceed, go; influence, *G* 90; initiate, *G* 985; occur, *Pe* 64; **m. to** portend, *G* 1197, rouse, *G* 1157

me(y)ny, mayny *n.* company, household, retinue; body of workmen, *Pe* 542

miche, mirþe, miry *see* **much(e), merþe, myry**

mislyke, mys- *v.impers.* displease

misschapen *adj.* deformed, evil

mistrauþe *n.* lack of faith

misy *n.* marsh, *G* 749

Mizael *n.* Mishael

mo *compar. adj. & adv.* more (*usu. in number*); **þe mo** the greater (benefit), *Pe* 340

mod(e) *n.*[1] anger, temper; mind, mood, *Cl* 713, *G* 1475; message, thought, *Cl* 6135; *fig.* nature, character, *Pe* 738

mode *n.*[2] melody, *Pe* 884

moder *n.* mother

moder-chylde *n.* mother's son

mod(e)y *adj.* proud; brave, *Cl* 1303

moȝt(e)(n), moȝtez *see* **may**

mokke *n.* muck, filth, *Pe* 905

mol *see* **mul**

molaynes *n.* bit-studs, *G* 169

mold(e) *n.* earth; *pl.* clods (*or possess.* of earth), *Pe* 30, *Pat* 494, lands, *Cl* 454

mon, man *n.* man; servant; **vche m.** everyone; **no m.** nobody; *gen.* **man(n)ez, monnez** man's, human; *pl.* **men(ne)** men, people

mon, man, men, me *indef. pron.* one, *Pe* 165, 194, *etc.*, *Cl* 180, 183, *etc.*, *Pat* 43, *G* 565, 1077, *etc.*

mon *v.* must, *G* 1811, 2354

mone *n.*[1] moon; month, *Pe* 1080; **(an)vnder m.** on earth, in existence; completely, *Pe* 923

mon(e), moon *n.*[2] moaning, lamentation, *Cl* 373, *G* 737; grief (*i.e.* loss), *Pe* 374

moni(e), mony(e) *adj. & pron.* many (a); **m. on** many a one, *G* 442

monkynde *see* **mankynde**

mon-sworne *n.* perjury

mony(e) *see* **moni(e)**

monyfolde *adv.* greatly, many times

monyth *n.* month

moon, moote *see* **mon(e)** *n.*[2]**. mot(e)**

more *n.* moor; earth, *Cl* 385

more, mare *compar. adj. & adv.* greater, larger; more; further, *Cl* 48; moreover, *Pe* 565; **most(e)** *superl. adj.* largest, biggest, greatest; *superl. adv.* most. *Cf.* **much(e), mukel**

Morgne (la Faye) *n.* Morgan le Fay

mornande *presp.* mourning, lamenting

morn(e), moroun *n.* morning; next day

morne *see also* **mo(u)rne**

mornyf *adj.* sorrowful

mornyng, -ing *n.* morning

mornyng *see also* **mo(u)rnyng(e)**

moroun *see* **morn(e)**

morteres *n.* candles

most(e) *see* **more, mot**

mot *auxil.v.* (**most(e)** *pa.t.*) may, must; *pa.t.* must; would have to, *Pat* 55

mot(e) *n.*[1] mote, speck; stain, spot, blemish, *Pe* 726, *etc.*, *Cl* 556; **not a m.** not a jot, *G* 2209

mote *n.*[2] dispute, quarrel, *Pe* 855

mote *n.*[3] moat; castle, *G* 635, *etc.*; court, (walled) city, *Pe* 142, *etc.*, *Pat* 422

mote, motez *n.*[4] notes of the horn

mote *v.* argue, *Pe* 613

moteles, -lez *adj.* spotless

moul *n.* earth, *Pe* 23. *Cf.* **mul**

moun *see* **may**

mountaunce *n.* amount, size

mountaynez *n.* mountains

mount(e) *n.* mountain, hill; **bi m.** among the hills, *G* 718

mounte *v.* amount, *Pat* 332; increase, *Pe* 351

mounture *n.* mount, horse, *G* 1691

mourkene *v.*[1] grow dark, *Cl* 1760

mourkne *v.*[2] rot, *Cl* 407

mo(u)rne *v.* lament, grieve; repent, *Pat* 508

mo(u)rnyng(e) *n.* sorrow; **in m. of** oppressed by, *G* 1751

mouþe, m(o)uth(e), mowþe *n.* mouth; voice

mowe *see* **may(e)**

much(e), miche, mych *adj., adv. & pron.* big, great, large, abundant, strong, *Pe* 604, *etc.*, *Cl* 22, *etc.*, *Pat* 70, *G* 182, *etc.*; a lot (of), much, *Pe* 244, *etc.*, *Cl* 182, *etc.*, *G* 558, *etc.*; **þus m.** as much as this, as follows; **much quat** many things; *adv.* much, greatly, very. *See also* **more, mukel**

muckel *n.* size, *G* 142

mudde *n.* mud

muged *pa.t.* drizzled, lay damp, *G* 2080

mukel *adj.* large, great; *adv.* greatly, *Pat* 324. *See also* **much(e), more**

mul, mol *n.* dust

mulne *n.* mill

mun *n.* mouth

munster, mynster *n.* church, temple

munt *see* **mynt, mynte**

muryly *see* **myryly**

mused *pa.t.* doted, wandered in mind, *G* 2424

mute *n.* pack of hounds; sound (of a hunt), *G* 1915

muth(e), mwe *see* **mouþe, meue**

my, myn(e) *possess. pron. & adj.* my; mine

mych *see* **much(e)**

myddelerde *n.* the earth

myddes, myddez *n.* midst. *Cf.* **inmyddes**

mydmorn *n.* mid-morning, 9 a.m.

mydnyȝt *n.* midnight

myd ouer vnder *n.* well on in the afternoon, *G* 1730*n*

myerþe *see* **merþe**

myȝt(e), maȝt *n.* might, power, strength; **at my m.** to the best of my ability

myȝt(ez) *see also* **may**

myȝty *see* **maȝty**

myke *n.*[1] crutch (forked support for lowered mast), *Cl* 417

mykez *n.*[2] (friends); chosen, *Pe* 572*n*

mylde *adj.* merciful; mild, gentle, *Pe* 961, 1115; *as n.* gentle ones, *Pe* 721
myle *n.* mile
mylke *n.* milk
mylke *v.* milk, *Cl* 1259
mynde *n.* mind, heart, spirit; intention, *Cl* 1502; memory, *G* 1283, 1484; **in m. hade** remembered, *G* 1283; **gotz in m.** is questionable, *G* 1293
myn(e), mynez *see* my, myn(n)e
mynge *v.* draw attention to, *G* 1422; think, *Pe* 855
mynne *adj.* less(er), *G* 1881
myn(n)e *v.* remember, think about; remind, declare; *impers.* **me mynez** I think, *Cl* 25
mynster *see* munster
mynstra(l)sy(e), -cie *n.* minstrelsy
mynt, -u- *n.* aim; feint, *G* 2345, *etc.*; purpose, intention, *Pe* 1161
mynte *v.* (**mynte, munt** *pa.t.*) aim (a blow), swing, *G* 2262, 2274, 2290; intend, purpose, *Cl* 1628
mynystred *pa.t.* served
myre *n.* mire; swamp
myri, myrþe *see* myry, merþe
myrþez *v.trans.* rejoices, gladdens, *Pe* 862
myry, mery, meré, mi(y)ry, myri *adj.* merry, pleasant, good-humoured, bonny, *etc.*; fine, beautiful, handsome, *Pe* 23, 158, *etc.*, *Cl* 417, 783, *etc.*, *G* 142, 153, *etc.*
myryly, meryly, muryly *adv.* happily, cheerfully; playfully, *G* 2345; splendidly, *G* 740
mys *see* mys(se)
mysboden *pp.* ill used, mistreated, *G* 2339
mysdede *n.* sin
myself(e), myseluen *pron.* myself; me, *Pe* 414, *Cl* 1572
myserecorde *n.* mercy, *Pe* 366
mysetente *pp.* misunderstood, distorted, *Pe* 257
myslyke *see* mislyke
mys(se) *n.* offence, fault; loss, grief, *Pe* 262, 364
mysse *v.* (**myst** *pp.*) lose, lack, miss; fail to obtain, *Cl* 189
mysseȝeme *v.* neglect, *Pe* 322
mysseleue *n.* misbelief, *Cl* 1230
myssepayed *pp.* displeased
myst, mist *n.* mist
myst *see also* mysse
myste *n.* spiritual mysteries, *Pe* 462
mysterys *n.* mysteries, *Pe* 1194
myst-hakel *n.* cape of mist, cap-cloud, *G* 2081n
myte *n.* mite (small coin); **not a m.** not a jot, *Pe* 351
myþe *v.* conceal, *Pe* 359

Nabugo *n.* Nebuchadnezzar
Nabugodenozar, Nabigodenozar *n.* Nebuchadnezzar
Nabuzardan, Nabizardan *n.* Nebuzaradan
naf *v.* have not, *G* 1066; **nade** *pa.t. & pa.subjunc.* had not
naȝt(e)(s) *see* nyȝt(e)

naked *adj.* naked, bare; *as n.* (bare) flesh, *G* 423, 2002
nakerys *n.* drums; **nakryn** *g.pl. or adj.* of drums
name, nome *n.* name
nappe *v.* sleep
nar *v.* are not; **nas** was not; **nere** *pa.subjunc.* were not, *Cl* 21, *Pat* 244
nase *n.* nose
nature, natwre *n.* nature
nauel, naule *n.* (navel); stomach, insides
nauþeles, naw-, nowþelese *adv.* nevertheless, *Pe* 877, *etc.*; *also* **neuerþelese, -ce,** *Pe* 912 *etc.*, *G* 474
nauþer, naw-, nou- *adj.*, *adv. & conj.* neither, either, nor
nawhere *see* nowhere
nay *adv.* no, nay
nay(ed) *pa.t.* refused, said no, *Cl* 65, 805, *G* 1836n
naylet *pp.* nailed, studded
naylez *n.* nails
nayte *v.* use; *pp.* **nayted** celebrated, repeated (*a pun*), *G* 65
naytly *adv.* well, properly
ne, nee *adv. & conj.* not; nor; or
nec *see* nek(ke)
nece *n.* niece, *Pe* 233
nede *n.* need, *Pe* 1045, *Cl* 1163; *pl.* **nedez** affairs, business, *G* 2216
nede *v.impers. in* **hit nedes** is necessary; (**hem**) **nedde** *pa.t.* was necessary (to them), *Pe* 1044
nede(s), (-z) *adv.* of necessity
nedles, -z *adj.* useless
nee *see* ne
neȝ(e), negh(e) *v.* approach; come to, reach
neȝ(e), neghe *see also* nyȝe
neked *n.* (a) little
nek(ke), nec *n.* neck
nel, nem(e), nemme *see* nyl, nym(e), neuen
nente *adj.* ninth, *Pe* 1012
ner(e) (*orig.compar. of* nyȝe) *adj.*, *adv. & prep.* near(er), nearly; **nerre** *compar.* nearer
nere *see also* nar
nesch *adj.* soft; *as n.* what is pleasant, *Pe* 606
neue *n.* fist, hand
neuen, nemme *v.* name, call, mention
neuer *adv.* never; not at all, *Pe* 333, 376, *etc.*, *Cl* 820, 862, *etc.*, *G* 376, 399, *etc.*; **n. bot** only, *G* 547; **n. onez** not one person's, *Pe* 864; **n. so** however, *Pe* 571, *Cl* 1330, *Pat* 156, 391, 420, *G* 2129; **n. þe les**(se) never (not at all) less, undiminished, *Pe* 852, *etc.*, *Cl* 215, nevertheless (*cf.* nauþeles) *Pe* 900, *etc.*
neuermore *adv.* never, *Cl* 191
n(e)w(e) *adj.* new, fresh; *adv.* newly, anew; **newes** *gen. sg.* (*as n.*) new thing, *G* 1407; **n. fryt** first fruits, *Pe* 894; **New Ȝere, Nw(e) Ȝer(e)** New Year
next(e) *adv. & prep.* next (to), immediately
nice, nys(e) *adj.* foolish; fastidious; wanton
nieȝ *see* nyȝe
nieȝbor *n.* neighbour
nif, nyf *conj.* if not, unless
nikked, -y- *v.* said no, *G* 706n, 2471

Niniue, Nuniue, Nynyue *n.* Nineveh
nirt *n.* cut, nick
nis, niye, niȝȝt *see* **nys, ny(ȝ)e, nyȝt(e)**
no *adj. & adv.* no
nobelay, nobleye, noblé *n.* nobility (of conduct)
noble, nobel(e) *adj.* noble; *and as n.*
nobot *adv.* only
Noe *n.* Noah
noȝt *adv. & pron.* nothing; not (at all); **for n.** in vain. *See also* **bot**
noȝ(t) *see also* **not**
noȝty *adj.* wicked
nok(e) *n.* nook, corner; point, angle, *G* 660
nolde *see* **nyl**
nom(e)(n) *see* **name, nym(e)**
no(n)(e) *adj.* no, any; **non(e)** *pron.* none, nothing, no one
nonez *pron.* **for the n.** indeed
norne, -u- *v.* ask, urge, *Cl* 803, *G* 1771; say, declare, *Cl* 65, 669; propose, *G* 1669*n*; offer, *G* 1823; call, *G* 2443; **n. aȝaynez** refuse, repulse
norture, nurture *n.* nurture, upbringing, good breeding
norþ(e) *adj. & n.* north
norþ-est *n.* northeast
nos *n.* opening
not, noȝ(t) *adv.* not
not *v.* know not, *G* 1053
note *n.*[1] task, activity, business, matter (*sometimes blended with n.*[2]); place, piece of work, *Pe* 922
note *n.*[2] note (musical), tune, *Pe* 879, 883, *Cl* 1413, *G* 514; fame, renown, *Cl* 1651; reputation, custom, *Cl* 727
note(d) *pp.adj.* well-known, famous
notyng *n.* using, partaking of
noþyng *adv.* not at all, *G* 2236
noþyng, noþynk *n.* nothing
noumbles *n.* numbles (offal of deer)
noumbre *n.* number
nouþe, nowþe *adv.* now
nouþer *see* **nauþer**
now(e), nov *adv. & conj.* now; now that, since, *Pe* 283, 377, 389, *G* 2296, 2420; if (now), *Cl* 721; **ryȝt n.** immediately
Nowel *n.* Christmas; the cry 'Nowel'
nowhere, nawhere *adv.* nowhere, anywhere
nowþe, nowþelese *see* **nouþe, nauþeles**
noyce, noyse *n.* noise, sound; music
noye, nye, nwye, nuye *v.* trouble; harass; injure
nummen, Nuniue, nurne(d), nurture *see* **nym(e), Niniue, norne, norture**
nuyez, nuyed *see* **noye**
nw(e) *see* **n(e)w(e)**
nwy(d) *see* **ny(ȝ)e, noye**
ny(ȝ)e, niye, nwy *n.* trouble, difficulty, vexation; bitter cold, *G* 2002
nye(d), nyf *see* **noye, nif**
nyȝe, neȝ(e), nieȝ, neghe *adv. & prep.* nigh, nearly; near. *See also* **ner(e)**
nyȝt(e), naȝt(e), niȝyt *n.* night; **on n.,** **on nyȝtes** at night; **at forþ naȝtes** late at night
nykked *see* **nikked**

nyl, nel, nylt *v.* (**nolde** *pa.t.*) will not
nym(e), nymme, neme *v.* (**nem, nom(e)** *pa.t.*, **nomen, nummen, inome** *pp.*) take, receive; undertake, *G* 91; *pp.* trapped, refuted in argument, *Pe* 703
Nynyue *see* **Niniue**
nys, nis *v.* is not, *Pe* 100, 951, *G* 1266
nys(e) *see* **nice**
nyteled *pa.t.* made a disturbance

o, oo! *interj.* oh!
o *see also* **of**
obes *v.* (**obeched** *pa.t.*) do obeisance (to), *Pe* 886, *Cl* 745
odde *adj.* odd; *as n.* odd one, single one, *Cl* 505
oddely *adv.* singularly, *Cl* 698; entirely, *Cl* 923
odour *n.* fragrance, *Pe* 58
of, o *prep.* of; about, *Pe* 925, *etc.*, *Cl* 26, *etc.*, *G* 94, *etc.*; from, (away) from, out of, *Pe* 31, 334, *etc.*, *Cl* 596, 855, *etc.*, *Pat* 188, 391, *etc.*, *G* 183, 1087, *etc.*; (made) out of, *Pe* 110, *etc.*, *Cl* 1276, *etc.*, *Pat* 438, *etc.*, *G* 121, *etc.*; with, *Pe* 119, *etc.*, *Cl* 1404, *etc.*, *G* 172, *etc.*; because of, through, *Pe* 11, *etc.*, *Cl* 848, *etc.*, *Pat* 443, *etc.*, *G* 86, *etc.*; by (agent), *Pe* 248, *Cl* 243, 1059, *Pat* 386, *G* 64; in respect of, *Pe* 74, *etc.*, *Cl* 92, *etc.*, *Pat* 23, *etc.*, *G* 143, *etc.*; (thank, *etc.*) for, *G* 96, 755, 975, *etc.*
of *adv.* off, *Pe* 237, 358, *Cl* 630, *etc.*, *G* 773, *etc.*
offys *n.* office, position, *Pe* 755
oft(e) *adv.* (**ofter** *compar.*) often, many times
oghe, oȝe, owe *v.* (**aȝt(e), oȝte** *pa.t.*) have, *G* 1941; own, *G* 767, 843, 1775; owe, *Pe* 543; (*pres. & pa.t.*) ought, *Pe* 1139, *Cl* 122, *G* 1526; *impers. Pe* 341, 552
oȝt *n.* anything, something
oke *n.* oak
olde *adj.* (**alder** *compar.*, **aldest** *superl.*) old; long-established, *G* 1124; **for o.** on account of age, *G* 1440
olipraunce *n.* ostentation
olyue *n.* olive
on *prep. & adv.* on, upon; in, *Pe* 97, 425, *etc.*, *Cl* 271, 327, *etc.*, *Pat* 133, *G* 1722, 1730, *etc.*; at, *Pe* 45, 243, *Cl* 578, *G* 47, 479, *etc.*; about, *Pe* 436, 771, *G* 683, 1800, *etc.*; **on a day** a (each) day, *Pe* 510, **on ȝer** a year, *Pe* 1079; **on huntyng,** *etc.* a-hunting, *etc.*, *G* 1102, 1143; **on lyue** alive, on earth (*or intensive:* indeed)
on(e) *adj.*[1] & pron. one, (a), *Pe* 9, 551, *etc.*, *Cl* 112, 152, *etc.*, *Pat* 312, 355, *G* 30, 206, *etc.*; one (and the same), *Cl* 716, 718, *Pat* 39; *pron.* one, *Pe* 293, 557, *etc.*, *Cl* 25, 42, *etc.*, *Pat* 34, *G* 137, 223, *etc.*; **þat o.** the one; **at o.** at one, united; **onez** of one, *Pe* 864
on(e) *adj.*[2] & adv. alone; merely, *Pat* 354; single, *Pat* 208, *G* 2249, 2345; **hym (oure,** *etc.*) **o.** (by) himself, ourselves, *etc.*; **myn one** myself, *Pat* 503; **by myn one** by myself, alone, *Pe* 243
onelych, only *adv.* only; alone, *Pe* 779
onende *see* **anende**
ones, -z *adv.* once; **at o.** together, at once; **at þys o.** on this occasion, here and now. *See also* **on(e)** *pron.*

onewe *adv.* anew
onferum *adv.* from a distance
onhede *n.* unity
onhelde *pp.* huddled
onhit *pp.* seized
only *see* **onelych**
onlyue *adj.* alive, *Cl* 356; *cf.* **alyue, lyf**
onstray *adv.* out of course, in a changed direction
onsware, answar *n.* answer
onsware, answ(a)re *v.* answer
on-vnder *see* **an-vnder**
onyʒed *adj.* one-eyed
oo *see* **o**
oquere *adv.* anywhere, *G* 660
or *conj.* or; than, *G* 1543; (*cf.* **oþer** *conj.*)
ordaynt *pp.adj.* ordained
ordenaunce *n.* ordinance, plan
ordure *n.* filth
orenge *n.* orange
ores *n.* oars
organes *n.* wind instruments
orient, oryent(e) the orient, the East, *Pe* 3, 82; *as adj. Pe* 255
orisoun *n.* prayer
oritore *n.* chapel
ornementes, vrnmentes *n.* ornaments
orp(p)edly *adv.* boldly, quickly
oryent(e), oryʒt *see* **orient, aryʒt**
ossed *pa.t.* showed
oste *n.* host
ostel *see* **(h)ostel**
oþer *adj. & pron.* other; second, *Cl* 235, *G* 1020, 2350; another, the other, *Cl* 267, *G* 501, 628; **þat o.** the other, *Pe* 955, *Cl* 299, *etc.*, *Pat* 515, *G* 110, *etc.*; *pl.* others, *Pe* 585, *etc.*, *Cl* 25, *etc.*, *Pat* 176, *etc.*, *G* 64, *etc.*; **an o.** otherwise, a (quite) differing thing, *G* 1268; **non o.** nothing else; **ayþer o., vchon o.** *see* **ayþer, vchon**
oþer, auþer, or *adv. & conj.* or (else); otherwise; **o. . . . o. (or)** either . . . or
oþerquyle, oþerwhyle *adv.* at other times, *G* 722; sometimes, *Pat* 121
oþerwayez *adv.* otherwise
oþez *n.* oaths
ouer *prep. & adv.* over, above, across, upon; too, *Pe* 473
oueral *adv.* all over, *G* 150; in all parts, *G* 630
ouerborde *adv.* overboard
ouerbrawden *adj.* covered over
ouerclambe *pa.t.* climbed over
ouerʒede *pa.t.* passed, went by
ouerloked *pa.t.* looked over their heads, *G* 223
ouerseyed *pp.* passed
ouertake *v.* (**-tok,** *pa.t.,* **-tan,** *pp.*) overtake, *Cl* 1213, *Pat* 127; understand, *G* 2387
ouerte *adj.* plain
ouertorned *pa.t.* passed by
ouerture *n.* neck-opening, *Pe* 218
ouerpwert *adj. & adv.* crosswise, at right angles, *Cl* 316, 1384; *prep.* across, *G* 1438
ouerwaltez *v.* overflows, *Cl* 370; *pp.* **ouerwalt** overthrown, *G* 314
our(e) *possess.adj.* our
oure *see also* **(h)oure**

out *see* **out(e)**
outþorst *pa.t.* burst out
outcomlyng *n.* stranger
outdryf *v.* drive out, *Pe* 777
out(e) *adv.* out; whatsoever, in existence, *Cl* 1046; far and wide, *G* 1511; *prep.* **out of** out of, from, *Pe* 3, 1163, *Cl* 287, *etc.*, *Pat* 137, *etc.*, *G* 802, *etc.*; deprived of, away from, *Pe* 642; past, beyond, *Cl* 656 (**hyʒe o. of age** advanced in age); expired, *Cl* 442. *See also* **day(e), dryue**
outfleme *adj.* driven out
outkast *pp.* cast out
outryʒte *adv.* directly out (of), *Pe* 1055
outsprent *pa.t.* gushed out, *Pe* 1137
outtaken *prep.* except
outtrage *adj.* extraordinary
outtulde *pp.* thrown out
ouþer *pron.* either, *Cl* 795
owe *see* **oghe**
owen, owne *see* **aune**
ox(e) *n.* ox

pace *n.* passage, *Pe* 677
pacience, pacyence, Pacyence *n.* patience, long-suffering; Patience (*personified*), *Pat* 33
pacient *adj.* patient, long-suffering
pakke *n.* gathering, company, *Pe* 929
pakked *pa.t.* packed
Palastyn *n.* Palestine
palays, palayce *n.*[1] palace
palays *n.*[2] fence, palisade, *G* 769
pale *v.* show pale, *Pe* 1004
palle *n.*[1] cloth, robe
palle *n.*[2] wooden platform, *Cl* 1384n
pane *n.* fur facing, edging; side, wall, *Pe* 1034
papejayes, -ez *n.* parrots
paper, papure *n.* paper
par ma fay *see* **fay**
paradys(e), paradis(e) paradise, heaven; the Earthly Paradise, the Garden of Eden, *Pe* 137, 321, *Cl* 238, 1007 (*see also Pe* 9n, 65n)
parage *n.* lineage
paramorez *n.* lovers, love
parauenture, paraunter, peraunter *adv.* perhaps
parchmen *n.* parchment
pared *pa.t. & pp.* cut, shaped
parformed *pa.t.* performed, brought to pass
parfyt, perfet *adj.* perfect
parget *n.* plaster
parlatyk *adj.* paralytic
part *n.* part, share
part *v.* divide, *Cl* 1107; *intrans.* separate, part, *G* 2473; descend, *Cl* 242
partlez *adj.* deprived, *Pe* 335
partrykez *n.* partridges
passage *n.* passage, journey
passe *v.* (**passed, past(e)** *pa.t. & pp.*) pass, go, travel; finish, end; cross, *Pe* 299, *G* 2071; surpass, *Pe* 428, 753, *Cl* 1389, *G* 1014; go free, *Pe* 707
Pater *n.* Paternoster, Lord's Prayer, *Pe* 485, *G* 757
patrounes *n.* masters

paume *n.* palm, hand; flat antler, *G* 1155
paunce *n.* abdominal armour, *G* 2017
paunch *n.* stomach, *G* 1360
paune *n.pl.* claws, *Cl* 1697
pay(e) *n.* satisfaction, pleasure, *Pe* 1, 1164, *etc.*; pay(ment), *Pat* 99, *G* 2247; **makes her paye** pays their fee
pay(e) *v.* please, satisfy, pay
payne *n.* penalty, punishment, *Pe* 664, *Cl* 46, *etc.*; pain, hardship, sorrow, *Pe* 124, 954, *Cl* 190, *Pat* 525, *etc.*, *G* 733
payne *v.reflex.* take pains, endeavour, *G* 1042
paynted, -t *pa.t. & pp.* painted, *Pe* 750, *G* 800; portrayed, *G* 611
payre *n.* pair
payre *v.* be blunted, deteriorate; *pp.* wasted, *Pe* 246
payttrure *n.* breast-harness
pechche *n.* fault
pece *see* **p(y)ece**
pelure *n.* fur
penaunce, Penaunce *n.* penance; Penance (*personified*), *Pat* 31
pendaunt, -d *n.* pendant
penez *n.* pens (of animals), *Cl* 322
pené, peny *n.* (**penies, penyes** *pl.*) penny; *pl.* money
penitotes *n.* peridots, chrysolites (green gems)
penne *n.* (writing) pen, *Cl* 1546, 1724
penned *pp.* imprisoned, confined, *Pe* 53*n*
penne-fed *adj.* fed in a pen
pensyf *adj.* sorrowful
penta(u)ngel pentangle (*see G* 625*n*)
pented *pa.t.* belonged, pertained
peple *n.* people; *pl.* peoples, races, *Cl* 242
peraunter *see* **parauenture**
Perce *n.* Persia
per(e) *n.* peer, equal, *Pe* 4, *Cl* 1214, 1336, *G* 873
perelous *adj.* perilous
perez *n.* pear trees, *Pe* 104
perfet *see* **parfyt**
peril(e), peryl(e) *n.* peril, danger; doubt, *Pe* 695; **at alle peryles** whatever the consequences, *Pat* 85
perle *n.* pearl
perré *n.* jewellery, precious stones
Perses *n.* Persians
persoun *n.* person
pertermynable *adj.* supreme in judgement, *Pe* 596*n*
pertly *adv.* plainly, openly, publicly
peruing *n.* periwinkles, *G* 611*n*
peryl(e) *see* **peril(e)**
pese *n.*[1] pea, *G* 2364
pes(e), Pes *n.*[2] peace; Peace (*personified*), *Pat* 33
peté *see* **pité**
Phares *n.* Peres
pich *n.* pitch, *Cl* 1008
piched *see* **pyche**
pike, pyke *v.* gather, get, *Pe* 573; crop, *Pat* 393; peck, *Cl* 1466; *pp.* polished, cleansed, *G* 2017, adorned, *Pe* 1036. *See also* **pyked** *adj.*
pinacle, pine *see* **pynakle, pyne** *n.*
pipe *v.* pipe (*of birds*), *G* 747

pipes, pypes *n.* pipes
pité, peté, Pitée, pyté, pyty *n.* pity; compassion *or* piety, *G* 654*n*; sorrow, *Pe* 1206; Pity (*personified*), *Pat* 31
pito(u)sly, pytosly *adv.* piteously; compassionately
place *n.* place; house, dwelling, city, domain, *Pe* 405, 679, *etc.*, *Cl* 72, 146, *etc.*, *Pat* 68, 349, *etc.*, *G* 252, 398, *etc.*; space, room, *G* 123
planed *adj.* planed, smoothed
planetez *n.* planets
plant(t)ed *pa.t.* established
plat *adj.* flat; *adv.* absolutely, *Cl* 83
plat *pa.t.* struck
plate *n.* (metal) plate; piece of armour
plater *n.* platter
plattyng *n.* striking
play *n.* play, sport, enjoyment
play *v.* play, amuse oneself (*also reflex.*); rejoice, be happy, *Pe* 261
playferes *n.* playmates, companions
playn *adj.* smooth; bare, *Pat* 439; *adv.* plainly, clearly, *Pe* 689
playn *n.* plain, meadow, field
playned, playnez *see* **pleny**
pleny, playne *v.* lament, mourn; complain, *Pe* 549, *Pat* 376 (**on:** against)
playnt *n.* complaint, *Pe* 815
plede *v.* plead
plek *n.* piece of ground
plesaunce *n.* pleasure, pleasing, *G* 1247
plesaunt *adj.* courteous, obliging, *G* 808; pleasing, lovely, *Pe* 1
plese *inf.* please; **plesed** *pa.t.subjunc.* would please, *Pat* 376
plete *v.* claim, *Pe* 563
pleyned *see* **pleny**
plonttez *n.* newly-planted shrubs or trees, *Pe* 104
plow *n.* plough
plyande *presp.adj.* waving
plye *v.* incline, tend, *Cl* 196; join, be attached, *Pe* 1039; be contained, enclosed, *Cl* 1385
plyt *n.* situation, condition, *Pe* 1015, *Cl* 111, 1494, *Pat* 114, *G* 733; array, grouping, *Pe* 1114; predicament, *Pe* 647
plyȝt *n.* condition, *Pe* 1075; danger, *G* 266; guilt, *G* 2393
pobbel *n.* pebble, *Pe* 117
polaynez *n.* knee pieces (*of armour*)
pole *n.* (pool); water-course, *Pe* 117; *pl.* **powlez** seas, depths
polle *n.* (hair of) head
polment *n.* pottage, broth
polyce, ice *v.* polish; *fig.* make clean, bright
polyle *n.* poultry
polyst *see* **polyce**
pomgarnades *n.* pomegranates
poplande *adj.* foaming
porchase, -ce *v.* strive (for), *Pe* 439; buy, *Pe* 744
pore *see* **pouer(e)**
porfyl *n.* embroidered border, *Pe* 216
porpos(e), pur- *n.* purpose, intention, *Pe* 267, 508, *G* 1734; (aim), quarry, *Pe* 185*n*
porpre, porpor, purpre *n. & adj.* purple

Porros *n.* Porus
port *n.*[1] port, harbour
port *n.*[2] gate, *Cl* 856
portalez *n.* portals, gateways
portrayed, pourtrayd, purtrayed, *pa.t. & pp.* devised, designed, *Cl* 700; formed, fashioned, *Cl* 1465, 1536; adorned, decorated, *Cl* 1271
poruay *v.* equip oneself with, *Pat* 36; settle on, *Cl* 1502
postes *n.* pillars
potage *n.* pottage
poudred, powdered *pp.* scattered, *Pe* 44, *G* 800
pouer(e), pore *adj.* poor, wretched; *as n.* the poor, *Cl* 127; poor man, *Cl* 615; *adv.* poorly, *Cl* 146. *See also* **power**
pouert(é), Pouert *n.* poverty; Poverty (*personified*), *Pat* 31
Poule, Saynt *n.* St Paul
poursent, pourtrayd, powdered *see* **pursaunt, portrayed, poudred**
power, pouer *n.* power
powlez *see* **pole**
poyned *n.* wristband, *Pe* 217
poynt(e) *n.* point; point in time, moment, *Cl* 628, *Pat* 68; point of doctrine, *Pe* 594; instance, *Pe* 309; high point, height, *Cl* 1502, 1677; condition, *Pat* 35; good condition, *G* 2049; virtue, *Pat* 1, 531, *G* 654; question, *G* 902; strain (of music), *Pe* 891; **vch a p.** everything, *Cl* 196
poynte *v.* describe in detail, *G* 1009
poynted *pp.* tipped
poyntel *n.* stylus
poysened *adj.* poisoned
pray *n.* booty, prize
pray(e) *v.* pray, ask, beseech; invite, *Cl* 72
prayed *pa.t.* plundered, *Cl* 1624
prayer(e) *n.*[1] prayer
prayere *n.*[2] meadow, *G* 768
prayse *v.* praise; compliment, *G* 2072; esteem, value, *Cl* 146, *G* 1850; *pp.adj.* valued, prized, *Pe* 1112; **to p.** praiseworthy, estimable, *Pe* 301, *Cl* 189, *G* 356
prec(e), -s *n.* press, crowd; crowding, *Pe* 1114
prece, -s *v.* hurry, press forward; press, crush, *Cl* 1249
prech(e) *v.* preach
precio(u)s, presyous *adj.* precious, *Pe* 36, *etc.*, *Cl* 1496; noble, *Pe* 192; rich, *Cl* 1282; in value, *Pe* 4
pref *n.* (test of experience); **is put in p.** is shown to be, *Pe* 272
prelates *n.* prelates, chief priests
pres *see* **prece** *n. & v.*
pres(e) *n.* worth, *Pe* 419; *as adj.* precious, *Pe* 730 (*cf.* **prys**)
presed *see* **prece**
presens(e) *n.* presence
present(e) *n.* presence, *Pe* 389, 1193
presoneres *see* **prisoner(e)s**
prest *adj.* eager, prompt; *adv.* quickly, *Pat* 303
prest(e) *n.* priest
prestly *adv.* promptly, readily
presyous *see* **precious**

preue *adj.* valiant, *G* 262; resolute, steadfast, *Pat* 525
preué, priuy, pryuy *adj.* special, own, *Pe* 12, 24; discreet, *G* 902; **-ly** *adv.* in private, *G* 1877; apart, *Cl* 238; mysteriously, *Cl* 1107; **pryuyest** *superl.* nearest, most confidential, *Cl* 1748
preue, proue *v.* prove, show, test, demonstrate; discover, *Pe* 4; acknowledge, *Cl* 1748
pride, priyde *see* **pryde**
prik, -y- *v.* gallop, *G* 2049; incite, *G* 2437
prince *see* **prynce**
pris *see* **prys**
prisoner(e)s, presoneres *n.* prisoners
priuy *see* **preué**
profecie, professye *n.* company of prophets, *Cl* 1308; prophecy, *Pe* 821, *Cl* 1158
proferen *v.* (**profered, profert** *pa.t.*) offer; propose, *Pe* 1200; address, *Pe* 235; project, *Cl* 1463; *reflex.* present (oneself), *Pat* 41
professye, profete *see* **profecie, prophete**
proper *adj.* noble, fine
property, properté *n.* attribute, *Pe* 446; special virtue, *Pe* 752
prophete, profete *n.* prophet
prosessyoun *n.* procession
proud(e), prowde *adj.* (**pruddest** *superl.*) proud; splendid, *G* 168, 601; high-mettled, *G* 2049; **proudly, prudly** *adv.*
proued *see* **preue**
prouince, prouynce *n.* province
prowes *n.* prowess, valour
pruddest, prudly *see* **proud(e)**
pryce *see* **prys(e)**
pryde, pri(y)de *n.* pride; eminent position, *Cl* 1227
pryk *see* **prik**
prymate *n.* head, chief
pryme *n.* the first canonical hour (6 a.m.); sunrise, *G* 1675
prynce, prince, prynse *n.* prince, nobleman, sovereign, king
prynces *n.* princess, lady, *G* 1770
pryncipal(e) *adj.* princely, royal
pryncipalté *n.* sovereignty
prys(e), pryce, pris *n.*[1] value, *Pe* 193, *G* 79, 1277, 1850; excellence, nobility, *Pe* 419, *G* 912, 1249, 1630; esteem, *Cl* 1124; renown, *G* 1379; **of p.** valuable, *Pe* 272, 746, *G* 615, 2364, excellent, noble, *G* 1770, 2398; *as adj.* excellent, *G* 1945; as excellent, *Cl* 1117; *adj. as n.* chief, *Cl* 1308, 1614; **your p.** your worthy self, *G* 1247
prys *n.*[2] 'capture' (*call on horn*), *G* 1362, 1601
pryse *v.* prize, esteem; **to p.** worthy, *Pe* 1131
prysoun *n.*[1] prison, *Pat* 79
prysoun *n.*[2] prisoner, *G* 1219
pryuély, pryuy(est), pryuyly *see* **preué**
pulle *v.* (**pullen** *pa.t.*) pull
pure *adj. & adv.* pure, perfect; noble, *Cl* 1570, *G* 262, *etc.*; *adv.* perfectly, *G* 808; **þe p. poplande hourle** the foaming sea itself, *Pat* 319; **pur(e)ly** *adv.* completely, entirely, fully, perfectly; clearly, *Pe* 1004
pure *v.* purify

pured *pp. & adj.* refined, *G* 633, 912; purified, *G* 2393; trimmed (to one colour), *G* 154, 1737

pur(e)ly, purpose, purpre *see* **pure, porpos(e), porpre**

pursaunt, poursent *n.* precinct, enclosing wall

pursued *pa.t.* made an attack, *Cl* 1177

purtrayed *see* **portrayed**

puryté *n.* purity

put *v.* put, set, place; **p. to** reduced to, *Pat* 35; **p. in** set on, *Pe* 267; **is p. in pref** is shown to be, *Pe* 272

puttyng *n.* putting

pyche *v.* (**py3t(e)** *pa.t. & pp.*, **pyched, piched** *pp.*) set, place, fasten; strike, stick, *G* 1456, 1734; occupy, *Cl* 83; array, dress, decorate, *Pe* 192, 205, *etc.*

p(y)ece *n.* piece; (*of armour*), *G* 2021; being, person, *Pe* 192, 229

pyes *n.* magpies

py3t(e) *see* **pyche**

pyked *adj.* spiked, *G* 769

pyke(d) *see also* **pike**

pyle *n.* stronghold, *Pe* 686

pyled *pa.t. & pp.* pillaged

pyleres *n.* pillars

Pymalyon *n.* Pygmalion

pynakle, pinacle *n.* pinnacle

pynakled *pp.adj.* pinnacled, with pinnacles, *Pe* 207

pyne, pine *n.* pain, suffering, torment, anguish; annoyance, *G* 1812; penance, *Pat* 423; pains, trouble, *Pe* 511, *G* 1985; difficult(y), *G* 123

pyne *v.*[1] confine, *Pat* 79; *pp.* **pyned** fenced in, *G* 769

pyne *v.*[2] *reflex.* take pains

pyned *pp.adj.* wasted, *Cl* 1095

pynkardines *n.* precious stones (?cornelians)

pyonys *n.* peonies, *Pe* 44

pypes *see* **pipes**

pypyng *n.* music of pipes

pysan *n.* gorget, throat-armour, *G* 204

pyté, pyty *see* **pité**

pyth *n.* toughness, *G* 1456

pytosly *see* **pito(u)sly**

quaked *pa.t.* trembled, *G* 1150

quat(so) *see* **what(so)**

quatsoeuer *pron.* whatsoever

quauende *adj.* beating, surging, *Cl* 324

quayle *n.* quail, *Pe* 1085

quaynt(yse) *see* **coynt, coyntyse**

qued *n.* evil

quel *see* **whyl(e)**

queldepoyntes *n.* quilted seats

quelle *v.* kill, put to death, destroy; end, *G* 752

queme *adj.* fine, pleasant

quen, w(h)en *adv. & conj.* when

quenches *v.* quenches, extinguishes

quene, whene (*G* 74, 2492) *n.* queen

quere *v.* discover, *Cl* 1632

quere(so) *see* **wher(e)**

queresoeuer, querfore *see* **w(h)eresoeuer, wherfore**

querré *n.* 'quarry', heap of game, *G* 1324

query *n.* complaint

quest *n.* search for game, *G* 1150, 1421; pursuit, *Pat* 39

quethe *n.* sound, utterance, *G* 1150

quettyng *n.* sharpening, *G* 2220

queþ**en, que**þ**er(soeuer)** *see* **whe**þ**en, whe**þ**er**

quik *see* **quyk**

quikken *pres.subjunc.* form, develop, *Pat* 471

quikly, quil(e) *see* **quyk, whil(e)**

quit-clayme *v.* renounce

quit(e), quo(m) *see* **whyt(e), who**

quos *pron.* whose

quoso *see* **whoso**

quoþ**, co**þ**e** *pa.t.* said

quoynt, quoyntis, -yse *see* **coynt, coyntyse**

quyk, quik *adj. & adv.* alive, living; lively, restive, *G* 177; lifelike, vivid, *Pe* 1179; *as pl.n.* living creatures, *Cl* 567; *adv.* quickly, *G* 975; **-ly** *adv.* quickly

quy, quyl(e) *see* **why, whil(e)**

quyssewes *n.* cuisses, thigh-pieces, *G* 578

quyte *v.* pay, reward; requite, repay

quyt(e), qwyte *see also* **whyt(e)**

raas *see* **race**

rabel *n.* rabble

rac *see* **rak**

race, raas *n.* headlong course, rush; attack, blow, *G* 2076; **on r.** headlong, *G* 1420; **of r.** in rushing headlong, *Pe* 1167

rach *n.* (**rach(ez), rachchez** *pl.*) hound

rachche *v.* (**ra3t** *pa.t.*) go, *Cl* 619, 766 (*cf.* **reche** *v.*[1], **rayke**)

rad *adj.* frightened, afraid, *Cl* 1543, *G* 251. *See also* **rad(ly)**

radde *see* **red(e)**

rad(ly) *adv.* quickly, promptly, *Cl* 671, 797, *Pat* 65, 89, *etc.*, *G* 367, 862, *etc.*

rafte *see* **reue**

raged *adj.* ragged, trailing, *G* 745

Ragnel *n.* Ragnel (a devil), *Pat* 188

ra3t *see* **rech(e), rachche**

rak, rac *n.* (**rakkes** *pl.*) cloudbank, storm-cloud, *Pat* 139, 176, *G* 1695; storm, *Cl* 433

rake *n.* water-course, *G* 2144, 2160

rakel *adj.* hasty

rakentes *n.* chains

rakkes *see* **rak**

ramel *n.* muck, *Pat* 279 (*see* 269*n*)

ran *see* **ren(n)e**

rande *n.* edge, *G* 1710; bank of stream, *Pe* 105

rank *see* **ronk**

rankor *n.* wrath

rape *n.* blow, *Cl* 233

rape *v.* rush, hurry; *reflex.* *G* 1309

rapely *adv.* hastily, *G* 2219; quickly, *Pe* 1168; rashly, *Pe* 363

rasch *adj.* rash

rased *pa.t.* snatched, *G* 1907

rasez *v.* charges, *G* 1461

rasores *n. gen.* razor's, *G* 213

rasped *pa.t. & pp.* scratched

rasse n.¹ ledge, *Cl* 446
rasse n.² water-course, channel, *G* 1570
ratted adj. ragged
rapeled pp. anchored, entwined, *G* 2294
raue v.¹ go astray, *Pe* 665
raue v.² rave, *Pe* 363
rauen n. raven
rauthe, rauþe see **rawþe**
rauyste pp. ravished, enraptured
raw adj. raw (*of silk*), *Cl* 790
rawe n. row; hedgerow, *Pe* 105, *G* 513
rawþe, rauthe, rauþe n. pity, *Cl* 972, *Pat* 21, *etc.*; repentance, *Cl* 233; a grievous thing, *G* 2204
raxled pa.t. stretched (myself), *Pe* 1174
ray n. ray (of light)
rayke v. go, depart; *reflex. G* 1735; **out r.** break cover, *G* 1727; **raykande** presp. flowing, sweeping, *Pe* 112, *Cl* 382
rayled pp. arrayed, set; spread, *G* 745; pa.t. *G* 952
rayn n. rain
rayne n. rein, *G* 457, 2177
rayne v. (**raynande** presp.,adj.) rain
rayn-ryfte n. break in a rain-cloud
rayse v. raise
raysoun, reysoun, resoun, Resoun n. (faculty of) reason, *Pe* 52; Reason (*person.*), *Pe* 665; wisdom, *Cl* 328; understanding, sense, *Cl* 1633; reason, cause, *Pe* 268, *Pat* 191; argument, *Cl* 2; words, speech, discourse (*also pl.*), *Pe* 716, *Cl* 184, 194, *G* 227, 392, 443; **bi r.** correctly, *G* 1344, by rights, *G* 1804
re(a)me n. realm, kingdom. *Cf.* **ryalme**
rebaudez n. dissolute men
rebel adj. rebellious, disobedient
rebounde pa.t. bounded, leapt, *Cl* 422
recen see **rekken**
rechate v. sound the recheat (to call the hounds together)
reche n. smoke, *Cl* 1009
rech(e) v.¹ (**raȝt** pa.t. & pp.) reach (out), *G* 432; reach, extend *Cl* 1691, *G* 183; reach, arrive at, *Cl* 890, 906; attain, *G* 1243; obtain, *Cl* 1766; offer, give, *Cl* 561, 1369, 1739, *G* 66, 1804, *etc.*; confer upon, *G* 2297
rech(e) v.² (**roȝt** pa.t.) care, *Pe* 333, *Cl* 465, *Pat* 460
rechles adj. carefree, *G* 40
recorde n. record, testimony
recorde v. record, *Cl* 25; repeat, *G* 1123
recouerer n. safety
recreaunt adj. cowardly
red(de), redden see **red(e)** v.
red(e) adj. red
rede, redy adj. ready; willing, obedient, *Cl* 294; alert(?), *Pe* 591
red(e) v. (**radde, redden** pa.t., **red(de)** pp.) advise, guide; read, interpret, *Pe* 709, *Cl* 7, 194, *etc.*; direct, decree, *Pat* 406; declare, *G* 443; manage, *G* 373, 2111
redles, rydelles adj. without counsel, helpless; as n. *Pat* 502; **for r.** for lack of advice, *Cl* 1595
redly, redy see **red(y)ly, redé**

red(y)ly adv. quickly, soon; without hesitation, *G* 373, 392
refet n. refreshment, *Pe* 1064
refete v. nourish, refresh, *Pe* 88; pp. *Pat* 20
reflayr n. scent, fragrance, *Cl* 1079
refourme v. restate, *G* 378
refrayne v. restrain
regioun n. region, country
regne see **re(n)gne**
regretted pp. grieved for, *Pe* 243
reȝtful adj. righteous
rehayte v. urge on, exhort; cheer, encourage, *Cl* 127
reherse, -c- v. repeat, mention
reiatéz see **rialté**
reken adj. lovely, noble, *Pe* 5, 92, 906, *Cl* 1082; righteous, pious, *Cl* 10 (*or adv.*), 738, 756; **-ly** adv. fitly, worthily, *Cl* 1318, *G* 39; politely, courteously, *Cl* 127, *G* 251, 821
rekken, recen v. reckon; tell, *Pe* 827; **r. vp** reckon up, go through, *Cl* 2
rele v. (**relande** presp.) reel, roll, *Pat* 147, 270, *G* 304; swerve, *G* 1728; sway (in combat), *G* 2246; *reflex.* swagger(?) *G* 229
relece v. release, deliver
reles n. remission, end
releue v. succour, *Pat* 323
relusaunt adj. shining, gleaming, *Pe* 159
relygioun n. the (Jewish) Church, *Cl* 1156; **renkez of r.** men in holy orders, *Cl* 7
relykes n. relics, sacred treasures
reme v. cry out, lament
reme see also **re(a)me**
remembred pa.t. *reflex.* remembered
remen see **reme** v.
remene v. recall, *G* 2483
remnaunt n. remainder
remorde v. bewail, lament, *G* 2434; pp. oppressed, *Pe* 364
remwe v. remove, take away; change, *G* 1475; **remued** pp. removed; remote, separated, *Cl* 1673
Renaud(e), Reniarde, Reynarde the fox, *G* 1728n, *etc.*
renay v. refuse; renounce, *Pat* 344
renden v. (**rended, rent** pp.) rend, tear
re(n)gne n. kingdom
rengne v. reign, rule
Reniarde, renischche see **Renaud(e), runisch**
renk, ring (*Cl* 592), **rynk** n.¹ (**renk(k)ez, -es** pl.) man, knight
renk n.² field of combat; **?me r. to mete** to challenge me to a duel, *G* 2206n
ren(n)e v. (**ran, runnen** pa.t., **runne(n)** pp.) run, flow; continue, *Cl* 527; be current, *G* 310, 2458; operate, *Pat* 511; **be runne** may have mounted up, *Pe* 523
renoun n. renown, fame, honour
renowle v. renew
rent, renyschly see **renden, runisch**
reparde pp. withheld, *Pe* 611
repayre v. be present, *Pe* 1028, *G* 1017
repente v.impers. in **ȝif hym repente** if it should grieve him, i.e. if he repents, *Pe* 662
reprené v. reproach

repreued *pa.t.* reproved, rebuked, *G* 2269
request *n.* request; **make r.** ask, *Pe* 281
require *v.* ask, *G* 1056
rere *v.* (**rer(e)d** *pa.t.*, **rered, rert** *pp.*) rise; raise, *Cl* 873, *G* 353; rouse, *Pat* 188; *pp.* supreme, *Pe* 591
res, resse *n.* rush; torrent, *Pe* 874
resayt *n. collect.* receiving stations, *G* 1168
resayue *v.* receive
rescoghe, rescowe *n.* rescue, *G* 2308; **matz r.** rescues, *Pe* 610
reset(te) *n.* refuge, shelter; habitation, *G* 2164
resonabele, resounable *adj.* reasonable, sensible
resoun *see* **raysoun**
respecte *n.* comparison (**of**: with), *Pe* 84
respite, respyt *n.* respite, delay, *G* 297; relief, reprieve, *Pe* 644
resse *see* **res**
restay, restey *v.* hold back, restrain, *Pe* 716, 1168; turn back, *G* 1153; persuade, *G* 1672; *intrans.* pause, *Pe* 437
rest(e) *n.* rest, repose; **withouten r.** endlessly, *Pe* 858
restlez *adj.* unceasing
restore *v.* restore, return; replace, *G* 2283
rest(t)(e) *v.* (**rest(ed)** *pa.t.*, **restted** *pp.*) rest; stand, *Cl* 738
retrete *v.* reproduce, *Pe* 92
reue *n.* reeve, bailiff
reue *v.* (**rafte** *pa.t. & pp.*) rob, take away
reuel *n.* revelry, revelling
reuel *v.* revel
reuer *n.* river, *Pe* 1055; river bank, meadow, *Pe* 105
reuerence, reuerens *n.* reverence, honour
reuerence *v.* greet, salute
reward(e) *n.* recompense, return; desert, *Pe* 604
rewfully *adv.* ruefully, sorrowfully
rewled, Reynarde *see* **rule** *v.*, **Renaud(e)**
reynyez *n.* loins, *Cl* 592
reysoun, rial *see* **raysoun, ryal**
rialté, rialty, reiaté *n.* royalty; *pl.* royal dignities, *Pe* 770
riboudrye *n.* debauchery
rich(ch)e, -y-, -u- *v.* prepare; deck out (*infl. by* **rich** *adj.*); proceed, move forward, *G* 8, 367, 1898; direct, *G* 1223; decide(?) *G* 360n; turn, *G* 303
rich(e), rych(e) *adj.* fine, noble, costly, splendid, glorious, *etc.*; wealthy; precious, *Pe* 646; *as n.* great man, *Cl* 1321, nobles, *Cl* 1208, *G* 66, *etc.*, noble steed, *G* 2177; *adv.* richly, splendidly, *Cl* 1411; **-ly** *adv.* richly, brightly, *Cl* 1045, plentifully, *G* 163, nobly, *G* 931, pompously, arrogantly, *G* 308
ridlande, rydelande *presp. & adj.* sifting, sprinkling, winnowing, *Cl* 953, *Pat* 254n
riftes *n.* fissures, clefts
rigge, rigt *see* **rygge, rygt(e)**
rimed hym *pa.t.* cleared his throat(?), drew himself up(?), *G* 308
ring *see* **renk**
ripe, rype *adj.* ripe; mature, *Cl* 869
ris(e) *see* **rys(e)**

robbed *pa.t. & pp.* robbed; *pp.* stolen, *Cl* 1142
robbors *n.* robbers
roborrye *n.* robbery
roché *adj.* rocky, *G* 2294
roche *n.* rock
rocher *n.* rocky bank
rode *n.*[1] rood, cross
rode *n.*[2] road, *Pat* 270
rod(e) *see also* **ryde**
roffe *n.* (**rouez** *pl.*) roof
rof-sore *n.* cut, gash, *G* 2346
rogh(e), rog(e), ruge *adj.* rough; cruel, *Pe* 646; **for r.** because of the turbulence, *Pat* 144
roghlych *adj.* rough, harsh
rogly *adj.* fortunate(?), *Cl* 433n
rogt *see* **reche** *v.*[2]
rok *n.* (**rokkes, -z** *pl.*) rock; castle, *Cl* 1514
rokked *pp.* rocked, *G* 2018n
rollande *presp.adj.* wavy
rol(l)ed *pa.t.* rolled; sagged, flapped, *G* 953
rome *v.* wind one's way, *G* 2198
romye *v.* cry out, *Cl* 1543
ronez *n.* bushes, thickets, *G* 1466
ronge *pa.t.* (**r(o)ungen** *pa.t.pl.*) rang
ronk, rank *adj.* proud, haughty; violent, *Cl* 233; impetuous, *Pe* 1167; full-grown, *Cl* 869; luxuriant, *Pe* 844, *G* 513; wanton, *Cl* 760; *as n.* pride, *Pat* 298
ronkled *pp.* wrinkled, *G* 953
ronkly *adv.* proudly
rop *n.*[1] rope, *Pat* 105, 150; cord, *G* 857
rop *n.*[2] gut, intestine, *Pat* 270
rore *v.* roar
ros *see* **rys(e)**
rose *n.* rose, *Pe* 269, 906; *gen. or adj.* of the rose, *Cl* 1079; **Rose** *Roman de la Rose*, *Cl* 1057
rose *v.* praise, *Cl* 1371
rost(t)ed *pp.* roasted
rote *n.*[1] root, *Pe* 420, *Cl* 619, *Pat* 467, *G* 2294
rot(e) *n.*[2] rot, decay, *Pe* 26, *Cl* 1079
rote *n.*[3] custom; **bi r.** with ceremony, *G* 2207
rote *n.*[4] stringed musical instrument, kind of violin *Cl* 1082
rote *v.* rot, decay, *Pe* 958, *G* 528
ropeled[1] *pp.* cooked, *Cl* 59
ropeled[2] *pa.t.* hurried, *Cl* 890
roper *n.* rudder
ropun *n.* redness
roue, rouez *see* **ryue** *v.*, **roffe**
roum *n.* room
roun *n.* secret, mystery; **in r.** inscrutably, *Pat* 511
roun, rowne *v.* speak privately, whisper, *Pat* 64, *G* 362; **rownande** *presp.adj.* whispering, *Pe* 112
roun *see also* **roun(de)**
rounce *n.* horse
roun(de) *adj.* round; **on r.** around, *Cl* 423, *Pat* 147
roungen *see* **ronge**
r(o)urd(e) *n.* noise, sound; voice, *G* 2337; clamour, cry, *Cl* 390
rous *n.* praise, fame, *G* 310
roust *n.* rust, *G* 2018
rout *n.* jerk, *G* 457

route *n.* company, *Pe* 926
routes *v.* snores, *Pat* 186
rowe, rowwe *v.* row
rownande, rowned *see* **roun** *v.*
rowtande *adj.* rushing
rowtes *n.* bands, crowds
ruch(ch)e *see* **rich(ch)(e)**
ruddon *n.* redness
rudede *pp.* reddened, reflected red, *G* 1695
rudelez *n.* (window?) curtains, *G* 857
rudnyng *n.* reddening, redness
rueled *pa.t.* poured
ruful *adj.* piteous, *Pe* 916; terrible, *G* 2076; *adv.* **rewfully,** sorrowfully
rugh(e), ruȝe *see* **rogh(e)**
rule *n.* rule, law
rule *v.* (**rewled** *pa.t.*) rule, control; **rewled hym** conducted himself, *Cl* 294
rungen *see* **ronge**
runisch, renischche *adj.* strange, outlandish, *Cl* 96, 1545; rough, wild, *G* 457; **-ly** *adv.* roughly, violently; **renyschly** strangely, in outlandish words, *Cl* 1724
runne(n), rurd *see* **ren(n)e, r(o)urd(e)**
rusched *pa.t.*[1] rushed, poured, *Cl* 368
rusched *pa.t.*[2] swished, *G* 2204, 2219
ruþen *v.* arouse, *Cl* 895, 1208; *reflex.* bestir oneself, *G* 1558
ruyt *v.* hasten
rwe *v.* pity; **r. on** take pity on; *impers.* repent, *Cl* 290, 561
rwly *adv.* pitifully
ryal(le), rial, ryol *adj.* royal; splendid, glorious; *adv. or adj. Cl* 1082; **-ly** *adv.* royally, splendidly
ryalme *n.* realm, kingdom
rybaudes *n.* villains
rybbe *n.* rib
rybé *n.* (**rubies** *pl.*) ruby
ryche *n.* kingdom, *Pe* 601, 722, 919
rych(e) *see also* **rich(e), rich(ch)(e)**
rychely *see* **rich(e)**
rychez *n.* wealth, *Pe* 26
ryd(d)(e) *v.* take away (from), *G* 364; part, *G* 2246; **r. of** clean off, *G* 1344
ryde, ride *v.* (**rod(e)** *pa.t.*) ride
rydelande, rydelles *see* **ridlande, redles**
rydyng *n.* riding
ryf *adj.* plentiful, abundant
ryg(e) *n.* storm, tempest, *Cl* 354, 382
rygge, rigge *n.* back(bone), *Pat* 379, *G* 1344, 1608
ryȝt *adv.* right, just; exactly; properly, correctly, *Cl* 1346, *G* 373; duly, *Pat* 326; **r. noȝt** anything at all, *Pe* 520; **r. non** none at all, *G* 1790
ryȝte *adj.* right, just; right (*as opposed to* left), *Pat* 511; justified (by grace), *Pe* 672
ryȝt(e), riȝt, Ryȝt *n.* justice (just judgement), *Pe* 591, 665, 721*n* (*person.*), *Pat* 19, 323, 493, *G* 2346; right (conduct), *Pe* 496, 622, *Pat* 431; righteousness, morality, *Cl* 194; justice, right, (entitlement), *Pe* 580, 703, 708, 1196, *Cl* 2; obligation, *G* 1041; claim, *G* 2342; prerogative, *G* 274; right (justification by

grace), *Pe* 684, 696, 720; **by r.** correctly, *Cl* 1633; **r. hade** was right (to do), *Cl* 1318; **on r.** (*cf.* **aryȝt**) indeed, truly, *Cl* 1513
ryȝtez *adv.* precisely, *Cl* 427
ryȝt hym *pa.t.reflex.* proceeded, *G* 308
ryȝtwys *adj.* righteous, just; *as n. Pe* 689; **-ly** *adv.* rightly, *Pe* 709
rymez *n.* membranes, *G* 1343
ryne *v.* touch, *G* 2290
ryng *n.* (**rynk,** *G* 1817, 1827) ring
ryngande, rynkande *adj.* ringing, resounding, *Cl* 1082, *G* 2337
rynging *n.* ringing
rynk *see* **renk, ryng**
rynkande, ryol *see* **ryngande, ryal**
rypande *presp.* examining, *Cl* 592
rype *see* **ripe**
rypez *v.* ripens
rys *n.* twig; **bi r.** in the wood, *G* 1698
rys(e), ris(e) *v.* (**ros, rysed** *pa.t.*) rise; grow, *G* 528; rise, come into view, *Pe* 103; **r. vp** stand up, *Pe* 191, 437
ryth *n.* ox
rytte *pa.t.* cut, *G* 1332
ryue *adv.* abundantly, *G* 2046 (*cf.* **ryf**)
ryue *v.* (**roue** *pa.t.*) cut

sabatounz *n.* steel shoes
sacrafyce, sacrafyse, sacrefyce, sakerfyse *n.* sacrifice
sad(d)(e) *adj.* long, *Cl* 1286; great, advanced, *Cl* 657; grave, dignified, *Pe* 211, 887, *Cl* 640; solemn, *Cl* 595; gloomy, *Cl* 525
sade *see* **say**
sadel *n. & v.* saddle
sadly *adv.* firmly, *G* 437, 1593; heavily, *Pat* 442; deliberately, *G* 437; long enough, *G* 2409
saf, saue *adj.* safe, *Pat* 334; redeemed, *Pe* 672, *etc.*; **sauer** *compar.adj.* safer, *G* 1202. *See also* **vouche**
saf, saue *prep. & conj.* except (for), except that
saffer *n.* (**safyres** *pl.*) sapphire, *Pe* 118, 1002
sage *adj.* wise
saghe, saȝe(s), -z *see* **sawe**
saȝ *see* **se(ne)**
saȝt(e) *adj.* at peace; *in* **set(t)e s.** reconcile, be reconciled, *Pe* 1201, would have reconciled, *Pe* 52
saȝtlyng *n.* reconciliation
saȝttel *v.* (**saȝtled** *pa.t. & pp.*) become reconciled; become calm, *Pat* 232; settle, *Cl* 445
sake *n.*[1] charge; fault, *Pat* 84, 172; **s. of felonye** criminal charge, *Pe* 800
sake *n.*[2] sake
sakerfyse *see* **sacrafyce**
saklez *adj.* guiltless
sakred *pp.* consecrated
Salamon, Salomon *n.* Solomon
sale *n.* hall
salue *v.* greet, *G* 1473
salure *n.* salt-cellar
Samarye *n.* Samaria
same *adj. & pron.* same; **of þe s.** in the same way, to match

same(n) adv. together, Cl 400, etc., Pat 46, G 50, etc.; **al(le)** s. with one accord, Pe 518, G 363, 673

samen, samne v. (**samned** pa.t. & pp.) assemble, bring (be brought) together

samen-feres n. fellow-travellers

samne(d) see **samen** v.

sample n. example, exemplum, Cl 1326; parable, Pe 499

sanap n. napkin, overlay

sancta sanctorum n. holy of holies

sange, -o- n. song

sant see **Sayn(t)** n.¹

sapyence n. wisdom

sardiners n. cornelians

sardonyse n. sardonyx

Saré n. Sarah

sarre(st) see sore

Satanas n. Satan

sat(e) see **sitte**

sathrapas n. satraps, governors

satteled pa.t. settled, descended

satz see **say(e)**

sauce, sawse n. sauce

saudan n. sultan

saue v. save, spare

saue see also **saf**

sauement n. safety

saueour, sauer see **sauio(u)r, saf**

sauere, sau(y)our v. apprehend, know, Cl 581; smell, Pat 275; season, Cl 825; pp. flavoured, G 892

sauerly adv. feelingly, G 1937; in comfort, G 2048; adj. adequate, satisfactory, Pe 226n

sauez see **sawe**

sauio(u)r, saueour, sauyour n. saviour. See also **sauere**

saule see **sawle**

saundyuer n. sandiver, glass-gall

sauo(u)r n. smell, Cl 510, 1447; taste, Cl 995

sauoured see **sauere**

sauter n. psalter

sauteray n. psaltery (stringed instrument)

sauyour see **sauio(u)r, sauere**

sauyté n. safety

sawe, saȝe, saghe n. (**saȝez, -s, sauez, sawez, -s** pl.) speech, statement, saying; words; (spoken) prayer, G 1202

sawle, saule, sawele n. soul

sawse see **sauce**

sayl n. sail

sayled pa.t. sailed, floated

saym n. grease

sayned pa.t. & pp. blessed, Cl 746, 986; reflex. cross oneself, G 761, 763, 1202

Sayn(t), Sant n.¹ Saint, St

sayn(t) n.² girdle, G 589, 2431

say(e) v. (**seggez, says, say(e)z, sa(y)tz** pres., **sayd(e)(n), sade** pa.t., **sayd** pp.) say, tell, declare; proclaim (of a book, with suggestion of read aloud), Pe 593, G 690

say(t)z see **say(e)**

scale n. surface, Pe 1005

scape v. escape

scarre v. frighten, terrify, alarm; be provoked, react fiercely, Cl 598

scaþe, schaþe, skaþe n. harm, injury, Cl 151, G 2353; punishment, Cl 600; evil, sin, Cl 21, 196, etc.; a pity, G 674

scaþel adj. harmful

scayled pa.t. scaled, climbed

scelt, schad(d)(e) see **skelt(en), schede**

schade n. shade

schaded pa.t. cast shadow

schadow n. shadow

schadowed pa.t. cast shadows, Pe 42

schafte n. shaft; ray, beam (of light); spear, G 205

schafted pa.t. shone low, set, G 1467

schaȝe n. thicket

schal(e) v. (**schalt** pres2sg., **schal, schul, schyn, schin** prespl.) shall, will, must; **schuld(e)(n)** pa.t. would, ought to, had to; was about to, Pe 1162

schalk(e) n. (**schalk(k)ez** pl.) man

scham(e), schome n. shame

schame v. be ashamed, embarrassed

schankes, schonkes, -z n. legs

schap n. (**schappes** pl.) shape

schape v. (**schop, schaped** pa.t., **schapen, schaped** pp.) fashion, make, G 213, 662, 1210; recount, G 1626; ordain, Cl 742, Pat 247, G 2138, etc.; endeavour, Cl 762; befall, Pat 160

schaped pp. (= **chaped**) mounted (with), G 1832

scharp(e) adj. & adv. sharp, keen; swift, Cl 475; intense, Cl 1310; as n. blade, G 424, 1593, etc.; adv. loudly, Pe 877

schaterande presp. dashing, breaking

schaþe see **scaþe**

schaued pa.t. scraped; **schauen** pp. scraped, shaven (smooth)

schawe see **schewe**

schede v. (**schad(d)(e)** pa.t.) sever, G 425; fall, be shed, Pe 411, G 506, 727, 956; shed, Pe 741; fall, extend, Cl 1690

(s)chelde n. shield; shoulder (of boar), G 1456; slab (of meat), Cl 58, G 1611, 1626

schende v. (**schended, schent(e)** pp.) destroy; disgrace, punish, Pe 668, Cl 47, 580; batter, Pat 246

schene adj. lovely, beautiful, bright; as n. brightness, sun, Pat 440, bright weapon, G 2268; fair maiden, Pe 166, 965

schent(e) see **schende**

schep n. sheep

schepon n. shippen, cattle-shed

schere n. see **cher(e)**

schere v.¹ (**scher** pa.t., **schorne** pp.) cut

schere v.² meander, Pe 107

schere-wykes n. groin

schet pp. enclosed

schewe, scheue, schawe v. show, reveal, display, set forth; produce, offer, G 315, 619, 2061; utter, Cl 662, 840; intrans. (also reflex.) show, appear, Cl 170, 553, G 420, etc.; **to s.** in appearance, G 2036

schin see **schal(e)**

schinande presp.adj. shining

schirly adv. completely (cf. **clanly**), G 1880

scho pron. she

scholes *adj.* shoeless
schome *see* **scham(e)**
schomely *adv.* shamefully
schyne *v.* (**schinande** *presp.*, **schon, schynde, schyned** *pa.t.*) shine
schon *see* **schyne**
schonied *pa.t.* shunned, avoided
schonkes, -z, schop *see* **schankes, schape**
schor *n.* (**schowrez** *pl.*) shower, *Cl* 227, *G* 506
schore *n.* bank (of stream); cliff, rock, *Pe* 166, *G* 2161
schorne *see* **schere**
schort *adj.* short
schortly *adv.* hastily, suddenly
schote *v.* (**schot(e), schotten** *pa.t.*) shoot; shoot, rush, spring, *Pe* 58, *Cl* 850, *G* 317, *etc.*; jerk, *G* 2318
schout *n.* shout
schowen, schowrez *see* **schow(u)e, schor**
schowted *pa.t.* roared, rang out, *Pe* 877
schow(u)e, schwue *v.* (**schowen** *pa.t.*, **schowued** *pa.t. & pp.*) push, press, thrust; **s. to** push forward, *G* 1454; **of mensk s.** driven from honour, *Cl* 1740
schrank(e) *pa.t.* shrank, winced, *Cl* 850, *G* 2267, 2372; sank, *G* 425, 2313
schrewe *n.* villain
schrewedschyp *n.* wickedness
schrof *pa.t.* confessed
schroude-hous *n.* ?place of shelter, *Cl* 1076
schrowde *n.* garment, clothing
schryfte *n.* confession
schrylle *adj.* shrill
schrylle *adv.* sharply, brightly, *Pe* 80
schul, schuld(e)(n) *see* **schal(e)**
schulder *n.* (**schulderez, -s, schylderez** *pl.*) shoulder
schunt *n.* sudden deflection, *G* 2268
schunt *pa.t. & pp.* moved aside, *Cl* 605; started aside, flinched, *G* 1902, 2280
schwue, schyire *see* **schow(u)e, schyr(e)(e)**
schylde *v.* shield, protect, *Pat* 440; prevent, *Pe* 965, *G* 1776
schylderez *see* **schulder**
schym *adj.* bright, *Pe* 1077
schymeryng *n.* shimmering, *Pe* 80
schyn *see* **schal(e)**
schynder *v.* sunder, break (apart)
schyp, schip *n.* ship
schyr(e)(e), schyire *adj. & adv.* (**schyrrer** *compar.*) bright, shining, white, fair; *as n.* white flesh, *G* 1331, 2256
sckete *see* **skete**
s(c)lade *n.* valley
s(c)laȝt *n.* slaughter, *Pe* 801, *Cl* 56n; *pl.* strokes, *Pat* 192
scole *n.* cup, *Cl* 1145
scoleres *n.* scholars
scomfyted *pa.t.* (**scoumfit** *pp.*) discomfited, disconcerted
scopen *pa.t.* scooped, *Pat* 155
scowtes *n.* jutting rocks, *G* 2167
scowte-wach *n.* guard, watchman
scoymus, skoymos *adj.* scrupulous; **is s. of** feels repugnance at
scrof *adj.* rough, *Cl* 1546

scrypture *n.* inscription, written characters
scue, scurtez *see* **skwe, skyrtez**
scylful *adj.* righteous, *Cl* 1148
scylle *see* **skyl(le)**
se, see *n.* sea
se, see *v. see*, **se(ne)**
seche *pron.* such, *G* 1543
sech(e) *v.* (**soȝt(e), soȝtten** *pa.t.*, **soȝt** *pp.*) seek, look for, make for; come, go, *Cl* 29, 510, *etc.*, *Pat* 116, *G* 685, 1052, *etc.*; attempt, move, *Cl* 201; try, strive, *Cl* 1286, *Pat* 197; invite, *Pat* 53; **s. fro** leave, *Pat* 116, *G* 685, 1440; **þe water soȝte** was going into the water, *Pat* 249
secounde *adj.* second
sed(e) *n.* seed; offspring, *Cl* 660
seele, seet, seete *see* **sele, sitte, sete**
seg(g)e *n.*[1] seat, *Pat* 93; siege, *Cl* 1185, *G* 1, 2525
segg(e) *n.*[2] man, knight, person; sir, *G* 394; *pl.* men, people; **vche (a) s.** everyone; **alle seggez** everyone
seggez *see also* **say(e)**
segh(e) *see* **se(ne)**
Segor *n.* Zoar
seȝ(e)(n) *see* **se(ne), seye**
seker *see* **siker**
sekke *n.* sackcloth
seknesse *n.* sickness
selcouth *n.* marvel, wonder
selden *adv.* seldom
sele, seele *n.* good fortune, happiness
self, seluen *adj.* same, very, *Pe* 203, *G* 751; **þe s. sunne** the sun itself, *Pe* 1076, **þe S. God** God Himself, *Pe* 1046; *as n.* self, himself, *Pe* 1054, *Cl* 243, 786, *etc.*, *G* 51, 1616, *etc.*; yourself, *Pat* 413; oneself, *Cl* 579
sellen *v.* sell
selly *adj.* (**sellokest** *superl.*) marvellous, *Pat* 353, *G* 1439, 1962; strange, *G* 2170; *as n.* (a) wonder, marvel, *Pat* 140, *G* 28, 239, 475; **selly(ly)** *adv.* exceedingly, *G* 963, 1194, 1803
seluen *see* **self**
selure *n.* canopy, *G* 76
sely *adj.* innocent, blessed
Sem *n.* Shem
sem *see* **sem(e)**
semb(e)launt *n.* appearance, *G* 148; face, *Pe* 211; sign, expression, *G* 468; demonstration (of regard), *G* 1658; friendly welcome, *Cl* 131; demeanour, *Pe* 1143, *Cl* 640, *G* 1273; kindness, *G* 1843
semblé *n.* assembly, throng
sembled *pp.* assembled
seme *adj.* seemly, *Pe* 1115, *Cl* 549, 1810, *G* 1085; *adv.* becomingly, *Pe* 190; *cf.* **semly(ch)**
sem(e) *n.* ornamental strip of material inserted in, or laid over, a seam; border, *Pe* 838; blemish, flaw, *Cl* 555
seme *v.* seem, appear; *impers.* be fitting *or* proper, become, suit, *Cl* 117, 793, *G* 73, 679 (*sc.* to be), 848, 1005, 1929
semly(ch), semely *adj. & adv.* (**semloker** *compar.*) seemly, fitting, *G* 348, 1198; fine, handsome, fair, lovely, *Pe* 34, 45, 789, *Cl*

209, 262, *etc.*, *G* 672, 685; *compar.* more beautiful, *Cl* 868, *G* 83 (*sc.* gem); *as n.* þat S. that fair (Lord), *Cl* 1055, the handsome (knight), *G* 672, those lovely (ladies), *Cl* 870; *adv.* becomingly, in a seemly manner, *Cl* 1442, *G* 622 (**semlyly**), 865, *etc.*; sweetly, *G* 1658, 1796

sen *see* **se(ne)**

sendal *n.* silk

sende *v.* (**sende** *pa.t.*, **sendez** *pa.t.2s.*, **sende** *pp.*) send

sene *adj.* visible, *Pe* 1143; outward, *G* 148; plain, *G* 341; *see also* **se(ne)** *v.*

se(ne), **se(e)** *v.* (**segh(e)**, **se3(e)(n)**, **sa3**, **sy3(e)** *pa.t.* **sen(e)** *pp.*) see; **on to s.** to look upon (at), *Pe* 45; *see also* **sene** *adj.*

sengel *adj.* alone, *G* 1531; **-ey** *adv.* apart, *Pe* 8

serched *pa.t.* examined, *G* 1328

ser(e) *adj.* various; different, *G* 2417; diverse, *Pat* 12; several, *G* 822; single, separate, particular, *Cl* 507, *G* 761, 1985; *adv.* severally, *G* 632; **sere twyes** on two different occasions, *G* 1522

serelych, **serly** *adv.* severally, individually

sergauntez, **serjauntes** *n.* servants, *Cl* 109; officers, *Pat* 385

serges *n.* candles

serjauntes *see* **sergauntez**

serlepes, **serlypez** *adv.* in turn, *G* 501; *as adj.* single, *Pe* 994

serly *see* **serelych**

sermoun *n.* speech; account, *Pe* 1185

sertayn *adv.* certainly, for sure

seruage *n.* servitude, bondage

serua(u)nt *n.* servant

serue(n) *v.*[1] serve; suffice, *Cl* 750; avail, be of use, *Pe* 331

serue *v.*[2] deserve, *Pe* 553, *G* 1380

seruyse, **-ce**, **-ise** *n.* service; (*in church*), *G* 751, 940 (*and cf. Cl* 1152); (*of a meal*), *Cl* 1401, *G* 130

sese *v.*[1] cease, stop; fail, *Cl* 523

sese *v.*[2] seize, snatch, take possession (of); touch, take, *G* 1825; put in possession, *in pp.* **sesed in** made possessor of, *Pe* 417

sesoun(ez) *see* **se(y)soun**

set *adj.* set, appointed, *Cl* 1364

sete *adj.* excellent, *G* 889

sete, **seete** *n.* seat, throne; sitting, *Cl* 59n; **wenten to s.** took their places, *G* 72, 493

sete(n) *see* **sitte**

set(t)e *v.* (**set(te)(n)** *pa.t.*, **set(te)** *pp.*) set, put, place; sit, seat (*pass. & reflex.*), *Cl* 1401, *G* 437, 1083, *etc.*; strike (blow, etc.), *G* 372, ?*Cl* 1225; prepare, *Pat* 193, ?*Cl* 1225; lay the table, *G* 1651; make, put, *G* 1883; establish, found, build, *Pe* 1062, *Cl* 673, 1015, *G* 14; invent, *G* 625; *reflex.* endeavour, devote (oneself), *Cl* 1453, *G* 1246; achieve, *Pat* 58; esteem, value, *Pe* 8, 307, 811, *Cl* 1710, *G* 1250; *pp.* (had) arrived, *Cl* 986, ingrained, *G* 148, determined, *Pat* 487, beset (by), *Pat* 46; **s. at li3t, lyttel** make light of, disregard, *Cl* 1710, *G* 1250; **s. hym on** *reflex.* charge at, *G* 1589; **s. in asente** agree, *Pat* 177; **s. on** choose, *Cl* 469; **s. on his hede** call down on him, *G* 1721; **s. sa3t(e)** reconcile, be recon-

ciled, *Pe* 1201, (*pa.t.subjunc.*) would have reconciled, *Pe* 52; **s. solace** find pleasure, *G* 1318; **s. sy3t toward** turn toward, *Cl* 672. *See also* **set**

settel *n.* seat

seþe *v.* (**soþen** *pp.*) boil

seue, **seve**, **sewe** *n.* broth, pottage

seuen *adj.* seven

seuentenþe *adj.* seventeenth

seuenþe *adj.* seventh

seuer *v.* separate, part, depart

seve *see* **seue**

sewe *v.* sew

sewe *see also* **seue**

sewer *n.* servant waiting at table, *Cl* 639n

sewrté *n.* security

sex(te) *adj.* six(th)

seye *v.* (**seyed** *pa.t.*, **se3en** *pp.*) go, come, pass

se(y)soun *n.* season; time, *G* 1958, 2085; **hy3 s.** festival, *Pe* 39

sidbordez, **sidebordez** *n.* side-tables, lower tables

side, **si3t** *see* **syde**, **sy3t(e)**

siker, **seker**, **syker** *adj.* true, firm, *G* 403; trustworthy, *G* 96, 111, 115, 2048, 2493; sure, *G* 265; *adv.* surely, *G* 1637

siker *v.* promise, pledge

silk(e) *see* **sylk(e)**

sille *n.* floor; **on s.** in the hall, *G* 55

sister-sunes *n.* nephews, sister's sons

sitte, **-y-** *v.* (**sat(e)**, **seet**, **sete(n)** *pa.t.*, **seten** *pp.*) sit

siþen *see* **syþen**

siue *n.* sieve, *Cl* 226

skarmoch *n.* skirmish

skaþe *see* **scaþe**

skayned *pp.* grazed

skeles *n.* dishes, *Cl* 1405

skelten, **scelt** *pa.t.* (**skelt** *pp.*) launch, *Cl* 1186, 1206; revile, *Cl* 827; hasten, *Cl* 1554

skere *adj.* innocent, pure, *G* 1261

skete, **sckete** *adv.* quickly, sharply

skewe *see* **skwe**

skowtez *v.* scouts, searches, *Cl* 483

skoymos *see* **scoymus**

skwe, **scue**, **skewe** *n.* sky, cloud

skyfte *v.* apportion, *Pe* 569; *pp.* changed, *Cl* 709, alternated, *G* 19

skyg *adj.* fastidious

skyl(le), **scylle**, **skyly** *n.* reason, (faculty of) judgement, *Pe* 312, *Cl* 151; mind, attitude, *Cl* 827; reason, argument, *Pe* 674, *Cl* 823, *G* 1296, 1509; meaning, *Cl* 1554; excuse, *Cl* 62; judgement, decree, *Cl* 569, 709

skylly *adj.* wise, *Cl* 529

skyre *adj.* bright, clear

skyrmez *v.* darts about

skyrtez, **scurtez** *n.* skirts, lower parts of a saddle or garment

skyualde *n.* division, separation, *Cl* 529

slade, **sla3t(es)** *see* **s(c)lade**, **s(c)la3t**

slake, **sloke** *v.* come to an end, stop, *Pe* 942; die away, *G* 244; **slokes** *see G* 412n

slauþe *n.* sloth

slayn(e) *see* **slow(e)**

sle3e *adj.* intricate, subtle; **-ly** *adv.* *G* 1182n

sleȝt *see* **slyȝt**
sleke *v.* quench
slente *n.* slope, hill; **by s. oþer slade** somewhere or other, *Pe* 141
slepe *n.* sleep; **(vp)on s.** asleep
slepe *v.* (**slepande** *presp.*, **sleped, slepte** *pa.t.*, **slepe** (*G* 1991) *pa.t.subjunc.*) sleep
slepyng-slaȝte sudden heavy sleep, *Pe* 59n
sloberande *presp.* slobbering
slode *see* **slyde**
slokes *v. see G* 412n
slot *n.* hollow at base of throat
slouen *see* **slow(e)**
sloumbe-s(e)lep(e) *n.* heavy sleep
slow, slowen, slouen *pa.t.* (**slayn(e)** *pp.*) slew, killed
sluchched *adj.* soiled
slyde *v.* (**slode** *pa.t.*) slide, slip
slyȝt *adj.* slim, slender, *Pe* 190
slyȝt, sleȝt *n.* skill; stratagem, device, *Pat* 130, *G* 1854, 1858; skilled demonstration, *G* 916
slyp *n.* blow, *Cl* 1264
slyppe *v.* (**slypped, slypte** *pa.t.*, **slypped** *pp.*) slip; escape, *Cl* 1785, *G* 1858; slip, fall, *Pat* 186, *G* 244
smach *n.* flavour, taste, aroma
smachande *presp.* smelling
smal(e) *adj.* small, *Pe* 90; slender, slim, *Pe* 6, 190, *G* 144, 1207; fine, *Cl* 226, *G* 76
smart *adj.* sharp, bitter
smartly *adv.* sharply, *Cl* 711; promptly, *G* 407
smelle *n.* smell
smeten *see* **smyte**
smeþely *adv.* gently, *G* 1789
smod *n.* filth
smolderande *adj.* stifling
smolt *adj.* gentle, *G* 1763
smolt *v.* go, set off, *Cl* 461; escape, *Cl* 732
smoþe *adj.* smooth, *Pe* 6, 190; pleasant, friendly, *G* 1763; **smoþely** *adv.* easily, *Cl* 732, deftly, *G* 407
smylt *adj.* sieved, sifted, fine
smyte *v.* (**smeten** *pa.t.pl.*, **smyten** *pp.*) smite, strike; fall, *G* 1763
snart *adv.* swiftly, sharply, *G* 2003
snaw(e) *n.* snow
snayped *pa.t.* cut, stung, *G* 2003
snitered *pa.t.* showered, *G* 2003
snyrt *pa.t.* snicked, touched, *G* 2312
so *adv. & conj.* so, thus, in this way; such (a); with *indef.pron.* so ever, *Cl* 100, 422, *etc.*, *G* 384, 1107, *etc.*; then, *Pe* 1187, *G* 218; *conj.* as; **sone s.** as soon as
soberly *adv.* reverently, solemnly, gravely
sobre *adj.* sober, serious, *Pe* 391, 532
Sodamas, Sodomas *n.* Sodom
sodanly, sodenly *adv.* suddenly
soffer(ed), soffraunce *see* **suffer, suffraunce**
soft(e) *adj.* soft, gentle, mild; *adv.* softly, quietly, comfortably
soft(e)ly, softly *adv.* softly, quietly; meekly, *Pat* 529
soghe *v.*[1] sow, spread, *Pat* 67
soghe *v.*[2] *impers.* (it may) hurt, *Pat* 391

soȝt(e), soȝtten *see* **seche**
sojorne *n.* sojourn, stay
sojo(u)rne *v.* stay; *pp.* lodged, *G* 2048
sok *n.* sucking
sokored *pp.* succoured
solace *n.* pleasure, joy; entertainment, *G* 1985
solased *pa.t.* entertained
solde *pa.t.* sold
solem(p)ne *adj.* solemn, dignified
solempnely *adv.* ceremoniously, solemnly
solem(p)neté *n.* solemnity, dignity; high position, *Cl* 1678; festival, *Cl* 1757
solie, soly *n.* throne
somer *n.* summer, spring
somones, som(m)oun *n.* summons; **mad s.** summoned, *Pe* 539
sonde *n.*[1] embassy, sending, command, *Pe* 943; message, *Cl* 781n; message, messenger, *Cl* 53
sonde *n.*[2] shore, *Pat* 341
sondezmon *n.* messenger
sone *adv.* immediately, quickly, soon; **s. so** as soon as
sonet *n.* music
sonetez *n.* sennets, fanfares
songe, sange *n.* song
songe(n), sonkken, sonne *see* **syng(e), synk, sunne**
sop(e) *n.* mouthful, morsel
soper *n.* supper
sore *adj.* (**sarrest** *superl.*) painful, grievous; diseased, afflicted, *Cl* 1111; *adv.* (**sarre** *compar.*) sorely, grievously; hard, *Pe* 550
soré *adj.* sorry, *G* 1826, 1987
sor(e) *n.* pain, sorrow
sorȝ(e), sorewe *n.*[1] sorrow, misery: imprecation, *G* 1721; contrition, *Pe* 663
sorȝe *n.*[2] filth, *Cl* 846, *Pat* 275
sorquydryȝe *see* **sourquydry**
sorsers *n.* sorcerers
sorsory *n.* sorcery
sortes *n.* lots
soth(e), soþ(e) *adj. & adv.* true; *adv.* truly, in truth, indeed; for a fact, *G* 348; **-ly** *adv.* truly (*see also* **soþly** *adv.*[2])
soth(e), soþ(e) *n.* truth
sothfol *adj.* true
sotte *n.* fool
sotyle *adj.* fine, transparent, *Pe* 1050
soþ(e) *see* **soth(e)**
soþefast *adj.* true
soþ(e)ly, sothely *adv.*[1] truly
soþen *see* **seþe**
soþly, sothly *adv.*[2] softly, *Cl* 654n, *G* 673n
souerayn *n.* lord; *as adj.* sovereign
soufre *n.* sulphur
souȝed, swe(y) *pa.t.* soughed, moaned, *Cl* 956, *Pat* 140; sounded, *Pat* 429
soumme, sowme *n.* number, quantity
soun *n.* sound, noise; voice, *Pe* 532, *Pat* 429; report, *Cl* 689; *see also* **sun**
sounande *presp.adj.* sonorous, *Pe* 883
sounde *adj.* sound, safe, well; undamaged, *Cl* 1795; *as n.* safety, *G* 2489
sounder *n.* herd (of wild pig), *G* 1440
souned *pa.t.* sounded

souped *pp.* supped, eaten supper, *Cl* 833

sour(e) *adj.* bitter; disagreeable, disgusting, *Cl* 192, *G* 963; *as n.* leaven, *Cl* 820

sourquydry, surquidré, sorquydryʒe *n.* pride

sowlé, sovly *adj.* unclean

sowme *see* **soumme**

soyle *n.* soil, ground

space *n.* time; distance, *Pe* 1030; respite, delay, *Cl* 755; opportunity, *Cl* 1774; **in s.** soon, in due course; **in þat s.** there and then

spak *adv.* readily, *Pat* 104

spakest *superl.adj. as n.* sharpest, wisest, *Pat* 169

spakk *see* **speke**

spakly *adv.* quickly

spare *adj.* spare, reserve, *Pat* 104; bare, *Pat* 338; restrained, tactful, *G* 901

spare *v.* spare; *intrans.* hold back, *Cl* 755, 1245

sparlyr *n.* calf (of leg)

sparred *pa.t.* sprang, rushed

sparþe *n.* battle-axe

spec *n.* speck

spece *see* **spyce**

spech(e) *n.* speech, conversation, discourse, words; *pl.* expressions, *G* 1261, 1778

special, specyal *adj.* special, specially chosen, *Cl* 1492; precious, *Pe* 235, 938

specialté *n.* partiality, affection, *G* 1778

sped(e) *n.* aid, *Cl* 1607; success, *G* 918; speed, *G* 1444; **a s. whyle** a short time, *Cl* 1285

spede *v.* (make) prosper, bless, quicken, further; cause, *Cl* 551; succeed, *Cl* 1058, *G* 410; *reflex.* hasten, *G* 979

spedly *adv.* happily, *G* 1935; quickly, *Cl* 1729

speke *v.* (**speked, spakk, speke, speken** *pa.t.,* **spoken** *pp.*) speak, say, declare

spelle *n.* speech, words, discourse

spelle *v.* tell, say, *Pe* 793. *G* 2140

spende, spenet *pa.t.* (**spend** *pp.*) fastened, *Pat* 104*n*; clasped, *Pe* 49; *intrans.* clung, *G* 158; *pp.* fastened, *G* 587

spende *v.* (**spent** *pp.*) spend; utter, *G* 410; **of speche s.** speech uttered about (*i.e.* tell of), *Pe* 1132

spenné *n.* ?fence, thorn hedge. *Possibly same as next*

spenne *n.* piece of land; **in s.** there, *G* 1074

spenne-fote *adv.* with feet together, *G* 2316*n*

spere *n.* spear

sperre *v.* strike, spur, *G* 670

spied *see* **spye**

spitous, spetos *adj.* abominable, *Cl* 845; cruel, *G* 209

spitously *adv.* contemptuously, maliciously

sponne *pa.t.subjunc.* would shoot up, *Pe* 35

sprez, spures, -z *n.* spurs

spornande *presp.* stumbling, *Pe* 363 *(fig.)*

spot(t)(e) *n.* spot, blemish, *Pe* 12, *etc.*, *Cl* 551; place, location, *Pe* 13, *etc.*; (*these senses perhaps combined in* **wythouten s.** *Pe* 12*n*, 24, *etc.*); **-lez** spotless, *Pe* 856; **-ty** spotty, *Pe* 1070

spoyle *v.* plunder, *Cl* 1774; seize, *Cl* 1285

sprad(de), sprang(e) *see* **sprede, spryng**

sprawlyng *n.* struggling

sprede *v.* (**sprad(de)** *pa.t.*) spread, extend; be overspread, *Pe* 25

sprenged *pa.t.* (dawn) broke, *G* 1415

sprent *pa.t.* leapt, *G* 1896

sprete *n.* bowsprit

sprit *pa.t.* jumped, *G* 2316

spryng *v.* (**sprang(e)** *pa.t.*) spring, leap (forth), shoot up; spread, *Cl* 1362; leap, rise, ascend, *Pe* 61; grow, *Pe* 453*n*; jump, fall, *Pe* 13

spryngande *presp.adj.* flourishing, *Pe* 35

spumande *presp.adj.* foaming

spured *pa.t.* (**spur(y)ed** *pp.*) asked

sput *v.* (*pres.subjunc.*) spit, *Pat* 338

sputen *pa.t.* uttered, *Cl* 845

spyce, spyse, spece *n.* creature, being, *Pe* 235*n*, 938; spice, *G* 892; spice-bearing plant, *Pe* 25, 35, (*collect.*) 104; spiced cakes, *G* 979

spye, -i- *v.* inquire, investigate, discover; look for, *G* 1896

spylle *v.* (**spylled, spylt** *pa.t.*) destroy, kill; scatter, spill, *Cl* 1248

spyrakle *n.* breath

spyryt *n.* spirit

spyse *see* **spyce**

spyserez *n.* spice sellers

spyt *n.* anger, *Cl* 755; (doing) injury, *G* 1444; evil deed, *Pe* 1138

stabeled *pa.t.* stabled, *G* 823

stable *adj.* steadfast, *Pe* 597

stable *v.* set, place, *Pe* 683; establish, *Cl* 1334, 1652, 1667, *G* 1060

stablye *n.* ring of beaters, *G* 1153

stac *see* **steke**

stad(de) *pp.* placed, fixed; set down, *G* 33; provided, armed, *G* 2137; **watz (wern) s.** found himself (themselves), *Cl* 806, *G* 644

staf *see* **staue**

staf-ful *adj.* cram-full, *G* 494*n*

stage *n.* degree, *Pe* 410

stal(e) *n.*[1] place, *Pe* 1002, *Cl* 1506

stalked *pa.t.* walked (warily), *Pe* 152, *G* 237; strode, *G* 2230

stal(l)e *n.*[2] standing position; **in s.** erect, *G* 104, 107

stalle *v.*[1] check, stop, *Cl* 1184; bring to a stand, *Pe* 188

stalle *v.*[2] (**stalled** *pp.*) install, *Cl* 1334; situate, *Cl* 1378

stalworth *adj.* (**stalworþest** *superl.*) strong, mighty; immovable, *Cl* 983; *as n.* bold knight, *G* 1659

stamyn *n.* prow

stanc *n.* (**stangez** *pl.*) pool, *Cl* 439, 1018

standen, standez, standes *see* **stonde**

stange *n.* pole, *G* 1614

stangez, stank *see* **stanc, stynke**

stape *adj.* advanced, *Pat* 122

stare *n.* power of sight, *Cl* 583

stare *v.* stare, *Pe* 149, *Cl* 389, 787; shine, glitter, *Pe* 116, *Cl* 1506; **starande** *presp.adj.* glittering, *G* 1818

start(e) *v.* start, jump, leap

statut *n.* agreement

staue, staf *n.* staff; club, *G* 2137

staue, stawe, stowe *v.* stow, place, lodge

stayned *pp.* stained, coloured
stayre *adj.* steep, *Pe* 1022
stayre *n.* rung (of a ladder), *Pat* 510n
stayred *adj.* arranged as steps, *Cl* 1396
sted(de), stud *n.* place; high place, *Cl* 389; **in s.** there, *G* 439
sted(e) *n.* steed, horse
steke *v.* (**stac, stek(en), stoken** *pa.t.*, **stoken** *pp.*) shut (up), enclose; cling (to), *G* 152; restrain, *Cl* 754; fasten, lock, *Cl* 884; *pp.* fixed, fastened, locked, *Pe* 1065, *Cl* 1524, *G* 33, 782; crammed (**of:** with), *G* 494; imposed on, *G* 2194. *Cf.* **stik**
stel *see* **stele** *v..*
stel-bawe *n.* stirrup
stel(e) *n.*[1] steel; armour, *G* 570
stele *n.*[2] handle, *G* 214, 2230; upright (of a ladder), *Pat* 510n
stele *v.* (**stel(en)** *pa.t.*) steal, creep; take by surprise, *Cl* 1778; **stollen** *pp.adj.* secret, *Cl* 706, surreptitious, *G* 1659
stel-gere *n.* armour
stem(m)e *v.* stop, delay, pause
stepe *n.* step, *Cl* 905; footstep, foot, *Pe* 683
stepe *see also* **step(p)e**
step(p)e *adj.* bright, brilliant, *Pe* 113, *Cl* 583
steppe *v.* (**stepe, stepped** *pa.t.*) step, walk; ascend, *Cl* 1396
stere *v.* guide, control, govern; restrain, *Pe* 1159
sterne *n.*[1] rudder, *Pat* 149
sternes, -z *n.*[2] stars, *Pe* 115, *Pat* 207
sterop, stirop *n.* stirrup
sterrez *n.* stars
steuen *n.*[1] voice, *Cl* 770, *Pat* 73, 307, *G* 242, 2336; sound, noise, *Pe* 1125, *Cl* 1203, 1402, 1524, 1778
steuen *n.*[2] time, time of meeting, appointment, *Cl* 706, *G* 1060, 2008, 2194, 2213, 2238; **at s.** for a meeting, *Pe* 188
steuen *n.*[3] command, *Cl* 360, 463
stif(fe), styf(fe) *adj.* (**stifest, styf(f)est** *superl.*) bold, brave, *G* 34, 260, *etc.*; rigid, *Cl* 983; firm, *Pe* 779, *G* 431, 846; unflinching, *G* 294; strong, *Cl* 255, *Pat* 234, *G* 214, 322, *etc.*; powerful, *G* 176, 1364; vigorous, *G* 104
stifly, styfly *adv.* firmly, *Cl* 157, 352, 1652, *G* 606; boldly, *G* 287, 1716
stiȝtel, styȝtel *v.* rule, be in command, *G* 104, 2213; master, *G* 2137; direct, ordain, *Pat* 402; **s. þe vpon** limit yourself to, *G* 2252; *pp.* directed (**with:** by), *Cl* 90
stik *v.* (**stykked** *pa.t.*) put, fasten, *Cl* 157, 583. *Cf.* **steke**
stille, stylle *adj. & adv.* (**stiller** *compar.*) still; quiet(ly); silent(ly); motionless; silent, dumb, *Cl* 1523; private, secret(ive), *Cl* 589, 706, *G* 1659; in peace and quiet, *G* 1367, *etc.*; in private, *G* 1085, 2385; at rest, *Pe* 683
stilly, stylly *adv.* quietly; stealthily, *Cl* 1778
stirop, stod(e)(n) *see* **sterop, stonde**
stoffed *pp.* filled, *Cl* 1184, lined, padded, *G* 606
stoken *see* **steke**
stokkes, stok(k)ez *n.* (punishment) stocks, *Cl*

46, 157, *Pat* 79; blocks of wood, *Cl* 1343, 1523, *etc.*; *sg.* tree stump, *Pe* 380n
stollen *see* **stele** *v.*
stomak *n.* stomach
ston *see* **ston(e)**
stonde, stande *v.* (**stod(e)(n)** *pa.t.* **standen** *pp.*) stand; be present; remain, *Pe* 597; put up with (from), take (from), *G* 294, 2286; shine, *Pe* 113; **s. alofte** stand out, *G* 1818
stonde *see also* **sto(u)nd(e)**
ston(e) *n.* stone, jewel; rock, *Pe* 822, *G* 2166, 2230, *etc.*; pavement, *G* 2063; **by stok oþer s.** anywhere at all, *Pe* 380
stonen *adj.* (made of) stone, *Cl* 995
ston-fyr *n.* flint-sparks
stonge *pa.t.* stung, struck, *Pe* 179
ston-harde *adv.* firmly
ston-stil *adj.* stone-still
stonye *see* **stoune**
stoped *pa.t.* closed up
stor(e) *adj.* powerful, *G* 1923; stern, harsh, *G* 1291
store *n.* supply, number, *Pe* 847
stote *v.* halt, stop, *Pe* 149
sto(u)nd(e) *n.* time; hour, time of hardship, torment, *Cl* 1603; blow, *Cl* 1540; **bi stoundes** at times
stoundez *v.* stupefies, *Pat* 317n
stoune, stowne, stonye *v.* astound, stun
stout(e) *adj.* strong, bold, mighty
stoutly *adv.* strongly, loudly; securely, *G* 1614
stowed, stowned *see* **staue, stoune**
strake *v.* (**strakande** *presp.*) sound (on horn)
stratez *see* **stre(e)te**
stra(u)nge, stronge (*Cl* 1494, *G* 1028) *adj.* strange; unnatural; foreign; visiting
stray *adj. or adv.* distracted, in bewilderment, *Pe* 179
stray *v.* stray; slip away, *Pe* 1173
strayn(e), streny *v.* strain; control, *G* 176; constrain, *Pe* 128, *Pat* 234; lead, make go, *Pe* 691; *reflex.* exert oneself, *Pe* 551
strayt *adj.* close-fitting, *G* 152
strayt *adv.* closely, severely, *Cl* 880, 1199
streche *v.* go, make one's way; **on s.** touch, cling to, *Pe* 843
stre(e)te *n.* (**stre(e)tez, stratez** *pl.*) street; highway, *Cl* 77
streȝt *adj.* (stretched); smooth, *G* 152; constricting, *Pat* 234; narrow, *Pe* 691
strem *n.* stream current
stremande *presp.adj.* streaming (with light), *Pe* 115
strenkle *v.* dispel
strenþe, strenkþe, strenghþe *n.* strength, power, intensity; force, *Cl* 880
streny *see* **strayn(e)**
stresse *n.* affliction, anguish, *Pe* 124
stretez, strike *see* **stre(e)te, stryke**
strok(e) *n.* stroke
strok(e) *see also* **stryke**
stronde *n.* shore; bank of stream, *Pe* 152
strong(e) *adj.* (**stronger** *compar.*) strong, powerful; steadfast, *Pe* 476; great, *Pat* 305; severe, *Cl* 1227, 1540. *See also* **stra(u)nge**
strot *n.* wrangling

strothe *n.* wooded marsh (*attrib.*), *G* 1710

stroþe-men *n.* fen-dwellers, men of earth, *Pe* 115*n*

strye *v.* destroy

stryf *n.* strife, contention; struggle, *Pe* 776; resistance, *G* 2323

stryke, strike *v.* (**strok(e)** *pa.t.*) strike; pierce, *Pe* 1125; come, go, *Pe* 570, 1186*n*; fly, *G* 671

stryndez *n.* currents

stryþ(þ)e *n.* stance

stryue *v.* (**stryuande** *presp.*) strive, contend

stubbe *n.* tree stump, *G* 2293

stud *see* **sted(de)**

studie *v.* gaze (to see), ponder

study *n.* thought

sturez *see* **styry**

sturn(e) *adj.* grim, formidable, *G* 334, 494, *etc.*; massive, *G* 143, 846, *etc.*; loud, *Cl* 1402; *as n.* redoubtable knight, *G* 214; **-ly** *adv.* fiercely

styf(est), styffe, styffest *see* **stif(fe)**

styfly *see* **stifly**

styȝe *n.* path, *Pat* 402

styȝe *pa.t.* climbed, *Cl* 389

styȝtel, stykked, stylle, stylly *see* **stiȝtel, stik, stille, stilly**

styngande *presp.adj.* stinging

stynke, stynkke *v.* (**stank** *pa.t.* **stynkande** *presp.*) stink

stynt *v.* (**stynt** *pp.*) cease, stop (**of:** from, *Pe* 353)

styry, sture *v.* (**styryed** *pa.t.*) stir; *trans.* brandish, *G* 331

styþly *adv.* strongly, *G* 431

such(e), seche (*G* 1543) *adj. & pron.* such

sue, sve, sw(y)e *v.* follow, pursue; proceed, go, *Cl* 87

suffer, soffer *v.* suffer, endure; allow, *G* 1967

suffraunce, soffraunce *n.* sufferance, patience

suffyse *v.* be adequate, *Pe* 135

sulp(en) *v.* (**sulpande** *presp.*, **sulped** *pp.*) defile, pollute

sum *n.* total; **of al and s.** in full, *Pe* 584

sumkyn *adj.* some (kind of), *Pe* 619

sum(me) *adj. & pron.* some; *adv.* partly, *G* 247 (*contr.* **al** wholly, *G* 246)

sum(m)oun *see* **somones**

sumned *pp.* summoned, *G* 1052

sumquat *adv.* somewhat, a little, *G* 86

sumquat *n.* something, *Cl* 627*n*, *G* 1799

sumquyle, -whyle *adv.* formerly, once (upon a time); sometimes, *G* 720, 721

sumtyme *adv.* formerly, once, at one time; at some time, *Pe* 760; sometime; *Cl* 582

sun, son, soun, sun(n)e *n.* son

sunderlupes *adv.* severally

sunkken *see* **synk**

sunne, sonne *n.* sun; **s. bemez** beams of the sun, *Pe* 83

suppe *v.* sup, drink

supplantorez *n.* usurpers

sure *adj. & adv.* sure, *Pat* 117; firm, *Pe* 1089; reliable, *G* 588; *adv.* firmly, *Pe* 222

surely *adv.* surely, firmly; reliably, *G* 1883

surfet *n.* transgression

surkot *n.* surcoat, gown

surquidré *see* **sourquydrye**

sustnaunce *n.* sustenance

sute, swete *n.* kind, suit; **of (a) s., of self s., of folȝande s., in s.** to match (in colour or pattern), *Pe* 203, 1108, *Cl* 1457, *G* 191, 859, 2518; **of his hors s.** matching that of his horse, *G* 180

sve, swalt(e) *see* **sue, swelt**

swanez *n.* swans

swange *n.* middle, hips

swange *pa.t.* worked, toiled, *Pe* 586

swange *see also* **swynge**

swangeande *presp.* swirling, *Pe* 111

swap *n.* blow, *Cl* 222

swap *v.* strike a bargain, exchange (?), *G* 1108

sware *adj.* square; squarely built, *G* 138

sware *v.* answer

swarmez *v.* swarms

swart *adj.* black

swat *pa.t.* sweated, laboured, *Pe* 586

swayf *n.* swinging blow

swaynes *n.* servants

swayues *v.* sweeps

swe *see* **souȝed, sue**

sweande *presp.adj.* driving, propelling, *Cl* 420 (*cf.* **sweȝe**)

sweft(e) *see* **swyft(e)**

sweȝe, swey *v.* (**sweȝe(d), sweyed** *pa.t.*) go, *Pat* 72; come, *Cl* 788; swing, *G* 1429; drop, *Pat* 151, *G* 1796; *trans.* bring, *Pat* 236

swelme *n.* heat (of suffering), *Pat* 3

swelt *v.* (**swalt(e)** *pa.t.*) perish, die, *Pat* 427, *Pe* 816, 1160; *trans.* destroy, *Cl* 332

swemande *adj.* grievous

sweng *n.* labour, *Pe* 575

swenge *v.* (**swenged** *pa.t.*) swing; rush, hasten, *Cl* 109, 667, *G* 1439, 1615; start, *G* 1756

swepe *v.* hurry, rush, *Cl* 1509; sweep, drift, *Pat* 341; sweep by, flow, *Pe* 111; *trans.* swoop on, catch, *Pat* 250

swere *v.* (**swer(e)** *pa.t.*) swear

swete *adj. & adv.* (**swetter** *compar.*, **swettest** *superl.*) sweet, lovely, fair; pure, unsoiled, *Cl* 1810; kind, courteous, *Cl* 640, *Pat* 280; delicious, *Cl* 1521; *as n.* sweet lady, *Pe* 240, *G* 1222; dear (one), *Pe* 325, 763, 829; dear (sir), *G* 1108, 2237; *adv.* sweetly, pleasantly; kindly, graciously, *Pe* 717; *compar.* gentler (one), *Pat* 236; **me were swetter to** I would rather, *Pat* 427*n*

swete *n.* life-blood, *Pat* 364

swete *see also* **sute**

swetely *adv.* kindly, graciously, *Pe* 717; happily, *G* 2034

swetnesse *n.* sweetness

swetter, swettest *see* **swete**

sweþled *pa.t.* or *pp.* wrapped, *G* 2034

sweued *pa.t.* whirled, swept

sweuen *n.* sleep, dream, *Pe* 62; *pl.* *G* 1756

swey *see* **souȝed, sweȝe**

sweyed *see* **sweȝe**

swoghe *adj.* deathly, *G* 243

swolȝ *n.* throat, *Pat* 250

swolȝed *pa.t. & pp.* swallowed, *Pat* 363; killed, *Cl* 1268

swone *n.* swoon

swowed *pa.t.* fell asleep, *Pat* 442

swyed *see* **sue**

swyerez *n.* squires, young knights

swyft(e), sweft(e), *adj. & adv.* swift(ly)

swyftly *adv.* swiftly

swymme *v.* (**swymmed** *pa.t.*) swim

swyn *n.* swine, boar

swynge *v.* (**swange** *pa.t.*) rush, *Pe* 1059, *G* 1562

swypped *pa.t.* escaped

swyre *n.* neck

swype(e), -ly *adv.* quickly, swiftly; very, *Cl* 816, 1283, *etc.*; greatly, *Cl* 354, 1176, *etc.*; strongly, earnestly, very much, *G* 1479, 1860, 1866, 2034; **as s.** at once

swypez *v.* burns, *Pat* 478

Syboym *n.* Zeboim

syde *adj.* wide, large, *Pat* 353; long, *G* 2431

syde, side *n.* side; direction, *G* 659, 2170; *pl.* surroundings, regions, *Cl* 956, 968

syence, cience *n.* learning; *pl.* different kinds of knowledge, *Cl* 1289

syfle *v.* blow; *reflex. G* 517

sy3(e) *see* **se(ne)**

sy3t(e), si3t *n.* sight, vision; look, glance, *Cl* 672, 1005; appearance, *Cl* 1406; **in s.** plainly, *Pat* 530, *G* 28; **se(e) wyth (in) s.** see (with one's own eyes), set eyes on

syked *pa.t.* (**sykande, sykyng** *presp.*) sighed

syker *see* **siker**

sykerly *adv.* securely, *Pat* 301

sykyng *n.* sigh, sighing, *G* 1982; *as presp. Pe* 1175, *G* 753

syled *pa.t.* passed, went

sylk(e), silk(e) *n.* silk; piece of silk, *G* 1846

syluer *n.* silver

syluerin, -en *adj.* silver, of silver; *as n.* **þe s.** the silver (dishes), *G* 124

symbales *n.* cymbals

sympelnesse *n.* sincerity, *Pe* 909

symple *adj.* (**symplest** *superl.*) meek, humble; guileless, *Cl* 746; plain, *G* 503, 1847

syn *see* **sypen**

synful *adj.* sinful; *as n. Cl* 716

syng(e) *v.* (**songe(n)** *pa.t.*) sing; sing the service, *Cl* 7

synglerty *n.* uniqueness, *Pe* 429

synglure *n.* uniqueness, *Pe* 8

syngne *n.* sign

syngnettez *n.* seals, *Pe* 838

synk *v.* (**synkande** *presp.*, **sunkken** *pa.t.*, **sonkken** *pp.*) sink; penetrate, *Cl* 689, *Pat* 507

synne *adv.* since, after, then, *Pat* 229, *G* 19

synne *n.* sin

synne *v.* sin

Syon *n.* Zion

syre, Syre *n.* lord; my Lord, *Pat* 413

syt(e) *n.* grief, sorrow; misfortune, *Pat* 517

sytole-stryng *n.* string of the cithern (type of guitar), *Pe* 91

sytte(n), (-s), (-z) *see* **sitte**

sype *n.*¹ scythe, *G* 2202

sype *n.*² (**sype(s), -z** *pl.*) time, period; *pl.* times, occasions; periods of time, *Cl* 1686; groups (of five), *G* 656

sypen, sipen, syn *adv. & conj.* after, afterwards, next, then, since; because

ta *see* **ta(ke)**

tabarde *n.* jerkin

tabelment *n.* tier (of foundation), *Pe* 994

table *n.* table; tier (of foundation), *Pe* 1004; cornice, *G* 789; **þe Rounde T.** the court of Arthur

tabornes *n.* tabours, small drums

tach(ch)e, tacche *v.* fasten, attach; *pp.* (*fig.*) implanted, *Pe* 464

ta3t *see* **tech(e)**

ta(ke) *v.* (**takes, -z, totz** *pres3s.*, **take(z), tatz** *imperat.*, **tok, toke(n)** *pa.t.*, **take(n), tan, tone** *pp.*) take; seize, capture, catch, *Cl* 836, 943, *etc.*, *Pat* 78, 229, *G* 1210; acquire, receive, get, *Pe* 539, 552, *etc.*, *G* 1396, 2243, 2448; give, offer, *Pe* 1158, *G* 1966; commit, *G* 2159; go, *Pe* 513; discover, find, *Cl* 763, *G* 2488, 2509; *pp.* situated, found, *G* 1811; **a counsayl hym takes** makes a plan, *Cl* 1201; **t. for** recognize as, *Pe* 830; **in theme t.** give an account of, *Pe* 944; **t. in vayne** spend in folly, *Pe* 687; **t. on honde** undertake, *G* 490; **t. to** take upon, *G* 350, 1540; *see also* **ille**

takel *n.* tackle, *Pat* 233; **takles** *pl.* gear, *G* 1129

tale, talle *n.* tale, story; account; statement; words, speech, conversation; message, *Pat* 75

talent *n.* wish, purpose

talentlyf *adj.* desirous

talk(e) *n.* speech, *Cl* 735, *G* 1486

talke *v.* talk, speak, say

talkyng *n.* conversation, *G* 917, 977

talle *see* **tale**

tame *adj.* tame; *as n.* tame animals

tan *see* **ta(ke)**

tapit *n.* tapestry, *G* 77, 858; carpet, *G* 568

tap(p)e *n.* tap, blow

Tarce *n.* Tarshish

tars *n.* rich fabric (*from Tharsia*)

tary *v.* tarry, linger; *trans.* delay, *G* 624

tatz *see* **ta(ke)**

tayl *n.*¹ tail

tayles *n.*² numbers (tallies), *G* 1377n

taysed *pp.* driven, *G* 1169

tayt *adj.* merry, *G* 988; attractive, *Cl* 871; well-grown, *G* 1377

tayt *n.* pleasure, *Cl* 889; sport, folly, *Cl* 935

teccheles *adj.* faultless, *G* 917

Techal *n.* Tekel

tech(e) *n.* sign, *Cl* 1049; spot, stain, *Pe* 845, *G* 2436, 2488; defilement, *Cl* 943; sin, *Cl* 1230

tech(e) *v.* (**ta3t** *pa.t.*) teach; direct, show, *Pe* 936, *Cl* 676, *G* 401, 1069, *etc.*

tede *see* **ty3ed**

tee *v.* (**towen** *pp.*) go, proceed, *Cl* 9, 1262, *Pat* 87, 416; *pp.* come, *G* 1093; **towen in twynne** severed (from each other), *Pe* 251

tel *see* **tyl(le)**

telde *n.* house, dwelling

telde *v.* raise, set up; **t. vp** build up, increase, *Cl* 1808

telle *v.* (**tolde** *pa.t.*) tell, speak, say; relate, describe, *Pe* 134; express, utter, *Pe* 815, *Pat* 358; recite, *G* 2188

teme, theme *n.* subject; **in t. layde** discussed, *Pat* 37; **in t. con take** described, *Pe* 944

teme *v.*[1] conceive, *Cl* 655

teme *v.*[2] **t. to** belong to, *Pe* 460, *Cl* 9, *Pat* 316

temple, tempple *n.* temple

tempre *v.* temper, moderate

temptande *presp.adj.* afflicting, *Cl* 283

tempte *v.* test

tender *adj.* tender, *Pe* 412, *Cl* 630; susceptible, liable, *G* 2436

tene *adj.* troublesome, *G* 1707; perilous, *G* 2075; angry, *Cl* 1808

tene *n.* anger, vexation, trouble, pain, grief, *Pe* 332, *G* 547, 1008; harm (inflicted), *Cl* 1232, *G* 22

tene *v.* torment, harass; punish, *Cl* 759; *intrans.* suffer torment, *G* 2501

tenfully *adv.* sorrowfully, bitterly

tenor *n.* purport

tent *v.* attend to; attend on, accompany, *Cl* 676; tend, *Pat* 498

tent(e) *n.* care, notice, *Pe* 387; **in t.** in a mind, *G* 624

tenoun *n.* joint, joinery; **of riche t.** admirably joined, *Pe* 993

tenþe *adj.* tenth

teres *n.* tears

terme *n.* limit, border, *Pat* 61; beginning, *Pe* 503; appointed time, *Cl* 1393; appointment, *G* 1671; trysting place, *G* 1069; period, *Cl* 239, 568; duration, *Pat* 505; word, expression, *Cl* 1733, *G* 917; **in termez** expressly, plainly, *Pe* 1053

terne *n.* lake

teþe *see* tothe

teueled *pa.t.* contended, *Cl* 1189

teuelyng *n.* striving, endeavour, *G* 1514

th- *see also* þ-

thaȝ *see* þaȝ

Thanes *n. see Cl* 448n

that, thay *see* þat, þay

the *see* þe, þou

theme, then(ne), ther(e), these, thik *see* teme, þen(e), þer(e), þis, þik(ke)

this, thow *see* þis, þou

t(h)rone *n.* throne

thus, thys, tid, til(le), tit(e) *see* þus, þis, tyd, tyl(le), tyd

titleres *n.* hounds (*specif.* those kept in reserve at a relay), *G* 1726

to *adv.* to, up, there; too, *Pe* 481, 492, *etc.*, *Cl* 22, 182, *etc.*, *Pat* 128, 425, *G* 165, 719, *etc.*

to *prep.* to, into, towards, at; against, *Cl* 1230; in, *Pat* 58; from, *Cl* 1586; for, *Pe* 507, 508, *etc.*, *Cl* 204, 309, *etc.*, *Pat* 98, *G* 420, *etc.*; as, *Pe* 759; as regards, *Cl* 174, 315, *etc.*; according to, *Cl* 1604; until, *Cl* 1032, *Pat* 317, *etc.*, *G* 71, *etc.*; in order to, *Pe* 507, *etc.*, *Cl* 107, *etc.*, *Pat* 97, *etc.*, *G* 43, *etc.*; as to, *G* 291; **to mede** as a reward, *Pat* 55; **to meruayle** (as) a marvel, amazing, *G* 1197; **for to** in order to; **gripped to, laȝt to,** *etc.* took hold of, *G* 421, 433, *etc.*

to *n.* toe, *Cl* 1691, *Pat* 229

tocleue *v.* cleave asunder

toclose *adv.* together, *Cl* 1541n

tocoruen *see* tokerue

todrawe *v.* dispel, *Pe* 280

tofylched *pa.t.* pulled down

togeder(e) *adv.* together

toȝe *adj.* tough, *Cl* 630

to-ȝere *adv.* this year, *Pe* 588n

toȝt *adj.* hardy, *G* 1869; **made hit t.** made it firm, made an agreement of it, *Pe* 522

tohewe *v.* cut down

tok(e)(n) *see* ta(ke)

token *n.* token; **in t. of** as a symbol of, *Pe* 742

tokened *pa.t.* signified, *Cl* 1557

tokenyng *n.* sign; **in t.** to signify, as a sign, *G* 2488

tokerue *v.* (**tocoruen** *pa.t.*) divide, *Cl* 1700; cut to pieces, *Cl* 1250

tolde, tole(s), tolk(e) *see* telle, tool, tulk

tolouse, tulé, tuly *n.* rich red fabric (from Toulouse), *G* 77, 568, 858

Tolowse *n.* Toulouse, *Cl* 1108n

tom *n.* leisure, time; opportunity, *Cl* 1153; interval, *Pat* 135

tomarred *pp.* spoiled, disfigured, *Cl* 1114n; (*cf.* **marre** *v.*[1])

tomorn(e) *adv.* tomorrow (morning)

tomurte *pa.t.* broke

tone *see* ta(ke)

tong(e) *n.* tongue

tool, tole *n.* (cutting) tool; weapon

top *n.* hair of the head, *Pat* 229

topasye, topace *n.* topaz; *pl. Cl* 1469

toppyng *n.* forelock, *G* 191

topreue *v.* prove conclusively, *Pat* 530

tor *n.* (**torres, -z, toures, towres** *pl.*) tower, stronghold; towering cloud, *Pe* 875n, *Cl* 951

tor *see also* tor(e)

toraced *pp.* pulled down, *G* 1168

tor(e) *adj.* difficult

torent(e) *pa.t. & pp.* tore (torn) apart

toret *pp.* (*for* **toret-ed**) with embroidered hem, *G* 960

toriuen *see* torof

Torkye *n.* Turkey

tormenttourez *n.* torturers

tornayeez *see* to(u)rnaye

torne *pp. & adj.* torn, *Cl* 1234, *Pat* 233, *G* 1579

torne *see also* t(o)urne

torof *pa.t.* (**toriuen** *pp.*) *intrans.* tore asunder, *Cl* 964; *trans.* tore, *Pat* 379; *pp.* shattered, *Pe* 1197

torres *see* tor

tortors *n.* turtle-doves, *G* 612

toruayle *n.* task, trouble

tote *v.* peep, *G* 1476

totez *n.* points (toes) of the shoes

totered *pa.t.* tottered

tothe *n.* (**teþe** *pl.*) tooth

totorne *pp.adj.* torn, ragged

totz, touch *see* ta(ke), towche

toun(e) *n.* town, city; court, *G* 31, 614; homestead, *Cl* 64; **out of t.** away, *G* 1049

tour *n.* entourage, *Cl* 216

toures *see* tor

to(u)rnaye *v.* double back, *G* 1707; joust, tourney, *G* 41

t(o)urne, torne *v.* turn; repent, *Pat* 506, 518; return, *G* 1099; go, make one's way, *Cl* 64, *G* 2075; **t. to hele** become sound, *Cl* 1099; *pp.* changing, turbulent, *G* 22

tournez *n.* deeds, acts, *Cl* 192

tow *see* **tweyne**

towalten *pa.t.* overflowed, burst forth, *Cl* 428

toward(e) *prep.* toward(s); *also* **to … warde** *Pe* 820, *G* 1200, *and cf.* **fro me warde,** *Pe* 981

towch(e), tuch *n.* touch, *Pat* 252; deed, action, *Cl* 48; covenant, *G* 1677; tone, strain, *G* 120; hint, *G* 1301

towche, touch *v.* touch; taste, *Cl* 245; reach, *Cl* 1393; tell, relate, *Cl* 1437, *G* 1541

towe *v.* take, *Pat* 100

towen *see* **tee**

towrast *adj.* awry, *G* 1663

towres *see* **tor**

tramme *n.* gear, tackle, *Pat* 101; device, plot, *G* 3

tramountayne *n.* north

trante *v.* twist, dodge, *G* 1707

tras *n.* course, way; **trone a t.** made (their) way, *Pe* 1113

traschez *n.* rags, ragged clothes, *Cl* 40

trased *pp.* set, *G* 1739

trauayl(e) *n.* labour, *Pe* 1087, *Pat* 505; journey, *G* 2241

trauayle *v.* labour, work, *Pe* 550, *Pat* 498; *pp.* had a hard journey, *G* 1093

traunt *n.* cunning practice, *G* 1700

trauthe, traupe *see* **trawpe**

traw(e), trave, trow, trow(e) *v.* believe, think, be sure; trust, *G* 2238; hope, *Cl* 388

trawpe, trawep, trauthe, -pe *n.* (word of) honour, *Cl* 63, 667, *Pat* 336, *G* 394, 403, *etc.*; pledge, *G* 2348; loyalty, integrity, *Cl* 236, *G* 626, 2470; righteousness, *Cl* 723; truth, *Pe* 495, *Cl* 1490, 1736, *G* 1050; **in t., with t.** truly, *Cl* 1703, *G* 1057, 1108

trayle *v.* trail, follow a trail, *G* 1700

trayled *pp.adj.* ornamented (with a pattern of trailing foliage), *Cl* 1473

traysoun, tresoun *n.* treason

trayst *adj.* sure

trayto(u)r *n.* traitor; *gen.pl.* *Cl* 1041

traryp(e)ly *adv.* ?ferociously, grievously, *Cl* 907, 1137

tre *n.* tree; wood, *Cl* 1342; *pl.* trees, *Pe* 1077, *Cl* 1041; planks, *Cl* 310, *Pat* 101 (**on po tres** on board)

trede *v.* walk

treleted *pp.* with (lace) lattice work, *G* 960

trendeled *pa.t. reflex.* rolled, *Pe* 41

tres *see* **tre**

tresor(e) *n.* treasure, *Pe* 331, *Cl* 866; price, value, *Pe* 237

tresorye *n.* treasury, *Cl* 1317

tresoun *see* **traysoun**

tresour *n.* treasurer, *Cl* 1437

trespas *v.* (**trespast** *pp.*) sin, transgress

tressour *n.* hair-fret, *G* 1739

trestes, -z *n.* trestles

trewest *see* **trwe**

trichcherye, tricherie, trecherye *n.* treachery

tried, trifel *see* **tryʒe, tryfle**

troched, trochet *pp.adj.* crocketed

tron(e) *see* **t(h)rone, trynande**

trot *n.* trot, run

trow, trowe(e) *see* **traw(e)**

Troye *n.* Troy

true *n.* truce, *G* 1210

true *see also* **trwe**

trulofez, truly *see* **trw(e)luf, trw(e)ly**

trumpen, -s, -z *n.* trumpets

trusse *v.* pack (up), stow away

trwe, true *adj.* (**trewest** *superl.*) true, correct, right; faithful, virtuous, trustworthy; firm (*fig.*), *Pe* 822; *as n.* *Cl* 702, *G* 2354; *adv.* firmly, truly, *Pe* 460

trw(e)luf *n.* true love; **trulofez** *pl.* true-love flowers, *G* 612

trw(e)ly, truly, *adv.* truly, faithfully

tryed *see* **tryʒe**

tryfle, trifel *n.*[1] trifle, pleasantry, *G* 108, 1301; idle talk, *G* 547; detail, *G* 165, ?960 (*see next*)

tryfle *n.*[2] trefoil, ?*G* 960 (*cf.* *n.*[1])

tryfled *adj.* ornamented with trefoils, *Cl* 1473

tryʒe *v.* (**tryed, tried** *pp.*) test, *Pe* 311n; *pp.* tried judicially, *Pe* 707, *G* 4; *adj.* chosen, choice, fine, distinguished

trylle *n.* quiver, *Pe* 78

trynande *presp.* going, *Cl* 976; **tron(e)** *pa.t.* went, *Pe* 1113, *Cl* 132, *Pat* 101

tryst(e) *v.* believe, depend (**perto:** upon that), *G* 2325; rely on, *G* 380; **mukel to t.** greatly to be depended on, very trustworthy, *Pat* 324

tryste *adv.* faithfully, *Pe* 460

trystor, -er *n.* hunting station

trysty *adj.* faithful, *Cl* 763

trystyly *adv.* faithfully, *G* 2348

tuch *see* **towch(e)**

tulé, tuly *see* **tolouse**

tulk, tolk(e) *n.* (**tulk(k)es** *pl.*) man, knight

tulket *pa.t.* sounded, *Cl* 1414

tult, turne(d) *see* **tylte, t(o)urne**

tuschez *n.* tusks

Tuskan *n.* Tuscany

twayne *see* **tweyne**

twayned *pp.* separated, parted, *Pe* 251

twelfpe *adj.* twelfth

twelmonyth *n. & adv.* twelvemonth, year; *adv.* a year hence, ago

twelue *adj.* twelve

twenty-folde *adv.* twenty times

tweyne, twayne, two, tow *adj.* two

twiges *n.* twigs, branches

twyez, twy(e)s *adv.* twice

twynande *presp.* entwining; **twynnen** *pp.* plaited, *G* 191

twynne *adj. as n.* two; **in t., on t.** in two, apart

twynne *v.* part, be separated, *Cl* 402, *G* 2512

twynne-hew *adj.* two-coloured

twynne, twys *see* **twynande, twyez**

tyd, tyt, tid, tit(e) *adv.* quickly, at once; **a(l)s, also t.** as quickly as possible, very quickly, immediately; **tytter** *compar.* sooner, *Pat* 231

tyde *n.* time, occasion; time of year, season, *G* 585, 2086; **hyȝe t.** festival

tydez *v.* befalls, is due to, *G* 1396

tyffe *v.* prepare, *G* 1129

tyȝed, tyȝt, tede *pp.* joined together; fixed, fastened, *Pe* 464, 1013

tyȝt *v.* (**tyȝt(e)** *pa.t.* **tyȝt** *pp.*) intend, *G* 2483; manage, succeed, *Cl* 1108; grant, appoint, *Cl* 1153; set forth, *Pe* 1053; spread, *G* 568, 858; come, *Pe* 503, 718; *reflex.* go on one's way, *Cl* 889

tykle *adj. as n.* uncertain, *Cl* 655

tyl(le), til(le), tel *conj. & prep.* until; **t. . . . þat** until; *prep.* to, *Pe* 676, *Cl* 882, 1174, *G* 673, 1979; **lykne t.** resemble, *Cl* 1064; **folȝe t.** serve, *Cl* 1752

tylte *v.* (**tult** *pa.t.*, **tylt** *pp.*) tumble; knock, *Cl* 1213; lean, *Cl* 832

tymbres *n.* timbrels, tambourines, *Cl* 1414

tyme *n.* time, period, occasion; **by tymez** on occasions, *G* 41

tymed *pp.* timed

tynde *n.* branch, *Pe* 78

tyne *n.* moment, *Pat* 59

tyne *v.* (**tynt** *pa.t.*) destroy, finish, *Cl* 775, 907; lose, *Pe* 332, *Cl* 216, *Pat* 500, 505

tyned *pa.t.* shut, enclosed, *Cl* 498

Tyntagelle *n.* Tintagel

type *v.* throw; **t. down** overthrow, *Pat* 506

typped *adj.* consummate, extreme, *Pat* 77n

tyrauntez *n.* evil men, *Cl* 943

tyrauntyré *n.* tyranny

tyrue *v.*[1] strip (**of:** off), *Cl* 630, *G* 1921

tyrue *v.*[2] overturn, *Cl* 1234

tyt *see also* **tyd**

tytel, tytle *n.* right, *G* 480, 626

tytelet *pp.* inscribed as a title, *G* 1515

tytter *see* **tyd**

tyþe *adj.* tenth

tyþyng, tyþynges, -ez *n.* tidings, information

tyxt(e) *n.* text; (actual) words, *Cl* 1634; passage, *Pat* 37; heading, rubric, *G* 1515; **temez of t.** subject matter, *G* 1541

þ' *see* **þe**

þad *see* **þat** *demonstr.*

þaȝ, þaȝ *conj.* though; even though; even if; if, *Pe* 368, *Cl* 743, *G* 496, 2282, 2307, 2427

þanne *see* **þen(n)(e)**

þar *v.* need, *G* 2355

þare, þore *adv.* there, then, on that occasion; in that respect, *G* 2356

þat *conj.* that, so that; *see also* **bi, for, with**

þat, that, þad (*G* 686) *demonstr.adj. & pron.* (**þo, þos(e)** *pl.*) that, the; *pl.* those, the; **þat ilk(e)** the same; **þat on, þat oþer** the one, the other. *See also* **þo, þos(e)**

þat *rel.pron.* who(m), which, that; what, that which, *Pe* 327, 521, *etc.*, *Cl* 652, 898, *etc.*, *Pat* 178, 336, *G* 291, 391, *etc.*

þay, thay *pron.* (**hem, him, hom, hym** *acc. & dat.*) they

þayr *possess.adj.* their

þayres *pron.(possess.)* theirs

þe, þ', the *def.art.* the

þe, the *adv.w.compar.* (so much) the (farther,

etc.), *Pe* 127, *etc.*, *Cl* 296, *Pat* 6, 34, *etc.*, *G* 87, *etc.*

þe *relat. pron.* who, *Pat* 56

þe *see also* **þou**

þede *n.* land, country, *Pe* 483, *G* 1499

þeder *see* **þider**

þef *n.* thief, *Pe* 273, *G* 1725

þefte *n.* theft

þen(e), þenn(e), then(ne), þanne *adv. & conj.* then, *Pe* 155, 277, *etc.*, *Cl* 15, 53, *etc.*, *Pat* 7, 33, *etc.*, *G* 116, 301, *etc.*; than, *Pe* 134, 555, *etc.*, *Cl* 76, 168, *etc.*, *Pat* 8, 48, *etc.*, *G* 24, 236, *etc. See also* **er(e)**

þenk(ke), þynke (*Cl* 749) *v.* (**þoȝt(en)** *pa.t.*, **þoȝt** *pp.*) think, consider, remember; intend, *Pe* 1151, *Cl* 304, 711, *etc.*, *G* 331, 1023; decide, *Cl* 138; **þ. (vp)on** bear in mind, *Pe* 370, *Cl* 819, *Pat* 294, *G* 2052, 2397. *See also* **þynk(k)(e)**

þenne *adv.* thence, *Cl* 1089

þerabof *adv.* above (it), *Cl* 1481. *Pat* 382

þeraboute *adv.* (working) at it, *G* 613; thereabouts, *Cl* 1796, *G* 705; round it, *G* 2485

þerafter *adv.* after(wards), behind, *G* 671; again, *G* 2418

þeralofte *adv.* on it, *G* 569

þeramongez *adv.* with it, *G* 1361

þeranvnder *adv.* underneath, *Cl* 1012

þeras *see* **þer(e)as**

þerat(t)e *adv.* at that, at it, to it, there

þerby, þerbi *adv.* near there, around it, *Cl* 1034; on them (the trumpets), *Cl* 1404, *G* 117

þerbyside, -syde *adv.* beside it, *G* 1925; near by, *Cl* 673

þer(e), þer(e) *adv. & conj.* there; then, on that occasion, *Cl* 203, 216, *Pat* 135, *etc.*; *conj.* where, when, as, *Pe* 26, 30, *etc.*, *Cl* 158, 238, *etc.*, *Pat* 37, *etc.*, *G* 195, 334, *etc. See also* **þare**

þer(e)as *conj.* where; in which, *Cl* 24; as, *Pe* 129

þerfor(e), þerforne *adv.* therefore, for that reason; for it, *G* 1107

þerin(ne), þerine *adv.* therein, in it, in them, there, in that place; in that (course), *Pe* 1168; *relat.* in which, *G* 17

þerof *adv.* thereof, of it; from it, from them, from there, *Pe* 1069, *Cl* 1499, 1507; because of that, *Cl* 972

þeron *adv.* on there, on that, on it; in them, *Cl* 1719; for it, *Pe* 645; of it, *Pe* 387

þerouer *adv.* above

þeroute *adv.* out, out of it (them); outside; out of doors, *Pe* 930, *Cl* 807, *G* 2000, 2481; overboard, *Pat* 153, *etc.*

þerto *adv.* at it, there, to it (them), *Pe* 664, *Cl* 1394, *G* 219, *etc.*; with these, *Pe* 833; to (do) that, *Pe* 172; for that, *Pe* 1140; for that purpose, *Cl* 701; accordingly, *G* 757

þertylle *adv.* to it, to that place, there

þerþurȝe *adv.* through it, *Pat* 354

þerue *adj.* unleavened, *Cl* 635

þervnder *adv.* underneath (it)

þervpone *adv.* upon it, *Cl* 1665

þerwyth, þerwith *adv.* with (by) it, with them; at this, about this, *Cl* 138, 1501, *G* 1509; through it, by means of it, *Pat* 60; thereupon, *Cl* 528, *Pat* 232, *G* 121

þes(e) *see* þis
þester *n.* darkness
þewed *pp.* endowed with virtue, *Cl* 733
þewes, -z *n.*[1] noble qualities, virtues; courteous manners
þewes *n.*[2] thieves, *Cl* 1142
þi *see* þy
þider, þeder, þyder *adv.* thither, to it, there
þiderwarde *adv.* in that direction
þik(ke), þike, þyk(ke), **thik** *adj. & adv.* (þik(k)er *compar.adv.*) thick(ly), close(ly), dense(ly); burly, thick-set, *G* 138, 175; frequent, *Cl* 952; hard, fast, *G* 1702; with (such) clatter, *Cl* 1416; insistently, *G* 1770; *compar.* more closely, *Cl* 1384, more intensely, *Pat* 6
þing(es), þingez, þink(ez) *see* þyng(e)
þink(kez) *see also* þynk(k)(e)
þirled, þurled *pa.t.* pierced, *Cl* 952, *G* 1356
þis, þise, þys(e), þysse, **this, thys** *adj. & pron.* (þis(e), þes(e), þyse, **these** *pl.*) this; the (usual), *Pe* 42, 505, *Cl* 428, *G* 1139n, *etc.*; = þis is *G* 2398
þiself *see* þyself
þo *adj. & pron.* those, the; *pron.* them, *Pe* 557; (five) such, *Pe* 451n
þof, þoȝ *conj.* though
þoȝt(e) *n.* thought
þoȝt(en) *v. see* þenk(ke), þynk(k)(e)
þole *v.* endure; allow, *G* 1859
þonk(e), þonc *n.* thank(s)
þonk(ke) *v.* thank
þoo *adv.* then, *Pe* 873
þore, þorȝ *see* þare, þurȝ(e)
þorne *n.* (þornez *pl.*) thorn(s), *G* 2529; thorn bush, *G* 1419
þorpes *n.* villages
þos(e) *adj. & pron.* those; them, *Pe* 515
þou, þow, **thow** *pron.* thou; þe, **the** *acc. & dat.* thee
þowsande(z), þousandez *n.* thousands
þrad *pp.* punished, *Cl* 751
þral *n.* serf, fellow, *Cl* 135
þrange *adv.* grievously, *Pe* 17
þrast *n.* thrust, onslaught, *G* 1443
þrat(ten) *see* þret(e)
þrawen, þrawez *see* þrow(e)
þre *adj.* three
þred *n.* thread; limit, *G* 1771
þrefte *adj.* unleavened, *Cl* 819
þrenge *see* þrynge
þrep(e) *n.* contradiction, dispute, *Cl* 350; contest, *G* 2397; insistence, *G* 1859
þrepe *v.* contend, *G* 504
þrepyng *n.* strife, quarrelling
þresch *v.* (thresh, thrash); strike, *G* 2300
þret(e), þrat *n.* compulsion, force, *Pat* 55, 267, *G* 1499
þrete *v.* (þrat(en) *pa.t.* þreted *pp.*) urge, *G* 1980; urge on, *Cl* 937; threaten, *Cl* 680, *G* 1725, 2300; attack, *G* 1713; rebuke, *Cl* 1728; wrangle, *Pe* 561
þretty, þretté *adj.* thirty
þreuenest *see* þryuen
þrich *n.* rush, *G* 1713
þrid *see* þryd(de)

þro *adj.* eager, earnest, *G* 645, 1751; fierce, *G* 1713 (*as n.*), 2300, proud, noble, *Pe* 868; stubborn, impatient, *Pe* 344; packed, hectic, *G* 1021
þro *adv.* eagerly, earnestly, *G* 1867, 1946; thoroughly, fully, *Cl* 1805; violently, *Cl* 220; quickly, *Cl* 590
þro *n.* anger, resentment, *Cl* 754, *Pat* 6, 8
þrobled *pa.t.* (þrublande *presp.*) crowded
þroly *adv.* violently, quickly; earnestly, *G* 939
þrong(e) *n.* throng, crowd
þrong(en) *see also* þrynge
þrote *n.* throat
þrow(e), þraw *v.* (þrwe(n) *pa.t.* þrawen, þrowen *pp.*) throw; rush, fly, *Cl* 590, *Pat* 267; fall violently, *Cl* 220; crowd, *Cl* 879; roll, *Pe* 875; þ. **forth** give vent to, *Pat* 8; þrawen, þrowen *pp. & adj.* laid, *G* 1740; twisted, drawn up, *G* 194; turned, *Cl* 516; crowded, packed, *Cl* 504, 1384; dense, *Cl* 1775; muscular, *G* 579
þrowe *n.* time, while, *G* 2219
þrublande (þrobled *pa.t.*) crowding, jostling
þrwe(n) *see* þrow(e)
þrych *v.* (þryȝt *pa.t. & pp.*) oppress, *Pe* 17; push down, flatten, *G* 1443; crowd, *Cl* 1687; *pp.* pushed, brought (with difficulty), *Pe* 670; pierced, *Pe* 706; imprinted on, *G* 1946; packed, in a throng, *Pe* 926; crowded, iammed, *Cl* 135
þryd(de), þryde, þrid *adj. & pron.* third
þrye(s), þryse, þryez *adv.* thrice, three times
þryf *see* þryue
þryftyly *adv.* in a seemly manner, *Cl* 635
þryȝt *see* þrych
þrynge, þrenge *v.* (þronge, þrong(en) *pa.t.*) press, crowd; go, pass, hasten; rush, *Cl* 180; þ. **after** follow, serve, belong to, *Cl* 930, 1639
þrynne *adj.* three; **in þ.** in three words, *Cl* 1727
þryuande *presp.adj.* worthy, *Cl* 751; hearty, *G* 1980; -**ly** *adv.* heartily, abundantly, *G* 1080, 1380
þryue, þryf *v.* (þryued *pa.t.subjunc.*, *Pat* 521) thrive, flourish; **so mot I þ. as** as I hope to prosper, upon my soul, *G* 387
þryuen *pp.adj.* (þreuenest, þryuenest *superl.*) fine, noble; fair, lovely
þuȝt *see* þynk(k)(e)
þulged *pa.t.* indulged, bore (with), *G* 1859
þunder *n.* thunder
þunder-þrast *n.* thunderbolt
þurȝ(e), þorȝ *prep. & adv.* through, throughout; because of, by means of, through, *Pe* 413, 640, *etc.*, *Cl* 236, 241, *etc.*, *Pat* 257, 284, *etc.*, *G* 91, 998, *etc.*; beyond, *G* 645, 1080; *adv.* through, *G* 1356
þurȝout *adv.* throughout, everywhere
þurȝoutly *adv.* completely, *Pe* 859
þurled *see* þirled
þus, **thus** *adv.* thus
þwarle *adj.* intricate, *G* 194
þwong *n.* thong, lace
þy, þyn, þi(n) *possess.adj. & pron.* thy, thine
þyder *see* þider
þyȝez *n.* thighs

þyk(ke), þyn *see* þik(ke), þy
þyng(e), þing, þink, þynk *n.* thing, matter, something; person, *Pe* 771, *G* 1526
þynk(k)(e), þink *v.impers.* (þo3t, þu3t *pa.t.*) (me) þynk, (me) þynkkez, *etc.* it seems (to me, *etc.*); *sometimes crossed with* þenk(ke), *esp. in pa.t.*; seem good (to you), *G* 1502
þynke *see also* þenk(ke)
þys(e) *see* þis
þyself, þiself, þyseluen *pron.* thyself
þysse *see* þis

uengaunce, uenged, ueray, uerayly, uesture, uisage, uoched *see* vengaunce, venge, ver(r)ay, verayly, vesture, vysayge, vouche
uyage *n.* journey, *G* 535
uyne *see* vyne

valay *n.* valley
vale *n.* valley
vanist *pa.t.* vanished
vanyté *n.* vanity, folly
vayl *v.* (vayled *pa.t.*) be effective, *Pe* 912; be of service, be used, *Cl* 1151; be of value, *Cl* 1311
vayles *n.* veils, *G* 958
vayn(e) *adj.* vain, useless; **in v.** in folly, *Pe* 687; at nought, *Pe* 811
vayned *see* wayne
vayneglorie *n.* pride
vayres *n.* truth, *G* 1015
vch(e), vuche, iche *adj.* each, every, (all); *also* vch(e) a; v. wy, haþel, lede, *etc.* everyone
vch(e)on(e) *pron.* each one, every one; v. . . . oþerez each one . . . the other's
veluet *n.* velvet
vengaunce, uengaunce, vengiaunce *n.* vengeance, retribution
venge, weng *v.* (uenged, venged, wenged *pa.t.*) take vengeance, punish; avenge; *reflex. Pat* 71
ven(k)quyst *pa.t.* (venkkyst *pp.*) overcame
venture *n.* hazard, peril, *G* 2482
venym *n.* venom, poison
venysoun *n.* venison
ver *n.* spring, *G* 866n
veray *see* ver(r)ay
verayly, uerayly *adv.* truly
verce *n.* verse
verdure *n.* green(ness)
vere *v.* turn, *Pe* 177, 254
vergyn, vyrgyn *n.* virgin; **v. flour** virginity, *Pe* 426
vergyn(y)té *n.* virginity
Vernagu *n.* Vernagu, *Pat* 165n
ver(r)ay, ueray *adj.* true; *as adv.* truly, faithfully, *Pat* 333
vertu(e) *n.* virtue; power, *Pat* 284
vertu(o)us *adj.* potent, *Cl* 1280, *G* 2027n
vessel, vessayl *n.* vessel; vessels (*collective*)
vesselment *n.* vessels (*collective*)
vesture, u- *n.* clothing; *pl.* vestments, *Cl* 1288
veued *see* wayue
vewters *n.* keepers of hounds, *G* 1146
vgly *adj.* (vglokest *superl.*) ugly, gruesome, *Cl*

892, *G* 441; threatening, *G* 2079; oppressive, *G* 2190
v3ten *n.* early morning
vice, vyse *n.* vice
vilanous *adj.* ill-bred, *G* 1497
vilanye, vyla(y)ny(e) *n.* ill-breeding, discourtesy, *Cl* 863, *G* 345; *shifting towards* degeneracy, villainy, wickedness, sin, evil, *Cl* 544, 574, *Pat* 71, *G* 634, 2375
vilté *n.* vileness, *Cl* 199
vmbe *adv. & prep.* (a)round, about
vmbebrayde *pa.t.* greeted, accosted, *Cl* 1622
vmbeclypped *pa.t.* encircled, ringed, *G* 616
vmbefolde *v.* envelop, *G* 181
vmbegon *pp.* encompassing, *Pe* 210
vmbegrouen *adj.* covered, grown over
vmbekeste *v.* (vmbekesten *pa.t.pl.*) cast about, search around, *Cl* 478, *G* 1434
vmbelappe *v.* interlace, *G* 628
vmbely3e *v.* surround, *Cl* 836
vmbepy3te *pp.* arrayed about, *Pe* 204, 1052
vmbeschon *pa.t.* shone around, *Pat* 455
vmbestounde(s) *adv.* sometimes; some time (or other), *Pat* 122
vmbesweyed *adj.* surrounded, *Cl* 1380
vmbete3e *pa.t.* enclosed, *G* 770
vmbetorne *adv.* round, *G* 184
vmbeþour *adv.* around the outside, *Cl* 1384
vmbewalt *pa.t.* surrounded, *Cl* 1181
vmbeweued *v.* enveloped, *G* 581
vmbre *n.* shadow
vnavysed *pp.adj.* thoughtless, *Pe* 292
vnbarred *pp.* unbarred
vnbene *adj.* cheerless, *G* 710
vnblemyst *pp.adj.* unblemished
vnbly3e *adj.* unhappy, *G* 746; dismal, *Cl* 1017
vnbrosten *adj.* unbroken
vnbynde *v.* separate, divide, *G* 1352
vncely *adj.* ill-fated, hapless, *G* 1562
vncheryst *pp.adj.* uncared for
vnclannes(se) *n.* uncleanness, impurity
vnclene *adj.* unclean, impure
vncler *adj.* indistinct
vnclose *v.* disclose, *Cl* 26; open, *Cl* 1438, *G* 1140
vncortayse *adj.* discourteous
vncoupled *pa.t.* uncoupled
vncowþe, vncouþe *adj.* unknown, strange
vndefylde *pp.adj.* undefiled
vnder *adv.* below, underneath, *G* 158, 742, 868; down, *G* 2318n
vnder *n.* the third hour (9 a.m.), *Pe* 513; **myd ouer vnder** well on in the afternoon, *G* 1730n
vnder *prep.* under; dressed in, *G* 260; **v. God, v. heuen, v. mone,** *etc.*, on earth
vnder3ede *pa.t.* understood, *Cl* 796
vndernomen *pa.t.* understood, *Pat* 213
vnderstonde *v.* understand; **to v.** that is to say, *Pe* 941
vndertake *v.* discern, understand, *G* 1483
vndo *v.* (vndyd *pa.t.*) cut open, *G* 1327; destroy, *Cl* 562
vneþe *adv.* hardly, scarcely
vnfayre *adj. or adv.* horrible, hideous(ly), *Cl* 1801, *G* 1572

vnfolde v. open, *Cl* 962; disclose, *Cl* 1563
vnfre adj. ignoble, *Cl* 1129
vngarnyst adj. not properly dressed, *Cl* 137
vnglad adj. unhappy
vngoderly adj. base, vile
vnhap n. misfortune
vnhap v. unfasten, *G* 2511
vnhappen adj. ill-fated, accursed
vnhardeled pa.t. unleashed, *G* 1697
vnhaspe v. disclose, *Cl* 688
vnhole adj. unsound, insane, *Cl* 1681
vnhonest adj. impure, *Cl* 579
vnhuled see **vnhyle**
vnhyde v. reveal, *Pe* 973
vnhyle v. (**vnhuled** pp.) uncover
vnknawen adj. unknown, unexplored, *Cl* 1679
vnkyndely adv. unnaturally, discourteously, *Cl* 208
vnlace v. cut up, *G* 1606
vnlapped adj. unbound, *Pe* 214
vnleuté n. faithlessness, *G* 2499
vnlouked pa.t. opened, *G* 1201
vnlyke adj. different, *G* 950
vnmanerly adv. discourteously
vnmard adj. undefiled, *Cl* 867
vnmete adj. monstrous, *G* 208; unfitting, *Pe* 759
vnneuened pp.adj. not mentioned, *Cl* 727
vnnynges n. signs, *Pat* 213
vapynne v. unbolt, open, *Pe* 728
vnresounable adj. unreasonable
vnrydely adv. confusedly, *G* 1432
vnryȝt n. wrong, crime, *Cl* 1142
vnsaueré adj. disagreeable, *Cl* 822
vnslayn pp.adj. not killed
vnslyȝe adj. incautious, *G* 1209
vnsmyten adj. unharmed, unpunished
vnsounde adj. diseased, corrupt, *Cl* 575; ragged (clothes), *Pat* 527
vnsounde n. misfortune, trouble, *Pat* 58;
vnsoundely, vnsoundyly adv. mortally, harshly, *Cl* 201; menacingly, *G* 1438
vnsparely adv. in plenty, *G* 979
vnspurd pp. (he being) unasked, *i.e.* without asking him, *G* 918
vnstered adj. undisturbed, *Cl* 706
vnstrayned pp.adj. untroubled (**of**: by), *Pe* 248
vnswolȝed pp.adj. unconsumed, *Cl* 1253
vnto, vnte prep. to; as, *Pe* 772
vntrawþe n. perfidy, dishonesty (see **trawþe**), *G* 2383, 2509
vntrwe adj. untrue, false; unfaithful
vntwyne v. destroy, *Cl* 757
vntyȝtel see **dele**
vnþewez n. faults, vices
vnþonk n. disfavour, displeasure
vnþryfte n. wickedness
vnþryftyly adv. wickedly, improperly
vnþryuande presp.adj. unworthy, ignoble, *G* 1499
vnþryuandely adv. meanly, *Cl* 135
vnwar adj. ignorant, foolish
vnwaschen adj. unwashed
vnwelcum adj. unwelcome
vnworþelych adj. shameful, *Cl* 305

vnworþi, -y adj. unworthy, *G* 1244; of little worth, *G* 1835
vnwyse adj. foolish
vnwytté adj. ignorant
vouche, uoche, wowche v. summon, *Pe* 1121; make, affirm, *Pat* 165; give, hold, *Cl* 1358; **w. ... saf** bestow, *G* 1391
vowes n. vows
voyde v. leave, *G* 345; clear, rid, *G* 1342, 1518; disappear, *Cl* 1548; annihilate, destroy, *Cl* 1013, *Pat* 370; **v. away** put aside, *Cl* 744; pp.adj. **voyded** (**of**) free (from), *G* 634
vp, vp(p)e adv. up; open, *Cl* 1263, *G* 820, 1192, etc.; away, *G* 1874; aroused, *Cl* 834
vpbrayde v. (**vpbrayde** pp.) upbraid, reproach, *Pat* 430; throw up, raise, *Cl* 848, *G* 781
vpcaste pp. proclaimed, *Cl* 1574
vpe, vpen see **vp, vpon** adj.
vpfolden adj. extended, *Cl* 643 (cf. **folde vp** *Pe* 434)
vphalde v. hold up, *G* 2442
vphalt pp.adj. drawn up, high, *G* 2079
vplyfte v. lift, *G* 505; pp.adj. raised, *Cl* 987
vpon, vpen, open adj. open, *Pe* 183, 198, 1066, *Cl* 453, 501, 882, *G* 2070
vpon adv. on, *Cl* 141, 1427, *G* 2021; in, *Cl* 1049; on it, on them, *Pe* 208, *Cl* 1276, *G* 1649
vpon(e) prep. on, upon; at, *Cl* 893, *G* 9, 37, etc.; by, *Cl* 578, *G* 47; in, *Pe* 545, *Cl* 902, *Pat* 12; into, *Pe* 59, *G* 244; of, *Pe* 370; for phrases see also **ende, hyȝ(e), longe, stiȝtel, wyse,** etc.
vpon, open v. open, *Cl* 1600, *G* 1183
vponande presp.adj. opening, *Cl* 318
vppe see **vp**
vprerde pa.t. raised up
vpryse v. (**vpros, vprysen** pa.t.) rise, get up
vpset pp. raised up, *Pat* 239
vp-so-down adv. upside-down
vpwafte pa.t. flew up, *Cl* 949
vpynyoun n. opinion
vrnmentes, vrþe see **ornementes, erþe**
vrþ(e)ly adj. earthly
Vryn n. (gen.) (of) Urien, *G* 113
vrysoun n. band of silk, *G* 608n
vsage n. custom
vse v. practise; use, *Cl* 11; spend, *Cl* 295; have relations with, *G* 2426; reflex. have sexual relations, *Cl* 267
vsellez see **vsle**
vsle n. (**vsellez** pl.) ash
Vter n. Uther (Pendragon), *G* 2465
vtter adv. outside, out
vtwyth adv. outwardly, on (from) the outside
vuche, vus see **vch(e), we**
vycios adj. vicious, depraved
vyf, vyuez see **wyf**
vygour n. power, *Pe* 971
vyl adj. vile, repugnant, *Cl* 744
vyla(y)ny(e) see **vilanye**
vyle v. disgrace, *Cl* 863
vyne, uyne n. vineyard
vyolence n. violation, *Cl* 1071
vyoles n. incense dishes, *Cl* 1280
vyrgyn see **vergyn**

vysayge, uisage *n.* face, *Pe* 178; appearance, *G* 866
vys(e) *n.* face, *Pe* 254, 750
vyse *see also* **vice**

wace *see* **be(ne)**
wach(e) *n.* vigil, state of wakefulness, *Cl* 1003; sentry, *Cl* 1205
wade *v.* (**wod** *pa.t.*) wade, *Pe* 143, 1151, *G* 2231; go (down in), *G* 787
waft(e) *see* **wayue**
wage *n.* pledge, foretaste, *G* 533; *pl.* wages, payment, *G* 396
wage *v.* ?continue, ?bring reward, *Pe* 416
waged *pp.* fluttered
waȝez *see* **wawez**
wake *v.* (**wok(e), waked** *pa.t.*, **waked** *pp.*) stay awake, watch, *Pat* 130; stay up late revelling, *G* 1025; *trans.* guard, *Cl* 85
waken *v.* (**wak(e)ned(e)** *pa.t. & pp.*) waken, arouse; *intrans.* waken, wake up, arise; shine, blaze, *G* 1650; *subjunc.* would wake up, *G* 1194
wakker *compar.adj.* weaker, *Cl* 835
wakkest *superl.adj.* weakest, *G* 354
wal *see* **wal(le)**
wale *v.* (**waled, walt** *pp.*) choose, *Cl* 921, *G* 1276; look for, *G* 398; distinguish, *Pat* 514; perceive, *Pe* 1000, 1007; take, *G* 1238; *pp.* chosen, *Cl* 1734
wale, walle *adj.* choice, noble, excellent, delightful, *Cl* 1716, 1734, *G* 1010, 1403, 1712; **w. chere** urbane manner, *G* 1759
walk(e) *v.* (**welke** *pa.t.*) walk; *reflex. Pe* 711; travel, *G* 1521
walkyries *n.* sorceresses, *Cl* 1577
wallande *presp.adj.* welling, surging
wal(le) *n.* wall. *See also* **wale** *adj.*
walle-heued *n.* (**welle-hedez** *pl.*) fountain, spring
walled *pp.* walled, *Cl* 1390
walour *n.* valour
walt *pa.t.* (**walte** *pp.*) (cast); tossed, *G* 1336; threw, *Cl* 501; *pp.* taken, removed, *Pe* 1156. *See also* **wale, welde** *& cf.* **walte** *v.*
walte *v.* flow, *Cl* 1037; pour, *Cl* 364
walter *v.* roll; pour, flow, *Cl* 1027, *G* 684
walterande *presp.adj.* rolling, wallowing
wamel *v.* feel sick
wan *see* **wynne** *v.*
wande *n.* staff, *G* 215; bough(s), *G* 1161
wane *adj.* lacking, *G* 493
waning *n.* reduction, *Pe* 558 (*cf.* **woned** *pp.*)
wanlez *adj.* without hope
wap *n.* blow; **at a w.** at a stroke, in one moment, *Pat* 499
wappe *v.* strike, swish, *G* 1161, 2004; **w. vpon** fling open, *Cl* 882
war *v. reflex.* beware, see to it
war *see also* **war(e)**
warde *see* **toward(e)**
warded *pp.* guarded
war(e) *adj.* aware, wary, cautious, alert; ware! (*hunter's cry*), *G* 1158; **be by hem w.** take warning from them, *Cl* 712; **be w. of** be

aware of, perceive; **-ly** *adv.*; **warloker** *compar.adv.* more cautiously, *G* 677
ware *v.* spend, use, *G* 402, 1235; pay back, *G* 2344
ware *see also* **be(ne)**
warisch *v.* (**waryst** *pp.*) protect, *Cl* 921; *pp.* recovered, *G* 1094
warlaȝes *n.* wizards, *Cl* 1560; **warlowes** *gen. sg.* the Devil's, *Pat* 258*n*
warlok *n.* fetter, *Pat* 80
warloker, warly *see* **war(e)**
warlowes *see* **warlaȝes**
warm(e) *adj. & adv.* warm; *adj. or adv. Pat* 470
warne *v.* warn, order
warnyng *n.* warning
warp(e)(n) *v.* (**warp(ped), werp** *pa.t.*) (cast); toss, *Cl* 444; put, *G* 2025; utter, say, *Pe* 879, *Cl* 152, 213, 284, *Pat* 356, *G* 224, 1423, 2253
warþe *n.* shore, *Pat* 339; ford, *G* 715
wary *v.* condemn, curse
waryed *pp.adj.* cursed
waryst *see* **warisch**
wasch(e) *v.* (**wesch(e)** *pa.t.*, **waschen(e)** *pp.*) wash
wassayl *interj.* good health!
was(se) *see* **be(ne)**
wast *n.* waist, *G* 144
waste *n.* wasteland, *G* 2098
wast(e) *v.* (**wast** *pa.t.* **wasted** *pp.*) destroy, *Cl* 326, 431, 1178, *Pat* 475; waste, *Cl* 1489
wasturne *n.* wilderness
wate, waþe *see* **wyt** *v.*[1], **woþe**
wat(t)er *n.* (**watt(e)rez, -s, wateres** *pl.*) water; flood(s), *Cl* 323, *etc.*; stream, *Pe* 107, 230, *etc.*, *Cl* 1380, 1776, *G* 715, 1595, *etc.*; tears, *G* 684
Wawan, Wawen *see* **Gaua(y)n**
wawez, waȝez *n.* waves; *fig.* water, *Pe* 287
wax *n.* wax, *Cl* 1487
wax *v.* (**wax(ed), wex(en)** *pa.t.*, **waxen** *pp.*) become, grow; grow (*of a plant*), *Pat* 499, *G* 518; increase, *Cl* 375, 397, *etc.*, *G* 997; stream, pour, *Pe* 649
waxen *adj.* of wax, *G* 1650
waxloxes *n.* lumps of wax, *Cl* 1037
way *adv.* away; **do w.** stop, *Pe* 718, *G* 1492
way(e) *n.* way, path; **by þe w. of** according to, *Pe* 580
wayferande *adj.* wayfaring
wayke *adj.* weak, feeble, *G* 282. *Cf. also* **wakker, wakkest**
waykned *pa.t.* weakened, grew feeble, *Cl* 1422
waymot *adj.* peevish
wayne *v.* (**vayned** *pp.*) bring, *Pe* 249, *Cl* 1616, *G* 264, 1032; send, *Pe* 131, *Cl* 1504, *Pat* 467, *G* 2456, 2459; restore, *Cl* 1701; direct, *G* 984. *Cf.* **wayue, weue** *v.*[1]
wayte *v.* watch, look; take care, make sure, *Cl* 292; search, *Cl* 99; study, *Cl* 1552; **w. after** watch over, *Pat* 86
wayth *n.* catch, game, *G* 1381
wayue *v.* (**wayued, waft(e)** *pa.t.*) wave, *G* 306, make to wave, *Pat* 454; flow to and fro, *Cl* 422; pull, close, *Cl* 857; **w. vp, w. vpon** push open, *Cl* 453, *G* 1743. *Cf.* **wayne, weue** *v.*·

we (**loo**) *interj.* alas!

we *pron.* (**vus** *acc. & dat.*) we

webbez *n.* tapestries, *Pe* 71

wed *pa.t.* went mad, *Cl* 1585

wedde *v.* wed, marry

wedded *pp.adj.* wedded, *Cl* 330

weddyng *n.* wedding, marriage-ceremony

wede *n.* garment, clothing; *pl.* clothes; **heʒe w., bryʒt w.** armour

weder *n.* weather, storm; fine weather, *G* 504*n*; air, sky, *Cl* 475, 847, 1760; *pl.* storms, *Cl* 948

weete *see* **wete**

weʒe, weye *v.* weigh, *Cl* 719; weigh (anchor). *Pat* 103; (carry), bring, *Cl* 1420, 1508, *G* 1403

weʒtes *n.* scales

wekked *see* **wykked**

wel *adv.* (**better** *compar.*, **best** *superl.*) well, certainly; much, *Pe* 145, *Pat* 114, 132, *G* 1276, *etc.*; very, *Pe* 537, *Pat* 169, *G* 179, 684; admittedly, *G* 1847; generously, *G* 1267; *as n.* good fortune, happiness, *Pe* 239, 1187, *G* 2127 (*cf.* **wele**); **w. nere** very nearly, *Pat* 169

wela *adv.* very

welawynnely *adv.* very joyfully, *Cl* 831 (*cf.* **wela, wynne**)

welcom, welcum *adj.* (**welcomest** *superl.*) welcome

welcume *v.* welcome, greet

welde *v.* (**walt** *pa.t.*) rule, govern; enjoy, use, possess, have, *Cl* 644, 705, 835, *Pat* 16, 464, *G* 231, 835, 837, 1064, 1528, *etc.*; pass (time). *G* 485

welder *n.* ruler

wele *n.* happiness, good fortune, prosperity; wealth, costliness; *as n.* precious one, *Pe* 14; *pl.* delights, *Pe* 154

welgest *superl.adj.* strongest, *Cf.* **wylger**

wel-haled *adj.* well pulled-up, *G* 157

welke *see* **walk**(**e**)

welkyn *n.* (the) sky

welle *n.* spring, fountain

welle-hedez *see* **walle-heued**

welnygh, welneʒ(**e**) *adv.* almost; **w. now** (*lit.* almost now) just now, *Pe* 581

welt *pa.t.* revolved, *Pat* 115

welwed *pp.adj.* withered

wely *adj.* blissful, *Pe* 101; *see also* **wyse**

wemlez *adj.* flawless, *Pe* 737

wemme *n.* flaw, blemish, *Pe* 221, 1003

wen *see* **quen**

wench *n.* girl; concubine, *Cl* 1423, 1716

wende *n.* turning, *G* 1161

wende *v.* (**wende, went**(**e**), **wenten** *pa.t.* **went** *pp.*) go; turn, *Pat* 403 (**of:** from), *G* 2152; **watz went** had come, *G* 1712

wene *v.* (**wende, went** *pa.t. Pe* 1148, *G* 669, 1711) suppose, think, believe; know; doubt, *Pe* 1141

wener *compar.adj.* lovelier, *G* 945

weng(**ed**) *see* **venge**

Wenore *n.* Guenevere, *G* 945

went(**e**), **wenten** *see* **wende, wene**

wenyng *n.* hope

wepe *v.* (**wepande** *presp.*, **weped** *pa.t.*) weep; *trans.* weep, lament, *Pat* 384

weppen *n.* weapon

werbeland *presp.adj.* shrill, whistling, *G* 2004

werbles *n.* trills, *G* 119

were *n.* defence, *G* 1628. *See also* **werre**

were *v.*[1] (**wer**(**e**)(**d**) *pa.t.*) wear, *Pe* 205, *Cl* 287, *G* 1928, 2037, 2358

were *v.*[2] (**wer**(**ed**) *pa.t.*) defend, *G* 2041; protect, shelter, *Pat* 486; keep out, *G* 2015; *reflex.* excuse oneself, *Cl* 69

wer(**e**)(**n**) *see* **be**(**ne**)

werk(**e**) *n.* (**werk**(**k**)**es, -z** *pl.*) work, labour, activity; creation, *Cl* 198, *Pat* 501; deed, practice, *Cl* 305; conduct, *Cl* 589; workmanship, *G* 2367; construction, *Cl* 1390; ado, *Cl* 1725; *pl.* structure, *Cl* 1480; labour(s), *Cl* 136, 1258; deeds, *G* 1515, 2026(?); ornamentation, *G* 216, 1817, 2432; embroidery, *G* 164, 2026(?)

werkmen *n.* workmen, labourers, *Pe* 507

werle *n.* circlet, *Pe* 209*n*

wern *see* **be**(**ne**)

werne *v.* refuse, *G* 1494, 1495, 1824

wernyng *n.* refusal, resistance, *G* 2253

werp *see* **warp**(**e**)(**n**)

werre, were *n.* war, fighting. *See also* **were**

werre *v.* fight, *G* 720

wers, worre, wors(**e**) *compar.adj.* (**werst, worst** *superl.*) worse; (socially) inferior; *as n. Cl* 80; **þe w.** the worst (of it), *G* 1588, 1591

wertes *see* **wort**

wery *adj.* weary

weryng *n.* wearing; **in w.** through being worn, *Cl* 1123

wesaunt *n.* gullet, *G* 1336

wesch(**e**) *see* **wasch**(**e**)

west(**e**) *n.* west; west wind, *Pat* 469

westernays *adj.* reversed, awry, *Pe* 307*n*

wete, weete *adj.* wet

wete *v.* wet, *Cl* 1027

weterly *adv.* clearly, truly, *G* 1706

weþer *see* **w**(**h**)**eþer**

weue, veue *v.*[1] proffer, give, *G* 1976, 2359; pass, *Pe* 318; *pp.* brought, *Pe* 976. *Cf.* **wayue, wayne**

weue *v.*[2] (**weuen** *Pe* 71, *pa.t.pl.* or *pres.pl.*, **wouen** *pp.*) weave

wex(**en**), **weye** *see* **wax, weʒe**

whal *n.* (**whallez** *gen.sg.*) whale

whallez bon *n.* ivory (from walrus), *Pe* 212

wham *see* **who**

wharred *pa.t.* whirred, *G* 2203

what, whatt, quat *interrog. & indef. pron. & adj.* what; why, *Pe* 1072, *Pat* 197, *G* 563; *interj.* why!, oh!, *etc.*, *Cl* 487, 845, *etc.*, *G* 1163, 2201*n*; *indef.* whatever, *Pe* 523, *G* 1073

whatkyn *adj.* whatever kind of, *Cl* 100

whatso, qu- *pron.* (*also* **w**(**h**)**at, qu- ... so**) whatever; what, *Pat* 243, *G* 255

whatt *see* **what**

whederwarde *adv.* in what(ever) direction

wheder, whyder *adv.* whither, where, *Cl* 917, *Pat* 200. *See also* **wheþer**

when, whene *see* **quen, quene**

whenso *adv.* whenever

wher(e), qu- *adv. & conj.* where; wherever, *Cl* 444, *G* 100; **whereso, quer(e)so** wherever. *See also* **wheþer**

wherfore, querfore *adv.* for which reason; *interrog.* why?

w(h)eresoeuer, queresoeuer *adv.* wherever

whete *n.* wheat, *Pe* 32

whette *v.* (**whette** *pa.t.*) sharpen, whet; grind

wheþen, qu- *adv.* whence (ever)

wheþer, wheder *adv.* yet, nevertheless, *Pe* 581, 826, *Cl* 570, *G* 203

w(h)eþer, qu-, where (*Pe* 617) *interrog.adv. introd. direct qu.*, *Pe* 565, **w. wystez þou euer** did you ever know?, *Pe* 617, **w. þis be** is this?, *G* 2186; *pron. & conj.* whichever, *shifting to* whether, *Pe* 130, 604, *Cl* 113; whether, *Cl* 583, etc.; **q. . . . so** *adj.* (to) whichever (man), *G* 1109; **queþersoeuer** *pron.* whichever, *Pe* 606

whichche *n.* chest (*i.e.* ark), *Cl* 362

whiderwarde-soeuer *adv.* to whatever place, *G* 2478

whil(e), whit *see* **whyl(e), whyt(e)**

who, quo *interrog. & indef. pron.* (**quom, wham** *dat.* (*rel.*)) who, whoever; you who, *Pe* 344; **as q. says** like one who says, *Pe* 693

whoso, quoso *pron.* whoever, if anyone

why, wy, quy *adv.* why; *interj.* why!, oh!

whyder *see* **wheder**

whyle *adv.* once, formerly, *Pe* 15

whyle, quyle, quile *n.* time, while; moment; **þe w.** *adv.* for the time, *conj.* while; **þe . . . q., þat . . . w.** during, *G* 940, 985

whyl(e), wyl(e), whil(e), quyl(e), quel *prep. & conj.* while, as long as; until, *Pe* 528, *Cl* 1686, *G* 536, 1072, 1180, *etc.*

whyssynes *n.* cushions, *G* 877

whyt(e), whit, quit(e), quyt(e), qwyte *adj. & n.* white

wich, wych *pron. & adj.* what, of what sort, *Cl* 169, 1060, 1074, *G* 918; **w. . . . so euer** whichever, *Pat* 280

wiȝt *see* **wyȝt(e)**

wil, wyl(le), wol *v.* (**wolde(z), woled** *pa.t.*) will, be willing, wish (for), desire, intend; **wolde** *pa.t.* was about to, *Pat* 424; would say, meant, *Cl* 1552; *in pres. sense* would, wish(es) to, *Cl* 1140, *etc.*

wit *see* **wyt**

with, wyth *prep.* (together) with; among, *G* 49; against; towards, *Cl* 849, *G* 1926, 2220; for, *Cl* 56; in comparison with, *Pat* 300; in respect of, *G* 418; by, through (*agent or instr.*), *Pe* 806, *etc.*, *Cl* 90, 91, 111, 1142, 1178, *etc.*, *Pat* 2, *etc.*, *G* 314, 384, 681, 949, 1119, 1153, 1229, *etc.*; (tired, afraid) of, *G* 1573, 2301 (*or* within); **w. hymseluen** with him, *G* 113, inwardly, *G* 1660; **w. þis, w. þat** thereupon; *see also* **lyt(t)el**

withinne, wythinne *adv. & prep.* within, inside, inwardly, among

withnay *v.* refuse, reject, *Pe* 916

withoute(n), wythoute(n) *adv. & prep.* without; outside

wittnesse, wyttenesse *n.* witness; evidence, testimony, *Cl* 1050

wlate *v. impers.* (disgust); be disgusted, feel loathing, *Cl* 305, 1501

wlatsum *adj.* loathsome, disgusting

wlonk, wlonc *adj.* fine, handsome, splendid, lovely; cordial, *Cl* 831; *as n.* **þat, þe w.** purity, pure conduct, *Cl* 1052, noble man, *G* 1988; *predic. adj. or adv.* proud(ly), presumptuous(ly), *Pe* 903, splendid(ly), *G* 2022

wo *n.* woe, misery, suffering; (fear of) harm, *Pe* 154; *adj.* sorrowful, *Cl* 284

wod *see* **wade, wod(e)**

wodbynde *n.* woodbine (climbing plant), *Pat* 446, *etc.* *See also* **bynde**

wod(e) *adj. & adv.* (**wodder** *compar.*) mad; angry, furious, *Cl* 204; (of waves, *etc.*) furious, raging, *Cl* 364, *Pat* 162; *adv.* fiercely, *Pat* 142

wod(e) *n.* wood, forest

wodcraftez *n.* woodcraft, hunting skills, *G* 1605

wod-schawez *n.* groves

wodschip *n.* fury

wodwos *n.* men of the woods, satyrs, *G* 721

woȝe, woghe *n.*[1] wrong, harm, *Pe* 622, *G* 1550

woȝe, wowe *n.*[2] wall, *Pe* 1049, *Cl* 832, 839, *etc.*, *G* 858, 1180, 1650

wok *see* **wake**

wolde *n.* possession, *Pe* 812

wolde(z), wol(ed) *see* **wil**

wolen *adj.* woollen, *Pe* 731

wolfes, wolues *n.* wolves

wolle *n.* wool, fleece, *Pe* 844

wombe *n.* belly, stomach

wommon *see* **wymmen**

won *n.* custom, *Cl* 720

won, wony(e) *v.* (**wonez, won(ie)s, wony(e)s** *pres.*, **wonyande** *presp.*, **wonde, won(y)ed** *pa.t.*, **wonde, wonyd, wont(e)** *pp.*) live, dwell; remain, *Cl* 362, *G* 50, 257, 814; **wont(e)** *pp.adj.* accustomed, *Pe* 15, 172, *Cl* 1489

won *see also* **won(e)**

wonde *v.* shrink, hesitate

wonde, woned *see* **won**

wonder *adj.* wonderful; *adv.* amazingly, wonderfully, exceedingly

wonder, wunder *n.* wonder, amazement; marvel, *Pe* 584, *Pat* 244, 256, *G* 29, 147, *etc.*; ?disaster, *G* 16; *collect.* marvels, *Cl* 1390; **haue w.** be amazed, be surprised

wonderly *adv.* amazingly, greatly; in an awesome manner *Cl* 570

won(e) *n.* dwelling, house; town, city, *Pe* 1049, *Cl* 891, 928, *Pat* 69, 436; (animal's) stall, *Cl* 311; pleasure, *Cl* 1238; multitude, company, *G* 1269; *pl. as collect.* abode, *Pe* 917, *etc.*, *Cl* 779; *G* 685, 1051, *etc.*; lands, *Cl* 841; **to w.** **wonne** brought in, harvested, *Pe* 32

woned *pp.* decreased, subsided, *Cl* 496

wonen *see* **wynne**

wonez, wonies *see* **won**

wonne *adj.* dark, *Pat* 141

wonne(n) *see also* **wynne**

wonnyng *n.* dwelling, *Cl* 921

wons *see* **won**

wont *n.* lack, *G* 131

wont *v.impers.* lack, be wanting
wont(e) *pp. see* **won**
wonyande, wony(e)(s), wony(e)d *see* **won**
worch(e) *see* **wyrk(k)(e)**
Worcher *n.* Creator
worchyp, worchip *v.* worship, *Pat* 206; honour, *G* 1227. *See also* **wor(s)chyp**
word(e) *n.* word, speech; *pl.* words, statement(s); command, *Cl* 348; fame, *G* 1521
worded *pp.* spoken, *Pat* 421
wordlych *adj.* earthly, *Cl* 49
wore, work *see* **be(ne), wyrk(k)(e)**
world(e) *n.* world, earth; nature, *G* 504, 530, 2000; prosperity, *Cl* 1298; **no worldez goud** no goodness in the world (at all), *Cl* 1048; **worldez kynde** mankind, mortal men, *G* 261; **w. wythouten ende** for ever; **in þis (of þe) world,** *etc.*, on earth (*intensive*), *Pat* 202, *G* 238, 871, *etc.*, at all, *Pe* 65n, 293
worme *n.* worm, *Pat* 467; snake, *Cl* 533; dragon, *G* 720
worre *see* **wers**
wor(s)chyp, wor(s)chip, wourchyp *n.* honour, dignity; reverence, *Cl* 1592; value, (honour of) possession, *G* 984, 2432
wors(e), worst *see* **wers**
wort *n.* (**wortes, wertes** *pl.*) plant, *Pe* 42, *Pat* 478, *G* 518
worth(e), -þe *v.* become; be; happen, befall (to); **is worþen to** has become (one of), *Pe* 394; **to noȝt w.** be destroyed, *Pat* 360; **worþe** *pres.subjunc.* let it (there, *etc.*) be, *Pe* 362, *Cl* 727, 925, *G* 1302, *etc.*
worþe, -th *adj.* worth, *Pe* 451, *Cl* 1244, *G* 1269, 1820
worþely(ch), worþilych, worþ(y)ly, worthyly *adj.* (**worþloker** *compar.*) noble, honoured; splendid, fine; glorious, *Pe* 1073; *as n.* precious one, *Pe* 47
worþly *see also* **worþyly**
worþy, worþé, worthé *adj. & adv.* noble (*& as n.*); worthy, *Pe* 616, *Cl* 84; virtuous, *Cl* 718; able, *Pe* 100; fitting, *G* 819; of value, valuable, *G* 559, 1848; *adv.* courteously, *G* 1477
worþyly, -ily, -th-, worþly (*Pe* 1133) *adv.* fittingly, becomingly, *Pe* 1133, *G* 72, 144; courteously, *G* 1759; honourably, *G* 1386, 1988
wost(e), wot(e) *see* **wyt** *v.*[1]
woþe, waþe *n.* danger
wounde *n.* wound
wouen, wounden, wourchyp *see* **weue** *v.*[2], **wynde, wor(s)chyp**
Wowayn, Wowen *see* **Gaua(y)n**
wowche, wowe, wrache *see* **vouche, woȝe, wrake**
wraȝte *pa.t.* suffered, was tormented, *Pe* 56
wrak, wrek *pa.t.* (**wroken** *pp.*) took vengeance; *pp.* driven out, removed, *Pe* 375
wrake, wrache *n.* vengeance, retribution
wrakful *adj.* vengeful, bitter
wrang(e), wrank, wronge *adj., adv. & n.* twisted, awry, *Cl* 891n; perverted, *Cl* 268; evil, *Pat* 384; (put in the) wrong, *G* 1494; *adv.* unjustly, wrongly, *Pe* 488, 614; amiss,

badly, *Pe* 631; *n.* wickedness, misdeed, *Cl* 76, *Pat* 376
wrappez *v.* (**wrapped** *pp.*) wrap, envelop; *reflex.* (*pres25g.*) wrap (dress) yourself, *Cl* 169
wrast *adj.* loud, *G* 1423
wrast *v.* (**wrast(en)** *pa.t.*, **wrast** *pp.*) (wrest); pluck, *Pat* 80; force, *Cl* 1166; resound, *Cl* 1403; *pp.* turned, disposed, *G* 1482; **w. out** thrust out, *Cl* 1802
wrastel *v.* (**wrastled** *pa.t.*) wrestle, struggle
wrath(þe) *n.* wrath, anger; (cause for anger), offence, *Pe* 362
wrath *v.* (**wrathed** *pa.t. & pp.*) become angry, *Cl* 230, 690, *etc.*, *Pat* 74, 431, *etc.*, *G* 1509; *trans.* anger, *Cl* 719, 828; trouble, *G* 726, 2420
wrech(che) *n.* wretch
wrech(ed) *adj.* wretched, *Pe* 56, *Pat* 258
wreȝande *presp.* denouncing, vilifying, *G* 1706
wrek *see* **wrak**
wrenchez *n.* deceits, *Cl* 292
writ *see* **wryt**
wro *n.* nook, *G* 2222; passage, *Pe* 866
wroȝt(e)(z), wroȝten *see* **wyrk(k)(e)**
wroken, wronge *see* **wrak, wrang(e)**
wrot *pa.t.* dug, *Pat* 467
wroth(e), wroþe *adj.* (**wroþer** *compar.*) angry; fierce, *Cl* 1676, *G* 1706, 1905; at variance, enemies, *Pe* 379 (*cf. Pat* 48)
wroth *see also* **wryþe**
wroþ(e)ly *adv.* (**wroþeloker** *compar.*) angrily, fiercely; (more) harshly, *G* 2344
wrux(e)led *adj.* adorned, arrayed, *Cl* 1381, *G* 2191
wryste *n.* wrist
wryt, writ *n.* writing; scripture, *Pe* 997, *Cl* 657; **holy w.** the Bible
wryte *v.* (**wryten** *pp.*) write; *reflex. Pe* 1033
wryþe *v.* (**wroth** *pa.t.*) writhe; wriggle, *Cl* 533, *G* 1200; labour, toil, *Pe* 511; turn aside, *Pe* 350; **w. so wrange away** blunder so badly, *Pe* 488; *trans.* twist, torture, *Pat* 80; turn, *Cl* 821
wunder, wunnen, wy, wych *see* **wonder, wynne** *v.*, **why, wich**
wychecraft *n.* witchcraft
wychez *n.* wizards, *Cl* 1577
wyd(e) *adj. & adv.* wide, broad; **on w.** round about, *Cl* 1423
wyddered *pp.adj.* withered, *Pat* 468
wydoez *n.* widows, *Cl* 185
wyf, vyf *n.* (**wyuez** *gen.sg.*, **wyues, -z, vyuez** *pl.*) woman, lady, wife
wyȝ(e) *n.* being, person, man, knight, servant, sir, *Pat* 492, *G* 252, *etc.*; **vch w.** everyone; **no w.** no one
wyȝt(e) *n.* creature; person, *G* 1792; maiden, *Pe* 338, 494
wyȝt(e), wiȝt *adj.* strong, *G* 261, 1762; valiant, *Pe* 694; piercing, *Cl* 119; **þe wyȝtest** the strongest current, *G* 1591; *adv.* quickly, *Cl* 617, *Pat* 103; **wyȝtly** swiftly
wyket *see* **wyk(k)et**
wykez *n.* corners, *G* 1572
wyk(ke) *adj.* bad, wickd; disagreeable, difficult, *Cl* 1063n
wykked, wekked *adj.* wicked

wyk(k)et *n.* door
wyl *see* **wil, wyl(le)**
wylde *adj.* wild; *as n.* wild animal(s)
wyldren *n.* wild places, *Pat* 297
wyldrenesse *n.* wild country, *G* 701
wyle, wylé *see* **whil(e), wyly**
wylfulnes *n.* wilfulness, obstinacy
wylger *compar.adj.* stronger. *Cf.* **welgest**
wyl(le) *adj.* wild, wandering, *Pat* 473, *G* 2084
wylle *n.*¹ will, mind, temper, *Pe* 56, *Cl* 200, 232, *etc.*, *Pat* 298, *G* 57, 352; will, wish, desire, pleasure, *Pe* 131, *Cl* 309, *etc.*, *Pat* 16, *etc.*, *G* 255, *etc.*; **at w.** abundant(ly), *G* 1371; **bi ȝoure w.** if you please, *G* 1065; **with (a) god w.** willingly, gladly, *G* 1387, *etc.*
wylle *n.*² error, perversity, *Cl* 76
wylle *v. see* **wil**
wylne *v.* wish, *Pe* 318
wylnyng *n.* wish, *G* 1546
wylsfully *adv.* perversely, ?lustfully, *Cl* 268
wylsum *adj.* out-of-the-way, *G* 689
wylt *pp.* escaped, *G* 1711
wyly, wylé *adj.* wily; *as n.* this wily one, *G* 1905; *adv.* cunningly, cleverly, *Cl* 1452
wylyde *adj.* skilful, *G* 2367
wymmen *n.pl.* women; **wommon** *gen.pl.* of women, womanly, *Pe* 236
wyn, wyne *n.* wine
wyndas *n.* windlass
wynd(e) *n.* wind; speech, message, *Pat* 345
wynde *v.* (**wounden** *pp.*) turn, *Cl* 534; come round, *G* 530; *pp.* bound, *G* 215
wyndow(e) *n.* window
wyndowande *presp.adj.* scattering in the wind
wyne *see* **wyn**
wynge *n.* wing
wynne *adj.* delightful, lovely; precious, *Pe* 647
wynne *n.*¹ joy, *G* 15, 1765
wynne *n.*² gain, advantage, *G* 2420
wynne *v.* (**wan, wonnen** *pa.t.*, **won(n)en, wonne, wunnen** *pp.*) win, obtain, gain, get; beget, *Cl* 112, 650; bring, *Pe* 32, *Cl* 617, *G* 831, *etc.*; win over, persuade, *Cl* 1616, *G* 1550; reach (*also reflex.*) *Pat* 237, *G* 402, 1569, 2231; *intrans.* win, *G* 70; go, come, *Pe* 107, 517, *Cl* 140, 882, *etc.*, *G* 461, 1365, *etc.*
wynnelych *adj.* gracious, *Cl* 1807; pleasant, *G* 980
wynter *n.* winter
wynt-hole *n.* windpipe
wypped¹ *pp.* wiped, polished, *G* 2022
wypped² *pa.t.* whipped, slashed, *G* 2249
Wyrale *n.* Wirral (in Cheshire)
wyrde *n.* fate, destiny; Providence
wyrk(k)(e), work, worch(e) *v.* (**wroȝt-(e)(z), -en** *pa.t.*, **wroȝt** *pp.*) do, act, perform; commit, *Pe* 622, *etc.*, *Cl* 171, *etc.*, *Pat* 513, *etc.*; bring about, accomplish, *Cl* 663, *etc.*, *G* 22, *etc.*; make, create, *Pe* 638, *etc.*, *Cl* 5 *etc.*, *Pat* 206, *G* 399, *etc.*; work, labour, *Pe* 511, 525, *etc.*, *Cl* 1287
wyrled *pa.t.* whirled, circled, *Cl* 475
wyschande *presp.* longing for, *Pe* 14; **wysched** *pa.t.* wished, *Pat* 462
wys(e) *adj.* wise, clever; skilful, *Pe* 748, *G* 1605; *as n. Cl* 1319, 1741

wyse *n.* manner, way, state; array, *Pe* 133, *G* 2456; **in feȝtyng w.** in battle array, *G* 267; **in wely w.** blissfully, in a blissful state, *Pe* 101; **on basteles w.** in the manner of a tower on wheels, *Cl* 1187n; **on a wonder w.** miraculously, *Pe* 1095; **vpon a grett w.** magnificently, *G* 2014; **vpon a ser w.** diversely, individually, *Pat* 12; **vpon spare w.** discreetly, *G* 901
wyse *v.* (**wysed** *pa.t.*) show, be visible, *Pe* 1135; send, *Cl* 453
wysse *v.* guide, *G* 549, 739; instruct, enlighten, *Cl* 1564, *Pat* 60
wyst(e)(n), wystez *see* **wyt**
wysty *adj.* desolate, *G* 2189
wyt, wytte, wyte *n.* mind, reason, intelligence, understanding, wisdom; meaning, *Cl* 1630; sense, *G* 677; *pl.* senses, *Cl* 515, *G* 640, *etc.*
wyt, wyte, wit *v.*¹ (**wot(e), wate, wost(e)** *pres.*, **wost(e) wystez, wyst(e)(n)** *pa.t.*) know, understand, be sure; perceive, learn
wyte *v.*² blame, *Pat* 501; **to w.** blameworthy, *Cl* 76
wyte *v.*³ look, *G* 2050
wyter *adv.* clearly, *Cl* 1552
wytered *pp.* informed, *Cl* 1587
wyterly *adv.* clearly, surely
wyth *see* **with**
wythal *adv.* in addition, *Cl* 636
wythdroȝ *pa.t.* removed, *Pe* 658
wythhalde *v.* (**withhelde, wythhylde** *pa.t.*) withhold, restrain, check
wythinne, wythoute(n) *see* **withinne, withoute(n)**
wytles *adj.* foolish, *Pat* 113; distracted, *Cl* 1585
wytte, wyttenesse *see* **wyt, wittnesse**
wyþe *adj.* mild, *Pat* 454
wyþer *adj.* opposite, *Pe* 230
wyþer *v.* **w. wyth** oppose, resist, *Pat* 48
wyþerly *adv.* rebelliously, *Pat* 74; fiercely, implacably, *Cl* 198
wyues, wyuez *see* **wyf**

ydropike *adj.* dropsical, *Cl* 1096
yȝe *n.* (**yȝen** *pl.*) eye
yle, ymage *see* **ille, image**
Ynde *n.* India; **ble of Y.** dark blue, indigo, *Pe* 76
ynde *adj.* dark blue, indigo, *Cl* 1411, *Pe* 1016
yot *pa.t.* ran, fell (like a tear), *Pe* 10
yo(u)r(e), yowre, ȝowre *possess.adj.* your
yourez, yowrez, ȝourez *pron.* yours
yourself, yow-, yowre-, ȝour-, yo(u)r-seluen *pron.* (you) yourself
yow *see* **ȝe**
yre, ire *n.* ire, anger
yrn(e) *n.* iron, *G* 215; weapon, *G* 2267; pl. armour, *G* 729
Ysaye *n.* Isaiah
yuore *n.* ivory, *Pe* 178
yþez *n.* waves
Ywan, Aywan *n.* Iwain

Zedechyas *n.* Zedekiah
Zeferus *n.* Zephyrus, the West Wind

Bibliography

Ackerman, Robert W. 1964. "The Pearl-Maiden and the Penny." *Romance Philology* 17: 615–23.

Anderson, J. J., ed. 1969. *Patience*. Manchester.

———, ed. 1977. *Cleanness*. Manchester.

Andrew, Malcolm, and Ronald Waldron, eds. 1987. *The Poems of the Pearl Manuscript*. Rev. ed. Exeter.

Auerbach, Erich. 1953. *Mimesis*. Translated by Willard Trask. Princeton.

Augustine. 1958. *On Christian Doctrine*. Translated by D. W. Robertson, Jr. New York.

Barthes, Roland. 1972. *Mythologies*. Translated by Annette Lavers. New York.

———. 1967. *Writing Degree Zero*. Translated by Annette Lavers and Colin Smith. New York.

Bateson, Hartley, ed. 1918. *Patience*. 2nd ed. Manchester.

Baughan, Denver E. 1950. "The Role of Morgan le Fay in Sir Gawain and the Green Knight." *Journal of English Literary History* 17: 241–51.

Benson, Larry D. 1965. "The Authorship of St. Erkenwald." *Journal of English and Germanic Philology* 64: 393–405.

Berlin, Normand. 1961. "*Patience*: A Study in Poetic Elaboration." *Studia Neophilologica* 33: 80–85.

Bishop, Ian. 1957. "The Significance of the 'Garland Gay' in the Allegory of *Pearl*." *Review of English Studies* 8: 12–21.

———. 1968. *Pearl in Its Setting: A Critical Study of the Structure and Meaning of the Middle English Poem*. Oxford.

Blanch, Robert, ed. 1966. *Sir Gawain and Pearl: Critical Essays*. Bloomington, Ind.

Blenker, Louis. 1968. "The Theological Structure of the Pearl." *Traditio* 24: 43–75.

———. 1971. "The Pattern of Traditional Images in *Pearl*." *Studies in Philology* 68: 26–49.

Bloomfield, Morton. 1958. "Symbolism in Medieval Literature." *Modern Philology* 66: 73–81.

Bogdanos, Theodore. 1983. *Pearl: Image of the Ineffable*. University Park, Pa.

Bone, Gavin. 1937. "A Note on Pearl and the Duke of Howlat." *Medium Ævum* 6: 169–70.

Borroff, Marie. 1962. *'Sir Gawain and the Green Knight': A Stylistic and Metrical Study*. New Haven.

———, trans. 1967. *Sir Gawain and the Green Knight*. New York.

Brewer, D. S. 1966. "Courtesy and the Gawain Poet." In *Essays in Memory of C. S. Lewis,* edited by John Lawlor. London.

Brown, Carleton F. 1904a. "The Author of the *Pearl,* Considered in the Light of His Theological Opinions." *PMLA* 19: 115–45.

———. 1904b. "Note on the Question of Strode's Authorship of *The Pearl.*" *PMLA* 19: 146–48.

Brown, J. T. T. 1902. *Huchown of the Awle Ryale and His Poems.* Glasgow.

Buchanan, A. 1932. "The Irish Framework of Gawain and the Green Knight." *PMLA* 47: 315–38.

Burrow, J. A. 1965. *A Reading of "Sir Gawain and the Green Knight."* London.

Cargill, Oscar, and Margaret Schlauch. 1928. "The Pearl and Its Jeweller." *PMLA* 43: 105–23.

Carson, Mother Angela. 1965. "Aspects of Elegy in the Middle English Pearl." *Studies in Philology* 72: 17–27.

Cawley, Arthur. 1976. *Pearl.* New York.

Chambers, Edmund K. 1945. *English Literature at the Close of the Middle Ages.* London.

Chambers, R. W. 1923. "Long Will, Dante, and the Righteous Heathen." *Essays and Studies of the English Association* O.s. 9: 50–69.

Chapman, C. O. 1931. "The Musical Training of the Pearl Poet." *PMLA* 46: 177–81.

———. 1932. "The Authorship of the *Pearl.*" *PMLA* 47: 346–53.

———. 1939. "Numerical Symbolism in Dante and the Pearl." *Modern Language Notes* 54: 256–61.

Clark, John W. 1941. "The Authorship of *Sir Gawain and the Green Knight, Pearl, Cleanness, Patience,* and *Erkenwald* in Light of Vocabulary." Ph.D. dissertation, University of Minnesota.

———. 1949. "Observations on Certain Differences in Vocabulary between *Cleanness* and *Sir Gawain and the Green Knight.*" *Philological Quarterly* 28: 261–73.

Conley, John. 1955. "Pearl and the Lost Tradition." *Journal of English and Germanic Philology* 54: 332–47.

———. 1970. *The Middle English Pearl: Critical Essays.* Indiana.

Cook, Albert S. 1908–09. "*Pearl.*" *Modern Philology* 6: 197–200.

Coulton, G. C. 1906–07. "In Defense of the Pearl." *Modern Language Review* 2: 39–43.

———. 1938. *Medieval Panorama.* Cambridge.

Davenport, W. A. 1978. *The Art of the Gawain Poet.* London.

Day, Mabel. 1919. "The Weak Verb in the Works of the Gawain Poet," *Modern Language Review* 14: 413–15.

———. 1931–32. "Strophic Division in Middle English Alliterative Verse." *Englische Studien* 66: 245–48.

———. 1934. "Two Notes on Pearl." *Medium Ævum* 3: 241–42.

Diekstra, F. N. M. 1974. "Jonah and *Patience*: The Psychology of a Prophet." *English Studies* 55: 205–17.

Earl, James W. 1972–73. "Saint Margaret and the Pearl Maiden." *Modern Philology* 70: 1–8.

Ebbs, John Dale. 1958. "Stylistic Mannerisms of the Gawain Poet." *Journal of English and Germanic Philology* 57: 522–25.

Einarsson, Stefan. 1937. "Old and Middle English Notes." *Journal of English and Germanic Philology* 36: 183–87.

Elliott, R. W. V. 1951. "Pearl and the Medieval Garden: Convention or Originality?" *Les Langues Modernes* 45: 85–101.

Emerson, Oliver F. 1921–22. "Imperfect Lines in Pearl and in the Rimed Parts of Sir Gawain." *Modern Philology* 19: 131–41.

———. 1922. "Some Notes on Pearl." *PMLA* 37: 52–93.

———. 1927. "More Notes on Pearl." *PMLA* 42: 807–31.

Engelhardt, George J. 1955. "The Predicament of Gawain." *Modern Language Quarterly* 16: 218–25.

Everett, Dorothy. 1959. *Essays in Middle English Literature*. London.

Everett, Dorothy, and Naomi D. Hurnard. 1947. "Legal Phraseology in a Passage in Pearl." *Medium Ævum* 16: 9–15.

Faigley, Lester L. 1978. "Typology and Justice in St Erkenwald." *American Benedictine Review* 29: 381–90.

Fick, Wilhelm. 1885. *Zum mittelenglischen Gedicht von der Perle: Eine Lautuntersuchung*. Kiel.

Field, P. J. C. 1971. "A Rereading of *Gawain*." *Studies in Philology* 68: 255–69.

Finch, Casey. 1987. "Immediacy in the *Odes* of William Collins." *Eighteenth-Century Studies* 20: 275–95.

Finch, Casey, and Peter Bowen. 1990. "'The Tittle-Tattle of Highbury': Gossip and the Free Indirect Style in *Emma*." *Representations* 31 (Summer): 1–18.

Fischer, Joseph. 1901. *Die Stabende Langzeile in den Werken des Gawain-Dichters*. Bonn.

Fletcher, Jefferson B. 1921. "The Allegory of the Pearl." *Journal of English and Germanic Philology* 20: 1–21.

Foley, Michael M. 1973–74. "A Bibliography of *Purity* (*Cleanness*)." *Chaucer Review* 8: 324–34.

———. 1974. "Gawain's Two Confessions Reconsidered." *Chaucer Review* 9: 73–79.

Fox, Denton, ed. 1968. *Twentieth-Century Interpretations of 'Sir Gawain and the Green Knight.'* Englewood Cliffs, N.J.

Friedman, John B. 1981. "Figural Typology in the Middle English *Patience*." In *The Alliterative Tradition in the Fourteenth Century*, edited by Bernard S. Levy and Paul E. Szarmach. Kent, Ohio.

Gardner, John, trans. 1965. *The Complete Works of the Gawain-Poet*. Chicago.

Garrett, Robert Max. 1918. "The *Pearl*: An Interpretation." *Studies in English* 4: 42–61.

Gatta, John, Jr. 1973–74. "Transformation Symbolism and the Liturgy of the Mass in *Pearl*." *Modern Philology* 71: 243–56.

Gollancz, Sir Israel, ed. 1891. *Pearl*. London.

———. 1907. In *The Cambridge History of English Literature*. Vol. 1, ch. 15. London and New York.

———, ed. 1924. *Patience*. 2nd ed. London.

————, ed. 1932. *Saint Erkenwald*. Reprinted from Select Early English Poems (4), 1922. London.

————, ed. 1940. *Sir Gawain and the Green Knight*. Introduction by Mabel Day and Mary S. Serjeantson. Early English Text Society, Ordinary Series (210). London.

————, ed. 1974. *Cleanness*. Translated by D. S. Brewer. Cambridge.

Gordon, E. V., ed. 1953. *Pearl*. Oxford.

Green, Richard Hamilton. 1962. "Gawain's Shield and the Quest for Perfection." *Journal of English Literary History* 29: 121–39.

Greene, W. K. 1925. "The Pearl: A New Interpretation." *PMLA* 40: 814–27.

Greenwood, Ormerod. 1956. *Sir Gawain and the Green Knight: A Fourteenth-Century Alliterative Poem Now Attributed to Hugh Mascy, Translated in Original Metre*. London.

Greg, W. W. 1932. "Continuity of the Alliterative Tradition." *Modern Language Review* 27: 453–54.

Hamilton, Marie P. 1955. "The Meaning of the Middle English *Pearl*." *PMLA* 70: 805–24.

Hart, Elizabeth. 1927. "The Heaven of Virgins." *Modern Language Notes* 42: 113–16.

Heisermann, A. R. 1965. "The Plot of Pearl." *PMLA* 80: 164–71.

Hieatt, Constance. 1965. "*Pearl* and the Dream-Vision Tradition." *Studia Neophilologica* 37: 139–45.

Higgs, Elton D. 1974. "The Progress of the Dreamer in *Pearl*." *Studies in Medieval Culture* 4: 388–400.

Hill, Ordelle G. 1967. "The Late-Latin *De Jona* as a Source for *Patience*." *Journal of English and Germanic Philology* 66: 21–25.

————. 1968–69. "The Audience of *Patience*." *Modern Philology* 66: 103–9.

Hillmann, Sister Mary V. 1941. "*Pearl*: Inlyche and Rewarde." *Modern Language Notes* 56: 457–58.

————. 1943. "The *Pearl*: west ernays (307) and fasor (431)." *Modern Language Notes* 58: 42–44.

————. 1944. "*Pearl*: lere leke (210)." *Modern Language Notes* 59: 417–18.

————. 1945. "Some Debatable Words in *Pearl* and its Theme." *Modern Language Notes* 60: 241–48.

————, ed. and trans. 1961. *The Pearl*. New York.

Hoffman, Stanton de Voren. 1960. "The *Pearl*: Notes for an Interpretation." *Modern Philology* 58: 73–80.

Horstmann, Carl, ed. 1881. *De Erkenwalde*. In *Altenglische Legenden*. Heilbronn.

Howard, Donald R., and Christian K. Zacher, eds. 1968. *Critical Studies of 'Sir Gawain and the Green Knight.'* Notre Dame, Ind.

Hulbert, J. R. 1918–19. "The Sources and St. *Erkenwald* and the *Trental of Gregory*." *Modern Philology* 16: 485–93.

————. 1921. "The West Midland of the Romances." *Modern Philology* 19: 1–16.

————. 1931. "A Hypothesis Concerning the Alliterative Revival." *Modern Philology* 28: 405–22.

————. 1950–51. "Quatrains in Middle English Alliterative Poems." *Modern Philology* 48: 73–81.

Jackson, Isaac. 1913. "Sir Gawain and the Green Knight Considered as a Garter Poem." *Anglia* 37: 393–423.

Johnson, Lynn. 1984. *The Voice of the Gawain Poet*. New York.

Johnson, Wendell S. 1953. "The Imagery and Diction of The Pearl: Toward an Interpretation." *English Literary History* 20: 161–80.

Kean, Patricia M. 1965. "Numerical Composition in Pearl." *Notes and Queries* 12: 49–51.

————. 1967. *The Pearl: An Interpretation*. London.

Keiser, Elizabeth. 1980. "The Festive Decorum of *Cleanness*." In *Chivalric Literature*, edited by Larry D. Benson and John Leyerle. London.

Kelly, T. D., and J. T. Irwin. 1973. "The Meaning of *Cleanness*: Parable as Effective Sign." *Mediaeval Studies* 35: 232–60.

Knigge, Friedrich. 1885. *Die Sprache des Dichters von Sir Gawain and the Green Knight, der sogenannten Early English Alliterative Poems, und De Erkenwalde*. Marburg.

Knightley, William J. 1961. "Pearl: 'The hy3 seysoun.'" *Modern Language Notes* 76: 97–102.

Knowles, David. 1961. *The English Mystical Tradition*. London.

Kooper, Erik. 1982. "The Case of the Encoded Author: John Massey in *Sir Gawain and the Green Knight*." *Neuphilologische Mitteilungen* 83: 158–68.

Kottler, Barnet, and Alan M. Markman. 1966. *A Concordance to Five Middle English Poems*. Pittsburgh.

Krappe, H. H. 1938. "Who Was the Green Knight?" *Speculum* 13: 206–15.

Lewis, C. S. 1964. *The Discarded Image*. Cambridge.

Luttrell, C. A. 1962. "The Medieval Tradition of the Pearl Virginity." *Medium Ævum* 31: 194–200.

McAlindon, T. 1970. "Hagiography into Art: A Study of *St. Erkenwald*." *Studies in Philology* 67: 472–94.

McAndrew, Bruno. 1957. "The *Pearl*: A Catholic Paradise Lost." *American Benedictine Review* 8: 243–51.

MacCracken, H. N. 1910. "Concerning Huchown." *PMLA* 25: 507–34.

McGilliard, John C. 1969. "Links, Language, and Style in the Pearl." In *Studies in Language, Literature, and Culture of the Middle Ages and Later: Studies in Honor of Rudolph Willard*, edited by E. Bagby Atwood and Archibald A. Hill. Austin, Texas.

McNamara, John Francis. 1968. "Responses to Ockhamist Theology in the Poetry of the *Pearl*-Poet, Langland and Chaucer." Ph.D. dissertation, Louisiana State University.

Macrae-Gibson, O. D. 1968. "*Pearl*: The Link Words and the Thematic Structure." *Neophilologus* 52: 54–64.

Madden, Sir Frederick, ed. 1839. *Syr Gawayne*. London.

Madeleva, Sister Mary. 1925. *Pearl: A Study in Spiritual Dryness*. New York.

Means, Michael H. 1972. "The 'Pure' Consolatio: *Pearl*." In *The Consolatio Genre in Medieval English Literature*. Gainesville, Fla.

Medary, Margaret. 1916. "Stanza-Linking in Middle English Verse." *Romantic Review* 7: 243–70.

Meisel, Perry. 1984. "Freud's Reflexive Realism." *October* 28: 43–59.

Menner, Robert J., ed. 1920. *Purity: A Middle English Poem.* Yale Studies in English, 61. New Haven.

———. 1926. "Four Notes in the West Midland Dialect." *Modern Language Notes* 41: 451–58.

———. 1922. "Sir Gawain and the Green Knight and the West Midland." *PMLA* 37: 513–26.

Migne, J.-P. 1878–90. *Partologiae Cursus Completus.* Series Latina. Paris.

Milroy, James. 1971. "*Pearl*: The Verbal Texture and Linguistic Theme." *Neophilologus* 55: 195–208.

Moorman, Charles. 1955–56. "The Role of the Narrator in *Pearl.*" *Modern Philology* 53: 73–81.

———. 1966. *The Pearl Poet.* New York.

———, ed. 1977. *The Works of the Gawain-Poet.* Jackson, Miss.

Morris, R., ed. 1864. *Early English Alliterative Poems in the West Midland Dialect of the Fourteenth Century.* London.

Morse, Ruth, ed. 1975. *St Erkenwald.* Cambridge.

Mynors, R. A. B. 1939. *Durham Cathedral Manuscripts.* Oxford.

Nietzsche, Friedrich. 1956. *The Birth of Tragedy* and *The Genealogy of Morals.* Translated by Francis Golffing. Garden City, N.J.

Northup, Clark S. 1897. "The Metrical Structure of the Pearl." *PMLA* 12: 326–40.

———. 1904. "Recent Studies of the Pearl." *PMLA* 19: 154–215.

Oakden, J. P. 1930–35. *Alliterative Poetry in Middle English.* Vol. 1. Manchester.

———. 1968. "The Liturgical Influence in *Pearl.*" In *Chaucer und seine Zeit: Symposium für Walter F. Schirmer,* edited by Arno Esch. Tübingen.

Osgood, Charles G., ed. 1906. *The Pearl.* Boston.

Patch, Howard. 1950. *The Other World, According to Descriptions in Medieval Literature.* Cambridge, Mass.

Pearsall, Derek. 1955. "Rhetorical Description in *Sir Gawain and the Green Knight.*" *Modern Language Review* 50: 129–34.

Pearsall, Derek, and Elizabeth Salter. 1973. *Landscapes and Seasons of the Medieval World.* London.

Peterson, Clifford. 1974. "The *Pearl*-Poet and John Massey of Cotton, Cheshire." *Review of English Studies* 25: 257–66.

———, ed. 1977. *Saint Erkenwald.* Philadelphia.

Piehler, Paul. 1971. *The Visionary Landscape: A Study in Medieval Allegory.* London.

Pilch, Herbert. 1964. "Das mittelenglische Perlegedicht: Sein Verhältnis zum Rosenroman." *Neuphilologische Mitteilungen* 65: 427–46.

Quinn, William A. 1984. "The Psychology of *St Erkenwald.*" *Medium Ævum* 3, No. 2: 180–93.

Reichardt, Paul Frederick. 1971. "The Art and Meaning of the Middle English *St Erkenwald.*" Ph.D. dissertation, Rice University.

———. 1984. "Gawain and the Image of the Wound." *PMLA* 99: 154–61.

Richardson, F. E. 1962. "Pearl: A Poem and its Audience." *Neophilologus* 56: 308–16.

Robertson, D. W., Jr. 1950a. "The 'Heresy' of *The Pearl*." *Modern Language Notes* 65: 152–55.

———. 1950b. "The Pearl as Symbol." *Modern Language Notes* 65: 155–61.

———. 1951. "The Doctrine of Charity in Mediaeval Literary Gardens." *Speculum* 26: 24–49.

Røstvig, Maren-Sofie. 1967. "Numerical Composition in *Pearl*." *English Studies* 48: 326–32.

Savage, Henry L., ed. 1926. *Saint Erkenwald*. Yale Studies in English, 72. New Haven.

———. 1956. *The Gawain-Poet: Studies in His Personality and Background*. Chapel Hill, N.C.

Schaubert, Else von. 1923. "Der englische Ursprung von Syr Gawayn and the Green Knight." *Englische Studien* 57: 331–446.

Schleusener, Jay. 1971. "History and Action in *Patience*." *PMLA* 86: 959–65.

Schofield, William H. 1904. "The Nature and Fabric of the *Pearl*." *PMLA* 19: 154–215.

———. 1909. "Symbolism, Allegory, and Autobiography in *The Pearl*." *PMLA* 24: 585–675.

Schotter, Anne Howland. 1983. "Vernacular Style and the Word of God: The Incarnational Art of *Pearl*." In *Ineffability: Naming the Unnameable from Dante to Beckett*, edited by Anne Howland Schotter and Peter S. Hawkins. New York.

Schumacher, Karl. 1914. *Studien über den Stabreim in der mittelenglischen Alliterationsdichtung*. Bonner Studien zur Englischen Philologie, 11. Bonn.

Serjeantson, M. S. 1927. "The Dialects of the West-Midlands." *Review of English Studies* 3: 54–67, 186–203, 319–331.

Shoaf, R. A. 1975. "Dante's Colombi and the Figuralism of Hope in the Divine Comedy." *Dante Studies* 93: 27–59.

———. 1981. "God's Malyse: Metaphor and Conversion in Patience." *Journal of Medieval and Renaissance Studies* 11: 261–79.

———. 1983. *Dante, Chaucer, and the Currency of the Word: Money, Images, and Reference in Late Medieval Poetry*. Norman, Okla.

Sklute, Larry M. 1973. "Expectation and Fulfillment in *Pearl*." *Philological Quarterly* 52: 663–79.

Spearing, A. C. 1962–63. "Symbolic and Dramatic Development in *Pearl*." *Modern Philology* 60: 1–12.

———. 1966. "*Patience* and the *Gawain*-Poet." *Anglia* 84: 305–29.

———. 1970. *The Gawain-Poet: A Critical Study*. Cambridge.

Speirs, John. 1957. *Medieval English Poetry: The Non-Chaucerian Tradition*. London.

Stern, Milton R. 1955. "An Approach to *The Pearl*." *Journal of English and Germanic Philology* 54 (October): 684–92.

Stone, Brian D., trans. 1959. *Sir Gawain and the Green Knight*. Harmondsworth, U.K.

————, trans. 1971. *The Owl and the Nightingale, Cleanness, St Erkenwald.* Harmondsworth, U.K.

Taylor, Paul B. 1971. "Commerce and Comedy in Sir Gawain." *Philological Quarterly* 50: 1–15.

————. 1974. "Gawain's Garland of Girdle and Name." *English Studies* 55: 6–14.

Thomas, P. G. 1922. "Notes on *Cleanness.*" *Modern Language Review* 17: 64–66.

Tolkien, J. R. R., and E. V. Gordon, eds. 1925. *Sir Gawain and the Green Knight.* London.

Turville-Petre, Thorac. 1977. *The Alliterative Revival.* Cambridge.

Tuve, Rosemund. 1974. *Seasons and Months: Studies in a Tradition of Middle Ages Poetry.* Reprint of the 1933 edition. Cambridge.

Vantuono, William. 1972. "The Question of Quatrains in *Patience.*" *Manuscripta* 16: 24–30.

————. 1987. *The Pearl Poem in Middle and Modern English.* Maryland.

Vasta, Edward. 1967. "*Pearl*: Immortal Flowers and the Pearl's Decay." *Journal of English and Germanic Philology* 66: 519–31.

Villette, J. 1940. *L'Ange dans L'Art Occident du XII–XVI Siècle.* Paris.

Warner, G. F., ed. 1889. *The Buke of John Maundeuill.* London.

Watts, V. E. 1963. "*Pearl* as *Consolatio.*" *Medium Ævum* 32: 34–36.

Williams, David. 1970–71. "The Point of *Patience.*" *Modern Philology* 68: 127–36.

Wilson, Edward. 1976. *The Gawain Poet.* Leiden.

Zavadil, J. B. 1962. "A Study of the Meaning in *Patience* and *Cleanness.*" Ph.D. dissertation, Stanford University.

Compositor: Maryland Composition
Text: 9/11 Baskerville
Display: Baskerville
Printer: Haddon Craftsmen, Inc.
Binder: Haddon Craftsmen, Inc.